W9-ABU-093

Date: 12/29/11

**803 QUI
Quinn, Edward,
A dictionary of literary and
thematic terms /**

A DICTIONARY OF

Literary and Thematic Terms

Second Edition

EDWARD QUINN

Facts On File

An imprint of Infobase Publishing

A Dictionary of Literary and Thematic Terms, Second Edition

Facts On File, Inc.
An imprint of Infobase Publishing
132 West 31st Street
New York NY 10001

Library of Congress Cataloging-in-Publication Data
Quinn, Edward, 1932–
    A dictionary of literary and thematic terms / Edward Quinn—2nd ed.
      p. cm.
    Includes index.
      ISBN 0-8160-6243-9 (hc : alk. paper) 1. Criticism—Terminology. 2. Literature—Terminology. 3. Literature, Comparative—Themes, motives, etc.—Terminology. 4. English language—Terms and phrases. 5. Literary form—Terminology. I. Title.
      PN44.5.Q56 2006
      803—dc22   2005029826

Text design by Sandra Watanabe
Cover design by Cathy Rincon

Printed in the United States of America

MP FOF 10 9 8 7 6 5 4 3 2 1

This book is printed on acid-free paper.

Contents

Preface
v

Literary and Thematic Terms
1

Index
453

Preface

This book offers the student or general reader a guide through the thicket of literary terms. Unlike traditional books of this type, however, it takes an expanded view of the term *literary*. One cause of this expansion is the new way of talking about and teaching literature that has emerged since the late 1960s under the general heading of "theory." Theory often deals with subjects that seem at best only peripherally related to what we think of as literature, but some of its insights have provided us with new tools to understand the processes of reading, writing, interpreting, and (alas, to a relatively insignificant extent) enjoying literature. This book provides discussions of the major terms begotten by theory, always with the goal of relating them to literary study.

Another form of expansion is reflected in the title word *thematic*. This is the first book of literary terms to include within it discussions of major literary themes, such as death, love, and time, and also of themes that have a particular significance for our age, such as AIDS, alienation, and anti-Semitism. Still another expansion of "literature" is its extension to include film, television, and other forms of popular culture, thus the appearance of terms such as *macguffin, sitcom,* and *rap.*

These updatings and innovations, however, should not obscure the fact that most of the entries in this book have been in existence for centuries, some of them—those relating to Aristotle—as old as 2,500 years. Like other living things, the literary tradition continues to evolve and expand, enriching the lives of all those lucky enough to come to know it. To that end, this book offers itself as a modest guide.

The subtitle of this new edition might well be labeled, "From Academic Discourse to Zines" since these are the first and last new entries in the book. However, while these two appropriately suggest the ever expanding range of what constitutes "literary" terms, they also indicate the somewhat shifting, deceptive nature of these terms. At first glance, *academic discourse* appears to be a rusty relic of an ivory-towered past, while *zines* seems to embody the essence of a computer-generated future. But as the entries themselves indicate, academic discourse has recently become a hotly "contested site," while the zines phenomenon is more than

75 years old. This is a sobering reminder, as another new entry, *liberal / conservative imagination*, demonstrates in the political sphere, that the old trickster *time* never tires of keeping us off balance. Time also offers a convenient device to categorize the thematic entries new to this edition, which include traditional, rooted-in-the-past entries such as individualism, skepticism, Odysseus/Ulysses; timely present-oriented themes such as nuclear war, terrorism and prison literature, and those subjects that slip through the chronological cracks, like alcohol, baseball, and vampirism.

Among new entries that bespeak the future are those dedicated to the various ethnic American literatures, many of which are just beginning to find their voices, but which, we can safely assume, will grow in importance and recognition as our country continues the great experiment of seeking renewal through immigration.

My thanks to Gail Quinn for typing this manuscript under combat conditions and Deirdre Quinn for pitching in at a critical point. Thanks again to Karl Malkoff, this time for offering his slow-witted friend a crash course in Computers 101. Continued thanks to Jeff Soloway of Facts On File for his patience, encouragement, and sound advice.

Thanks also to Liam and Adam Kirby, Caitlin, Kieran and Declan, Maya, and Shannon Quinn for being the grandest of grandchildren. Finally, a special debt to Barbara Gleason, whose patience, tact, and support kept the ship afloat even after it had sprung a few leaks.

a

Abbey Theatre   The Dublin home of the Irish National Theatre Company, where some of the most celebrated plays of the 20th century first appeared. On its opening night, December 26, 1904, the Abbey presented four short plays: William Butler Yeats's *Cathleen Ni Houlihan* and *On Baile's Strand*, Lady Augusta Gregory's *Spreading the News*, and John Millington Synge's *In the Shadow of the Glen*. This premiere set a standard that the company was to maintain for the next two decades. The company presented Synge's *The Playboy of the Western World* (greeted by rioters protesting the play as "a libel of the Irish character") in 1907 and his powerful tragedy *Deirdre of the Sorrows* in 1910. The twenties saw the presentation of Sean O'Casey's great tragicomic achievements: *The Shadow of a Gunman* (1923), *Juno and the Paycock* (1924), and *The Plough and the Stars* (1926), the latter causing another riot at the theater.

Although never matching the great achievements of its early years, the Abbey, which burned down in 1951 and reopened in 1966, continues to produce plays and players of unusually high quality, maintaining its status as one of the premier theaters in Europe.

Hugh Hunt's *The Abbey: Ireland's National Theatre, 1904–1978* (1979) offers a historical overview of the Abbey's productions, politics and personalities. Adrian Frazier's *Behind the Scenes* (1990) is a witty and provocative reading of the Abbey's early years viewed from the perspective of NEW HISTORICISM.

Absolute, the   In philosophy, the principle of fundamental reality that underlines and sustains the various forms it assumes in the world. Although the idea of an unconditioned Absolute is as old as Plato, the term is associated with 19th-century German idealist philosophy, most notably in the work of G. W. F. Hegel. Hegel maintained "the Absolute is spirit; this is the highest definition of the absolute." For Hegel, the role of great art—for example, Greek tragedy—was to provide the average person with an approach to the Absolute that was more accessible than philosophy.

Samuel Taylor Coleridge adopted this principle in developing his theory of literature, a theory in which NATURE appears as the Absolute. Coleridge's conception assumed a dominant place in 19th-century literary theory. Among reactions in the early years of the 20th century to Coleridge's ROMANTICISM, the movement known as the NEW HUMANISM, led by the scholars Irving Babbitt and Paul Elmer More, called for a rejection of transcendental, idealist terms, of which the Coleridgean Absolute was a major example.

Jacques Derrida, the principal exponent of DECONSTRUCTION, criticized Western thought for operating on the basis of LOGOCENTRISM, the belief that there exists an Absolute, a "logos" that transcends the limitations of language.

The scholar Robert Calasso used the term *absolute literature* to describe writings that reveal a search for an absolute. (*See also* GODS.)

Paul Elmer More's *The Demon of the Absolute* (1928) constitutes a strong indictment of the Absolute; Robert Harland's *Superstructuralism* (1987) provides a thoughtful analysis of Derrida's argument. Robert Calasso's study is *Literature and the Gods* (2001).

abstract expressionism   *See* ACTION PAINTING.

absurd   Ridiculous or unreasonable, a definition that has been extended to characterize human life. In the 20th-century philosophy of EXISTENTIALISM, the French writer Albert Camus employed the term to describe the futility of human existence, which he compared to the story of Sisyphus, the figure in Greek mythology condemned for eternity to push a stone to the top of a mountain only to have it roll back down again.

In the wake of two world wars, the principle of absurdity found fertile soil in the imaginations of modern writers. An early example is the fiction of Franz Kafka, peopled with guilt-ridden, alienated, grotesquely comic characters. In the 1950s a group of playwrights created a new form of drama, which the critic Martin Esslin named "the theatre of the absurd," to describe plays that abandoned traditional construction and conventional dialogue. These plays were notable for their illogical structure and the irrational behavior of their characters. Chief among the absurdist playwrights was Samuel Beckett, whose *Waiting for Godot* (1953) and *Endgame* (1957) had a revolutionary impact on modern drama. In *Waiting for Godot,* two tramps wait for Godot, who sends a message every day that he will meet them tomorrow. They pass the time engaging in comic stage business, trying to remember where they are and how they got there—as one character puts it, "Anything to give us the illusion we exist." The second act repeats the first with slight variations; Godot never arrives, and the two tramps continue to wait.

Other "absurdists" include Eugene Ionesco (*Rhinoceros,* 1960) and Arthur Adamov (*Ping Pong,* 1955) in France, Harold Pinter (*The Caretaker,* 1959) in England, and Edward Albee (*The American Dream,* 1961) in the United States.

In FICTION, two of the best known novels of the 1950s and '60s, Joseph Heller's *Catch-22* (1961) and Gunther Grass's *The Tin Drum* (1959), captured the absurdist theme and style.

Albert Camus's *The Myth of Sisyphus* (1955) is an extended treatment of the absurd applied to human existence. Martin Esslin's *The Theatre of the Absurd* (1961) is a landmark study of its subject; its third edition (1980) includes the author's reservations about the popularization of the term.

academic discourse   A general term for the written language used by college and university faculty members. Some academics hold that the term should be plural, reflecting the range and variety of linguistic conventions that separate, for example, writing in psychology from that in art history. But despite wide differences in vocabulary and style, there are some agreed-upon features common to most academic prose, notably professional terminology (*see* JARGON) and rather strict criteria in determining the proof of an argument. In other words, academic discourse traditionally tends to subordinate rhetoric to logic, maintaining the appeal to reason as the highest standard of discursive language use.

Occasionally that standard is questioned or challenged by the scholars themselves. One example concerns the Shakespearean scholar Stephen Greenblatt, an exemplary practitioner of academic discourse in the books and articles he has written in connection with NEW HISTORICISM. In 2004, Greenblatt published a popular biography of Shakespeare (*Will in the World*), in which he speculates about his subject, not only rather loosely by academic standards, but substantially contradicting the thrust of his earlier works on Shakespeare's plays, producing a generally negative reaction among his academic peers. On the other hand, nonacademic reviewers and general readers have responded very positively to the biography, applauding the author for having "liberated Shakespeare from the professors and returning him to the people." The controversy illustrates the differences generated by different discourses, and the perils of attempting a crossover from one to the other.

In COMPOSITION STUDIES, academic discourse serves as a reminder of the gap between the expectations of the traditional college teacher and the student. The latter, particularly in a BASIC WRITING course, frequently feels overwhelmed by the attempt to mimic or imitate academic discourse in a writing assignment. The effort to sound "academic" usually results in a greater failure than had the student used his/her own "voice." One consequence has been a growing pedagogical interest in the WRITING ACROSS THE CURRICULUM movement in an attempt to introduce beginning writers to the forms and conventions of the major academic disciplines.

Marjorie Garber looks at the pros and cons of academic discourse in her *Academic Instincts* (2001).

academic fiction *See* CAMPUS NOVEL.

Académie française Powerful French academy founded in 1635 by Cardinal Richelieu, chief minister during King Louis XIII's reign, and still a force in contemporary French culture. The Académie continues to exercise its authority, overseeing and attempting to control developments in the language. Its most recent efforts, a measure of its linguistic conservatism, have been directed against the employment of loan words from other languages. The group also bestows various awards and prizes for distinguished literary achievements.

The Académie consists of 40 members, all prominent intellectuals and formerly all-male until 1980, when the novelist Marguerite Yourcenar was elected its first female member.

Academy An olive grove near Athens where Plato and his followers established a school (called the Academy) for the study of philosophy. *Academy* or *academe* are general terms for the university or the academic community. The name is alluded to in a line from the Roman poet Ovid, "And pursue truth in the groves of academe," which serves as the ironic epigraph to Mary McCarthy's satiric CAMPUS NOVEL *The Groves of Academe* (1952).

Academy Awards Annual awards given by the American Academy of Motion Picture Arts and Sciences. The symbol of the award is an "Oscar" (the origin of the name is disputed), a gold-plated statuette of a sword-bearing knight standing on rolls of film. The awards cover 23 categories of filmmaking, including Best Picture, Best Director, Best Foreign Language Film, four acting awards (Best Leading Actor and Actress, Best Supporting Actor and Actress), two writing awards (Best Original Screenplay, Best Adaptation), two music awards (Best Song, Best Original Score), two short films awards (Best Animated Film, Best Live), two documentaries (Best Feature, Best Short Subject), and awards for art direction, cinematography, costume, design, editing, sound, sound effects, visual effects, and makeup.

The awards ceremony, usually occurring in March of the year following the films' original showing, is the world's most widely viewed television event. Though almost always seen in retrospect as disappointing and overly long, the ceremony never fails to attract a large audience, lured by its potpourri of glamour, humor, and suspense. Despite their popularity, the awards have been frequently criticized for the voters' tendency to select personal favorites and blockbuster films rather than making quality judgments. The blockbuster preference is presumably related to the belief that the success of such films is always "good for the industry." Critics cite as evidence the fact that the two winners of the largest number of awards— 11 each—were for two epical films, *Ben-Hur* (1959) and *Titanic* (2001).

Emanuel Levy's *Oscar Fever* (2001) offers a serious, intelligent history of the awards.

accent   A regular recurring stress in a line of verse. In poetry written in English, the order and number of accented syllables determine the METER of a line or an entire poem. For example, if the order of stress is an unaccented syllable followed by an accented one, the two syllables constitute an iambic FOOT. A line containing five such feet is in iambic pentameter, as in this line from Alexander Pope:

˘   /   ˘   /   ˘   /   ˘   /   ˘   /
The proper study of mankind is man.

acrostic   A poem in which the first letter in each line spells out a word. A well-known example is the notoriously sentimental MOTHER acrostic. The form's low repute as a literary device is reflected in John Dryden's satiric poem "MacFlecknoe" (1682), in which he advises his hapless adversary to:

Leave writing plays, and choose for thy command
Some peaceful province in Acrostic land.
There thou mayest wings display and altars raise,
And torture one poor word ten thousand ways.

act   The major division of a DRAMA. The ELIZABETHAN five-act structure derives from the Roman playwright Seneca. Modern drama allows for considerable variation in the number of acts within a play, although the majority of contemporary plays are written in two acts. Many plays have adapted the EPIC THEATER structure of Bertolt Brecht, which substitutes a series of episodes, or self-contained incidents, for the act structure.

action   The sequence of events in a novel or play. Aristotle's definition of tragedy as "an imitation of an action" underscores his contention that action rather than character is the central element in a tragic play. What he seems to emphasize is not simply what the characters do but also what underlies their specific acts. The tragic action, for example, appears to be a threefold movement, characterized by the critic Kenneth Burke as the "purpose, passion and perception" of the tragic protagonist: the tragic hero begins with a specific purpose, undergoes a trial by suffering (passion), and emerges with a fuller, although tragic, sense of his own identity (perception). The idea of speech as a form of action is a major principle of SPEECH ACT THEORY.

Kenneth Burke analyzes the tragic rhythm of action in his *A Grammar of Motives* (1945).

action painting   A term coined by the critic Harold Rosenberg to describe a central principle of the Abstract Expressionist art movement that developed in the 1940s and '50s. The goal of action painting was to capture the act of *creating* the painting: the painting itself was to be seen simply as the representation of the act of producing it. Jackson Pollock's technique of dripping paint as he walked over his canvas is a prime example of action painting.

Such painting is "expressionist" in that it is an expression of the artist in action. It is "abstract" in that it represents not a picture of the world but something that comes into existence in the act of making it. The emphasis in action painting is not on the eye but on the hand. The movement of the line within the painting involves its viewers, inviting them to become part of the process of creation.

The principle of action painting was incorporated into the work of the NEW YORK SCHOOL of poetry. One member of the school, Frank O'Hara, a museum curator and friend of many abstract expressionist painters, described the appeal of the new art movement: "Poetry was declining/Painting advancing/We were complaining/it was '50." The influence of action painting on the New York School is evident in O'Hara's attempt to present directly the poet in the process of composing.

Harold Rosenberg's essays are collected in his *Act and the Actor* (1970). Jerome Klinkowitz has studied the impact of action painting on subsequent artistic, literary, and critical movements in *Rosenberg/Barthes/Hassan* (1988).

actor-manager   The designation for a leading actor who is also the manager of a theater or repertory troupe. In the French theater the tradition was established by Molière, who in addition to acting and managing his troupe, was also its chief playwright.

In the English and American theater, the tradition of the actor who also served as director and producer was dominant from the end of the 17th century to the beginning of the 20th. Among the most celebrated actor-managers were David Garrick in the 18th century, Henry Irving and, in America, Edwin Booth in the 19th. Among fictional actor-managers, the genial Mr. Crummles, in Charles Dickens's *Nicholas Nickleby* (1839) is memorable.

A moving homage to the actor-manager tradition is captured in the play, and later film, *The Dresser* (1981), which skillfully depicts the relationship of the actor-manager and his dresser as paralleling that of King Lear and his Fool.

Actors' Studio   *See* METHOD ACTING.

adage   *See* PROVERB.

adaptation   The employment of material in one medium or genre for use in another as, for example, when a novel is made into a film. Many of Shakespeare's plays are adaptations of prose narratives, and those plays have become in turn the SOURCE of countless novels, poems, films, operas, and ballets. Adaptation is one form of the practice contemporary theorists refer to as INTERTEXTUALITY.

adultery   One of the major themes in the history of literature, a recurrent feature of TRAGEDY, COMEDY, ROMANCE, and the NOVEL. Marriage and the family have constituted the linchpin of the social order, guaranteeing society's survival and continuity. In this context adultery may have served a dual and contradictory role: both as threat to society and as safety valve, an outlet for the oppressive features of marriage. The literature of adultery reflects this ambivalence from the beginning. In Homer's *Iliad,* the adulterous relation of Paris and Helen is the catastrophic cause of the Trojan War, while the New Testament account of the woman taken in adultery, with Jesus' injunction that punishment of the woman belongs only to "he who is without sin," underscores the ubiquity of the sin along with the need for compassion.

Medieval romances, such as those surrounding the ARTHURIAN LEGEND or the story of Tristan and Iseult, often emphasize the destructive nature of adulterous passion. In medieval and Renaissance comedy, particularly FARCE, the emphasis frequently falls on cuckoldry, usually with the suggestion of adultery as a form of justified revenge; Machiavelli's *Mandragola* (1518) is a representative example. Shakespeare offers a distinctive variation on the tradition, focusing on *imagined* cuckoldry, a theme that forms the basis not only of such farces as *The Merry Wives of Windsor* and romances like *The Winter's Tale* but also, most memorably, the tragic action of *Othello*.

According to the critic Tony Tanner, adultery was a particularly fertile theme for the 19th-century novel, providing the opportunity to explore the instability of marriage at the historical moment when marriage was beginning to be seen in conflict with the desire for individual freedom. Undoubtedly this development was also intensely connected to the changing definitions of the nature and roles of women. In novels such as Flaubert's *Madame Bovary* (1856–57), Tolstoy's *Anna*

Karenina (1875–77) and Hawthorne's *The Scarlet Letter* (1850), the centrality of the woman and the complexity of her role anticipate this shift in mood. Although the heroines of all three of these novels commit adultery and are punished as social outcasts, they also achieve an authentic sense of self from the adulterous experience and the suffering that follows it.

Among 20th-century novelists, John Updike is noted for his concentration on the theme. Updike's approach is distinguished by his representation of adultery as a spiritual transgression instead of a social threat. In focusing on this spiritual or religious dimension, he follows his progenitor, Nathaniel Hawthorne. *The Scarlet Letter,* in fact, forms the basis of three novels by Updike (*A Month of Sundays,* 1975; *Roger's Version,* 1986; and *S,* 1988) in which the perspectives of the three main characters of the Hawthorne novel (Arthur Dimmesdale, Roger Chillingworth, and Hester Prynne) are recreated in contemporary terms.

The influence of the "myth of adultery" is traced in Denis de Rougemont's *Love in the Western World* (1940). Tony Tanner's *Adultery in the Novel* (1979) examines the theme in key 19th-century European novels. Donald Greiner's *Adultery in the American Novel* (1985) looks at the uses of the theme in the works of Nathaniel Hawthorne, Henry James, and John Updike.

adventure story   A type of fiction that usually includes suspense, excitement, physical danger, travel to exotic settings, and an intrepid hero/heroine. In many of these respects, the adventure story is kin to the ROMANCE, but the adventure story relies on a series of exciting episodes unified by the theme of a search for a lost person, place, or object. The prototype of the form is Homer's *Odyssey,* in which the hero faces a series of threatening situations as he attempts to voyage home.

The adventure story is one of the staples of CHILDREN'S LITERATURE, such as Robert Louis Stevenson's *Treasure Island* (1883). In film, the form is a key element of the SERIAL.

advertising   Although the history of advertising dates back to classical times, it did not emerge as a powerful force in society until the industrial age in the 19th century. Literature and advertising share a common purpose, to have its audiences engage in the WILLING SUSPENSION OF DISBELIEF. However, where literary work asks you merely to accept the temporary illusion that its characters are real and its events really happening, the advertisement asks you to carry its illusion into the real world by buying its product or electing its candidate.

In *Advertising Fictions* (1988), Jennifer Wickes looks at the relationship of advertising and literature through the lenses of three writers, Charles Dickens, Henry James, and James Joyce, whose novels, she suggests, represent three stages in the interaction of advertising and literature: advertising's borrowing from literature, its emergence as a perceived threat, and its ultimate triumph. She begins with a seminal example, a jingle written on a bottle of shoe polish , made by the Warren factory in London, as "one of the first examples of an individually packaged product with a textual accompaniment." When Charles Dickens was forced to work as a child, he was employed at Warren's, pasting those labels on bottles. As a young man, Dickens later wrote advertising copy for Warren's. Thus, at an early age he became conscious of advertising's power, assigning it a significant role in his novels and employing it in their sales campaigns. In *The Old Curiosity Shop* (1841), for example, the shop, which deals with relics of a dead past, is itself a relic, symbolized by the fact that it has no sign advertising itself. Little Nell, the novel's heroine, moves from the shop to become a model, used to advertise Mrs. Jarley's waxworks museum. The author's attitude toward advertising is evident in the name he gives the advertising copywriter, Slum. But Dickens's own reliance on advertising is evident in his use of it in his financially successful reading tours in which the texts of his novels become the advertisements for his readings.

To illustrate the second phase when advertising emerges as a formidable threat to literature, Wickes sees Henry James as an author sensitive to the impending "usurpation and displacement of literature that loomed on the horizon." A specific example of that threat is the figure in James's *The Ambassadors* (1903) of Chad Newsome, whose idyll in Europe must end. He is being called back to America to assume a critical role in the family business by becoming the head of the advertising department. Chad readily abandons his lover for the lure of advertising, which he describes as "an art. . . and infinite like all the arts. . . in the hands, naturally, of a master."

The third stage of interaction, Wickes maintains, finds a reversal of the earlier relationship. Now literature borrows the language of advertising in the vocabulary and thought of one of the 20th century's most celebrated characters, Leopold Bloom, the central figure of James Joyce's *Ulysses* (1922). Bloom is an advertising canvasser, soliciting ads for local newspapers. In the process, he has absorbed the language and slogans of advertising, of which, as his INTERIOR MONOLOGUE reveals, he is a walking repository. As a result, according to Wickes, the novel "performs a tango with advertising and is set to its music." Wickes's point is a striking one, but for many readers, the notion that the language of advertising dominates the rich linguistic tapestry that is *Ulysses* would seem to be overstating the case. Closer to the truth is her general proposition· Advertising's rise to power has been accompanied by a comparable decline in the influence of literature.

aestheticism In French and English literature, a 19th-century movement that maintained art need serve no moral or ethical purpose (*see* ART FOR ART'S

SAKE). In the preface to his novel *Mademoiselle de Maupin* (1838), the French poet and novelist Thèophile Gautier proclaimed the only purpose of art was to be beautiful. The French SYMBOLIST poets attempted to translate that principle into practice.

In England the major texts of the aesthetic movement were Swinburne's *Poems and Ballads* (1866) and Walter Pater's *Studies in the History of the Renaissance* (1873), which concludes with the famous invitation to "burn with a hard gem-like flame" in the "desire for beauty, the love of art for its own sake." The best-known advocate of aestheticism was Oscar Wilde, who at the end of his life lamented in *De Profundis* (1905), "I treated art as the supreme reality and life as a mere mode of fiction." FORMALISM represents a modified, less extreme form of aestheticism.

R. V. Johnson's *Aestheticism* (1969) is an accessible treatment of the movement.

aesthetics   A branch of philosophy that explores the theory of the beautiful and the nature of art. As a separate field of study, it did not begin until the mid-18th century, but the questions it deals with date back at least to Plato and Aristotle. Among these questions are those relating to art as imitation, or MIMESIS, to the function of the artist in society, and to the impact of art on its audience.

The term *aesthetic distance* refers either to the artist's or the audience's relation to the art object. A satirical novelist such as Evelyn Waugh, for example, appears to be more removed from his characters and their fate than a romantic novelist such as Sir Walter Scott.

NEW CRITICISM emphasized the need for a certain detachment in order to understand without being swept away by the tide of emotion. A similar principle is implicit in Bertolt Brecht's ALIENATION EFFECT and in the concept of DEFAMILIARIZATION.

affective fallacy   A term in NEW CRITICISM used to describe the error, from a New Critical perspective, of analyzing a work of literature in terms of its impact upon a reader. The critics William Wimsatt and Monroe Beardsley coined the term to call attention to the distinction between the text of a work and "its results in the mind of its audience." For Wimsatt and Beardsley, any attempt to locate the meaning of a work within the mind of the reader "ends in impressionism and relativism."

A corollary fallacy, according to the same authors, the so-called INTENTIONAL FALLACY, lies in any attempt to see the meaning of a work as residing in the intention of the AUTHOR. For the New Critics, true meaning resided in "the text itself," the language of the poem or story.

One of the principal developments of a more recent critical school, READER RESPONSE CRITICISM, in the words of Jane Tompkins, "defines itself in direct opposition to the New Critical dictum issued by Wimsatt and Beardsley."

"The Affective Fallacy" is included in Wimsatt's *The Verbal Icon* (1954); Jane Tompkins's critique is featured in her critical anthology *Reader Response Criticism* (1980).

African-American literature   Long overlooked, the rich tradition of oral and written African-American literature had its beginnings in the songs, spirituals, and folktales of slaves working in the fields. By the late 18th century, a few slaves and former slaves, given the opportunity to read and write (an opportunity denied by law in many Southern states), published poetry. Notable among these were Jupiter Hammon and Phillis Wheatley, both slaves whose poems reflect a strong religious tone. In the early years of the 19th century a number of slaves, aided and encouraged by abolitionists, published autobiographical accounts of their experiences as slaves. These SLAVE NARRATIVES played a significant role in the anti-slavery movement that preceded the Civil War. In 1859, Harriet Wilson's *Our Nig; or, Sketches from the Life of a Free Black* was the first novel by an African-American writer to be published in the United States.

In the years following the Civil War, African-American literature began to reflect the frustrations and fears of a people who in large part continued to suffer from widespread discrimination and segregation. The poetry of Paul Laurence Dunbar and the prose of Charles Chesnutt touch upon these themes, as do autobiographical works such as Booker T. Washington's *Up from Slavery* (1901) and James Weldon Johnson's novel *The Autobiography of an Ex-Colored Man* (1912).

In the 1920s, the vast migration from the rural South to the urban North in the years leading up to and following World War I resulted in the HARLEM RENAISSANCE, the term for the period of outstanding literary activity centered in the Harlem section of New York City. During this period, Harlem served as a magnet for talented young black artists, writers, and musicians. Among the most memorable are the poets Langston Hughes (*The Weary Blues,* 1926), and Countee Cullen (*The Black Christ,* 1929), and the novelists Jean Toomer (*Cane,* 1923), Claude McKay (*Home to Harlem,* 1928), Arna Bontemps (*God Sends Sunday,* 1931), and Zora Neale Hurston (*Their Eyes Were Watching God,* 1937). Another distinguishing feature of these writers was their incorporation of the rhythms and themes of blues and JAZZ.

In the period preceding the Civil Rights movement of the 1960s, African-American literature was dominated by three novelists: Richard Wright, Ralph Ellison, and James Baldwin. Wright's *Native Son* (1940), Ellison's *The Invisible Man* (1952), and Baldwin's *Go Tell It on the Mountain* (1953) matched passion with eloquence and literary skill in their depictions of the African-American experience. In the wake of the Civil Rights movement a new generation of writers emerged, establishing in unequivocal fashion the centrality of the African-American experience in the consciousness of all Americans. In the hands of writers such as Maya Angelou (*I Know Why the Caged Bird Sings,* 1969), Ishmael Reed (*Mumbo Jumbo,* 1972), Alice Walker (*The Color Purple,* 1982), the playwright August Wilson (*Fences,* 1987), and the Nobel laureate Toni Morrison (*Beloved,* 1987), African-American literature has moved out of the ghetto onto the national stage.

The Norton Anthology of African American Literature, edited by William L. Andrews *et al.,* and *The Oxford Companion to African American Literature,* edited by Henry Louis Gates and Nellie Y. McKay (both 1997), provide comprehensive introductions to the African-American literary tradition.

Age of Johnson   In English literary history, the second half of the 18th century, a period dominated by the poet, critic, editor, and lexicographer Dr. Samuel Johnson. Traditionally regarded as a merely transitional phase in the movement from NEOCLASSICISM to ROMANTICISM, the age now commands more respect for a unique literary character of its own. The critic Northrop Frye has argued that a more accurate title for the period would be the Age of Sensibility, to emphasize that the poetry of Robert Burns, Thomas Gray, William Cowper, and William Blake offered a form of literature rooted in feeling and, in the case of Blake, the sense of the poet as a visionary. The poetry of the period also represents the movement toward nature and the power of the human mind when in contact with nature.

The great nonfiction prose works of the era were Gibbon's *Decline and Fall of the Roman Empire* (1776–87) and Boswell's *Life of Johnson* (1791). In drama the comedy of manners (*see* COMEDY) flourished in the hands of Richard Brinsley Sheridan (*The School for Scandal,* 1777) and Oliver Goldsmith (*She Stoops to Conquer,* 1773). The development of the NOVEL, begun earlier in the century, was enriched by Tobias Smollett's *Humphrey Clinker* (1771) and Laurence Sterne's *Tristram Shandy* (1760–67), one of the great comic novels in English.

The age also saw the production of two works that have been extremely influential in the development of modern RHETORIC, George Campbell's *The Philosophy of Rhetoric* (1776) and Hugh Blair's *Lectures on Rhetoric* (1783).

James Sambrook's *The Eighteenth Century: The Intellectual and Cultural Context of English Literature, 1700–1789* (1986) provides an invaluable introduction to the ideas and attitudes of the era. Northrop Frye's appeal for an "age of sensibility" is contained in his *Fables of Identity* (1963).

aging   The literature of aging and old age differs from nonliterary accounts of the process in its emphasis on individual experience, describing what it is like for a particular person at a particular point in time. As a result, taken as a whole, it is filled with contradictions and paradoxes, which see age, on the one hand, as the culmination of a rich and rewarding life, and on the other, as deterioration and dependence.

The dichotomy is well represented by two figures in Homer's *The Iliad*: Nestor, the aged Greek general, is renowned for his eloquence, wisdom, and sense of justice, all acquired in the experience of his long life. In contrast, Anchises, as a young man celebrated for his beauty, the lover of Aphrodite, now is weak, blind, having to be carried from the burning walls of Troy by his son, the Trojan hero Aeneas.

Between the heroic (Nestor) and the pathetic (Anchises) views of age stands the tragic. And that is embodied with unparalleled power in Shakespeare's portrait of King Lear. As the play opens, Lear is every inch the king, an imperious old man habituated to a lifetime of power, now demanding protestations of love from his three daughters. Thwarted by his youngest daughter, Cordelia, who refuses to play a hypocritical game, he unleashes his pent-up fury in rash, angry words—invoking the gods in his denunciation of her candor. When he discovers the true nature of his other daughters, he begins to lose his identity. "Who is it who can tell me who I am?" That is a question he must answer for himself as he undergoes the painful lessons of one who "has ever but slenderly known himself." In the process he becomes a "poor, naked wretch," who achieves insight in madness. But his suffering and the wisdom derived from it are finally eclipsed by the unanswerable question he poses to the dead body of Cordelia. "Why should a horse, a dog, a rat have life and thou no life at all?" He dies having learned what it means to be human, having paid an awful price in the process.

At the polar opposite of the view of age in *King Lear* is Robert Browning's depiction in *Rabbi Ben Ezra*:

> *Grow old along with me*
> *The best is yet to be*

The Rabbi urges us to use the limitations, the aches and pains of age, as spurs to participate in life, but always in the recognition that there is a divinity that shapes our ends.

In the 20th century the religious coda is less in evidence as we are enjoined to experience life fiercely, in Dylan Thomas's words, to "not go gently into that good night." A memorable representative of this conviction is Zorba in Nikos Kasantzakis's *Zorba the Greek* (1946; tr. 1952), whose passionate commitment to life leaves him open to all experience, including death.

A less romantic view of age—one closer to contemporary experience—is meticulously portrayed in the last two volumes of John Updike's Rabbit tetralogy, *Rabbit is Back* (1981) and *Rabbit at Rest* (1990), while the depiction of the protagonist of Marilynne Robinson's *Gilead* (2004), a Protestant minister of a small congregation in Iowa, now in his seventies, suggests the continuing value of religious belief in imbuing the life of an aged person with a sense of the beauty of existence.

Barbara Frey Waxman's *From the Hearth to the Open Road* (1990) is an interesting feminist study of aging in contemporary literature.

agitprop   The use of literature to promote a political or ideological goal. The term—a fusion of *agitation* and *propaganda*—derives from the early years of the Soviet regime in Russia. The Soviets instituted a policy of agitation and propaganda to encourage popular participation in the goals of the Communist government. Using songs, films, and plays, agitprop agents brought the party line to towns and villages throughout the Soviet Union. In the 1920s and '30s, forms of agitprop spread throughout Europe and the United States. A celebrated American example of the form is Clifford Odets's *Waiting for Lefty* (1935), a passionate pro-labor union drama focusing on a taxi drivers' strike.

agon   A Greek word for struggle or conflict. In classical drama, it denotes the portion of the play, both in tragedy and comedy, in which two characters, each one supported by members of the CHORUS, engage in heated debate. The agon was a feature of both comedy and tragedy.

The term is generally used in contemporary criticism as a synonym for a competitive struggle, particularly in the criticism of Harold Bloom, who depicts literary history in terms of the conflict between a "strong" poet and a significant predecessor whom the strong poet feels he must, in the reenactment of an Oedipal struggle, displace.

Harold Bloom's *Agon: Towards a Theory of Revisionism* (1982) is a collection of essays employing his theory.

AIDS   In the relatively brief period since its outbreak in the early 1980s, AIDS (acquired immunodeficiency syndrome) has resulted in the production of a large body of literature. Most of this work has formed the central theme of contemporary GAY LITERATURE. As the disease achieves the dimension of a worldwide epidemic, however, a small but increasing proportion of AIDS literature is being written by nongays.

Much of the early AIDS literature was angry, direct, and combative, striving to overcome the hostility, superstition, and fear that greeted the disease. While more recent literature has retained this angry tone, it has been tempered by infusions of comedy and the themes of love, compassion, and remembrance.

Among the early accounts of the disease was Armistead Maupin's *Tales of the City,* originally serialized in the San Francisco *Chronicle,* published in book form in 1984, and later dramatized on public television, and Larry Kramer's play *The Normal Heart* (1985), the first play to bring AIDS to the attention of the general public. The outstanding chronicler of the disease in fiction is Paul Monette, who died of AIDS in 1995. Monette's memoirs *Borrowed Time* (1988) and *Becoming a Man* (1992), and his novels *Afterlife* (1990) and *Halfway Home* (1991), affirm the strengths of homosexual love in the face of death. Monette is also the author of a moving collection of poems celebrating the life of his deceased lover, *Love Alone: Eighteen Elegies for Rog* (1988).

In drama, the AIDS crisis forms the center of the most acclaimed American play in many years, Tony Kushner's *Angels in America* (1989), a two-part drama that touches on a broad range of themes with AIDS playing a central role. Outstanding among nonfiction accounts of the disease is Randy Shilts's *And the Band Played On* (1987).

Among the nongay literature of AIDS, a notable example is Alice Hoffman's *At Risk* (1988), the account of an eleven-year-old girl's contracting AIDS from a blood transfusion.

In film, the epidemic has been captured in *Longtime Companion* (1990) and *Philadelphia* (1993). In the latter film 53 AIDS infected people were employed in bit parts; by the end of 1994, 43 of them had died, a gruesome reminder of the close connection between fiction and fact.

AIDS: The Literary Response, edited by Emmanuel Nelson (1992), is a collection of critical essays examining the literature of the crisis from a variety of perspectives. *Confronting AIDS Through Literature,* edited by Judith Laurence Pastore (1993), provides a variety of views on using literature as a means of understanding the disease and its ramifications.

alazon   A Greek term meaning impostor. The alazon is a stock figure in COMEDY, frequently taking the form of the miles gloriosus (the BRAGGART WARRIOR) or the learned bore ("the pedant"). He sometimes figures in the comic plot as one of the suitors of the heroine and is frequently set up in contrast to his opposite, the EIRON. Modern versions of the alazon figure include the figures of the professor in Chekhov's *Uncle Vanya* (1899) and Captain Boyle in Sean O'Casey's *Juno and the Paycock* (1924).

alcohol A prominent feature in DRAMA, alcohol is a constitutive aspect of its very foundation. In his *Poetics*, Aristotle asserts that drama emerges from hymns in praise of Dionysus, the god of wine. (*See* APOLLONIAN/DIONYSIAN). Drinking and drunkenness plays a central role both in comedy, from Rabelais' *Gargantua* (1534) to W.C. Fields, and in tragedy, from Euripides' *Bacchae* (c. 405 B.C.) to Eugene O'Neill's *Long Day's Journey into Night* (1940).

In addition to his portrayal of collective drunkenness as one aspect of the occult powers accorded to followers of Dionysus, Euripides depicts the peril of individual drunkenness in his *Alcestis* (438 B.C.), in which Heracles' inebriated state almost leads to catastrophe.

The reverse side of the warning about the evils of alcohol forms the climax of Rabelais' *Gargantua and Pontagruel* (1532–64), in which the pilgrimage to the Oracle of the Holy Bottle leads to the oracular message, "Drink."

Shakespeare's notable drinkers, Sir Toby Belch in *Twelfth Night* and Falstaff in his three plays, also celebrate the state of inebriation. More realistically, the Drunken Porter in *Macbeth* sees drink as playing an equivocal role in one area: "Lechery, Sir, it provokes and unprovokes; it provokes the desire, but it takes away the performance."

Another notable imbiber is Sidney Carton, in Charles Dickens's *A Tale of Two Cities* (1859), who before sacrificing his life to save another declares, "It is a far, far better thing I do than anything I have ever done."

But despite its long lineage, alcohol does not "come of age" until the 20th century, when writers begin to examine the major role it plays in the lives of their characters. This is particularly true of modern American literature, where an astonishingly high number of the best writers have been outright alcoholics or extremely heavy drinkers. One reason for this phenomenon, it has been suggested, was Prohibition, which turned drinking into a defiant, rebellious act. Whatever the reason, the names of writers who came of age during the Prohibition years and became addicted include F. Scott Fitzgerald, Ernest Hemingway, William Faulkner, Sinclair Lewis, John Steinbeck, John Cheever, Norman Mailer, Ring Lardner, Dashiell Hammet, Thomas Wolfe, Malcolm Lowry, the playwrights Eugene O'Neill and Tennessee Williams, the poets Hart Crane, Theodore Roethke, James Dickey, John Berryman, and Robert Lowell.

Many of these writers engaged the subject of alcoholism in their writing. Among the finest explorations of the experience is Malcolm Lowry's *Under the Volcano* (1947), which records the disintegration of an alcoholic British consul in Mexico. The hallucinatory visions and voices he experiences are interwoven throughout the novel, suggesting analogies between the alcoholic's disintegration and that of Europe on the brink of World War II.

Another powerful and illuminating account of the alcoholic experience written by one who knew it at firsthand, is Eugene O'Neill's *The Iceman Cometh* (1939, pub. 1946), in which reformed drinker Hickey forces the alcoholic habitues of Harry's Bar to recognize their pathetic self-deceptions as "pipe dreams." But at the play's conclusion he confesses that he himself has killed his faithful wife and is going to turn himself in. When he leaves, the drinkers fall back into their self-deceptive illusions.

Notable novels written by writers who were not themselves problem drinkers are Graham Greene's study of an alcoholic priest hunted by an anticlerical government in 1930s Mexico, *The Power and the Glory* (1940), and Saul Bellow's *The Victim* (1947), in which the alcoholic Albee uses drink to achieve an abandonment, a loss of self that he thinks of as heroic, while his counterpart Levenson overcomes his fear of failure, which for him has been embodied in the person of Albee.

Two films dealing with alcoholism are Billy Wilder's *The Lost Weekend* (1947) based on a novel by Charles Jackson, and Mike Figgis's *Leaving Las Vegas* (1995).

Thomas B. Gilmore's *Equivocal Spirits: Alcohol and Drinking in Twentieth-Century Literature* (1987) is an excellent account of the ways in which "literature may confirm, intensify, dramatize, extend, and occasionally even challenge" scientific studies of alcoholism.

alexandrine   In PROSODY a line of six iambic feet (12 syllables). The standard line in traditional French verse, it is rarely used in English. A notable exception: Edmund Spenser's *The Faerie Queene*, which consists of nine-line stanzas, the first eight in iambic pentameter, with the ninth line an alexandrine.

alienation   The sense of estrangement from society or the self, identified in philosophy, the social sciences, and literature as a central feature of modern life. This pervasive use of the term derives from the 19th-century German philosophers G. W. F. Hegel and Karl Marx. For Hegel, alienation is the inevitable condition arising from the gap between human consciousness and the natural world, between the inner world and the outer world. Marx adapted the term to describe the condition of workers in industrialized, capitalist society, deprived of the satisfaction of experiencing their work as a meaningful expression of themselves. Reduced to viewing the fruits of their labor as objects and commodities, modern workers, according to Marx, experience alienation not only within themselves but also among one another because of the competitive ethos of capitalism. In the 20th century, social thinkers such as C. Wright Mills (*White Collar: The American Middle Classes*, 1951) and Herbert Marcuse (*One Dimensional Man: Studies in the Ideology of Advanced Industrial Society*, 1964), and psychologists such as Eric Fromm (*The Sane Society*, 1965) developed these terms further.

The Marxist sense of the term, however, has played a relatively minor role in literary history. As represented in literature, alienation tends to come closer to the Hegelian definition with its emphasis on the disparity between the self and the world, consciousness and the objects of consciousness. In its literary form, alienation emerges as a major theme with the birth of ROMANTICISM. Even here, however, it invokes an earlier time, for the icon of alienation in the Romantic period is doubtless Shakespeare's Hamlet. The introspective prince, alienated from his world and the role of avenger thrust upon him, is also alienated from himself, and acutely conscious of his condition. It is this painful self-consciousness that characterizes much of modern poetry, from the English Romantics and French Symbolists to T. S. Eliot's *The Waste Land* (1920) and the CONFESSIONAL POETRY of Robert Lowell and Sylvia Plath. Central to much of this poetry is not only a repudiation of modern culture but also an agonized self-estrangement that has come to serve as the signature of the modern artist.

In fiction, the alienated figures of 19th- and 20th-century literature— Dostoyevsky's Underground Man (*Notes from Underground,* 1864), Melville's Bartleby (*Bartleby the Scrivener,* 1850), Tolstoy's Ivan Ilych (*The Death of Ivan Ilych,* 1886), Kafka's Joseph K. (*The Trial,* 1925), Ellison's *Invisible Man* (1952), Salinger's Holden Caulfield (*The Catcher in the Rye,* 1951), and Camus's *The Stranger* (1942)— are only a few of the many figures haunted by the shallowness and hypocrisy of modern life. But on another level, these works point to a more profound malaise: the sense that human existence lacks any coherence or purpose, that life is finally ABSURD. The close association of this mood with the EXISTENTIALISM of Sartre and Camus is not accidental. In the wake of World War II, the alienation theme had merged with the larger current of existentialist thought and feeling.

In drama the alienated figure emerges in the tortured characters of Henrik Ibsen, the richly ironic tragicomic figures of Anton Chekhov, the haunted family of Eugene O'Neill's *Long Day's Journey Into Night* (1940), the film *personae* of James Dean, Jean-Paul Belmondo, and the young Marlon Brando, and, perhaps most explicitly, in the formulation from Sartre's *No Exit* (1945), "Hell is other people." *See* MODERNISM.

For a major study of literary alienation, see Erich Heller's *The Disinherited Mind* (1952). For a discussion of the existentialist connection see William Barrett's *Irrational Man: A Study in Existentialist Philosophy* (1958). The collection *Man Alone: Alienation in Modern Society* (1962), edited by Eric and Mary Josephson, is an anthology of classic writings on the subject.

alienation effect   A term coined by the German dramatist Bertolt Brecht to describe a desired detachment on the part of both actors and audience to prevent them from becoming emotionally involved in the action of the play. From Brecht's perspective the practice of being swept away in complete identification with the characters produces a reaction that is highly emotional but insufficiently critical and reflective. As a result, Brecht employed such features as placards, music, and personal asides designed to remind the audience that they are watching a play. His aim, part of his commitment to MARXIST CRITICISM, was for the audience to examine the social and economic causes that lay beyond the actions and conditions in his plays. Ironically, playwrights in the West have adopted these techniques while they were rejected in countries under Communist control. *See* EPIC THEATER.

Martin Esslin's *Brecht: The Man and His Work* (1960) offers an excellent survey of Brecht's achievement as a dramatist.

allegory   A type of NARRATIVE in which the surface story reflects at least one other meaning. Traditional allegory frequently employs PERSONIFICATION, the use of human characters to represent abstract ideas. Medieval MORALITY PLAYS were allegories in which abstractions such as Mankind, Good Deeds, Penance, and Death appeared as characters.

Another type of allegory uses the surface story to refer to historical or political events and persons. Jonathan Swift's *Tale of a Tub* (1704), for example, provides a satirical allegory of the REFORMATION. In his *Anatomy of Criticism* (1957), Northrop Frye distinguishes between a continuous allegory, such as *The Faerie Queene* (1590–96), which maintains the allegorical meaning throughout the narrative, and intermittent allegory, such as in *The Scarlet Letter* (1850), where it "may be picked up and dropped at pleasure."

By the 19th century, allegorical technique had begun to fall from favor. Symbolism, another method of representing an alternative meaning, became the preferred form. Symbolism and allegory sometimes overlap, but there is an important distinction between the two. A symbol bears a natural relation to the events of the story: the whale in Herman Melville's *Moby Dick* (1851) is both a whale and a mysterious force. In allegory, the surface story is often an arbitrary excuse for the secondary meaning.

As a result, in the age of MODERNISM symbolism came to be preferred to the seemingly antiquated technique of allegory. More recently allegory has made a comeback, in theory if not in practice: DECONSTRUCTION argues that the arbitrary quality of allegory is an accurate reflection of the character of language itself. That is, deconstructionists see the idea of a "natural" relation between a word and the object to which it refers as a comforting illusion. For them, the reality is closer to that depicted in allegory.

An additional use of the term is as the second of the FOUR LEVELS OF MEANING in medieval exegeses of biblical and literary texts.

Northrop Frye discusses allegory in his *Anatomy of Criticism* (1957). C. S. Lewis's *The Allegory of Love* (1936) provides a clear discussion of the traditional sense of the term. Paul DeMan's *Allegories of Reading* (1979) reflects the deconstructionist sense.

alliteration   The repetition of stressed initial sounds in a group of words that are closely connected to one another. A common feature of traditional poetry and, to a lesser extent, of prose, alliteration is a distinctive feature of OLD ENGLISH poetry, as in this line from *Beowulf:* "From a friendless foundling, feeble and wretched." Alliteration also plays an important role in MIDDLE ENGLISH literature, as in this line from *Sir Gawain and the Green Knight:* "The battlements broken down and burnt to brands and ashes." Modern poets use it sparingly, or in a mocking, ironic context.

Christopher Ricks's *Allusion to the Poets* (2002) is a stimulating treatment of the subject.

alternative history   *See* COUNTERFACTUAL FICTION.

allusion   A reference within a literary text to some person, place, or event outside the text. Allusions that refer to events more or less contemporary with the text are called *topical* allusions. Those referring to specific people are *personal* allusions. An example of a topical allusion is the reference of the drunken porter in *Macbeth* to "an equivocator . . . who committed treason enough for God's sake . . ." This is a reference to Father Henry Garnet, a Jesuit priest who justified equivocation (a form of lying) during his trial for treason in connection with the Gunpowder Plot of 1605. An example of personal allusion is William Butler Yeats's reference to "golden thighed Pythagoras" in his poem "Among School Children."

Other uses of an allusion might be to summarize an important idea (as in the concluding line from *King Kong:* "It was Beauty killed the Beast"), or to point to an ironic contrast between contemporary life and a heroic past (as in James Joyce's classical parallels in *Ulysses* [1922], in which the heroic deeds in the *Odyssey* are implicitly contrasted to the banal details of everyday life in modern Dublin).

In film, *homage* is the term for one director's allusion to another's work.

ambiguity   In ordinary usage the term refers to a lack of clarity in a situation or in an expression. In language use it is generally regarded as an error or flaw. This view of the term was dominant until the publication of William Empson's *Seven Types of Ambiguity* (1930), a work that had a powerful impact on the development of NEW CRITICISM and of subsequent literary theory (*see* INDETERMINACY).

Empson used the term to describe a literary technique in which a word or phrase conveys two or more different meanings. He defined ambiguity as "any verbal nuance, however slight, which gives room for alternative reactions to the same piece of language." Included among the "seven types" is the traditional meaning of the term, but the chief interest of the book lies in examples of the ways in which ambiguity can enhance the experience of poetry.

An example of Empson's analysis is his discussion of a line from Shakespeare's Sonnet 73. In the poem the speaker compares his advancing age to a tree in early winter and the boughs of that tree to "Bare ruined choirs where late the sweet birds sang." The reference here is to the abandoned Catholic monasteries where choir boys once sang. Here is Empson's analysis:

> The comparison is sound because ruined monastery choirs are places to sing, because they involve sitting in a row, because they are made of wood, . . . because they are now abandoned by all but the grey walls coloured like the skies of winter, because the cold and narcissistic charm suggested by the choir boys suits well with Shakespeare's feeling for the object of the Sonnets [the young gentleman to whom the sonnets are addressed], and for various sociological and historical reasons (the Protestant destruction of monasteries, fear of puritanism) . . . and many more relating the simile to its place in the Sonnet, must all combine to give the line its beauty, and there is a sort of ambiguity in not knowing which of them to hold most clearly in mind.

Seven Types of Ambiguity represents the first sustained analysis of the phenomenon of multiple meaning, or PLURISIGNATION.

Empson's considerable contribution to 20th-century criticism is discussed in Christopher Norris's *William Empson and the Philosophy of Literary Criticism* (1978).

American renaissance   A term for a period of American literature that saw a remarkable outburst of creativity in American letters. The American critic F. O. Matthiessen first employed the term to describe the major works of Emerson (*Essays*, 1841, *Poems*, 1847); Thoreau (*Walden*, 1854); Hawthorne (*The Scarlet Letter*, 1850); Melville (*Moby Dick*, 1851), and Whitman (*Leaves of Grass*, 1855). Now the term is used to describe the entire American literary output in the 30 years preceding the Civil War. Critical to the development of literature and thought in the period was the movement known as TRANSCENDENTALISM, a rich mixture of Romantic ideas and American individualism.

In addition to the outstanding figures listed above, the period also boasted four poets, venerated in their own time and even today looked upon as important figures in the development of American poetry: Henry Wadsworth Longfellow (*The Song of Hiawatha,* 1855), Oliver Wendell Holmes ("The Wonderful One Hoss Shay," 1858), John Greenleaf Whittier (*Voices of Freedom,* 1846), and James Russell Lowell (*The Biglow Papers,* 1848). Unlike these poets, Edgar Allan Poe was almost completely neglected in his time, yet he made the greater impact on literary history. Poe's poetry and criticism proved to be an important influence on the French SYMBOLIST poets, and his fiction helped to create two unique genres, the DETECTIVE STORY and HORROR FICTION.

Other important developments in the period were the publication of SLAVE NARRATIVES and of Harriet Beecher Stowe's fictional indictment of slavery *Uncle Tom's Cabin* (1852).

F. O. Matthiessen's study, generally considered a seminal work of American literary criticism, is *The American Renaissance: Art and Experience in the Age of Emerson and Whitman* (1941). Writing from a feminist perspective, Charlene Avallone has challenged Matthiessen's exclusion of women writers in "What American Renaissance? The Gendered Genealogy of a Critical Discourse" in *PMLA* (October 1997), 1102–20. In *Beneath the American Renaissance* (1980), David Reynolds maintains that the major authors were heavily indebted to the popular culture of the period.

anagnorisis   In DRAMA, a term describing the moment of discovery or recognition by the protagonist. In TRAGEDY such a moment frequently accompanies the PERIPETEIA, the reversal or downturn of his fortune, as in Oedipus's discovery of his true identity in Sophocles's *Oedipus Rex*. In COMEDY, the recognition leads to the happy ending, a connection parodied at the conclusion of Oscar Wilde's *The Importance of Being Earnest* (1895), where Jack, who has been pretending that his name was Ernest, discovers that Ernest really is his name.

anagogical   *See* FOUR LEVELS OF MEANING.

analogy   A comparison based upon a similarity between two things. As a figure of speech, analogy functions as an extended SIMILE or METAPHOR. As a mode of thought, it refers to the process of reasoning from parallel examples, for example, the common Renaissance belief that the four HUMORS in a person's body—blood, phlegm, choler, and bile—are analogous to the four elements in nature: earth, air, fire, and water.

anapest   A metrical FOOT containing two unaccented syllables followed by an accented syllable, as in this line from William Cowper:

ᵕ ᵕ / ᵕ ᵕ / ᵕ ᵕ / ᵕ ᵕ /
With a turf on my breast, and a stone on my head

22

anaphora In RHETORIC, a figure of speech in which a word or words are repeated, usually at the beginning of successive sentences or lines of verse. William Blake's "London" provides an example:

> *In every cry of every man*
> *In every infant's cry of fear*
> *In every vice, in every ban*
> *The mind-forg'd manacles I hear.*

anarchism Political creed advocating the elimination of governmental authority in favor of the voluntary association of individuals or groups. This sense of the term originated in the mid-1800s, first coined by the French political philosopher Pierre Proudhon. Earlier the term had been used, as it is still used today, to characterize groups who promote social chaos by TERRORISM or other violent means. In fact, anarchism has assumed a variety of forms that include nonviolent, pacifist groups as well as the more aggressive forms that involved anarchist communism and anarchosyndicalism, the alliance of anarchism and the trade union movement in France.

Among literary figures associated with anarchism, the outstanding figure is Leo Tolstoy, who advocated a Christian-based form of nonviolent resistance to the state. As for the more aggressive terrorist form of anarchism, the best-known writer to examine it is Joseph Conrad. In two penetrating, powerful novels, *The Secret Agent* (1907) and particularly *Under Western Eyes* (1911), he explores the impenetrable conflict of revolutionary violence and authoritarian despotism. Conrad's repudiation of anarchism is based on a profound belief in a natural order, always threatened, in his eyes, by the anarchist impulse.

According to the critic David Kadlec, the common association of anarchism with leftist movements has led to the failure to see the important impact of anarchist principles, on literary MODERNISM and American PRAGMATISM. Kadlec maintains that, despite their political differences, anarchists and pragmatists were as one in rejecting the notion of "foundations," the idea of a bedrock, underlying truth that supports social existence, creating an atmosphere on both sides of the Atlantic that had a powerful impact on modern writers. Ezra Pound and James Joyce , for example, saw in the anarchist rejection of "first principles" a political and philosophical context for the radical new poetic and narrative forms that distinguish their work. In America, on the other hand, the links between anarchism and creative writers were the philosophical pragmatists William James and John Dewey, who shared a common bond with "anarchism of the good kind." The poets Marianne Moore and William Carlos Williams, for example, struggled against the debasement of language, which they saw as the inevitable social result of an outmoded economic system, causing them to "make it new" in Pound's phrase, to break with traditional poetic forms. Kadlec also invokes the figure of Zora Neale Hurston, whose training as a cultural anthropologist enabled her to see through the artificial categories of "race." As Janie Crawford, the heroine of Hurston's novel *Their Eyes Are Watching God*, puts it, "We're uh mingled people," thus pointing to the cultural, not "natural," basis of racial identity.

George Woodcock's *Anarchism* (1962) is a clear and objective analysis. David Kadlec's *Mosaic Modernism: Anarchism, Pragmatism, Culture* (2000) details the case for the alignment of anarchism and pragmatism and their employment by certain modern artists.

anatomy   In literature, the thorough analysis of a significant subject involving the division of the subject into its constituent parts. Writers in the English Renaissance adapted the medical sense of the term in order to probe a particular subject. For example, Robert Burton's *Anatomy of Melancholy* (1621) constitutes an exhaustive analysis of the melancholic HUMOR.

In his *Anatomy of Criticism* (1957), Northrop Frye defines the term as "a form of fiction . . . characterized by a great variety of subject matter and a strong interest in ideas."

androgyny   The combination of male and female characteristics. The word itself combines the Greek words for male (*andros*) and female (*gynous*). The literary tradition rests on the myth, recorded in Plato, of an ancient unified being of whom male and female are displaced halves seeking in sexual contact a long lost union.

In its literary adaptation, androgyny assumes a number of forms. One is the motif of boy-girl twins. Shakespeare's *Twelfth Night,* Dickens's unfinished novel *The Mystery of Edwin Drood* (1870), Poe's "The Fall of the House of Usher" (1838), and John Barth's *The Sot-Weed Factor* (1974) employ opposite-sex twins as embodiments of androgynous ideals.

Another form is the motif of a woman disguised as a man (in Shakespeare's comedies), or man disguised as a woman (Thomas Branson's *Charley's Aunt,* 1892; Billy Wilder's *Some Like It Hot,* 1959). Still another is the androgynous hero: Leopold Bloom in James Joyce's *Ulysses* (1922), Orlando in Virginia Woolf's *Orlando* (1928), and the hero/heroine of Gore Vidal's *Myra Breckinridge* (1968). These novels and others exemplify what the critic Carolyn Heilbrun calls "the androgynous ideal," based not upon the polarization of men and women, but on their integration.

FEMINIST CRITICISM has created a new sensitivity about the presence of androgyny in less obvious forms, for example in that most unlikely of places, the life of Ernest Hemingway. The critic Mark Spilka has argued that Hemingway's strenuously masculine exploits, such as bullfighting and big game hunting, were efforts to repress an attraction to androgyny deeply rooted in the writer's childhood.

Carolyn Heilbrun's *Toward a Recognition of Androgyny* (1973) traces the theme from Greek myth to modern literature. For the question of Hemingway's androgyny see Mark Spilka's *Hemingway's Quarrel with Androgyny* (1990).

Anglo-Irish literature   In the most general sense, literature written in English, rather than Gaelic, by Irish authors. In its narrower and more common sense, literature written largely by Irish Protestants loyal to the English throne during the "Protestant Ascendancy" in Ireland, the period from the late 17th century until the end of English rule in 1921. During that period many of the most distinguished authors in English literature were born in Ireland, a fact that appears to have little influence on the work of George Farquahr, Richard Steele, Laurence Sterne, Richard Brinsley Sheridan, Oliver Goldsmith, Oscar Wilde, and George Bernard Shaw. With the exception of Shaw, all appeared to identify themselves as Englishmen.

Others, such as Edmund Burke and Jonathan Swift, while not identifying themselves as Irish, passionately denounced the oppressive features of English rule. Still others, such as the novelist Maria Edgeworth, the poet James Clarence Mangan, and the song composer Thomas Moore, drew upon Irish culture and themes to define their work.

By the late 19th century a new group of Anglo Irish had arisen, impatient with England's refusal to grant Home Rule and defining themselves as Irish. Chief among these figures was William Butler Yeats, who returned to Celtic mythology as the inspirational source of his poetry. Yeats in turn influenced Lady Augusta Gregory, John Millington Synge, Sean O'Casey, and a host of talented writers who wrote for the ABBEY THEATRE. Their work spearheaded what came to be known as the IRISH RENAISSANCE. The establishment of the Irish republic in 1921 marked the end of "Anglo Irish" as a meaningful term, even in the six counties that constitute the Unionist state of Ulster (Northern Ireland). Distinguished Ulster poets such as John Montague, Seamus Heaney, and Derek Mahon identify themselves as Irish.

Denis Donoghue's *We Irish* (1986) discusses the term's "identity problem."

Anglo Norman   In English literature, the period following the Norman invasion of England in 1066 until the middle of the 14th century. Most of the literature of the period was either in Latin or in the Norman dialect of French. Among important works were Geoffrey of Monmouth's *Historia Regum Britanniae* (*History* *of the Kings of England,* c. 1135), part legend, part history, an important source of material relating to King Arthur, and the *Ancrene Riwle* (*Rule for Anchoresses,* c. 1200) for young women preparing to enter the cloister.

Another religious genre popular in the period involved the recounting of mystical experiences. Major mystical authors include Richard Rolle (*Meditations on the Passion,* c. 1340) and Dame Julian(a) of Norwich (*Revelations of Divine Love*). Dame Julian(a) recorded the mystical experiences she underwent while suffering from a severe illness.

By the middle of the 14th century, the language we know as MIDDLE ENGLISH had evolved sufficiently to serve as a vehicle for the first great English poet, Geoffrey Chaucer.

Richard Wilson's *Early Middle English Literature* (revised edition, 1968) surveys the literature from 1066 to 1300, and D. M. Stenton's *English Society in the Early Middle Ages* (1952) depicts the social background.

Anglo Saxon   *See* OLD ENGLISH.

angry young men   A term applied to a group of English writers, whose novels and plays in the 1950s featured protagonists who responded with articulate rage to the malaise that engulfed postwar England. The best known example of the work these writers produced is the angry working-class hero of John Osborne's drama *Look Back in Anger* (1956). In fiction, the term has been applied to Kingsly Amis's *Lucky Jim* (1953), John Braine's *Room at the Top* (1957), and Allan Sillitoe's *Saturday Night and Sunday Morning* (1958) and *The Loneliness of the Long Distance Runner* (1959).

Kenneth Allsop's *The Angry Decade* (1958) is an incisive account of the period.

angst   A German word meaning "dread," used by the 19th-century theologian Søren Kierkegaard to describe the combination of guilt and fear that accompanies the loss of religious faith. This sense of the word is alluded to in the last name of the protagonist of John Updike's Rabbit tetralogy—*Angstrom*. *See* EXISTENTIALISM.

Kierkegaard's analysis forms the core of his *The Concept of Dread* (1844).

animated films   Films in which thousands of cartoon drawings, each slightly different from the next, are photographed by a special camera to give the illusion of movement. In the formative years of animation these films required the labor of hundreds of illustrators. Today the work is done largely with a computer.

Since the 1930s, animated films have been dominated by one name, Walt Disney, the creator of cartoon characters, such as Mickey Mouse and Donald Duck, and full length animated classics such as *Snow White and the Seven Dwarfs* (1937), *Pinocchio* (1940), and *Fantasia* (1940) that achieved worldwide fame. Long after his death the company that bears his name continues to produce successful animated films, including the innovative *Who Framed Roger Rabbit* (1988), in which cartoon and human characters appear to be interacting with one another.

anonymous discourse   The French theorist Michel Foucault's term, used to assert the idea that a verbal utterance does not indicate a "thinking, knowing, speaking subject" but a totality, "which reflects not an individual's intention, that is to say, meaning. In other words we speak a language whose definitions have been imposed upon us." What Foucault is suggesting is that in the way we think and talk about a given topic, we have internalized a range of discourses that are, like the power they serve, anonymous.

Foucault's analysis appears in his *Archaeology of Knowledge* (1972).

antagonist   The chief opponent of the main character in a play or novel. The main character, whether HERO or VILLAIN, is called the PROTAGONIST. Thus the antagonist in *Hamlet* is the villainous King Claudius, while the antagonist in *Macbeth* is the righteous Macduff.

anthology   A collection of essays, poems, or plays usually sharing a similar subject, period of time, or place of origin. Among the most important anthologies in English literature is Thomas Percy's *Reliques of Ancient English Poetry* (1765), which created a popular taste for traditional English and Scottish ballads. Important anthologies in the history of American culture are the six *Eclectic Readers* (1836–57), compiled by William Holmes McGuffey. These "McGuffey Readers" were enormously successful school textbooks (over 100 million copies sold in the 19th century). They included excerpts from the major English writers, chosen to communicate moral lessons to their readers.

anthropology   The study of human societies from physical, cultural, and social perspectives. Anthropology and literary studies have increasingly overlapped in the 20th century. Anthropology and literature first united in the early years of the century when a group of classical scholars at Cambridge University (*see* CAMBRIDGE RITUALISTS) employed James Frazier's anthropological study *The Golden Bough* (1890–1915) to argue that classical myth, literature, and religion had their origins in primitive rituals (*see* MYTH CRITICISM). Frazier's study took on added significance when T. S. Eliot cited it as a source of *The Waste Land* (1922). The second great influence of anthropology on literary study has been STRUCTURALISM, specifically the work of the French anthropologist Claude Lévi-Strauss. Lévi-Strauss's study of primitive society, in which he noted the universal tendency to classify and order according to some principle—for example, the contrast between *raw* and *cooked* (*The Raw and the Cooked,* 1964)—provided one of the key elements of structuralism for literary critics, the notion of BINARY OPPOSITION as basic to human thought.

Central to the contemporary relation of literature and anthropology is the current view of ETHNOGRAPHY, or anthropological description. In the world of cultural anthropologists such as Clifford Geertz, ethnographers have become increasingly aware of the extent to which the conventions of narrative shape and alter their descriptions, or that their descriptions tell a story. Furthermore, some ethnographers, in striving for what Geertz terms "thick descriptions," have called for a greater reliance on literary techniques in order to convey the actual experiences of the societies they study. In turn, Geertz's own ethnographies have served as models for practitioners of NEW HISTORICISM.

James Clifford's *The Predicament of Culture* (1988) looks at the relation of ethnography and art.

anticlimax   In fiction or drama, a falling off in intensity and interest following a serious high point. The term has a pejorative connotation when used to indicate a flaw in a narrative or play, unless a writer is employing it for a humorous effect. An apparent anticlimax can be, on closer examination, a brilliant enhancement of the scene. An example is the Drunken Porter scene following the murder of Duncan in *Macbeth,* which begins with an inebriated gatekeeper responding to a loud knocking on the gate to admit the noblemen Macduff and Lennox to the castle. On the surface the scene's comic tone seems inappropriate at such a solemn moment, but, as analyzed by Thomas De Quincey in his famous essay "On the Knocking at the Gate in *Macbeth*" (1823), the scene manages to intensify the tragic tone by suggesting that the murder has transformed Macbeth's castle into hell, while at the same time suggesting a kind of redemption with the entrance of Macduff.

anti-hero   The principal character in a play or novel who exhibits qualities the opposite of those usually regarded as "heroic." The anti-hero may be cowardly, weak, inept, or simply unlucky. Here is the description of the anti-hero of E. Annie Proulx's *The Shipping News* (1993):

> . . . failure to speak clearly; failure to sit up straight; failure to get up in the morning; failure in attitude; failure in ambition and ability; indeed in everything. His own failure.

Although occasionally present in earlier literature, the anti-hero has proven to be a staple of modern literature, much of which is written, in Northrop Frye's phrase, in the "ironic mode." Frye describes the ironic mode as one in which "the characters exhibit a power of action inferior to the one assumed to be normal by the reader or audience." (*See* HERO; IRONY.)

The modern prototype (he even uses the term *anti-hero* to describe himself) is the anonymous, first-person narrator of Fyodor Dostoevsky's *Notes from Underground* (1864). Locked in his room, the underground man records his rage and humiliation as he rails against the prevailing belief in human reason and scientific progress. His progeny have been many. As the critic Victor Brombert points out, "Nineteenth and twentieth century literature is . . . crowded with weak, ineffectual, pale, humiliated, self-doubting, inept, occasionally abject characters . . ." Notable recent examples include the narrator of Ralph Ellison's *Invisible Man* (1952) and Jean-Baptiste Clamence, the "judge–penitent," confessing his sins in Albert Camus's *The Fall* (1954).

The anti-heroic strain also adapts itself well to comedy with its inherent impulse to debunk the pretensions to greatness that heroism implies. Here Shakespeare sets the tone in Falstaff's "catechism" on honor from *Henry IV Part 1*, where the old knight asserts that "honor" is a mere word that he'll have none of. In the 20th century, the anti-heroic comic figure finds two perfect proponents in Jaroslav Hasek's *The Good Soldier Schweik* (trans. 1930) and in Joseph Heller's *Catch-22* (1961). Both Schweik and Yossarian, Heller's anti-hero, attack the heroic ideal at its heart, the field of military valor. Similarly, the weak, neurotic, bespectacled figure embodied by Woody Allen in his films always implies a critique of the pretentious, beautiful people with whom he associates.

Victor Brombert's *In Praise of Anti-Heroes* (1999) eloquently discourses on the relation of the anti-hero to the spirit of our time. Northrop Frye's account of low mimetic and ironic modes is developed in his *Anatomy of Criticism* (1957).

anti-Semitism   In literature, the representation of Jews in terms of certain negative stereotypes. In Western culture, anti-Jewish prejudice, although present in a few classical writers, is primarily rooted in the New Testament. The Gospels in fact introduce the figures who were to become the basis of enduring individual Jewish stereotypes: Herod, the slaughterer of children; and Judas, the betrayer (for a price) of Christ. But a far more potent stereotype, the depiction of the Jews as a race of "Christ-killers," produced a legacy that has distorted, as few events have, the history of the West. Particularly ironic is that, like Jesus himself, the authors of the Gospels were Jews.

By the late middle ages, these biblical descriptions had developed into literary stereotypes. The image of Jews as child murderers constitutes the main action of "The Prioress's Tale" in *The Canterbury Tales* (1380–1400); the association of Jewish behavior with both treason and avarice surfaces in the MORALITY PLAYS, and the representation of Jews as responsible for the crucifixion is a recurring feature of MYSTERY PLAYS. Medieval Europe also gave birth to anti-Semitic legends such as the story of the wandering Jew.

In English Renaissance drama, two plays by its two greatest dramatists helped to perpetuate the myth of the Jew as arch-villain. Christopher Marlowe's *The Jew of Malta* (1590) catered to a current of anti-Semitism, but the other play, Shakespeare's *The Merchant of Venice* (1595), has given birth to a host of controversial and conflicting interpretations in print, on stage, and in society as a whole. On the one hand, Shylock, the play's fierce, Christian-hating moneylender, is a stereotypical villain who launched a thousand anti-Semitic progeny; on the other, he is one of Shakespeare's greatest dramatic achievements whose "Hath not a Jew eyes" speech echoes through time as a searing denunciation of anti-Semitism. He is, in the critic Harold Bloom's words, "a permanently equivocal trouble to all of us."

In the 18th century anti-Semitism appears regularly in the writings of Voltaire, whose celebrated commitment to tolerance apparently did not include Jews and Catholics.

The 19th-century novel maintained the "villain Jew" stereotype in the characters of Fagin in *Oliver Twist* (1837–39) and Svengali in George Du Maurier's *Trilby* (1894). Much more subtle are the references to rich and greedy Jewish bankers in the novels of Honoré de Balzac and Henry James.

The attempt to represent a pro-Semitic point of view is evident in Sir Walter Scott's *Ivanhoe* (1820) and George Eliot's *Daniel Deronda* (1876), but the Jewish characters in these novels, while positive, are equally stereotypical. No one, it seemed, could get it right until June 16, 1904, the fictional date when Leopold Bloom left his house to walk the streets of Dublin in James Joyce's *Ulysses* (1922). Bloom is not defined by his Jewishness; it is merely one facet of his unique, memorable, complex character.

Twentieth-century writers charged with harboring anti-Semitic attitudes include the poet Ezra Pound and the French novelist Louis-Ferdinand Céline, both of whom were active supporters of Fascist regimes and were outspoken in their denunciation of Jews. A name recently added to this list is that of Paul De Man, one of the leading exponents of DECONSTRUCTION.

The long tradition of "polite" anti-Semitism in France has been examined recently by the critic Jeffrey Mehlman, who has argued that this attitude is reflected in the lives and writings of four prominent 20th-century literary figures: the novelist André Gide, the playwright Jean Giraudoux, and the prominent critical theorists Maurice Blanchot and Jacques Lacan. Mehlman makes it clear that most of the evidence for these attitudes derives from the writings of these men before the Nazis transformed social snobbery into an unimagined horror—that is, before anyone was aware of the extremes to which anti-Semitism might be put. Nevertheless, Mehlman suggests that those attitudes contributed to an atmosphere that made possible the HOLOCAUST.

Edgar Rosenberg's *From Shylock to Svengali* (1960) traces the history of anti-Semitism in English literature. Jeffrey Mehlman's study is *Legacies of Anti-Semitism in France* (1983). The question of Paul De Man's wartime writings is debated in the journal *Critical Inquiry* v. 15 (summer, 1989).

anti-Stratfordian theories   A general term for the belief that someone other than William Shakespeare wrote the plays attributed to him. The chief candidates for the authorship of the plays have been Sir Francis Bacon, the 17th-century essayist and philosopher; the dramatist Christopher Marlowe; and Edward de Vere, 17th earl of Oxford. Bacon's candidacy was advanced as early as 1769 and was supported in the 19th century by Mark Twain among others. The supporters of Marlowe are not deterred by the fact that Marlowe was murdered in 1593, a year in which Shakespeare was just beginning his career; they have argued that Marlowe's death was staged and that he continued to live abroad, conveying the plays to Shakespeare's company through an intermediary. The most popular recent candidate has been the earl of Oxford, whose claim, like Marlowe's, is considerably undermined by Oxford's death in 1604; many of Shakespeare's greatest plays were written after that date.

The assumption shared by most anti-Stratfordians is that Shakespeare, a commoner with only a grammar school education, could not have written these great plays, a position that exhibits a touching faith in the virtues of the aristocracy.

Frank Wadsworth's *The Poacher from Stratford* (1958) offers a comprehensive account of the controversy.

antistrophe In classical Greek drama, a response by a section of the CHORUS to a previous strophe (a stanza of verse). Both strophe and antistrophe were written in the same METER.

aphaeresis *See* SYNCOPE.

aphorism A brief, elegant statement of a principle or opinion, such as "God is in the details." An aphorism is similar to an EPIGRAM, differing only in the epigram's emphasis on WIT.

apocalypse Literally, the last book of the BIBLE, the Book of Revelation according to John. The more general sense, reflected in the adjective apocalyptic, is a type of literature that is prophetic or focused on the end of the world. Among English poets associated with the apocalyptic strain, the outstanding figures are William Blake, many of whose works—including his *Milton* (1801) and *Jerusalem* (1804)—are apocalyptic visions, and William Butler Yeats, whose "The Second Coming" is among the most celebrated poems of the 20th century.

The creation of the atomic bomb in 1945 has moved the apocalyptic form closer to realism. (*See* SCIENCE FICTION; NUCLEAR WAR. *See also* "LEFT BEHIND" NOVELS.)

Frank Kermode's *The Sense of an Ending* (1967) is a study of apocalyptic fiction.

apocope *See* SYNCOPE.

apocrypha Works of the Old and New Testament not admitted to the CANON by the Catholic Church, or works rejected by Jews or Protestants for doubtful validity.

In literature, the term is applied to works whose authorship is questionable. An example of an apocryphal play is *Edward III*, a history play that many scholars believe was written partly by Shakespeare.

Apollonian/Dionysian Contrasting terms coined by the 19th-century German philosopher Friedrich Nietzsche. For Nietzsche, the Apollonian (after the god Apollo) stands for order, rationality, and moral behavior, while the Dionysian (after Dionysus, the god of wine) represents the spontaneous, irrational, and amoral spirit of life. Nietzsche employs these terms in his *The Birth of Tragedy* (1872), in which he argues that Greek tragedy is essentially Dionysian, rooted in powerful and primitive emotions, and that the Apollonian element is a later accretion. This position directly contradicted the prevailing view of Nietzsche's time, but has been confirmed by later studies.

aporia   The Greek word for complexity, used in classical philosophy to describe a debate in which the arguments on each side are equally valid. In DECONSTRUCTION the term describes the impasse, the inner contradiction that, according to deconstructionist critics, lies at the heart of any TEXT, thus rendering its meaning always indeterminate. The "answer" to the question "Which comes first, the chicken or the egg?" is an example of an aporia.

apostrophe   A figure of speech in which a speaker turns from the audience to address an absent person or abstract idea. It differs from a soliloquy in that the speaker of an apostrophe need not be alone on the stage. An example occurs in the second act of *Hamlet*, when the Prince turns from a conversation with Rosencrantz and Guildenstern to declare:

> What a piece of work is a man, how noble in reason, how infinite in faculties, in form and moving how express and admirable, in action how like an angel, in apprehension how like a god: the beauty of the world, the paragon of animals—and yet, to me, what is this quintessence of dust?

The apostrophe also figures prominently in lyric poetry, as in William Blake's "Tyger":

> *Tyger, tyger, burning bright*
> *In the forest of the night,*
> *What immortal hand or eye*
> *Could frame thy fearful symmetry?*

appearance/reality   A recurring theme in literature, the distinction between what appears to be and what is has taken on a wide variety of forms. Its classical statement occurs in the Myth of the Cave in Plato's *Republic:* Plato's parable pictures people chained in a cave and facing a wall. They can see only shadows cast by objects in the light of a fire within the cave. Most people remain within the cave, but a few venture outside where they finally look up to see the sun, the true source of light. This movement from appearance to reality is based on a philosophy of idealism, the belief that ultimate reality resides in ideas, not in matter. Plato's views exerted a strong influence in the literature of the RENAISSANCE; in Shakespeare's tragedies, for example, appearance is the outer "clothing" that disguises the inner reality. In the first act of *Hamlet*, the prince's mother rebukes him for continuing to wear black in mourning for his father: "Why seems it so particular with thee?" Hamlet casts his reply in terms of inner reality versus outer show:

Seems, madam? Nay it is. I know not "seems."
'Tis not alone my inky cloak, good mother,
Nor customary suits of solemn black. . . .
        These indeed seem,
For they are actions that a man might play;
But I have that within which passes show
These but the trappings and the suits of woe.

In later periods the alternative view—that the sum of appearances *is* reality—begins to emerge in such works as the philosophy of Benedict de Spinoza and the poetry of William Wordsworth, who locates the principle of reality in the experience of nature. Other Romantic poets, notably Samuel Taylor Coleridge, adhere to the principle that the imagination shapes and defines reality.

In the 20th century, the doctrine of PHENOMENOLOGY asks that the question of "the real" be *bracketed* (set aside) in order to provide a precise description of experience. One extreme reaction to this concept is the view of the ABSURD which, in the words of John Yolton, is the "denial of reality to the only reality left, the reality of lived human experience." *See also* "AS IF" FICTIONS.

John Yolton's "Appearance and Reality" in *The Dictionary of the History of Ideas* (1968), edited by Philip Wiener, is an admirable summary of the terms.

apron stage   A stage that is thrust out into the audience on three sides, creating closer contact than is the case with a PROSCENIUM stage. The apron stage was a common feature of Elizabethan theaters, such as Shakespeare's GLOBE THEATRE.

Arab-American literature   The first wave of Arab-American immigration, largely Christians from Syria and Lebanon, began in the 1880s and continued into the 1920s. The second wave, about half of them Muslims, arrived after World War II and continues to the present day.

An early and important force in Arab-American literature is Ameen Rihani, a Lebanese-born scholar and diplomat, whose *The Book of Khalid* (1911), a novel written in free verse records the struggles and triumphs in the immigrant experience. The most important early work of Arab-American literature is Kahil Gibran's world-famous *The Prophet* (1923), a meditative prose poem, extolling love as the central fact of the human condition. In America alone, this book, which has been translated into 13 languages, has sold over more than 4 million copies.

Some later Arab-American writers include the talented William Peter Blatty, author of *The Exorcist*, and Vance Bourjaily, but neither chose to examine the ethnic experience in their work. The major breakthrough occurred with the publication of *Grape Leaves* (1982) an anthology of Arab-American poetry, which included work by three outstandingly talented poets, Samuel Hazo, D. H. Melhem, and Etel Adnan. Recent notable novelists include Naomi Shihab Nye. Equally talented is Diana Abu-Jabere; *Arabian Jazz* (1994), a work whose feminist perspective casts a cold eye on male dominance in both Arab and American societies, but her main character represents the best of both worlds, a Palestinian refugee who loves jazz.

Evelyn Shakir's "Arab-American Literature" surveys the subject in *New Immigrant Literatures in the United States* (1996), ed. Alpana Sharma Knippling.

Arcadia   An idealized PASTORAL setting. Arcadia is a mountainous region in Greece, celebrated as a rustic setting in classical and Renaissance literature. Sir Philip Sidney's *Arcadia* (1587, 1590) is an elaborate, pastoral prose-romance that exerted a strong influence on English Renaissance literature.

archetypal criticism   *See* MYTH CRITICISM.

archive   A place for storing documents or records. In literary studies, the correspondence, manuscripts, and personal papers of important writers are stored in major libraries. One example is the T. S. Eliot archive at Princeton University, which has been sealed until 2020. The Eliot archive forms the background to Martha Cooley's novel *The Archivist* (1998).

The term takes on new meaning in the work of the theorist Michel Foucault, who uses *archive* to denote the accumulated body of definitions that dominates a particular field of knowledge. For Foucault, the word AUTHOR, with its connotations of an autonomous, creative individual ("the genius"), is an example of the archival nature of language in literary studies.

Michel Foucault's treatment of the archive is developed in his *Archaeology of Knowledge* (1972).

argument   In RHETORIC, the line of reasoning designed to demonstrate the truth or falsity of a particular position; in literature, a brief summary of the plot or subject matter of a narrative or play, such as the Argument preceding Samuel Taylor Coleridge's *The Rime of the Ancient Mariner* (1798).

Aristotelian criticism   A type of criticism deriving from Aristotle's *Poetics*, probably the most influential analysis of literature ever recorded. Aristotle defined literature as imitation (MIMESIS); gave an account of the origins, development, and structure of drama; distinguished between comedy and tragedy; and introduced the concept of CATHARSIS and the UNITIES.

Aristotelian critical principles inform much of the thinking of the CHICAGO SCHOOL of modern criticism.

Armenian-American literature Until the 11th century, Armenia was an independent nation in western Asia. From that time, Armenia was continuously colonized by Ottoman Turks, who ceded part of the country to Russia in the late 19th century. Divided between two warring empires (Russian and Ottoman) during World War I, Turkish Armenians were subject to genocidal massacres, the worst of which occurred in 1915. In the wake of the genocide, the Armenian diaspora brought 100,000 immigrants to the United States. Since then, the number of immigrants swelled to the point that there are now 750,000 Armenian Americans.

The ghost that haunts Armenian-American literature is the "ethnic inheritance of genocide," in which 1 million Armenians were killed by Turkish rulers between 1890 and 1915. The best known of these works is Michael Arlen's *Passage to Ararat* (1975), which recounts the author's attempts to fix the identity of his father (who disguised his Armenian roots) and therefore of himself. Winner of the National Book Award, *Passage to Ararat* describes Arlen's trip to the genocide memorial in present-day Armenia and an imagined dialogue with his dead father, with whom he makes his peace.

The most celebrated of Armenian-American authors, is the playwright and novelist William Saroyan. Saroyan writes extensively on non-Armenian subjects, but he frequently returned to his ethnic roots, notably in his novel *Rock Wagram* (1951) and in three plays, *An Armenian Trilogy*, written in the last years of his life. In these works Saroyan focuses on the theme of family and ethnic identity.

Other major Armenian novels are Peter Sourian's *The Gate* (1965) and Peter Najarian's *Voyages* (1971), both of which deal with the legacy of genocide. These novels invoke primarily a patrilineal world. The contrasting feminine perspective is captured in Carol Edgarian's *Rise the Euphrates* (1994).

Among important contemporary Armenian-American poets are David Kherdian (*The Nonny Poems,* 1974) and Peter Balakian (*Reply From Wilderness Island*, 1988).

Two important surveys of Armenian-American literature are Margaret Bedrosian's *Magic in the Pine Ring* (1991) and Khachig Tololyan's "Armenian-American Literature" in *New Immigrant Literatures in the United States* (1996), ed. Alpana Sharma Knippling.

Arnoldian criticism The critical writings of the 19th-century poet and critic Matthew Arnold, or subsequent criticism derived from Arnold. Arnold introduced a number of terms that have enjoyed wide currency: HEBRAISM/ HELLENISM, PHILISTINE, SWEETNESS AND LIGHT, and the TOUCHSTONE principle. He was an early exponent of cultural criticism, seeing literature as "a criticism of life" and defining culture as "the best that has been thought and said." Arnold's definition has often been quoted and, in the field of contemporary CULTURAL STUDIES, contested for its apparent limitation of culture to "high" culture.

art for art's sake   The argument that art should be autonomous and not compelled to serve a specific social or moral purpose. The phrase was used in 19th-century France and England as a slogan of AESTHETICISM.

In its Latin form, *ars gratia artis*, the phrase has been used as a motto appearing at the beginning of all Metro Goldwyn Mayer films.

art/nature   *See* NATURE/ART.

Arthurian legend   The term for the large body of material relating to King Arthur and his court. Whether or not there was an actual, historical King Arthur, existing sometime in the sixth century A.D., remains a subject of debate among historians. The legendary figure appears to have originated in Celtic (either Irish or Welsh) folklore, spreading to England, and from there to the European continent.

By the 12th century, the legend was sufficiently established for Geoffrey of Monmouth to include Arthur in his *History of the Kings of Britain* (1136) and to single him out as the greatest of these monarchs. Geoffrey's account portrayed Arthur's court in Camelot as a model of the ideal knightly society. Geoffrey's version of the legend was adapted by the Norman writer Wace in his *Roman de Brut* (c. 1155). Wace's version introduced the motif of the Round Table, at which Arthur's knights gathered, its shape ensuring that no one would have a privileged position over the others. In the hands of the TROUVÈRE poet Chrétien de Troyes, the legend became immortalized in the stories of the pursuit of the Holy Grail, and the love affair of Sir Lancelot and Queen Guinevere. The popularity of Chrétien's innovations gave birth to a number of long verse romances that elaborated the legend further, placing the stories within the COURTLY LOVE tradition.

In the 15th century, Sir Thomas Malory, in good English fashion, toned down the love interest to celebrate Arthur as a wise and just ruler. Malory's *Morte D'Arthur* (edited and published in 1485 by the English printer William Caxton) details the reign, the death, and the promised return of the "once and future king." Malory's version consists of eight romances that, taken together, make up the story as it has come down to later generations. It recounts the story of Arthur's ascension to the throne after pulling the sword Excalibur from a stone; his famous victories; his court at Camelot; the feasts of the Knights of the Round Table; the love affair of Lancelot and Guinevere; the quest for the Grail; the treachery of Arthur's illegitimate son, Sir Mordred; Arthur's death; and his final resting place on the island of Avalon.

In the 19th century, Alfred, Lord Tennyson's retelling of the legend, *The Idylls of the King* (1859–85), enjoyed enormous popularity, resulting in a revival of medievalism in art and literature, particularly among the PRE-RAPHAELITES. In the 20th century, the publication of T. H. White's *The Once and Future King* (1958) brought the legend to a wide audience. White's book was adapted by Alan Jay Lerner and Frederick Loewe as the musical *Camelot* (1960), a version of the legend that has become identified with the administration of John F. Kennedy.

Margaret Reid's *The Arthurian Legend* (1970) is a chronological account of the various versions of the legend since 1485.

artist/hero   The portrait-of-the-artist novel is a species of literature that has been popular since the late 18th century. A major theme of such fiction is the idea of the artist as a split self, one who is both a human being and, in the words of the psychologist Carl Jung, "one who allows art to idealize its purpose through him . . . who carries the unconscious, psychic life of mankind." Pulled in two directions, the artist may respond either by a passionate commitment to the experience of life, converting the experience into art, or by insulating himself from life, becoming a "priest of art."

The artist/hero theme is rooted in, and a central conception of, ROMANTICISM. The Romantics created two types of artist/hero, the "sensitive plant" and the BYRONIC HERO. The first type is the ineffectual dreamer, too refined for the tawdry reality of ordinary life; the second type is the passionate rebel, mocking both God and man. Goethe's artist-heroes include both types, the sensitive Werther and the defiant Faust.

Charles Dickens departs from this tradition in *David Copperfield* (1849–50), presenting his novelist/hero as an unexceptional figure, a transparent window through which we view the novel's other, very colorful characters. In the stories of Henry James, such as "The Jolly Corner," the artist is rendered as a detached observer who withdraws from life in order to capture it in the lens of his art. The danger of such withdrawal is the theme of Thomas Mann's *Death in Venice* (1910), in which elemental forces long suppressed by the artist's self-discipline erupt and bring about his death.

The 20th century's most significant example of the genre is James Joyce's *A Portrait of the Artist as a Young Man* (1916), whose flawed hero, Stephen Dedalus, is as much pretender as artist until he encounters the warmth and humanity of Leopold

Bloom in *Ulysses* (1922). Nevertheless, Stephen's creed, formulated as the determination to "forge in the smithy of my soul the uncreated conscience of my race"—to recreate one's culture so that its moral essence will be made clear—stands as the paradigmatic statement of the function of the artist in the 20th century.

Maurice Beebe's *Ivory Towers and Sacred Founts* (1964) provides a history of the theme with chapters on Honoré de Balzac, Henry James, Marcel Proust, and James Joyce.

Asian-American literature   The increased immigration of people from all sections of Asia has resulted in a redefinition of this term. As originally conceived (and reflected in the well-known 1974 collection *AIIIEEEEE: An Anthology of Asian American Writers*), the term referred only to Chinese, Japanese and Filipino Americans. Since then it has been broadened to include Korean, Indian, Pakistani Americans as well as authors from other areas of Southeast Asia. (*See* ETHNIC LITERATURE.)

aside   In drama, a comment by a character directed to the audience, not intended to be heard by the other characters on stage. The use of the aside affects the role of the audience in the play. In a realistic drama the aside can be jarring since it breaks the illusion, reminding the audience that they are watching a play. In nonrealist drama, particularly light comedy, it can help to draw the audience into the action and heighten its sense of participation.

"as if" fictions   A philosophical principle affirming the usefulness of acting on the basis of an assertion known to be untrue. This idea, associated with the German philosopher Hans Vaihinger, operates on the assumption of the irrationality of life and the conclusion that human thought is not capable of comprehending reality. Given the inherent limitations of the human intellect, Vaihinger endorses the validity of ideas he calls fictions. "An idea whose theoretical untruth . . . is admitted is not for that reason practically valueless and useless, for such an idea, in spite of its theoretical nullity may have great practical importance."

While not directly influencing specific writers, Vaihinger's theory helped to create an atmosphere in which the literature of MODERNISM, with its emphasis on the validity of subjective experience, could flourish. It also opens the door to the validity of seeing MYTH as contributing to the well-being of society. *See* FAIRY TALES.

The English version of Vaihinger's *The Philosophy of "As If,"* translated by C. R. Ogden, was published in 1924. Charles Glicksberg's *Modern Literary Perspectivism* (1970) contains a description of Vaihinger's principles.

assonance   A form of RHYME in which the vowels rhyme, but not the consonants. Examples: *kite-bike; rate-cake*.

Astor Place riot   An outbreak at the Astor Place Opera House in New York in 1849. The riot was the violent outcome of a rivalry between two leading Shakespearean actors of the time, the American Edwin Forrest and the English William Charles Macready. Forrest was the first native born American actor to qualify as a star in the 19th-century sense of the term. Macready, on the other hand, was the very model of a British gentleman: careful and cerebral.

During a performance on tour in England, Forrest received a slight which he attributed to Macready. As a result, when Macready returned for his third tour of the U.S., the fuse was lit. In May 1849, he arrived in New York to complete his tour. The popular penny press made the most of the quarrel between the two, but what really fueled the fire was the opportunity it offered certain local politicians who used the quarrel to solidify the power of the Nativist Party. The Nativists—later to emerge as the Know Nothing Movement—seized upon the feud to make it an "American" issue. They claimed that Macready was a symbol of English arrogance and snobbery.

One of the ringleaders in this effort was E. Z. C. Judson, better known then, and now, as Ned Buntline, one of the originators of the DIME NOVEL and the creator of the legend of Buffalo Bill. Buntline and Tammany Hall politicians organized a demonstration to take place at the "aristocratic" Astor Place opera house recently constructed in a neighborhood made fashionable by the presence of John Jacob Astor's residence nearby.

On the evening of May 10, some 10,000 to 15,000 people massed in front of the theater, while inside Macready was performing *Macbeth*. In an attempt to control the mob, the New York State Militia was called out. In the ensuing chaos, the soldiers were given orders to open fire. The results: approximately 22 killed and over 100 people wounded. Macready in disguise had to escape the theater and, later that evening, the city.

The incident has formed the basis of Richard Nelson's drama *Two Shakespearean Actors* (1990) and played a major role in the theatrical superstition that *Macbeth* is an unlucky play.

Richard Moody's *The Astor Place Riot* (1958) offers a meticulously detailed account of the event.

atmosphere   *See* MOOD.

aubade   A poem in which lovers complain of the appearance of dawn, which requires them to part. The form achieved great popularity in medieval France and was employed by Chaucer in *Troilus and Criseyde* and by Shakespeare in *Romeo and Juliet*.

audience   The spectators at a play, film, or television show. In each case the role of the audience differs: At a play, the audience's responses, or lack thereof, are immediately communicated to the actors, which may alter to some degree their performance; filmgoers frequently respond more to the visual effects than to the story, while television viewers can exercise the option of switching to another channel, which radically qualifies their commitment to a WILLING SUSPENSION OF DISBELIEF.

Theatrical history records a number of incidents in which the audience's reaction resulted in a riot. (*See* ABBEY THEATRE; ASTOR PLACE RIOT.)

In writing about literature, "audience" is often used as a synonym for "reader." One celebrated example is Walter J. Ong's essay, "The Writer's Audience is Always a Fiction," in which he maintains that an experienced writer is able "to fictionalize in his imagination an audience," based upon his reading of earlier writers "who were fictionalizing in their imagination audiences they had learned."

Walter Ong's essay is reprinted in *An Ong Reader*, ed. Thomas Farrell and Paul Soulcup (2002).

Augustan age   The term refers to two periods of literary history.

1. The reign of the Roman emperor Caesar Augustus (27 B.C.–A.D. 14). In this period Latin literature was in its so-called Golden Age, as represented by the poetry of Virgil, Ovid, and Horace.

2. Writers in England in the first half of the 18th century invoked a parallel with Rome to describe the literature of their period. They promoted the writings of Alexander Pope, Jonathan Swift, Joseph Addison, and Richard Steele not only for their intrinsic merits but also as models of "correct" literature as defined by the doctrines of NEOCLASSICISM.

The period also saw the development of a distinctly nonneoclassical form, the NOVEL. Major practitioners of the newly developed genre included Daniel Defoe (*Robinson Crusoe*, 1719; *Moll Flanders*, 1722); Samuel Richardson (*Pamela*, 1740–42; *Clarissa*, 1747–48), and Henry Fielding (*Joseph Andrews*, 1742; *Tom Jones*, 1749).

John Butt's *The Augustan Age* (1956) captures the spirit of the era; Ian Jack's *Augustan Satire* (1952) focuses on the satiric production of the period. Michael McKeon's *The Origins of the English Novel, 1600–1740* (1987) explores the development of the novel with particular attention to the social and cultural contexts.

auteur A term used in film criticism expressing the idea that the "author" of a film—the individual who exercises personal control in the making of a film—is the director. More specifically the term describes a director who has developed an identifiable style and a consistent set of themes in his or her work. The term originally was employed by NEW WAVE film critics of the 1950s, who applied it to Howard Hawks and Alfred Hitchcock, until then regarded as entertaining but not "serious" filmmakers. The re-estimation of Hawks and Hitchcock as auteurs spearheaded the movement to view popular film directors and their films as suitable subjects of criticism.

The dominant film theory of the '60s and '70s, auteurism more recently has had to withstand the challenges of SEMIOTICS and POSTSTRUCTURALISM, two schools with pronounced antipathy to any emphasis on individual authorship.

The best known American auteurist critic is Andrew Sarris, for many years the film critic of *The Village Voice*.

Andrew Sarris's *The American Cinema: Directors and Directions 1929–1968* (1968) fully develops his auteurist theory.

author A term traditionally used to describe the person who originates a piece of writing. Like many other literary terms in recent years the "idea of the author" has been the subject of an increasingly rigorous analysis, which is to say—in the language of contemporary THEORY—"author" has been "theorized."

Theorists see the term as intimately related to authority. In the middle ages, "auctores" were those figures, such as Aristotle, who were the fundamental "authorities" on their subjects. As the world grew more complex in the Renaissance, respect for "authority" weakened in favor of valuing individual initiative. One example might be the development in Protestantism of the emphasis on individual interpretation of the Bible, a central issue of the REFORMATION; another, the emphasis in CAPITALISM on the individual entrepreneur as opposed to the collective economy of feudalism. In this climate "author" came to be associated with a creative person honored less as an authority than as an example of individual creativity and freedom.

In one respect, however, the notion of authority clung to the term. Defining the author as the "creator" of a work implied that its meaning derived from its creator, that in seeking to arrive at a meaning readers should attempt to recapture the author's intention. In the mid-20th century the NEW CRITICISM launched an attack on this conception, categorizing this thinking as an example of the INTENTIONAL FALLACY.

But an even more radical challenge was raised by the partisans of POSTSTRUCTURALISM. They argued that the notion of the author as an autonomous, individual creator should give way to a less powerful conception: the author as a culturally conditioned "subject" who participates in the production of a text but is merely one among many who contribute to its multiple meanings. Roland Barthes rendered this position dramatically in his celebrated essay "The Death of the Author." Barthes argued that reference to the author as the originating point of a text maintains the illusion of determinate meaning as opposed to the reality of INDETERMINACY, the principle that there is no such thing as a "correct" interpretation of a literary text.

Just as the 19th-century philosopher Nietzsche had, in announcing "the death of God," depicted a world from which order and meaning had fled, so Barthes wished to remove the text's creator: "The removal of the Author . . . is not merely an historical fact, it utterly transforms the modern text." The negation of the author results in the increased significance of the reader who is the "destination" of the text: "The reader is the space on which all the quotations that make up a writing are inscribed without any of them being lost; a text's unity lies not in its origin but in its destination."

Barthes's position was modified in turn by Michel Foucault, who defined the author as a function of the relations between the reader and the text. Foucault appears to agree with Barthes in calling for an end to the "author" conceived of as an individual who is the origin and, in the capitalist tradition, the "owner" of a piece of writing. In its place is the writer-as-subject, a creature of cultural institutions and the practice of DISCOURSE.

Behind the revolutionary rhetoric of Barthes and Foucault lies a call for unlimited openness in the interpretation of texts, a resistance to any kind of critical CLOSURE. Their attack on the traditional conception of the author is a specific example of the general program of POSTSTRUCTURALISM with its critique of individual identity and its insistence on the instability of meaning.

For another approach to the question of authorship, *see* IMPLIED AUTHOR/READER.

Roland Barthes's "The Death of the Author" is included in his *Image, Music, Text* (1977); Michel Foucault's "What Is an Author?" is reprinted in *The Foucault Reader* (1984). For a critique of their positions and an historical account of the term, see Donald Pease's "Author" in *Critical Terms for Literary Study*, edited by Frank Lentricchia and Thomas McLaughlin (1990).

autobiography   The story of a person's life written by him- or herself. Autobiographical writing embraces a number of forms including MEMOIRS, DIARIES, and LETTERS, but the form proper usually involves the interaction of character and external event over a substantial span of a person's life.

The model of future autobiographies is the *Confessions of Saint Augustine* (c. A.D. 400), a passionate and intellectually powerful account of his life, culminating in his conversion to Christianity. Among the notable autobiographies of the Renaissance were Benvenuto Cellini's colorful story of his life and times, and Saint Theresa of Avila's intense and moving rendering of a life devoted to God. Outstanding 18th-century examples of the form include Jean Jacques Rousseau's *Confessions* (1766–70), paradoxically candid and self-justifying, and Benjamin Franklin's *Autobiography* (1771; 1784–85; 1788), a model of clear, unpretentious prose. In the 19th century Cardinal Newman's *Apologia Pro Vita Sua* (1864), one of the century's finest examples of English prose, and John Stuart Mill's *Autobiography* (1873), with its classic account of a youthful emotional breakdown, are outstanding. The 20th century has seen a proliferation of autobiographies of the "tell all" variety by celebrities of every type. Among more serious examples of the form are Sean O'Casey's, written in the third person, and Simone de Beauvoir's five-volume account of her life. In the United States, undoubtedly the most significant autobiography of the post-war period has been *The Autobiography of Malcolm X* (1965), written by Alex Haley and based upon taped interviews with the American civil rights leader.

Roy Pascal's *Design and Truth in Autobiography* (1960) and John Pilling's *Autobiography and Imagination* (1981) are recent studies of the form.

auto sacramental (sacramental play)

auto sacramental (sacramental play)   A type of drama performed in Spain on the feast of Corpus Christi from the 16th through the 18th centuries. Corpus Christi (body of Christ) is a Roman Catholic feast honoring the sacrament of the Eucharist, celebrated on the Thursday after Trinity Sunday, which is 60 days after Easter Sunday. The *auto*, a one-act drama, featured mythic, allegorical, or historical characters; the action concluded with the manifestation of a Communion host and chalice. The aim of many of the *autos* was to draw analogies between secular stories of love and adventure and the divine mystery of the Eucharist.

Its greatest practitioner was Pedro Calderón de la Barca (1600–81), who wrote more than 70 of these plays in his lifetime.

Alexander Parker's *The Allegorical Drama of Calderón: An Introduction to the Autos Sacramentales* (1943) provides a history of the genre.

avant-garde

avant-garde   A French term originally used to describe the vanguard of an army, adapted to art and literature to describe various movements in the 19th and 20th centuries that called for experimentation and repudiated the established conventions of their times. The term implies that true artists are ahead of their times, establishing new frontiers of thought and expression. In the 19th century, the Romantics and later the SYMBOLIST poets were avant-garde; in the 20th century, the avant-garde has included the proponents of IMAGISM, PROJECTIVISM and, more recently, language poetry (*See* LANGUAGE POETS). Often an avant-garde's criticism of prevailing forms of literature extends to a criticism of society as a whole—as, for example, the BEAT movement's objections to American culture in the 1950s.

Baconian theory *See* ANTI-STRATFORDIAN THEORIES.

bad faith In the EXISTENTIALISM of Jean-Paul Sartre, the act of self-deception in which one evades an authentic or self-defining choice by remaining unaware that such a choice exists, or by depicting oneself as determined by external forces. *See* DETERMINISM.

bad quarto Term applied to certain early editions of Shakespeare's plays that exhibit various forms of corruption, including omissions, insertions, and garbled passages. The common assumption is that the bad quartos represent the "stolen and surreptitious copies," referred to in the Preface to the FIRST FOLIO, the first collected edition of Shakespeare's plays.

Some textual scholars have effectively refuted this view in relation to at least one of the so-called bad quartos, the 1608 edition of *King Lear*, which is now accepted as a legitimate text, based on Shakespeare's early draft of the play.

Steven Urkowitz's "Good News about Bad Quartos," appears in *Bad Shakespeare*, ed. Maurice Charney (1988).

ballad Originally a song associated with dance, the ballad developed into a form of folk verse narrative. The majority of folk ballads deal with themes of romantic passion, love affairs that end unhappily, or with political and military subjects. The story usually is in dialogue form, in direct and unsparing language, arranged in quatrains with the second and fourth lines rhyming. An example is the final stanza to the Scots ballad "Bonny Barbara Allen":

> *O mother, mother, make my bed!*
> *O make it saft and narrow!*
> *Since my love died for me today*
> *I'll die for him to-morrow.*

Ballads were popular throughout medieval Europe. In the 18th century, the publication of Bishop Thomas Percy's *Reliques of Ancient English Poetry* (1765) created a vogue both in England and Germany for folk verse. The ballad form was imitated by Romantic poets, signaled by the publication of William Wordsworth and Samuel Taylor Coleridge's *Lyrical Ballads* in 1798.

T. F. Henderson's *The Ballad in Literature* (1912; reprinted 1966) provides a history of the British folk ballad.

banality of evil   A phrase from the subtitle of a book by Hannah Arendt describing the war crimes trial of Adolph Eichmann, the man responsible for the transportation of Jews from all over Europe to the Nazi death camps. Arendt argued that, far from being an inhuman monster, Eichmann was all too human, a dull, unimaginative, banal bureaucrat. His evil was not the result of some profound pathological mystery, but of the fact that he was a man who, living within an evil system, never examined his life. He was "banal" (in the sense of "commonplace") because he lived his life automatically.

A literary parallel is evident in the conflicting interpretations of the character of Iago in Shakespeare's *Othello*. Is Iago a Satanic figure whose "motiveless malignity" (Samuel Taylor Coleridge's phrase) is an index of his diabolic nature? Or is he an unscrupulous but rather ordinary man who is merely the stage manager of Othello's own self destruction? As these two examples from life and literature demonstrate, the issue touches on a fundamental question: the nature of EVIL.

Hannah Arendt's *Eichmann in Jerusalem: A Report on the Banality of Evil* (1963) is a controversial account of the Eichmann trial; Stanley E. Hyman's *Iago: Some Approaches to the Illusion of His Motivation* (1970) offers a full discussion of the character from a variety of perspectives.

bard   Among ancient Celtic tribes the bard played an important role as the preserver and recounter of cultural lore. In modern times the term functions as a synonym for any poet, often with particular reference to Shakespeare.

Two analysts of POPULAR CULTURE, John Fiske and John Hartley, have argued that the role of the ancient bard in modern society has been assumed by television. Television, like the bard, is an oral medium whose messages are not the product of an individual author, but instead form the mythology of the culture "which delivers to the members of that culture a confirming, reinforcing version of themselves."

Fiske and Hartley's analysis appears in *Reading Television* (1978).

bardolatry   A term used to describe an excessive devotion to Shakespeare. In the literature of the late 18th century there developed a sense of the greatness of Shakespeare's work that viewed him as the precursor of ROMANTICISM. The enthusiasm of some so exceeded the norms of admiration that Shakespeare became, in the words of the great actor David Garrick, echoing *Romeo and Juliet*, "the God of our idolatry."

An example of a bardolater in 20th-century literature is the figure of James Tyrone in Eugene O'Neill's *Long Day's Journey Into Night* (1940).

baroque   In art, architecture, music, and literature, a highly ornamental style that flourished in 17th-century Europe. More significant in art and music than in literature, the baroque style is associated with the Italian poet Giambattista Marino (see MARINISM) and the Spanish poet Luis de Gongora (see GONGORISM).

In English literature, baroque elements are present in the elaborate conceits of metaphysical poetry, particularly the poetry of Richard Crashaw. Typical of Crashaw's baroque sensibility is this poem in which the crucified Christ's blood is conceived of as a garment.

On Our Crucified Lord, Naked and Bloody

They have left thee naked, Lord, O that they had!
This garment too, I would they had denied;
Thee with thyself they have too richly clad,
Opening the purple wardrobe of thy side.
O never could be found garments too good
For thee to wear, but these, of thy own blood.

For a wide-ranging study of the term, see Wylie Sypher's *Four Stages of Renaissance Style: 1400–1700* (1955).

baseball   The growth of sports as a social and cultural force—propelled by increased leisure time and the pervasive presence of television—has produced a world that has become increasingly "soccer-crazed." But in the United States, and increasingly in Japan, the sport that most writers are attracted to is baseball. Its literary appeal lies in its rich store of myth, ritual, and history, most of which is absorbed by Americans in their early years, when the imagination is most impressionable.

Originally the subject of juvenile fiction, exemplified by the fine novels of John R. Tunis (*The Kid from Tomkinsville*, 1940; rep't., 1987), baseball has emerged since the 1950s as an important literary theme in American literature. One earlier exception is Ring Lardner's satirical short pieces collected under the title *You Know*

Me, Al (1916), but the first serious adult novel is Bernard Malamud's *The Natural* (1952). Malamud took the traditional story of the young rookie who becomes a star and transformed it into the mythic mode of MAGIC REALISM, thus suggesting the symbolic possibilities inherent in the "great American pastime." Following Malamud's lead, Robert Coover explored the "baseball as the world" metaphor in *The Universal Baseball Association, J. Henry Waugh, Prop.* (1968) and Philip Roth added his parodical view in *The Great American Novel* (1973). Meanwhile in a traditional realistic vein, Mark Harris produced insightful, intelligent treatments of the game with *The Southpaw* (1953) and *Bang the Drum Slowly* (1956).

The '70s and '80s saw an explosion of adult baseball fiction, in which more than 30 novels dealing with the subject appeared. Among these are two that deal with the famous Black Sox gambling scandal of 1919, W. P. Kinsella's *Shoeless Joe* (1982) and Eric Rolfe Greenberg's *The Celebrant* (1981), a novel keyed to the career of the great pitcher Christy Mathewson, which concludes with the 1919 debacle.

A powerful novel touching on the sport is William Kennedy's *Ironweed* (1983), the story of a professional ball player, haunted by the memory of a tragic accident. An outstanding example of integrating baseball within the general frame of a wide-ranging social and philosophical novel is the 60 page prologue to Don DeLillo's *Underworld* (1997). The prologue has been so highly regarded that it has recently been published as a separate book, *Pafko at the Wall* (1997). It places within a fictional context what many consider the greatest game ever: the 1951 pennant winning victory of the New York Giants over the Brooklyn Dodgers in the last half of the ninth inning on a home run by Bobby Thomson. Throughout the rest of the novel, the home run ball assumes iconic status, while the game itself is juxtaposed with the fact that on the same day, October 3, 1951, the Soviet Union detonated a hydrogen bomb. Thus October 3, 1953, provided the occasion for "two shots heard round the world."

Another significant theme in baseball history relates to the discriminatory practice in which black players were prevented from participating in the major leagues, resulting in the formation of the Negro League, whose distinctive and exciting form of play is celebrated in William Brashler's *The Bingo Long Traveling All-stars and Motor Kings* (1973). Jackie Robinson's heroic breakthrough as the first black player in the major leagues forms the subject of Eliot Asinof's *Man on Spikes* (1998) and plays a significant role in Pete Hamill's *Snow in August* (1997). Baseball has also inspired some excellent poetry, not least from the distinguished poet Marianne Moore, who was a dedicated Brooklyn Dodgers fan.

basic writing   In COMPOSITION STUDIES, a term used to describe the writing of students with little or no experience in writing an essay. In the 1970s, a period in which college open admissions programs admitted students who would not ordinarily have qualified, the term was originally applied to the writing of students who were essentially beginning writers, despite being high school graduates. The term was designed to locate the problem in the educational system rather than in the writers themselves, the point being they were not bad writers, any more than students taking a beginning class in German were bad speakers of German —they were beginners. In the ensuing years this focus has been lost with the result that basic writing has been closely identified with remediation, along with the implication that basic writing is inferior, as opposed to beginning writing.

Mina Shaughnessy's *Errors and Expectations* (1973) is the foundational text in the field.

bathos   A term used to describe a writer's failure to elicit a strong emotion, inadvertently producing laughter or ridicule.

Battle of the books   A reference to debates that raged in England and France in the late 17th and early 18th centuries over the relative merits of ancient and modern writers. The strict NEOCLASSICAL position maintained for many years in French literature, favored the ancients. So too did Jonathan Swift, whose *Battle of the Books* (1697) satirized the modernist position.

beat   Term for a group of American writers who came into prominence during the 1950s and offered a radical critique of middle class American values. "Beat" has been variously defined as an abbreviated form of "beaten down" or of "beatific." The word also suggests the "beat" of JAZZ, whose improvisation and free association were mimicked in beat writing. Centered in New York and San Francisco, the beats celebrated individual freedom, Zen Buddhism, and the free use of drugs; they attacked the conformity, complacency, and commercialism of the "tranquilized fifties." Beat poets popularized the practice of reading poetry in cafes and jazz clubs.

The most prominent members of the group were the poet Allen Ginsberg and the novelist Jack Kerouac. Ginsberg's 1956 poem *Howl* (its celebrated opening line: "I saw the best minds of my generation destroyed by madness, starving hysterical naked") became the most popular poem of its time.

Kerouac's *On The Road* (1957), famously written on a continuous roll of teletype paper, depicts a world of dropouts from conventional society bonding to form a new, mystical community, an America rooted in its individualistic, westward-looking past.

Other major beat writers included the poets Lawrence Ferlinghetti (*A Coney Island of the Mind*, 1958) and Gregory Corso (*Gasoline*, 1958) and the novelist

William Burroughs (*Naked Lunch*, 1962). The full impact of the beat movement was to be seen less in literature than in the general culture, specifically in the hippie and student movements of the 1960s.

Gregory Stephenson's *The Daybreak Boys: Essays on the Literature of the Beat Generation* (1990) contains a collection of critical essays on the major beat writers.

belles lettres (fine letters) A term used to describe either impressionistic or highly cultivated writing or simply as a synonym for literature in general. In its adjectival form (*belletristic*) it carries a pejorative connotation, suggesting writing in which formal elegance far outweighs substance.

Berliner Ensemble Theatrical company established in East Berlin in 1949 by the playwright Bertolt Brecht. A committed communist, Brecht readily accepted the invitation of the postwar East German government to set up a repertory company that would produce Brecht's own plays. It also offered Brecht the opportunity to implement his theoretical conceptions, such as EPIC THEATRE and the ALIENATION EFFECT.

best seller A book sold in large numbers either at the time of publication or over a long period of time. Frank McCourt's *Angela's Ashes* (1997) is an example of the first type; *The Bible*, the all-time best seller, an example of the latter type.

bestiary A form of medieval literature in which the actions and/or characteristics of animals provided the basis for moral and religious homilies. The form originated in a Greek collection the *Physiologus* (second century A.D.), later translated into Latin. The stories were adapted in medieval monasteries in the form of beautifully illustrated books.

Bible, the In addition to its status as a sacred text, the revealed word of God for millions of Jews and Christians, the Bible is, in the words of Robert Alter and Frank Kermode, "probably the most important single source of all our literature." Past generations of readers knew its language and stories, songs and poems intimately. On the American frontier in the 18th and 19th centuries, it was often the only book in the house, read or listened to, by every member of the family. The loss of that intense biblical awareness in modern society has created a significant culture gap dividing us from our ancestors.

As a literary source, the Bible no longer informs modern literature as it did the works of Edmund Spenser, John Milton, and William Blake, but its "hidden" presence at a structural level is still pervasive. In an exemplary modern text, James Joyce's *Ulysses*, the Bible operates, as Robert Alter points out, as "a fundamental allusive matrix for Joyce's novel . . . with its hero Leopold Bloom, the new messiah himself, clinging to a sincere if muddled vision of love and harmlessness in a world of old hatreds and stubborn strife." Moreover, recent years have seen a growing appreciation of the power and the beauty of the Bible, not just as a powerful source but as a text in itself.

Doctrinal, as opposed to literary, interpretation was a central issue of the 16th-century Protestant REFORMATION. Determined to free themselves from the perceived tyranny of the Catholic tradition, the reformers adopted a philological approach, reading the texts, and basing their translations on the original Hebrew and Greek as opposed to the Catholic tradition of using the Latin VULGATE version as the standard. By the 19th century, this philological approach had evolved into the HIGHER CRITICISM, introducing a more skeptical atmosphere in biblical studies, intensified even further when scientific discoveries, notably DARWINISM, seriously undermined efforts to read the text as literal truths. The decline in the literal acceptance of the Bible left the door open for the literary response. Even among those who continue to adhere to literal renderings, there is a growing interest in reading the Bible as literature (*see* "LEFT BEHIND" NOVELS).

But on the scholarly level the literary approach is not free of religious factionalism.

The principal contention relates to the traditional division of the Bible into the Old and New Testaments. For many Jews, this designation implies not only a specious unity, but a subordination of the "Old" to the "New." This is particularly true in the practice of FIGURAL INTERPRETATION, in which events and persons in the Old Testament are seen as prototypes of New Testament figures. For an increasing number of mainly Jewish scholars, the Old Testament should be more properly designated as the Hebrew Bible, which itself is not a unified text but in Robert Alter's words, "a loose anthology that reflects as much as nine centuries of Hebrew literary activity."

For the New Testament, the chief obstacle to a historical or literary understanding is the relation among the SYNOPTIC GOSPELS. The result from a literary point of view is to experience the story from four different vantage points. Even here, however, such an obstacle can be viewed by readers as an invitation to PERSPECTIVISM.

Most prominent of those who adhere to a unified view of the entire Bible have been Erich Auerbach, whose pathbreaking *Mimesis* (1953) demonstrated the critical roles played by the Bible in the development of REALISM in Western literature, and Northrop Frye, whose *The Great Code* (1980) and *Words With Power*

(1990) argue that the Bible is written in the language of myth and metaphor, and that its basic structures are mirrored in all of Western literature.

The Literary Guide to the Bible, ed. Robert Alter and Frank Kermode (1987) is an admirable attempt to represent the full range and detail of contemporary biblical literary criticism. Robert Alter's *Canon and Creativity* (2000) contains an excellent account of Joyce's use of the Bible. William Schniederwind's *How the Bible Became a Book* (2004) looks at the oral origins of the biblical stories.

bibliography   Most commonly, a list of books and articles appended to a work implying that the author has consulted most or all of these works.

Another use of the term describes a full-length book devoted to a subject, a period, or an author. *The New Cambridge Bibliography of English Literature* (1969–77) is a five-volume bibliography of writings on British literature from the Old English period to the present day; *American Literary Scholarship: An Annual* (1963–   ) is a yearly bibliography that includes evaluations of the works listed. There are even bibliographies of bibliographies, as, for example, *Black Access: A Bibliography of Afro-American Bibliographies* (1984).

In still another sense of the term, *bibliography* acts as a synonym for TEXTUAL CRITICISM, a type of scholarship focusing on the physical features of manuscripts and books that may yield important insights into a literary work. For example, scholars have been able to reconstruct the actual practices used in the printing of Shakespeare's FIRST FOLIO in 1623. As a result, we have a much firmer understanding of the extent to which the printed texts of the plays accurately reflect what Shakespeare wrote.

bildungsroman (education novel)   A German term for a type of novel that focuses on the development of a character moving from childhood to maturity. Sometimes known as a COMING OF AGE novel, the form usually charts a movement from innocence to knowledge. Prominent examples include Goethe's *The Sorrows of Young Werther* (1774), Charles Dickens's *David Copperfield* (1849–50), James Joyce's *A Portrait of the Artist as a Young Man* (1916), and Günter Grass's *The Tin Drum* (1959).

binary opposition   In STRUCTURALISM, a basic linguistic principle in which each of two opposing terms implies the other: presence/absence; raw/cooked; male/female. As analyzed by the structuralist anthropologist Claude Lévi-Strauss, these basic contrasts underlie a society's cultural expressions, particularly its myths.

According to poststructuralist theorists (see POSTSTRUCTURALISM), binary opposites invariably reveal the assumption of the superiority of one term over the other with profound social and intellectual consequences. For example, in all patriarchal cultures, the assumed superiority of men to women plays a basic role in the cultural life of the society. Some of these consequences have been explored in FEMINIST CRITICISM, as in the fact that, in oppositions such as active/passive or subject/object, the second term has traditionally associated with the feminine.

biography   The written history of someone's life, with attention not only to the events but to the character and personality of the subject. An early example of the form is Plutarch's *Parallel Lives*, a study of the comparable careers of Greek and Roman statesmen. In the middle ages, biography consisted only of hagiography (the lives of saints) or of moralized accounts of royalty, as in John Lydgate's *Fall of Princes* (1420).

The RENAISSANCE emphasis on the individual found expression in the recording of particular lives. One of the earliest examples in English is *The Life of Sir Thomas More* (1560), written by More's son-in-law, William Roper. The 18th century saw the production of what is probably the greatest biography in English, James Boswell's *The Life of Samuel Johnson* (1791). Boswell's example influenced the development of literary biography in the 19th century, which was generally uncritical about its subjects. In the early 20th century, this attitude was radically overturned by Lytton Strachey, a member of the BLOOMSBURY GROUP, whose *Eminent Victorians* (1918) introduced an ironic and irreverent tone to the form.

Twentieth-century biography has also employed psychoanalytical insights in attempting to understand the subject. Although many early attempts to apply a Freudian perspective to the lives of their subjects have dated badly, recent work displays a more sophisticated grasp of the principles of PSYCHOANALYTICAL CRITICISM.

Among distinguished modern literary biographies are Leon Edel's five-volume biography of Henry James (1953–72), Richard Ellmann's *James Joyce* (1959), and David Riggs's *Ben Jonson: A Life* (1989).

Leon Edel's *Literary Biography* (1957) offers a meditation on the topic by a leading practitioner.

Blackfriars Theatre   A former Dominican monastery in London that became the headquarters of a company of child actors in 1576. This company was suppressed in 1608, thus providing Shakespeare's company, the King's Men (*see* CHAMBERLAIN'S/KING'S MEN) with an indoors winter home to complement their public theater, the GLOBE THEATRE. Writing for a more select audience,

Shakespeare employed a new type of drama—the romances, *Cymbeline*, *The Winter's Tale* and *The Tempest*.

Along with all the other theaters in London, the Blackfriars was closed by order of Parliament in 1642. In 1653, the vacant theater received a tribute from the writer Richard Flecknoe:

> *Poor house that in days of our grandsires*
> *Belongst unto the mendiant friars*
> *And where so oft in our father's days*
> *We have seen so many Shakspears plays.*

Black Mountain Poets   *See* PROJECTIVISM.

blank verse   The term for verse written in unrhymed iambic pentameter, unrhymed lines of about 10 syllables, in which the accent falls on the even numbered syllables. Since its introduction into English poetry in the 16th century, it has become the standard form for English drama in verse.

blazon   A lyric poem, typically a SONNET, in which the poet praises the beauty of his beloved, detailing her specific features: eyes, hair, cheeks, and usually her "fair" complexion. Shakespeare defied this tradition and the clichés it invoked by describing his loved one in less idolatrous terms:

> *My mistress eyes are nothing like the sun*
> *Coral is far more red than her lips red*
> *If snow be white, why then her breasts are dun*
> *If hairs be wires, black wires grow on her head*

Despite Shakespeare, the tradition soldiered on, notably in Lord Byron's "She Walks in Beauty like the Night." But Shakespeare's more realistic approach is reflected in Rodgers and Hart's "My Funny Valentine."

Bloomsbury group   A circle of English writers, artists, and philosophers with a shared set of values who frequently socialized at the homes of the novelist Virginia Woolf and her sister Vanessa Bell, located in the Bloomsbury section of London. The group flourished from 1906 to the 1930s, achieving prominence in the 1920s. Among its members were the economist John Maynard Keynes, the novelist E. M. Forster, the biographer Lytton Strachey, and the philosopher Bertrand Russell.

Although the group endorsed no official doctrine, they placed a high value on aesthetics, the cultivation of taste, unconventional sexual attitudes, and the importance of friendships. Many of these attitudes reflected the ethical teaching of the Cambridge philosopher G. E. Moore, who held that personal friendship and rich aesthetic experience were among the highest aims in life.

Leon Edel's *Bloomsbury: A House of Lions (1979) recaptures the spirit of the group.*

body, the In literature the human body has been a primary subject, though often approached indirectly. Insofar as the great humanist ideal of Western literature has been the human spirit, much of that literature appears to suppress or denigrate the body. From Plato on, the main tradition has regarded the body as the "prison house" of the soul, perhaps because the body is identified with mortality, while the soul has been seen as "immortal."

Nevertheless, the body occupies a central place in literature. In classical literature, the body—chiefly, a mark on the body—is closely related to identity: the scar of Odysseus, the club foot of Oedipus, the heel of Achilles, and the wound of Philoctetes play critical roles in their stories. They are emblems of the characters' frailty, but also keys to their identity. Even in the Christian era, in which the emphasis on the spiritual would appear to be completely dominant, the Incarnation of Christ—"The Word made flesh," as John's Gospel puts it—and the fact that Christ's flesh and blood serves as the substance of the Eucharist, suggests a connection between the divine and the corporal.

Some critics have argued that the body occupies the central place in at least one literary genre, comedy. They maintain that while tragedy speaks to the human spirit, comedy celebrates the corporeal, the physical being, driven by the instinct for survival or, the next best thing, reproduction by means of sexuality. A prime example, the figure who "embodies" the idea of comedy, is Shakespeare's Falstaff. In the two *Henry IV* plays, however, Falstaff's body moves from health to disease, signaling his ultimate rejection by his friend Prince Hal, as he assumes the crown.

Recently the concept of the body has assumed a central place in FEMINIST CRITICISM. Operating on the thesis that the female body has been "constructed" by a patriarchal culture, a culture that sees the woman as the object of the male *gaze*, feminists have taken a close look at the rendering of the woman's body in literature and the arts. They argue that, primarily in film and the visual arts, but also in literature, the traditional representation of the female body leaves the viewer in a privileged, dominant position.

Operating from a different stance, a group of French feminists have seen a close relationship between the body and WOMEN'S WRITING (*écriture feminine*).

Peter Brooks's *Body Work* (1993) is a study of "the body as an object and motive of narrative writing." *Literature and the Body* (1988), edited by Elaine Scarry, is a collection of essays exploring the subject from a feminist perspective.

bombast   Inflated or exaggerated language. Bombast usually denotes a boasting character such as the BRAGGART WARRIOR figure of classical and Renaissance comedy.

book   Usually a written or printed bound volume. Until the introduction to Europe of the printing press, all books were manuscripts. The regular appearance of the printed book in the 16th century ushered in widespread literacy in succeeding centuries, creating enormous changes in society (*see* ORALITY/LITERACY).

   The technical production of books involves the use of a number of terms that are employed in literary studies, particularly in the field of TEXTUAL CRITICISM. Among these are the terms for the approximate size of the book: A *leaf* is a single sheet, printed on both sides. Folded over once, it becomes a *folio* of two leaves, or four pages; folded twice, it is a *quarto* of four leaves, or eight pages; folded three times it is an *octavo* of eight leaves, or sixteen pages. Of course, the actual size of a book depends upon the size of the original sheet.

Boulevard theaters   A group of theaters on the Boulevard du Temple in Paris in the late 18th and early 19th centuries. The 1944 French film *The Children of Paradise* (*Les Enfants du Paradis*) is a celebrated tribute to these theaters.

bourgeois   In a strict sense, an adjective meaning "middle class" but frequently used disparagingly to suggest a person or attitude that is conventional or unimaginative. In Marxist terminology it takes on an even more disparaging definition, referring to the oppressive capitalist class and its ideology. Its pre-Marxist sense is reflected in the title of Molière's *Le Bourgeois Gentilhomme* (*The Would-be Gentleman* 1670), a satiric comedy about a relentless social climber.

bowdlerize   To edit out material deemed salacious or offensive. The term derives from Sir Thomas Bowdler, who published an edition of Shakespeare's plays (*The Family Shakespeare*, 1818). Bowdler's intention was to offer a text "in which nothing is added to the original; but those words and expressions are omitted which cannot with propriety be read in a family."

   The term *bowdlerization* now commonly refers to instances of editorial squeamishness.

braggart warrior (miles gloriosus)   In classical comedy, a STOCK CHARACTER who boasts of his military valor, but is usually shown to be a coward. Shakespeare's Falstaff is a type of braggart warrior, as is Captain Boyle in Sean O'Casey's *Juno and the Paycock* (1924).

brat pack   Name given to a group of young writers who enjoyed brief fame in the 1980s. They included Jay McInerney (*Bright Lights, Big City*, 1984), Bret Easton Ellis (*Less Than Zero*, 1985) and Tama Janowitz (*Slaves of New York*, 1986). Unlike the Frank Sinatra–led "rat pack," from which the term derives, these writers did not associate with one another but shared the same setting in their works, the fast track world of discos, drugs, and "getting over" that defined the decade.

breviary   A prayer book containing the Divine Office, which Catholic priests are required to recite daily. The medieval Book of Hours was a secular version of the breviary. The novel *The Very Rich Hours of Count von Stauffenberg*, by Paul West, about the leader of the 1944 attempt to assassinate Adolf Hitler, takes the form of a Book of Hours.

bricoleur   A term coined by the French Structuralist Claude Lévi-Strauss to describe someone who assembles disparate objects to produce a tool that serves a particular purpose. Applying the term to literature, some critics argue that *bricoleur* is a more accurate description of a writer than AUTHOR, in that it suggests not creation out of nothing but instead the rearranging of existing material. See INTERTEXTUALITY.

Brook Farm   A utopian community established in West Roxbury, Massachusetts in 1841. Brook Farm represented, at least in its first phase, an attempt to put into practice some of the principles of TRANSCENDENTALISM, together with newly emerging ideas of Socialism. George Ripley was the leader of the community. Among its prominent supporters were the early feminist Margaret Fuller and Nathaniel Hawthorne, whose novel *The Blithedale Romance* (1852) is based upon the history of the experiment. Brook Farm was disbanded in 1846 after a fire destroyed its main building.

Edith Roelker Curtis's *A Season in Utopia* (1961) is a history of Brook Farm.

bucolic verse   *See* PASTORAL.

Bunraku   The modern term for the puppet theater of Japan. The use of puppets for dramatic presentation is a Japanese tradition extending back more than a thousand years. Its golden age occurred in the late 17th century, when the great Japanese dramatist Chikamatsu Monzaemon began writing for the puppet theater. The plays, employing large dolls that require three people to manipulate each one, frequently deal with tragic subjects. Chikamatsu Monzaemon's *The Love*

Suicides at Sonezaki (1703) is one of the most celebrated examples of the genre. *See also* KABUKI; NŌ.

An Anthology of Japanese Literature, edited by Donald Keene (1955), contains Keene's eloquent translation of *The Love Suicides at Sonezaki*.

burlesque   1. A type of literature or drama designed to mock a serious work or an entire GENRE. As a form of PARODY, burlesque is usually distinguished from satire by its broad comic effects and its willingness to depart from serious criticism of its subject in favor of simple entertainment. As a result, burlesque is a frequently employed element of popular literature and film.

Notable 18th-century burlesques include John Gay's *The Beggar's Opera* (1728), a burlesque of Italian opera, and Richard Brinsley Sheridan's *The Critic* (1779), a send-up of HEROIC DRAMA. Contemporary examples of burlesques include *Monty Python and the Holy Grail* (1975), a spoof of the ARTHURIAN LEGEND, and *Airplane!* (1980), which targets airplane disaster films.

2. In America, a type of comic entertainment featuring slapstick comedy and striptease acts. American burlesque houses flourished from the late 19th century through World War II. The most famous striptease artist was Gypsy Rose Lee, whose career was chronicled in the Broadway musical and film *Gypsy* (1957). Other films dealing with the subject include *Lady of Burlesque* (1942) and *The Night They Raided Minsky's* (1968).

John Jump's *Burlesque* (1972) surveys the literary term. Robert Clyde Allen's *Burlesque and American Culture* (1991) analyzes the theatrical form as a POPULAR CULTURE phenomenon.

busker   In England a term used to describe a street performer in London during the late 19th and early 20th centuries. In the 1938 film *St. Martin's Lane* (American title: *The Sidewalks of London*), Charles Laughton gives a memorable portrayal of a Cockney busker.

For an account of Laughton's performance, see Simon Callan's *Charles Laughton; A Difficult Actor* (1987).

buskin   A boot, also known as a cothurnus, rising to the calf, worn by actors in Greek tragedies. Originally the boot had a thin sole, but additional layers were added in later periods of Greek drama, presumably to give the actors a more stately and dignified appearance. Conversely, actors in comedies wore the "sock," a low heeled, slipper-like shoe. As a result, in the Renaissance, *buskin* and *sock* became metaphors for tragedy and comedy. An example of this use is Philip Massinger's tragedy *The Roman Actor* (1626), which speaks of "the Greeks to whom we owe the first invention, both of the buskined scene and humble sock."

Byronic hero   A term for the dark, brooding, rebellious and defiant hero associated both with the character of George Gordon, Lord Byron and the heroes of many of his poems and plays. In the 19th century the Byronic hero became a major feature of ROMANTICISM, its internally conflicted, alienated, and demonic strain at once attractive and dangerous.

The Byronic hero owed something to the villain of the GOTHIC NOVEL and the suggestion of diabolism related to the FAUSTIAN THEME. His literary descendants include Edward Rochester in Charlotte Brontë's *Jane Eyre* (1847) and the figure of Jeffrey Aspern in Henry James's *The Aspern Papers* (1888).

Peter Thorslev's *The Byronic Hero* (1962) offers a defense of Byron and a discussion of his influences.

C

Cabala   *See* KABBALAH.

cacophony   In verse or prose, a discordant, harsh sound. One form of cacophony arises from the arrangement of words designed to make the reading of them difficult. Paul Fussell gives the following example from Alexander Pope: "When Ajax strives some rock's vast weight to throw." The effect of the s sounds (*Ajax, strives, some*) creates for the reader the same sense of heavy labor that the line describes.

Paul Fussell's *Poetic Meter and Poetic Form* (1965) offers insightful comments on cacophany.

cadence   In verse and prose, the rhythmic rise and fall of a line as opposed to the regularity of METER. Cadence is a prominent feature of poetry written in FREE VERSE and of formal prose.

caesura   In poetry written in English, a pause within a line of verse, indicated in SCANSION by a double slash (| |). A caesura normally occurs near the middle of a line, but in many poems the position of the caesura varies from line to line, as in this example from W. H. Auden's "Lullaby":

> *Lay your sleeping head | | my love*
> *Human | | on my faithless arm.*

Calvinism   The religious doctrines and practices derived from John Calvin's *Institutes of the Christian Religion* (1536). The most distinctive feature of Calvinism is its concept of predestination, the belief that the salvation or damnation of each person is predetermined by God and not within human control. Originating in Geneva, the movement spread to Scotland and England, where the Puritans brought it to America.

Among the literary figures whose works exhibit strong Calvinist tendencies are the English poet Edmund Spenser and the Puritan poets Anne Bradstreet and Edward Taylor. *See* PURITANISM.

Cambridge Ritualists   Term referring to a group of scholars from various disciplines at Cambridge University in the late 19th and early 20th centuries, who explored the origins of ancient Greek religion and its ties to literature and art. The event that brought the group together was the publication of James Frazier's monumental, 12 volume anthropological study *The Golden Bough: A Study in Magic and Religion* (1890–1915). With Frazier's example in mind, the Cambridge group—Arthur B. Cook, Francis Cornford, Jane Harrison, and Gilbert Murray—explored the ritual origins of Greek mythology, the marvelous transformation of primitive rites into tales of the Homeric gods, and still further, into the great achievements of classical Greek drama. Among their most important works from the standpoint of literature and drama are Jane Harrison's *Prolegomena to the Study of Greek Religion* (1903) and *Themis* (1912); Francis Cornford's *The Origin of Attic Comedy* (1914); and Gilbert Murray's *The Classical Tradition in Poetry* (1922), which includes Murray's "Hamlet and Orestes" (1914), the first example of applying MYTH CRITICISM to Shakespeare. Murray traces the formation of Hamlet and the Orestes of Aeschylus' *Oresteia*, characters deeply rooted in the mythology of Western civilization. Both figures are developments of the "myths of seasonal gods in that prehistoric and worldwide ritual battle of summer and winter, of life and death, which has played so vast a role in the mental development of the human race."

The work of the Cambridge Ritualists had a profound impact on early 20th-century writers, such as James Joyce, T. S. Eliot and William Butler Yeats. One expression of this debt is Eliot's tribute in the "notes" to *The Waste Land* (1922).

camp   A term in GAY LITERATURE and culture referring to a style that favors artifice and various forms of "posing." Believed to derive from the French word *camper* (to pose), the term appears in Christopher Isherwood's novel *The World in the Evening* (1956), divided into low camp and high camp. The novelist and critic Susan Sontag brought the term to general attention in her essay "Notes on Camp" (1965), which defined camp as "a certain form of Aestheticism . . . [operating] not in terms of beauty, but in terms of degree of artifice, of stylization." Examples of camp include Busby Berkeley film musicals (*Gold Diggers of 1933*), Tiffany lamps, and the epigrams of Oscar Wilde.

Camp Ground, edited by David Bergman (1993), is a collection of essays on the topic.

campus novel   A novel set at a college or university, in which academic life assumes not merely a background role (as it does, for example, in many murder mysteries) but is a determining factor in the lives of its characters. Campus novels may be divided between those dealing with students' experiences and those that focus on the faculty. Campus novels involving students began as outgrowths of 19th-century prep school fiction, such as *Tom Brown's Schooldays* (1857).

Early student-oriented campus novels include accounts of student life at Harvard and Yale at the turn of the 20th century. Owen Wister's *Philosophy 4* (1903) looks at undergraduate life at Harvard at the turn of the 20th century, while Owen Johnson's *Stover of Yale* (1911) emphasizes the importance of a caste system at the school.

More recent examples are Philip Roth's *When She Was Good* (1967), which looks at graduate student life, and Tom Wolfe's *My Name Is Charlotte Simmons* (2004), a less than benign look at the contemporary college campus.

Faculty-oriented campus fiction emerged in the late 1940s, when writers began teaching creative writing at colleges. Among interesting—and interlocking—satires are Mary McCarthy's *The Groves of Academe* (1952) and Randall Jarrell's *Pictures from an Institution* (1954). McCarthy's novel takes aim at a small, progressive women's college, bearing a strong resemblance to Sarah Lawrence College in New York, where McCarthy taught in the late 1940s. Anticipating by some 30 years the issue of POLITICAL CORRECTNESS, she depicts a professor who, being fired for incompetence, rallies his colleagues' support by claiming he's being dismissed for having been a Communist. Jarrell, who also taught at Sarah Lawrence, targets Gertrude Johnson, a writer who comes to a small, progressive women's college.

An even better-known satiric portrayal of academic life is Kingsley Amis's *Lucky Jim* (1955), whose protagonist, an unlovely, lazy lecturer at a provincial university, is more lucky than good. David Lodge's *Changing Places* (1975) is a delightfully satiric look at professors on an exchange program, a timid Englishman who comes to the earthly paradise of a campus not unlike Berkeley, and a go-getting American, Morris Zapp, who arrives at a redbrick university that bears a resemblance to Lodge's University of Birmingham. *Small World* (1984) continues their adventures.

John Updike explores the dilemma of a Harvard Divinity student in *Roger's Version* (1986). The political motif of *The Groves of Academe* is ironically mirrored in Philip Roth's *The Human Stain* (2000), where the protagonist, a dean at a small liberal arts college, has his life wrecked as a result of spurious charges of racism.

John O. Lyons *The College Novel in America* (1962) covers the topic from the 19th century to the 1950s.

canon The literary use of the term derives from its employment in Christianity to denote those works of the Bible and the early Fathers of the Church that were "authentic," or consistent with Church doctrine as it was being developed in the fourth century A.D. In literature, the term applies to the recognized works of a particular writer or to a body of works acknowledged as "classics," for example, "the canon of Western literature."

In the 1980s the idea of a "canon" of major literary works came under severe criticism by those who argue that the term "classic" has been reserved almost exclusively for writers who are white, Western males (the adjective "dead" is sometimes added to this description). As a result, say the canon's critics, women, minority, and third world writers have been systematically overlooked and ignored. These critics argue that the selection of certain writers as "great" is a consequence of the inbred attitudes or unconscious prejudices of the literary establishment, past and present. The defenders of the canon argue that the manifest superiority of canonical works is attested by the continuous recognition of their greatness over centuries.

Central to this debate is the question of the validity of literary VALUE JUDGMENTS in general, although the canon's critics are less critical of value judgments per se than they are of the specific judgments that have been made. The debate involves a number of thorny questions, not the least of which is the possibility of establishing criteria for measuring literary greatness.

One consequence of the debate is that recent years have seen a concerted effort to revise the reading list in required literature courses at American and British universities. Many of these courses now include works by Asian, African, and Latin American writers as well as by women writers from all spheres. This issue has become interwoven within the larger controversy surrounding the question of POLITICAL CORRECTNESS and MULTICULTURALISM.

Another view argues that studying the history of the canon provides a necessary clarification of the debate. The original use of the canon in schools was to provide models of standard written vernacular. In the 20th century, emphasis fell on the interpretation of literature as a means of apprehending its transcendent and universal value. Lost in the process was the historical experience out of which the work was produced and in which it is seen or read. From this perspective, the question of the canon is really a debate about the future of literary education, its aims and its function within society. A notable contributor to this view is Gerald Graff, who has argued for "teaching the conflicts": that the basis for any new curriculum should be the very issues that underlie the debate over the canon.

The fullest treatment of the question is the collection *Canons*, edited by Robert von Halberg (1985). The focus on literary education is adopted in John Guillory's "Canon" in *Critical Terms for Literary Study* (1990), edited by Frank Lentricchia and Thomas McLaughlin. Henry Louis Gates's *Loose Canons: Notes on the Culture Wars* (1992) addresses the debate from the perspective of an African-American scholar. Gerald Graff's views are contained in his *Beyond the Culture Wars: How Teaching the Conflicts Can Revolutionize American Education* (1986). Harold Bloom's *The Western Canon* (1994) is a forceful, somewhat idiosyncratic defense of the old canon.

canto   A major section of a long poem. Dante's *Divine Comedy*, for example, consists of three separate narratives: the "Inferno," the "Purgatorio" and the "Paradiso." Each of these is divided into 33 cantos. Thus, with the addition of an introductory Canto, the entire work consists of 100 cantos.

In the 20th century, Ezra Pound's major work is a poem consisting of over 100 cantos entitled simply *The Cantos* (collected and published in one volume in 1971).

caper film   A type of crime film that focuses on the intricate details of an elaborately planned robbery. Early examples of the form are John Huston's *The Asphalt Jungle* (1950) and Charles Crichton's *The Lavender Hill Mob* (1951). The latter set the standard for comic treatments of the subject, admirably pursued in Mario Moncelli's *Big Deal on Madonna Street* (1960) and George Roy Hill's *The Sting* (1973).

capitalism   An economic system based upon the investment of privately owned wealth (capital) to produce new wealth. Capitalism emerged in 16th-century England, powerfully assisted by the theological principles of CALVINISM. In Elizabethan drama, celebrations of the merchant class are evident in plays like Thomas Dekker's *The Shoemaker's Holiday* (1599), but in general dramatists of the period frequently attack the new urban commercial class, not least because of the association of trade with Puritans, committed Calvinists and vocal enemies of the theater. Ben Jonson's satiric comedies contain searing indictments of the new class. Shakespeare characteristically offers us both the positive and negative aspects of commercialism in the figures of Antonio and Shylock in *The Merchant of Venice* (1596).

By the end of the 17th century the distrust of materialistic and commercial values appears to give way to hopeful optimism as England assumed a leading role as a commercial and colonial power. In the first half of the 18th century, the dream of unlimited progress on the wings of commerce and science achieves its clearest expression in the novelist Daniel Defoe's works on economics (*The Complete English Tradesman*, 1726–27; *A Plan of the English Commerce*, 1728).

With the Romantic period, disenchantment with the capitalist world begins to appear, epitomized in William Blake's description of the "Satanic mills" appearing in the first wave of the Industrial Revolution. The evils of industrialism become the key theme in the work of Thomas Carlyle. Carlyle's *Sartor Resartus* (1833) sees the economic laws emerging in the industrial era as a grave threat to the maintenance of a truly human society.

The fiction of the period echoed Carlyle's critique: in the comprehensive picture of bourgeois society in Honoré de Balzac's *The Human Comedy* (1842–50); in Charles Dickens's memorable indictment of dehumanizing industrialism in *Hard Times* (1854); in Melville's brilliant, mystifying short novel *Bartleby the Scrivener* (1853), which bears the resonant subtitle "A Story of Wall Street."

The mid-19th century also gave birth to Karl Marx's critique of capitalism (*see* MARXIST CRITICISM), but even without a commitment to Marxist ideology, writers of this period and the early 20th century tended to view the economic system as a symptom of social and moral chaos, part of a larger picture of cultural decay. The literary tradition from William Wordsworth to Ezra Pound rests upon a critique of industrial society on moral, rather than economic, grounds. Even a committed socialist like Bernard Shaw offers, in the figure of Andrew Undershaft (*Major Barbara*, 1905) an unrepentant munitions maker who wins the day rhetorically by offering a vision of the social order more coherent and logically compelling than his high-minded adversaries.

On the other hand, the principles of REALISM and NATURALISM imply a radical critique of capitalism. The MUCKRAKER novels of Frank Norris (*The Octopus*, 1901) and Upton Sinclair (*The Jungle*, 1906) expose not simply the specific practices but the capitalist system as a whole. The proletarian novel of the 1930s (*see* PROLETARIAN LITERATURE) puts the case against capitalism with a passion intensified by the suffering of the Depression. In the 1940s the capitalist critique from the left is compellingly reflected in Arthur Miller's *Death of a Salesman* (1949) and from the right in Ayn Rand's popular novel, later a successful film, *The Fountainhead* (1943).

The acceptance of capitalism in American culture is an accomplished fact by the end of World War II. The postwar years see the emergence of the business novel, the most distinguished of which is John P. Marquand's *Point of No Return* (1949), whose hero attempts to bring his corporate career into relation with his personal values. The '50s produced a rash of popular business novels, the best known of which is Sloan Wilson's *The Man in the Gray Flannel Suit* (1955), a study in conformity based upon William Whyte's sociological studies, later published in Whyte's *The Organization Man* (1956).

Among distinguished novels of recent years dealing with a corporate ambience are Joseph Heller's *Something Happened* (1974), with its powerful evocation of fear as a motivating principle in the corporate world, and William Gaddis's *JR*

(1975), a satire focusing on a child capitalist. Tom Wolfe's portrait of one of the new "Masters of the Universe," the Wall Street broker, occupies the center of his satirical *The Bonfire of the Vanities* (1987).

The most consistent chronicler of the world of bankers, brokers and lawyers has been Louis Auchincloss. In more than 20 novels he has discerningly depicted, in Gore Vidal's words, "the collapse of the Puritan ethical system and its replacement by . . . nothing."

John McVeagh's *Tradefull Merchants: The Portrait of the Capitalist in Literature* (1981) examines the image of the businessman in English literature. Wayne Westbrook's *Wall Street in the American Novel* (1980) looks at the financial world. Gore Vidal's discussion of Louis Auchincloss is included in Vidal's *Matters of Fact and Fiction* (1974).

captivity narratives   In American literature, the accounts of white settlers who had been captured by American Indians during the Indian wars from the late 17th to the 19th centuries. The earliest of these, dating from the Colonial period in New England, was Mrs. Mary Rowlandson's account of being held prisoner for three months in 1676. Although she provides a chilling account of privation and suffering, which included the death of her child, she makes it clear that she had to endure no more suffering than the Indians themselves underwent. Her story, *The Sovereignty and Goodness of God: Being A Narrative Of The Captivity And Restauration of Mrs. Mary Rowlandson* (1682), was reprinted many times throughout the 18th century.

By the 19th century these narratives provided the basis for quasi-fictional accounts with a pronounced racist coloration, such as Royal Stratton's *The Captivity of the Oatman Girls*, which tells its readers that "the footfalls of the pioneering, brave Anglo Saxon is hard upon the heels of the savage." Edwin Jones's *Memories of a Captivity Among the Indians of North America* is a rarity: an unbiased account of the experience of John Tanner, captured at the age of nine who lived for 30 years with the Ojibwa Tribe. When offered the chance to return to white society, he refused.

Eric Sundquist's "The Frontier and American Indians," in the *Cambridge History of American Literature*, vol. 2, ed. Sacvan Bercovitch (1995), contains an important discussion of post-Colonial captivity narratives.

caricature   A term, usually applied to drawing, for an exaggerated description of an individual. In literature caricature usually serves a comic purpose, as in the plays of Ben Jonson, in which a particular trait becomes an overwhelming feature of a character's personality. Jonson's *The Alchemist* (1610), for example, features characters whose names contribute to their caricature: the sensualist, Sir Epicure Mammon, the hypocritical Puritan, Tribulation Wholesome, and the con men, Subtle and Face. Another master of literary caricature was Charles Dickens, whose novels abound with characters distinguished by their individual eccentricities.

The term sometimes carries a pejorative connotation when a critic uses it to stress the one-dimensional nature of a character.

carnival   A term used by the Russian theorist Mikhail Bakhtin to explore the subversion of authority and official culture in popular entertainment and festivals. Using the medieval carnivals—celebrations such as the Feast of Fools or Mardi Gras—as his prime example, Bakhtin argues that the bawdy, irreverent, scatological humor of these festivals testified to a rejection of the dominant medieval IDEOLOGY of church and state.

For Bakhtin the impulse to carnival, essentially an impulse to freedom, is reflected best in its literary form in the NOVEL. He sees the novel as rooted in the democratic world of the carnival where everyone, regardless of how eccentric, has a voice. This babble of voices, which Bakhtin calls HETEROGLOSSIA, characterizes a certain type of novel (exemplified by Dostoevsky) in which the full range of human nature is revealed. *See also* DIALOGISM.

Mikhail Bakhtin's *Rabelais and His World* (1968) and *Problems of Dostoevsky's Poetics* (1984) develop the concepts of carnival and heteroglossia.

Caroline   Relating to the reign of Charles I, King of England from 1625 until his beheading in 1649. It was during Charles's reign that the Puritan-controlled Parliament rebelled against the crown, establishing Parliament rule in England from 1642 to 1660.

Among the edicts Parliament issued when it came to power in 1642 was a decree closing all theaters in England. Prior to that date theatrical activity in the reign of Charles had been vigorous but qualitatively uneven. Caroline drama never achieved the eminence of the preceding JACOBEAN era. In fact, much of the court drama of the period consisted of pretentious, elaborately staged attempts to update the courtly love tradition. Nevertheless, the Caroline age witnessed the plays of two major English dramatists, Philip Massinger (*A New Way to Pay Old Debts*, 1632) and John Ford (*'Tis Pity She's a Whore*, 1633).

The lyric poetry of the era, known popularly as "Cavalier Poetry," specialized in witty, elegant love lyrics. Among the better known cavalier poets are Sir John

Suckling, Richard Lovelace, Edmund Waller, Thomas Carew, and the finest poet of the group, Robert Herrick (*see* CARPE DIEM).

F. S. Boas's *An Introduction to Stuart Drama* (1946) covers both the Jacobean and Caroline stages; Robin Skelton's *The Cavalier Poets* (1970) includes analyses of these poets' most important poems.

carpe diem (seize the day)   A Latin term expressing the idea of taking advantage of the present moment. In literature, the term refers to a type of poetry in which the poet implores the beloved to seize pleasure rather than to be "coy." Two outstanding examples of the type date from the 17th century, Robert Herrick's "To the Virgins, To Make Most of Time" and Andrew Marvell's "To His Coy Mistress."

In his novel *Seize the Day* (1956), Saul Bellow employs the motif ironically: A disastrous day in the life of the main character becomes the occasion for his spiritual rebirth.

catachresis   In RHETORIC, the misuse—usually deliberate—of a word or phrase. Traditionally regarded as a flaw, it can also apply to a striking and original usage, such as the reference in John Milton's "Lycidas" to "blind mouths," in which what appears to be a mixed metaphor is in fact a creative condensation of meaning. Milton's phrase is in a description of corrupt clergy: men who, instead of offering a vision and feeding their flock, are blind and interested only in feeding themselves.

In the sense that it applies to a misapplied word, catachresis bears a family resemblance to other examples of misapplication such as MALAPROPISM, OXYMORON, and PARADOX.

catastrophe   In TRAGEDY, the final phase—the denouement—of the tragic action. In *Henry IV, Part II*, Shakespeare uses the term comically in the sense of "rear end": "I'll tickle your catastrophe."

catharsis   In classical Greek, a word meaning "purgation" or "cleansing." In his *Poetics*, Aristotle defines TRAGEDY as "an imitation of an action . . . through pity and fear effecting the proper catharsis of these emotions." The chief question in connection with the meaning of the term is whether "catharsis" describes the experience of the audience or whether it refers to the action of the play itself, the purification or cleansing required to atone for prior guilt. Most students of drama favor the former interpretation, while those who employ MYTH CRITICISM tend to employ the latter view. Both groups agree, however, that the two views

69

are mutually compatible, not contradictory. Tragedy may reenact an archetypal pattern of guilt and atonement and, in so doing, recreate those emotions in the audience.

Recent studies include Adnan Abdulla's *Catharsis in Literature* (1985) and Stephen Halliwell's *Aristotle's Poetics* (1986).

Cavalier Poets   A group of poets connected to the court of Charles I of England, who supported the King during the English Civil Wars (1641–49). The king's followers were called *Cavaliers* while his Parliamentary opponents were known as *Roundheads*. The Cavalier poets created a fluent, sophisticated body of love lyrics in which the theme of CARPE DIEM ("Seize the day!") played a prominent role. Among the best known of the group are Richard Lovelace, Sir John Suckling, Thomas Carew, Edmund Waller, and Robert Herrick. *See also* CAROLINE.

Celtic literature   Literature produced by the Celtic speaking peoples of Western Europe and the British Isles, notably the Irish, Scottish, Welsh, Manx (the natives of the Isle of Man), and, in France, the Bretons (natives of Brittany).

In 18th-century England, a literary movement known as the Celtic Revival spurred an intense interest in Celtic literature, culminating in the literary forgeries attributed to the Celtic poet OSSIAN.

censorship   The practice of examining and suppressing writing or performances on political, moral, or religious grounds. Political censorship has been and continues to be characteristic of totalitarian regimes. Moral censorship generally relates to the issue of PORNOGRAPHY. Religious censorship is exemplified by the Vatican's INDEX LIBRORUM PROHIBITORUM, a listing of forbidden books. A notable example of religious censorship is the FATWA directed against the novelist Salman Rushdie by the religious government of Iran.

center/decenter   Key terms in DECONSTRUCTION and POSTSTRUCTURALISM. In these theories, "center" represents a firm foundation upon which rests a perception, a conception, or simply an order of words. The task of the poststructuralist is to show how this "center" is not a natural condition but a social construction rooted in a binary system of opposing terms in which one term has gained ascendancy over the other—for example, the traditional preference of male over female or speech over writing (*see* PHALLOCENTRISM, LOGOCENTRISM).

In analyzing these values, poststructuralists attempt to "decenter" them, dislodge them from their status as truths "that go without saying." The problem, though, is that decentering, once begun, has no end because it cannot simply replace one center with another. Thus the deconstruction of a literary text is a bottomless well that never achieves CLOSURE, only the stalemate characterized as APORIA.

A further irony is that the agent of centering/decentering is not the traditional "centered" SELF, but the decentered SUBJECT who has neither control nor freedom. In the view of the psychoanalytic poststructuralist Jacques Lacan, the subject's chief motive is the desire for a centered selfhood, but this is impossible to achieve because it is rooted in a fantasy represented as the union with the mother.

***

Interpreting Lacan (1983), edited by Joseph H. Smith and William Kerrigan, is a useful collection of essays on Lacan's ideas.

cento   *See* COLLAGE.

chain of being   An 18th-century metaphor depicting all existence as an interlocking chain, a gradation of existence from the lowest to the highest. At one end of the chain was God, extending down from above the orders of angels, to human beings, to animals, to animate and inanimate objects, to nothing. Humans occupied the center of the chain midway between God and nothingness. The concept stretches back to Plato's *Republic* and *Timaeus*, the Scholastic philosophy of the MIDDLE AGES, and the NEOPLATONISM of the Renaissance. It reached its culmination in the theory of the 18th-century philosopher Gottfried Leibniz. For Leibniz the conception of the chain of being reinforced his thesis that this was the best of all possible worlds, a concept satirized by Voltaire in *Candide* (1759).

The most elegant literary expression of the chain concept is in Alexander Pope's *Essay on Man* (1734).

***

A. S. Lovejoy's *The Great Chain of Being* (1936) contains a definitive account of the history of the idea.

Chamberlain's/King's Men   The two names of the acting company of which Shakespeare was a member and for which he wrote his plays. The Lord Chamberlain's Men was formed in 1594 under the patronage of Henry Carey, (Lord Hunsdon), Lord Chamberlain from 1585 to 1596 and under his son George until 1603. With a powerful patron to protect them from the antitheatrical city authorities, the company prospered, spurred by the popularity of Shakespeare's dramas. The two star performers were Richard Burbage, who excelled in the leading tragic roles, and Will Kempe, the principal comic actor. In 1599 the players erected their own playhouse, the GLOBE THEATRE, on the outskirts of London.

They soon became the leading acting troupe in London, although the company narrowly escaped extinction in 1601. In that year, the company put on a production of Shakespeare's *Richard II* on the eve of an abortive attempt by the earl of Essex to seize the throne from the aging Queen Elizabeth. In the investigation that followed the unsuccessful uprising, the actors testified that they had been paid by the followers of Essex to put on *Richard II* (the play has an abdication scene in it), but the company itself was exonerated.

With Elizabeth's death in 1603, the company came under the patronage of the new king, James I. With a royal protector, they continued to play at the Globe, but they also gave private performances for the king. In 1608, they were able to lease the BLACKFRIARS THEATRE, a private indoor playhouse. The players continued to perform there until 1642, when the Puritan-dominated Parliament decreed that "publike Stage-Plays shall cease and bee forebone."

Twenty years earlier, however, John Heminges and Henry Condell, two actors in the company, had ensured its immortality by collecting Shakespeare's plays and overseeing the publication of the FIRST FOLIO (1623).

An informative study of the Chamberlain's / King's Men is Andrew Gurr's *The Shakespearian Playing Companies* (1996).

chanson de geste (song of deeds) A medieval narrative poem detailing the heroic exploits of a legendary hero. Of the 80 extant chansons, the majority date from the 12th century, celebrating the battles of Emperor Charlemagne (A.D. 742–814). Despite their historical base the chansons were highly fictionalized and fantasized accounts. The most famous is the *Chanson de Roland* (c. 1100), recounting the heroic deeds of Roland, Charlemagne's nephew, whose valiant death against great odds exemplified the heroic virtues of loyalty and courage. The chansons had a powerful impact throughout Europe, spawning imitations in Italy, Spain, and Germany.

chapbook A pamphlet of 16 or 32 pages sold in England from the 16th to the 19th century by peddlers ("chapmen"). The contents might include accounts of crimes, romances, ballads, or sermons. The original account in England of the story of Dr. Faustus appeared in a chapbook. Other well-known chapbooks were the Elizabethan "cony-catching pamphlets," exposés of the Elizabethan underworld that purported to offer an insider's view of the way con men and pickpockets went about their trade.

character A person depicted in a NARRATIVE or DRAMA. Traditional fiction usually includes a physical description of a character's appearance, but many modern and postmodern novels dispense with the physical description and focus on the state of mind or motivation of the character. One form of description is sometimes evident in the character's name. Charles Dickens refined this technique by using names that suggest rather than directly describe the character, such as Scrooge, Murdstone, and Pecksniff. Some modern writers use names that function as ALLUSIONS, often either biblical (Ahab and Ishmael in *Moby Dick*) or mythological (Dedalus in *A Portrait of the Artist as a Young Man*).

A basic distinction between types of characters is that between "flat" and "round." Flat characters tend to be minor figures, who remain unchanged throughout the story. Round characters—those seen in a more rounded fashion—usually change in the course of the story. A comparable distinction exists between STOCK CHARACTERS and those that are "three-dimensional." Some critics point out, however, that even highly individualized and fully rounded characters are variations of certain archetypal figures (*see* MYTH CRITICISM).

The influence of Freudian psychology has played a powerful role in the depiction of, and response to, characters in 20th-century literature. The role of the UNCONSCIOUS and the employment of techniques such as the INTERIOR MONOLOGUE and MAGIC REALISM have provided a more complex conception of the internal lives of characters.

Among important critical treatments of character are E. M. Forster's *Aspects of the Novel* (1917) and John Bayley's *The Characters of Love: A Study in the Literature of Personality* (1960).

character, the   A form of literature consisting of a brief sketch of a general type of person, such as a "boaster" or a "malcontent." The Greek writer Theophrastus originated the form in the third century B.C. In 17th-century England, Joseph Hall (*Characters of Virtues and Vices*, 1608) and Sir Thomas Overbury (*Characters*, 1614) adapted and popularized the form.

chase, the   In FILM, the exciting, sometimes comic scene of pursuit, which has been an enduring feature of movies from the earliest days to the present. Chases are an integral aspect of film because they embody the essence of the medium, sometimes described as "the art of action."

The chase played a central role in *The Great Train Robbery* (1903), which established its place in the WESTERN. In silent films the chase was a pervasive ingredient in comedies, indeed the indispensable element in Mack Sennett's Keystone Kops series. Usually occurring near the conclusion of the film, the chase provided the final, farcical highlight preceding the resolution of the plot.

In addition to Westerns and comedies, chases have become a common device in action and detective films. Notable in this category is the San Francisco chase in *Bullitt* (1968), and the under-the-el chase in *The French Connection* (1971). In some cases the chase has been expanded to embrace the central action of the film, notably in *Odd Man Out* (1947), *The Chase* (1966) and *The Fugitive* (1993).

Among the literary antecedents of the film chase, the prototype is the classic pursuit through the sewers of Paris in Victor Hugo's *Les Misérables* (1862). In *The Power and the Glory* (1940), Graham Greene supplies a religious interpretation to the theme: it depicts a priest who is being hunted by an anti-clerical Mexican government. The original American title of the novel was *The Labyrinthine Ways*, an allusion to "The Hound of Heaven" (1893), a poem by Francis Thompson in which the speaker describes his pursuit and ultimate capture by Christ:

> *I fled Him, down the nights and down the days;*
> *I fled Him, down the arches of the years;*
> *I fled Him, down the labyrinthine ways. . . .*

chiasmus   In RHETORIC, the inversion of words from the first half of a statement in the second half. A famous example is John F. Kennedy's "Ask not what your country can do for you; ask what you can do for your country." The critic Louis Montrose employs chiasmus in his definition of NEW HISTORICISM as "the history of texts and the textuality of history."

Chicago renaissance   A period in early 20th-century American literary history when a significant number of important writers, including Theodore Dreiser, Edgar Lee Masters, Carl Sandburg, and Sherwood Anderson, lived in and wrote about Chicago. The spirit of the movement was captured in the literary magazine *Poetry*, founded in 1912 by Harriet Monroe and still in existence today.

The Chicago writers both celebrated and deplored their city, seeing it bursting with raw energy and optimism, reflected in Carl Sandburg's phrase, "hog butcher to the world." On the other hand, they condemned the evils of industrialization and commercialism, memorably exposed in Upton Sinclair's *The Jungle* (1906). The earliest expression of the renaissance was Theodore Dreiser's *Sister Carrie* (1900), the first half of which is set in the city. Later Chicago-based works include Sandburg's *Chicago Poems* (1916) and James T. Farrell's Studs Lonigan trilogy (1932–35).

The term has also been applied to a flourishing literary activity among African-American writers who settled in the city as a result of the migration of southern blacks to the large cities of the Midwest during the 1930s and '40s. The most prominent of these writers was Richard Wright, whose *Native Son* (1940) captured the struggle of the black man in the Depression years. Other Chicago-based writers of the '40s and '50s were the poet Gwendolyn Brooks (*Annie Allen,* 1949), the novelist Margaret Walker (*Jubilee,* 1966) and the playwright Lorraine Hansberry (*A Raisin in the Sun,* 1959).

Chicago school   A critical movement centered at the University of Chicago from the 1930s to the 1960s that adopted an Aristotelian approach to literary texts. Despite their basic adherence to Aristotle's *Poetics,* the Chicago school maintained an essentially pluralist view of criticism, arguing for a variety of critical perspectives on literature. Their basic principles were spelled out in the collection of essays *Critics and Criticism: Ancient and Modern* (1952), edited by the group's leader, Ronald Crane. Among their Aristotelian characteristics was an emphasis on GENRE as the basis of analyzing a literary work. In addition to Crane, other prominent Chicago critics included W. R. Keast, Richard McKeon, Elder Olson, and Norman Maclean (later celebrated as the author of *A River Runs Through It,* 1976).

Although the Chicago critics had a limited influence, their tradition survives in later generations of critics associated with the university, particularly Wayne Booth, whose work on the rhetoric of literature was instrumental in the development of READER RESPONSE CRITICISM.

Chicano/Chicana literature   *See* HISPANIC-AMERICAN LITERATURE.

children's literature   Literature designed to be read by children. Apart from nursery rhymes and FAIRY TALES, children's books were largely educational and edifying until the middle of the 18th century. John Newberry's *A Little Pretty Pocket Book* (1744) was the first book in English designed to entertain rather than educate a child. In the 19th century adventure stories for boys became popular with Johan Wyss's *The Swiss Family Robinson* (1812–13), Robert Louis Stevenson's *Treasure Island* (1882) and *Kidnapped* (1886), and Mark Twain's *The Adventures of Tom Sawyer* (1876). Among 19th-century novels for girls, celebrated examples include Louisa May Alcott's *Little Women* (1868) and Johanna Spyri's *Heidi* (1880).

Among children's classics of the early 20th century, Beatrix Potter's *The Tale of Peter Rabbit* (1902), Kenneth Grahame's *The Wind in the Willows* (1908) and A. A. Milne's *Winnie the Pooh* (1926) are outstanding. The mid-century was marked by the popularity of E. B. White's *Charlotte's Web* (1952) and C. S. Lewis's "The Narnia Chronicles," a series of books published in the 1950s.

Recent years have seen an emphasis on the importance of children's need to experience tragedy in literary form. Opposed to the traditional view that children should be shielded from tragic experience, many now argue for books that are not simply more "realistic" but "tragic" in the traditional sense, designed to evoke in their audience a spiritual cleansing (CATHARSIS). An example of this type of fiction is William Armstrong's *Sounder* (1969), a novel in which the evils of a segregated society result in the physical defeat but moral victory of the principal characters. (*See also* FAIRY TALE.)

Carolyn Kingston's *The Tragic Mode in Children's Literature* (1974) offers a thoughtful analysis of the subject.

Chinese-American literature

In the 1840s the first substantial number of Chinese immigrants arrived on the West Coast. They came to work on the transcontinental railroad or in mining camps. A steady stream of immigration continued until 1924, when new immigration laws radically reduced the number of Asian immigrants. In the meantime most immigrants had settled in large cities, congregating in "Chinatowns," which became areas of curiosity and stereotyping for mainstream Americans.

The first prominent Chinese-American writer was Lin Yutang, born in China in 1895, who immigrated in 1930 after the Chinese civil war. He achieved great popularity, introducing Chinese modes of thought and culture to Americans, frequently employing a humorous, light touch, as in *The Chinese Way of Life* (1959). Similarly, Louis Chu's *Eat a Bowl of Tea* (1961) offers a comic approach to the serious question of the male Chinese immigrant's plight issuing from the immigration laws that prevented women from entering the country.

An angrier, more critical approach is evident in Frank Chin's *The Chickencoop Chinamen* (1972), a sharply satirical look back in anger at mainstream Asian and traditional Chinese culture. His novel *Donald Duk* (1991), however, takes a somewhat more optimistic look at the problem.

The Chinese-American work that broke through the boundary of "Chinatown" is Maxine Hong Kingston's *The Woman Warrior* (1976), a semi-autobiographical account of a Chinese-American woman coming to grips with her identity, trying to reconcile the stories of women warriors with the traditional patriarchal oppression in Chinese culture.

David Harry Hwang's 1979 drama *F.O.B. (Fresh Off the Boat)* focuses on the experiences of new immigrants from Hong Kong who "don't act like they're fresh off the boat," a fact that causes identity problems for some ABCs (American-born Chinese). The struggle for identity among women immigrants is the central subject of the best-selling novels by Amy Tam, *The Joy Luck Club* (1989) and *The Kitchen God's Wife* (1991).

Notable recent novels by Chinese Americans include Ha Jin's *Waiting* (1999), a tragi-comic account of life in China during the Cultural Revolution, and *War Trash* (2004), the experience of a Chinese P.O.W. in the Korean conflict. Lon

Chang's *Inheritance* (2004) deals with the impact of a woman's suicide on her two daughters, extending to her Chinese-American granddaughters.

Shan Qiang He's "Chinese Asian-American Literature" is a succinct summary of the subject in *New Immigrant Literatures in the United States* (1996), ed. Alpana Sharma Knippling. San-Ling Cynthia Wong's *Teaching Asian American Literature* (1993) brings feminist theory to bear on the topic.

chorus   In Greek drama, a group of actors who observe and comment on the action of the play. According to Aristotle, Greek tragedy developed from choral performances. The function of the chorus in Greek drama is to reflect the traditional views of society, views that are usually inadequate to comprehend the full implication of the tragic action.

Shakespeare uses a single-person chorus to introduce and comment on the action in *Romeo and Juliet, Henry V, Pericles,* and *The Winter's Tale.* A collective chorus is effectively employed in T. S. Eliot's play *Murder in the Cathedral* (1935).

In MUSICALS, the term refers to a group of performers who sing or dance, or both, sometimes playing a collectively important role in the action, as in *A Chorus Line* (1975).

Christ   In literature, both a historical and symbolic figure whose image has consistently changed over 20 centuries. The religious historian Jaroslav Pelikan has charted these changes, ranging from the earliest view of Jesus as teacher and prophet through the medieval conception of the Son of God, the Renaissance view of the Universal Man, the Enlightenment ideal of the Teacher of Common Sense, the Romantic image of the Poet of the Spirit to the modern representation of Christ as Liberator, healer of the oppressed.

Along with the direct usages captured in religious writing are the symbolic representations of the Christ figure. At the heart of these conceptions is the view, articulated in MYTH CRITICISM, of the Christ archetype, the sacrificial agent whose suffering and death atones for the sins of the community. Tragic figures such as Hamlet, Conrad's Jim (*Lord Jim*, 1890), Faulkner's Joe Christmas (*Light in August*, 1932), and Ignazio Silone's Pietro Spina (*Bread and Wine*, 1936) exemplify the Christ figure as tragic hero.

Among direct representations of the Christ figure, the most notable is the "Grand Inquisitor" episode in Dostoyevsky's *The Brothers Karamazov* (1879–80), which depicts Jesus endorsing human freedom, opposing the Inquisitor's belief that most of humankind wants security, not freedom. This sense of Jesus as "liberator" was also invoked in Tolstoy's novel *Resurrection* (1899) and in 20th-century social protest novels such as John Steinbeck's *The Grapes of Wrath* (1939).

A similar view of Christ pervades the more self-consciously allegorical *A Fable* (1954) by William Faulkner, and, in a mocking, satiric vein, *Giles Goat Boy* (1966) by John Barth.

Nikos Kazantzakis's *The Last Temptation of Christ* (1954), adapted into a controversial film by Martin Scorsese in 1988, represents a spiritually conflicted Christ.

These shifting conceptions suggest that the archetypal power of the Christ figure remains powerful despite the diminished religious faith of the modern age.

Jaroslav Pelikan's *Jesus through the Centuries* (1985) is a cultural history of the significance of Christ's life. Edwin Moseley's *Pseudonyms of Christ in the Modern Novel* (1962) and Theodore Ziolkowski's *Fictional Transfigurations of Jesus* (1972) analyze major treatments of Christ in fiction.

chronicle play   A term for plays dealing with English history that were written during the ELIZABETHAN and JACOBEAN periods. The term derives from the fact that many of these plays used as their sources Raphael Holinshed's *Chronicles of England, Scotland and Ireland* (1577–87) and, to a lesser extent, Edward Hall's *The Union of the Two Noble and Illustrious Families of Lancaster and York* (1548). Shakespeare made use of both works in writing his English history plays.

Some writers occasionally use the term to describe modern history plays, notably George Bernard Shaw in his *Saint Joan: A Chronicle Play* (1923).

Ciceronian style   The style identified with the Roman orator and statesman Cicero. In 16th-century England, humanists searching for an appropriate style for formal written English looked to Cicero as their model. The style was highly rhetorical with elaborately constructed sentences. One of its finest exemplars was the theologian Richard Hooker, as in this sentence from his *The Laws of Ecclesiastical Polity* (1593):

> If we define that necessary unto salvation whereby the way to salvation is in any sort made more plain, apparent and easy to be known, then there is no part of true philosophy, no art of account, no kind of science rightly so called, but the scripture must contain it.

In the 17th century there was a marked turn away from the Ciceronian style to the SENECAN STYLE, which, in turn, developed at the end of the 17th century into modern English prose.

English Renaissance Prose (1997), edited by Neil Rhodes, is a collection of essays discussing the evolution of English prose from the early 16th to the late 17th centuries.

cinéma verité (film truth)   A type of DOCUMENTARY filmmaking that employs handheld cameras and portable sound equipment, enabling the filmmakers to capture the reality of the situation being filmed.

circumlocution   A roundabout, usually evasive, use of language. The formal term in rhetoric is periphrasis. In his novel *Little Dorrit* (1855–57), Charles Dickens satirizes the bureaucratic delays of government agencies in his depiction of the Circumlocution Office: "In short all business of the country went through the Circumlocution Office, except the business that never came out of it; and its name was legion."

J. Hillis Miller's *Charles Dickens: The World of His Novels* (1958) discusses the role of circumlocution as a symbol of evil.

city, the   In literature, the theme of the city has acquired contradictory connotations: on the one hand, learning, fellowship, and human achievement; on the other, worldliness, corruption, and crowds. At the heart of this ambivalence is the recognition that the city—its virtues and its vices   is a human creation and, as such, a testament to the best and worst of the human race.

The city has served as a literary topic since antiquity, achieving its fullest exposition in Saint Augustine's *The City of God*. Written following the fall of Rome in A.D. 410, Augustine's description of the two cities, the heavenly city and the city of this world, powerfully locates the idea of the city at the center of human experience.

Although the evils of city life had been the subject of satire by Aristophanes, Horace, and Juvenal in classical times, and Ben Jonson in Renaissance London, the virtues of city life were also extolled. With the coming of industrialization, however, the negative images of urban life intensified. The crowding of the cities—rife with poverty, crime, and diseases, together with the spectacle of deserted villages and exploited countrysides—unleashed a powerful anti-urban theme burgeoning in the late 18th century and continuing to the present day.

Romanticism, with its profound commitment to nature, viewed the city as an alien and alienating place—the seat, in Wordsworth's phrase, of "getting and spending" and of Blake's "mind-forg'd manacles."

In the 19th-century novel, the city assumes a preeminent role. The Paris of Victor Hugo, Honoré de Balzac, and Émile Zola; the London of Charles Dickens (particularly his *Bleak House*, 1852); the St. Petersburg of Dostoyevsky (*Crime and Punishment*, 1886); the New York of Herman Melville (*Pierre*, 1852) serve not merely as scenic backdrops but as characters, active forces that alter and shape the lives of their inhabitants.

A significant feature of many of these novels is the motif of the young man or woman from the provinces, determined to make his or her mark in the big city. This encounter of innocence and experience is dramatized in the form of a BILDUNGSROMAN, an education novel, or as ironic tragedy.

Both traditions adhere in 20th-century literature with the added dimension of the city as the site of modern EPIC. Distinguished examples include Marcel Proust's *Remembrance of Things Past* (1913–27), James Joyce's *Ulysses* (1922), Alfred Doblin's *Berlin Alexanderplatz* (1929), James T. Farrell's *Studs Lonigan: A Trilogy* (1935), Lawrence Durrell's *Alexandria Quartet* (1961) and, in verse, William Carlos Williams's *Paterson* (1946–58).

Notable films that capture the feel of modern cities include *Summertime* (Venice, 1955); Fellini's *Roma* (Rome, 1972); *Under the Roofs of Paris* (Paris, 1930); *Odd Man Out* (Belfast, 1947); *The Third Man* (Vienna, 1949); and *Taxi Driver* (New York, 1976).

Diana Festa-McCormick's *The City as Catalyst* (1979) examines the urban theme in 10 novels of the 19th and 20th centuries; John H. Johnston's *The Poet and the City* (1984) selectively surveys urban poetry from the classical period to the present.

class As a term, social class is relatively recent, dating back to the 19th century, although the phenomenon it describes is ancient. The most famous employment of the term belongs to Karl Marx, who postulated the existence of three classes: the land-owning old aristocracy; the bourgeoisie, the owners of the financial and manufacturing "means of production"; and the proletariat, who own only their own labor. Marx also designated two sub-classes, the petit bourgeoisie, made up of shopkeepers, service professionals, and small farmers, and the lumpenproletariat, the outcasts of society. Among these contending classes conflict is inevitable, but, according to Marx, the dominant class is the bourgeoisie, having successfully infiltrated all of society with its IDEOLOGY, the conviction that bourgeois values are the only reasonable ones.

In most novels, the literary form in which the interactions of the classes are most pronounced, social class functions not as an abstract category but as a dynamic presence, at times explicitly, at other times unexpressed but taken for granted. Examples of the latter process are the novels of Jane Austen, whose fine discriminations of character are framed within the context of the intrusion of bourgeois values into the lives of the landed gentry in early 19th-century England.

From a Marxist perspective, most of the literature of the 19th and 20th century exhibits an endorsement of bourgeois values. Marxists cite as bourgeois even those novels, such as those of Charles Dickens, that focus on social problems, but call for only moderate reforms and celebrate a common humanity that transcends class distinctions.

Novels that embody a working class ideology include Émile Zola's *Germinal* (1885), which depicts the lives of striking miners; Jack London's *The Iron Heel* (1907), in which ruthless capitalists seize control of the United States government; D. H. Lawrence's *Sons and Lovers* (1913), a vivid account of the lives of workers in an English mining town; James T. Farrell's *Studs Lonigan* trilogy (1932–35), a portrayal of life in the Chicago slums; and John Steinbeck's *The Grapes of Wrath* (1939), depicting the lives of migrant laborers in the midst of the 1930s depression.

By the 1960s, Marx's categories no longer reflected the reality of class structures. The rise of an international youth culture in Europe and America is one example. The distinctions of dress, dialect, and cultural preferences that were the hallmarks of class distinctions disappeared as young people from all classes celebrated and imitated working class icons, such as the Beatles and the Rolling Stones. The subsequent collapse of Communist regimes in Eastern Europe further supported the suspicion that the Marxist analysis of class was oversimplified and outmoded, but a satisfactory alternative has not as yet received general acceptance.

Mary Eagleton and David Pearce's *Attitudes to Class in the English Novel* (1979) examines the issue in terms of Victorian and 20th-century fiction. Raymond Williams's *Keywords* (1976) contains a historical definition of the term. Fredric Jameson's *Postmodernism, Or, the Cultural Logic of Late Capitalism* (1992) analyzes the current situation.

classicism   A term covering a variety of uses but chiefly referring to qualities associated with the literature and culture of Greece and Rome. Among those qualities are symmetry, harmony, control, and reason. In this sense classicism stands in opposition to ROMANTICISM.

The Renaissance rediscovery of classical literature led to the development in the 17th and 18th centuries of NEOCLASSICISM, the conscious imitation of the forms, and what were believed to be the rules, of classical literature. The first half of the 20th century saw to some extent a return to classical principles, at least in academic circles where the NEW CRITICISM upheld the classical principles of restraint and order. One notable example is T. S. Eliot's defense of James Joyce's *Ulysses* from the charge that it was "undisciplined": Eliot argued that it is a true "classicist" text, using classical myth as "a way of controlling, of ordering, of giving a shape and a significance to the immense panorama of futility and anarchy which is contemporary history."

T. S. Eliot's essay "*Ulysses*, Order, and Myth" is reprinted in *The Modern Tradition* (1965), edited by Richard Ellmann and Charles Feidelson.

climax   The turning point in a DRAMA or work of fiction. Although usually located near the end of a NARRATIVE or play, the climax occasionally occurs earlier, as in Mark Antony's address to the crowd at the midpoint of Shakespeare's *Julius Caesar*.

closet drama   A play designed to be read either silently or in a group, not performed. "Closet" in this sense means private library or study.

Among notable examples of the type are John Milton's *Samson Agonistes* (1671), Lord Byron's *Manfred* (1817), and Percy Bysshe Shelley's *Prometheus Unbound* (1820).

close-up   In film, a SHOT in which the camera appears to be so close that the subject, even if it is a relatively small object like the head of a person, fills the entire screen. Close-ups are frequently used to focus the audience's attention on the reactions or emotions of a specific character. They may also be employed to call attention to an important detail.

The pioneer director D. W. Griffith was the first to use the close-up as an important element in film. Among other celebrated examples of the close-up technique in film history are Carl Dreyer's The *Passion of Joan of Arc* (1928), Alfred Hitchcock's *Rear Window* (1954), and Michelangelo Antonioni's *Blow-up* (1966). In the latter two films the technique serves as a self-conscious, thematic commentary on the nature of film itself.

Thomas Harris's "*Rear Window* and *Blow-up*: Hitchcock's Straight Forwardness and Antonioni's Ambiguity" (*Literature/Film Quarterly*, V. 15, 1987) offers an interesting analysis of the technique.

closure   The ending or point of resolution in a literary work. The term becomes problematic in connection with many modern and contemporary works that are distinguished by their open-endedness or apparent lack of closure. Such works seem to ask the reader or viewer to complete them. Closure in this context refers not so much to the technical ending of a story as to a sense of completeness or wholeness experienced by the reader.

Marxist critics have emphasized the need to move beyond the formal structure of the text to examine the work's ideology. From this perspective the ending of a work occurs when the reader determines its function in society. Similarly, from the standpoint of READER RESPONSE CRITICISM, the reader's feelings determine closure. It is an operating assumption of DECONSTRUCTION that critical closure, in the sense of arriving at a determinant meaning of a text, is neither possible nor desirable.

Barbara Herrnstein Smith's *Poetic Closure: A Study of How Poems End* (1968) is an admirable analysis of closure in poetry; Frank Kermode's *The Sense of an Ending* (1967) looks at the human need to impose endings as a way of sustaining the illusion of order; David Richter's *Fable's End* (1974) draws a distinction between plot-oriented novels and those with a thesis, maintaining that the latter "close" when the author's point has been made.

cockney school of poetry   A derisive term first employed in 1817 to describe the poetry of Leigh Hunt, John Keats, Percy Shelley and William Hazlitt. The term *cockney* alluded to the fact that the writers were all Londoners, some of whose rhymes were thought to reflect a cockney pronunciation.

code   In linguistics, the shared understandings that make communication possible. In literature, the term also refers to certain principles of behavior—for example, the conduct of heroes in Ernest Hemingway's fiction. The "Hemingway Code," a phrase coined by the critic Philip Young, refers to a pattern of behavior that is stoic, resigned, unillusioned, and dignified. All of these virtues are exemplified in the character of the old fisherman in Hemingway's *The Old Man and the Sea* (1952). Another code characteristic is courage, defined by Hemingway as "grace under pressure."

Philip Young's *Ernest Hemingway: A Reconsideration* (1966) discusses the code at length.

codex   A book that contains manuscripts.

collaborative learning   A pedagogical practice that emphasizes learning in small groups. Rooted in the principle of SOCIAL CONSTRUCTION, collaborative learning argues that students learn more effectively by exchanging and developing ideas with their peers than by the isolated efforts of individuals to absorb facts handed down by a teacher. This approach is evident to a significant extent in COMPOSITION STUDIES where such activities as peer tutoring, collaborative authorship, and the emergence of writing centers, amplify the writing curriculum as an important learning resource.

Kenneth Bruffee's *Higher Education, Independence, and the Authority of Knowledge* (1993) is an exemplary treatment of that subject.

collage   In art, an arrangement of disparate materials pasted on a surface. The term is sometimes used in literature to refer to the technique of incorporating bits and pieces of other writing within a story or poem. One version of a collage is a cento, a poem made up entirely of lines from other poems.

collation   In TEXTUAL CRITICISM, the meticulous comparison of two copies of the same text to determine variations between the two.

Colonial period (American literature)   American literature begins with the first accounts of the colonies of Virginia and New England. Among the early tales of voyages to Virginia is one of a ship wrecked in a storm in the Bermudas. The survivors of the wreck, cast away on a strange island, rebuilt their ship and eventually sailed to Jamestown. The account of their castaway experience provided Shakespeare with source material for *The Tempest*. Conditions in the early Virginia colony rendered it an inauspicious place for literature. Not so in New England, where Puritan industry and discipline saw the establishment of the first college (Harvard), the first printing press, and the first newspaper. The literature that emerged in New England was of a largely religious character. One notable exception was a satire against the Puritans, *New English Canaan* (1637), written by Thomas Morton, a former colonist who had been banished by the authorities for his dissolute, loose-living ways. On a much loftier ethical plane was Roger Williams's *The Bloudy Tenent of Persecution for Cause of Conscience* (1644), an earnest if ineloquent plea for the separation of church and state. The second generation colonists, among whom can be included the two finest poets of the period, Anne Bradstreet and Edward Taylor, also created a new genre: the CAPTIVITY NARRATIVE. But the most important cultural development of the early 18th century was "the Great Awakening," the religious revival spearheaded by Jonathan Edwards, a theologian who had a lasting impact on American thought. Edwards is best known for his SERMON "Sinners in the Hands of an Angry God" (1741), famous for its fire and brimstone character.

Darrel Abel's *American Literature: Colonial and Early National Writing* (1963) provides a detailed history of the period.

colophon   A publisher's logo and identifying information appearing on the title page of a book.

Comédie-Française   The national theater company of France founded in 1680 by royal decree. The company is famous for the consistently high quality of its ensemble performances and its repertory of classical French drama. Among its greatest actors was the legendary Sarah Bernhardt, whose performance in the lead role of Racine's *Phèdre* marks a high point in the history of French theater.

comédie larmoyante (tearful comedy)   A type of 18th century DRAMA that contained tearful, sentimental scenes in which virtuous characters triumph over adversity. The creator of the form was Pierre Claude Nivelle de la Chausée, whose plays influenced the success of SENTIMENTAL COMEDY in England in the early 18th century.

comedy   A type of DRAMA that celebrates or satirizes the follies of characters. (For a description of comedy in fiction, *see* COMIC NOVEL.) Although the comic impulse is a universal human trait, the particular form of dramatic comedy has been traced, as has TRAGEDY, to its origins in the primitive celebrations of spring designed to ensure a prosperous seed time and the health and longevity of the community. This is a view that has been readily adapted and convincingly described in MYTH CRITICISM. The mythic approach helps to explain comedy's emphasis on the social and the collective as opposed to tragedy's focus on the isolated individual. Socially, comedy can be seen from two perspectives. One employs the idea of CARNIVAL, the collective assertion of freedom in the face of the repressive structures of society. Comedy in the carnival mode thumbs its nose at the powers that be, whether they be gods or governments. An alternative view sees comedy as an essentially conservative force, providing a release through a ritualized SCAPEGOAT figure whose ultimate repudiation permits the restoration of the society's traditional values.

   Classical comedy dates to the fifth century B.C. The sole extant examples of this "Old Comedy" are 11 plays of Aristophanes, all of them characterized by extravagant plots and biting satire of individuals and institutions. These plays consist of a debate between two characters; an address to the audience by the CHORUS, representing the author's point of view on topical issues; and a series of broad comic scenes, followed by a wedding or feast to conclude the action. In the course of the play, characters would deliver scurrilous invective against various well-known people. One such target was Socrates, ridiculed in Aristophanes' *The Clouds* (423 B.C.) as a fraud and atheist. The best known of Aristophanes' comedies, *Lysistrata* (411 B.C.), is a striking example not only of Old Comedy, but also of comedy in general. It depicts the successful efforts of Athenian women to put an end to the Peloponnesian War by refusing to have sex with their husbands while the war lasts. In the triumph of love over war or, more precisely, sex over death, the play sounds a basic comic principle.

   Aristophanes' last play, *Plutus* (388 B.C.), is the sole surviving example of "Middle Comedy," a form that employed parody and satire of classical myth.

   By the end of the fourth century B.C., Middle Comedy had given way to "New Comedy," a form employing stock characters such as the EIRON and ALAZON, and plots focusing on domestic issues involving young lovers, clever servants, and greedy old men. The great figure of New Comedy in Greece is Menander. Imported to Rome in the second and third centuries B.C., New Comedy received further development at the hands of Plautus, the author of 21 extant plays, and Terence, credited with six surviving plays. The other popular comic form, FARCE, developed in Sicily and southern Italy and achieved its Renaissance expression in the COMMEDIA DELL'ARTE.

As fashioned by Plautus and Terence, New Comedy formed the basis of Renaissance and modern comedy. As Northrop Frye suggests in his summary of New Comedy, its core consists of a "comic Oedipus situation. Its main theme is the successful effort of a young man to outwit an opponent and possess the girl of his choice. The opponent is usually the father (*Senex*) and the psychological descent of the heroine from the mother is also sometimes hinted at."

Forms of New Comedy are evident throughout Europe. In Italy, Niccolò Machiavelli's *Mandragola* (1518) provided a particularly cynical version of the formula. English comic dramatists integrated New Comic principles with the folk tradition of medieval drama, a tradition that allowed for the mixing of the sacred and the profane, the tragic and the comic. A notable example of the latter is *The Second Shepherd's Play* (late 14th century), a MYSTERY PLAY that fuses the Nativity with a comic plot involving the stealing of sheep. Out of these classical and medieval roots Shakespeare fashioned a diverse range of comic forms. Such plays as *The Comedy of Errors* are direct applications of Roman models, while *As You Like It* and *A Midsummer Night's Dream* transpose the New Comic plot to the "green world," a setting that incorporates the theme of nature as a regenerating force, invoking the echo of comedy as a ritual celebration of rebirth.

New Comedy is given another twist in the plays of Molière, who uses the form to launch attacks on social and religious hypocrisy in such plays as *The Misanthrope* (1666) and *Tartuffe* (1669).

The RESTORATION period in England saw the development of the comedy of manners, a form that feeds on dazzling wit and the creation of an artificial world. Although temporarily eclipsed in the 18th century by SENTIMENTAL COMEDY, the comedy of manners has proven a remarkably resilient genre, reappearing in the comedies of Oscar Wilde and in a host of prominent 20th-century playwrights. By the end of the 19th century, TRAGICOMEDY, a type of drama that had flourished during the Renaissance, appeared in a new and weightier form.

Modern tragicomedy has taken two forms: tragedies laced with comic characters and scenes, such as Sean O'Casey's *Juno and the Paycock* (1924), and comedies that end unhappily. The master of the latter form is Anton Chekhov, whose *Uncle Vanya* (1899), *The Three Sisters* (1901), and *The Cherry Orchard* (1904) explore a psychological and social malaise whose pathos is rooted in its characters' acute self-consciousness. Although their unhappy endings would seem to violate a basic comic law, Chekhov insisted that his plays were sad but comic.

Chekhov's plays, echoed in different ways by George Bernard Shaw, Arthur Schnitzler, and Luigi Pirandello, led to the 20th-century phenomenon in which many "serious" plays were written in the comic mode. Writing in the era of EXISTENTIALISM, playwrights of the Theater of the ABSURD created new descriptions for their work, such as *tragic farce*, designed to underline the meaninglessness of human existence, most notably expressed in Samuel Beckett's *Waiting for Godot* (1951). Beckett may have defined the paradox of tragic farce most accurately in his comment, "There is nothing funnier than unhappiness." But Absurdist theater and Beckett in particular seemed to have created a dead end, leaving subsequent dramatists nowhere to go, resulting in a return to more immediate social and political issues in recent comic drama.

In films, the great silent film comedians—Charlie Chaplin, Buster Keaton, and Harold Lloyd—gave way to the Marx Brothers' farces and the SCREWBALL COMEDY of the 1930s, the romantic sparring of Spencer Tracy and Katharine Hepburn, the Alec Guinness comedies of the '40s, the wry, observant "moral tales" of Eric Rohmer, the exuberance of Federico Fellini, and the wit of Woody Allen, all testifying to the infinite variety of the comic.

Robert Corrigan's *Comedy: Meaning and Form* (1965) offers a valuable collection of the most significant criticism. Northrop Frye's seminal discussion is included in his *Anatomy of Criticism* (1957). Harry Levin's *Playboys and Killjoys* (1987) examines comedy in theory and practice.

comic novel   Any list of important comic novels is certain to include some of the greatest novels ever written. Beginning with Cervantes's *Don Quixote* (1605–15), the comic mode has played a fundamental role in the history of the novel. Novels have always mirrored the societies in which they were written, thereby providing an apt venue for satire or IRONY. Novels also allow for fully developed characters and actions, demonstrating that folly is a fundamental human trait intermixing in complicated ways with more admirable characteristics. This is the signature of the great comic novelists, notably Jane Austen, whose wit and irony are only components of a wider, more comprehensive view of her characters and their world. In this respect she expands the rich comic sphere of the 18th-century novel, exemplified by Henry Fielding's *Tom Jones* (1749) and Laurence Sterne's *Tristram Shandy* (1759–67). The comic fun of these two novels lies in their energy and inventiveness, but they lack the complexity of feeling that Austen creates. Charles Dickens is capable of employing both styles. His *The Pickwick Papers* (1837) continues the witty, episodic tradition of the 18th century, while his rendering of the character of Mr. Micawber in *David Copperfield* (1850) suggests a more complex figure, his basic decency entwined with, and to some extent dependent upon, his foolishness.

In the 20th century, the comic novel is dominated by the work many regard as the century's greatest, James Joyce's *Ulysses* (1922). Its leading character, Leopold Bloom, a modern-day Ulysses, wanders the streets of Dublin and exhibits those qualities of decent humanity and foolishness with unparalleled depth, communicated through the device of the INTERIOR MONOLOGUE.

The best known comic novel of the second half of the century is Joseph Heller's *Catch-22* (1961), an antiwar, antibureaucracy satire.

Bernard Schilling's *The Comic Spirit* (1965) explores the theme of "tolerant laughter" in five comic novels.

comic relief   A humorous scene in tragic DRAMA or fiction that has the effect of temporarily altering the mood of the play and thereby relieving the tension. The term is a misnomer insofar as it suggests a lessening of the tragic effect. As employed by Shakespeare in the gravediggers' scene in *Hamlet*, the drunken porter episode in *Macbeth*, and the commentary of the Fool in *King Lear*, comedy intensifies the tragedy by permitting us to see the tragic action from an alternative point of view. The gravedigger's comment that he began digging graves on the same day that "our last king overcame Fortinbras . . . that very day that young Hamlet was born, he that is mad and sent to England" reconceives the entire action of the play from the perspective of the common man.

Another form of comic relief occurs with the ironic juxtaposition of the comic and tragic. A master of this technique in fiction is the American short story writer Flannery O'Connor, whose comic characters frequently meet tragic ends. In her best-known story, "A Good Man Is Hard to Find," for example, the main character undergoes a transformation from a comically smug manipulator into a tragic, but redeemed, figure a moment before she is murdered.

Susan Snyder's *The Comic Matrix of Shakespeare's Tragedies* (1979) analyzes the interplay of comedy and tragedy with subtlety and precision.

coming of age   A sociological term for the movement of an individual from childhood or adolescence to adulthood. In primitive societies, coming of age is marked by a prescribed ritual in which the young person, after undergoing a test or submitting to a painful procedure, becomes a member of the tribe. In literature, this tradition is reflected in stories that mark a child's passage from innocence to experience or knowledge, in which the child usually pays the price of pain or disillusionment.

The process is a major theme of such major 19th-century works as Charles Dickens's *Great Expectations* (1860–61), Mark Twain's *Adventures of Huckleberry Finn* (1884), and Henry James's *What Maisie Knew* (1897). Notable examples in 20th-century literature include those short stories of Ernest Hemingway that focus on the character of Nick Adams, J. D. Salinger's *Catcher in the Rye* (1951), and Harper Lee's *To Kill a Mockingbird* (1960). The theme also constitutes an important chapter in any novel characterized as a BILDUNGSROMAN, a type of novel that includes coming of age.

The Rite of Becoming, edited by Arthur and Hilda Waldhorn (1966), is a collection of stories and commentary on the theme.

commedia dell'arte   A form of popular comedy that developed during the 16th and 17th centuries in Italy, from which it spread throughout Europe. The commedias were performed by professional strolling players who improvised the dialogue while assuming the roles of certain stock characters. The most popular of these were the *zanni*, or clowns, many of them trained acrobats whose tricks and derring-do delighted audiences. A typical plot involved the efforts of *Pantalone*, a parent or guardian, and his friend the *dottore* to marry off a ward or daughter, Isabella, to a rich suitor. But the young woman connives with her maid, Columbine, to outwit the older generation and marry the young hero, Flavio. Aiding their efforts and dominating the play are the other servants, the *zanni*, whose names have been celebrated in theatrical history: *Arlecchino* (Harlequin), *Pedrolino* (Pierrot), and *Scaramuccia* (Scaramouche).

The influence of commedia dell'arte was pervasive. Italian performers toured every major country in Europe, sometimes setting up permanent theaters in capital cities, thereby contributing significantly to the development of comic drama in Europe. Their most important influence was in France, notably in the comedies of Molière. Traces of their influence are evident in Shakespearean comedies such as *Love's Labour's Lost* and *Twelfth Night*.

By the beginning of the 18th century, the appeal of this form of comedy had begun to fade, but its legacy lives on in popular puppet plays, such as the Punch-and-Judy show.

Scenarios of the Commedia Dell'Arte (1967), translated by Henry Salerno, offers a comprehensive collection of the plots used by one of the theatrical companies. K. M. Lea's *Italian Popular Comedy* (1962) includes a discussion of the commedia's influence on Elizabethan drama.

commonplace book   A notebook in which a writer stores ideas, quotations, news items, stories, and other material for possible future use. An early example of a commonplace book is Ben Jonson's *Timber* (1640), in which he recorded his ideas on literary theory and expressed his deep, but not uncritical, admiration of his great contemporary, Shakespeare.

common reader   A term used to designate people who read widely for pleasure, as distinct from people whose reading is a function of their profession. In the 18th century, Samuel Johnson clarified the distinction when he spoke of "the common sense of readers uncorrupted with literary prejudices." Virginia Woolf echoed Johnson in *The Common Reader* (first series, 1925; second series, 1932): she identifies her ideal reader as an educated, non-scholarly, "common" reader, a category in which she included herself. In his essay "The Common Reader," the critic Frank Kermode discusses the decline of this type of reader since Woolf's day.

Frank Kermode's *An Appetite for Poetry* (1989) contains his essay on the common reader.

Commonwealth period   In England, the years between the execution of King Charles I (1649) and the restoration of the monarchy (1660). Another name for this period is the *Interregnum*. During this time, Parliament ruled the country under the leadership of Oliver Cromwell, the Puritan leader and commander of the English army. The writers most closely associated with the period are John Milton and Andrew Marvell, both of whom served as Latin secretaries (international diplomacy was conducted in Latin) for the commonwealth government.

Marvell's "An Horatian Ode upon Cromwell's Return from Ireland" (1650) is considered one of the great political poems in English. Milton wrote a number of tracts supporting the commonwealth government, notably *Eikonoklastes* (1649), a defense of the execution of Charles I.

Among other outstanding works of the period is Thomas Hobbes's classic statement of political philosophy, *Leviathan* (1651).

In literary history, the age is best known for the closing of all theaters in 1642 by the Puritan-controlled Parliament. The reason given was that plays were "spectacles of pleasure too commonly expressing mirth and levity." In 1644 the Globe Theatre, where Shakespeare's company had performed his dramas, was demolished. The theaters were reopened in 1660 at the beginning of the RESTORATION period.

comparative literature   The study of relationships among literatures of different languages or eras, or between literature and the other arts. Embracing a broad range of methodologies and subjects, comparative literature may focus on specific authors (Mark Spilka's *Dickens and Kafka: A Mutual Interpretation*, 1963), genres (George Steiner's *The Death of Tragedy*, 1961), broad international studies

(Ernst Robert Curtius's *European Literature in the Latin Middle Ages*, 1954), themes (Robert Rogers's *The Double in Literature*, 1970), or cross-cultural treatments of feminist issues (Rey Chow's *Woman and Chinese Modernity: The Politics of Reading between East and West*, 1991).

competence/performance   In LINGUISTICS, a term used to distinguish the innate capacity to speak one's natural language, usually before the age of three, according to rules we are not consciously aware of (competence) and the actual utterances we make that derive from this knowledge (performance). These terms, developed by the linguist Noam Chomsky, have been adapted to literary study to characterize the implicit understanding of literary connections on the part of a competent reader. Such a reader, for example, will respond to the TONE of a text without making a conscious effort to do so. The analogy breaks down, however, in that Chomsky is describing an innate, biological competence, while the reader's competence is acquired through experience.

Noam Chomsky developed his theory in his *Syntactic Structures* (1957).

complaint   A type of poem in which a speaker laments his or her unhappy condition or bemoans the general condition of life. A popular feature of medieval or Renaissance poetry, the complaint might involve a lamentation for a lost or unrequited love, as in Sir Thomas Wyatt's "They Flee From Me" and the Earl of Surrey's "Complaint of a Lover Rebuked," or it might represent a cry against "the wretched world" as the seat of "filth and fowle iniquitie," as in Edmund Spenser's *Complaints* (1591).

Another popular form in this period was the narrative complaint, in which historical or mythological figures recounted the twist of fortune which led them to a tragic end. Among the best known of these are the complaints included in John Lydgate's *Falle of Princes* (1431–38) and a collection of miscellaneous Tudor verse called *A Mirror for Magistrates* (1554), in which the ghosts of famous figures relate their sad tales.

Another example of the form is "A Lover's Complaint," notable because it was attributed to Shakespeare in his lifetime and included in the first edition of his *Sonnets* (1609).

John Peter's *Complaint and Satire in Early English Poetry* (1956) provides a comprehensive account of the form.

complication   In dramatic construction, the part of a play that traditionally follows the EXPOSITION and precedes the CLIMAX. In the complication the

91

intentions and purposes of the main characters encounter obstacles that must be overcome.

composition studies   The term for the academic field that focuses on the teaching of writing in American schools and colleges. As a practical discipline, composition refers to a range of activities that include the achievement of literacy, the transmission of the cultural heritage, the preparation of students' skills for use in the workplace, and the use of writing as a mode of personal expression and identity.

In its historical development, composition studies has been closely allied to, and in some cases identical with, RHETORIC. Like rhetoric, it is both a practical and a theoretical discipline. Its theoretical character has been complicated by the introduction of various branches of recent THEORY, including CULTURAL STUDIES, feminism, and POSTSTRUCTURALISM. As in literary study, these theoretical perspectives have brought about profound changes in composition's self-definition and sense of purpose. Traditionally focused on the written "products" of students in terms of correctness of grammar and style, composition developed into a conception of writing as "process" or as "transaction" and, most recently, as a complex network of interweaving social, political, and individual components. As a result, the field now includes pedagogical practices that include collaborative writing—writing done by two or more students, each one assuming specific responsibilities—and a heavy emphasis on repeated revisions.

Composition studies now operates as an interdisciplinary study and an eclectic practice. Like its view of writing, it is itself always in "process," performing a critical, largely misunderstood role by those who see it as limited to the correction of students' grammar.

Louise Wetherbee Phelps's "Composition Studies" in *Encyclopedia of Rhetoric and Composition* (1996), edited by Theresa Enos, offers an admirable summary of the field.

computers   *See* CYBERPUNK, HYPERTEXT, INTERACTIVE COMPUTER FICTION.

conceit   A term for a particularly fanciful metaphor. In the Renaissance, the term carried the general notion of a clever, witty expression. In the 18th and 19th centuries, *conceit* became a disparaging term used to describe poetry that was too clever or fanciful for its own good. In this negative sense, critics of the time applied it to the 17th-century metaphysical poets. In the first half of the 20th century, T. S. Eliot and other advocates of NEW CRITICISM rehabilitated the REPUTATION of the Metaphysicals and celebrated many of their elaborate conceits. Eliot saw these conceits as instances of a unified sensibility that later poetry lacked (*see* DISSOCIATION OF SENSIBILITY). Here are two examples of conceits by

John Donne, the foremost metaphysical poet. The first is from a lighthearted love poem that focuses on a flea that has bitten both lovers:

> *Mark but this flea, and mark in this,*
> *How little that which thou deniest me is;*
> *Me it sucked first, and now sucks thee,*
> *And in this flea our two bloods mingled be . . .*

The second is from one of Donne's "Holy Sonnets," mingling in powerful fashion religious devotion and sexual passion. In this conceit, the speaker asks God to invade his soul like an army, pillaging and raping a besieged town:

> *Batter my heart, three personed God; for You*
> *As yet but knock, breathe, shine, and seek to mend;*
> *That I may rise, and stand, o'erthrow me, and bend*
> *Your force to break, blow, burn, and make me new.*
> *I, like an usurped town, to another due,*
> *Labour to admit You, but Oh, to no end;*
> *Reason, Your viceroy in me, me should defend,*
> *But is captived, and proves weak or untrue.*
> *Yet dearly I love You, and would be loved fain,*
> *But am betrothed unto Your enemy.*
> *Divorce me, untie or break that knot again;*
> *Take me to You, imprison me, for I,*
> *Except You enthrall me, never shall be free,*
> *Nor ever chaste, except You ravish me.*

Currently, *conceit* carries a neutral connotation. Conceits may be either good or bad depending upon their context, their purpose, or their ingenuity.

K. K. Ruthven's *The Conceit* (1969) offers an excellent treatment of the subject.

concordance   An alphabetical listing, along with the immediate context, of all the words in a work, such as the Bible, or in the complete works of a writer. Here for example is the entry for the word *unaccommodated* in *The Harvard Concordance to Shakespeare*, edited by Marvin Spevack (1969):

> unaccommodated man is no more but such a poor,
>   LR 3.04. 101 P

The listing indicates that Shakespeare used the word only once, in *King Lear*, Act 3, Scene 4, line 101. The "P" at the end indicates that the line is in a passage written in prose, rather than in verse.

concrete universal   The definition of literature in relation to its alleged capacity to represent universal concepts in terms of particular instances. Aristotle distinguished literature from history and from philosophy: History represents the particular in terms of the particular; philosophy treats universals in universal terms, while literature represents the universal in terms of the particular. Thus literature is superior to history and, while inferior to philosophy, it is more accessible to the average person.

Employed in the 19th century by some philosophers, the validity of the term was the subject of a debate by two leading figures in NEW CRITICISM, William Wimsatt and John Crowe Ransom. Wimsatt defended the use of the term, while Ransom, a practicing poet, insisted on the singular particularity of a poem, in that it represented a unique experience. *See* UNIVERSALITY.

For the Wimsatt-Ransom argument, see W. K. Wimsatt's *The Verbal Icon* (1954) and John Crowe Ransom's *Selected Essays* (1984).

confessional poetry   Name for a type of post–World War II American poetry in which the poet appears to reveal intimate details of his or her life and a fragile, fragmented sense of self. What renders the term confessional particularly appropriate are the intimations of personal guilt that pervade the work of these poets. A major practitioner of the form was Robert Lowell, whose book of poems *Life Studies* (1959) had a powerful influence on two younger poets, Sylvia Plath and Anne Sexton. Plath's *Ariel* (1965), a collection of brilliant, angry, suicidal revelations, proved to be prophetic: two years before their publication, she took her own life. The title of Sexton's first book of poetry, *To Bedlam and Part Way Back* (1960), is indicative of the personal anguish that motivated her poetry. (Like Plath, Sexton also took her own life.) An example is this painful passage from Sexton's "Briar Rose/Sleeping Beauty":

> *It is not the prince at all, but my father*
> *drunkenly bent over my bed,*
> *circling the bed like a shark,*
> *my father thick upon me*
> *like some sleeping jelly fish.*

Other prominent poets associated with the confessional form include Theodore Roethke and John Berryman. In Roethke's case, the confessional form emerged in the evocation of himself as a child, fearful and small, movingly recounted in poems such as "My Papa's Waltz." Berryman, whose alcoholism and self-destructive behavior culminated in his suicide, turned to the confessional form in his novel *Recovery* (1973) as well as in his last collection of poems, *Henry's Fate* (1977).

Karl Malkoff's *Crowell's Handbook of Contemporary American Poetry* (1973) outlines the development of the movement and the careers of the poets associated with it.

confidant(e)   The CHARACTER in a play or novel who is privy to the thoughts and feelings of the main character, similar to the CHORUS in classical drama. Examples include Horatio in *Hamlet*, and Jack Burden in Robert Penn Warren's *All the King's Men* (1946).

conflated text   In TEXTUAL CRITICISM, the result of combining variant texts to produce a single unified edition. Modern editions of many of Shakespeare's plays are conflated texts.

conflict   The struggle either within or between characters that is often the basis of the PLOT of a play or story. In its simplest form, such as in MELODRAMA, the conflict is usually between the HERO and the VILLAIN. In more complex works, such as Sophocles' *Antigone*, the conflict between two characters (Antigone vs. Creon) may embody the conflict between two ideas (duty to the gods vs. duty to the State). In others, such as Shakespeare's *Hamlet*, the external conflict (Hamlet vs. Claudius) may be overshadowed by the internal conflict (Hamlet vs. himself). Finally, the main conflict may lie in the opposition of the individual and his society, as in Ralph Ellison's *Invisible Man* (1952).

Connecticut wits   Name of a group of late 18th century American writers who attended Yale University around the time of the American Revolution. Most of the group lived in or near Hartford, Connecticut. The members represented conservative political and cultural values, endorsing the study of literature as a source of moral improvement. Stylistically, they were influenced by the English tradition of the Augustan age, the examples of Pope and Swift. They affected a satiric tone. Among their better-known practitioners were the poets John Trumbull, Timothy Dwight, who became president of Yale in 1795, and Joel Barlow, who later served as ambassador to France. As a group, despite their ideals and commitment, they never provided work of any lasting literary merit.

connotation   *See* DENOTATION/CONNOTATION.

consciousness   Recent decades have seen significant changes in the scientific study of human consciousness, seriously challenging the traditional view of consciousness as a dynamic combination of awareness, emotion, judgment, and action, organized into a distinctive whole. In its place, according to neuroscientist Steven Pinker, modern science maintains that the word *mind* is " nothing but the on-board computer of a robot made of tissue." Consciousness, presumably, is the software to the brain's computer. As the neurosurgeon protagonist of Ian McEwan's novel *Saturday* (2005) thinks to himself, ". . . the mind is what the brain, mere matter, performs."

In response, the novelist and critic David Lodge points out that a novel, *Saturday* for example, is a representation of consciousness, a fact overlooked by the neuroscientist. "Literature is a record of human consciousness, the richest and most comprehensive we have." He maintains that the novel offers the perfect vehicle for rendering human consciousness since reading and writing themselves are acts of imagined consciousness.

Entering into and giving life to a fictional CHARACTER are how writers go about creating the illusions of consciousness and how readers engage with and incorporate those illusions. Looking at a group of modern novels, Lodge explores various techniques in rendering consciousness.

A novelist intensely interested in representing consciousness was Henry James, who nevertheless recognized its difficulty: "To project yourself into a consciousness of a person eventually your opposite requires the audacity of genius." James attempted this projection, employing the FREE INDIRECT STYLE in which a third person narrator operates within the mind of a particular character. James Joyce took a large step further by employing the stream of consciousness, combining the interior world with a minutely detailed rendering of the objective world (*see* INTERIOR MONOLOGUE). The variety and ingenuity of novelists testify to the complexity of the task of a consciousness creating or, for the reader, "co-creating" another consciousness. In the dialogue created by the interaction of the consciousness and the fictional created consciousness lies a mystery that science has been unable to explain. (*See also* GENEVA SCHOOL.)

David Lodge's essays on the subject are collected in *Consciousness and the Novel* (2002). Daniel Dennett's *Consciousness Explained* (1991) is a scientific study that makes reference to literary criticism.

consonance   *See* RHYME.

consumption   A central position of Marxist-oriented criticism maintains that capitalism creates a "culture of consumption" both for its own economic enrich-ment and to disguise the emptiness and discontent of BOURGEOIS life. Using ADVERTISING as it chief tool, consumer culture repeats the message that happiness and self-realization are epitomized in the consumption of more and more com-modities. The result is succinctly summarized in the bumper sticker that ends "He who dies with the most toys wins."

Some feminist critics offer an alternative view, arguing that the Marxist analysis underrates the ingenuity of certain socioeconomic groups who reinterpret the "official story." A similar argument is made in connection with POPULAR CULTURE.

content   Traditionally in literary study, the subject matter of a play, poem, or narrative, as distinguished from its FORM. The subject matter of Walt Whitman's "When Lilacs Last in the Dooryard Bloomed" is the death of Abraham Lincoln; its form is an elegiac poem. A basic principle of modern literary criticism is that form and content are inextricably intertwined. As a result, discussions of the subject matter of literary texts frequently focus on THEME, which allows for the interplay of content and form.

context   In its most common use, a term referring to the part of a statement in which a word or group of words is used, or the circumstances within which a word is used. The context is often regarded as essential to the meaning of such words.

In literary study, context also refers to the relevant historical and social conditions in which a text is written, set, or received. Arthur Miller's *The Crucible* (1953), for example, is a play written at the height of the McCarthy era, set in 17th-century Salem, and received by its original audience as a contemporary social comment.

A later form of NEW CRITICISM, formulated by the critic Murray Krieger, argued for an approach known as "contextualism" in which the poem itself was conceived of as a "closed context" independent of the historical and social conditions in which it was produced. NEW HISTORICISM, on the other hand, challenges the basic distinction between the text and context on the grounds that our knowledge of history comes to us as a written record, that is, a text. Thus when we refer to the "historical context" of a literary work we are in fact talking about another text.

Murray Krieger's *The New Apologists for Poetry* (1956) develops his idea of contextualism.

convention   A traditional assumption or practice in literature or DRAMA. Although some basic conventions survive through the centuries—for example, the assumption that a first person narrator in a story is telling the truth—others, such as having the villain in a melodrama speak in an ASIDE to the audience, become outmoded. Used too often, such a convention is eventually replaced by something regarded as more realistic (the villain turns out to be the handsome "nice guy" who had befriended the hero), but this convention ultimately dies of overuse and is in turn replaced by another. Conventions are necessary to all literature, since they are part of the unspoken contract between reader or audience and the literary work. In fiction, for example, the reader is asked to accept the point of view from which the story is told and its sequence (flashbacks, flash forwards, multiple narrators, etc.) In drama, the audience assumes that it is viewing the action from the "fourth wall." Critical also are the conventions that grow up around specific genres; detective stories, bedroom farces, postmodernist novels, and epic poems. Many conventions reflect the sense of DECORUM of a particular age, for example, the practice in Greek tragedy of having violent death occur offstage.

Repudiating existing conventions is characteristic of the AVANT-GARDE. Many modern breaks with convention, beginning with the DADA movement in 1916, have stressed the irrational, absurd, hallucinatory elements in life. Inevitably one generation's breakthroughs become a later one's convention. Thus the convention-defying credo of the dadaists "Dada Means Nothing" in time became the announced principle of the spectacularly popular sitcom *Seinfeld*, "the show about nothing." (*See also* WILLING SUSPENSION OF DISBELIEF.)

cony-catcher   An ELIZABETHAN term for a con man or trickster. The writer Robert Greene exposed their tricks in a series of popular cony-catching pamphlets in the 1590s.

Shakespeare used some of the information in them to depict the cony-catching figure of Autolycus in *The Winter's Tale*.

Corpus Christi (body of Christ)   In Christian ritual, a feast day in honor of the Eucharist celebrated on the Thursday following Trinity Sunday. In the MIDDLE AGES, the feast provided the occasion for the performance of religious plays based on the Bible. In England, such plays were known as MYSTERY PLAYS; in France, *Mystères*; and in Spain, *auto sacramentales*. (*See* AUTO SACRAMENTAL.)

cothurnus   *See* BUSKIN.

counterfactual fiction   Taking the principle of WILLING SUSPENSION OF DISBELIEF to an extreme, counterfactual fiction asks the hypothetical question "What if?" in order to explore what might have happened if certain historical events had turned out differently. One popular example, Richard Harris's *Fatherland* (1992), operates on the what-if assumption that Germany has won World War II. The novel opens in April 1964, six days before the celebration of Adolf Hitler's 75th birthday. The Author's Note following the end of the novel concludes with an appropriate line from the poet Dante Gabriel Rossetti: "Look in my face; my name is Might-have-been."

Counterfactual fiction differs from those novels, largely found within the SCIENCE FICTION genre, which invite speculation about future events, such as the possible consequences of NUCLEAR WAR. It also differs from time-travel novels, such as Jack Finney's *From Time to Time* (1995), in which the hero's attempt to prevent the sinking of the *Titanic* fails, thus leaving history unaltered.

A more recent example of the counterfactual genre is Philip Roth's *The Plot Against America* (2004), which explores the impact of the election of Charles Lindbergh as president in 1940 on the Jewish-American family of a young boy named Philip Roth.

What Ifs of American History (2000), edited by Robert Cowley, is an anthology of essays by historians exploring alternative history.

Counter-Reformation   The response of the Catholic Church to the REFORMATION.

coup de théâtre (stroke of theater)   A sudden development in the plot of a play that has a surprising or shocking effect. A recent example is the revelation of the gender of the mistress in David Hwang's *M. Butterfly* (1987).

couplet   In verse, a pair of contiguous lines, often rhymed. HEROIC COUPLET is the name given to a rhymed couplet written in iambic pentameter (*see* IAMB). Each of Shakespeare's sonnets concludes with a heroic couplet, as in this example from Sonnet 30:

> But if the while I think on thee, dear friend,
> All losses are restored and sorrows end.

The master of the heroic couplet, Alexander Pope, was also capable of mocking its hackneyed use:

> Where'er you find "the cooling Western breeze,"
> In the next line, "it whispers through the trees."

Maynard Mack's biography *Alexander Pope* (1985) contains an informative account of Pope's use of the couplet.

courtesy books   In the RENAISSANCE, a guide to proper behavior for aspiring courtiers. At their best, as for example, in Baldassare Castiglione's *The Courtier* (trans. 1561), the books examined fundamental ethical questions as well as conventional behavior. The witty exchanges between Beatrice and Benedick in

Shakespeare's *Much Ado About Nothing* may be based, to some extent, on passages from *The Courtier*.

courtly love   An attitude toward love, and a corresponding code of behavior, reflected in medieval lyric poetry and romances. In both its social and literary guises, courtly love came to exert an extraordinary influence throughout Western Europe. A representative model of courtly love is the male lover, a young knight such as Lancelot or Tristan, who vows total obedience to his lady, usually a married woman, whom he idealizes. This passion for an unattainable ideal throws the lover into emotional torments which he transcends by noble deeds done in his lady's name. Thus perfect devotion ennobles the lovers, rendering them faithful servants of the god of love. The religious language of this description suggests that, in the courtly love tradition, erotic love is the equal of divine love; it may be more accurate to say that erotic love here emerges as analogous to religious love, the human approximation of the infinitely greater love that God exhibits for all things.

Courtly love developed in the late 11th century in the courts of southern France, in the poetry of the TROUBADOURS and TROUVÈRES. From there it spread throughout France and many other European countries. A celebrated example of the form is Chrétien de Troyes' romance *Lancelot, or The Knight of the Cart* (late 12th century) and Sir Thomas Malory's *Morte D'Arthur* (1485).

The term itself was coined in 1883 by the French medieval scholar Gaston Paris and developed by C. S. Lewis in his *The Allegory of Love* (1938). Although there is some dispute about the validity of the Paris-Lewis definition of the term, there is general agreement that the ideals of courtly love had a powerful influence on the literature of the Renaissance and on 19th-century ROMANTICISM. Courtly love represented the first expression of the belief that sexuality is the consequence, not the cause, of love, and that sexual love is a noble passion that enhances and enriches the lives of those who experience it. *See* LOVE.

Irving Singer's *The Nature of Love*, Vol. 2 (1984) contains a discussion of courtly love and its relation to the later Romantic conception.

crisis   A decisive point in a story or play. The crisis may be external, the moment when the opposition of conflicting forces is most intense, or it may be internal, when a character is forced to make a decisive choice. For related terms, *see* CONFLICT.

Criterion, The   An influential literary quarterly published in England from 1922 to 1939. Edited by T. S. Eliot, whose most famous poem *The Waste Land* appeared in its first issue, the journal helped to propagate the principles of NEW CRITICISM. In addition to publishing leading English and Irish writers, such as Virginia Woolf and William Butler Yeats, *The Criterion* provided an outlet in English translation for the work of several outstanding Europeans, including the novelist Marcel Proust and the poet Paul Valéry.

critical theory   *See* FRANKFURT SCHOOL.

criticism   A general term for the analysis, interpretation, and evaluation of LITERATURE. One aspect of criticism—the examination of its underlying assumptions and the presentation of its principles and procedures—is characterized as literary theory, which has assumed increasing importance in literary study since the 1960s. (For an account of this field, *see* THEORY.)

Distinct from, but related to, literary theory is practical criticism, which usually deals with a specific work or writer. Practical critics may be divided into two groups. The first is reviewers of books, films and plays, writing in newspapers, magazines, and publications such as *The New York Times Book Review*, whose primary purpose is to judge the nature and value of a recent or recently reissued work, while also offering an interpretation of the work. The audience for such reviewers are potential readers or viewers seeking some guidance to the work under consideration.

The second group of practical critics are usually university-connected academics who write book-length studies, published by university presses, or essays in specialized journals, which are read by other specialists. The subjects of these studies are generally not new works, but those associated with the CANON, or less important works that nevertheless throw light on some aspect of literary history. In this type of criticism, the emphasis falls on interpretation rather than evaluation, although the simple selection of the work as a subject implies a positive sense of its value.

These critics also function as reviewers of one another's work in specialized journals. In some cases an individual may function both as a general reviewer and as a scholarly critic. The English critic Frank Kermode, the Irish critic Dennis Donoghue, and the American Alfred Kazin are prolific reviewers and at the same time scholars who have published book-length studies on specialized subjects. Another class of critics and reviewers are practicing poets, novelists, and playwrights who regularly write critical essays and reviews. Included among this group are the novelists John Updike, Gore Vidal, and Susan Sontag, and the playwright Tom Stoppard.

crux   In literary scholarship, *crux* refers to a puzzling word or phrase that has given rise to a variety of interpretations. John Milton's elegy "Lycidas" contains a celebrated example: While attacking the Anglican clergy and outlawed Jesuit priests covertly proselytizing in England, the poet suggests a form of retaliation: "But that two handed engine at the door/ Stands ready to smite once and will smite no more." Some scholars have suggested that the engine in question is an axe or sword, others have thought it to be a reference to the two houses of Parliament, but a definitive answer continues to elude them.

Sometimes a crux arises from differences between two early versions of a work. In the last scene of Shakespeare's *Othello*, the 1622 quarto version of the play reads, "Like the base Indian, threw a pearl away. . ." while the 1623 FIRST FOLIO version, which was printed from the quarto, renders the line "Like the base Judean, threw a pearl away . . . ." Some editors, assuming the line refers to Judas, the betrayer of CHRIST, choose Judean; others, arguing for the quarto reading, cite a legend. Probably a compositor in the print shop inverted the second letter since the i and j were used interchangeably, and the same font would have been used for both *n* and *u*. However, this explanation still leaves open the question as to which reading reflects Shakespeare's final intention.

cultural criticism   An interdisciplinary approach that looks at literature as the expression of a particular national or cultural tradition. In traditional literary studies, culture is considered the "background" to literature, important but subsidiary to the text itself. In cultural criticism, the aim is to call into question the distinction between the TEXT and the CONTEXT by suggesting that the text and context are intimately entwined and to offer a critique of prevailing assumptions as to what constitutes "culture." (*See* NEW HISTORICISM.)

cultural studies   An interdisciplinary movement that focuses on POPULAR CULTURE, placing it in a socio-historical context. The movement originated in Great Britain in the 1960s and spread to the United States in the 1980s. Taking as its province all forms of cultural expression from advertising to RAP lyrics, cultural studies looks at these various forms as "texts" to be analyzed in a manner usually reserved for serious or "high" literature.

Examining popular cultural forms and their interaction with their audience, conceived either collectively or individually, cultural studies critics assume a variety of approaches. Some choose to analyze the practices of institutions, such as publishers, movie studios, or record companies as they produce their products. Others focus on the negotiations these "culture industries" engage in with their audiences as they search for a successful "format." Still others look at the uses to which individuals within the audience put these forms.

The majority of these critics, particularly those in Great Britain, share a Leftist or Marxist orientation. They argue that the distinction between high and popular culture is at heart political, designed to reinforce traditional class structures within society. This political orientation, associated with a founding father of the movement, Raymond Williams, has combined, not always harmoniously, with the tenets of POSTSTRUCTURALISM. This connection has produced yet another approach—the use of linguistics and semiotics to analyze popular culture and the distinction between "high" and "popular" culture in terms of BINARY OPPOSITION, a structuralist principle that critiques the traditional preference for high over popular culture. As a consequence, a recent development in cultural studies has been the inclusion of both high and popular culture, implying their equal status as cultural objects.

Cultural Studies (1992) edited by Lawrence Grossberg, Carey Nelson, and Paula Treichler is a wide-ranging anthology of writing in the field. Raymond Williams's *Culture and Society* (1958) and Richard Hoggart's *The Uses of Literacy* (1957) are two of the founding works of the movement.

curtal sonnet Term coined by the Victorian poet Gerard Manley Hopkins to describe a sonnet of 10 and a half lines rather than the 14 lines of the usual sonnet. A curtal sonnet contains a sestet (rhyming abcabc) followed by a four-½ QUATRAIN (dbcde), as in Hopkins's celebrated poem "Pied Beauty."

cut In film, the movement from one SHOT to another, for example, a shift from a medium close-up (the human figure seen from the chest up) to a close-up (the human figure seen from the neck up).

In the editing of a film, *cut* refers to the practice of splicing two shots together.

cyberpunk A form of SCIENCE FICTION in which the world of high-tech computer networks (cyberspace) dominates life in the near-future. The term is an amalgam of *cybernetics*, the science that links control processes in human and electronic systems, and *punk*, the youth culture phenomenon characterized by angry rejection of the norms of traditional behavior. The leading figure in the genre is William Gibson, whose novel *Neuromancer* (1984) established the form. His more recent work, *Idoru* (1996), set in Tokyo in the 21st century, explores the nature of stardom or celebrity in a world in which technology has effaced the line between the virtual and the real.

The French film director Jean-Luc Godard anticipated the form in his 1965 film *Alphaville*, in which the villain rules intergalactic space through his computer, Alpha 60.

cycle   A group of poems, plays, or novels that share a common theme, hero, or era. The medieval MYSTERY PLAYS, linked by their common biblical source, are an example of a dramatic cycle. The narratives of the CHANSON DE GESTE and the ARTHURIAN LEGEND are other medieval romance cycles. *See also* SAGA.

cynics   Originally a group of Greek philosophers (fifth century B.C.), who identified the strength of the individual will and the virtue of self-control as the ultimate good. In their emphasis on individualism, the cynics set themselves up against the accepted beliefs of their society, particularly the belief in the essential goodness of human beings.

The adjective *cynical* has often been applied to writers who evoke a dark, satiric view of human nature, such as Jonathan Swift and Ambrose Bierce, the author of *The Devil's Dictionary* (1906).

dactyl A metrical foot consisting of one stressed syllable followed by two unstressed syllables, as in the word *courtesy*, or in the following example by Alfred, Lord Tennyson:

/ ˘ ˘ / ˘ ˘ /
Into the valley of death

/ ˘ ˘ / ˘
Rode the six hundred

dada A movement of writers and artists that rejected conventional modes of art and thought in favor of consciously cultivated, deliberate nonsense. According to its founder, Tristan Tzara, "DADA MEANS NOTHING"—nothing, in this context, standing for the principle that the gratuitous, irrational, unconditioned element in life is the true source of freedom and creativity.

The movement began in Zurich in 1916, the name *dada* (it means "hobby horse") selected randomly from the dictionary. It flourished until 1923, attracting among its adherents the sculptor Hans Arp, the artists Man Ray and Marcel Duchamp, the composer Erik Satie, and the writers Jean Cocteau, Louis Aragon, and André Breton. Breton was to lead the break with dada that resulted in the formation of SURREALISM in 1924.

Though dada produced little or no memorable literary work, the movement made an important contribution to the modern conception of literature. In attacking the traditional hierarchy of values based on reason and logic, dada helped to free the modern artist from the restrictions of past conventions and to unlock the power of the UNCONSCIOUS.

John Erickson's *Dada: Performance, Poetry, and Art* (1984) provides a historical and analytical view; Manuel Grossman's *Dada* (1971) considers the movement's history and influence.

dance of death *(danse macabre)* In art and literature, the depiction of a procession in which the figure of a skeleton, representing death, leads a group of

people to their graves. The image, a recurrent feature of medieval art and literature, is powerfully reenacted in Ingmar Bergman's film *The Seventh Seal* (1956).

Allusions to the dance appear in Goethe's *Faust* (1808), Bryon's *Don Juan*
(1819–24), and Conrad's *Heart of Darkness* (1902).

Johan Huizinga's classic study *The Waning of the Middle Ages* (1924) provides a vivid
account of the "death dance."

Darwinism   The ideas growing out of the findings of Charles Darwin in his *On
the Origin of Species* (1859), which argued that life is governed by the principle of
"survival of the fittest," that evolution favors the species best equipped to survive
in a given environment. He also maintained that a literal interpretation of the
Bible does not accord with the biological facts concerning the origins of life.
Darwin's evolutionary theory burst upon the 19th century with explosive force,
particularly in Darwin's native England. His theory offered an explanatory narrative that gave society a new way to conceive of human history, introducing the
threatening idea that chance, rather than design, played a major role in the plot.
The theory led to a wide range of social, political, and cultural implications that
offered fertile soil for the imagination of Victorian novelists and poets. Among
these were George Eliot, who struggles to discover the connection of biological
fact to human morality; Charles Dickens, who, in the words of the critic George
Levine, "reads Darwin within a fully comic vision . . . to reveal a world prolific
and dynamic in the production of endless and sometimes grotesque varieties
of life"; and Anthony Trollope, who shares with Darwin a view of the world,
as Levine suggests, "pervasively imperfect." In the case of Joseph Conrad, the
general political assumption that Darwinism supports evolution, not revolution,
is contradicted particularly in his novel *Under Western Eyes* (1911). There, Levine
maintains, "Conrad takes his Darwinian reality as evidence that revolution is
everywhere and inevitable."

George Levine's analysis appears in his *Darwin among the Novelists* (1988).

dasein   A term used by the German philosopher Martin Heidegger to describe
the distinctively human way of being in the world. Dasein literally means "being
there," and Heidegger employs it to avoid the notion—implicit in terms like "self"
or "man"—of an isolated private entity set off from the objective world. "Being
there" underscores the fact that human consciousness is always "situated," always
a consciousness *of* something. This conception forms an important principle of
EXISTENTIALISM. In literature, the concept supports the view that the meaning of
a literary work emerges from the exchange between reader and text.

date of a literary text   Although in the majority of cases the date of a literary text is equated with the date of its first publication, the date becomes more problematic when dealing with works written before the invention of the printing press or even later in DRAMA when plays might be performed years before publication.

The chronology of Shakespeare's plays, for example, poses problems for scholars interested in his development as a playwright. One half of his plays were printed in his lifetime, although not in the order in which they were written. The other half did not appear in print until the FIRST FOLIO of 1623, seven years after his death. In 1774 the scholar Edmund Malone published *An Attempt to Determine the Order in Which Shakespeare's Plays Were Written*. Since that time, scholars have slowly formed a general picture of Shakespeare's career, beginning with the *Henry VI* plays around 1589 and concluding with *Henry VIII* in 1613.

The scholarly approach to dating a literary text is to establish a *terminus a quo*, a point before which the text could not have been written, and a *terminus ad quem*, after which it could not have been written. To that end they collect external and internal evidence. For external evidence they examine records and writings of the period that might contain a reference to the text. Internal evidence relies on stylistic features or allusions in the text to contemporary events. An example of the latter is the reference by the Gatekeeper in *Macbeth* to "the equivocator that lies like the fiend." This is an allusion to the trial of the conspirators to the Gunpowder Plot of 1605. Another example is the reference to the impending return of the earl of Essex from Ireland in the Prologue to *Henry V*. Essex left England for Ireland on March 27, 1599, and returned on September 28, 1599. Shakespeare must have written the lines in that Prologue within those dates.

Richard Altick's *The Art of Literary Research* (3rd ed. 1981) summarizes the subject succinctly.

Dead Sea scrolls   *See* QUMRAM MANUSCRIPTS.

death   As a literary theme, death is most prominent in TRAGEDY, although it also plays a central role in LYRIC and NARRATIVE forms and even, implicitly at least, in COMEDY.

In Greek tragedy, death is the inevitable limit to the portion of life allotted at one's birth, the obstacle that can never be overcome. As a celebrated ODE in Sophocles' *Antigone* expresses it, man is the greatest wonder of the world, who has accomplished many marvelous feats, "only against death has he secured no refuge."

Ironically, although mortality occupies a central role in classical tragedy, the act of dying takes place offstage. What makes death specifically tragic in these plays is its violent or suicidal character as opposed to, say, the representation of the death of Socrates in Plato's *Phaedo*. The *Phaedo* describes how Socrates, accepting the unjust death penalty imposed upon him by the Athenian court, dies cheerfully, a martyr to philosophical inquiry. His death stands as a model of human dignity and control in facing one's end.

The classical tragic view was fundamentally altered in the West by the emphasis in Christianity on the immortality of the soul. Within the medieval Christian view, death was less important as a fact in itself than as the end of the opportunity for salvation. Death was familiar, universal, and collective, the great leveler that led kings and beggars, hands linked together, in its DANCE OF DEATH.

With the Renaissance, the growing sense of individualism revived the pre-Christian sense of death as the end of individual existence. The essays of Montaigne, particularly "That to Philosophize is to Learn How to Die," articulated the need to confront one's own death not in the context of an afterlife, but instead within the fabric of one's daily existence. Montaigne's influence is powerfully present in the soliloquies of Prince Hamlet, whose reflections in Shakespeare's play can be seen as a process of "learning how to die."

The Renaissance also saw the development of the association of death with sexual LOVE. The love/death connection (in German, *liebestod*), perhaps a residue of religious guilt, or perhaps rooted, as Freud has suggested, in the desire for the unindividuated, womblike union with the mother, assumes a major role in the literature of the period. The association of love and death is evident in romantic tragedies such as *Romeo and Juliet*, in which Death is represented as Romeo's rival for the love of Juliet, and in the love poems of John Donne, in which the pun on "die" as a reference to orgasm (echoed in the French term *le petit mort*) suggests the intimate relationship of *eros*, sexual love, and *thanatos*, the death wish.

The poetic infatuation with death achieved an even greater degree of intensity in the movement known as the GRAVEYARD SCHOOL, whose mournful elegies achieved a vogue in the late 18th century. With the advent of ROMANTICISM the obsession with the theme of mortality continued, notably in the poetry of Percy Bysshe Shelley, whose elegy on the death of John Keats (*Adonais*, 1821) contains a prophetic vision of his own death.

Shelley's poems represented what the critic Mario Praz has called the "Romantic agony," the aesthetic that pairs death with beauty. This association is evident in the poetry of Alfred, Lord Tennyson, Emily Dickinson, Christina and Dante Rossetti, and Algernon Swinburne. This tradition continued in the early work of William Butler Yeats, but in his later years Yeats celebrates heroic freedom over death in the famous lines from his epitaph poem "Under Ben Bulben":

Cast a cold eye
On life, on death.
Horseman, pass by.

By general consent the greatest rendering of dying in modern literature is Tolstoy's *The Death of Ivan Ilych* (1886), often cited as the pre-eminent example of literary EXISTENTIALISM. Other distinguished renderings of death and dying include Thomas Mann's novella *Death in Venice* (1912) and James Joyce's short story "The Dead" (1916).

The theme reappears in the CONFESSIONAL POETRY of Sylvia Plath, in which suicide is a major theme, in the death-haunted plays and novels of Samuel Beckett, and in the literature of AIDS, notably in Tony Kushner's *Angels in America* (1989).

Distinguished film treatments of the theme include Ingmar Bergman's *The Seventh Seal* (1956) and *Cries and Whispers* (1973) and Akira Kurosawa's *Ikiru* (1960), while Luchino Visconti's *Death in Venice* (1971) and John Huston's *The Dead* (1987) are memorable film versions of the Mann and Joyce stories.

Philippe Ariès's *The Hour of Our Death* (1981) offers a social history, while Sherwin Nuland's *How We Die* (1994) examines the subject from a contemporary physician's point of view. Benjamin Kurtz's *The Pursuit of Death* (1930) on Shelley, and Johan Ramazani's *Yeats and the Poetry of Death* (1990) are excellent individual studies.

débat   A form of dialogue in medieval literature in which two figures, sometimes allegorized, engage in a verbal contest. The classical source of the form are the ECLOGUES of Theocritus and Virgil. The Eclogues were PASTORAL poems featuring song contests among shepherds. As adapted in the MIDDLE AGES, the *débat* form consisted of an introduction, a description of the background of the dispute, the contest itself, and the appeal to a judge.

In English literature, the best known examples are *The Owl and the Nightingale* (c. 1220), in which two birds, the symbols of love and religion, debate their respective values. The form was adapted to drama in Henry Medwall's *Fulgens and Lucrece* (1490–1500), considered the first secular play in English.

decadence   An aspect of the ART FOR ART'S SAKE movement, maintaining the view that late 19th-century civilization was in a state of decay comparable to the last years of the Roman Empire. At such a time, the movement maintained, the artist should cultivate his senses and reject that which is "natural," both in the ecological and moral sense of the word.

Adherents of decadence held that art should be artificial, and that the artist should experiment with new sensations, including sexual deviation and drug use, all in the name of achieving a distinctive artistic vision.

The French SYMBOLIST poets, particularly Charles Baudelaire, Paul Verlaine, and Stéphane Mallarmé, were the original sources for these ideas. They were taken up in England by poets such as Arthur Symons, Ernest Dowson, and Lionel Johnson, and by Oscar Wilde, whose novel *The Picture of Dorian Gray* (1891) captures the spirit of the movement.

Richard Gilman's *Decadence: The Strange Life of an Epithet* (1979) traces the use and misuse of the term over the past two centuries.

decenter   *See* CENTER/DECENTER.

deconstruction   Although in popular use a term synonymous with "destruction" or "debunking," deconstruction also has a more precise, if highly complex, reference. As used in literary criticism, philosophy, and more recently, legal studies, it focuses on the inherent, internal contradictions in language and interpretation. As formulated by the French thinker Jacques Derrida, deconstruction is a fundamental critique of certain intellectual assumptions that underlie Western thinking. According to Derrida, Western thought and culture have been organized around unacknowledged presuppositions—"centers"—that both structure and restrict meaning. These centers appear as self-evident truths that lie outside the system of language. One example might be "the human spirit," a phrase that implies the existence of transcendent reality, as do such terms as "God" or "consciousness," that forms the basis of meaning. Derrida calls this belief LOGOCENTRISM, the assumption of an ultimate ground or referent for language.

Against the logocentric conception Derrida argues that meaning is not generated by some extralinguistic presence, but by absence—that is, by the differences between one word and another. Thus it is difference (not the traditional "identity" of the word and its object) that distinguishes language. In other words, language is rooted not in a positive relation of words to the world but instead in a relation of differences of one element to the other. Language does not reveal things as they are; it imposes categories on the world. Meaning is a function of the fact that our pictures of reality are the products of these linguistically derived categories.

In America in the 1970s these ideas were taken up and applied to literature by the "Yale critics": Paul De Man, J. Hillis Miller, Geoffrey Hartman, and, at one time on the periphery of the group, Harold Bloom. Adapting and applying some of Derrida's ideas, they helped to create an atmosphere in which deconstruction became the center of an intense controversy. In general the American deconstructionist movement is not a theory but a method—partly philosophical, partly literary—of reading texts. In this respect, as in others, deconstruction is directly opposed to STRUCTURALISM, which attempts to discover the underlying grammar of literature. The deconstructive method zeroes in on a specific text, much in the manner of the "close reading" approach that characterized NEW CRITICISM. But deconstructionists aim, in Hartman's words, "to see *through* literary forms to the way language . . . makes or breaks meaning."

Central to this method is Derrida's concept of *différance*, a word he coins to distinguish it from simple *différence* (difference). Derrida employs the word in both senses of the French verb *différer*, which means both to *differ* and to *defer*. The sense of "differ" in the term refers to Saussure's view that the meaning of words is a function of differences and that these differences are "negative," that is, distinguished by what they are not. The sense of *defer* applies to the belief that meaning is never really present but always deferred because the "meaning" is simply more words leading to a cycle of words about words. Operating from this principle, deconstructionists scrutinize the contradictory elements in a text until they reach an APORIA (an impasse), the point at which the text's contradictory meanings are shown to be irreconcilable. Thus the text is revealed as a house divided against itself, which cannot stand close scrutiny. The result is an illustration of the indeterminacy of meaning.

Attacked as an irresponsible game, a denial of common sense, or empty nihilism, deconstruction—in the narrower sense of a critical school—appears to be on the wane. Its decline has been hastened by the revelation that its chief American practitioner, Paul De Man, had written some 200 articles for two pro-Nazi newspapers during the German occupation of Belgium in World War II. As a result, some critics of deconstruction have made efforts to link deconstructive criticism to totalitarian thought. But despite its decline, many of deconstruction's ideas—particularly those related to the "decentering" of the subject and the rejection of the idea of a single meaning—have been incorporated into the mainstream of academic critical thinking. The question of whether that influence will spread outside the universities into the world of general readers remains open.

Vincent Leitch's *Deconstructive Criticism: An Advanced Introduction* (1983) examines the literary movement. For a critical view of the general position, see David Lehman's *Signs of the Times: Deconstruction and the Fall of Paul De Man* (1991).

decorum   In the 16th and 17th centuries, an important critical term calling for conformity to literary convention within GENRES, and, in the representation of characters, to accepted social standards. For example, decorum dictated that an EPIC had to be written in the grand, heroic style and that a noble character should speak in verse while a peasant's speech would be in prose. Seventeenth-century neoclassicists considered decorum to be a crucial barometer of good literature.

Although the principle seems to have disappeared in the less formal literary and social atmosphere of modern times, examples occasionally emerge: some critics and audiences who believe performers in a Shakespearean play should speak the lines with a traditional upper-class British accent are, implicitly, invoking the principle of decorum.

deep focus   In film, the inclusion of objects both close to and far from the camera in the same shot without loss of focus. The deep focus lens was developed in the late 1930s and first used with stunning success by the cinematographer Gregg Toland in Orson Welles's *Citizen Kane* (1941).

defamiliarization   A principle associated with RUSSIAN FORMALISM which asserts that one function of art and literature is to disturb its audience's routine perception of reality. The term (in Russian *ostranenie*) was coined by the critic Viktor Shklovsky, who argued that in disrupting our everyday sense of what is real and important, art puts us in touch with our deepest experiences. The techniques of defamiliarization include placing characters and events in unfamiliar contexts, FOREGROUNDING dialects and slang in formal poetry, and employing unusual imagery.

Some recent critics have argued that science fiction, with its freedom from the constraints of representing the probable and the realistic, exemplifies the doctrine of defamiliarization.

Viktor Shklovsky's essay appears in *Russian Formalist Criticism: Four Essays in Criticism* (1965), edited by Lee Lemon and Marion Rees. Robert Scholes discusses the concept in his *Structuralism and Literature* (1974).

deism   A philosophical and religious position that developed, largely in England and France, in the 18th century as part of the ENLIGHTENMENT. Deism held that belief in God was consistent with human reason, but not with the beliefs of specific religions that claim truth on the basis of divine revelation. Thus most Deists rejected Christianity's claim that the BIBLE contained the revealed word of God.

Influenced by the discoveries of scientists from Copernicus to Newton, Deists argued that although God had initiated "the great clock" of the universe, the Deity had withdrawn from any involvement with it or with the activities of human kind.

In literature, Deistic elements appear in the poetry of Alexander Pope. Pope himself remained a practicing Christian all his life, but his *Essay on Man* ("Know then thyself, presume not God to scan/The proper study of Mankind is Man.") is considered a deistic poem, as is James Thompson's *The Seasons* (1730).

In American literature, the best known deistic work is Thomas Paine's *Age of Reason* (1794–95).

demythologizing   The argument, associated with the German biblical scholar Rudolph Bultmann, that most of the New Testament is beyond comprehension for a modern audience because it is expressed in the language of MYTH. Bultmann maintained that the real meaning of the Gospels lay, for example, not in the literal acceptance of Christ's resurrection, but in accepting it as a symbolic act with implications for all humanity. In formulating his position, Bultmann acknowledged his debt to EXISTENTIALISM, as propounded by the German philosopher Martin Heidegger.

In a more general sense the term refers to any attempt to look for an underlying meaning in a mythological story, for example, Sigmund Freud's reading of the story of Oedipus as an instance of the OEDIPAL COMPLEX.

Bultmann's *New Testament and Mythology* (1953) contains the most complete account of his position.

denotation/connotation   A pair of terms referring to the distinction between the literal, dictionary definition of a word and the associations it has acquired in use. For example, the denotation of the word *politician* is one who is professionally engaged in politics, while its connotation suggests one whose primary interest is personal or partisan gain. Connotations of words are reflections of the inherent RHETORIC of language and play a critical role in literature, particularly in poetry. It is the connotation of a word that leads back to its use as a METAPHOR. For example, the connotation of the word *foot* suggests something at the bottom, which leads to its metaphoric use in *foot of the hill*, or *footnote*.

denouement   The clarification of the complications of the PLOT in a NARRATIVE or DRAMA. The denouement normally occurs close to the end of the story, following its climax. One exception is the traditional DETECTIVE STORY in which the climax (the revelation of the murderer's identity) and the denouement (the clarification of the plot) often occur simultaneously.

description   In fiction, the words that describe the physical aspects of a story and its characters. The opening of Charles Dickens's *Bleak House* (1852) includes a memorable example of descriptive writing:

> Fog everywhere. Fog up the river, where it flows among green aits and melons; fog down the river, where it rolls defiled among the tiers of shipping . . . fog lying out on the yards, and hovering in the rigging of

great ships, fog drooping on the gunwales of barges and small boats. And hard by Temple Bar near Lincoln's Inn Hall, at the very heart of the fog, sits the Lord High Chancellor in his High Court of Chancery.

desire   A term that, in the sense of "wanting" or "needing," implies a lack or emptiness that seeks fulfillment. In the Western religious tradition desire represents a restlessness rooted in a craving for union with God. In the nonreligious view desire has been seen as resting upon the aim of becoming a god, characterized by the philosopher Nietzsche as "the will to power." In the religious view, on the other hand, union with God requires not will, but the *surrender* of will.

Alternatively, desire may be seen as a psychological rather than spiritual process, rooted in self-preservation or in the need to see oneself reflected in another and to have that recognition be reciprocated. The latter impulse, frequently viewed as underlying romantic LOVE, has made this sense of desire an important focus of recent FEMINIST CRITICISM. The feminist critique argues that this and other conceptions of desire or love are essentially phallocentric, framed in masculine terms. (*See* PHALLOCENTRISM.)

For the psychoanalytic theorist Jacques Lacan, desire and language are intertwined in the longing for wholeness, sanity, and meaning, a longing that can never be fulfilled. *See* PSYCHOANALYTICAL CRITICISM.

A contemporary analysis of the term is Judith Butler's "Desire" in *Critical Terms for Literary Study*, 2nd edition, edited by Frank Lentricchia and Thomas McLaughlin (1995).

detective story   A type of fiction in which a crime or series of crimes is solved by a detective, either an amateur or a professional, and, if the latter, either a policeman or a "private eye" (private investigator). The basic formula (upon which an infinite number of variations may be spun) consists of a murder or disappearance that leads to additional murders; a cluster of baffling clues that invites the reader to match wits with the detective; a number of plausible suspects; a detective who employs rigorous logic and creative intuition in solving the crime; a sidekick, spouse, servant, or, in the case of the private eye, secretary to provide comic relief.

The earliest example of the genre is thought to be Edgar Allan Poe's *Murders in the Rue Morgue* (1841). The most celebrated of all fictional detectives is undoubtedly A. Conan Doyle's Sherlock Holmes, who made his first appearance in 1887 in *A Study in Scarlet*. Not only did Conan Doyle establish the prototype of the detective who induces evidence by his extraordinary powers of observation; he also created, in Dr. Watson, the sidekick whose ordinary intelligence serves as a foil for the detective's superior intellect.

Notable among the immediate descendants of Sherlock Holmes is G. K. Chesterton's Father Brown (*The Innocence of Father Brown*, 1911), who added a theological dimension to the form.

In the 20th century the detective story has taken two distinctive paths. The American form features the private eye figure pioneered by Dashiell Hammett and Raymond Chandler. Hammett's Sam Spade (*The Maltese Falcon*, 1930) and Chandler's Philip Marlowe (*The Big Sleep*, 1939) established a distinctively American hero: the hardboiled private detective, a cool, sceptical-bordering-on-cynical veteran of life who holds fast to a private code of honor despite the temptations of money and love.

Both *The Maltese Falcon* and *The Big Sleep* were made into successful films starring—not coincidentally—Humphrey Bogart as Spade and Marlowe. The critical and popular success of these films contributed profoundly to the formation of FILM NOIR and to memorable recreations of the genre in Roman Polanski's *Chinatown* (1974) and Carl Franklin's adaptation of Walter Mosely's *Devil in a Blue Dress* (1996).

In a lighter vein, Hammett also created the team of Nick and Nora Charles (*The Thin Man*, 1934), a sophisticated couple who solve murders whenever they are not drinking martinis in elegant restaurants. Also highly successful as films, *The Thin Man* series popularized the light comic version of the form.

The other strain of 20th-century detective fiction is identified largely with England, although there have been notable contributions from the United States and France. The greatest name in this tradition is Agatha Christie, who dominated the genre in the '20s and '30s, the period known as the golden age of mystery writing. Among the celebrated detectives of the time: Christie's Hercule Poirot and Miss Marple; S. S. Van Dine's Philo Vance; Dorothy Sayers's Lord Peter Wimsey; Margery Allingham's Albert Campion; Ngaio Marsh's Superintendent Alleyn; and Georges Simenon's Inspector Maigret. These sleuths operate within worlds distinguished by ingenious plots, misleading clues, and surprise endings.

Since World War II, the major development in detective fiction has been the shift to the police precinct. In response to the demand for more realism, authors and filmmakers have explored the world of the working police officer in a format known as the "police procedural." In fiction the best known examples are Ed McBain's 87th precinct novels and Joseph Wambaugh's studies of the Los Angeles police department. Notable films with a precinct orientation include Jules Dassin's *Naked City* (1948) and Dennis Hopper's *Colors* (1987).

Among television series, *Dragnet* (1952–59), *Hill Street Blues* (1981–87), and *NYPD Blue* (1993–2004) were successful examples of the precinct form. An outstanding British contribution is the *Prime Suspect* series (1992–2004), featuring Helen Mirren as the harried and harassed chief inspector. Another outstanding television contribution is Dennis Potter's lovingly ironic homage to the genre, *The Singing Detective* (1987).

For a survey of 20th-century American detective fiction see Robert A. Baker and Michael T. Nietzel's *Private Eyes: One Hundred and One Knights* (1985). The English scene is surveyed in Julian Symons's *The Detective Story in Britain* (1978). A classic study of the genre is W. H. Auden's "The Guilty Vicarage" in his *The Dyer's Hand* (1962).

determinism   The view that all events in the universe, including those of human history, are determined by the conditions that produced them. In theology the view is expressed as predestination, the belief that God has predetermined the fate of each individual soul (*see* CALVINISM).

In literary studies the issues implied by determinism have been expressed in the debate over the relative importance of character-vs.-fate in the analysis of TRAGEDY. In the 19th century scientific determinism played a key role in the formulation of NATURALISM. In the 20th century the idea of free choice as the defining characteristic of human existence is a central principle of EXISTENTIALISM, while much of modern THEORY implies a linguistic determinism, although one that issues, in DECONSTRUCTION at least, in a form of free PLAY.

deus ex machina (the god from the machine)   In classical drama a mechanical device was used to lower a god onto the stage at a critical point in the play. The god's appearance usually served to untangle the plot and rescue the hero. By extension, the term refers to any arbitrary plot device that resolves a dilemma in a story or play. The appearance of the cavalry at a critical point in a WESTERN film is an example of deus ex machina.

diachronic/synchronic   Two terms designed to reflect two approaches to the study of language. To look at language diachronically is to study its historical development, while the synchronic approach analyzes a language system at a given moment in its history. The terms are associated with the French linguist Ferdinand de Saussure, who advocated the synchronic approach to the study of language, a position that had a significant impact on the development of STRUCTURALISM.

Dial, The   A quarterly American journal advocating the principles of TRANSCENDENTALISM published from 1840 to 1844. Its first editor was the early feminist Margaret Fuller. She was succeeded as editor by Ralph Waldo Emerson, who contributed his own "Lectures on the Times" as a regular feature of the journal.

–1929, first as a monthly, later
came a distinguished literary and
re the poets E. E. Cummings and
ınd Thomas Mann, and the critic
Chagall were among the artistic

ı spoken by members of a class or
ıulary, syntax, conversational style,
ıny contemporary writers attempt
:sorting to the distracting practice
lect writing around the turn of the
ım Stephen Crane's rendering of a
(1893): "Wid a home like dis an' a

ıg at the truth through debate or
ıpict Socrates' skillful questioning,
by the 19th-century German phi-
the process that governs historical
ıus transformed into a new, higher
n turn adapted by Karl Marx, who
:tions of the capitalist system. (See

rk of the Russian theorist Mikhail
:terance is a contribution to a con-
tinuing human dialogue—that is, it is both a response to past uses of the language
and an occasion for future uses: "The word in living conversation is directly, bla-
tantly oriented toward a future answer word: it provokes an answer, anticipates
it and structures itself in the answer's direction."

Within this abstract conception, Bakhtin explored particular forms of dialogism exhibited in the NOVEL. In his view, the novel is inherently dialogic in that it
incorporates a broad range of human voices, some associated with the characters,
others with the author, and still others apparently unconnected and free floating.
Included within this medley are the voices of authority (such as the author's),
but they are consistently undermined, contradicted, and enriched by the voices
of subversion, which Bakhtin characterizes as CARNIVAL. All these voices interact
and collide to create a polyglot universe, in which there is no "last word," only a
continuing dialogue.

117

Bakhtin's principles are best exemplified in his *The Dialogic Imagination* (1981), which contains a detailed and comprehensive introduction by the book's editor, Michael Holquist. David Lodge's *After Bakhtin* (1990) offers a highly readable application of Bakhtin's theories.

dialogue, the   In addition to being a feature of fiction and drama which represents characters' speech, the dialogue is also a type of literature in which two or more people engage in a discussion. Among the earliest and greatest examples of the form are the *Dialogues of Plato* (fourth century B.C.), which depict Socrates as the intellectual gadfly employing a question/answer technique with his interlocutors.

In the RENAISSANCE, the Platonic precedent encouraged the use of the form for a variety of purposes: Erasmus's *Colloquies* (1516) were used to teach Latin to school children throughout Europe; Erasmus's English friend, Sir Thomas More, employed the dialogue for polemical purposes in his *Dialogue Concerning Heresies* (1528), and Baldassare Castiglione's influential *The Courtier* (1518) employed a series of dialogues to shape a definition of the ideal courtier in a cultured society.

A measure of the continued importance of the form in the 17th and 18th centuries is its use in such serious works as Galileo's *Concerning the Two World System* (1632) and David Hume's *Dialogues Concerning Natural Religion* (1779).

By the 19th century the form had fallen into disuse, a development, according to one view, that reflects the increasing dominance of literate over oral forms of literature (*see* ORALITY/LITERACY). Nevertheless the dialogue has made occasional reappearances in modern literature, notably in the poems of the French poet Paul Valéry. Valéry's *L'Idée Fixe* (1932) consists of imagined dialogues with 20th-century physicists in an attempt to apply their ideas to the mind of the individual. Another celebrated modern use of the form is William Butler Yeats's "Dialogue of the Self and the Soul."

In its general sense as a synonym for conversation, dialogue has assumed increasing importance in theories of literature that emphasize the interaction between reader and text, as, for example, in HERMENEUTICS or READER RESPONSE CRITICISM. It also plays a crucial role in Mikhail Bakhtin's conception of DIALOGISM.

Michael Macovski's *The Dialogue and Literature* (1994) surveys the various uses of the form.

diary   A daily account of events recorded by an individual, usually personal in nature. Often used synonymously with the term *journal*, it is distinguished from the latter by its more intimate and informal tone. Famous diarists include Samuel Pepys in the 17th century and Anaïs Nin in the 20th century. Undoubtedly the most compelling diary of modern times is Anne Frank's *Diary* *of a Young Girl*, published in 1952, written while she was hiding from the Nazis during World War II.

Among novels cast in diary form, George Bernanos's *Diary of a Country Priest* (1937) is a modern classic.

diction   The choice of words in a work of literature. The general categories of diction are formal, as in the novels of Henry James; colloquial, as in the essays of Calvin Trillin; and slang, as in Richard Price's *Clockers* (1992), a novel set in a ghettoized housing project.

didactic literature   Usually used as a disparaging term to describe literature so intent on instructing or moralizing that it interferes with or overwhelms the artistic experience of the work. What constitutes didacticism varies with historical periods. In modern times the term has been applied to the principles of SOCIALIST REALISM as practiced in the Soviet Union.

diegesis/mimesis   Contrasting terms used to indicate the difference between literature in which the AUTHOR or NARRATOR is presumed to be speaking (as in descriptive passages in fiction—diegesis) and that in which a character speaks (as in drama or in the dialogue portion of fiction—mimesis). Complicating the use of the latter term is that MIMESIS also can refer to literature's presumed ability to reflect the real world—as, for example, the audience's sense at Conor McPherson's play *The Weir* (1998) that they are sitting in a real pub, listening to the character's stories. But when paired with diegesis, the term assumes a more limited role relating to the analysis of types of NARRATIVE.

The traditional 19th-century novel placed a greater emphasis on the author's voice and therefore on his authority as an omniscient narrator. Around the turn of the century, particularly in the practice of Henry James, there was a shift in emphasis in the writing of fiction from exposition (diegesis) to direct representation (mimesis)—from "telling" to "showing."

Since James's time, the practice of interweaving dialogue or monologue (mimesis) and description (diegesis) in the same passage has become common. Here, for example, is a passage from James Joyce's *Ulysses* (1922), as Leopold Bloom prepares breakfast for his wife Molly:

Another slice of bread and butter: three, four,: right. She didn't like her plate full. Right. He turned from the tray, lifted the kettle off the hob and set it sideways on the fire. It sat there, dull and squat, its spout stuck out. Cup of tea soon. Good. Mouth dry.

The first sentence is a description rendered through Bloom's INTERIOR MONOLOGUE. In the second sentence the use of the past tense ("didn't") suggests an authorial narrator, speaking through the consciousness of the character in FREE INDIRECT STYLE. The third sentence ("Right.") refers us back to Bloom's monologue. The fourth and fifth sentences are straight authorial descriptions. The final fragments ("Cup of tea soon. Good. Mouth dry.") place us back in Bloom's stream of consciousness.

As this passage illustrates, the complex mix of diegesis and mimesis has become one of the distinguishing features of modern and postmodern fiction.

David Lodge provides an illuminating discussion of the technique in *After Bakhtin* (1990).

dieresis   In verse, a pause in a line when the end of a word and the end of a foot coincide; in RHETORIC, the division of an entity into its component parts. A parodical example is the Gravedigger's analysis of "act" in Shakespeare's *Hamlet*: "An act hath three branches: it is to do, to act, to perform."

différance   *See* DECONSTRUCTION.

dime novel   Popular 19th-century paperback novels usually sold in America for 10 cents. The first successful dime novel was *Malaeska, The Indian Wife of a White Hunter* (1860) by Ann Sophia Stephens. The appeal of these novels was that they were "action packed" with steely-eyed heroes, despicable villains, and maidens in distress. Among the most successful of these was *Buffalo Bill, King of the Border Men* (1869) by Ned Buntline, the pseudonym of E. Z. C. Judson.

Daryl Jones's *The Dime Novel Western* (1978) offers a history of the genre.

dimeter   A line of verse consisting of two feet. (*See* METER.)

director   In DRAMA and film the person charged with the overall responsibility for the performance. In the case of a play, the director coordinates and supervises the actors, the design, the costumes, the lighting and, most important, the acting, in the services of the play's objective, a goal that the director must determine in collaboration with the other figures. In this respect he or she must succeed in communicating the vision to everyone involved in the production.

The modern concept of a director evolved from an earlier period when the AUTHOR, certainly in the case of Molière and possibly in the case of Shakespeare, served as the company's director. In later years when the tradition of the ACTOR-

MANAGER of a company held sway, the dominant tendency was to present the play as a showcase for the star. Perhaps the most significant figure in the emergence of the modern sense of the term was Konstantin Stanislavski, the director of the MOSCOW ART THEATRE.

In FILM the director is similarly responsible for all of the activity that goes into the shooting of the film. With the growth of the STUDIO SYSTEM, the director's control of a film was largely limited to the actual filming. Like the actors, writers, and technicians, he or she was an employee of the studio with limited opportunity to exercise creative control. With the decline of the studios, the director assumed more autonomy, a movement accelerated by the AUTEUR theory of filmmaking, which equated the director with the author of a literary work. As a result, the film director has come to assume greater prominence than a theater director, the latter being still seen as subordinate in importance to the playwright.

Wendy Lasser's *A Director Calls* (1997) is a detailed study of a director in action.

dirge A funeral song lamenting someone's death. Two famous examples from Shakespeare are: "Full fathom five" in *The Tempest* and "Fear no more the heat of the sun" in *Cymbeline*, which contains the memorable couplet:

Golden lads and girls all must,
As chimney-sweepers, come to dust.

discourse An extended treatment of a subject, as in *Discourses*, Sir Joshua Reynolds's lectures on painting delivered at the Royal Academy of Art in the 18th century. In traditional literary study, the term "poetic discourse" suggests a language specific to the genre of poetry.

Discourse also refers to a specific form of language, as in ACADEMIC DISCOURSE, which refers to the type of language employed in the writings of university professors. Similarly we speak of *medical discourse*, *legal discourse*, or *military discourse*. According to the French theorist Michel Foucault (*The Archaeology of Knowledge*, 1972), the discourse of a given institution or discipline governs the production of knowledge within it. For example, the language of literary criticism emphasizes interpretation, a practice that is seen as "naturally appropriate" to criticism. Foucault would argue that, far from being "natural," such a practice is rooted in a historical development where choices were made to exclude some things and emphasize others. Thus the emphasis on interpretation tended to abstract and idealize literature, isolating it from the historical conditions within which it was produced and with which it interacted.

Growing out of Foucault's work, the aim of the study of discourse is, in the critic Paul Bové's words, "to describe the surface linkages between power, knowledge, institutions, intellectuals, the control of populations and the modern state."

A representative selection of Foucault's ideas is available in *The Foucault Reader*, edited by Paul Rabinow (1984). Paul Bové's essay "Discourse" appears in *Critical Terms for Literary Study* (1990), edited by Frank Lentricchia and Thomas McLaughlin.

discourse analysis   In LINGUISTICS, the study of speech or writing longer than a single sentence. Discourse analysis usually focuses on the structures of conversations, anecdotes, jokes, storytelling, or other forms of narrative. As related to the study of fiction, discourse analysis appears as NARRATOLOGY, the structural analysis of novels and stories.

discovery space   A term for the curtained area running the entire width of the rear of the Elizabethan stage, used for unveiling certain interior scenes where the characters are "discovered," or in place, as the curtain is parted. The discovery space is regarded as a more plausible alternative to the belief that the open Elizabethan stage contained an "inner stage," an interior acting area set back from the rear of the stage.

disintegrators   Term for a group of 19th and early 20th century scholars who maintained that a substantial number of the 37 plays in the Shakespearean CANON represents Shakespeare's revisions of other writers' works. The basis for the disintegration theses were the results of verse tests designed to offer statistical analyses of specific metrical elements in each play, lending the appearance of scientific rigor to the proceedings. The most responsible and restrained of the disintegrators was J. Dover Wilson, who argued that in the early plays, the *Henry VI* trilogy, for example, Shakespeare revised pre-existing material. Many scholars accept the idea that in the beginning of his career, Shakespeare may have participated in the revising of older plays, a common practice of playwrights in the Elizabethan theater.

E.A.J. Honigmann's *The Stability of Shakespeare's Text* (1965) offers an interesting, corrective view of the controversy.

dissociation of sensibility   A phrase coined by T. S. Eliot to describe the separation of feeling and thought. According to Eliot, prior to the middle of the 17th century, poets exhibited a capacity to easily integrate feeling and thought. This was particularly true of METAPHYSICAL POETRY. The Metaphysicals had been criticized for yoking together wildly divergent images in their poems, as when John Donne compared two separated lovers to the twin legs of a compass in his poem "The Anniversary." But Eliot argued that this reconciling of opposites, in this case love and science, was characteristic of poetry and indicative of the poetic SENSIBILITY:

> The ordinary man's experience is . . . fragmentary. The latter falls in love, or reads Spinoza, and these two experiences have nothing to do with each other or with the noise of the typewriter or the smell of cooking. In the mind of the poet these experiences are always forming new wholes.

For Eliot, the Metaphysicals were the last group to exhibit a consistently unified sensibility. Since their time the impact of scientific rationalism had created a division between thought ("truth") and feeling ("poetry"), resulting in the assignment of literature to the emotional, nonrational sphere of human existence.

Eliot's thesis was adopted by many adherents of the NEW CRITICISM, among whom it enjoyed unusual authority. In recent years it has been seen more as special pleading on Eliot's part, an example of his desire to turn the clock back to a time before the mid-17th century.

Eliot's essay "The Metaphysical Poets" appears in his *Selected Essays* (1932); for a penetrating critique of his thesis, see Frank Kermode's *The Romantic Image* (1957).

dissolve   In FILM, an overlapping transition between two scenes; as one scene fades out, the other fades in. A quick dissolve sets up sharply contrasting scenes; a slow dissolve can be used to suggest the passage of time. A "ripple dissolve" involves the blurring of the first scene as it slowly disappears, a technique frequently used to introduce a FLASHBACK.

Dissolves are an effective means of communicating a relationship between two images, often used in television commercials to build an association of ideas in the mind of the viewer.

dithyramb   Originally a hymn sung by a chorus at Greek festivals honoring the god Dionysus. The term now describes any impassioned and structurally irregular lyric poem. Historically, the dithyramb enjoys great significance because of Aristotle's claim, in his *Poetics*, that the dithyramb was one of the roots out of which TRAGEDY emerged.

documentary   In FILM and television, the presentation of factual events designed to inform or persuade its audience. The documentary usually relies on realistic techniques to emphasize the view of the presentation as truthful. Included within the genre are nature, travel, historical, ethnographic, science, current events, and propaganda films.

The father of the film documentary is the American Robert Flaherty, whose *Nanook of the North* (1922), a depiction of Eskimo life, provided an extraordinary look at a remote culture. Flaherty reinforced *Nanook*'s theme, the battle of human beings against the elements of nature, in his other great documentary, *Man of Aran* (1934), a study of the lives of fishermen in a remote island off the coast of Ireland.

A radically different use of the form appears in the work of Leni Riefenstahl, who created two powerful Nazi propaganda films, *Triumph of the Will* (1935), a mythic rendering of the 1934 Nazi Party congress held in Nuremburg, and *Olympiad* (1938), a sumptuously photographed record of the Berlin Olympics of 1936.

The 1930s saw another innovation in the form with the introduction of *The March of Time*. Shown in movie theaters from 1935 to 1951, *The March of Time*, produced under the aegis of *Time* magazine, was a cinematic version of a monthly newsmagazine.

World War II produced a rich vein of propaganda documentaries, a number of which, such as the British *Desert Victory* (1943), the Soviet *Stalingrad* (1943), Frank Capra's series *Why We Fight* (1942–45), and John Huston's *The Battle of San Pietro* (1945) transcended the propaganda genre.

In the postwar years the documentary took on the characteristics associated with Italian NEOREALISM and with CINEMA VERITÉ, or "Direct Cinema." Direct Cinema aimed at capturing the experience of an individual or social group. Notable examples include Lionel Rogosin's *On the Bowery* (1957), a powerful study of the lives of derelicts, and Frederick Wiseman's *Titicut Follies* (1968), a painful portrait of life in a state hospital.

In the '60s, documentaries explored a new social phenomenon, the rock concert. Donn Allen Pennebaker's *Monterey Pop* (1968), Michael Wadleigh's *Woodstock* (1969), and Albert and David Maysles' *Gimme Shelter* (1970) captured the energy and spirit of a generation.

A number of outstanding European documentary films have attempted to come to terms with the horror of the HOLOCAUST, notably Alain Resnais's *Night and Fog* (1955), Marcel Ophuls's *The Sorrow and the Pity* (1969), and Claude Lanzmann's *Shoah* (1985).

In television, documentaries frequently have taken on the form of investigative reports, a tradition that began with the Edward R. Murrow–Fred Friendly series *See It Now* (1951–58), famous for a number of programs on McCarthyism. One of these McCarthy documentaries became the subject of a film documentary, *Good Night and Good Luck* (2005), directed by George Clooney. Later

Murrow and Friendly produced a notable single documentary, *Harvest of Shame* (1960), an account of the plight of migrant workers.

The 1970s saw the innovation in television of the "docudrama," dramatized versions of historical events. Among many examples are *King* (1978), a biography of Martin Luther King, and *Holocaust* (1978).

Richard Meran Barsam's *Nonfiction Film: A Critical History* (1972) is a scholarly and analytical account that draws attention to the relationship of documentaries to nonfictional prose.

doggerel   Crude, shallow verse, sometimes consciously employed for comic effect, as in the poems of the English poet John Skelton (1460–1529). (*See* SKELTONICS.)

domestic tragedy   A form of tragedy in which the protagonists are middle or working class people whose downfall takes place within a family relationship. The term underscores the contrast between these tragic characters and those in Classical and Renaissance plays, men and women of royal blood, whose fate has consequences for the community as a whole. Domestic tragedy made its first appearance on the Elizabethan stage in such plays as the anonymous *Arden of Feversham* (1591), in which a wife and her lover murder the woman's husband and are caught and executed for the crime; and Thomas Heywood's *A Woman Killed with Kindness* (1603), in which the husband of an adulterous wife denies her access to her children after he discovers her affair.

The form reemerged in the 18th century with the success of George Lillo's *The London Merchant* (1731), in which the murder of a merchant and the repentance and execution of the murderer constitute the main action. The success of Lillo's play led to imitations in Germany, notably G. E. Lessing's *Miss Sara Sampson* (1755), the first example in German drama of a tragedy focused on a middle class family.

American drama in the 1940s saw a remarkable resurgence of middle class family tragedy with Tennessee Williams's *A Streetcar Named Desire* (1947), Arthur Miller's *Death of a Salesman* (1948), and Eugene O'Neill's most important play, *A Long Day's Journey into Night* (1940, produced, 1956).

Don Juan theme   A theme originating with the idea of Don Juan as a compulsive seducer, later transformed into the figure of the laughing, scoffing rebel, and most recently seen as a joyless, reflective intellectual.

The earliest example of the story is Tirso de Molina's *El burlador de Sevilla y convidado de piedra* (*The Trickster of Seville and the Stone Guest*, c. 1626), which includes the two essential features of the story, the predatory seducer and the avenging statue of the man Don Juan has murdered. The next great version of the legend, Molière's *Don Juan* (1665), added atheism and hypocrisy to Don Juan's offenses. During the same period in Restoration England, Thomas Shadwell produced *The Libertine* (1676), a formless but spirited rendering of the legend that was extremely popular in its time.

But the most influential of the versions of Don Juan was Mozart's *Don Giovanni* (1787), the world's most imitated opera, its LIBRETTO by Lorenzo Da Ponte providing an adequate vehicle for the sublime music.

The Romantic Age transformed the great lover from a scoffing libertine to a lonely, unhappy rebel in search of, but never achieving, an ideal, of which women were the symbol. In this role he is seen, as in Christian Grabbe's play *Don Juan and Faust* (1829), as the spiritual kin of Goethe's hero. Lord Byron's *Don Juan* (1818–23) contributed further to the great fame of the figure, although Byron's work, an epic poem, has little in common with the plays that preceded it. What it does add to the legend is the idea of a passive figure, more seduced than seducing.

In 1844 appeared the Spanish writer José Zorilla's *Don Juan Tenorio*, a play that has assumed the status of a religious feast, performed every November in Spanish-speaking countries.

George Bernard Shaw turned the legend on its head in *Man and Superman* (1905) with its memorable third act scene "Don Juan in Hell." Shaw represented Don Juan as a "superman," a servant of the "life force" marked by a restless quest for perfection.

The Swiss dramatist Max Frisch gave Shaw's figure a negative twist in *Don Juan and the Love of Geometry* (1968), where the Don is an intellectual in a vain quest for an ordering principle in life.

Notable film versions include a 1926 swashbuckler starring John Barrymore, and Joseph Losey's opulent production of *Don Giovanni* (1972).

Oscar Mandel's *The Theatre of Don Juan* (1963) contains commentaries along with excerpts from various theatrical versions of the theme.

doppelgänger (the double) German word used to describe a character whose divided mind or personality is represented as two characters. A famous, if melodramatic, example is Robert Louis Stevenson's *Dr. Jekyll and Mr. Hyde* (1886). A psychologically more subtle treatment is Joseph Conrad's *The Secret Sharer* (1912) in which a young captain in charge of his first ship secretly harbors a young man until such time as the captain proves himself capable of command. Other examples include Edgar Allan Poe's story "William Wilson" (1839) and Fyodor Dostoyevsky's novel *The Double* (1840). Brian Friel put the device to effective comic use in his play *Philadelphia, Here I Come* (1964), in which the lead character's double (played by a second actor) ironically comments on the action.

Robert Rogers's *The Double in Literature* (1970) surveys the use of the device from the perspective of psychoanalysis.

downstage/upstage   In a PROSCENIUM stage, downstage indicates the front and upstage the rear. In a scene in which upstage and downstage characters engage in a dialogue, the upstage actor has the advantage, since the downstage actor's back is to the audience—hence the term *upstaged*, meaning to be put at a disadvantage.

drama   In its broadest sense, any work in which actors assume roles before an audience, either in a theater or on radio or television. Drama is a major literary GENRE, frequently subdivided into the categories of TRAGEDY, COMEDY, and TRAGICOMEDY. Further subdivisions include MELODRAMA, FARCE, pantomime, and the various genres of FILM. (*See also* CLOSET DRAMA, RADIO DRAMA, TELEVISION DRAMA.)

dramatic illusion   A term for the "illusion of reality" that is the basis of theatrical REALISM. The supposition of realistic drama is that the audience is gazing into a real room with one wall removed, sometimes known as the "fourth wall convention." Thus the costumes, speech, movements, and props in the play should correspond exactly to the world being represented so that the audience will succumb to the illusion that it is watching real people, not a play. The convention of the dramatic illusion was challenged by Bertolt Brecht in his defense of the EPIC THEATER and the ALIENATION EFFECT.

dramatic monologue   A type of lyric poem in which a person speaks to a silent audience and, in the course of doing so, reveals a critical aspect of his own character. The acknowledged master of this form was Robert Browning. Browning's "My Last Duchess" (1845), in which a nameless Duke, proudly showing off his art collection, exposes himself as the callous murderer of his late wife, is the finest dramatic monologue of its time. Browning extended the form further in *The Ring and the Book* (1869), a verse novel cast as 12 lengthy monologues.

In the 20th century the best known example of the form is T. S. Eliot's "The Love Song of J. Alfred Prufrock" (1915). The American poet Frank Bidart has recently revived the form using historical figures, as in his "The War of Vaslav Nijinsky" (1981).

Robert Langbaum's *The Poetry of Experience* (1957) examines the form in detail.

dramatism   A term coined by the American critic and theorist Kenneth Burke to describe his use of drama as a model of human behavior. For Burke, human beings act on two levels, the literal and the symbolic. Insofar as we are animals our actions are literal, essentially responses to stimuli, but we are also symbol-using, meaning-making animals for whom language is a mode of action.

Language is, in other words, a form of "symbolic action"; therefore, when we ascribe a particular motive to an act, we are like a playwright setting that action within a certain "frame." This frame can be analyzed from any one of five perspectives, which Burke calls the "pentad." The pentad offers the following ways of looking at any action, literal or symbolic:

Act (What happened?);
Scene (What was the context?);
Agent (Who did it?);
Agency (How was it done?);
Purpose (Why was it done?).

Any one of these terms may be combined with any other to offer a perspective that Burke terms a "ratio." An "agent-scene" ratio, for example, would explore the relationship between the actor and one of a wide range of possible "scenes" in which the act occurred, such as the geographical place, the historical moment, or the type of civilization. Each choice alters the interpretation. Thus, emphasizing any particular "ratio" produces "a truth," as opposed to "the truth."

Extending the dramatic metaphor even further, Burke argues that "a poem is an act, the symbolic act of the poet who made it—and of such a nature that, in surviving as a structure, or object, it enables us as readers to re-enact it."

Burke's dramatism has had less direct impact in literature than in sociology, where it is regarded as a basic tool in analyzing the SOCIAL CONSTRUCTION of reality. Nevertheless, for many of his followers, Burke stands as one of the forerunners of contemporary THEORY and a great critic in his own right. *See* SPEECH ACT THEORY.

An anthology of Burke's writing containing an introduction that explains his contribution to sociology is *On Symbols and Society* (ed. Joseph Gusfield, 1989). William Rueckert's *Kenneth Burke and the Drama of Human Relations* (1963) gives a detailed analysis of dramatism. Frank Lentricchia's *Criticism and Social Change* (1985) treats Burke's contribution to contemporary criticism and theory.

dramatis personae   The list of characters in a play, usually appearing in a theater program or at the beginning of a printed version of the play.

dramatization   The rendering of a story or event as a play. *See* ADAPTATION.

dramaturge   An adviser employed by a theater company who assists in choosing the plays the company will present. The dramaturge sometimes also assists the director in determining an interpretation of a play to be presented.

drâme bourgeois (bourgeois drama)   A term coined by the 18th-century French philosopher and playwright Denis Diderot to describe a type of drama that focused on the domestic problems of middle class families. In these plays, Diderot wished to explore the impact of social conditions on the lives of his characters, in a manner that reflected the seriousness of tragedy, but without that form's unhappy endings. His talent as a playwright was limited, but his critical principles exerted considerable influence on the development of European drama in the 18th and 19th centuries. For related terms, see DOMESTIC TRAGEDY; MELODRAMA.

Diderot's Collected Essays, edited by L. G. Crocker (1966), contains his most important essays on the theater.

drawing room comedy   A type of drama, particularly popular in the first half of the 20th century which focused on the lives of sophisticated, upper middle-class types. The drawing room often served as the setting of such plays as in Noël Coward's *Blithe Spirit* (1941).

dream   Since classical times two opposing views of the dream have prevailed. The first is to regard a dream as irrational (the "crazy dream") and insignificant. Mercutio's account in Shakespeare's *Romeo and Juliet* summarizes this view:

> *I talk of dreams;*
> *Which are the children of an idle brain,*
> *Begot of nothing but vain fantasy;*
> *Which is as thin of substance as the air,*
> *And more inconstant than the wind.*

Countering this view of dreams as pointless and illusory is the tradition—of far greater use to storytellers and writers—of the dream as prophetic or symbolic. In this view, dreams, though illusory, are a source of a wisdom beyond reason, a truth of the imagination.

The medieval expression of this view took the form of the DREAM VISION, a narrative poem, in which the narrator describes a dream that has clearly allegorical implications. Examples of this type range from the 13th-century *Roman de la Rose* of Guillaume de Lorris to Chaucer's *The Book of the Duchess* (1369) and William Langland's *Piers Plowman* (1366–99). In this form, the effect of the dream is to restore the awakened dreamer to a new sense of harmony with his world. A famous modern example would be L. Frank Baum's *The Wizard of Oz* (1900; film version 1939), which concludes with Dorothy's recognition of the value of her Kansas home.

In Elizabethan drama, the dream functioned both as a plot device and as a means of adding an air of mystery and the supernatural to the action. To these, Shakespeare added the use of dreams as metaphors for the meaning of the play—as, for example, in *A Midsummer Night's Dream*, in which the very title suggests the relation between the dream and other illusory forms such as drama and romantic love. In the play, the character Theseus makes the connection among these three phenomena:

> *The lunatic, the lover and the poet*
> *Are of imagination all compact.*

In this comment Theseus is deprecating the poet and the lover by equating them with the madman, but unwittingly he is testifying to the experience of the play as a whole, which suggests that its "dream world" of fairies, magic, and transformations yields a truth, "something of great constancy" as Theseus's bride, Hippolyta, says in correcting his view.

What Shakespeare hinted at was made explicit in the plays of his near-contemporary, the Spanish dramatist Pedro Calderón de la Barca. Calderón's *Life Is a Dream* (1635) explores the theme that "all men dream the lives they lead," a conception closely allied to Calderón's (and Shakespeare's) other great theme: THEATRUM MUNDI, or "the world as a stage." Both "life is a dream" and "the world as a stage" suggest the basic religious proposition that human values are transient and deceptive and, conversely, that the apparent illusion of the dream or play may reflect a higher truth.

The modern view of the dream is an outgrowth of the central role of dreams in Sigmund Freud's theories, as expressed in his *The Interpretation of Dreams* (1900). Here and throughout his work, Freud maintained that a dream is an expression by an individual's UNCONSCIOUS of a wish or fear that is partially suppressed and therefore employs symbols that must be interpreted in order to be understood (*see* DREAMWORK).

This conception has had a profound effect on modern literature because of Freud's implied assertion that the literary artist is a kind of dreamer whose unconscious wishes or fears constitute the hidden meaning of a poem or story. (*See* PSYCHOANALYTICAL CRITICISM.)

The literary work that employs the Freudian conception of the dream to greatest effect is James Joyce's *Finnegans Wake* (1939). Presented as the dream of H. C. Earwicker, the owner of a Dublin pub, Joyce's novel suggests that the language of dreams is a fusion (and confusion) of tongues and free association. More difficult to interpret than any dream, it is written, not for dreamers, but, in Joyce's words, for "the ideal reader suffering from ideal insomnia."

Marjorie Garber's *Dream in Shakespeare* (1974) covers the variety of uses of dreams and dreamworlds in his plays. Charles Rycroft's *The Innocence of Dreams* (1979) adapts and updates the Freudian theory.

dream vision   A type of medieval literature in which the narrator, in a dream, observes allegorical or actual figures whose behavior illustrates some truth of life. The prototype of the form is Guillaume de Lorris's *Roman de la Rose*, a long 13th-century poem that recounts his dream of love, in which he observes the courtship of a maiden. Chaucer employed the form in a number of works: *The Book of the Duchess* (1369) is a combined elegy and dream vision, commemorating the death of Blanche, the Duchess of Lancaster and wife of John of Gaunt, Chaucer's patron. The dream in *The Parliament of Fowls* (c. 1375) concludes with a parliament of birds discussing a variety of views of the nature of love. The prologue to his *The Legend of Good Women* (c. 1380) contains a dream vision that operates as the framing device of the individual stories that follow it.

Another notable English dream vision poem is William Langland's *Piers Plowman* (1366–86), a series of dream vision episodes that focuses on the proper conduct of a Christian life against a background of 14th-century English society. Another famous 14th-century dream vision poem is *The Pearl*, in which a lost pearl comes to stand for a daughter who has died in infancy.

dreamwork   Sigmund Freud's term for the transformation of the hidden or latent meaning of a dream into the form that is remembered and reported by the dreamer. A dream is a combination of the "day residue," an immediate situation in daily life, together with a powerful motive dating back to childhood. The latter has been long suppressed from consciousness, but in sleep it manages to escape the "censor," the unconscious. In order to succeed, however, the escape must take on disguised forms, two features of which are *condensation*—the compression of two or more desires or fears into a single image—and *displacement*—the shifting of feeling from one object or person to another.

Here is an excerpt from a dream analyzed by Freud:

> The dreamer sees three lions in the desert, one of which is laughing, but she is not afraid of them. . . . The occasion of the dream was a sentence in the dreamer's English exercise: "The *lion's* greatest adornment is her

131

mane." Her father used to wear a beard which encircled his face like a *mane*. The name of her English teacher is Miss *Lyons*. An acquaintance of hers had sent her a book of the ballads of *Loewe* (Loewe-lion). These, then, are the three lions. . . . The lion is like the lion in *A Midsummer Night's Dream*, who is unmasked as Snug the joiner; and of such stuff are all the dream-lions of which one is not afraid.

Characteristically, Freud's analysis includes literary allusions, underscoring his view that dreams and literary works are, as Shakespeare points out in *A Midsummer Night's Dream*, "of imagination all compact."

Freud's *The Interpretation of Dreams* (1900) contains his most complete treatment of dreams and dreamwork.

drinking *See* ALCOHOL.

dumb show In Elizabethan drama, a mimed scene depicting an episode occurring outside the time sequence of the play. The dumb show was employed by a number of dramatists including Thomas Kyd (*The Spanish Tragedy*, 1589) and John Webster (*The Duchess of Malfi*, 1613). By far the best known example is the introductory segment to the play-within-the-play in Shakespeare's *Hamlet*.

Dieter Mehl's *The Elizabethan Dumb Show* (1965) is the definitive study.

dybbuk In Hasidic Jewish folklore, the soul of a dead person that, as a punishment for past sins, wanders aimlessly until it can enter the body of a living person. Once it does, that person becomes possessed, as if by a devil. The folktale formed the basis of the Russian Jewish writer S. Ansky's *The Dybbuk* (1920), a tragedy in which a young woman is possessed by a dybbuk, the soul of a young man who died after completing a pact with the devil. The play, one of the most celebrated in the Yiddish theater, has been widely performed in Europe and America.

Joseph C. Landis has translated the play into English in his *The Dybbuk and Other Great Yiddish Plays* (1966).

dystopia *See* UTOPIA.

early modern period   A recent term used by some scholars and historians to replace the more traditional term RENAISSANCE. The choice of "early modern" emphasizes those features at the end of the period (the 17th century) that antici- pate the themes of MODERNISM, as opposed to the term *Renaissance*, which, with its meaning of "rebirth," tends to focus on the beginnings of the period (the 15th and 16th centuries).

early Tudor   In English literature, the period from the accession of Henry VII in 1485 to the beginning of the ELIZABETHAN reign in 1558.

The major historical event of the period was the decision of Henry VIII to break with Rome and establish the Church of England, a move that had profound consequences for the subsequent history of the nation. The period also saw the introduction of HUMANISM to England. The outstanding humanist of the age, Sir Thomas More, created its most significant prose work, *Utopia* (1516).

In poetry, the age is distinguished by the lyrics of Sir Thomas Wyatt, the first English poet to employ the sonnet form, and Henry Howard, Earl of Surrey, whose translation of Books II and IV of Virgil's *Aeneid* (1554–57) represents the first use of BLANK VERSE in English. Another pioneer writer of the age was George Gascoigne, whose *Supposes* (1566) is the first prose comedy in English and a major source of Shakespeare's *Much Ado About Nothing*. Another feature of the era was the development of the theatrical form known as the INTERLUDE.

C. S. Lewis's *English Literature in the 16th Century* (1954) provides a highly readable and provocative analysis of the nondramatic work of the time; David Bevington's *Tudor Drama and Politics* (1968) deals with the interaction of plays and politics in the period.

eclogue   A PASTORAL poem, traditionally featuring shepherds engaged in dia- logue, as in Edmund Spenser's *The Shepherd's Calendar* (1579). Since the 18th cen- tury the term has been divorced from its pastoral setting and has come to refer to a poem in which a dialogue or monologue provides the vehicle for serious reflection, as in W. H. Auden's *The Age of Anxiety: A Baroque Eclogue* (1948).

ecocriticism   An approach to literature from the perspective of environmentalism. An aspect of the broader field of Environmental Studies, ecocriticism focuses on nature writing: classics, such as Henry David Thoreau's *Walden* (1854), and contemporary works, such as Annie Dillard's *Pilgrim at Tinker Creek* (1974) and John McPhee's *Coming into the Country* (1977). An interesting example of ecocriticism is Joseph Meeker's *The Comedy of Survival* (1974), a study of comic theory in relation to the environment.

A more ambitious goal for this type of criticism is laid out by Karl Kroeber in *Ecological Literary Criticism* (1994). Drawing on recent findings in biological science, Kroeber argues that the romantic poets' experience of nature anticipated the current view in biological science that an "individual organism is not definable except through its interactions with its environment." Romantic self-consciousness, instead of being the source of alienation, was uniquely suited to an intersubjective attunement to nature.

Another ecocritical view is evident in Jonathan Bate's *The Song of the Earth* (2000). Bate employs a phenomenological approach indebted to the philosopher Martin Heidegger, who sees the connection of nature with literature as "the poetry of dwelling" with the earth.

The Ecocriticism Reader (1996), edited by Cheryll Glotfelty and Harold Fromm, is the first anthology of critical essays on the topic.

Edwardian   In English history and literature, the reign of King Edward VII (1901–10). It was a period characterized by a reaction against Victorianism (*See* VICTORIAN) and by the first stirrings of MODERNISM. Although it was a relatively tranquil time, the increasing discontent of the lower classes asserted itself in the formation, in 1900, of the socialist British Labour Party. The Edwardian era also saw the birth of the Woman's Suffrage Movement (1905). Under the leadership of Emmeline Pankhurst, the Suffragettes, as they were known, adopted a militant campaign that included violence in their efforts to obtain full voting rights for women, which were finally won in 1918.

In poetry the era saw the birth of IMAGISM; in drama, the plays of George Bernard Shaw and the founding of the ABBEY THEATRE; and in fiction, the novels of Joseph Conrad, H. G. Wells, and E. M. Forster. Conrad's *Heart of Darkness* (1902) and *Nostromo* (1905) were complex analyses of the moral consequences of imperialism. Wells, best known for his SCIENCE FICTION, also wrote social novels, of which the most accomplished is *Tono-Bungay* (1908), a critical look at Edwardian values. Forster's *Howards End* (1910) depicts the interaction of the English leisure class with the commercial middle class.

The period is usually seen as ending with the outbreak of World War I.

Samuel Hynes's *The Edwardian Turn of Mind* (1968) captures the tone and substance of the period.

eiron A STOCK CHARACTER in classical comedy, whose pose as a self-deprecating, humble figure enables him to outwit his opponents, particularly the ALAZON or boaster. The real life prototype of the eiron was the philosopher Socrates, who always professed his own ignorance while exposing the faulty thinking of others. The eiron is a basic figure in comedy, often portrayed as the good friend of the hero. The type is also recognizable today in the homespun humorist, such as Will Rogers or Andrew Rooney, or Peter Falk's dirty-raincoat-clad detective in the television series Columbo.

élan vital (vital impulse) According to the French philosopher Henri Bergson, the force that drives the process of evolution in life, the generative motor of the instinct for preservation. One manifestation of this impulse is treated in Bergson's famous treatise *Laughter: An Essay on the Meaning of the Comic* (1900). George Bernard Shaw anticipated and developed Bergson's "creative evolution" concept in some of his plays, notably *Man and Superman* (1905). Shaw presents a detailed account of Bergson's theories in his "Preface" to *Back to Methusaleh* (1921).

elegy A lyric poem meditating on the death of an individual or on the fact of mortality in general. The reflection on death usually leads to a resolution in which the speaker asserts a general truth. Distinguished examples of elegies include Thomas Gray's "Elegy Written in a Country Churchyard" (1750) and Alfred, Lord Tennyson's *In Memoriam* (1880). Modern examples include W. H. Auden's "On the Death of W. B. Yeats" (1939) and Paul Monette's tribute to a lover who died of AIDS, *Love Alone: Eighteen Elegies for Rog* (1988). A poignant modern elegy is Frank O'Hara's tribute to Billie Holiday "The Day Lady Died." (1959).

A particular type, the PASTORAL elegy, involves the representation of the dead person as a shepherd. The pastoral elegy originated among Sicilian poets writing in Greek in the second and third centuries B.C. Notable examples in English are John Milton's *Lycidas* (1637) and Percy Bysshe Shelley's *Adonais* (1821).

P. M. Sacks's *The English Elegy* (1985) provides a survey of the form.

Elizabethan   The literature of the 45-year reign of Queen Elizabeth I (1558–1603) encompasses two literary periods: the end of the EARLY TUDOR era in the 1560s and the extraordinary age that bears her name. The term *Elizabethan* is sometimes used to embrace literary activity up to the death of Shakespeare (1616), but the latter part of Shakespeare's career properly belongs to the JACOBEAN era.

Elizabethan literature is characterized by an intense national pride and a sense of optimism expressed in rich, at times ornate, language. It was a period of linguistic experimentation and discovery, reflected in the magisterial prose of Richard Hooker's *The Laws of Ecclesiastical Polity* (1594) and the mannered experiments of John Lyly's EUPHUISM.

In poetry the age witnessed the epic achievement of Edmund Spenser's *The Faerie Queene* (1590–96) and the flowering of the Elizabethan sonnet, particularly those written by Edmund Spenser, Sir Philip Sidney, and Shakespeare. Sidney is also responsible for *An Apologie for Poetrie* (1595), a defense of literature from Puritan attack and an early example of literary criticism in English.

But the glory of the age lay in its popular drama. Among the early Elizabethans the outstanding playwrights are Christopher Marlowe and Thomas Kyd. Marlowe, who died at age 29, produced two of the greatest plays in the language, *Doctor Faustus* (1588–92) and *Edward II* (1592–93). Kyd wrote *The Spanish Tragedy* (1578), a very successful tragedy of revenge, and a play, now lost, based on the Hamlet theme. Among the later Elizabethans, the works of Thomas Dekker (*The Shoemaker's Holiday*, 1599), George Chapman (*Bussy D'Ambois*, 1603), and Thomas Heywood (*A Woman Killed with Kindness*, 1603) are notable.

Shakespeare displayed his genius in romantic comedies, histories and tragedies such as *A Midsummer Night's Dream* (1595), *Henry V* (1599), and *Romeo and Juliet* (1598).

The death of the 70-year-old queen in 1603 ushered in a new royal family, the Stuarts, a new century, and a new tone in literature. *See* JACOBEAN.

A lively and original survey of the period is C. S. Lewis's *English Literature in the Sixteenth Century, Excluding Drama* (1954). For the drama, see Muriel C. Bradbrook's *Themes and Conventions of Elizabethan Tragedy* (1935) and Alan Dessen's *Elizabethan Drama and the Viewer's Eye* (1977).

emblem   A pictorial and poetic device containing a motto, an engraving that symbolically depicts the motto, and a short verse that comments on the motto and the engraving. In the 16th and 17th centuries, many of these were collected and published in book form.

Rosemary Freeman's *English Emblem Books* (1948) surveys the form from 1586 until the end of the 17th century.

emendation   In textual scholarship, a term used to describe a correction of a text. The aim of an emendation is to remove an error believed to have crept into a text in the process of its being either transcribed or printed. A celebrated emendation is from Shakespeare's *Henry V*, where the description of the dying Falstaff in the original published text reads, "his nose was as sharp as a pen and a table of greenfields." Lewis Theobald, an 18th-century editor of the play, changed it to "a' [he] babbl'd of green fields." The idea that a dying man would be babbling strikes most readers as a logical correction.

empathy   The capacity to enter into the experience of another. Empathy is a more intense version of sympathy, the compassionate understanding of another's feelings. In literary study empathy can be considered from the perspective of the writer or the reader. ROMANTICISM emphasized the writer's capacity for empathy while recently, under the influence of READER RESPONSE CRITICISM, attention has focused on the reader's role in creating empathy.

empiricism   In philosophy, the doctrine that experience is the basis of all knowledge. Empiricism is closely allied to the scientific method in that they both employ the principle of inductive reasoning—moving from the particular to the general—as their logical basis. The traditional philosophical opposite of empiricism is rationalism. Literary scholarship tends to be heavily empirical in its orientation, while literary theory has been for the most part rationalistic.

end-stopped line   A line of verse that concludes with a pause coinciding with the completion of a phrase or clause. The HEROIC COUPLET, perfected by Alexander Pope, usually employs it, but the end-stopped line is used in many other verse forms, as in these lines from Emily Dickinson:

> *Because I could not stop for Death—*
> *He kindly stopped for me—*
> *The carriage held but just ourselves*
> *And Immortality.*

The term for the opposite of the end-stopped line, the run-on line, is ENJAMBMENT.

enjambment   In verse, the continuation without pause from one line or couplet to the next. It is frequently employed in BLANK VERSE drama, lending a realistic conversational rhythm to the characters' speech, as in these lines from Shakespeare's *Macbeth*:

> *There is none but he*
> *Whose being I do fear; and under him*
> *My genius is rebuked, as it is said*
> *Mark Antony's was by Caesar.*

The opposite of enjambment is the END-STOPPED LINE.

Enlightenment, the   An intellectual movement in 18th-century Europe celebrating human reason and scientific thought as the instruments of emancipation, sweeping away the superstition and ignorance that appeared to be the legacy of the past. The period is also known as the "Age of Reason" since it was committed to the belief that, in the words of the 18th-century philosopher John Locke, "Reason must be our last judge and guide."

With reason as their guide, the Enlightenment thinkers believed in a future of unlimited possibilities. The idea of progress in all spheres of human activity was a central tenet of Enlightenment thought. The Enlightenment also stood for tolerance, human rights (Thomas Jefferson's *Declaration of Independence* is an Enlightenment document), scientific inquiry, and scepticism. It called for the rejection of religion based upon scriptural revelation in favor of DEISM, which posited a Divine creator, but one who remained aloof from human affairs.

Among the major figures of the Enlightenment were Voltaire and Diderot in France, Immanuel Kant and G. E. Lessing in Germany, Cesare Beccaria in Italy, John Locke in England, and David Hume in Scotland.

Many of the general assumptions regarding the period have been challenged by recent scholars, some influenced by Michel Foucault's conception of DISCOURSE, suggesting that reason also served as an instrument of repression during this period. Other anti-Enlightenment sentiment is reflected in the rejection of the ideal of objectivity in thought. (*See* RHETORIC.)

Peter Gay's *The Enlightenment* (1973) offers a valuable overview of the period.

envoy (envoi)   A short stanza affixed to the end of certain poems, usually as an address to an individual. In "The Complaint of Chaucer to His Purse," the poet affixed an envoi to the newly crowned king, Henry IV:

> *O conqueror of Brutus Albioun,*
> *Which that by line and free eleccioun*
> *Been verray [true] king, this song to you I sende:*
> *And ye, that mowen [may] alle our harmes amende,*
> *Have minde upon my supplicacioun.*

In this case, the envoy achieved its purpose: Henry substantially increased Chaucer's pension.

envy One of the most pervasive of human vices, envy is distinct from jealousy, the fear of losing something that one has. Envy involves desiring what someone else has, to such an extent that it leads to hatred of the other. It plays a central role in the biblical stories of the FALL, Cain and Abel, Joseph's brethren, and the parable of the laborers in the vineyard. Aristotle describes and discusses it in his RHETORIC. In the MIDDLE AGES, it ranked second only to Pride among the SEVEN DEADLY SINS. In Edmund Spenser's *The Faerie Queen* (1590–96), envy plays a powerful role, closely associated with the "Blatant Beast," Spenser's symbol of intractable evil. In John Milton's *Paradise Lost* (1667), envy of Christ and later of man is a motivating force in Satan's revolt and his temptation of Adam and Eve.

Shakespeare's *Othello* is a play about jealousy insofar as it is Othello's play, but insofar as it is Iago's, its main theme is envy. Iago is envious not only of Othello but also of his rival, the handsome Michael Cassio. As Iago, in a moment of self-revelation puts it, Cassio "hath a beauty in his life that makes mine ugly." Envy of this kind is not merely the desire for something else but a mirror revealing the self-hatred of the envious.

A celebrated semi-comical treatment of envy is Robert Browning's "Soliloquy in a Spanish Cloister" (1842), a DRAMATIC MONOLOGUE, in which the speaker, inflamed with envy of the unflappable goodness and happiness of a fellow monk, schemes of ways to try to ensure the damnation of the good man. As in the example of Iago, envy here evolves from the desire to replace the other to the desire to destroy the other.

For the theorist and critic René Girard, envy is the great repressed emotion in life, specifically in the form he calls MIMETIC DESIRE, desiring someone not for his or her self, but because this person is loved by another. Thus, envy creates an eternal triangle in which the Other is the mediator between the lover and the love object. In other words, the lover imitates (hence the term, *mimetic*) the desire of the third person. Literary examples include Cervantes's Don Quixote and Flaubert's Emma Bovary, two characters famous for borrowing their desires from romantic books, their need to be somebody else. In *A Theatre of Envy: William Shakespeare* (1991), Girard explores the prevalence of mimetic desire in Shakespeare's plays, whose actions are readily enhanced by techniques of disguise, mistaken identity, and other examples of the unreliability of the eyes in perceiving reality.

The topic takes on an ironic connotation in an entirely new context in the Soviet novelist Yuri Olesha's *Envy* (1927). As the publication date indicates, the setting is the newly established Soviet Union, pitting two remnants, spiritually speaking, of the old regime against a successful, confident Communist who represents the machine world of the future. Although the novel clearly deplores the loss of human values that attends the triumph of the machine, the Communist bureaucrat is presented as a decent person sincerely committed to the new society. This ambivalent view of the socialist ideal was still tolerated in the Soviet Union in the 1920s before the Stalinists took control of Russian literature under the banner of SOCIALIST REALISM.

Joseph Epstein's *Envy* (2003) is an elegant discussion of the subject.

epic In its original sense, the term refers to a long NARRATIVE poem that focuses on a heroic figure or group, and on events that form the cultural history of a nation or tribe. The epic hero undergoes a series of adventures that test his valor, intellect, and character. Among the conventions of the epic are the author's invocation to the muse, the opening of the action in the middle of things (in medias res) and the long lists, or catalogues, of ships, armies or, as in John Milton's *Paradise Lost*, devils.

In modern times, epic has come to denote a work in prose, verse, theater, or film that exhibits action on a large scale and treats a significant historical event. Such works are usually referred to as belonging to the epic tradition.

Within the original sense of the term, critics tend to distinguish between primary and secondary epics. Primary epics are direct expressions of the culture they depict, composed orally for performance before an audience. Secondary epics are written compositions that use the primary form as a model. Homer's *Iliad* and *Odyssey* are primary epics, while Virgil's *Aeneid* and Milton's *Paradise Lost*, both of which use Homer as their model, are secondary epics.

While Homer's works are the best known of the primary epics, they are by no means unique. Others include the Anglo-Saxon *Beowulf* (eighth century), the German *Nibelungenlied* (13th century) and the Yugoslavian epics recorded by the scholar Milman Parry (see ORALITY/LITERACY). Recent anthropological work has resulted in the recording of *The Mwindo Epic*, a lengthy narrative sung and recited by members of the Nyanga tribe of Zaire (now the Democratic Republic of Congo). This work exhibits many features of the classical primary epic—a miraculously born hero with supernatural powers, whose adventures include both subterranean and celestial journeys.

Works that operate within the epic tradition include novels such as Cervantes's *Don Quixote* (1605–15), Herman Melville's *Moby Dick* (1851), Marcel Proust's *Remembrance of Things Past* (1913–27), and poetry such as Lord Byron's

Don Juan (1816), Walt Whitman's *Leaves of Grass* (1855), Ezra Pound's *Cantos* (1920–72) and William Carlos Williams's *Paterson* (1946–58).

In a special category belong those modern experiments that consciously invoke classical models, both in celebration of the past and in ironic commentary on the present. Major achievements in this form include James Joyce's *Ulysses* (1922), each chapter of which is intricately modeled on an episode of the *Odyssey*, and Nikos Kazantzakis's *The Odyssey: A Modern Sequel* (1938), which continues the Homeric story from the return of Ulysses until his death.

EPIC THEATER, a form associated with the playwright Bertolt Brecht, represents another application of the epic.

In film, the term is frequently used to describe lengthy, expensive, biblical, or historical spectacles, of which *Ben Hur* (1926; second version, 1959), serves as a model. But it has also been applied, perhaps with greater justice, to D. W. Griffith's *Birth of a Nation* (1915), Abel Gance's *Napoleon* (1927), Sergei Eisenstein's *Alexander Nevsky* (1938), and Sergei Bondarchuk's eight-hour version of *War and Peace* (1966–67).

Outstanding applications of the epic tradition in television drama include Alex Haley's *Roots* (1977) and the Ken Burns documentary *The Civil War* (1990).

C. M. Bowra's *Heroic Poetry* (1952) provides a learned account of the classical epic. *The Mwindo Epic* (1969) was edited by Daniel Biebuyck and Kahomo Mateene.

epic theater   A type of drama developed by the playwright Bertolt Brecht and the German director Erwin Piscator, designed to discard the "theater of illusion," the traditional acceptance by an audience that the events they are watching on stage are actually taking place. In its place, Brecht argued for a form of theater in which actors and audience would be always aware that they were enacting or watching a play. This ALIENATION EFFECT, as Brecht termed it, attempts to produce a more thoughtful and less emotional response in the audience.

In his notes to his opera *Mahagonny*, Brecht detailed some of the differences between epic theater and dramatic theater:

Dramatic Theater	Epic Theater
plot	narrative
implicates the spectator in a stage situation	turns the spectator into an observer, but
wears down his capacity for action	arouses capacity for action
provides him with sensations	forces him to decide

Brecht's emphasis on an audience aroused to action is a reflection of his Marxist view of drama as an agent of social change. Among Brecht's plays illustrating his theory, *Mother Courage and Her Children* (1941) exhibits both "dramatic" and "epic" qualities.

For the full text of Brecht's remarks, see *Brecht on Theatre* (1964), edited by John Willett.

epicureanism A philosophy that advocated intellectual pleasure and freedom from pain as the greatest good. Often misunderstood as an endorsement of sensual pleasure, epicureanism, as articulated by Epicurus, the Greek philosopher for whom it is named, celebrates practical wisdom and the achievement of tranquillity as its ultimate goal.

Edward Surtz's *The Praise of Pleasure* (1957) traces the Epicurean influence on Sir Thomas More's *Utopia* (1516).

epideictic In RHETORIC one of the three forms of classical oratory. Epideictic oratory is reserved for special occasions such as funerals or weddings, the goal of which is to praise the subject. Abraham Lincoln's Gettysburg Address (1863) is a memorable example of the form.

epigram A witty phrase or short poem. In ancient Greece the term referred to an inscription on a monument. It assumed a literary status when the Roman poet Martial called his short, satirical poems *Epigrams* (first century A.D.). In its modern sense, epigram usually refers to the type of WIT for which Oscar Wilde is famous—for example, "I can resist everything but temptation."

epigraph A quotation used at the beginning of a text designed to illustrate its title or designate its theme. In a recent example, the line "In the valley of the lilies, Christ was born across the sea," from Julia Ward Howe's "The Battle Hymn of the Republic" (1862), forms the epigraph of John Updike's novel *In the Valley of the Lilies* (1996).

epilogue In drama, a final speech addressed to the audience soliciting its approval for the play. Famous examples from Shakespeare's plays are Puck's appeal for applause at the conclusion of *A Midsummer Night's Dream*, and Prospero's epilogue to *The Tempest*, which concludes with these lines:

> *As you from crimes would pardon'd be*
> *Let your indulgence set me free.*

epiphany   An appearance or manifestation of a deity. In Christianity, the term refers to the appearance of the infant Jesus to the three Magi, celebrated on the 12th day of Christmas, January 6.

James Joyce used the term to describe the artistic revelation of the inner radiance of an object or event. Joyce's short stories contain epiphanies, lyrical moments of insight that encapsulate the essence of the tale. Probably the best known of his epiphanies, however, occurs in his autobiographical novel *A Portrait of the Artist as a Young Man* (1916):

> Her slateblue skirts were kilted boldly about her waist and dovetailed behind her. Her bosom was as a bird's soft and slight, slight and soft as the breast of some darkplumaged dove. But her long and fair hair was girlish: and girlish, and touched with the wonder of mortal beauty, her face.

This vision of a girl wading in the surf becomes a moment of truth for the novel's young hero, a realization that he will become an artist, a servant of beauty.

David Lodge's *The Art of Fiction* (1992) offers a lively account of the use of the epiphany in modern literature.

episodic novel   A novel that features a significant number of loosely connected incidents, each one more or less self-contained. The traditional examples of the episodic novel are the PICARESQUE narratives that marked the beginning of the novel form. The episodic form has experienced something of a revival in postmodernist novels such as John Barth's *The Sot-Weed Factor* (1960) and Thomas Pynchon's *V.* (1963).

episteme   The Greek word for knowledge, adapted by the French poststructuralist Michel Foucault to describe a conceptual framework that underlies a culture's DISCOURSE, its linguistic rules and connections, at a given point in history. Foucault maintained that the 17th century, for example, represented a period of "epistemic shift" in Western Europe, a movement from analogical thought (seeking resemblance between the human and the natural) to scientific thinking (emphasizing the separation of the knowing subject from the known object). In this respect, if in no other, Foucault's theory bears some resemblance to T. S. Eliot's conception of the DISSOCIATION OF SENSIBILITY.

In Foucault's view, the discourses of various disciplines, such as economics or natural history, reflect this shift, opening up new forms of knowledge but at the same time shutting down or foreclosing other possibilities. Thus every episteme exhibits examples of insight and blindness. For a comparable term *see* IDEOLOGY.

For a clearly written account of Foucault's ideas see Richard Harland's *Superstructuralism* (1987).

epistemology   The study of knowledge, what it means to know something and how we acquire knowledge. The two broad theories of knowledge are empiricism and rationalism. The empiricist maintains that knowledge exists when what we know corresponds to observable reality. The rationalist holds that since we can only know ideas, knowledge consists of a system of logical, coherent ideas.

The question of the elusive nature of truth, such as that relating to APPEARANCE/REALITY, plays a prominent role in literature. It takes a specifically epistemological turn in modern texts such as Henry James's *What Maisie Knew* (1897), in which the young protagonist is forced to confront the knowledge of her parents' sexual transgression. A strikingly "epistemological" writer is the Italian dramatist Luigi Pirandello, whose *Right You Are If You Think You Are* (1917) suggests the relative nature of truth, a theme echoed in Akira Kurosawa's celebrated film *Rashomon* (1951), in Jean Genet's play *The Balcony* (1960), and in Philip Roth's novels *Deception* (1991) and *Operation Shylock* (1994).

epistle   In literature, a poem written in the form of a letter. The genre originated in the Latin poetry of Horace and Ovid. In the form derived from Horace, the epistle addresses a literary, philosophical, or social theme, but does so in a familiar, relatively casual style. Poets in the Renaissance and the 18th century adapted this form, best exemplified in Alexander Pope's *Epistle to Dr. Arbuthnot* (1735), a brilliant satire of life and letters in 18th-century England.

epistolary novel   Fiction written in the form of a series of letters. Epistolary fiction dates back to the early development of the English novel, particularly the work of Samuel Richardson, whose *Pamela* (1740) and *Clarissa* (1747–48) established its basic forms. In *Pamela* the letters are written by the major character, recording her experiences; in *Clarissa* a number of characters exchange letters. Richardson's success created a vogue of epistolary fiction in the late 18th century. The appeal of the epistolary form was that it combined simple, direct language with the opportunity to explore the emotions of the characters.

In recent years the epistolary form has been revived to the extent that a significant portion of a novel may be given over to an exchange of letters—notably, in John Barth's *Letters* (1979), Alice Walker's *The Color Purple* (1982), and A. S. Byatt's *Possession* (1990).

A memorable film based upon the epistolary idea is Max Ophuls's *Letter From An Unknown Woman* (1948).

epitaph   Literally an inscription on a tomb, by extension any verse or prose commenting on a dead person. The epitaph on Shakespeare's tomb, thought to have been written by Shakespeare himself, discourages any future sexton from removing his bones to make room for another corpse:

Good friend, for Jesus sake forbear
To dig the dust enclosed here
Blessed be the man that spares these stones,
And curst be he who moves my bones.

epithalamion   A poem written on the occasion of a wedding, usually celebrating the virtue and beauty of the bride. A popular form in the RENAISSANCE, the best known example is Edmund Spenser's "Epithalamion" (1595), written for his own wedding. A modern example is John Ciardi's "I Marry You" (1958).

epithet   A word or phrase that functions as part of someone's name, such as "Ivan the Terrible" or "Richard the Lion-Hearted," or that describes a noun, such as Homer's "wine-dark sea." The latter is known as a Homeric epithet, with its characteristic use of a compound adjective. Another famous Homeric epithet is "rosy-fingered dawn."

erotic literature   A type of literature that includes explicit sexual details as its central feature. It differs from PORNOGRAPHY insofar as the latter aims primarily at sexual arousal. It differs from the traditional literature of LOVE in its focus on sexual details, although the distinction between the two appears to have been obscured, if not erased, in many modern works. Some contemporary FEMINIST CRITICISM focuses on erotic literature as an index of sexual attitudes in various historical periods.

Pleasure and Danger: Exploring Female Sexuality (1984), edited by Carol S. Vance, is a controversial collection of essays that deal with the relation of sexuality and pleasure to feminist principles.

escapist literature   Works intended or read as diversion and light entertainment. The term implies a distinction between serious and popular literature, particularly genres such as detective fiction, Harlequin romances, and adventure stories. For another view of some escapist literature, *see* FAIRY TALE.

esemplastic A term coined by the Romantic poet and critic Samuel Taylor Coleridge to describe the shaping power of the poetic imagination. *See* IMAGINATION/FANCY.

essay Variously defined, the term is generally used to describe a prose composition, usually from two to 20 pages, dealing with, or taking off from, a specific topic. Its form reflects the meaning of the French word (*essayer*) from which it is derived: "to try" or "to attempt." As a result, the essay proper is usually informal in tone and exploratory and tentative in its conclusions. It does not aspire to be the last word on its subject, but instead to reflect the private musings of a particular individual. This is the type of essay written by the man who coined the term and who is still regarded as its greatest practitioner, Michel de Montaigne (1533–92).

In the hands of Montaigne's English contemporary, Francis Bacon (1561–1626), the essay became more dogmatic and impersonal. Since that time there have been two traditions for the essay, the formal and the familiar. The popularity in the 18th century of the periodicals, *The Tatler* (1709–11) and *The Spectator* (1711–14), contributed to the development of both forms. The 19th century saw the emergence of a number of outstanding essayists, including Thomas De Quincey, Charles Lamb, Ralph Waldo Emerson, John Ruskin, and Walter Pater.

Among influential examples of modern literary essays are Henry James's *The Art of Fiction* (1894), D. H. Lawrence's *Studies in Classic American Literature* (1923), Virginia Woolf's *The Common Reader* (1925), and the collected essays of T. S. Eliot. Postmodern writers such as Jorge Luis Borges (*Labyrinths*, 1962) and Guy Davenport (*Tatlin!*, 1974) have developed a hybrid form, part essay, part fiction, designed to test the boundaries between fact and fiction.

The most significant examples of the essay adapted to verse are Alexander Pope's *Essay on Criticism* (1711) and his *Essay on Man* (1733).

essentialism The principle that natural, underlying essences exist in all peoples and things. Essentialism is opposed on the one hand to EXISTENTIALISM, with its principle that "existence precedes essence" and, on the other, to poststructuralist theories that stress the primacy of language. Essentialism is a central feature of traditional HUMANISM, which assumes that human beings contain a defining inner core or spirit that elevates them above the rest of creation.

In FEMINIST CRITICISM the issue of essentialism has generated significant controversy. Some feminists, particularly Julia Kristeva and Helene Cixous, have attempted to define and affirm a female essence as reflected in a non-patriarchal language rooted in a basic bond with the mother (*see* PSYCHOANALYTICAL CRITICISM). More traditional feminists have characterized this position as essentialist and, as such, an unwitting capitulation to the dominant patriarchal position that posits the woman as "other" and implicitly inferior. The debate has brought about a sharpened awareness of the need to distinguish between biological differences and those that are culturally defined.

Feminist Literary Criticism (1991), edited by Mary Eagleton, is a collection of essays that includes a discussion of the controversy from both sides.

establishing shot   In FILM, a SHOT, usually from a distance, that establishes the environment in which the action of a sequence is about to take place. An establishing shot may communicate an attitude toward the subject, as in the worshipful opening shot of the New York skyline in Woody Allen's *Manhattan* (1979). An eight-minute, ironic establishing shot forms the opening of Robert Altman's *The Player* (1992), in which the director introduces the chief character, satirizes the film industry, summarizes the plot (in the form of a "pitch" by a screenwriter), and includes references to other famous establishing shots, notably one in Orson Welles's *Touch of Evil* (1957).

eternal return   A belief that time is cyclical, held by the Greek philosopher Heraclitus, by the medieval philosopher Scotus Erigena, and, in modern philosophy, by Friedrich Nietzsche. The scholar Mircea Eliade has argued that preliterate archaic societies were a historical; that is, they subscribed to a view that human acts acquired meaning only insofar as they re-enacted acts consecrated originally by gods or heroes. An ancient ritual is a repetition of its first, sacred archetype. In this view TIME is cyclical rather than the linear, historical progression that dominates Western thought. *See* ORALITY/LITERACY.

Mircea Eliade develops his thesis in *Cosmos and History: The Myth of the Eternal Return* (1954).

ethical criticism   People have always debated the ethical effect of reading literature. The belief that exposure, in Matthew Arnold's phrase, to "the best that has been thought and said" would inevitably improve the character of a reader, has usually been the basic justification of a literary education. Conversely, many hold that reading the "wrong" literature can have a deleterious effect on a person's moral character. Such a view underlies, for example, the proscription against PORNOGRAPHY.

On the other hand, some see the belief in the moral or immoral power of reading literature as oversimplified. Those who argue for literature as a purely aesthetic experience, such as the proponents of the ART FOR ART SAKE'S movement, or English AESTHETICISM, insist that literature exists entirely for itself, that it asks nothing of us other than appreciation of its formal beauty.

On this question professional literary critics occupy similarly opposing positions. From the perspective of FEMINIST or MARXIST CRITICISM literature's fundamental impact is socio-political and its ethical ramifications are filtered through that primary fact. In the words of the Marxist critic Fredric Jameson, "The political has taken precedence over the ethical in the old fashioned sense of the word." From this point of view, literature helps to reaffirm attitudes or ideologies, but its ethical impact on any given individual is too complex to be measured.

Nevertheless, a number of recent critics have attempted to reassert the ethical power of literature. Basing their work on the tradition of philosophical ethics, these critics argue that in exploring the value of self-knowledge and relatedness with others, literature offers not only a model of moral behavior, but also the experience of engaging in ethical reasoning. A novel by Jane Austen or George Eliot, for example, demands of its readers subtle ethical discriminations as a condition of understanding the action.

For Northrop Frye, the ethical effect of literature resides in its ability to free the imagination of the reader, while the criticism of literature is ethical in its recognition of the validity of pluralist interpretations. For J. Hillis Miller, a proponent of DECONSTRUCTION, the act of reading is itself ethical insofar as we are willing to undermine our own initial interpretations of a text.

It would seem that finally there is no answer to the question of the ethical impact of literature. Perhaps the best response is that of the poet Marianne Moore in her poem "Poetry":

> *I, too, dislike it: there are things that are important beyond all this fiddle.*
> *Reading it, however, with a perfect contempt for it, one discovers in*
> *it after all, a place for the genuine.*

Among the best known of the ethical critics is Wayne Booth, whose *The Company We Keep: An Ethics of Fiction* (1988), offers a comprehensive view of the subject. Fredric Jameson's view is contained in his *Marxism and Form* (1971); Northrop Frye's views are contained in *Anatomy of Criticism* (1957), and J. Hillis Miller's in *The Ethics of Reading* (1987) and *Versions of Pygmalion* (1990).

ethnic literature   The definition of the term *ethnic*—"characteristic of a religious, linguistic, racial, national, or cultural group"—points up its difficulty. So broadly defined, it becomes impossible to distinguish the term from others, such as *race, religion,* or *nationality*. As a result, arbitrary definitions are necessary. In the United States, for example, the term refers to immigrant groups, exclusive of African Americans, Native Americans, and Hispanic Americans. Thus American ethnic literature refers to the stories, plays, and poems of European and Asian groups immediately prior to, and after, their immigration to the United States.

The immigrant experience plays a central role in this literature, often reflected through the perspective of a particular writer's generation. First-generation ethnic writers frequently focus on the contrast of values and beliefs in the old country and those in their new home. One example of this type is Abraham Cahan's *The Rise of David Levinsky* (1917), a portrait of a Russian Jew who emigrates, becomes a successful businessman, but in the process loses the deep religious connections that forged his basic identity.

Second-generation writers tend to emphasize the conflicting loyalties and estrangement from their parents that spring from the process of "Americanization." A representative example is Harry Mark Petrakis's *Lion at My Heart* (1959), set in Chicago's Greek-American community, detailing the conflict between father and son over the son's desire to marry someone outside the community.

Another notable example is Amy Tan's *The Joy Luck Club* (1989), a moving account of the gap between the experience of Chinese-American immigrant women and their daughters, growing up in the United States. *See also* AFRICAN-AMERICAN LITERATURE, ARAB-AMERICAN LITERATURE, ARMENIAN-AMERICAN LITERATURE, CHINESE-AMERICAN LITERATURE, GREEK-AMERICAN LITERATURE, HISPANIC-AMERICAN LITERATURE, INDIA/PAKASANI-AMERICAN LITERATURE, IRISH-AMERICAN LITERATURE, ITALIAN-AMERICAN LITERATURE, JAPANESE-AMERICAN LITERATURE, JEWISH-AMERICAN LITERATURE, KOREAN-AMERICAN LITERATURE, and NATIVE AMERICAN LITERATURE.

Ethnic Perspectives in American Literature, edited by Robert Di Pietro and Edward Ifkovic (1983), is a collection of essays surveying the field.

ethnography   In cultural anthropology, the written description of the culture of a particular social or ethnic group. In recent years, ethnography has exhibited the influences of STRUCTURALISM and POSTSTRUCTURALISM. The specific form this influence has taken is in the consciousness of the rhetorical and literary character of ethnographic accounts. The result has been that cultural anthropology has begun to examine some of its own assumptions regarding the accuracy and objectivity of ethnographic description. In the words of anthropologist Clifford Geertz, "What we call our data are really our own constructions of other people's constructions of what they and their compatriots are up to."

Further complicating the issue is the question of the extent to which the form itself embodies narrative conventions associated with literature. A striking example of this innovation is James Boon's demonstration of the parallels between the structuralist anthropologist Claude Lévi-Strauss and the French symbolist poets Charles Baudelaire and Stéphane Mallarmé. Examples are the emphasis on the underlying unity of mental and sensory experience described in Baudelaire's poem "Correspondances" and Lévi-Strauss's descriptions in his *Mythologies*.

The connection between literary and ethnographic studies has been further strengthened by NEW HISTORICISM, which is heavily indebted to the work of Michel Foucault, a leading figure in the critique of anthropology associated with POSTSTRUCTURALISM.

Clifford Geertz's discussion forms a part of his *The Interpretation of Cultures* (1973). James Boon's study is *From Symbolism to Structuralism* (1972).

ethos   In RHETORIC, the ethical character that a speaker projects in his efforts to persuade an audience. The term is used in literary study to refer to a governing principle in an institution, idea, or movement, as in "the ethos of capitalism" or "the ethos of the Beat generation."

euphony   A pleasing, agreeable sound, traditionally associated with lyric poetry. The combination of words connoting serenity and nature along with the use of long vowels (o, u) and liquid consonants (l, m, r) contribute to a euphonious effect, as in Shakespeare's "But look, the morn in russet mantle clad."

The opposing term to euphony is CACOPHONY.

euphuism   A late 16th-century, highly mannered style developed by John Lyly in his *Euphues: The Anatomy of Wit* (1578) and *Euphues and His England* (1580). Features of the style included samplings of alliteration, antitheses, balanced constructions, and analogies drawn from natural history. In the 1580s, euphuism became a fad at the English court of Elizabeth I. By the 1590s, however, Shakespeare parodied the style in the Tavern Scene of *Henry IV, Part One*, where Falstaff speaks to Prince Hal in euphuistic prose: "for though the camomile the more it is trodden on the faster it grows, yet youth the more it is wasted, the sooner it wears. . . . for Harry, now I do not speak to thee in drink but in tears, not in pleasure but in passion, not in words only, but in woes also. . . ."

evaluation   *See* CRITICISM; VALUE JUDGMENT.

evil   In literature, a destructive force or condition broadly classified as either human (moral evil) or supernatural (metaphysical evil). In the former category lies the bulk of literary interest, focusing on the activities of an individual VILLAIN or on an injustice, such as slavery, inaugurated and perpetuated by human agency.

Also included in this category would be psychological evil—the self-destructive, conflicted impulses of a person who is his or her "own worst enemy."

Still another subdivision would be the BANALITY OF EVIL, a term coined by the 20th-century philosopher Hannah Arendt to describe those who are unquestioning servants of an evil system.

The concept of metaphysical or supernatural evil, on the other hand, attempts to provide an explanation for the existence of evil in the world: Either the divinity, the author of Good, has a mirror-image opposite—a Satan figure, the source of Evil—or the Divinity itself is part evil. The Devil figure has been a staple of literature from the temptation of Eve to the mocking Mephistopheles of Goethe's Faust, to Anne Rice's *Memnoch the Devil* (1995). The malevolent or apparently malevolent deity is evident in the Book of Job where Evil is designed as a test of the human spirit. A darker view is captured in Gloucester's despairing cry in Shakespeare's King Lear: "As flies to wanton boys are we to the Gods/They kill us for their sport."

On the border between supernatural and human evil are ambiguous figures such as Iago in Shakespeare's *Othello*. Iago's apparent lack of a motive for his actions, his "motiveless malignity," hints at a diabolism, but if he is a devil, he is an all-too-human one.

Evil in another sense is the subject of the French theorist Georges Bataille's *Literature and Evil* (1973). Writing in the tradition of the POÈTE MAUDIT, the writer as outlaw, Bataille identifies literature with evil, which he sees as the violent and erotic impulses that are suppressed in ordinary life. Thus his study focuses on writers, such as William Blake, the Marquis de Sade, and Charles Baudelaire, who explored the darkest sides of life aligned with madness and death. *See* ETHICAL CRITICISM.

William Myers applies Bataille's thesis in his study of Evelyn Waugh, *Evelyn Waugh and the Problem of Evil* (1991).

evolution *See* DARWINISM.

exegesis The analysis or interpretation of a portion of a TEXT, usually a passage or a key phrase. The term is used most often in interpretations of the Bible.

exemplum A tale designed to illustrate a moral lesson. The form was popular in the MIDDLE AGES. "The Pardoner's Tale" in Chaucer's *The Canterbury Tales* is a representative example. It is a story cast in the form of a sermon on the theme of money as the root of all evil.

existentialism A philosophical and literary movement, rooted in the 19th century, that came into prominence in the aftermath of World War II. This historical context helps to explain the broad appeal of the movement. Existentialism mirrored the spiritual crisis that had become palpable in the wake of the war: ALIENATION, the loss of sustaining religious beliefs, the sense of anxiety and guilt, the growing conviction that life was, at bottom, meaningless. All of these attitudes and ideas were given powerful and explicit voice in existentialist thought.

PHILOSOPHY

Central to existentialism is a critique of the traditional idea that within each human being there is an essence: a universal, defining characteristic that is independent of existence. In place of this conception of humanity as a shared collective essence, existentialism focuses on the fact that we create ourselves through our choices, that one's individual "essence" is nothing more than the sum total of one's existence. The existential formula expressing this conception is "Existence precedes essence."

One 19th-century progenitor of existentialism was Søren Kierkegaard, a Danish theologian who depicted the individual as estranged from God and needing to make an absurd "leap of faith." The other forerunner was Friedrich Nietzsche, the prophet of both existentialism and POSTMODERNISM, who proclaimed the "death of God." Kierkegaard and Nietzsche represent the two strains of the movement that were to persist into the 20th century, religious and humanistic existentialism. The religious strain attempted to demythologize the New Testament (*see* DEMYTHOLOGIZING), while humanistic existentialism celebrated the strength of the human mind, capable of confronting the ultimate meaninglessness of existence.

The subsequent development of existentialist thought grew out of the philosophical method called PHENOMENOLOGY, as developed by the German philosopher Edmund Husserl. Husserl's method consisted of a rigorous attempt to describe what happens when a subject perceives an object. (One example might be to describe what happens when a person reads the writing on a page.) Husserl's method was adopted by his pupil Martin Heidegger. In *Being and Time* (1927), Heidegger provides a phenomenological description of human existence which he calls DASEIN (being there). Dasein is a time-bound being who is aware of, and riddled with anxiety by, the knowledge of his own death. In the attempt to avoid that awareness, Dasein uses language to shield himself, thus living an "inauthentic" life, a life of denial characterized by depersonalizing generalizations. An example of the latter is the statement "all men are mortal," a truth rendered abstract and unreal by its universal formulation; in saying "all men" we arm ourselves against the reality of "I am mortal." Heidegger's arcane and difficult ideas, later to form the basis of HERMENEUTICS, were adapted and made more accessible by Jean Paul Sartre, whose work bridged the gap between literature and philosophy.

LITERATURE

As in philosophy, literary existentialism is also rooted in the 19th century, particularly in works by Fyodor Dostoyevsky, Herman Melville, and Leo Tolstoy that anticipated major existential themes. Dostoyevsky's *Notes from Underground* (1864) is a passionate monologue by an embittered, angry, self-destructive figure defiantly asserting his freedom in the face of a society increasingly controlled by technology. Melville's *Bartleby the Scrivener* (1853) recounts the fate of a man who pays the ultimate price for the assertion of his right to choose, and Tolstoy's *The Death of Ivan Ilych* (1884) portrays a man coming to terms with his own death.

These themes were articulated with deeply ominous overtones in the novels and stories of Franz Kafka ("Metamorphosis," 1915; *The Trial*, 1925) and Robert Musil (*The Man Without Qualities*, 1930–43), which struck a responsive chord in readers engulfed in the malaise that swept post-war Europe. In addition to Sartre's major philosophical work, *Being and Nothingness* (1943), his novels, such as *Nausea* (1939), and plays, such as *No Exit* (1945), brought to a wide audience his ideas that we are "condemned to be free," are defined by choice, and are in need of "commitment."

Sartre was joined in this effort by his compatriot Albert Camus in his novels (*The Stranger*, 1942; *The Fall*, 1956) and plays (*Caligula*, 1944), and by Simone de Beauvoir, whose *The Second Sex* (1949) presented these ideas from a feminist perspective.

Another outgrowth of literary existentialism was the development of the theater of the ABSURD.

Among American works influenced by existentialism, the most notable are Ralph Ellison's *Invisible Man* (1952), Saul Bellow's *Herzog* (1964), and Norman Mailer's *American Dream* (1965). The protagonists of these novels are in search of their true identities, undergoing the crisis of anxiety and loss of faith that are the existentialist preconditions for the discovery of the self. Among works that reflect the religious influence of Kierkegaard are Flannery O'Connor's short stories and her novel *The Violent Bear It Away* (1960), and Walker Percy's *The Moviegoer* (1961).

In film, existentialist ideas and moods are pervasive in Ingmar Bergman's early work, particularly *The Seventh Seal* (1956); in Michelangelo Antonioni's *L'Avventura* (1959); and in Akira Kurosawa's memorable version of *The Death of Ivan Ilych, Ikiru* (1960). In the comic vein, Woody Allen's films reflect these ideas in the anxiety-ridden, death-obsessed characters he plays.

The repudiation of existentialist ideas was signaled in France by the rise of the NEW NOVEL and the emergence of STRUCTURALISM and POSTSTRUCTURALISM, all of which reject the principle of autonomous selfhood.

William Barrett's *Irrational Man* (1958) gives an intelligent, clearly written overview of existentialist thought. Nathan Scott's *Rehearsals of Discompose* (1952) offers a religious interpretation of this literature. Sartre's *What Is Literature?* (1949) provides an interesting application of existentialism to literary criticism.

exordium   In RHETORIC, the introductory part of a formal speech. The aim of the exordium is to catch the attention of the audience. In Abraham Lincoln's "Gettysburg Address" (1863), his use of "fourscore" in place of "eighty" is an example of an attention-getting device within an exordium.

explication   A form of critical analysis that involves the "close reading" of a literary text. Close reading requires a careful examination of the language and structural features of a work, particularly of lyric poems. It is a characteristic feature of both NEW CRITICISM and DECONSTRUCTION. The term *explication* derives from the French phrase *explication de texte*, a French school exercise in which students are required to carefully analyze brief passages of literature.

exposition   The part of a play or fiction that sets up the main action, introduces the characters, explains the background, and anticipates the conflict. The author's challenge is to supply these elements without losing the interest of the audience or reader. The opening scene of Shakespeare's *Hamlet* is often cited as a model of highly effective exposition.

In composition the term is used to indicate a straightforward explanation of a topic in essay form. (*See* COMPOSITION STUDIES.)

expressionism   A movement in literature and art in the early 20th century that sought to go beyond REALISM on the one hand and IMPRESSIONISM on the other. For the expressionists, realists and impressionists were too concerned with the surface of reality and reproducing the appearance of things. Expressionism called for art to go beyond imitation, to plunge into the formless depths of the human psyche, represented by a range of artistic devices including symbolism, fantasy, and distorted representations of reality.

Although Germany was the center of expressionism in the years before and after World War I, it was the Swedish dramatist August Strindberg who anticipated the spirit of the movement. Strindberg's *To Damascus* (1898–1901), regarded by some as the first expressionist play, discards all the traditions of the realistic theater to present a drama in which every character represents a part of one soul in search of its own identity. Heavily influenced by Strindberg, German expressionist drama flourished from 1910 until 1929. The chief dramatist of this period was Georg Kaiser, who produced 24 plays between 1917 and 1923, all in the expressionist mode. In Kaiser's plays (notably *From Morn to Midnight*, 1912, and *Gas*, 1917), characters frequently embody abstractions, a reflection of the shattered modern consciousness shuttling from one extreme state to another in pursuit of unrealizable goals.

Kaiser's influence in the '20s was evident in the expressionist plays of Eugene O'Neill. *The Emperor Jones* (1920) and *The Hairy Ape* (1921) exhibit the expressionist influence in their intense subjectivism and stylized settings. Other examples of non-German expressionist drama are Elmer Rice's *The Adding Machine* (1925) and Sean O'Casey's *The Silver Tassie* (1929).

The influence of expressionism was also felt in German lyric poetry. Notable expressionist poets included Georg Trakl, August Stramm, and Georg Heym. Their experiments had a strong influence on the English poetic movement known as vorticism.

But the most enduring monuments of the movement lay in the then-new art form of FILM. Cinematic expressionism is distinguished by distorted effects of the camera and bizarre images in setting, makeup, and costume. Thematically, these films focus on the alienating pressures of modern urban society and the piercing truths that the mind discovers only when it is in a disordered and deranged state. Among the classics of expressionist film are Robert Wiene's *The Cabinet of Dr. Caligari* (1919), F. W. Murnau's *Nosferatu* (1922) and *The Last Laugh* (1924), and Fritz Lang's *Metropolis* (1927). The influence of these films is evident in many later films, particularly in the genre known as FILM NOIR.

R. S. Furness's *Expressionism* (1973) is a study of the movement in Germany and its influence on 20th-century literature; John Willett's *Expressionism* (1970) looks at the political and social contexts of the movement.

extravaganza   A spectacular theatrical entertainment usually employing music, dance, and elaborate sets. Extravaganzas were popular in England in the first half of the 19th century. James Robinson Planché's *The Island of Jewels* (1849) was the most celebrated example of the type.

As currently used, the term refers to any type of elaborate entertainment, such as stage performances at New York's Radio City Music Hall.

extrinsic/intrinsic study of literature   These terms refer to two ways of approaching a literary text: from the *outside*, for example in relation to the

AUTHOR's biography, or from a social, psychological, or philosophical perspective. Alternatively, it might be approached from the *inside*, examining the formal elements of the work, its language, style, images, metaphors, symbols, and underlying myth. The extrinsic/ intrinsic distinction first appeared in René Wellek and Austin Warren's 1942 study *A Theory of Literature*. In their analysis the authors argued for the superiority of the intrinsic over what they described as "the most widespread and flourishing methods of studying literature. . . its setting, its environment, its external causes."

While acknowledging the value of other disciplines in shedding light on a literary work, they maintained that intrinsic analysis dealt with the aesthetic features of the work. Wellek and Warren were clearly endorsing the NEW CRITICISM, poised at that time to take a commanding position in American literary criticism, and they were rejecting the legacy of 19th-century positivism, the attempt to bring the study of literature into line with scientific techniques.

In the 1970s and '80s, the emergence of THEORY, reasserted the claims of the "extrinsic," arguing that literature is a "social practice," an inescapable part of the society in which it was written and in which it was later read. Where New Critics had claimed a special sphere of literary language, theorists argued that all language stood at the same remove from reality, that the world is a TEXT. Thus "A Theory of Literature" gave way to Theory, and with it, the intrinsic to the extrinsic. But by the 1990s the influence of theory had begun to wane, as the aesthetic claim reassumed its traditional place, guaranteeing that some version of the extrinsic/intrinsic controversy would continue.

René Wellek's *The Attack on Literature* (1983) contains his response to later developments in critical theory.

Fabian society   A society founded in 1884 by a group of English intellectuals who advocated a modified form of socialism. Rejecting the idea of a socialist revolution, the Fabians advocated the gradual transformation of English government. The leading figures and spokespersons of the Society were Beatrice and Sidney Webb and George Bernard Shaw. Shaw edited *Fabian Essays* (1889), which led to the formation of the British Labor Party in 1900.

fable   A short NARRATIVE in prose or verse in which the action of the characters, usually animals, conveys a moral lesson. The earliest examples of the type are those associated with the name of Aesop (sixth century B.C.). Aesop was the chief source of the fables of Jean de La Fontaine, whose 17th-century collection in verse continues to represent the standard for the form. Fables are a recurrent feature of FOLKLORE, and they appear occasionally in other literary forms, particularly satire. Notable examples of the satiric fable are Chaucer's "Nun's Priest's Tale" from *The Canterbury Tales* and George Orwell's *Animal Farm* (1945).

H. J. Blackman's *The Fable as Literature* (1985) surveys the history of the form.

fabliau   Humorous, frequently bawdy, tales in verse popular in Europe during the MIDDLE AGES. Originating in France, where they satirized courtly romances and other aristocratic forms, fabliaux employed slapstick and broad humor sufficiently subversive to qualify as a form of CARNIVAL. Among the chief targets of these tales were the clergy and the institution of marriage.

   The fabliau was adapted for use by Boccaccio in his *Decameron* (1350) and by Chaucer, who used the form for the "Miller's Tale," the "Reeve's Tale," and the "Summoner's Tale" in his *Canterbury Tales* (1387–1400).

A lively translation of French fabliaux is available in Robert Hellman and Richard O'Gorman's *Fabliaux: Ribald Tales from the Old French* (1965).

Fabula/sjuzet   *See* STORY.

fade   In FILM, a shot that appears out of blackness (fade in) or moves into blackness (fade out).

fairy tale   A form of CHILDREN'S LITERATURE consisting of a short, fanciful story that may feature witches, dragons, wicked stepmothers, and fairy godmothers. Rooted in oral tradition and folk literature, the fairy tale is of ancient origin. *The Arabian Nights* (also known as *The Thousand and One Nights*) contains among its 264 tales a number of fairy tales of the Middle East. The most famous European collections are those of the brothers Grimm in Germany, Hans Christian Andersen in Denmark, and Charles Perrault in France. Perrault's collection contained a frontispiece with the words "*Contes de ma Mère l'Oye*" ("Tales of Mother Goose").

In "On Fairy Stories" (1947) J. R. R. Tolkien describes the four basic elements of fairy tales: fantasy—freedom from the domination of observed fact; escape—not an escape from the real world but a breakthrough into another reality; recovery—the return to ordinary life with a renewed spirit; and consolation, the happy ending (Tolkien uses the term *eucatastrophe*) that brings with it the promise of salvation. Tolkien's structural breakdown of the fairy tale corresponds to some degree with the "AS IF" FICTIONS of Hans Vaihinger. Another view of the value of fairy tales is that of the child psychologist Bruno Bettelheim.

Among sophisticated postmodern adaptations of the fairy tale are Donald Barthelme's novel *Snow White* (1967) and Stephen Sondheim's Broadway MUSICAL *Into the Woods* (1989).

Bruno Bettelheim's *The Uses of Enchantment* (1976) makes a strong argument for the importance of fairy tales in the emotional and intellectual development of young children. Tolkien's essay appears in his collection *Tree and Leaf* (1964).

fall, the   A term referring to the biblical story of ORIGINAL SIN and the subsequent expulsion from the Garden of Eden. By extension, the fall refers to the MYTH of the fallen state of humankind, an explanation for the universal human experience of the loss of innocence. In this respect it is the primal story, standing at the onset of human history. The Christian doctrine of the FORTUNATE FALL maintains that the fall of Adam and Eve, since it resulted in Christ's redemption of the world, exhibited the triumph of good over evil. The modern view, on the other hand, is that the fall is a metaphor for the nameless sense of guilt that grips many, if not all, people. This is the sense in which the term is used in such modern works as Joseph Conrad's *The Heart of Darkness* (1902), Albert Camus's

The Fall (1956), William Golding's *The Lord of the Flies* (1955), and Arthur Miller's *After the Fall* (1964).

Terry Otten's *After Innocence: Visions of the Fall in Modern Literature* (1982) offers a broad overview of the topic. Stephen Mitchell's *Philosophical Myths of the Fall* (2005) examines its use by modern philosophers.

false consciousness   *See* IDEOLOGY.

family romance   In psychoanalysis, the child's fantasy of being adopted by one's real parents. Literature gives expression to this idea in the recurrent story of the foundling, the child (frequently of noble birth) who is abandoned, then discovered and raised by simple people. With some variations, examples of the story include Oedipus in Greek legend, the biblical Moses, Perdita in Shakespeare's *The Winter's Tale*, Tom Jones in Henry Fielding's *Tom Jones* (1749), Tarzan in Edgar Rice Burroughs's *Tarzan of the Apes* (1914), and the interplanetary foundling Clark Kent in Jerry Siegel and Joe Schuster's *Superman* (1938).

fancy   *See* IMAGINATION/FANCY.

fantasy   A form of literature characterized by highly imaginative or supernatural events. As such, fantasy constitutes a broad category that includes literary types such as the FAIRY TALE, the FABLE, SCIENCE FICTION, and some versions of ROMANCE. Examples of fantasy include J. R. R. Tolkien's *The Lord of the Rings* (1954–56) and James M. Barrie's *Peter Pan* (1904).

A related term is the fantastic, referring to a literary type that mixes realistic and supernatural elements without offering an explanation to the reader. One form of the fantastic is the genre of MAGIC REALISM, particularly celebrated examples of which are Gabriel García Márquez's *One Hundred Years of Solitude* (1967) and Toni Morrison's *Beloved* (1987).

Eric Rabkin's *The Fantastic* (1976) examines both fantasy and the fantastic.

farce   A type of dramatic comedy characterized by broad, visual effects, fast moving action, and STOCK CHARACTERS, whose escapades lead them to, but never beyond, the brink of disaster.

Always a popular form, farce appears to be as old as DRAMA itself, a staple in folk plays, Greek drama, medieval, RENAISSANCE, and modern theater.

The 19th-century French farceur Georges Feydeau developed the form known as "Bedroom Farce," so named for action centering on the mishaps deriving from attempted seductions. This tradition has retained its popularity, particularly in the work of the English playwright Alan Ayckbourn (*The Norman Conquests*, 1973; *Bedroom Farce*, 1975).

The advent of the theater of the ABSURD has lent new meaning to the term. Using farce to represent the utter chaos and meaninglessness of life, absurdist dramatists have created a form sometimes characterized as "tragic farce." The term "tragic farce" was also employed by T. S. Eliot to describe Christopher Marlowe's *The Jew of Malta* (1590). Jean Renoir provides a brilliant example in his film *Rules of the Game* (1939), in which a long farcical sequence ends in the death of one of the characters.

Silent films ushered in the golden age of farce in the movies of Charlie Chaplin, Buster Keaton, Harold Lloyd, and, quintessentially, in Mack Sennett's Keystone Kops, in which the CHASE played a central role. With the advent of sound in films, farce and sharp wit were combined in the films of the Marx Brothers, whose *A Night at the Opera* (1935) contains a scene that may be said to sum up the essence of farce. This episode, in which an impossibly large number of people are jammed into a small stateroom, recalls the etymology of the term: the word farce derives from the French cooking term meaning "stuffing." Originally, the term referred to interludes of broad humor inserted (that is, "stuffed") into medieval religious dramas.

Albert Bermel's *Farce: From Aristophanes to Woody Allen* (1982) examines the genre in a wide variety of forms.

fatwa   An Arabic term meaning a religious ruling or decree. The term was brought to world attention in 1989 when the Iranian government of Ayatollah Khomeini issued a fatwa calling for the execution of the novelist Salman Rushdie. The decree was issued as a response to Rushdie's *The Satanic Verses* (1988), a novel regarded as insulting to Islam in general and to the prophet Mohammed in particular. Living under the threat of assassination since that time, Rushdie, an English citizen, has publicly apologized and declared himself to be a faithful Muslim. In 1998, after extended negotiations with the British government, Iranian authorities rescinded the death sentence.

Satanic Verses is an irreverent, satiric fantasy, containing a character loosely based on Mohammed, who is depicted as a confused and conflicted figure with doubts about his own faith.

The Rushdie File, edited by Lisa Apprignanesi and Sara Maitland (1990), provides a documentary history of the affair.

Faustian theme   The generic term for stories of people whose lust for absolute knowledge drives them to tragic extremes, symbolized by a pact with the Devil.

The legend is based upon the career of Johann Faust, a 16th-century German scholar who experimented with alchemy and magic. An account of his life that incorporated medieval legends of selling souls to the devil, published in 1587, provided the basis for Christopher Marlowe's *Tragical History of Dr. Faustus* (1588–92). Marlowe's play is notable for Faust's celebration of the beauty of Helen of Troy and for its powerful conclusion in which Faustus is dragged screaming into Hell.

Dr. Faustus was imitated by German writers of the 17th and 18th centuries, who emphasized the magical tricks of Faustus and downplayed the tragic aspects of the story. The adaptation of Gotthold Lessing in 1759 restored the serious tone, emphasizing Faust's lust for knowledge as his motive.

In Goethe's great drama (*Faust, Part One*, 1808, *Part Two*, 1832), Faust's story illustrates the basic unity underlying the variety and complexity of life. Its happy ending, in which Faust is saved because of his constant searching and striving, reflects the Romantic belief in the ultimate goodness of the human soul.

Following Goethe, scores of 19th-century writers attempted with little success to capture the essence of the figure. The most notable 20th-century rendering of the theme is Thomas Mann's *Doktor Faustus* (1947), in which the story is recast as a commentary on the German people's "pact" with Nazism. Some critics have also seen in Faust the embodiment of the scientist's arrogance that issued in the atomic age. The American poet Karl Shapiro, in "The Progress of Faust" (1946), describes Faust's reemergence "In an American desert at war's end."

Modern comic versions of the story include Stephen Vincent Benet's The *Devil and Daniel Webster* (1937) and Douglas Wallop's *The Year the Yankees Lost the Pennant* (1954), later transformed into the successful Broadway and film MUSICAL *Damn Yankees* (1957; 1958).

J. W. Smeed's *Faust in Literature* (1975) traces the history of the figure.

Federal Theater Project A theatrical enterprise, funded by the federal government during the Depression of the 1930s, designed to provide inexpensive, serious theater to people all over the United States. The project, which provided work for hundreds of actors, playwrights, directors, and stage technicians, operated in 40 states, playing to audiences in the millions.

feminine ending A term for an unstressed final syllable in a line of verse, which in a line of iambic pentameter usually counts as an extra syllable. Thus in Shakespeare's line

ˇ / ˇ / ˇ / ˇ / ˇ / ˇ
To be or not to be, that is the question

the eleventh syllable, -*tion*, is an example of a feminine ending. Feminine endings are a common feature in the BLANK VERSE of Renaissance English drama.

In a masculine ending, the accent falls on the final syllable.

feminist criticism   The application to literature of the principles of feminist theory. Since its emergence in the late 1960s, feminist criticism has undergone a series of significant developments, moving from a concentration on the representation of women in literature to the promotion and analysis of neglected women writers (GYNOCRITICISM) to a wide-ranging theoretical critique of traditional thought and social practice. The consistent strain throughout this process has been the focus on PATRIARCHY, rule by men, and its cultural correlate, PHALLOCENTRISM, identifying the phallus as the source of POWER. Thus feminist criticism sees itself as an extension of the social and political goals of feminism in general.

Although feminist criticism emerged in the late '60s, the book generally regarded as the most influential of its predecessors is Simone de Beauvoir's *The Second Sex* (1949), which discussed the relegation of women in literature and life to the category of the "Other." (*See* SELF/OTHER.) De Beauvoir, whose position as a prominent exponent of EXISTENTIALISM added prestige to her argument, cited literary representations of women as "Other" in the novels of Stendhal and D. H. Lawrence.

Mary Ellmann's *Thinking about Women* (1968) and Kate Millett's *Sexual Politics* (1970) developed de Beauvoir's approach further. Millett's book became a cause célèbre, particularly because of its characterization of the image of women in Norman Mailer's writing, prompting Mailer's response in *The Prisoner of Sex* (1971). Millett's book also represented a break with the critical tradition of the time, not only in its feminist subject matter but also in its abandonment of any pretense of objectivity. Millett was angry and made no attempt to hide it.

Millett also touched on an issue of central importance in feminist thought, the distinction between sex and gender. Sex is the biologically determined difference between men and women, while gender refers to the cultural differences, the product of social conditioning. This distinction was critical in reconsidering women writers who had traditionally been viewed as usurpers in the "male" domain of creativity.

In focusing on the problems faced by women writers and their treatment in literary history, feminists usually cite one critical text, Virginia Woolf's *A Room of One's Own* (1929). Woolf takes as the symbol of women who have been prohibited from freely exercising their creativity the hypothetical figure of "Shakespeare's sister," one who should have been the creative equal of her brother, but who never had the opportunity to express herself.

With this possibility in mind, feminists have uncovered a rich repository of long overlooked literature written by women. This recovery, however, has raised questions that have led to a broader theoretical debate involving questions such as the following: Will emphasis on a distinctive *écriture féminine* (WOMEN'S WRITING) result in the ghettoization of women's literature, allowing it existence as a subgenre but denying its entrance into the mainstream? Is there a danger of assuming a monolithic category of "women's literature" without recognizing the important historical and individual differences among women themselves?

Among those who raise the second question are black feminist critics, who have suggested that the feminist agenda has been written by middle class white women without regard to the black woman's double oppression of race and sex. Similarly, lesbian feminists have critiqued the heterosexual focus of early feminism. The novelist Alice Walker, for example, has coined the term *womanist* to describe a feminist "of color," and the French feminist Monique Wittig has argued that *lesbian* is the more appropriate term for a feminist than *woman* since it redefines the female sex in nonpatriarchal terms. While not necessarily endorsing Walker's and Wittig's specific suggestions, many feminists would agree on the need to break from the constraints of male-dominated DISCOURSE. *See also* ESSENTIALISM.

Monique Wittig's argument is in *The Lesbian Body* (1975); Alice Walker's is in *In Search of Our Mothers' Gardens* (1983); *The New Feminist Criticism*, edited by Elaine Showalter (1985), is a collection of important essays on the subject. Jacqueline Rose's *On Not Being Able to Sleep* (2003) is another important study.

Fenian cycle   In Gaelic literature, a collection of heroic tales, orally transmitted in the pre-Christian era, later transcribed by medieval monks. The Fenian cycle celebrates the deeds of Finn MacCool and his son Ossian, a poet. In the 18th century, poems attributed to Ossian enjoyed great popularity until they were exposed as forgeries. *See* OSSIAN.

feudalism   A social, political, and economic system that dominated Europe in the MIDDLE AGES. Feudal society was an elaborate hierarchical structure. In its ideal but not always actual form, all land was the property of the King, in whose name the highest ranking nobles held large tracts of lands known as fiefs. These were divided among lesser nobles, and further subdivided down to the single man or estate, ruled by the *seigneur* (lord). The lord in turn rented out his land to serfs or other peasants, who worked the land and owed fidelity and service to the lord.

In their emphasis on the forms and procedures of this hierarchical society, medieval ROMANCE and the CHANSON DE GESTE are two literary genres that rest upon the assumptions of feudalism.

fiction   A general term for any form of NARRATIVE that is invented or imagined as opposed to being factual. Thus Gore Vidal's *Lincoln* (1984) is a NOVEL, a form of fiction, while a biography of Lincoln would be considered nonfiction. The distinction is that although the novel is based on historical research, many elements—characters, scenes, speeches, and so on—are "made up," not represented as factual.

For those who view fact as synonymous with truth, the made-up character of fiction underscores its essential triviality. Defenders of fiction usually point out that the association of truth with fact belies the complexity and many-faceted aspects of truth. These critics sometimes invoke Shakespeare's Hamlet's observation, "There are more things in heaven and earth, Horatio, / Than are dreamt of in your philosophy."

Recently this question has become more complex as a result of the poststructuralist view, which sees all narrative—fiction and nonfiction—governed by principles of which their practitioners are frequently unaware. From this perspective, nonfictional prose—for example, narrative history or ETHNOGRAPHY—shares with fiction an underlying structure common to all stories: They are narratives constructed according to the rules of their genres, rather than transparent recordings of reality.

figural interpretation   The introduction in the first century A.D. by the early Church Fathers of the idea that figures and events in the Old Testament are prototypes of comparable people or actions in the New Testament. In the words of the scholar Erich Auerbach, figural interpretation "establishes a connection between two persons or events in such a way that the first signifies not only itself but also the second, while the second involves or fulfills the first. Thus, Abraham's sacrifice of Isaac was interpreted by the Fathers as a prototype of Jesus' sacrifice on the cross in which Isaac's near sacrifice is "fulfilled" in Jesus' actual sacrifice. For Auerbach, this type of interpretation represented a radical departure from the traditional classical rendering of historical events, since it introduces the concept of a divine plan governing reality. Many Jewish scholars, notably Harold Bloom, regard the terms *Old Testament/New Testament* as an expression of the long, historical subordination of the Hebrew Bible to the Christian Bible and see figural interpretation as another "instance of how the New Testament reduced the Hebrew bible to that captive work, the Old Testament." *See* BIBLE, THE.

Auerbach's discussion of figural interpretation appears in *Mimesis: The Representation of Reality in Western Literature* (1953). Harold Bloom's comment appears in the introduction to *The Gospels* (1988).

film A general term for a particular motion picture or for motion pictures in general. Synonyms for the latter sense of the term are *cinema* and *movies*, two terms whose connotations illustrate the ambivalent history of film. *Cinema* suggests that film is an art form, *movies* that it is popular entertainment. *Film* is a happy compromise, a term that can connote both art and entertainment.

As a photographic medium, film has developed a technical language to deal with its organization of space and time. Terms such as CLOSE-UP, CUT, DEEP FOCUS, DISSOLVE, ESTABLISHING SHOT, FREEZE FRAME, MONTAGE, and SHOT are essential in the vocabulary of film.

Films that tell a story are, like verbal NARRATIVEs, divided into two basic categories: fiction and nonfiction. Fictional films employ the traditional generic terms of literature and drama, such as comedy and romance, but film also has developed certain distinctive genres of its own such as FILM NOIR, the CAPER FILM, the SERIAL, and the SCREWBALL COMEDY. Film genres that derive from literary forms include the DETECTIVE STORY, the GANGSTER FILM, the HORROR FILM, SCIENCE FICTION, and the WESTERN. The major nonfiction category is the DOCUMENTARY film.

For a discussion of critical, theoretical approaches to film, *see* FILM THEORY.

Thomas and Vivian Sobchack's *An Introduction to Film* (1980) provides a comprehensive primer on the subject.

film noir A term coined by French film critics to describe a type of American film produced in the 1940s and '50s that was literally and figuratively "dark" (*noir*). Literally, the lighting of the noir film was dark; most of the action occurred at night, with an emphasis on the play of shadows and light. Figuratively, the noir film was dark in its representation of modern life as an urban wilderness, its hero a disillusioned drifter or (after World War II) an ex-GI whose war experiences had left him estranged from society and himself. In addition to this theme of ALIENATION, some have seen noir films, which usually ended unhappily, as critiques of an American culture that celebrated success.

The major influences on film noir were the American DETECTIVE STORY, particularly the novels of Dashiell Hammett and Raymond Chandler, and the cinematic techniques associated with German EXPRESSIONISM. A number of noir directors—Billy Wilder (*Double Indemnity*, 1944), Otto Preminger (*Laura*, 1944), Robert Siodmak (*The Killers*, 1946), and Fritz Lang (*The Big Heat*, 1953)—were Germans or Austrians who had fled their countries after the rise of Hitler. They had absorbed expressionism in their youth (Fritz Lang had been one of the foremost expressionist directors) and found the shadowy world of *noir* an ideal context for those techniques.

Another distinctive feature of the genre was that many of them were "B" films, produced on a low budget, lacking big name stars, designed to serve as the second feature in the "double feature" format of filmgoing in this period. Some examples of low-budget noir classics include Edgar Ulmer's *Detour* (1945), Rudolph Mate's *D.O.A.* (1950), and Samuel Fuller's *Pickup on South Street* (1953).

Elements of the genre have been retained in many subsequent, so-called neo-noir, films including Martin Scorsese's *Taxi Driver* (1976), Allan Pakula's *Klute* (1971), and John Dahl's *The Last Seduction* (1994).

Film Noir, edited by Alain Silver and Elizabeth Ward (3rd edition, 1988), offers a complete reference guide to the genre.

film theory   The theoretical discussion of the nature and meaning of FILM. In its early years the debate over the nature of film centered on the question of whether it offered viewers a "frame" or a "window." Viewed as a frame, film is conceived of as a visual work of art; as a window it becomes a powerful vehicle for representing reality. This debate between formalism (frame) and realism (window) dominated the first three decades of theory. Prominent formalists included the great Russian director Sergei Eisenstein (*Film Sense*, 1942, and *Film Form*, 1949) and Rudolph Arnheim (*Film as Text*, 1957). Among the realists, one of the best known theorists was André Bazin, the principal contributor to the French film journal *Cahiers du Cinema*. Founded in 1951, *Cahiers du Cinema* became the home of the French NEW WAVE movement in which such filmmakers as François Truffaut and Jean-Luc Godard developed the theories that underlay their films. Another important contribution to realist theory was Sigfried Kracauer's *Theory of Film: The Redemption of Reality* (1960), which argues that film is an ordered vision of real life not available to the naked eye. One offshoot of the New Wave was the development of the AUTEUR theory, which identified the director as the film equivalent of the AUTHOR of a literary work.

In the 1960s film theory moved in a significant new direction under the influence of SEMIOTICS, the application of the linguistic study of the SIGN to film. Christian Metz's *Film Language: A Semiotics of the Cinema* (1968) views film as a type of language, a series of codes or conventions that have become internalized by filmgoers. In recent years semiotics has incorporated cultural, political, and psychoanalytical concepts. These developments have led to the charge that film theory has strayed too far from home, becoming increasingly abstract and removed from the reality of the viewer's experience.

Dudley Andrew's *The Major Film Theories: An Introduction* (1976) offers an excellent overview of the subject. *Film Theory and Criticism*, 2nd edition (1979), edited by Gerald Mast and Marshall Cohen, is a wide-ranging anthology of critical essays.

fin de siècle (end of the century)   A French phrase referring to the mood of many European artists and writers in the last decades of the 19th century. Embracing the principles of DECADENCE and ART FOR ART'S SAKE, they proclaimed art's (and the artist's) freedom from the principles of morality, social justice, and the conventions of REALISM. They saw the role of the artist as a critic of society, aiming to shock the middle class (*épater les bourgeois*). In this respect they created the model for later expressions of the literary AVANT-GARDE.

First Folio   The first collected edition of Shakespeare's plays, published in 1623, seven years after the playwright's death. The book was published as a result of the efforts of John Heminges and Henry Condell, two of the principal actors of The King's Men, Shakespeare's theatrical company. The Folio included a total of 36 plays, half of which had never been published before. Without the work of Heminges and Condell and the publisher Isaac Jaggard, it is probable that such masterpieces as *Julius Caesar*, *Twelfth Night*, *Macbeth*, and *Antony and Cleopatra* would have been lost to later generations.

The prefatory material in the Folio includes a commendatory poem by Ben Jonson that includes his famous description of Shakespeare as "not of an age, but for all time."

Charlton Hinman's *The Printing and Proofreading of the First Folio of Shakespeare* (1963) provides a meticulous reconstruction of the actual process of printing the book.

flashback   In film, a change in the temporal sequence of the story so that it moves back to show events that took place earlier than those already shown. Orson Welles's *Citizen Kane* (1940) is an example of a film that makes extensive use of flashbacks, as five people who knew the protagonist recount their recollections of him.

Occasionally the flashback will involve a return to a scene that the audience has already witnessed. This type of flashback may be repeated a number of times, each time acquiring added significance as the plot progresses. A particularly effective example of this type is the Errol Morris documentary *The Thin Blue Line* (1988), which constantly flashes back to the crime that is the center of the film, each time from a slightly different angle.

Flying Dutchman   A ghostly ship that, according to legend, drifts aimlessly off the Cape of Good Hope. In the version of the legend followed by Richard Wagner in his opera *The Flying Dutchman* (1843), the ship is cursed, a consequence of an oath by the ship's boastful Dutch captain that nothing would prevent him from rounding the Cape. As a result, his ship is fated to spend eternity futilely attempting to complete the journey.

flyting   In Scottish literature, a competition in verse in which two poets exchange insults. The competition was popular in the 15th and 16th centuries. The term also refers to the exchange of abuse between characters in epic poetry. In contemporary African-American culture, the street competition known as "the dozens" bears a strong relation to the flyting tradition.

foil   In FICTION and DRAMA, a CHARACTER who functions as a contrast to a more important figure. Thus in DETECTIVE STORIES, the slow-witted police inspector serves to heighten the intelligence of the amateur sleuth who is the hero of the story. In *Hamlet*, the Prince speaks of "examples gross as earth" that spur him to action: the Player in "the player's speech"; Laertes, who impulsively tries to avenge his father's death; and Fortinbras, the warrior prince, who commits thousands of soldiers to their deaths "even for an eggshell."

folklore   Generally, any aspect of a culture's beliefs, practices, crafts, speech, legends, or stories that have been passed on orally from generation to generation. Folklore has been an integral part of literature from its inception. In the Western tradition alone, such central texts as Homer's *Iliad* and *Odyssey* appear to have been conceived and delivered originally as oral folk performances. In addition to works that constitute FOLKTALES, there is a pervasive presence of folkloric elements in written literature. C. L. Barber's *Shakespeare's Festive Comedy* (1959) offers a convincing example of the ways in which folk festivals and holidays can be integrated into the structure and content of later literature. (*See* MYTH CRITICISM.)

In the 20th century, folklore has played a critical role in the works of a wide range of writers such as the Irish poet William Butler Yeats, the Spanish poet Federico García Lorca, and the African novelist Chinua Achebe. Folklore also plays a significant role as a constituent element of MAGIC REALISM.

In contemporary criticism the connection between literature and folklore has been explored fruitfully in Albert Lord's *The Singer of Tales* (1960), a work that has been highly influential in recording the distinctive features of ORALITY/LITERACY.

Bruce Rosenberg's "Literature and Folklore" in *Interrelations of Literature* (1982), edited by Jean-Pierre Barricelli and Joseph Gibaldi, surveys the scholarly work in the field.

folktale   A story handed down orally from generation to generation that becomes part of the tradition of a group of people. Oral transmission allows for continuing development and alteration of the story. Once a folktale assumes a written form, it remains a folktale, but its form becomes fixed. The folktale may include a wide range of types including the FABLE, FAIRY TALE, LEGEND, and MYTH. *See also* ORALITY/LITERACY.

foot   A unit of METER consisting of two or more syllables, each of which is treated as accented (stressed) or unaccented (unstressed). The most common feet in English are:

IAMB	a·gáin
TROCHEE	pí·ty
ANAPEST	in·ter·cépt
DACTYL	dés·pe·rate
SPONDEE	bár·róom

Iamb, trochee, and spondee are two-syllable feet; dactyl and anapest are three-syllable feet. Other metrical feet (found in QUANTITATIVE VERSE and rarely in English) are:

AMPHIBRACH	col·léct·ed
AMPHIMACER	crí·ti·cíze
CHORIAMB	tíred of lífe

Amphibrach and amphomacer are also three-syllable feet. Choriamb contains four-syllables.

foregrounding   The use of language in such a way that it calls attention to itself, setting it off from the ordinary language of the text. One form of foregrounding would be the insertion of slang in the middle of a traditional style. An example is X. J. Kennedy's "The goose that laid the golden egg/Died looking up its crotch," in which the surprise of the slang phrase has a strong impact on the reader. Foregrounding is the English translation of the Czech word *aktualisace*, a term coined by Jan Mukarovsky of the PRAGUE SCHOOL, early advocates of linguistic STRUCTURALISM.

foreshadowing   The hint in a NARRATIVE of later developments. Foreshadowing may assume a variety of forms: Hedda's toying with a pistol early in Ibsen's play *Hedda Gabler* anticipates her eventual suicide, while the description of a graveyard with "five or six graves" foreshadows the fate of the traveling family in Flannery O'Connor's short story "A Good Man Is Hard to Find."

form   The organization of a work in terms of its overall design. In this sense, form is closely related to the term STRUCTURE. Since the advent of STRUCTURALISM, *structure* has replaced *form* as the more commonly used term. For many contemporary theorists, *form* implies a position of philosophical idealism, dating back to Plato, in which "thought" is seen as prior to, and independent of, "language." For traditional critics, however, form remains the preferred term. It is frequently invoked in the context of ORGANIC FORM, the argument associated with ROMANTICISM that a literary text is a living organism, like a tree, with a natural, internal form.

Despite the influence of contemporary theory, form also continues to be used frequently in conjunction with CONTENT, the latter taken to be the "what" as opposed to the formal "how" of a text. Critics generally agree that in determining the meaning(s) of a text, it is necessary to consider form and content as inextricably linked. The notion that form is simply an ornamental addition to content is one that has been discredited since the time of the NEW CRITICISM.

Another common use of the term is as a synonym for GENRE or type. Thus any text has a generic form as well as a specific one.

formalism   An approach to literature that analyzes its internal features (its STRUCTURE, TEXTURE, and IMAGERY, for example) and minimizes or ignores its relations to historical, social, political, or biographical factors. A formalist analysis of Henry James's *Washington Square* (1880), for example, might tend to focus on recurrent images, structural oppositions, and features such as FORESHADOWING, while ignoring such topics as 19th-century class consciousness, the role of women, and the relevance of the novel to the author's biography.

Formalism is most prominently associated with two important schools of 20th-century criticism, RUSSIAN FORMALISM and NEW CRITICISM. Russian formalists concentrated on defining the distinguishing features of literature as reflected in devices such as DEFAMILIARIZATION and FOREGROUNDING. The New Critics focused on elements of literary language such as AMBIGUITY, IRONY, TENSION, and TEXTURE.

Formalism: History, Comparison, Genre (1978), edited by L. M. O'Toole and Ann Shukman, is a collection of essays on the subject.

fortunate fall (felix culpa)   The doctrine that the fall of Adam and Eve was ultimately a victory for humankind in that it necessitated the redemption of the world by CHRIST. The redemption insured the possibility of salvation, eternal life in heaven—a far more exalted state than existence in the earthly paradise of Eden. The term was coined by the literary historian Arthur Lovejoy to describe a passage in Book XII of John Milton's *Paradise Lost*. Adam, told of the coming of Christ and the eventual fate of mankind, exclaims:

O Goodness infinite, Goodness immense
That all this good of evil shall produce
All evil turn to good . . .

In *Tragedy and the Paradox of the Fortunate Fall* (1958), Herbert Weisinger argues that this idea lies at the root of our experience of traditional tragedy, in which the facts of defeat and death are offset by the spiritual validation of the hero's life.

Arthur O. Lovejoy in his *Essays in the History of Ideas* (1948) sketches the development of the idea.

four levels of meaning   A method of interpretation employed in the MIDDLE AGES to explore the various levels of significance of a literary or biblical text. These four levels were characterized as follows:

literal   In the Bible, the historical event being described; in fictional texts, the story.

allegorical   Any person or event in the Old Testament who anticipates a figure in the New Testament; in literature, a truth applicable to all people.

tropological   In the Bible and literature, the moral meaning of the text.

anagogical   In the Bible and literature, the spiritual truth or mystical vision of the text.

In his famous Epistle X ("Letter to Can Grande"), Dante gives an example of fourfold EXEGESIS in the biblical story of the Exodus of the Jewish people from bondage in Egypt: literally, the exodus is a historical event; allegorically, a mirror of Christ's redemption of mankind; tropologically, an account of an individual's salvation; and anagogically, a picture of death as a passage leading to eternal life.

Medieval Literary Theory and Criticism (1988), edited by A. B. Scott and David Wallace, offers a detailed account of this interpretive practice.

fourteener   A line of iambic verse consisting of 14 syllables (seven feet), also known as heptameter. The form was popular in the early Tudor period (1500–60) of English literature, but by ELIZABETHAN times it had fallen into disuse, not before being briefly revived by George Chapman for his translation of the *Iliad* (1605). When alternated with a 12-syllable line, the 14 formed a METER known as POULTER'S MEASURE.

fratricide   The biblical story of Cain and Abel stands as the archetype of the literature of fratricide. As the primal murder, Cain's killing of Abel resonates throughout Western history, evoking a variety of responses that have enriched literature. One source of its appeal is the fact of brotherhood, a term that is a metaphor for profound human ties, as in "band of brothers." Thus, the rallying cry of the French revolution, "Liberté, Égalité, Fraternité," suggests that "Fraternite" (brotherhood) is one of the basic constituents of a just society. In this extended sense of brotherhood, civil war is often seen as the ultimate fratricidal conflict. Another source of the power of the theme is the shared blood of brothers, which, in fratricide, involves the shedding of shared blood. This suggests sacrificial roots to the fratricidal story, the possibility of its origins in primitive ritual, requiring a sacrifice to ensure the well-being of the community. Such could be the case in the myth from which Aeschylus derived his tragedy *Seven Against Thebes* (467 B.C.). The story of Eteocles and Polyneices, sons of Oedipus, who kill each other in battle, has its Roman corollary in the myth of Romulus and Remus, cofounders of Rome. Romulus slays his twin brother, Remus. Another work rooted in sacrifice involving fratricide is Shakespeare's *Hamlet*, where the act from which the action springs is the murder of King Hamlet by his brother, Claudius. In this case, however, the sacrificial figure is the murdered king's son, Prince Hamlet. In the last act of *King Lear*, Edgar, the legitimate son of the earl of Gloucester, kills his half brother Edmund in a ritualized duel that underscores that play's mythic past.

In his excellent study of the subject, the scholar and critic Ricardo Quinones explores the uses of the Cain-Abel story in later literature. He sees its development from a broad historical perspective. In the pre-ENLIGHTENMENT Christian era, Cain is the outcast, his descendants cursed, a threat to order and morality. With the Romantic era, however, as represented notably in Lord Byron's *Cain* (1831), Cain emerges a restless seeker after truth, the embodiment of the self-conscious, tormented, romantic hero, a rebel against the dead or dying religious strictures still governing society. As ROMANTICISM gave way to MODERNISM, Cain's self-consciousness produced a divided sense of self, leading to the DOPPELGÄNGER (the Double).

In *The Fratricides* (1963), Nikos Kazantzakis develops the extended use of "Brother" in his depiction of the Greek Civil War (1945–49). Although Kazantzakis's novel does include the killing of one brother by another, he uses the term to describe the victory of ideological fanaticism over the strong, fraternal ties in a remote mountain village. Other modern novels in which fratricide appears include James Baldwin's *Giovanni's Room* (1956), John Cheever's *Falconer* (1977) and Michael Ondaatje's *Anil's Ghost* (2000).

Ricardo Quinones's analysis is in his *The Changes of Cain* (1991).

Frankfurt school   The name given to a group of German intellectuals associated with the Institute for Social Research at the University of Frankfurt in the 1920s and '30s, and later in London and New York. After World War II, the Institute was reconstituted in Frankfurt.

Among the prominent figures associated with the School are the philosophers and social theorists Max Horkheimer, Theodore Adorno, and Herbert Marcuse, the psychologist Erich Fromm, and, on the fringe of the group, the theorist Walter Benjamin. The School is best known for its doctrine of "critical theory," a wide ranging neo-Marxist analysis of culture and society.

In literary studies the most important figures are Benjamin, Adorno, and the sociologist Leo Lowenthal. Benjamin has been an influential figure in the development of POSTMODERNISM. One of his best known essays, "The Work of Art in the Age of Mechanical Reproduction" (1935), is a pioneering study of the impact of film and photography on general questions of art and criticism. Adorno and Lowenthal are best known for their attention to POPULAR CULTURE. Adorno focused on the production of popular culture as a means of social control (*see* HEGEMONY), and Lowenthal on the reception of popular literature.

In recent years there has developed a "second generation" Frankfurt School, led by the social philosopher Jurgen Habermas.

Walter Benjamin's essays have been collected in his *Illuminations* (1968); Leo Lowenthal's *Literature, Popular Culture and Society* (1961) looks at the social implications of popular art. Andrew Arato and Eike Gebhardt have edited *The Essential Frankfurt School Reader* (1978), which contains excerpts from the works of the major figures of the movement.

free indirect style   In fiction, a technique that combines third person narration with the features of INTERIOR MONOLOGUE. The technique places the reader inside a character's mind, representing his or her thoughts in a vocabulary and dialect appropriate to the character while maintaining the implicit presence of the author through the use of the third person. A typical example is in Katherine Mansfield's short story "Miss Brill":

> Oh, how fascinating it was! How she enjoyed it! How she loved sitting here watching it all! It was exactly like a play. Who could believe the sky at the back wasn't painted. . . . They were all on the stage. They weren't

only the audience looking in, they were acting. Even she had a part and came every Sunday.

The advantage of the free indirect style is that it offers access to the character's mind without resorting to tags such as "she thought," which has the effect of placing the NARRATOR between the reader and the story.

The technique is sometimes used in conjunction with stream of consciousness. *See also* DIEGESIS/MIMESIS.

Dorrit Cohn's *Transparent Minds* (1978) considers this and other narrative techniques.

free verse   Lines of poetry written without a regular METER and usually without RHYME. Although scattered examples of free verse appear in earlier poetry, the great pioneer of the form was Walt Whitman, whose *Leaves of Grass* (1855) constituted a free verse manifesto. Similar principles were developed by the French SYMBOLISTS in initiating the *vers libre* (free verse) movement in the latter half of the 19th century. In the 20th century, free verse has become the dominant poetic form.

Free verse is aptly named in that it offers the poet the freedom to choose a unique rhythm for each poem, but it demands just as much, or more, craftsmanship on the part of the poet. Robert Frost described free verse disparagingly as "playing tennis without a net," but such a definition also implies a practice that makes the task harder, not easier.

Charles Hartman's *Free Verse: An Essay on Prosody* (1980) and Timothy Steele's *Missing Measures: Modern Poetry and the Revolt against Meter* (1990) are excellent studies of the form and history of free verse.

freeze frame   In film, a single photograph from a SHOT that is reproduced and spliced into a sequence. The result gives the effect of a frozen action. The device is frequently used to underscore a specific idea or attitude toward the subject. It is employed to great effect in François Truffaut's films *The 400 Blows* (1959) and *Jules and Jim* (1962), and in the final shot of *Butch Cassidy and the Sundance Kid* (1969), in which the two outlaws are frozen at the moment of their deaths.

Freudian criticism   *See* PSYCHOANALYTICAL CRITICISM.

Freytag's pyramid   A description of the structure of a five-act play as developed by the German playwright Gustav Freytag in his *Technique of Drama* (1862). Freytag's design features five movements: exposition, complication, climax, reversal, and denouement, each one arranged in a pattern of rising and falling action:

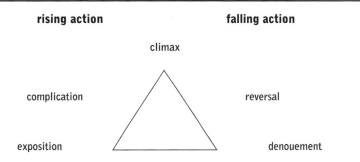

rising action   falling action

climax

complication   reversal

exposition   denouement

fugitive/agrarians   The name for a group of Southern writers, many of them faculty members of Vanderbilt University, who in the 1920s argued for a return to an agricultural society in the South. They viewed industrialization as a destructive force, destined to undermine and distort traditional Southern values. The group published their views, along with poetry and criticism, in *The Fugitive* (1922–25) and later in *The Southern Review* (1935–42). Among the early group were Allen Tate, John Crowe Ransom, and Robert Penn Warren, three of the leading exponents of what was to become the NEW CRITICISM.

futurism   A literary/artistic movement in early 20th-century Italy, calling for a rejection of the past and a celebration of modern technology. The movement was founded in 1909 by Tommaso Marinetti in Milan, born out of impatience with the resistance to change that characterized Italian culture at the time. Marinetti argued for a culture of efficiency, speed, and invention, modeled for him by American society. The Futurists proclaimed "the beauty of speed" and a poetics wedded to the glorification of the machine. They called for a reform of literature, art, and society, demanding new forms and themes. Eventually the Futurists moved beyond strictly literary concerns into the political and social spheres, becoming allied with fascism, which came to power in Italy in 1922.

In 1910, the movement spread to Russia, where it had a vogue because of its iconoclastic attitude toward the great Russian writers of the past. Among its Russian adherents was the well known Russian poet Vladimir Mayakovsky. As a result of Mayakovsky's efforts, Futurism assumed a kind of official status in the early years of the Soviet state but was rejected finally in favor of SOCIALIST REALISM.

Futurism produced very little literature of worth, but like DADA and SURREALISM, both of which it anticipated, many of its ideas were incorporated by later writers.

Russian Futurism Through Its Manifestoes, 1912–1928 (1988), edited by A. Lawton, is a collection of the Russian movement's declarations.

g ─────

gangster film A type of FILM that traces the career of a gangster. In the wake of the Prohibition Era, and with the emergence of the modern gang, the gangster assumed the status of a celebrity. As a result, he became the subject of three successful films that established the basic features of the genre: *Little Caesar* (1930), *Public Enemy* (1931), and *Scarface* (1932). All three films were suffused with urban violence, fast-paced action, and riveting main characters, portrayed respectively by Edward G. Robinson, James Cagney, and Paul Muni.

Church groups and others objected to the charismatic qualities of such portrayals, which resulted in later gangster films that emphasized the role of law enforcement officials, particularly the FBI. Nevertheless, the gangster-as-hero continued to appear in such Cagney films as *Angels with Dirty Faces* (1939) and *The Roaring Twenties* (1941).

The postwar gangster film took a psychoanalytical turn in *White Heat* (1949), which depicted Cagney's Cody Jarrett as an oedipally fixated psychotic. With the notable exception of *Bonnie and Clyde* (1967), the form suffered a decline in the 1950s and '60s.

The 1970s saw a powerful revival of the genre in the two *Godfather* films (1972, 1974), in which the heroic gangster is transformed into a corporate figure, the executive of a large and complex financial organization. (The 1990 sequel *Godfather III* elaborated further upon this metaphor, but the film itself was noticeably less successful).

Even the corporate gangster, however, reveals traces of what the critic Robert Warshow described as "The Gangster as Tragic Hero." Warshow's thesis is that the gangster film embodies the modern American sense of tragedy: "At bottom the gangster is doomed because he is under the obligation to succeed, not because the means he employs are unlawful. . . . This is our intolerable dilemma: that failure is a kind of death and success is evil and dangerous, is—ultimately—impossible."

Recent notable examples of the genre are *Miller's Crossing* (1990), *Goodfellas* (1991), and, from England, *The Long Good Friday* (1981). One interesting adaptation of the gangster film to another medium is Bertolt Brecht's satiric drama *The Resistible Rise of Arturo Ui* (1941), a rendering of Hitler's rise to power as a gangster story. A new era has been ushered in with the *Sopranos* series, which may come to be seen as the last of the great gangster films, "The Gangster as Tragicomic Hero."

John Baxter's *The Gangster Film* (1970) is a reliable reference work; Robert Warshow's essay appears in his *The Immediate Experience* (1962).

gay literature   Literature that focuses on sexual or romantic relationships between men. The history of gay literature is for the most part shrouded in coded language, disguised communication among gays, resulting from the social and legal suppression of homosexuality in Western society. With the notable exception of classical Greek culture, where it was accepted as a natural phase in a young man's development, homosexuality has been denounced in the Western tradition as an "abomination." As a consequence, homosexual literature remained largely either an underground or disguised expression until well into the 20th century.

There were, however, some exceptions. Among these were Christopher Marlowe's *Edward II* (1592–93), a play depicting the monarch's love for a courtier, Piers Gaveston, and its tragic consequence. Somewhat less clearly homoerotic are the sonnets that Michelangelo addressed to a number of young men in praise of male beauty. More complicated still are the SONNETS of Shakespeare, in which the poems addressed to a young nobleman together with those relating to the "dark lady" suggest the possibility of bisexuality on the part of the speaker, if not the author, of the poems. These two examples have generated a debate over whether these poems represent specifically homosexual feelings or manifestations of male friendship that, in the RENAISSANCE, fell within the definition of acceptable nonsexual discourse. The debate calls attention to the increasing awareness of the shifting historical denotations and connotations of homosexuality.

Similar controversies have been generated by the assertion that writers such as Walt Whitman, particularly in the "Calamus" section of *Leaves of Grass* (1855–92), and Herman Melville, in *Typee* (1846) and other novels, are portraying homosexual relations.

Openly gay literature begins in the 20th century with André Gide's *Corydon* (1911), an eloquent plea for the defense of homosexuality, but Gide was the exception. The rule was reflected in E. M. Forster's *Maurice*, a novel written in 1914 but, because of its explicit homosexuality, not published until 1971, years after the author's death. The real breakthrough came after World War II with the publication of Jean Genet's *Querelle de Brest* (1947), Gore Vidal's *The City and the Pillar* (1949), the posthumous translations (French, 1947; English, 1951) of the poems of the Greek poet Constantine Cavafy, and the poetry of the NEW YORK SCHOOL and the BEATS, particularly Frank O'Hara and Allen Ginsberg. Other writers to deal openly with homosexual themes included James Baldwin (*Giovanni's Room*, 1956), Christopher Isherwood (*A Single Man*, 1964), and James Purdy (*The Nephew*, 1960). Distinguished gay novels of the '70s include Andrew Holleran's *The Dancer from the Dance* (1979) and Edmund White's *Nocturnes for the King of Naples* (1978). David Leavitt's *Equal Affections* (1988) is a poignant account of a young gay man's coming to grips with his mother's death.

With the advent of AIDS, gay literature has encountered a subject as powerful and profound as the reality it represents. For a discussion of this theme, see AIDS.

David Berman's *Gaiety Transfigured* (1991) is a thoughtful examination of the major themes of gay literature.

gender   The classification, as for example in Latin grammar, of nouns and pronouns into masculine, feminine, or neuter. In a more general sense the term has been used as a synonym for a person's sex, but FEMINIST CRITICISM and contemporary THEORY have stressed the importance of distinguishing *gender* from *sex*. For feminists and others, sexual difference is biological, while differences of gender are products of culture and society. Feminists argue that patriarchal society (*see* PATRIARCHY), which has tended to assume that conventional (gender) differences arise from natural (sex) differences, has traditionally disregarded this distinction. It is precisely this oversight that feminist criticism seeks to expose as the source of the oppression of women. Feminist critics often focus on the ways in which literature has contributed to "gendering," a process by which social and cultural norms are depicted as natural.

On Gender and Writing (1983), edited by Micheline Wandor, is a collection of essays on the subject.

Geneva school   A group of critics associated with the University of Geneva in the 1940s and '50s, who employed the methods of PHENOMENOLOGY to examine a particular author's body of work in order to apprehend its distinctive "consciousness." For these "critics of consciousness," the task of the reader is to open him/herself to the author's consciousness, which is not the same as the author's intention. The authorial consciousness operates at a deeper level than conscious intention. It represents not the author's biographical, but instead his imaginative, self.

The leading figure of the Geneva School was Georges Poulet, for whom the writing and reading of literature were continuing, interactive acts of consciousness. Others include Jean Starobinski, whose *Jean-Jacques Rousseau: Transparency and Obstruction* (1957) is an impressive analysis of Rousseau's imagination. J. Hillis Miller, an American critic later associated with DECONSTRUCTION, was at one time a practitioner of the Geneva School. His *Charles Dickens: The World of His Novels* (1959) represents another notable application of consciousness criticism. *See* CONSCIOUSNESS.

Sarah Lawall's *Critics of Consciousness* (1968) provides an intelligent account of the Geneva School.

genre   A type of literature or FILM. In addition to referring to the basic generic types of POETRY, DRAMA, and FICTION, the term also denotes subdivisions such as TRAGEDY, COMEDY, ROMANCE, EPIC, or, in film, the WESTERN and DETECTIVE STORY.

Since classical times, genre has been a way of not only classifying but also analyzing literature. In *Hamlet*, Shakespeare satirizes the approach in Polonius's catalogue of the types of drama:

> The best actors in the world, either for tragedy, comedy, history, pastoral, pastoral-comical, historical-pastoral, tragical-historical, tragical-comical-historical pastoral. . . .

Polonius's effort reminds us that the lines between genres are often blurred and the effort to be too precise can lead only to confusion. Nevertheless, generic distinctions are often useful as a set of understandings that guide our responses to a work. Even when our expectations are not realized—when, for example, a "comedy" ends unhappily—we may experience the result either as a failure or as an interesting departure from the tradition. In either case, the generic norm remains the basis of our judgment.

Nevertheless, great writers tend to extend the definition of genre, or redefine it altogether. Shakespeare regularly incorporated comedy into his tragedies and "darkened," or made more somber or serious, the comedy of his PROBLEM PLAYS.

James Joyce, in *A Portrait of the Artist as a Young Man* (1916), characterizes the development of the writer as a progression from the LYRIC (self-expression) to the NARRATIVE (the artist acting as mediator for the audience) to the dramatic (invisible in his work, as a dramatist is in his play and as God is in creation). The remarkable feature of Joyce's analysis is the extent to which it foreshadowed his own progress from the autobiographical Portrait to his narrative "epic" *Ulysses* (1922) to his invisible presence in *Finnegans Wake* (1939).

Genre criticism begins with Aristotle, who divided literature into the basic categories of lyric, epic, and dramatic. In the RENAISSANCE and the age of NEOCLASSICISM, genres were thought to be fixed and governed by rules, such as those relating to tragedy. With the advent of ROMANTICISM and its emphasis on individual creativity, the approach to genres became considerably more flexible—as it did, for different reasons, with the development of REALISM. One theory by the French critic Ferdinand Brunietière, developed in the wake of Darwin's discoveries, argued that genres arose and declined according to a principle roughly analogous to Darwin's principle of natural selection.

In the 20th century, genre criticism was revived by the neo-Aristotelian CHICAGO SCHOOL of criticism, which argued that genre was the determining principle in arriving at the literary meaning of a text.

The most notable contribution in recent genre criticism is Northrop Frye's *Anatomy of Criticism* (1957). Although much of his criticism is rooted in MYTH CRITICISM, Frye's work is profoundly generic as well. Viewing genre from a historical perspective, Frye sees literary history as a movement from myth to modern literature based upon a development in which generic categories—tragic, comic, lyric, and epic—pass through five stages: mythic, romantic, high mimetic, low mimetic, and ironic.

Among literary theorists who have considered genre important, the most interesting perhaps is Mikhail Bakhtin, who views genre as a way of understanding the world. Thus, from Bakhtin's perspective, in the novel, truth is what emerges in the interaction between the individual and society.

Recent developments in literature and film, such as the nonfiction novel or the "docudrama," suggest a blurring of genres. Some critics see this development as a reflection of the influence of television, in which fact and fiction, news and entertainment, commercials and story blend into a homogenized mass. Others see it as confirmation of the view that the content is subordinate to the medium—in other words, that what is on TV is not as important as the fact that the TV is on.

Paul Hernadi's *Beyond Genre* (1972) explores the future directions of genre criticism; Alastair Fowler's *Kinds of Literature* (1982) is a theoretical treatment.

georgic   A poem with a rural or agricultural theme. The best known example is Virgil's *Georgics* (37–30 B.C.), which includes advice on topics such as animal husbandry and beekeeping.

ghost story   A story in which a ghost plays a prominent role. Ghost stories are a popular feature of folk literature in virtually all cultures. Henry James's *The*

Turn of the Screw (1899) is a classic of the genre. In this highly ambiguous tale, the reader never learns whether the "ghosts" in the story are real or the product of the NARRATOR's imagination.

Comic versions have resulted in a number of notable films, including René Clair's *The Ghost Goes West* (1935), in which a rich American buys an ancient Scottish castle and has it transported stone by stone to America, without realizing that it still harbors its resident ghost, and Joseph Mankiewicz's *The Ghost and Mrs. Muir* (1947), in which a young widow falls in love with the ghost of a salty sea captain.

ghostwriter   A person employed to write an article or book in the name of some other, usually well-known person. Autobiographies of celebrities and politicians are commonly ghostwritten.

Philip Roth's novel *The Ghost Writer* (1979) uses the term to reflect on the HOLOCAUST in depicting Anne Frank (literally, a "ghost writer") as an embittered survivor of a concentration camp, now living in America.

Gilded Age   A term for the post–Civil War era when rampant acquisitiveness became a prominent feature of American society. These were years of great changes in American society: technological advances such as the inventions of the telegraph and the telephone; the growth of industry; massive increases in immigrant populations; the rapid development of new urban centers like Chicago and San Francisco; and the feverish spread of speculation in land and on the stock market. The name derives from *The Gilded Age: A Tale of Today* (1873), a novel written by Mark Twain and Charles Dudley Warner. The novel satirizes unscrupulous land speculation and its connections with corrupt politicians. The social criticism built into this novel reflected the spirit of REALISM/NATURALISM that defined the literature of the age.

Richard Ruland and Malcolm Bradbury's *From Puritanism to Postmodernism* (1991) contains a concise account of the age. *The Gilded Age and After* (1972), edited by John De Nono, contains selected readings from the period.

global village   A term used by Marshall McLuhan to describe the results of the triumph of electronic culture over traditional print culture. According to McLuhan, television, along with other electronic modes of communication, will ultimately produce a "retribalization" of human society. The invention of the printing press in 1455 ushered in 500 years of the dominance of visual, linear, and literate modes of thought, in which the individual and isolated experience (such as reading) was given priority. Television returns us to an aural-tactile world of preliterate society in which the collective experience of the tribe supersedes that of the individual. When millions of people all over the globe are watching television (the differences in content are insignificant), they may be said to be inhabiting the same tribal village.

Many of these observations have been discredited as sweeping generalities. Nevertheless, McLuhan, who spent most of his career as a literary scholar, helped call attention to the impact of technology on human thought and to highlight important distinctions between literate and oral thinking (*see* ORALITY/LITERACY).

Marshall McLuhan's *War and Peace in the Global Village* (1968) explores the subject at length.

Globe Theatre   An ELIZABETHAN playhouse, the home of Shakespeare's company, the Lord Chamberlain's Men (later The King's Men). The playhouse was constructed in 1599 on the Bankside of the Thames River, just outside the London city limits. It burned down in 1614 during a production of Shakespeare's *Henry VIII,* an event that Shakespeare might have prophesied when in *The Tempest* (1612) Prospero spoke of the disappearance of "the great globe itself." Rebuilt the following year, the Globe was torn down in 1644, two years after the Puritan-dominated Parliament had ordered the closing of the theaters (*see* COMMONWEALTH PERIOD).

In 1995, after years of a painstaking campaign by the American actor Sam Wanamaker, a replica of the Globe was constructed on the London bankside, close to the original site. Since that time, initially under the direction of Mark Rylance, a resident company has been staging original and entertaining Shakespearean productions with great success.

gloss   An explanation or definition of a word or phrase. The gloss may appear as a footnote or in a margin. Sometimes glosses are collected in an appendix known as a glossary. An interesting example in fiction is Anthony Burgess's *A Clockwork Orange* (1962). The novel is narrated in an imagined teenage dialect called *nasdat,* for which Burgess supplies a glossary at the end of the novel.

gods, the   A general term in literature for the pagan gods—primarily, but not exclusively Greek and Roman—who have played a dominant role in Western literature since its inception. As depicted in Homer's *Iliad* and *Odyssey* and charted in Hesiod's *Theogyny* (700 B.C.) human history unfolded before the watchful eye of gods and goddesses who sporadically, often capriciously, interfered. The gods themselves were subject to the all-powerful Zeus, but even he was subject to Moira (fate). The result was a complex but ordered world in which the great

Greek tragedians, Aeschylus, Sophocles, and Euripides wrestled with fundamental questions of human existence.

Historically the ancient gods were assimilated into the monotheistic Judeo-Christian culture, their various powers redistributed to the three-person God and, to an extent, the Virgin Mary. But in literature the mythic appeal of the denizens of Mount Olympus proved to be irresistible. Although in much of Western literature in succeeding centuries the gods played more of a decorative and rhetorical role, there were notable exceptions. Among those was the greatest play of the English Renaissance, Shakespeare's *King Lear*. In *Lear*, the term *the gods* is used 26 times. In the ominous first act, Lear invokes the gods Apollo, Jupiter, and Hecate against Cordelia, while the bastard son, Edmund, after declaring "nature" his "goddess" pleads, "New gods stand up for bastards." Later in the play—specifically in the storm scenes—the gods are invoked on behalf of the good characters. Although these gods are not represented in the play, the human characters interpret their response from contrasting positions—profound pessimism ("As flies to wanton boys are we to the gods; /They kill us for their sport."); desperate hope ("The clearest gods who make them honors of men's impossibilities"); and recognition of man's tragic burden ("Upon such sacrifices, my Cordelia, /The gods themselves throw incense").

In *Literature and the Gods* (2001), the Italian critic Roberto Calasso celebrates "the return of the gods" to the Western literary imagination. Calasso locates the initial reappearance in late 18th century German Romanticism. The exemplary figure here is Friedrich Holderlin, the 19th century German poet who tried to capture the sensation of being alive, of being "in the moment," the source of which is grounded in the idea of the gods. Following Holderlin later in the century, Friedrich Nietzsche's *Birth of Tragedy* (1871) argued that tragedy arose out of the conflicting positions symbolized by the gods Apollo and Dionysus, where Apollo represents reason, restraint, and morality, and Dionysus, represents passion, frenzy, and amorality. Nietzsche's APOLLONIAN/DIONYSIAN summoned the gods, particularly Dionysus, back onto the stage of Western consciousness. Calasso argues that their presence continues to be felt wherever an artist in search of the ABSOLUTE appears. But even he acknowledges that in the contemporary world a profound revolution has occurred in which "the brain's analogical pole was gradually supplanted by the digital pole . . . ." As a result, "Zeus is the algorithm." *See also* MEDIOLOGY.

William Elton's *King Lear and the Gods* (1966) considers the role of the absent gods in the play.

golden age   A mythical era celebrated in classical and Renaissance literature. The myth of the golden age recounts a happy primitive state in man's prehistory, when justice, peace and love prevailed. The earliest reference appears in Hesiod's *Works and Days* (eighth century B.C.), which speaks of five prehistorical ages. In the transmission of the myth one of the ages (the "heroic") was dropped, reducing the number of ages to four. The first of these was the golden era, when men lived in harmony with nature and the gods and died painless deaths. The end of the golden age was followed by a series of progressively deteriorating eras: the silver, bronze, and iron ages.

The myth was transmitted from Greece to Rome, where it was given prominence by Virgil in his Eclogues. With the humanist revival in the Renaissance, the golden age motif was incorporated in the work of most of the major Renaissance writers, including Edmund Spenser and Shakespeare. Harry Levin has argued that the myth represents the human impulse to transcend the limits of history and time.

Harry Levin's *The Myth of the Golden Age in the Renaissance* (1969) is a learned and thoughtful study.

gongorism An ornate, highly mannered poetic style associated with the Spanish poet Luis de Góngora y Argote (1561–1626). An extreme example of BAROQUE poetry, Gongorism is filled with puns, paradoxes, and elaborate conceits. *See* MARINISM.

gothic novel A type of FICTION that employs mystery, terror or horror, suspense, and the supernatural for the simple purpose of scaring the wits out of its readers. The traditional setting, beginning with Hugh Walpole's *The Castle of Otranto* (1764), is a medieval (hence, "Gothic") castle, replete with secret passages, torchlit dungeons, and an occasional bat. The traditional plot, as in Anne Radcliffe's *The Mysteries of Udolpho* (1794), involves a beautiful heroine beset by dark shadows, strange noises, and a candle that keeps blowing out. These early gothic novels aimed at instilling terror. Later examples of the form, such as Matthew Lewis's *The Monk* (1796), moved beyond terror to horror, invoking demons, ghosts, and other supernatural paraphernalia in gory and subliminally erotic detail.

The form maintained its popularity from the 1760s to the 1830s. During that time it was imitated throughout Europe, influencing and being influenced by the age of ROMANTICISM. Satirized by Jane Austen in *Northanger Abbey* (1818), the form eventually fell out of favor, only to resurface in the 20th century as the HORROR FICTION and HORROR FILM. One particularly memorable example of the form, Mary Shelley's *Frankenstein* (1818), is also regarded as an early progenitor of SCIENCE FICTION.

Brendan Hennessy's *The Gothic Novel* (1978) offers a useful survey of the genre; Manuel Aguirre's *The Enclosed Space* (1990) places it in the context of all horror literature.

grammar   In LINGUISTICS, the study of the structural relationship of words in a sentence; more popularly, the system of rules that govern accepted standards of usage. The latter is known as "prescriptive grammar." "Transformational grammar" is a method of analysis developed by the linguist Noam Chomsky that explains how a limited number of grammatical rules can be transformed into a limitless number of sentences.

Still another meaning of *grammar* refers to the basic principles of a subject. This is the sense in which it was used in the 19th century by Cardinal Newman in his *A Grammar of Assent* (1870), an analysis of the nature of religious belief, and in the 20th century by Kenneth Burke in *A Grammar of Motives* (1945), an analysis of human motivation. (*See also* DRAMATISM.)

graphic novel   Term for a full-length novel of serious intent presented in the form of a comic book. Paradoxically, the best-known example of this form is not, in fact, a novel. It is Art Speigelman's *Maus* (1986), a harrowing memoir of his father's experience in Auschwitz. What contributes to the confusion about the genre of this work (it was originally listed in *The New York Times* best-seller list under "Fiction," but later at the author's request under "Nonfiction") is that the CHARACTERS are represented as cats, mice, dogs, and frogs, thus casting the brutal story in an allegorical mode.

Graphic novels evolved from the underground comics of the 1960s and '70s, notably the work of R. Crumb, regarded as the forerunner of the new form. Like Crumb's work, many of these novels offer autobiographical, ironic portraits of the artist-as-loser. They frequently focus on the main character's unhappy childhood, dysfunctional family, retreat from reality, and ultimate despair. A representative sample is Harvey Pekar's *American Splendor* (1976), later transformed into a critically acclaimed film.

Other successful graphic novels are Daniel Clowes's *Ghost World* (1998), dealing with two teenage girls coming of age in suburbia, and Chris Ware's *Jimmy Corrigan* (2000), an experimental text even by graphic novel standards. More recently, the form has expanded to embrace documentary work such as *Joe Palestine* (1995), a description of Palestinian refugee camps; *Safe Area Gorazde* (2000), an area in the Bosnian War where Serbs besieged Muslims over a three-year period; and Spiegelman's *In the Shadow of No Towers* (2004), a feverish and intense rendering of the experience in downtown Manhattan in the wake of 9/11.

Charles McGrath's amply illustrated article "Not Funnies" in *The New York Times Magazine* (July 11, 2004) offers an insightful introduction to the new genre.

graveyard school   A term for a group of 18th-century poets who focused on the theme of DEATH, the pain of bereavement, and the longing for immortality. Not a true school in the sense of an organized literary movement, these poets were united by their common themes. The best known of the group were Robert Blair ("The Grave," 1743), Edward Young (*Night Thoughts on Life, Death, and Immortality*, 1742–45), and Thomas Gray, whose "Elegy Written in a Country Churchyard" (1751) is an acknowledged masterpiece of the form.

Greek-American literature   Of all the immigrant groups that have come to America, none could look back upon their cultural heritage with greater pride than the Greeks. Unfortunately, the glorious era of classical Greece had been followed by centuries of tragic repression by and subjection to foreign rule. Gaining independence in 1829, Greece began the long process of renationalization. The first significant wave of immigrants to the United States consisted mainly of rural peasants intent on achieving economic and social gains in a strange land. Their struggle to articulate their experience was first achieved by Demetrios Michalaros in his collection of poems *Sonnet of an Immigrant* (1930). His poems served as a model for the next generation of poets, including Paul Nord (Nikos Laides) and Andonis Descavalles, both of whom wrote prolifically in English and Greek. Two poets who have also make major contributions to Greek literature as translators are Kimon Frair, best known for his impressive translation of Nikos Kazantzakis's *The Odyssey: A Modern Sequel* (1958) and for his anthology *Modern Greek Poetry* (1978), and Rae Dalven, whose many books include her translation of *The Complete Poems Of Cavafy* (1961).

In fiction, the best-known Greek-American figure dealing with the immigrant experience is Elia Kazan, the original director of such celebrated plays as *A Streetcar Named Desire* (1947) and *Death of a Salesman* (1949) and films as *On the Waterfront* (1954) and *East of Eden* (1955). Kazan was born in 1909 in Anatolia, in a section of modern Turkey that at the time contained a large Greek population. In the 1960s, frustrated with his career in Hollywood, he turned to fiction writing. His first novel, *America, America* (1962), recounts the story of Stavros, an Anatolian adolescent whose odyssey is completed when he arrives at Ellis Island. Kazan later picks up his story in *The Anatolian* (1962), in which Stavros is depicted somewhat severely as a social climber trying to charm his way to the top. In *Beyond the Aegean* (1994), the last volume of the trilogy, Stavros is back in Anatolia, hoping to cash in on the expected victory of the Greeks in the Greco-Turkish War (1921–22). The catastrophic outcome of the war for the Greeks finds a chastened Stavros happy to be back in his adopted country.

Another well-known chronicler in fiction of the Greek immigrant experience is Harry Mark Petrakis. Born in the Midwest, the son of an Eastern Orthodox priest, Petrakis developed as an important theme in his work the conflict, usually set in the Greek community of Chicago, between first- and second-generation family members. His first novel, *Lion At My Heart* (1959), for example, deals with the theme of intermarriage: a son's desire to marry a non-Greek woman triggers an unreconcilable rupture with his parents. In *The Odyssey of Kostas Volakis* (1963), the Greek immigrant father favors one son over another with tragic results. In *The Dream of Kings* (1966), an exuberant Greek father, Leonidas Matsoukas, filled with good intentions but a rascal at heart, fails to help his invalid son. In his portrayal of Matsoukas, Petrakis appears to be using as his model Zorba in *Zorba the Greek* (1946; tr. 1952).

In contrast to the intergenerational conflict in Petrakis, Konstantinos Lardas (*A Tree of Man* [1968]) offers an evocative, moving tribute to his immigrant grandfather. A highly unusual immigrant novel is Jeffrey Eugenides' Pulitzer Prize-winning *Middlesex* (2002), which records, as does Kazan's *Beyond the Aegean*, the catastrophic Greco-Turkish War, culminating in the massacre of Greeks in the port of Smyrna in 1922. A brother and sister manage to survive and make their way to America. Meanwhile the two have become lovers, a union that results in the birth of a hermaphroditic grandchild, who becomes the novel's protagonist.

Alexander Karanikas's "Greek American Literature" in *Ethnic Perspectives in American Literature* (1983) offers an overview of the topic. Richard Schickel's *Elia Kazan* (2005) is a widely acclaimed biography of the director and author.

grotesque, the   As a literary term, *grotesque* refers to a work in which abnormal or macabre characters or incidents are presented in a mix of comedy and pathos or horror. The incompatibility of this mix creates in the reader the kind of conflicted response that one makes to a "sick joke": on the one hand, funny; on the other, nauseating or horrifying.

Among famous works that have been characterized, at least in part, as grotesque are Rabelais' *Gargantua and Pantagruel*, Shakespeare's *King Lear* (in "King Lear and the Comedy of the Grotesque," the critic G. Wilson Knight argues that the play's comic elements produce a "sublime incongruity"), and Jonathan Swift's "A Modest Proposal," the brilliant satiric pamphlet advocating that children of the Irish poor be killed and eaten as a way of improving the economy.

But the grotesque has come into its greatest prominence in the 20th century. Among examples of the form are Franz Kafka's "The Metamorphosis," whose hero finds himself transformed into a giant insect; the brothel scene in James Joyce's *Ulysses* (1922); and "The Book of the Grotesque," the introductory chapter in Sherwood Anderson's *Winesburg, Ohio* (1919).

Group Theatre   The name of a New York–based, experimental theatrical company that flourished in the 1930s. The group was well known for its productions of plays dealing with socially significant issues such as labor unrest and racism. Two of the group's best known productions were Clifford Odets's *Waiting for Lefty* and *Awake and Sing* (both 1935).

Basing its acting principles on the model of the MOSCOW ART THEATER, the troupe developed many of the techniques later associated with the Method (*see* METHOD ACTING).

guilt   The search for the guilty one forms the action of the archetypal DETECTIVE STORY, Sophocles' *Oedipus Rex*, in which the detective, Oedipus, discovers that he himself is guilty of the death of his father and of incest with his mother. Guiltless guilt is perhaps best represented in Albert Camus's *The Stranger* (1942), in which the protagonist Meursault kills a man but is executed not for the killing but for his indifference to society's apparent values.

Between such polarities range the two dominant forms. In the 19th-century version guilt is the preliminary, purgatorial stage that leads to redemption. The sinner is rescued after experiencing genuine guilt. In the 20th-century psychological novel, heavily influenced by psychoanalysis, guilt itself is the VILLAIN, seen as repressed residue from childhood that needs to be expressed in order to free the individual.

In *The Literature of Guilt* (1988) critic Patrick Reilly argues that the redeemed sinner is a central figure of the 19th-century novel, evident in Victor Hugo's *Les Misérables* (1862), Charles Dickens's *A Christmas Carol* (1843) and *A Tale of Two Cities* (1859), George Eliot's *Silas Marner* (1861) and Fyodor Dostoevsky's *Crime and Punishment* (1866). In the 20th century, Reilly argues, writers rejected redemption, arguing in the words of Jean Paul Sartre, writing in the wake of World War II, "Evil is an appearance that knowing its causes does not dispel it . . . Evil cannot be redeemed." Among Reilly's detailed examples is Joseph Conrad's *The Heart of Darkness* (1902), the story of the idealist Kurtz who plunges into the perilous mystery of human evil and is damned in the process. The same is true of the story's narrator Marlow, who undergoes a similar voyage to encounter the heart of evil, namely Kurtz himself. In the end, Marlow echoes Kurtz's vision of what he encounters: "The horror, the horror!"

Another example is Albert Camus's *The Fall* (1954), in which the protagonist Jean-Baptiste Clamence, John the Baptist, who in discovering his own guilt, takes upon himself the role of judge/penitent, forcing others to acknowledge their guilt. Still another example is William Golding's *The Lord of the Flies* (1954) which inverts the 19th-century Romantic conviction that society corrupts the individual by suggesting that the individual carries the "beast" within him, which eventually corrupts society.

However, *The Literature of Guilt* overlooks the most important modern writer on the subject of guilt, Franz Kafka. Kafka's depiction of guilt in *The Trial* (1925), whose protagonist Joseph K. finds that he has been judged guilty without having done anything wrong, leaving the impression that, for Kafka, existence itself is guilt, to be is to be guilty.

gynocriticism In FEMINIST CRITICISM, the emphasis on literature written by women, as opposed to an earlier phase of feminist criticism that concentrated on the representation of women in literature written by men. Coined by the feminist scholar Elaine Showalter in 1978, gynocriticism is designed, in her words, to "stop trying to fit women between the lines of the male tradition and focus instead on the newly visible world of a female culture." Examples of formerly neglected novels that gynocritics have helped to publicize include Kate Chopin's *The Awakening* (1899) and Zora Neale Hurston's *Their Eyes Were Watching God* (1937).

Elaine Showalter's "Toward a Feminist Poetics," in *Women Writing and Writing about Women* (1979), edited by Mary Jacobus, contains the essence of her thesis.

hagiography   Writing of the lives of saints. By extension, the term now describes biographies that exhibit an uncritical, idealizing view of their subjects. One such example is the "campaign biography," a book written and published to coincide with a politician's campaign for a major office.

The Golden Legend is a 13th-century collection of popular tales concerning saints which became an important form of CHILDREN'S LITERATURE in the Middle Ages.

haiku   A type of Japanese poetry that captures the impression of a single object or aspect of nature. The traditional haiku consists of 17 syllables, arranged in three lines of five, seven, and five syllables, but there are numerous variations, especially in modern poems. Haiku has influenced a number of Western poets, particularly those associated with IMAGISM.

hamartia   In Aristotle's *Poetics*, an error committed by a tragic hero that leads to his downfall. The error may be a consequence of some inherent weakness of character or the result of a lack of knowledge (as in the case of Oedipus, who does not know that he has killed his father and married his mother). The term itself is a metaphor from archery that means "not hitting the bull's-eye."

In some English translations of the *Poetics*, *hamartia* has been defined as "tragic flaw," a phrase that has led to the misinterpretation that sees the "flaw" as the "cause" of the hero's downfall. Hamlet's indecision, for example, has been seen as his "tragic flaw," a view given wide circulation in Laurence Olivier's 1948 film version of the play, which opens with a voiceover comment, "This is the tragedy of a man who could not make up his mind." The notion of the tragic flaw suggests that the hero's deeds and his fate are always commensurate, an attitude that reduces the tragic mystery to a simple equation.

For an incisive treatment of the term, see Peter Alexander's *Hamlet: Father and Son* (1955).

Hamlet theme   "The Mona Lisa of literature," T. S. Eliot's epithet for *Hamlet*, acutely points to the mystery lying at the heart of each work. Despite the efforts of countless interpreters, the mysteries remain, not as problems to be solved but as experiences to absorb. In the case of *Hamlet*, almost every major Western audience has acknowledged the centrality of the play and its impact on them.

The story itself is based on a 12th century legend (from the perspective of MYTH CRITICISM, the story is much older than that, since it fits the archetypal pattern of the sacrificial dying god whose purpose is "to set right" a time that is "out of joint"). The play and its protagonist have created a modern archetype, the first modern man, that is to say, psychological man, the first work to explore the interior reality of a self-conscious mind.

It was the Romantic movement, sweeping through Europe in the late 18th and early 19th centuries, which first recognized itself in the play. That Romantic identification begot a phenomenon known as Hamletism. Hamletism was triggered by Johann Wolfgang von Goethe's comments in his BILDUNGSROMAN *Wilhelm Meister's Apprenticeship* (1795-96), in which Hamlet is described as one who has had an impossible burden imposed upon him, characterizing the Prince as a "delicate vase." In the process there developed a tendency to remove the character from the play, to see him through the mirror of 19th century Romanticism.

Triggered by Goethe's enthusiasm, younger German writers proclaimed an intense identification with the brooding, alienated, introspective prince, culminating in Ferdinand Freiligrath's 1844 poem "Deutschland Ist Hamlet," in which he attacks young Germans, himself included, for indecisiveness and excessive introspection.

Goethe's Hamlet-identification was carried to England by Samuel Taylor Coleridge, who saw the prince's tragedy as a case of action hindered by thought: "The native hue of resolution is sicklied o'er by the pale case of thought." Hamlet's tendency to intellectualize paralyzes him. Another Romantic, William Hazlitt, comes closer to the heart of the matter, "We are Hamlet."

Even in France, Hamletism (the term itself originates there) dominates the literature of the 19th century, taking the form of an obsession in the poetry and prose of Jules Laforgue.

Hamlet sits at the heart of one of the great novels of the 20th century, James Joyce's *Ulysses* (1922). In the novel's celebrated "library scene," young Stephen Dedalus discourses at length on the father/son relationship in the play. He identifies Shakespeare with the Ghost in the play, while Leopold Bloom, a cuckolded husband, hovers ghostlike over the scene. Laced with puns from *Hamlet*, Stephen's commentary establishes correspondences between Bloom/Stephen, the Ghost of King Hamlet/Hamlet and Ulysses/Telemachus. Thus, Joyce stakes his claim to stand aside Homer and Shakespeare.

In the words of the French poet Max Jacob, "Hamletism died in the First World War," signaled by T. S. Eliot's J. Alfred Prufrock:

> I am not the prince, nor was meant to be
> I'm an attendant lord. . .

The shift in identification from Hamlet to an "attendant lord" signaled a rejection of ROMANTICISM and, to Eliot and others, its self-centered egoism. The demotion from identification with Hamlet to "attendant Lord" takes a further downward step in Tom Stoppard's *Rosencrantz and Guildenstern Are Dead* (1969), in which the prince's hapless schoolfellows assume the center stage. These modern antiheroes, bearing more than a slight resemblance to the two tramps in Samuel Beckett's *Waiting for Godot* (1953), ask questions about their existence but go to their deaths without a clue.

Adding to its stature as a literary achievement is the play's preeminent place in the history of the theater. Beginning with Richard Burbage, the leading tragic actor in Shakespeare's company, the CHAMBERLAIN'S/KING'S MEN, the role of the prince has been the ultimate challenge for great actors from David Garrick to Sara Bernhardt to John Gielgud and Laurence Olivier.

Ruby Cohn's *Modern Shakespeare Offshoots* (1976) contains an extensive chapter on Hamlet's presence in modern literature. William Kerrigan's *Hamlet's Perfection* (1994) devotes a "polemical" chapter to "Hamlet in History."

happening   In DRAMA, an extemporaneous performance generated and developed by the interactions of players and audiences. In its ideal conception, a particular happening occurs only once; it can never be repeated. The writer Allan Kaprow coined the term in 1958.

Harlem Renaissance   Term for the flowering of African-American literature, music, and dance that took place in the 1920s in New York's Harlem district. In the wake of World War I, a half century after the abolition of slavery, many black intellectuals and artists perceived that the time had come for the final emancipation of African Americans, the recognition of their right to equal status in America's social and cultural life.

The progenitors of the movement were James Weldon Johnson, a diplomat, poet, and author of *The Autobiography of an Ex-Colored Man* (1912), and W. E. B. Du Bois, whose *The Souls of Black Folk* (1903) powerfully argued the case for social justice. These two figures constituted both the older generation and the lure that brought black artists to Harlem in the 1920s. The movement's manifesto appeared in Alain Locke's anthology *The New Negro* (1925), which called for the incorporation of the African artistic heritage as an enrichment of American culture.

Among those associated with the Renaissance were the novelists Jean Toomer (*Cane*, 1923), Claude McKay (*Home to Harlem*, 1928), Nella Larsen (*Quicksand*, 1928), and Wallace Thurman (*Infants of the Spring*, 1932); the poet Countee Cullen, and a host of artists, musicians, performers, and black intellectuals. The two outstanding writers of the movement were Langston Hughes and Zora Neale Hurston. Hughes, who was primarily a poet but eventually branched out into drama, fiction, and personal memoirs, was the most multitalented, while Hurston's *Their Eyes Were Watching God* (1937) is generally regarded as the greatest single product of the Renaissance.

The Great Depression signaled the end of the Harlem Renaissance, but not the process it began, which, as the critic Ann Douglas has argued, irrevocably changed American and, subsequently, all of Western culture. Douglas maintains that the movement began the interaction of black and white cultural forms that continues today to permeate all aspects of the arts.

Nathan Huggins's *Harlem Renaissance* (1971) offers a judicious history of the era. Ann Douglas's *Terrible Honesty: Mongrel Manhattan in the 1920s* (1995) is a brilliant, provocative reading that explores the interaction of the black and white cultures of the time.

Hebraism/Hellenism   Matthew Arnold's characterization of the two major formative influences in Western culture. "Hebraism" stands for the moral tradition of Judeo-Christianity; "Hellenism" for the intellectual and aesthetic inheritance of Greek civilization. As elaborated in his *Culture and Anarchy* (1869), Arnold's thesis called for a new synthesis of these two traditions in which literature would occupy the void created by the decline of religious faith in the modern world. From Arnold's perspective, literature offered an enlarged view of the idea of religion.

hegemony   A word meaning predominance, used by the Italian Marxist Antonio Gramsci to explain how a dominant CLASS gains and maintains its power. In Gramsci's analysis the ascendant class controls not only the economy but also the cultural and ideological spheres of its society. Thus it is able to persuade the lower classes to willingly support its agenda.

The consent of the subordinate class is won by a process of "incorporation." Incorporation involves concessions, or negotiated settlements, the results of which are always designed to reinforce the interests and security of the dominant class while meeting some of the demands of the others. Thus the hegemonic class maintains its leadership by embracing spheres more comprehensive than its own short-term economic gains. In his analysis, Gramsci is issuing a warning to fellow Marxists that any exclusively economic reading of a society usually will be inadequate.

Some theorists of POPULAR CULTURE argue that the concept of hegemony explains the process by which radical styles (such as the music or dress codes of young people) are quickly incorporated into the mainstream culture.

Antonio Gramsci's *Selections from the Prison Notebooks* (1971) develops his conception of the term; Raymond Williams explores the idea in *Marxism in Literature* (1977).

hendiadys   In RHETORIC, the use of a compound noun where an adjective and noun would be more usual. Shakespeare uses it often, as in "the dead waste and middle of the night" from *Hamlet*.

heptameter   A seven-FOOT metrical line, rarely used in English since the 16th century, at which time it was superseded by iambic pentameter (*see* IAMB). The heptameter is also known as a "FOURTEENER" for its 14 syllables.

hermeneutics   The theoretical examination of the understanding and interpretation of TEXTS. Originally used to refer to the interpretation of the BIBLE, hermeneutics eventually moved into a consideration of secular texts as well. In the 19th century, this textual concern resulted in the formulation of the so-called *hermeneutic circle*, the apparent PARADOX in which we cannot understand the whole of a work without understanding its parts but that the understanding of the parts presupposes some knowledge of the whole.

In the 20th century, the German philosopher Martin Heidegger and his disciple Hans-Georg Gadamer transformed hermeneutics from a problem of knowledge (epistemology) into a problem of "being" (ontology). In other words, understanding became not simply a question of knowing something, it also defined the human way of being in the world, which Heidegger calls DASEIN. One consequence of this transformation is to see understanding as necessarily rooted in *prejudice* (preconceptions) and in *time* (history). When we encounter a text from the past we unite our historically shaped preconceptions with the historically shaped preconception of the text. Out of this "fusion of horizons" emerges understanding. A 20th-century reader's interpretation of Dante's *Divine Comedy* (1310–14), for example, will represent a fusion of modern and medieval minds.

The interpretation that grows out of this understanding is never the kind of objective "truth" that is the hallmark of science. A classic text has no final meaning, but only a history of its interpretations. In this sense the meaning of a text is the history of its criticism.

This position has been contested by the American hermeneutic critic E. D. Hirsch, who sees it as an example of historical relativism. In his *Validity in Interpretation* (1967), Hirsch argues for a distinction between the *meaning* of a text and its *significance*. For Hirsch, the *meaning* resides in the intention of the author, while the *significance* represents the meanings acquired in the course of its history.

Another important figure in hermeneutics is the French philosopher Paul Ricoeur. Ricoeur makes a distinction between what he calls the "hermeneutics of suspicion" and the "hermeneutics of trust." The hermeneutics of suspicion views the "horizon" of a text—the tradition it reflects—as the source of error and mystification. This skeptical position is reflected in the thinking of such moderns as Friedrich Nietzsche, Sigmund Freud, and Jacques Derrida. The hermeneutics of trust argues that the classic text, although apparently "outdated," represents a provocative challenge to the assumptions of modern, particularly scientific "prejudices." For Ricoeur, hermeneutics should operate from a posture of trust, not suspicion.

In literary criticism hermeneutics underlies the contemporary critical schools associated with PHENOMENOLOGY, RECEPTION THEORY, and some versions of READER RESPONSE CRITICISM.

The best introductions to hermeneutics are Richard Palmer's *Hermeneutics* (1969) and Timothy Cruise's *A Teacher's Introduction to Philosophical Hermeneutics* (1991).

hermetic poetry   A term for the kind of obscure and difficult poetry that employs private allusions and symbols. First associated with the 19th-century French symbolists, the term is now used to describe poetry in which the sound qualities, the music, of a poem appear to be more important than the sense.

hero/heroine   The major figure in a DRAMA or NARRATIVE. In traditional usage the term implies qualities of valor and courage, but in modern literature it can as easily apply to characters who lack "heroic" qualities, a perspective ironically alluded to by Robert Musil in the title of his novel *The Man Without Qualities* (1930–43). As a consequence, some critics prefer the word PROTAGONIST to describe the main character in a modern novel.

In his *Anatomy of Criticism* (1957), Northrop Frye traces the history of Western literature in terms of the "diminishing power of the hero." As Frye represents it, as literature grows more "realistic," it presents the hero as progressively weaker. Thus in 20th-century literature, the hero is likely to be an ANTI-HERO.

heroic couplet   In verse, a pair of rhyming lines in iambic pentameter. In English poetry the form was used as early as Chaucer's *The Canterbury Tales* (1387–1400), but its most extensive use occurred in the RESTORATION and AUGUSTAN periods. The master of the form was Alexander Pope, who perfected the symmetrically balanced, self-contained unit known as the "closed" (that is, containing a complete thought) heroic couplet, as in the opening lines of his "Essay on Criticism":

> 'Tis hard to say, if greater want of skill
> Appear in writing, or in judging ill.

heroic drama   A type of drama popular in the RESTORATION period featuring heroes of exalted, epic dimensions. Written either in HEROIC COUPLETS or BLANK VERSE, these plays generally focused on the conflict between what John Dryden called "love and valour." Operatic and occasionally bombastic, they achieved popularity in the early years of the Restoration, but eventually fell into disrepute spurred by the duke of Buckingham's successful burlesque of the form, *The Rehearsal* (1671). Among the best known of the heroic plays are Dryden's *The Conquest of Granada* (1670–1), *Aureng-Zebe* (1675), and *All for Love* (1677), his adaptation of Shakespeare's *Antony and Cleopatra*.

Eugene Waith's *Ideas of Greatness: Heroic Drama in England* (1971) offers a valuable overview of the form.

heteroglossia   A term coined by the Russian theorist Mikhail Bakhtin, who saw language as made up of an endless variety of "languages," each one of which imposes its own perspective on reality. Every individual speaks a variety of these "languages"—the language of work, of prayer, of song, and so on—so that each person may be said to be heteroglot ("many tongued").

In the NOVEL, heteroglossia appears as a complex interweaving of dialogue and description (*see* DIEGESIS/MIMESIS). In the contemporary novel, idiolects, dialects, first-person NARRATORS, letters, excerpts, PARODIES, transcriptions, and PASTICHES all exemplify the principle of heteroglossia.

David Lodge's *After Bakhtin* (1990) provides an insightful account of Bakhtin's terms.

higher criticism   A 19th-century form of biblical scholarship that raised important questions about the origins and authority of the BIBLE. Based upon the work of "lower criticism," the restoring and editing of biblical texts, this form of analysis frequently operated on the assumption that there existed earlier, lost versions of the texts that have come down to us. As a result, it tended to devalue the existing biblical CANON.

***

The *Literary Guide to the Bible* (1987), edited by Robert Alter and Frank Kermode, provides a comprehensive survey of the Old and New Testaments.

Hispanic-American literature A term for the literature of Americans with a Spanish speaking heritage. In a general sense, there are two groups within this category: the Chicano/Chicana group, or Mexican Americans, and the Latino/Latina group, from Latin America or the Caribbean islands. Many people use the term Latino/Latina to refer to both groups, however.

Chicano literature extends back to 1848, the year in which the Treaty of Guadalupe Hidalgo ceded the lands of the Southwest to the United States. The newly Americanized Mexican residents continued to conduct their cultural affairs in Spanish for nearly a century. Chicano literature written in English first attracted attention with the publication in 1959 of Antonio Villareal's *Pocho*, a novel about a young Mexican American. Since that time, there has been an outpouring of fiction and poetry from this group. Outstanding examples include Rudolpho Anaya's *Bless Me, Ultima* (1972) and *Tortuga* (1979), two novels that combine mythic and folkloric elements with realistic sociopolitical themes, and Sandra Cisneros's *The House on Mango Street* (1985), an account of life in a Chicago barrio, told in the forceful and direct voice of a Chicana girl. Gary Soto (*The Elements of San Joaquin*, 1977) is an important poet, while Gloria Anzaldúa's *Borderlands* (1987) is a collection of essays and reflections on the identity crisis afflicting Mexican Americans.

The Latino novel came into prominence in 1990 when the Pulitzer Prize was awarded to Oscar Hijuelos for *The Mambo Kings Play Songs of Love*, a vibrant account of the music and lives of Cuban immigrants living in New York in the 1950s. Before that there had been two outstanding memoirs of growing up Puerto Rican in New York: Piri Thomas's *Down These Mean Streets* (1967) and Edward Rivera's *Family Installments* (1980). Equally tough-minded is Ernesto Quinonez' *Bodega Dreams* (2000) a raw, racy depiction of life in *El Barrio*. The Puerto Rican experience has fueled notable developments in poetry and theater. The Nuyorican Poetry movement has been an active group since the 1970s. The work of these New York–based Puerto Rican poets has been anthologized by two of the group's best known poets, Miguel Algarín and Miguel Piñero. Piñero is also the author of an acclaimed play *Short Eyes* (1975). An outstanding novelist and poet from the Dominican Republic is Julia Alvarez, whose novel *In the Time of the Butterflies* was nominated for the 1995 National Book Critics Circle Award. The title poem of her collection *The Other Side, El Otro Lado* (1995) recounts the conflicted emotions generated by a return visit to her native island. This is the conflict that lies at the heart of Hispanic-American literature, the sense of divided identity.

The Biographical Dictionary of Hispanic Literature in the United States (1990) contains biographical and thematic accounts of the major writers.

historical novel   A type of FICTION in which a significant historical event or era serves as a backdrop to a story that may include fictional or historical characters, or a mix of both. Most historical novels conform fairly closely to the conventions of ROMANCE rather than REALISM, although there have been exceptions to this rule, notably in Tolstoy's *War and Peace* (1869).

The father of the historical novel is Sir Walter Scott, many of whose novels focus on Scottish history. His American counterpart, James Fenimore Cooper, whose *Leatherstocking Tales* (1823–41) won him worldwide fame, was the progenitor of the WESTERN. Other 19th-century masters of the form were Victor Hugo (*Notre Dame de Paris*, 1831) and Alexandre Dumas (*The Three Musketeers*, 1844).

In the 20th century, the popularity of historical fiction continues to be strong, as exemplified by Margaret Mitchell's *Gone with the Wind* (1936), but a number of historical novels have made a larger demand on their reader's attention. Among these are two novels that penetrate the heart of the institution of slavery, William Styron's *The Confessions of Nat Turner* (1967) and Toni Morrison's *Beloved* (1987).

historical criticism   A critical approach that looks at literature from the perspective of the philosophical, ethical, political, and economic conditions of the time in which it was produced. Historical criticism is closely related to and reliant on scholarly research and for this reason is favored by academic scholars. Although eclipsed during the era of NEW CRITICISM (which maintained that historical criticism subordinated literature to history), the historical approach has experienced a resurgence in the form of MARXIST CRITICISM, NEW HISTORICISM, and other approaches that operate under the general heading of LITERARY HISTORY.

history of ideas   An interdisciplinary movement among American scholars designed to trace the history of specific concepts, as they are reflected in history and literature. The movement began with the publication of A. O. Lovejoy's *The Great Chain of Being* (1936), a survey of the belief in a hierarchical order in nature from classical times to the early 19th century. Four years later, Lovejoy founded *The Journal of the History of Ideas*.

With the publication of the multivolume *Dictionary of the History of Ideas* (1968), this approach expanded to include "studies of three different sorts: cross-cultural studies limited to a given century or period, studies that trace an idea from antiquity to later periods, and studies that explicate the meaning of a pervasive idea in the minds of its leading proponents." An example of the history of ideas in practice is Lovejoy's study of the doctrine of the FORTUNATE FALL.

In recent years, this approach has been challenged by contemporary theorists who argue that it is based on a naively referential view of language. Opposed to the History of Ideas is the perspective represented by Michel Foucault's *Archeology of Knowledge* (1972) in which analysis is focused not on the subject itself but on the ordering and controlling mechanisms that are built into the language of the subject, its DISCOURSE.

Despite this postmodernist critique, the history of ideas remains an important contributor to, and subdivision of, HISTORICAL CRITICISM.

For detailed examples of the theory and practice of the history of ideas, see Arthur O. Lovejoy's *Essays in the History of Ideas* (1949).

Holocaust Literally a large consuming fire, later adapted as a metaphor for the systematic Nazi program to exterminate the entire population of European Jews.

The literary attempt to represent this event has produced a large body of literature seeking to come to terms with a horror that defies comprehension. The chief challenge faced by writers of Holocaust literature is how to describe the experience without cheapening or exploiting it. A related problem arises from the prospect of converting monstrosity into aesthetic pleasure. Some have argued that Holocaust literature should be limited to diaries, memoirs, and other first-hand accounts, that rendering the experience in fictional and poetic forms amounts to blasphemy. Others maintain that literature deepens, rather than palliates, the significance of the Holocaust. A striking example of the latter are the novels of W. G. Sebald, particularly *The Emigrants* (1997) and *Austerlitz* (2001). The latter explores the experience of an emotionally crippled man who sets out to discover the fates of his parents, holocaust victims.

Among outstanding examples of Holocaust fiction are André Schwarz-Bart's *The Last of the Just* (1961), which places the Nazi effort in the historical context of European ANTI-SEMITISM; Jerzy Kozinski's *The Painted Bird* (1965); and Tadeusz Borowski's collection of short stories *This Way for the Gas, Ladies and Gentlemen* (1967). Two important poets whose experiences in the Nazi concentration camps have been transformed into powerful poetry are Paul Celan (*Collected Poems*, 1988) and Nelly Sacks (*O the Chimneys*, 1967).

Outstanding personal NARRATIVEs include Anne Frank's world-famous *Diary of a Young Girl* (1952) and Primo Levi's *Survival in Auschwitz* (1961).

In the field of DOCUMENTARY film, the Holocaust has been the subject of three unforgettable films: Alain Resnais's *Night and Fog* (1955), Marcel Ophuls's *The Sorrow and the Pity* (1969), and Claude Lanzmann's *Shoah* (1985). Memorable fictional films include Jan Kadar and Elmor Klos's *The Shop on Main Street* (1965), Vittorio De Sica's *The Garden of the Finzi-Continis* (1970), Lina Wertmuller's *Seven Beauties* (1976), and Alan Pakula's adaptation of William Styron's novel *Sophie's Choice* (1982). Undoubtedly the most successful Holocaust film is Steven Spielberg's *Schindler's List* (1993), adapted from a book by Thomas Keneally.

Lawrence Langer's *The Holocaust and the Literary Imagination* (1975) is a detailed study; Ilan Avisar's *Screening the Holocaust* (1988) analyzes the major films.

Homeric   Referring to the Greek epic poet Homer (fl. 850 B.C.), the author of the *Iliad* and the *Odyssey*. A Homeric epithet is a descriptive phrase that employs a compound adjective with a noun. The best known example from Homer's *Iliad* is "wine-dark sea."

Horatian ode   *See* ODE.

horizon of expectations   *See* RECEPTION THEORY.

horror fiction   Term used to describe literature that extended the tradition of the GOTHIC NOVEL with an emphasis on the macabre and the supernatural. The success of horror fiction lies in the thrill of fear.

One of the landmark horror stories is Edgar Allan Poe's "The Fall of the House of Usher" (1839), but probably the most influential of all horror fictions are Mary Shelley's *Frankenstein* (1818) and Bram Stoker's *Dracula* (1897), whose famous vampire serves as an archetype of seductive sexual power.

Modern practitioners of the genre include Dennis Wheatley (*The Devil Rides Out*, 1935) and H. P. Lovecraft (*At the Mountains of Madness*, 1936). Their contemporary successors include the highly successful Stephen King (*Carrie*, 1974; *The Shining*, 1972) and Anne Rice (*Interview with the Vampire*, 1976; *The Vampire Lestat*, 1985).

Stephen King's *Danse Macabre* (1981) provides an excellent introduction to the modern genre. David Punter's *The Literature of Terror* (1980) is a provocative attempt to redefine the genre. Manuel Aguirre's *The Closed Space* (1990) explores the relation of horror fiction to the symbol of the world as a "closed space."

horror film   The horror film achieved its earliest, and for many its greatest, realization in two masterpieces of German EXPRESSIONISM, Robert Wiene's *The Cabinet of Dr. Caligari* (1919) and F. W. Murnau's *Nosferatu* (1921), the latter the first of the vampire films. Three of the most famous examples of the form followed in the next decade: Todd Browning's *Dracula* (1931), with Bela Lugosi as the vampire; James Whale's *Frankenstein* (1931), with Boris Karloff as the monster; and *The Bride of Frankenstein* (1935), with Elsa Lanchester as the disappointed intended.

The '30s also saw the birth of the mythic monster *King Kong* (1933). The 1940s witnessed an outstanding example of the power of suggestion rather than direct representation in Jacques Tourneur's *Cat People* (1942).

Eclipsed in the early '50s by the SCIENCE FICTION film, horror made a comeback in Terence Fisher's *The Curse of Frankenstein* (1957) and his *Dracula* (1958), two remakes that added sensuality and social comment to the original stories.

The '60s were inaugurated by the film that has created more nightmares than any other, Alfred Hitchcock's fiendishly compelling *Psycho* (1960), and by Roger Corman's adaptations of Edgar Allan Poe's stories, beginning with *House of Usher* (1960). In 1968 George Romero's *Night of the Living Dead* spawned a horde of zombie movies, while Roman Polanski's *Rosemary's Baby* introduced the theme of witchcraft. Brian DePalma's *Carrie* (1976), Wes Craven's *A Nightmare on Elm Street* (1984), and Sean Cunningham's *Friday the 13th* (1980) are early examples of the high school horror film that dominated the field in the '80s and '90s. In 1991, Jonathan Demme's *The Silence of the Lambs* raised the genre to a new level by including a feminist protagonist holding her own against a patriarchal nightmare figure, Hannibal Lecter.

The Encyclopedia of Horror Movies (1985), edited by Phil Hardy, contains descriptions of more than 1,300 films.

hubris (hybris)   A Greek word for excessive pride, an arrogance that invites the retribution of the gods. The term is frequently employed in reference to Greek tragedies. It is related to, but distinct from another term, HAMARTIA.

humanism   Originally a term used to describe a set of attitudes and beliefs triggered by the RENAISSANCE interest in the literature and thought of Greece and Rome. One outgrowth of this interest was a developing commitment to the dignity of the individual, a concept subordinated in the collective-oriented consciousness of the MIDDLE AGES. Concurrently there developed a growing concern with secular life as opposed to the religious focus of medieval culture, although the original humanists, such as Thomas More and Erasmus, were profoundly religious and experienced no difficulty reconciling these beliefs with their Christian faith.

In succeeding centuries, however, humanism (represented by Alexander Pope's line "The proper study of mankind is man") exhibited an increasing secularism. Humanism came to be associated with an a-religious, if not anti-religious, position. Humanism also set itself up against the DETERMINISM associated with scientific thought. Humanists argued for the fundamental freedom of the individual as a core belief. Even generally pessimistic philosophies endorsed the humanistic ideals, as in Jean-Paul Sartre's assertion that "EXISTENTIALISM is a humanism."

POSTSTRUCTURALISM argues that the humanist belief in the free individual is an illusion, engendered either by language itself or, in the view of contemporary MARXIST CRITICISM, by bourgeois capitalist IDEOLOGY, which promotes the idea of freedom to further its own interests. Nevertheless the humanist tradition remains dominant in that area of study that bears its name, the humanities. *See* NEW HUMANISM.

For an excellent overview of early humanism, see C. S. Lewis's *History of English Literature in the Sixteenth Century* (1954) and Paul Kristeller's *The Classics and Renaissance Thought* (1955). For a Marxist, anti-humanist critique, see Terry Eagleton's *Literary Theory* (1983).

humors   In medieval and RENAISSANCE literature, a notion of character derived from medical beliefs of the time. The four humors within people were believed to be the subjective equivalents of the four elements in nature. As nature is made up of earth, air, fire, and water, so each individual exhibited a combination of blood, phlegm, choler, and bile. No one, except Jesus Christ, had ever had these humors in perfect balance. One's imbalance determined the general tendency of one's character. Thus, an overabundance of blood produced a sanguine personality; of phlegm, a phlegmatic personality; of choler, a hot-tempered person; of bile, a melancholic disposition.

Some ELIZABETHAN dramatists, Ben Jonson in particular, employed these categories to develop the comedy of humors, which represented characters dominated by their particular obsession. For Jonson, this focus gave a realistic edge to his comedies, enabling him to draw his characters from recognizable human types. One of the best examples of the comedy of humors is Jonson's *Bartholomew Fair* (1614), in which he creates a vivid, dazzling array of characters (the play contains 30 speaking parts), the dramatic equivalent of a Charles Dickens novel.

hyperbole   An exaggerated or extravagant expression not meant to be taken literally. Edmond Rostand's romantic drama *Cyrano de Bergerac* (1896) contains an entertaining example, in a scene in which Cyrano instructs someone how he might have commented on Cyrano's nose if he had wished to insult him:

> *You might have said*
> *Oh, a great many things. . . .-.*
> *Eloquent:When it blows, the typhoon howls,*
> *And the clouds darken. Dramatic:When it bleeds—*
> *The Red Sea. Enterprising:What a sign*
> *for some perfumer. . . .*
> *Simple:When do they unveil the monument?*

hypertext   A series of electronic features built into a computerized text, enabling the reader to choose alternatives to a straight linear reading of the text. In a hypertext version of a Shakespearean play, for example, the reader might have access to the text of the play and background information in both words and visual images, such as maps, charts and photographs, a glossary, reprints of the play's sources, visual reproductions of the costumes, and sets of famous theatrical presentations of the play, along with opportunities to "block," or determine the placement and movements of the actors in certain scenes. The material would be available either for systematic use or for random selection.

One of the striking features of hypertext, as this example illustrates, is that it interrupts the traditional reading of the main text. As a result, the reader is in effect creating his or her own text in which the actual words written by Shakespeare may or not play the central role. In effect, the reader "adapts" the play for his or her own purposes (*see* INTERACTIVE COMPUTER FICTION).

O. B. Hardison's *Disappearing Through the Skylight* (1989) discusses the term within a broad speculative framework.

hypotaxis   In RHETORIC, the process of arranging subordinate clauses in a complex sentence (as opposed to PARATAXIS, the arrangement of coordinate clauses).

i

iamb   A metrical FOOT consisting of one unstressed syllable followed by a stressed syllable, as in the word *alone*. In the words of the critic William Kerrigan, the iamb is "the heartbeat of English poetry." In English the most important iambic line is iambic pentameter, which consists of five iambic feet. Unrhymed iambic pentameter, also known as BLANK VERSE, is the basic METER of Shakespeare's plays and John Milton's *Paradise Lost*. Iambic pentameter in rhymed pairs of lines, known as HEROIC COUPLETS, is the meter of Chaucer's *Canterbury Tales* and much of the English poetry of the early 18th century, exemplified in Alexander Pope's famous lines from *The Rape of the Lock*:

> *The hungry judges soon the sentence sign,*
> *And wretches hang that jurymen may dine.*

identification   The process by which readers or viewers associate themselves with fictional characters, as in "She identified (herself) with Ilse in *Casablanca*," or with the performer of the role, "She identified (herself) with Ingrid Bergman."

Identification can be both a positive and negative process: positive, for example, in that it permits us to enter sympathetically into the world of people different from ourselves, thus promoting understanding. It can be negative when it encourages bizarre or self-destructive behavior. A famous literary example of the latter is Don Quixote, whose identification with the heroes of medieval romances causes him to lose touch with reality.

In Kenneth Burke's conception of RHETORIC, the chief rhetorical goal is not persuasion, but identification.

Burke's argument appears in his *A Rhetoric of Motives* (1950).

identity   According to the critic Northrop Frye, the fundamental theme in literature is the quest for one's identity. One recurrent form is the story of the foundling. From Moses to Superman, the account of the child of unknown parents has held a special fascination for audiences, even when parodied as it is in Oscar Wilde's *The Importance of Being Earnest* (1895). The more common form is the protagonist's self-recognition and the subsequent reversal of fortune that issues from that recognition. In his *Poetics*, Aristotle's term for the recognition is ANAGNORISIS and the reversal, PERIPETEIA.

Identity is a consistent theme in ethnic minority literatures and in FEMINIST CRITICISM. In the former case, the issue of identity frequently turns on the conflict within the children of immigrant parents torn between their ethnic origins and their aspirations to succeed in the new world. *See*, for example, HISPANIC-AMERICAN LITERATURE.

Northrop Frye's discussion of the identity theme is in his *Anatomy of Criticism* (1957).

ideology In its most common sense, a system of belief or political creed. MARXIST CRITICISM employs the term in a different sense, defining it as "false consciousness," a pervasive social process that reflects the HEGEMONY of the dominant class. Marxists argue that in capitalist societies ideology is hidden under the rubric of "common sense" or simply "the way things are."

In relation to literature, this hidden ideology is in evidence whenever there is an emphasis on FORMALISM or AESTHETICS as the governing principles of literature and art. Marxists generally regard limiting a text to its formal elements as an attempt to separate a poem or story from its social/historical context. Similarly, they view any reference to a text's universal or timeless qualities as an attempt to de-politicize or de-historicize literature.

The Marxist theorist Louis Althusser introduces a further development of the term, arguing that bourgeois ideology also works to convince the individual that he or she is a unified, autonomous SELF. According to this view, literature and film operating within the bourgeois framework reinforce this ideology by emphasizing personal and psychological themes, even when they are purportedly dealing with social issues.

Louis Althusser's position is developed in "Ideology and Ideological State Apparatuses" in *Lenin and Philosophy* (1971). Terry Eagleton's *Literary Theory* (1983) offers a lively defense of the Marxist thesis.

idiolect The distinctive feature of a particular person's language, as distinct from dialect, or the language of a group. For example, Holden Caulfield, the NARRATOR and main character of J. D. Salinger's *The Catcher in the Rye* (1950), speaks in the dialect of an American teenager circa 1950, but his idiolect is reflected in the special significance he gives to terms such as "old" (an epithet for anyone he has known for a long time) and "phoney" (a general term character-izing any behavior that is meretricious or hypocritical): "Then he and old Sally started talking about a lot of people they knew and it was the phoniest conversa-tion you ever heard in your life."

idyll   Usually a poem depicting a rural scene, suggesting tranquility and peace. Tennyson uses the term in his multivolumed series of poems *Idylls of the King* (1859–85) based on the ARTHURIAN LEGEND.

imagery   The patterns of images that are the verbal equivalents of sense expe-rience in a text or portion of a text. Every METAPHOR or SIMILE constitutes an image. Thus Macbeth's "ravell'd sleeve of care" visualizes an emotional condition in terms of an article of clothing. Taken together with all other references to clothing in Shakespeare's play, it constitutes a pattern of clothing imagery. From the perspective of NEW CRITICISM, the patterns of images in a poem, play, or novel offer the key to its TEXTURE. For others, the imagery discloses the moral vision of the author. For still others, it engages readers on the level of sense expe-rience, enabling them to "re-create" the text (*see* READER RESPONSE CRITICISM).

imagination/fancy   From the RENAISSANCE through the 18th century these two terms were basically synonymous, referring to the faculty of mind that is the source of both creativity and madness. The exchange between Theseus and Hippolyta in Act V of Shakespeare's *A Midsummer Night's Dream* reflects both these senses of the words as well as their interchangeability.

> Theseus: *The lunatic, the lover and the poet*
> *Are of imagination all compact. . . .*
> *And as imagination bodies forth*
> *The forms of things unknown, the poet's eye*
> *Turns them to shapes, and gives to airy nothing*
> *A local habitation and a name. . . .*
>
> Hippolyta: *But all the story of the night told over*
> *And all their minds transfigured so together*
> *More witnesseth than Fancy's images. . . .*

Theseus's critique of imagination as illusory and allied to madness is coun-tered by Hippolyta's reminder that "Fancy's images," nevertheless, can reveal a truth beyond reason.

The 18th century expressed the Theseus-Hippolyta debate in terms of the opposition of judgment/reason to imagination/fancy. But with the publication of his *Biographia Literaria* (1817), the Romantic poet and critic Samuel Taylor Coleridge introduced a crucial distinction between fancy and imagination. He argued that the terms described two separate poetic faculties. Fancy was a process of association, "a mode of memory," that reconceived the data of the senses in new and unusual arrangements. The operation of fancy was, for Coleridge, the signature of the "poetry of talent." But the "poetry of genius" involved the imagination, the faculty that transformed rather than rearranged, that "dissolves, diffuses, dissipates, in order to recreate." The imagination is thus a synthesizing force, creative and organic. In the 20th century Coleridge's conceptions were restated by the critic I. A. Richards. Richards translated Coleridge's theories into the language of modern psychology.

In the MYTH CRITICISM of Northrop Frye, the imagination is a collective human faculty creating an alternate world, the product of mankind's basic fears and desires. This imaginative world is self-perpetuating, having begun in myth, and evolving from it into literary forms that retain their archetypal, universal character.

In their reduction of the traditional creative self to a decentered "subject," some postmodernist critics and writers have proclaimed the "death of the imagination," an attitude summed up in the title of one of Samuel Beckett's "texts for nothing," Beckett's term for certain short pieces exhibiting his NIHILISM: "Imagination Dead Imagine" (1965).

R. L. Brett's *Fancy and Imagination* (1969) provides a brief history of the terms; I. A. Richards examines Coleridge's theories in *Coleridge on Imagination* (1935), and Northrop Frye's ideas are developed in his *Anatomy of Criticism* (1957). Richard Kearney's *The Wake of Imagination* (1988) looks at the history of the term from classical to postmodern times.

imagism A school of English and American poetry that flourished in the years prior to and during World War I. The school originated at a meeting in a London restaurant of the poets Ezra Pound, T. E. Hulme, and F. S. Flint that resulted in the formation of principles published in 1913. The Imagist creed enunciated three poetic goals: "1) to treat the 'thing' directly, whether subjective or objective; 2) to use absolutely no word that did not contribute to the presentation; 3) as regarding rhythm: to compose in sequence of the musical phrase, not in sequence of a metronome."

The first two principles represent the Imagists' reaction against the tradition of ROMANTICISM, which emphasized abstract ideas and to some degree ornamental language. The third principle concerning rhythm constituted an argument for FREE VERSE.

As for the term image, Pound defined it as "an intellectual and emotional complex in an instant of time . . . which gives that sense of sudden liberation . . .

which we experience in the presence of great works of art." (For a related term *see* EPIPHANY.)

In America the poet Amy Lowell promoted the movement, editing three anthologies titled *Some Imagist Poets* (1915–17), a development Pound disapprovingly characterized as "Amygism." Pound was reacting to what he saw as Lowell's emphasis on pictorial description rather than on his more rigorous definition of the term. Pound's purpose is best expressed in his famous two-line poem "In a Station of the Metro":

> *The apparition of these faces in the crowd*
> *Petals on a wet, black bough.*

Influenced by the Japanese HAIKU, this poem is not meant to be a simple description but to invoke the tension between its two images—the moment when, in Pound's words, "A thing outward and objective transforms itself, or darts into a thing inward and subjective." Imagist principles were important influences in the development of later poetic movements, particularly OBJECTIVISM and PROJECTIVISM.

J. B. Harmer's *Victory in Limbo: Imagism, 1908–1917* (1975) discusses the movement's transitional role in the development of modern poetry.

imitation   The principle that literature is fundamentally an imitation of reality. For a description of this conception, *see* MIMESIS.

implied author/reader   In NARRATOLOGY, two terms used to distinguish the author/reader "within" the TEXT from the author/reader "outside" the text. "Implied author" was coined by the critic Wayne Booth to describe the "second self" of the author, the one that exists only as the creative presence governing a NARRATIVE. Distinct from this internal author is the external or "real" author. For example, the actual author of *A Farewell to Arms* is Ernest Hemingway, an American novelist who achieved worldwide fame for living in a style that seemed to exemplify the "code" of the heroes of his novels. The implied author of this novel is neither Hemingway the man, nor Frederick Henry, the first-person narrator of the novel.

The implied author, as described by Booth, is a figure who "stands behind the scenes whether as stage manager, or puppeteer, or as an indifferent God. . . ." The critic and novelist David Lodge presents the distinction in the form of a question, "Is the implied author of a novel . . . the 'same' as the actual historical individual who sat at his desk and wrote it and who has his own life before and after that activity, or an identity who exists only at the moment of composition?"

Similarly, the "real" reader of a novel is anyone who reads it at a particular time. The "implied" reader, a term first used by Wolfgang Iser, a critic whose work is rooted in PHENOMENOLOGY, is the ideal hypothetical reader who enters into a partnership with the implied author in order to complete the work—that is, to read and understand it. In one sense, the task of the real reader is to become the implied reader. Reading forces the reader out of him/herself to assume various points of view.

In *A Farewell to Arms*, for example, the reader is asked to assume a critical view of abstract nouns like "glory" and "honor" that are used to justify war. The reader may also be asked to fill in the blanks, to complete an implied interpretation that any text may produce. As a result, the implied reader becomes a creative participant in the production of meaning. Actual readers fulfill these tasks in limitless numbers of ways, each of us bringing to the reading our own experiences, individually "concretizing" it, but each of us functioning within the framework established for the implied reader.

If the real reader rejects this role, either by being incapable of assuming it or by "seeing through" it, then the work will be incomplete. A reader may either lack sufficient knowledge or simply refuse to accept the "implied reader" role. Thus a reader of *A Farewell To Arms* who knows nothing about World War I may not be able to become an adequate implied reader. On the other hand, the reader may be, for example, a modern feminist such as Judith Fetterley, who would describe herself as a "resisting reader" of *A Farewell to Arms*, rejecting the implied reader role because of what she sees as its sexist, male orientation. In the one case the actual reader may assert "I don't understand"; in the other case she may say "I understand all too well." In either case a disjunction exists, created by the real reader's inability or refusal to accept the implied reader's role.

Conversely, a "real" author may refuse to accept the commonly held opinion of the identity of the implied author. William Blake's famous comment that in *Paradise Lost*, Milton was "of the devil's party" would doubtless be one that the historical John Milton would have vigorously denied.

The implied author/reader theory has played an important role in the development of READER RESPONSE CRITICISM and been subject to a wide range of refinements designed to offer more precise, but often more confusing, categories.

For other aspects of the subject, *see* AUTHOR, DIALOGISM, RHETORIC, RECEPTION THEORY.

Wayne Booth's *The Rhetoric of Fiction* (1961) offers the fullest, as well as the original, treatment of the "implied author." The second edition of this work (1983) includes an important postscript and a valuable bibliography. Wolfgang Iser's *The Implied Reader* (1974) provides a detailed description of the reader's role in fiction. David Lodge's *After Bakhtin* (1980) provides a highly readable account of these and other literary ideas. Judith Fetterley's *The Resisting Reader* (1978) views the reader's role from the perspective of FEMINIST CRITICISM.

impressionism   The success in the late 19th century of the impressionist school of painters—Claude Monet, Camille Pissarro, Pierre-Auguste Renoir, Edgar Degas, Édouard Manet, and others—inevitably had an impact on the literature of the period. Literary impressionism shares with the art movement the belief that reality is a synthesis of sense experiences, and that the distinction between subject and object is misleading. What is real is the object-as-experienced by a perceiver (*see* PHENOMENOLOGY).

In the impressionist literary style, emphasis falls on the creation of a mood or atmosphere reflecting a world filtered through an individual consciousness. To some extent this mood is created by a "painterly" style, an attempt to render images, reflections of light and sound, that represent the literary equivalents of Impressionist paintings.

Although examples of literary impressionism can be detected even earlier than the movement in art, its great period is more or less parallel to the art movement, from 1875 until World War I.

During that time, writers from a variety of countries made the pilgrimage to Paris to absorb the impressionist ambience. Among these were Oscar Wilde, James Joyce, Stefan George, Rainer Maria Rilke, Anton Chekhov, and Gabriele D'Annunzio. The most powerful influence of impressionism was indirect: It helped to infuse modern literature with a lyric element and the importance of capturing a passing mood in which character and scene, observer and observed are merged (*see* MODERNISM).

Maria E. Kronegger's *Literary Impressionism* (1973) is a useful guide.

incest   Sexual relations among family members is an all but universal taboo, a fact that contributes to its power as a literary theme. But beyond the shock value of incest, there lies, in psychoanalytical terms, the powerful interplay of primal feelings grouped under the heading of the OEDIPAL COMPLEX.

For Sigmund Freud and later practitioners of PSYCHOANALYTICAL CRITICISM, the connection of parent-child incest to the symbolic killing of the rival parent is a critical fact central to the development of the individual. Thus from a Freudian perspective, the Oedipal complex is pivotal in life as well as literature.

In classical Greece incest is characteristic of the gods as well of ill-fated humans, such as Oedipus. In the Old Testament incestuous behavior is depicted in the seduction of Lot by his daughters, in the story of Joseph and his stepmother, and in the relation of a son of David, Amnon, and his stepsister, Tammar.

Although many psychoanalytical interpretations of Shakespeare focus on hidden incestuous motifs, the only explicit example is in *Pericles*, where the evil King Antiochus is guilty of incest with his daughter. The best known example in English drama is John Ford's tragedy *'Tis Pity She's a Whore* (1633), which depicts the love of brother and sister sympathetically, although with no amelioration of the tragic consequences of incestuous passion. Jean Racine's *Phèdre* (1677), an adaptation of Euripides's *Hippolytus*, is a moving tragedy of stepmother-stepson incest.

With the emergence of the novel in the 18th century, incest assumes a minor role in Defoe's *Moll Flanders* (1722) and, in the view of some critics, a major role in Fielding's *Tom Jones* (1749), in which the fear that he has committed incest with his mother produces a moral transformation in Tom's character.

Among the English Romantic poets, incest between brother and sister is seen as an example of pure uncorrupted love in Percy Bysshe Shelley's poem "Epipsychidion" (1821) and Lord Byron's CLOSET DRAMA *Cain* (1821). The tradition of the superior character of brother-sister love is developed further in Herman Melville's *Pierre* (1852), Thomas Mann's short story "The Blood of the Walsungs" (1921), and Iris Murdoch's novel *A Severed Head* (1962).

In FILM, the theme of mother-son relations has been addressed in Louis Malle's *Murmur of the Heart* (1971) and Neil Jordan's *The Miracle* (1990), and of father-daughter incest in Roman Polanski's *Chinatown* (1974).

Violation of Taboo, edited by Donald Cary and R. E. C. Masters (1963), is an anthology of literary treatments of incest. Otto Rank's *The Incest Theme in Literature and Legend* (1912) is the classic study of the subject.

incunabula   A term for books printed before the year 1501. After the invention of the printing press ca. 1455, many books were published that resembled medieval manuscripts in size and form with typefaces based upon the handwriting of the time. As a result, these early books were large and ornate and are prized by rare book collectors.

indeterminacy   A term, sometimes referred to as "uncertainty," from modern physics that has been adapted by contemporary literary theorists. In science, the term is associated with the physicist Werner Heisenberg. Heisenberg's Indeterminacy Principle argues that the attempt to measure at the same time position/momentum and energy/time must result in an inaccuracy. In more general terms, Heisenberg's theory suggests that the very act of measuring these quantities alters them. This principle has been adapted in literary theory, particularly by deconstructionists, to argue that the act of interpretation alters the work it seeks to interpret. That is to say that, given the innate instability of language itself, a linguistic interpretation of a linguistic text is inescapably indeterminate (*see* DECONSTRUCTION, THEORY).

In *Joyce's Uncertainty Principle* (1987), Phillip Herring argues that James Joyce used uncertainty as a device designed to provoke the reader to further reflection.

Index librorum prohibitorum (Index of forbidden books) A list of books compiled by the Vatican that Roman Catholics were forbidden to read. The Index, as it was known, was updated and revised periodically from the 16th to the 20th centuries. As a result of strong criticism during Vatican Council II, the Index was abandoned in 1966.

Indian/Pakistani American literature As recent arrivals, post-1965, the development of literary cultures in these two communities is still in its infancy. Nevertheless, they have produced at least two outstanding writers from India, Bharati Mukherjee and Meena Alexander, and at least one from Pakistan, Zulfikar Ghose. Mukherjee is well known as the author of *The Middleman and Other Stories* (1988), a short story collection that won the National Book Critics Circle Award for fiction in 1988, and her novel *Jasmine* (1989), which attempts to help create an understanding of the Indian-American immigrant.: "The people I write about are culturally and politically several hundred years old. . . . They have shed old identities, taken on new ones, and learned to hide the scars." Meena Alexander expresses the immigrant dilemma in her memoir *Fault Lines* (1993). Speaking of the "multiple anchorages" she experiences, as one who has lived on three continents, ". . . it is a fiction—a very dangerous one—to think we can play endlessly in postmodernist fashion, because our ethnicity is located in our bodies and comes in as a pressure to resist this sort of fracturing." A younger Indian-American writer, Jhumpa Lahiri, the daughter of Indian parents won the Pulitzer Prize for her collection of stories *Intepreter of Maladies* (1997).

Zulfikar Ghose is a prolific author, born in 1935 in what is now Pakistan. Having witnessed the partition riots in the late 1940s, he is profoundly skeptical of nationalist claims and has lived most of his life in England, South America, and the United States. His connection to his native land is such that his autobiography is titled *The Confessions of a Native Alien* (1965). Nevertheless, he has written one novel about Pakistan in the 1950s, *The Murder of Aziz Khan* (1967), which exposes the machinations of the ruling class in that decade.

Gurleen Grewal's "Indian-American Literature" and Sunil Sharma's "Pakistani-American Literature" appear in *New Immigrant Literatures in the United States* (1996), ed. Alpana Sharma Knippling.

individualism   The social doctrine that the individual is the primary element of society, taking precedence over the collective. The doctrine makes its first significant appearance in the Western world among the Sophists of ancient Greece. It reemerged in the RENAISSANCE with the invention of the printing press. Private reading opened the doors to a wide range of perspectives for the individual reader. This activity, when directed to the reading of the BIBLE, played a critical role in the REFORMATION. In this heady atmosphere it became possible for some individuals to break through the confining structures of authority and law in order to "fashion a self." Insofar as Renaissance individualism was associated with unbridled egoism (*see* MACHIAVEL), it represented a profound threat to the social order. Shakespeare's major VILLAINS, Richard III, Iago, and Edmund in *King Lear*, are fierce individualists, proclaiming their defiance of the social status quo. On the other hand, Shakespeare, perhaps thinking of that Renaissance individualist whose writings were an important source for him, Michel de Montaigne, created the first "self-conscious" character in literature, Hamlet.

In *Myths of Modern Individualism*, the critic Ian Watt focuses on four archetypal individuals: Faust (*see* FAUSTIAN THEME), DON JUAN, Don Quixote, and Robinson Crusoe. The earliest of these is the 16th-century Faust, whose experiments in magic represent both the threat and the possible benefits of modern science. Notable in Christopher Marlowe's rendering of the myth (*The Tragical History of Doctor Faustus*, 1588) is Faust's refusal to disavow his individual identity even as he is dragged into hell.

Goethe's 19th-century version (*Faust, Part I*, 1808; *Part II*, 1832), on the other hand, reflects a greater tolerance of the individualist ethos as Faust is triumphantly welcomed into heaven. Thomas Mann's 20th-century version (*Doktor Faustus*, 1947) reverts to the 16th-century version, seeing the individualism of the Reformation ironically realized in the German people's pact with the evil of Nazism, the enemy of the individual.

Two names in American literature that dominate the discussion of individualism are Ralph Waldo Emerson and Henry David Thoreau. These two champions of the individual—Emerson, the theorist, and Thoreau, the theorist/practitioner—reflect a radical commitment to individualism. Emerson, whose assertion of the need for the individual's self-reliance, increased during his lifetime as he witnessed both in America and Europe the growth of commercialism and materialism and the conformity that they fostered. Thoreau extended Emerson's ideas of the links between the self and nature by building a hut in the woods (described in his best-known book, *Walden*, 1854) desiring to live a life of simplicity, independence, magnanimity, and trust, where he developed his idea, among others, of civil disobedience.

Emerson's and Thoreau's ideas continue to reverberate in American intellectual life, forming important elements in the development of William James's and John Dewey's PRAGMATISM. The critic Charles Mitchell cites two examples of the Emersonian influence on the American writers W. E. B. DuBois and William Carlos Williams. DuBois called for "a new interpretation of the word freedom. There must be left a wide individualism and yet no individualism must be allowed to infringe on others' freedom. . . ." Williams asserted in his poetry that the freedom of the modern poet is not freedom with its implication of sheer anarchy, but "liberty, disciplined power. . . . only in this way can that which is common, commonly possessed, be preserved among differences."

Charles E. Mitchell's *Individualism and Its Discontents* (1997) traces the influence of Emerson's ideas in the 20th century.

induction   A 16th-century term for an introduction or prologue to a play or poem. Thomas Sackville's induction to a COMPLAINT included in *A Mirror for Magistrates* (1563) is a fine example of mid-16th-century poetry. The opening of Shakespeare's *The Taming of the Shrew* (frequently omitted in modern productions) contains an induction relating to a drunken tinker, Christopher Sly.

industrial revolution   The social, economic, and cultural changes in English life brought about by the shift from home manufacture to large factories in the late 18th and 19th centuries. The social evils of the factory system were explored in a number of Victorian novels including Elizabeth Gaskell's *Mary Barton* (1848) and *North and South* (1855), and Charles Dickens's memorable study of life in a textile town, *Hard Times* (1854).

influence   In literary study the impact of events, ideas, or persons on subsequent literature. In this sense, the word contains the same somewhat vague character that it does in ordinary usage. When the influence on a given text is another, earlier text, the older text is frequently designated as a SOURCE.

The critic Harold Bloom employs a special use of the term. Bloom speaks of "the anxiety of influence," a condition in which "strong poets" view the great canonical writers as Freudian father figures who must be overcome by a process of first "misreading" and then "rewriting." In other words, a "strong" (that is, resisting) writer recognizes an earlier writer as the "father," the personal precursor, whom he or she is determined to surpass. Thus the act of writing becomes an AGON or contest with the predecessor, a continually renewed Oedipal struggle, in which the strong poet must proceed through six phases in order to achieve mastery.

Harold Bloom's theory is worked out in *The Anxiety of Influence: A Theory of Poetry* (1973).

inkhornism   An ELIZABETHAN term for a word or phrase that reflected a newly coined term, borrowed from another language, particularly Latin. The term was used to ridicule the pedantry and pomposity of the new coinages. In *Love's Labour's Lost*, Shakespeare satirizes inkhornism in the figure of the bombastic Don Armado, who at one point asks "Dost thou infamonize me among potentates?"

in medias res (in the middle of things)   A NARRATIVE convention in which a story begins in the middle of an important action rather than at its chronological beginning. The technique is associated with the classical EPIC, exemplified in Homer's *Iliad*, which begins not with the abduction of Helen or the Greek expedition to Troy, but with the anger of Achilles in the middle of the Trojan War. The practice is a common feature of modern literature and film, where it frequently involves the use of the FLASHBACK.

inscape/instress   Terms employed by the Victorian poet Gerard Manley Hopkins to describe certain features of nature. Hopkins uses *inscape* to single out the individuating character of a natural thing, that which distinguishes it from everything else, its "thisness." *Instress* is the force that gives a form to inscape, enabling it to be perceived by an observer. Hopkins's poetry strives to capture both qualities by representing creatures whose actions are at one with their nature, as in his poem "The Windhover" (1877):

> *I caught this morning morning's minion, king-*
> *dom of daylight's dauphin, dapple-dawn-drawn Falcon, in his*
> *riding*
> *Of the rolling level . . .*

The sound and rhythm of these lines duplicate the swerving flight of the windhover, noted for its ability to hover in the air. The poem attempts to function as the verbal equivalent of the windhover's essence and form, its inscape and instress.

Walter J. Ong's *Hopkins, the Self and God* (1986) provides a cogent analysis of the terms.

inspiration   In literary study, the traditional term for the source of a writer's creativity. The classical convention located a writer's inspiration in the MUSES. Since the Romantic period, writers have tended to focus on the faculty of the IMAGINATION as the source of poetic activity.

   Modern writers sometimes describe inspiration as a demonic spell, but they resoundingly assert that what is at work in the creative process is a combination of calculation and inspiration. As T. S. Eliot phrased it, "The idea, of course, simply comes, but upon arrival is subject to prolonged manipulation."

T. S. Eliot's comment is from his *The Use of Poetry and the Use of Criticism* (1933).

intentional fallacy   According to the New Critics W. K. Wimsatt and Monroe Beardsley, the fallacy of locating the meaning of a work of literature in the intention of its AUTHOR. Wimsatt and Beardsley argued that, in the majority of cases, it was neither possible nor desirable to search for the meaning in the author's intention. Instead, the meaning was to be determined from the TEXT itself, the words on the paper. They also listed as fallacious the attempt to determine the meaning from the experience of the reader. *See* AFFECTIVE FALLACY.

interactive computer fiction   A term for stories created in part by decisions made by the "reader," in this case the computer user. In order to proceed with the reading, the reader/user must solve problems requiring reasoning, guesswork, or intuition. As a result, the reader/user experiences an unusually high degree of involvement with the text. In the words of O. B. Hardison, "You do not read about an adventure. You have an adventure."

Among the best-known interactive stories is *Adventure*, a pioneer work that originated in the '60s and has undergone a number of updates and revisions; *Where in the World Is Carmen Sandiego?* (1986), a mystery novel; and *Mindwheel* (1984), by the well-known poet Robert Pinsky. In *Mindwheel*, the reader is asked to occupy the minds of a murdered rock star, a dead military dictator, a poet, and a scientific genius.

Some critics have viewed the growing popularity of this type of fiction as evidence that the age of the BOOK is coming to a close (*see* CYBERPUNK, HYPERTEXT).

O. B. Hardison considers some broad-ranging implications in his *Disappearing Through the Skylight* (1989).

interdisciplinarity   Insofar as it applies to literature, interdisciplinarity refers to the practice of approaching FICTION, POETRY and DRAMA from the standpoint of other disciplines such as psychology, sociology, or history. Alternatively, the term may refer to the use of literary texts in a nonliterary discipline. Both developments have become increasingly evident in recent years. Thus it is not unusual to encounter novels such as F. Scott Fitzgerald's *The Great Gatsby* (1925) or John Dos Passos's *U.S.A.* trilogy (1930–31) in a course on 20th-century American history. In many respects, the emergence of THEORY in the latter half of the

20th century virtually dictated an interdisciplinary approach—so much so that a backlash developed charging that too many interdisciplinary approaches lacked "intellectual coherence." On the other hand, others have argued that existing disciplines are too narrow and specialized to address the complexity of modern culture. They point to exceptional thinkers who have burst the bounds of a single discipline.

In America the best example of an interdisciplinary literary figure in the 20th century is Kenneth Burke, who began his career as a writer of poetry and fiction in the 1920s, moving into literary criticism in the 1930s and formal RHETORIC in the 1940s, which he transformed into a new RHETORIC by employing insights from anthropology, sociology, psychology, and semantics. Not surprisingly, Burke's work explores the interconnectedness of human affairs through the miracle of language. *See* DRAMATISM; SYMBOLIC ACTION.

Marjorie Garber's *Academic Instincts* (2001) takes a perceptive view of both sides of the interdisciplinarity argument.

interior monologue In FICTION, a NARRATIVE technique in which a character's intimate thoughts and impressions are related directly and immediately. For the reader the effect is, in the words of novelist and critic David Lodge, "like wearing earphones plugged into someone's brain, and monitoring the subject's impressions, reflections, questions, memories, and fantasies as they are triggered either by physical sensations or the association of ideas."

The term is sometimes used interchangeably with *stream of consciousness*, although increasingly there has been a tendency to define stream of consciousness as a type of fiction that represents a character's consciousness, and interior monologue as one form of that representation, others being free indirect discourse and simple first-person narration. (*See* FREE INDIRECT STYLE.)

The best-known example of interior monologue is Molly Bloom's soliloquy, the closing section of James Joyce's novel *Ulysses* (1922). Other novels featuring interior monologues include *Manhattan Transfer* (1925) by John Dos Passos, *To the Lighthouse* (1927) by Virginia Woolf, and *The Sound and the Fury* (1929) and *As I Lay Dying* (1930) by William Faulkner.

interlude A type of short play that achieved popularity in 16th-century England. The term traditionally has been used to describe a play brief enough to be performed between the courses of a banquet, but it now appears that "interlude" was widely used to refer to any kind of theatrical entertainment. The best known of the interlude authors was John Heywood, a poet and satirist as well as a playwright. Heywood's most successful interludes are *The Four P's* (1521), based on a medieval French FARCE, and *Johan Johan the Husband, Tyb His Wife and Sir John the Priest* (1533), a comedy of cuckoldry whose title is ironically echoed in the Peter Greenaway film *The Cook, the Thief, His Wife and Her Lover* (1990).

With the emergence of the public theaters near the end of the 16th century, interludes fell out of favor.

David Bevington's *From Mankind to Marlowe* (1962) provides an overview of the development of dramatic form during the 16th century.

internal rhyme   In VERSE, the rhyming of two or more words in a single line, as in Johnny Mercer's song "That Old Black Magic": "The mate, that fate had me created for."

interpolation   The insertion of lines into another text by someone other than the original AUTHOR of the TEXT. Well-known examples are the insertions into Shakespeare's *Macbeth* of lines and songs from *The Witch* a play by Shakespeare's contemporary, Thomas Middleton.

interpretation   The process of construing or constructing meaning in a TEXT. The difference between "construing" and "constructing" points up the difference between traditional and contemporary views of interpretation. Traditionally, the meaning of a text resides in the intention of the author or, as in NEW CRITICISM, within the "text itself." From these perspectives, the aim of interpretation is to extract or discern the meaning within. The opposing view rejects either the idea of a determinate meaning, as in DECONSTRUCTION, or the idea that the meaning is "within" the text. The latter view is the position of READER RESPONSE CRITICISM and RECEPTION THEORY, both of which argue that meaning is "constructed" by a reader in interaction with the text.

Another sense of interpretation refers to a performance of a play or film. The overall performance usually represents the director's interpretation, while an individual performance within the play may represent the actor's interpretation.

HERMENEUTICS is the study of the theory of interpretation, the principles governing the practice of interpreting.

For discussion of the relationship of interpretation to evaluation, *see* VALUE JUDGMENT.

intertextuality   A term associated with POSTSTRUCTURALISM, which rejects the idea of a TEXT as a single, autonomous entity created by a single author. Any given text is, instead, an assemblage of prior texts, in the words of Vincent Leitch, "a set of relations with other texts. Its system of language, its grammar, its lexicon drag along numerous bits and pieces—traces—of history so that the text resembles a cultural Salvation Army outlet. . . ."

The French critic Julia Kristeva coined the term, which she derived from the theory of DIALOGISM formulated by Mikhail Bakhtin. Dialogism posits the presence of a variety of "voices" in a text. These voices contribute to the text's pluralist nature—its shared identity with other texts. In effect Kristeva has added to dialogism the principle that all language is made up of prior uses of language.

Broadly speaking, there are two types of intertextuality: citation and presupposition. Citation includes not only direct quotation and allusion, but also literary conventions, imitation, parody, and unconscious sources. Presupposition involves assumptions regarding the reader, the situation being referred to, and its context. In Anthony Trollope's *The Eustace Diamonds* (1872), for example, the first two chapters are devoted to the character of Lady Eustace. At the beginning of Chapter Three, the narrator "begs his reader not to believe that that opulent and aristocratic Becky Sharp [Lady Eustace] is to assume the dignity of heroine in the following pages." The passage assumes (1) that the reader is aware of the convention of being directly addressed in a kind of authorial aside, (2) that it is reasonable to assume that if the opening chapters of a novel are devoted to a character, that character will be the "heroine," and (3) that the reader will be familiar with the character of Becky Sharp, the protagonist of William Makepeace Thackeray's *Vanity Fair* (1848).

Citational intertextuality is a prominent feature of postmodernist literature, which relies heavily on references to earlier styles and conventions, engages in extensive allusions that its knowing audience will recognize, and consistently calls attention to itself as being made up of other texts. In this respect intertextuality characterizes a cultural sense that everything has already been said, and that the ironic consciousness of this condition is a kind of mastery over it.

Julia Kristeva's theories are available in *The Kristeva Reader*, edited by Toril Moi (1986). *Intertextuality and Contemporary American Fiction* (1989), edited by Patrick O'Donnell and Robert Con Davis, offers essays on the theory and practice of intertextuality in literature, film, and television.

invention In RHETORIC, the process of discovering the information that will make up the body of the speaker or writer's presentation, formulating a thesis and finding good reasons to support the thesis.

As a term in literary study, invention is rarely used in modern criticism, although as employed in the RENAISSANCE and the 18th century it carried the force of a vague compliment to an author's imaginative ability.

Some recent writers have used the term as a kind of metaphor for the introduction of a new idea, as in Garry Wills's *Inventing America* (1978) and Harold Bloom's *Shakespeare and the Invention of the Human* (1998).

invocation   The appeal to the MUSE that is a convention of the EPIC poem. The poet is asking the muse for poetic inspiration and/or knowledge in order to proceed with his poem. The convention was established in the *Iliad* of Homer, who invoked the muses both at the beginning of the poem and to introduce his famous "Catalogue of the Ships."

In the Prologue to Shakespeare's *Henry V*, the Chorus invokes the muse in the opening line:

> *O for a Muse of fire, that would ascend*
> *The brightest heaven of invention.*

Irish-American literature   In its broad outline, the history of the Irish Americans can be summarized in a phrase: the movement from the "shanty" to, in 1960, the White House. The landmark along the way is the Great Hunger, the potato famine of 1847–1850, when more than a million "Banished Children of Eve" (the title of Peter Quinn's 1994 novel about these refugees) crowded into the large cities of the United States. There had been an earlier wave, in the 18th century, when thousands of Irish Protestants (many of them of Scotch descent) left Northern Ireland to seek their fortunes in the new world. This group quickly assimilated into mainstream Anglo-Saxon culture, numbering among their descendants many presidents before and since John F. Kennedy. But it was the 19th-century Catholic Irish, most of them impoverished peasants, who retained their ethnic identity well into the 20th century. The earliest authentic voice of this group was Finley Peter Dunne. In 1893, he created, in a series of newspaper sketches, his spokesman, Martin Dooley, an Irish immigrant bartender on the South Side of Chicago. Mr. Dooley, his language coated with a brogue, soon assumed the role of a national sage. Mr. Dooley's neighborhood produced another Irish-American voice, this one as serious and somber as Mr. Dooley was witty and sly. James T. Farrell powerfully depicted Irish tenement life in the Chicago slums. In his Studs Lonigan trilogy (1932–35) and his Danny O'Neill tetralogy (1936–53), Farrell looked at the Irish poor as imprisoned by poverty, to be sure, but even more, by their own fantasies and their need to be affirmed by others.

By the 1940s, the Irish had for the most part left poverty behind. Their rise had been fueled, in part by their skills in politics, assisted by their easy charm and way with words. The political Irish are captured in Edwin O'Connor's *The*

Last Hurrah (1956) and, with greater literary skill, in William Kennedy's novels focused on the Irish in Albany: *Legs* (1975), *Billy Phelan's Greatest Game* (1978), *Ironweed* (1983), *Quinn's Book* (1988) and *Very Old Bones* (1992). The last two of these novels deal with the Famine generation. The others are set in the years between 1920 and 1950.

After World War II, Irish Americans, along with millions of others, abandoned their urban enclaves and staked their claim on the embodiment of the American dream, the house in the suburbs. The view of prominent Irish-American journalists and novelists, such as Jimmy Breslin (*Table Money*, 1986), Pete Hamill (*Loving Women*, 1989) and the sociologist/novelist Andrew Greeley (*That Most Distressful Nation*, 1972) is that something died in Irish Americans when they moved to the suburbs; they had become homogenized, the children of Democratic ward politics had become right-wing Republicans, lured in that direction by a predominantly Irish-American Catholic hierarchy.

In a series of novels that explore the inner life of the suburban Irish, Alice McDermott depicts the quiet desperation underlying their personal lives. Conditioned by their culture, the characters in *That Night* (1987), *At Weddings and Wakes* (1992), and *Charming Billy* (1998) are flawed, often frozen, but beautifully realized human beings.

In this respect, McDermott is extending the work of Elizabeth Cullinan (*House of Gold*, 1970) Maureen Howard, *Bridgeport Bus* (1965), and Mary Gordon, *Final Payments* (1978), all three sensitive, critical recorders of postwar Irish-American society. All four may be seen as exploring the territory of the greatest Irish-American writer, Eugene O'Neill, whose crowning achievement, *Long Day's Journey Into Night* (1941, first produced in 1956) depicts the dissolution of an Irish-American family, each one of whom is tragically conflicted with, and mutually dependent upon, the others.

Something of a transitional figure in the loss of Irish identity is the extraordinarily gifted SHORT STORY writer and novelist, Flannery O'Connor. On the one hand, her fiction exhibits no references to things Irish. On the other, the major theme in her work is theological, specifically Catholic, a reminder that the Americanization of Irish Catholics has not as yet extended to their religious affiliation.

Other notable Irish-American achievements in DRAMA are William Alfred's evocation of an Irish community in Brooklyn, *Hogan's Goat* (1966), and John Patrick Shanley's *Doubt* (2004), a searing depiction of the church's response to the alleged molestation of a boy by a priest.

In the comic vein are two splendid PICARESQUE novels, J. P. Donleavy's *The Ginger Man* (1958), an American's adventure studying in Ireland, and John Kennedy Toole's cult classic *The Confederacy of Dunces* (1969), with its impossible, unforgettable protagonist Ignatius Reilly. Comedy and misery mingle memorably in Frank McCourt's memoirs *Angela's Ashes* (1996), *'Tis* (1999), and *Teacher Man* (2005) all three works perfect illustrations of the principle of another Irishman, Samuel Beckett: "There's nothing funnier than unhappiness."

Among historical novels, Thomas Flanagan's trilogy (*The Year of the French* [1979], *The Tenants of Time* [1988], and *The End of the Hunt* [1994]) traces the history of Ireland from 1798 to the death of Michael Collins in 1922.

In FILM, Edward Burns has caught the Irish-American suburbanites at the point where their children are developing a new moral code (*The Brothers McMullen*, 1995). Jim Sheridan's *In America* (2003) captures the experience of a different kind of immigrant family, one headed by an aspiring actor, coming to grips with life in a New York tenement.

Modern Irish American Fiction: A Reader (1989) offers a selection of recent work Charles Fanning's *The Irish Voice in America* (1990) is a useful survey.

Irish renaissance   A term used to describe the period (from about 1885 until the eve of World War II) when a number of Irish-born writers produced extraordinary achievements in *poetry*, *drama*, and *fiction*. This creative outburst was fueled in part by the revival of a national identity associated with the attempt to restore the Gaelic language, and by the movement to secure Home Rule (and later independence) from England. Among the artists associated with the period are four of the 20th century's greatest writers in their respective genres: William Butler Yeats (poetry), James Joyce (fiction), and John Millington Synge and Sean O'Casey (drama). (*See also* ABBEY THEATRE.)

irony   A term with a number of distinct references. Among its common uses in literary study are 1) as a rhetorical and literary device, 2) as a mode of literature, 3) as a way of perceiving life itself.

1. Irony refers to the technique of implying something very different from what one is ostensibly saying. The intention of an ironic statement can range from the comically light: "It is a truth universally acknowledged that a young man in possession of a good fortune must be in want of a wife" (Jane Austen, *Pride and Prejudice*) to the ominously dark: "Someone must have been telling lies about Joseph K. for without having done anything wrong, he was arrested one fine morning" (Franz Kafka, *The Trial*).

2. *Socratic irony* is a term used to describe Socrates' technique of feigning ignorance by asking innocent questions that would eventually trap his opponents in a debate. Implicit in Socratic irony is the notion of dissembling, pretending to be something one is not. This idea is also present in classical comedy in the

STOCK CHARACTER known as the EIRON. Disguising himself as a low-born or mentally incompetent figure, the eiron eventually triumphs over his opponent the ALAZON, the pompous braggart.

In classical tragedy irony is a structural feature of plays such as Sophocles' *Oedipus Rex*, in which the murderer Oedipus sets out to expose turns out to be himself. The term dramatic irony thus refers to any situation in which the audience has knowledge that the character lacks.

3. In the 18th and 19th centuries, irony underwent a transformation from a rhetorical and literary device to a broad-ranging, all-encompassing idea. In the words of critic Wayne Booth, "by the end of the Romantic period, it had become a grand Hegelian concept . . . or a synonym for romanticism; or even an essential attribute of God." This attitude, sometimes called Romantic or cosmic irony, developed from the belief that life is inherently a mix of opposites and that the most appropriate response to its double-edged nature is to assume the role of a detached, knowing spectator.

In the 20th century irony plays a central role in NEW CRITICISM, where the term is used to denote an essential characteristic of poetry, the capacity of poetic language to reconcile opposites. Thus, for example, in Cleanth Brooks's new critical reading of Keats's "Ode on a Grecian Urn," the ironic meaning of the poem is that "the frozen moment of loveliness is more dynamic than the fluid world of reality, *only* because it is frozen." In this sense irony means something very close to PARADOX.

In the MYTH CRITICISM of Northrop Frye, irony stands as a GENRE along with COMEDY, TRAGEDY, and ROMANCE, allied to the seasonal myths that Frye sees as underlying all of literature. In his scheme, irony is the myth of winter, a self-conscious genre in which heroism and meaningful action have been lost. In this sense it is the characteristic genre of the 20th century.

Wayne Booth's *The Rhetoric of Irony* (1974) is a selective and insightful analysis. Cleanth Brooks's analysis of Keats's poem appears in his *The Well Wrought Urn* (1947). Northrop Frye's use of the term appears in his *Anatomy of Criticism* (1957).

Italian-American literature

The major wave of Italian immigration occurred between 1890 and 1920. Most of these immigrants came from a peasant culture where literacy was the exception, not the rule. Italian-American fiction had to wait for a second generation, vigorously present in the novels of Pietro di Donato and John Fante.

Di Donato, born in New Jersey of immigrant parents, joined the Communist Party on the day two Italian immigrants, Sacco and Vanzetti, were executed for a crime they did not commit. His sense of outrage and passion informs his novel

Christ in Concrete (1939), a classic account of working-class immigrant life. John Fante's *Wait Until Spring, Bondini* (1938) and *Dago Red* (1940) depict immigrant workers and their families as they struggle to maintain their dignity, adapting to life in America. In contrast to these two working-class novelists, is the sophisticated poet John Ciardi, whose work includes a translation of Dante's *Divine Comedy* (1954).

The 1960s saw the emergence of the writer who was to have a profound influence on the image of Italian Americans throughout the world. Mario Puzo's *The Fortunate Pilgrim* (1965) depicted life in Little Italy with sensitivity and insight, but it was his novel *The Godfather* (1969), transformed by director Francis Ford Coppola into two of the most acclaimed achievements in film history, that created, in the words of the critic Fred Gardaphe, "a mythic filter through which Italian-American culture would henceforth be read." If so, that filter has been intensified by the films of the equally talented director Martin Scorsese *Mean Streets* (1970) and *Goodfellas* (1990). Following these powerful films is the enormously successful television series, *The Sopranos*. Where few would dispute the cinematic brilliance of these works, many Italian Americans are upset at the impression created by these films. Among the works, less sensational but truer to the reality of ordinary Italian Americans are three novels by women: *Umbertina* (1979) by Helen Barolini, *Paper Fish* (1980) by Tina de Rosa, and *Ghost Dance* (1986) by Carol Maso, all three exploring and explicating their culture from the experience of Italian-American women. In addition to her own creative writing, Barolini has made an important contribution in publicizing the work of a new generation of Italian women writers in her collection *The Dream Book* (1985).

Unquestionably the most important Italian-American novelist is Don DeLillo, whose work has not generally touched on the ethnic theme. However, in the penultimate section of his acclaimed novel *Underground* (1997), he depicts life in the Italian section of the Bronx in the early 1950s.

Fred L. Gardaphe's *Italian Signs, American Streets* (1996) surveys the development of Italian American literature.

j

Jacobean   English literature in the reign of James I (1603–25). (*Jacobean* is derived from the Latin word for *James*.) In contrast to the optimism and promise of the ELIZABETHAN era, Jacobean literature was colored by darker, doubting tones. The conflict between Parliament and King, carefully controlled under Elizabeth, grew perceptibly sharper during the reign of her successor, whose insistence on royal divine right exacerbated tensions.

The new atmosphere produced a literature distinct from, but no less brilliant than, the Elizabethan. In poetry, John Donne and his followers developed the unique style of METAPHYSICAL POETRY. In prose, the essays of Francis Bacon along with his scientific studies set the stage for scientific development later in the century. The drama of the period displayed the satiric comedy of Ben Jonson, the brooding tragedies of John Webster, the dark comedies of Shakespeare. But the greatest glory of the Jacobean era were Shakespeare's great tragedies: *Macbeth*, *Othello*, *King Lear*, and *Antony and Cleopatra*.

For an illuminating contrast of the two periods, see F. P. Wilson's *Elizabethan and Jacobean* (1945).

Jansenism   A 17th-century reform movement within the Catholic Church that had a significant impact on the intellectual life of the time. Jansenism took its name from a Dutch bishop, Cornelis Jansen, who argued that divine grace is not earned by good works but is arbitrarily bestowed by God on some and not on others. This doctrine, which hewed closely to the doctrine of predestination in CALVINISM, created a storm of controversy.

The movement had its intellectual center at PORT-ROYAL, a school that attracted a number of prominent intellectuals, among them Blaise Pascal, the mathematician and theologian. Pascal defended the cause of Jansenism against the attacks of the JESUITS in his *Provincial Letters* (1656–57), but despite his eloquence, the papal authorities condemned the movement, and, in 1709, the buildings at Port-Royal were demolished.

The term *Jansenist* has been applied to modern religious writers, such as the French novelist François Mauriac (*A Woman of the Pharisees*, 1941), who present characters apparently devoid of free will.

Japanese-American literature   Japanese Americans employ specific terms in order to identify each generation:

issei   first generation
nisei   second generation
sansei   third generation
yonsei   fourth generation

The first generation immigrated either to Hawaii or the Pacific Coast in the years between 1883 to 1924. In 1924, an exclusionary immigration law was enacted effectively cutting off the flow of immigrants from Asia. Then in 1942 came the central traumatizing event in the history of Japanese Americans—their relocation to internment camps, where they were confined until 1944. However painful the experience, it had one salutary effect: Internment unlocked dormant, unexpressed emotions and fueled a search for ethnic identity. on the part of nisei, sausei, and yonsei.

One of the first Japanese-American novels dealing with the impact of internment is Monica Sone's *Nisei Daughter* (1953; 1979), whose heroine, evacuated to a camp with her parents, leaves the camp only to discover that she's not accepted in white society. Particularly poignant is John Okada's *No No Boy* (1957; 1976), which portrays the effect of war and internment on a young nisei. Lured into rejecting the draft because of his unstable mother's fanatical devotion to Japan, Ichiro refuses to be drafted and is imprisoned. As a result, he invites the wrath of his nisei friends desperate to be accepted as American. He ends up totally alienated and despised. Yoshiko Uchida's *Picture Bride* (1987), a story of a woman who immigrates to America as part of an arranged marriage. (For a book of poems with the same title, see Cathy Song's *Picture Bride* [1983] in KOREAN-AMERICAN LITERATURE). The experience of three generations of Japanese Canadians is recounted in Joy Kogawa's *Obrason* (1981). Another notable Japanese-American work is Cynthia Kadahota's *The Floating World* (1989), a novel that captures the Japanese-American search for a true home in America.

Benzi Zhang, "Japanese American Literature" in *New Immigrant Literatures in the United States*, ed. Alpana Sharma Knippling (1996).

jargon   A term used to describe the specialized terminology of particular groups or professions. Generally used in a derogatory sense, it carries an implicit criticism that those who employ jargon do so in order either to exclude outsiders or to create the impression of complexity or profundity. Literary critics have often been accused of using jargon, particularly in recent years.

Many within and without the university complain that theory-influenced critics not only introduce too many new terms but that they encase them in unreadable sentences. John Mullan, a reviewer in the *London Review of Books*, after quoting an impenetrable sentence from a book under review asked, "Is there any good reason why such a book should be so hard to follow?" Marjorie Garber holds that "the history of jargon is the history of ideas in the making." Even if true, it still leaves Mullan's question unanswered.

Marjorie Garber's *Academic Instincts* (2001) devotes a chapter to the subject. John Mullan's comments appear in the May 5, 2005, issue of the *London Review of Books*.

jazz A form of MUSIC developed by African-American musicians containing distinctive rhythmic patterns and harmonies, in which improvisation plays an important role. The influence of jazz on literature is most apparent in AFRICAN-AMERICAN LITERATURE, particularly that associated with the HARLEM RENAISSANCE. Less apparent is the indebtedness to jazz rhythms of poets as different as T. S. Eliot and the BEAT writers. Jack Kerouac, for example, considered the jazz saxophonist Charlie Parker one of the major influences on his writing.

jealousy Although in general use a synonym for ENVY, in literature the term usually refers to a lover's or spouse's fear of infidelity. Thus, as a theme, jealousy is entangled with the theme of romantic LOVE, either as its perversion, or, as in some modern texts, its inevitable consequence. However represented, the most striking feature of, in Shakespeare's words, "the green-ey'd monster" is its obsessional nature: how it gradually consumes the life of its victim, converting him or her into a parody of a detective, hunting for clues, interpreting evidence, entrapping the real or imagined "criminal." The guilt or innocence of the suspected lover can play a critical role in the action of the story, as for example in Shakespeare's *Othello* or *The Winter's Tale*, but it may be of only marginal significance, as it is in many modern novels, where the emphasis is on the psychology of the jealous person. Such is the case in Alain Robbe-Grillet's *Jealousy* (1957), in which the nameless NARRATOR seems to have no other existence except to be the embodiment of jealousy. The French title of Robbe-Grillet's novel, *Jalousie*, emphasizes another recurrent feature of the jealous mind: the desire to see the act of infidelity. In the novel, the narrator views the suspected lovers through a louvre shutter, which in French is called a *jalousie*. This voyeuristic element is a recurrent feature of the jealousy theme. Thus Shakespeare's Othello demands that Iago provide him "ocular proof" of Desdemona's guilt.

A French novel with a distinctive view of the subject is Madame de La Fayette's *The Princess of Clèves* (1678), notable for its inclusion of two reactions to jealousy: The husband of the princess, obsessing over his wife's acknowledged love for another man, hires spies, and mistakenly concludes that she is unfaithful. He soon falls ill and dies. His wife, now that she is free and can marry the man she loves, refuses to do so because she does not believe that he will remain faithful. She chooses peace of mind over the pain of jealousy.

The psychology of jealousy achieved its most powerful rendering in Marcel Proust's *Remembrance of Things Past* (1913–27), in which the personal disintegration the jealous lovers undergo mirrors the collapse of their society. Among the more disturbing examples of jealousy at work is the account in Vladimir Nabokov's *Lolita* (1955), in which the narrator's jealousy is the culmination of the narcissism that underlies his passion for Lolita.

Rosemary Lloyd's *Closer & Closer Apart* (1995) examines the way jealousy "acts as a trope for both consuming and creating art and literature."

jeremiad   A scathing denunciation of the evils of a society. The term derives from the preaching of the Old Testament prophet Jeremiah, who was imprisoned for his outspoken criticism. In American history, the form is associated with the fierce sermons of 17th-century Puritan preachers in New England.

Examples of modern American jeremiads include H. L. Mencken's essays and James Baldwin's *The Fire Next Time* (1963).

Sacvan Bercovitch's *The American Jeremiad* (1978) ties the Puritan jeremiad to the development of American nationalism.

jest books   A collection of tales and extended jokes popular in 16th-century England. A well-known example is *An Hundred Merry Tales* (1526), a popular jest book alluded to in Shakespeare's *Much Ado About Nothing*. In that play, the witty Beatrice complains that her verbal sparring partner Benedick has slandered her by saying that "I had my wit out of the *Hundred Merry Tales*."

A famous descendant of the ELIZABETHAN jest books was *Joe Miller's Jests*, first published in 1739, which in various revised editions maintained its popularity until the end of the 19th century.

Jesuits   Members of the Society of Jesus, the Roman Catholic order of priests founded by Saint Ignatius Loyola in 1534. The best-known and most controversial of the Catholic orders, the Jesuits have been alternately praised for their intellectual discipline and condemned for their alleged duplicity and cunning.

The representation of Jesuits in literature reflects their controversial image. On the one hand they have been satirized by John Donne (*Ignatius His Conclave*, 1610), and by Voltaire (*Candide*, 1759); represented as inquisitors by Dostoyevsky (*The Brothers Karamazov*, 1879–80); portrayed by Thomas Mann, in the character of Leo Naptha, as brilliant but unstable (*The Magic Mountain*, 1927); and treated with dislike but begrudging respect in James Joyce's *A Portrait of the Artist as a Young Man* (1914). More recently they have served as models of inner anguish in two notable films, *The Mission* (1988) and *Black Robe* (1992).

In the 17th and 18th centuries, Jesuit colleges achieved considerable distinction for the plays written and produced there. Composed either in Latin or the vernacular, these plays were not limited to religious subjects but frequently embraced historical and classical themes. A few even ventured into political satire.

The Jesuit contribution to nondramatic literature is evident in the work of the ELIZABETHAN poet and martyr Robert Southwell and, most notably, in the experimental verse of Gerard Manley Hopkins, a major VICTORIAN poet.

In America, the Jesuit critics William Lynch (*Christ and Apollo*, 1958) and Walter J. Ong (*Orality and Literacy*, 1982) have made major contributions to their fields.

J. C. H. Aveling's *The Jesuits* (1981), a history of the Order, contains a chapter on literature.

Jewish-American literature   Although some Jews had settled in America as early as the 17th century, the great wave of Jewish immigration did not occur until the period from the 1880s to the 1920s, the vast majority from the ghettos of eastern Europe. Denied full citizenship there and subject to periodic persecutions (pogroms), they fled in search of freedom and economic opportunity. The literary text that commemorates that quest is the famous SONNET inscribed on the base of the Statue of Liberty. Its author, Emma Lazarus, herself a Jewish American, voiced a sentiment meant for all immigrants, but it had a special poignance for the Jews.

An early example of the literature that emerged from this migration is Abraham Cahan's *The Rise of David Levinsky* (1917), a novel tracing the career of a successful Russian-Jewish immigrant and the price he pays for his success.

A decade later came the works of Michael Gold (*Jews Without Money*, 1930), Henry Roth (*Call it Sleep*, 1934) and the playwright Clifford Odets (*Awake and Sing*, 1935), depicting the struggles of Jewish families in New York in the depths of the Great Depression.

The postwar renaissance of Jewish-American literature is triggered by the stories and novels of Bernard Malamud (*The Magic Barrel*, 1958; *The Assistant*, 1957) and Saul Bellow's pathbreaking *The Adventures of Augie March* (1953), a novel that announces in a vibrant, exuberant voice the essential "Americaness" of its Jewish protagonists. Their immediate heir is Philip Roth, whose intense subjectivity has moved from comedic satires of Jewish family life (*Goodbye Columbus*, 1959, *Portnoy's Complaint*, 1969) to passionate affirmations of Jewish identity (*American Pastoral*, 1997 and *The Plot Against America*, 2004).

Female writers include the notable short fiction writers Tillie Olsen (*Tell Me a Riddle*, 1967), Grace Paley (*Enormous Changes at the Last Minute*, 1974) and Allegra Goodman (*The Family Markowitz*, 1996). Another area of culture in which Jewish writers and performers have excelled is comedy. In theater, the rich tradition of Jewish wit and humor is evident in the plays of George S. Kaufman and Moss Hart, and of Neil Simon; in film the Marx Brothers, Mel Brooks, and Woody Allen; in radio and television Fanny Brice, Jack Benny, George Burns, Milton Berle, Jerry Seinfeld, Larry David; in STAND-UP Lenny Bruce, Mort Sahl, and Alan King.

Distinguished Jewish-American writers who have not generally focused on the Jewish experience include J. D. Salinger, Normal Mailer, Susan Sontag, and Arthur Miller, although Miller's drama *The Price* (1968) stands as an exception.

An important area of literary culture in which Jewish Americans have made significant contributions is literary and cultural criticism. The NEW YORK INTELLECTUALS, a group associated with the journal *Partisan Review*, made major contributions to literary culture in the post–World War II era, exemplified by such works as Alfred Kazin's *A Walker in the City* (1951), Lionel Trilling's *The Liberal Imagination* (1950), and most important from the standpoint of Jewish-American experience, Irving Howe's *The World of Our Fathers* (1976).

In their wake have come a new generation focused less on Jewish identity than on the Jewish religious legacy. The most prominent of these is the essayist, short story writer, and novelist Cynthia Ozick. The wide-ranging critic Harold Bloom has been a major force in biblical criticism as well as in secular canonical literature.

Mark Krupnick's guide to Jewish-American literature appears in *New Immigrant Literatures in the United States*, ed. Alpana Sharma Knippling (1996). Sanford Pinsker's *Jewish American Fiction* (1992) is a reliable survey.

jig   In the ELIZABETHAN theater, the jig referred both to a dance and to a brief musical that featured singing and dancing. Some of these appeared as the afterpiece of a play, the best known of which is "Mr. Attowell's Jigge." The earliest example of an Elizabethan jig is "Michael and Francis," a jig consisting of six short scenes, dealing, as did most jigs, with cuckoldry. Hamlet's dismissive reference to Polonius's taste in drama, "He's for a jig or a tale of bawdry," suggests that the humor was low-level slapstick.

C. J. Sisson summarizes the history in "Jig" in *The Reader's Encyclopedia of Shakespeare*, eds. O. J. Campbell and Edward Quinn (1966).

jingle   A short verse usually set to music, that catches the attention of even a casual listener. As a result, jingles have been a staple of radio and television ADVERTISING.

jongleur   A French term, the equivalent of the English juggler, describing a medieval wandering entertainer who sang, danced, juggled, and performed acrobatic tricks. Unlike the TROUBADOUR who composed his own works, the jongleur relied on others' compositions, which he disseminated through his travels.

jouissance   A French word with a number of literal meanings, including "bliss" or, in a specifically sexual sense, "orgasm." In *The Pleasure of the Text* (1973) the French critic and semiotician Roland Barthes employs the term to distinguish two responses to literature. One response is "pleasure," the satisfaction of having one's basic beliefs and expectations ratified by the text. The other is the shattering, unsettling and disorienting experience of "jouissance."

Complicating these distinctions is Barthes's paradoxical claim that the reader is conscious of both responses, moving from one to the other. In TRAGEDY, for example, the reader undergoes a process of steadily diminishing "pleasure" and increasing "jouissance."

Jungian criticism   *See* MYTH CRITICISM.

juvenilia   Literature written in an author's youth. An extraordinary example is the voluminous poetry and prose written by Emily, Charlotte, Anne, and Branwell Brontë, who as children created the strange worlds of Gondal and Angria, the seeds out of which *Jane Eyre* (1847) and *Wuthering Heights* (1847) later grew.

Kabbalah (Cabala)   A set of esoteric doctrines developed within Judaism between the third century B.C. and the 14th century A.D. Among the elements of the Kabbalah's teachings were the belief in a primordial man who is both male and female, in orders of angels, in a view of sin as separation from God, and in the attribution of special importance to certain numbers. Among the books that constitute the Kabbalah, the most important is the *Zohar (The Book of Splendor)*.

The American critic Harold Bloom has argued that the Kabbalah "revises" the Old Testament scriptures in a fashion parallel to the way a "strong poet" "revises" the poetry of his precursor. *See* INFLUENCE.

Harold Bloom's thesis is presented in his *Kabbalah and Criticism* (1975).

Kabuki   A form of Japanese theater that employs dance, music, and story. Its lavishly designed sets, costumes, and makeup all contribute to the popularity of the form, which has existed since the 17th century. Long regarded as inferior to its rival forms, the NŌ and BUNRAKU, Kabuki is an actor's theater. The actors, all men, some of whom are female impersonators, are more important than the play. The great Kabuki actors have large devoted followings, particularly the *onnagata*, or female impersonator.

kenning   In Old Germanic and Old English verse, a metaphor made up of a compound of two words, which became the standard phrase for a particular object. Thus the ocean was described as the "whale road," the sun as the "world cradle," and a ship as "horse of the sea."

keystone (cops) comedies   The slapstick comedies produced by the Keystone Film Company from 1912 to 1917. The company's director was Mack Sennett, whose comedies regularly featured the actors of the "Keystone Kops" a group of inept policemen who always participated in wildly comic CHASE scenes. Charlie Chaplin became a member of the company in 1913.

kitchen sink dramas Term used to describe a type of English REALISTIC DRAMA in the 1950s that focused on working-class life. Arnold Wesker's *The Kitchen* (1954), set in the kitchen of a restaurant, is the best-known example of the type.

Knickerbocker group A term for a group of writers living in New York in the first half of the 19th century. The name derived from "Diedrich Knickerbocker," the pseudonym used by Washington Irving for his *History of New York* (1809). In addition to Irving, the best known members of the group were James Fenimore Cooper (while he lived in the city), the poet William Cullen Bryant, and the playwright John Howard Payne, best remembered as the composer of the song "Home Sweet Home."

Koran The sacred text of the Islamic religion, believed to contain the revelations of Allah to the prophet Mohammed (ninth century A.D.), and thus the voice of Allah mediated through an angel. It contains histories, moral instruction, and civil laws. *See* FATWA.

Korean-American literature The end of the Korean conflict in 1953 brought a relatively small number of immigrants, many of them students, "war brides" or orphaned children adopted by American parents. After the passing of the 1961 immigration laws, large numbers from the general population arrived. The earlier group of immigrants included the novelist Richard Kim, whose *The Martyred* (1964) recounts the killing by North Korean soldiers of 12 Christian ministers.

The daughter of Korean immigrants, Kim Ronyoung, died in an accident in 1986 after having published *Clay Walls* (1986), a novel dealing with an immigrant family's struggle, adapting to life in Los Angeles in the prewar years. A most unusual novel is *Dictée* (1982), written in three languages and mixing prose and poetry, by Theresa Hak Kyung Cha. Shortly after the book's publication, the author was murdered.

The best-known Korean-American poet is Cathy Song, whose first collection is *Picture Bride* (1982). An outstanding Korean-American writer is Chang-rae Lee, born in Korea but raised in America. His novel *Native Speaker* (1995) recounts the experiences of a second-generation Korean working as a spy in the Korean-American community. In Lee's *A Gesture Life* (1999), a successful, retired

Japanese American discovers that his emotional life has been buried in a World War II experience involving a Korean "comfort woman," the unwilling sexual slave used to serve the Japanese army in World War II. In Mia Jun's *Translations of Beauty* (2004), a Korean family living in Queens, New York, struggles with the consequences of a terrible accident to a family member.

Jae-Nam Han "Korean-American Literature" in *New Immigrant Literatures in the United States*, ed. Alpana Sharma Knippling (1996).

Lake poets   A term for a group of early Romantic poets—William Wordsworth, Samuel Taylor Coleridge, and Robert Southey—who lived in the Lake District of Cumbria in Northwestern England. The term was originally employed by hostile critics (including Lord Byron) to characterize the rural and "uncouth" verse of the Romantic experimenters. It has come to represent the importance of nature as a theme in ROMANTICISM.

lampoon   A broad satirical piece that focuses on an individual. In verse form lampoons were popular in 18th-century England. In modern times, the term has been associated with magazines such as the *Harvard Lampoon* and its offshoot, the *National Lampoon*, which in turn has spawned the *National Lampoon* film series.

language poets   A contemporary school of American poets emphasizing a number of DEFAMILIARIZATION techniques, including the condensation and distortion of words, phrases, and sentences. The aim is to produce an awareness of language that will create a resistance to the existing codes that pervade contemporary culture. Thus language poets regard themselves as having a social and political, as well as artistic, purpose. Among the poets associated with this movement are Ron Silliman, Bob Perelman, and Lyn Hejinian.

The L-A-N-G-U-A-G-E Book (1984), edited by Bruce Andrews and Bob Perelman, is a convenient anthology; George Hartley's *Textual Politics and the Language Poets* (1989) places the movement in its social and political context.

langue/parole   Contrasting terms employed by the Swiss linguist Ferdinand de Saussure to distinguish language as an abstract system (langue) from a particular speech or utterance (parole) in that language. Underlying every use of a given language is a GRAMMAR or set of rules constraining its use. Saussure urged linguists to study these underlying linguistic structures, the langue,

235

an emphasis that proved to be profoundly influential in the development of STRUCTURALISM.

Ferdinand de Saussure employs the two terms in his *Course in General Linguistics* (1915).

Latino/Latina literature   *See* HISPANIC-AMERICAN LITERATURE.

law   Interest in the relation of law to literature has risen to such an extent that "Law and Literature" now constitutes an interdisciplinary field of its own. This development is a consequence partly of the recognition of the rhetorical and narrative characteristics of legal language and partly from the fascination that legal procedures hold for many readers and writers.

Questions of law—of justice, equity, and morality—are central human concerns, so that it is not surprising to see those questions raised in the great works of literature. In Greek tragedy, for example, the law plays a decisive role in the *Oresteia* of Aeschylus, where Orestes is tried for and found innocent of matricide, and in the *Antigone* of Sophocles, which centers on the conflict between religious and secular law.

Comparable legal questions are seen from a satiric perspective in the medieval beast fables centering on the trials of Reynard the Fox. Rendered in French, German, and Flemish, these accounts of Reynard's clever evasion of the law provide a detailed commentary on the legal systems of medieval Europe.

In the RENAISSANCE, François Rabelais maintains the satiric tradition in his *Gargantua and Pantagruel* (1532–64), where a judge explains how he carefully reviews every document of a case before rendering his decision by a roll of the dice. More profound, and more controversial, is the Renaissance text that continues to fascinate students of law and literature, Shakespeare's *The Merchant of Venice*. Is the treatment of Shylock in the courtroom scene of this play a consistent, or an ironic, application of Portia's "quality of mercy" speech? Critics have weighed in on this issue from both sides, armed with a knowledge of the history of English law. All commentators agree, however, on the importance of equity—the application of justice in circumstances not specifically covered by the law—as a central theme in literature.

Among the major 19th-century treatments of the law are Charles Dickens's *Bleak House* (1852) and Herman Melville's *Billy Budd* (1891). Dickens depicts the interminable case of Jarndyce vs. Jarndyce to highlight the absurdity of the endlessly delayed procedures of the English court system of his day. Melville recounts the tragic consequences (the execution of the innocent Billy Budd) of a system of law that removes itself from all natural or spiritual feelings in favor of a strict observance of the legal code.

Among 20th-century novelists, none provides a more penetrating conception and critique of the law than Franz Kafka, himself a lawyer. Kafka's *The Trial* (1914) is, first, a masterful critique of the legal system of the Austro-Hungarian empire, in which an individual's GUILT could lie in an "evil intent," as well as in a deed. Thus the novel's protagonist Joseph K. is arrested and executed "without having done anything wrong." But the novel also suggests that beyond this legal condition lies the larger question of existential guilt, guilt as a defining characteristic of human existence (*see* FALL, THE).

Kafka's conception of "universal guilt" acquires a critical significance in the work of Albert Camus. Camus's *The Fall* (1956) concerns a prominent lawyer who undergoes a moral crisis when he fails to save a drowning woman. As in Kafka, he is not guilty of a criminal act, but of moral indifference. Writing in the wake of the atrocities of World War II, Camus appears to be questioning both the legal system that permitted the growth of totalitarianism, and, on the individual level, the problem of "survivor guilt."

More recently, the practice of law and the mentality of lawyers has become a staple of popular literature, film, and television. Intensifying this popularity has been the practice of televising actual court cases, such as the O. J. Simpson trial, a development that some critics feel has blurred the distinction between popular entertainment and the law, to the detriment of the latter.

Theodore Ziolkowski's *The Mirror of Justice* (1997) is an informative history of legal development and the reflection of that history in literature. Robert Ferguson's *Law & Letters in American Culture* (1984) examines the interaction of literature and law in 19th-century America. Richard Weisberg's *Poethics* (1992) is "a guide book to Law and Literature theory and practice."

lay (lai) A verse ROMANCE popular in medieval France. The best known examples are the lais of Marie de France written in the late 12th century. Marie's lais are Celtic in origin, all of them centered on the theme of love.

In the 19th century the term was used to describe any poetic NARRATIVE. Sir Walter Scott's *The Lay of the Last Minstrel* (1805), for example, uses the narrative device of a tale told by an aging minstrel.

"Left Behind" novels Term referring to a series of novels, derived from the biblical APOCALYPSE, focusing on seven years leading up to the end of the world. The first book of the series, *Left Behind: A Novel of the Earth's Last Days* was published in 1995, its authors Tim LaHaye and Jerry Jenkins. Since then, the 12 novels of the series have sold more than 50 million copies. The series begins with an account of the "Rapture," the secret, brief return of CHRIST to the Earth, where he calls the faithful to their reward in heaven. Left behind are those Christ has not chosen, and they become enmeshed in a chaotic world of death and destruction known as the Tribulation. The world is now ruled by the anti-Christ, but his reign is overcome by the return of Christ, who assumes control of the world. The astonishing popularity of these books among evangelical Christians in the United States has caused concern among nonfundamentalist Christians, for its perceived religious distortions. Among secular observers, the series has been seen as a potent political and social weapon employed by the Christian right.

In her study of the Left Behind phenomenon, Amy Johnson Frykholm concentrates on representative readers of the series, finding not a "monolithic force" alienated from the larger secular culture but people exhibiting a range of attitudes rooted in the emotions of fear and desire, fear of being left behind as the apocalypse nears, and the desire to belong to "a post-rapture community of believers that binds together to share their suffering."

Amy Johnson Frykholm's analysis forms the basis of her *Rapture Culture: Left Behind in Evangelical America* (2004).

legend   A story rooted in fact but which has been elaborated over time so that it is largely fictional. The stories surrounding King Arthur and his court constitute a central legend of European literature. *See* ARTHURIAN LEGEND.

leitmotif (leitmotiv)   In music, particularly a Wagnerian opera, a repeated musical phrase associated with a character or idea. In literature, the term is used in similar fashion to refer to a phrase or image that suggests a particular THEME. The repeated sound of a breaking string in Chekhov's *The Cherry Orchard* (1904) is one example, the use of the music of George Gershwin on the soundtrack of Woody Allen's *Manhattan* (1979) is another.

lesbian literature   The representation of sexual or romantic relationships between women. The earliest examples of lesbian literature are the poems of Sappho (sixth century B.C.), whose residence on the Greek island of Lesbos gave birth to the term as well as the literary tradition.

The subsequent tradition of lesbian literature was dominated by the descriptions of male writers who, capitalizing on the titillation the subject aroused, characterized same-sex love as perversion. As with the history of GAY LITERATURE, the suppression well into the 20th century of explicit lesbianism allowed only disguised forms of lesbian love to be published. Gertrude Stein's short story "Miss Furr and Miss Skeene" (1922), with its subtle play on the word *gay*, is an example of a lesbian story that was evident only to insiders familiar with the term at the time. The best known openly lesbian novel in English was Radclyffe Hall's *The Well of Loneliness* (1928), which was banned in England for 20 years. The same year saw the publication of Djuna Barnes's *Ladies Almanac*, which featured a lesbian heroine, but it is Barnes's *Nightwood* (1936) that stands for many as the finest lesbian novel in English. Two other writers for whom lesbianism proved an important subject were Colette, whose popular *Claudine* novels included several lesbian episodes, and Virginia Woolf, whose *Orlando* (1928) was a tribute to her lover, Vita Sackville-West.

Such works were exceptions: Until very recently the majority of lesbian literature was written either in disguised terms or in a manner designed to associate lesbianism with unhappiness, frustration, and suicide. The turning point in American literature occurred in 1969 with the famous Stonewall riots, in which gay men and lesbians resisted a police raid on a Greenwich Village bar, leading to the formation of the civil rights movement for these two groups. The first literary manifestation was Rita Mae Brown's *Rubyfruit Jungle* (1973), which depicted a lesbian protagonist filled with pride and the love of life. In poetry the equivalent text was Adrienne Rich's *Twenty-One Love Poems* (1976). Since the '70s, lesbian literature has occupied an increasingly prominent place in contemporary literature and criticism.

Bonnie Zimmerman's *The Safe Sea of Women* (1991) surveys recent lesbian fiction. *The Persistent Desire* (1992), edited by Joan Nestle, is an anthology of fiction, poetry, and essays by lesbian writers.

letter   In the sense of a form of correspondence, the letter has played an important role in literary history. An early example is Dante's letter to the Can Grande, a public document that articulated the medieval conception of the FOUR LEVELS OF MEANING of a text. Other famous public letters include Pascal's *Provincial Letters* (1656–57), containing his defense of PORT-ROYAL.

The private correspondence of well-known authors provides insight into their writing and their lives, while at the same time providing their readers with the pleasures of eloquent prose.

For the use of letters as a device in fiction *see* EPISTOLARY NOVEL.

liberal/conservative imagination   *The Liberal Imagination* (1950) is the title of an important essay and book by the distinguished critic Lionel Trilling. Writing in the post–World War II era, when American liberalism, buoyed with the success of the Roosevelt and Truman administrations, appeared to be riding the crest of a wave, Trilling, himself a liberal, issued what, at the time, was a provocative dissenting opinion. His criticism focused not on the pragmatic, political agenda of his fellow liberals, but on the second term of his title, *imagination*, which he characterized as the deeper, broader engagement with reality to be found in the great modern writers, "Proust, Joyce, Lawrence, Eliot, Yeats, Mann (in his creative work), Kafka, Rilke, Gide. . . ." The works of these writers, he argued, are infused with a profoundly tragic sense of life, with a deep skepticism of the idea of progress that propels the liberal imagination. His solution was to integrate the imagination into liberal politics, letting some darkness into the bright, shining superficial future.

In one sense, Trilling's ideas may be said to have fallen on fertile soil with the emergence of the NEOCONSERVATIVE movement, in which prominent former liberals became important elements in shaping American foreign policy in Republican administrations. On the other hand, there are those who claim to hear Trilling from beyond the grave, echoing T. S, Eliot's J. Alfred Prufrock, "That is not what I meant at all."

Some 40 years after *The Liberal Imagination*, the critic Virgil Nemoianu examined the question of the conservatism of major 20th-century writers. He expanded Trilling's core of major figures who, while embracing the aesthetic values of MODERNISM, made clear their opposition to liberal democratic ideals. Among those he added to Trilling's list were Ezra Pound, William Faulkner, Evelyn Waugh, Samuel Beckett, Eugene Ionesco, and three prominent leftists who later changed sides, W. H. Auden, John Dos Passos, and Andre Malraux.

However, Nemoianu saw this development not as a rejection of liberalism, per se, but as an illustration of what he called the "Theory of the Secondary." In modern culture literature and the arts play a secondary role, relative to the primary thrust that dominates society. The primary is represented by the principle of historical evolution, which rests upon scientific progress. It falls to literature not to turn back the clock of social development but to contribute to the dialectic of history, checking the unimpeded force and control of the primary. In political terms, literature's role becomes that of the minority party; in literary terms, the tragic vision as opposed to the comic.

William Chace's *Lionel Trilling: Criticism and Politics* (1980) takes a critical but balanced view of *The Liberal Imagination*. Virgil Nemoianu's argument is contained in his *A Theory of the Secondary: Literature, Progress and Reaction* (1989).

libretto   An Italian term (meaning "little book") for the verbal text of an OPERA or the "book" of a MUSICAL. Notable operatic librettists include Lorenzo Da Ponte, who wrote the librettos for Mozart's *The Marriage of Figaro* (1786) and *Don Giovanni* (1787), and Arrigo Boito, the librettist of Verdi's *Otello* (1887) and *Falstaff* (1893).

light verse   Humorous or witty poetry that maintains a lighthearted tone. The term sometimes carries with it the notion of superficiality and lack of depth, but some light verse such as the Prologue to Chaucer's *The Canterbury Tales* or Alexander Pope's *The Rape of the Lock* ranks among the classics of English poetry.

Common types of light verse include LIMERICK and PARODY.

limerick   A form of light verse consisting of five anapestic lines rhyming *a-a-b-b-a*. The vogue for the limerick was created in 1846, when the humorist Edward Lear included examples in his *Book of Nonsense*. The origin of the form, as well as any connection it may have with the Irish county of Limerick, remains a mystery.

A well-known example is Oliver Wendell Holmes's limerick on the 19th-century clergyman Henry Ward Beecher:

The Reverend Henry Ward Beecher
Called a hen a most eloquent creature.
The hen, pleased with that,
Laid an egg in his hat
And thus did the hen reward Beecher.

Bennett Cerf's *Out on a Limerick* (1960) is a representative collection of traditional and modern limericks.

linguistics   The scientific study of language. Linguistics and literary study share a common bond, Shakespeare's Hamlet's "words, words, words." As a consequence, there has always been an overlapping of the two areas. In the classical period the study of language and literature was grouped under the heading of RHETORIC, a linkage that survived through the Renaissance. In the 19th and early 20th centuries, the study of literature was governed by PHILOLOGY, at that time an umbrella term for cultural, linguistic, and literary history.

By the beginning of the 20th century, linguistics had begun to develop as a separate discipline focusing on a rigorous analysis of language systems or on specific discourses. Among linguistic categories with specific relations to literature are the following:

phonology   The sound patterns of language. Modern linguistic research has engaged in a number of experiments designed to demonstrate the relative values speakers of a language assign to certain sounds. These studies reflect the importance of CACOPHONY, EUPHONY, and other sonic features of poetry.

syntax   The word order and structures in a sentence. Linguistic terms frequently are employed in analyzing a literary text from a syntactic point of view. For example, in his analysis of the opening paragraph of Henry James's *The Ambassadors* (1903), Ian Watt focuses on James's use of intransitive verbs, abstract nouns, subordinate clauses, and other distinctively syntactic features of this paragraph in order to describe its general effect on the reader.

style The distinctive verbal characteristics of a writer or group of writers. Linguistics enables us to give a descriptive basis to evaluative judgments using this term, as when we refer to a writer having a "sense of style."

STYLISTICS, the formal study of style, also makes us conscious of such features of style as diction, vocabulary, and syntax, all contributing to definitions of style as expressions of individual personalities.

Linguistics has played a key role in the development of contemporary THEORY. The work of the Swiss linguist Ferdinand de Saussure has provided the cornerstones for STRUCTURALISM and DECONSTRUCTION. In addition, Saussure coined a number of terms that are part of the currency of critical theory: SIGNIFIER/SIGNIFIED, LANGUE/PAROLE, DIACHRONIC/SYNCHRONIC. The other great 20th-century linguist, Noam Chomsky, has had less direct influence on literary study.

Jonathan Culler's "Literature and Linguistics" in *Interrelations of Literature* (1982), edited by Barricelli and Gibaldi, provides a survey of the topic. Roger Fowler's *The Languages of Literature* (1971) analyzes the contribution of linguistics to literary criticism.

list poem A type of poetry made up largely of long lists of people, places, and things. Lists in the form of catalogues of ships are a feature of the classical EPIC, a tradition that was given a new life in the exuberant catalogues of Walt Whitman's *Leaves of Grass*. Whitman in turn provided a model for the BEAT poet Allen Ginsberg, whose *Howl* includes a catalogue of modern alienation. A less apocalyptic modern example is John Hollander's "Movie Going," a catalogue of the now defunct movie theaters on the Upper West Side of Manhattan.

Lists also form the basis of some standard popular songs, such as Cole Porter's "Let's Do It" and "You're the Top" as well as Dave Frishberg's "Van Lingle Mungo," which contains a lyric consisting entirely of the names of BASEBALL players of the 1930s and '40s.

literacy *See* ORALITY/LITERACY.

literal In criticism, the simplest meaning of a TEXT. In the medieval conception of FOUR LEVELS OF MEANING, the literal is the first and most obvious level. A *literal translation* is one that adheres to the literal meaning—the letter, but not necessarily the spirit—of the original.

literati   A term, often employed ironically, describing members of the literary establishment: writers, critics, scholars, and publishers.

Edgar Allan Poe's "The Literati of New York City" (1845–46) is a series of 38 mostly satiric sketches that provide an insider's view of literary life in New York in the 1840s.

literary history   A term for the study of the history of literature. It is frequently synonymous with HISTORICAL CRITICISM or with its contemporary version, NEW HISTORICISM. Literary history differs from these in that it also includes a view, currently in the minority, that the history of literature can be treated independently of other forms of history.

A well-known example of this view is developed by the critic Northrop Frye in his *Anatomy of Criticism* (1957). Frye traces the "history" of the basic forms of tragedy, comedy, lyric, and epic as cyclical movements that pass through five phases: mythic, romantic, high mimetic, low mimetic, and ironic. Frye's position, rooted in MYTH CRITICISM, gained considerable support in the 1950s and '60s. More recently, it has been superseded by the New Historicist view that a literary text is inextricably interwoven with the culture in which it is produced.

literature   Usually understood to refer to "creative" works in the form of POETRY, FICTION, and DRAMA. One problem created by this sense of the term is that it excludes nonfictional works commonly regarded as part of literature, for example the essays of Michel de Montaigne and Francis Bacon, biographies such as James Boswell's *Life of Johnson*, histories such as Henry Adams's *Mont-Saint-Michel and Chartres*, and diaries such as those of Samuel Pepys and Anne Frank.

Some types of criticism, such as RUSSIAN FORMALISM and NEW CRITICISM, have attempted to limit literature to those texts in which language is used in a unique fashion. As articulated by the linguist Roman Jakobson, literary language is distinguished by its self-referential character. A variant of the principle of ART FOR ART'S SAKE, this perspective argues for literature's occupying a special realm removed from direct reference to life but illustrative of universal truths.

Implicit in this view as well is the notion that the term refers not merely to all novels, plays, and poems, but only to "serious" as opposed to "popular" examples of those forms. The assumption underlying this distinction is that popular literature is ephemeral entertainment, unworthy of inclusion within the domain of literature.

In recent years this sense of the term has undergone a radical redefinition. The chief source of the recent revision has been the development of POSTSTRUCTURALISM and the re-emergence of socio/political criticism.

Poststructuralists argue that all language is "self-referential" and rhetorical. Political critics, chiefly proponents of MARXIST CRITICISM, maintain that literature is only one among many other social practices with no claim to a special exalted status removed from the social and economic forces that govern society. As a result, these critics deny any claim to literature's distinctiveness on the grounds either of language or of aesthetic privilege. From their point of view, literature has come off its pedestal and entered the real world. This criticism has been challenged directly by critics such as Harold Bloom, and indirectly as well by those who maintain that what appears to be a major revolution in the definition of literature will in time prove to be a minor adjustment.

Redrawing the Boundaries, edited by Stephen Greenblatt and Giles Gunn (1992), explores recent developments in literary studies. Harold Bloom's *The Western Canon* (1995) offers an alternative view.

litotes   In RHETORIC, the assertion of an idea by denying its opposite. An ironic figure of speech, litotes achieves its effect by appearing to understate the case, as in "a not insignificant sum," which implies a large figure.

little magazine   A term for a MAGAZINE that focuses on experimental literature, sometimes identified with a specific movement or school. The word "little" refers to the fact that such magazines usually have a very small readership. The value of the little magazine is that it provides an outlet for fiction and poetry that is considered too AVANT-GARDE for a large audience.

An early American example was *The DIAL*, founded in 1840 as a vehicle for the ideas associated with TRANSCENDENTALISM. Among its earliest editors were Margaret Fuller and Ralph Waldo Emerson. An influential English little magazine was *The Yellow Book* (1894–97), which proclaimed the principles of AESTHETICISM and included among its contributors Oscar Wilde, Henry James, and Aubrey Beardsley, whose artistic designs broke new ground in art illustration.

Twentieth-century little magazines have flourished and withered with the changing of tastes. The most notable exception is *Poetry: A Magazine of Verse*, founded in 1912 and still in existence. Among prominent contemporary little magazines are *The Paris Review*, *Sewanee Review*, and *Grand Street*.

liturgical drama   A medieval proto-dramatic form. The Christian Mass was inherently dramatic, designed to re-enact the sacrifice of Christ. By the 10th century certain "scenes" were being presented as part of the Mass. The earliest known example is the *Quem Quaeritis* (Whom do you seek?) fragment, an addition to the Easter Sunday Mass that contains sung dialogue between monks representing the women who have come to CHRIST's tomb and the angels who announce the Resurrection.

Gradually these enactments were separated from the mass itself, although still performed in churches or monasteries. One of the best known examples was the *Presentation of the Virgin in the Temple*, performed at the cathedral in Avignon, France.

Until recently it was thought that medieval MYSTERY PLAYS evolved from liturgical drama, but recent evidence has shown that the two were coexistent.

O. B. Hardison's *Christian Rite and Christian Ritual* (1965) offers an original, convincing treatment of the subject.

logocentrism   In the principles of DECONSTRUCTION, the belief in an ultimate referral point outside of language that forms the basis of Western thought. As critiqued by Jacques Derrida, who coined the term, logocentrism lies at the root of the assumption that words "present" (in the sense of "make present") to the listener their referent, the object to which they refer. This assumption, also characterized by Derrida as the METAPHYSICS OF PRESENCE, results in the preference given to speech over writing, and in assigning meaning to the intention of the speaker.

Derrida derives his term from *logos*, a Greek word that means both "word" and "logic" or "reason." Logos is also the term used at the opening of the Gospel of John to describe Jesus Christ ("In the beginning was the Word"). For Derrida this identification of "Word" and "God" in one of the central texts of Western history is a stunning example of logocentrism, the desire to guarantee the authority of language by rooting it in the presence of a transcendent authority.

Another important aspect of logocentrism, one that is virtually synonymous with it, is "phonocentrism," that is, the preference for speech over writing as the basis of linguistic analysis. This speech-centered approach to language creates a bias in favor of presence, since in speech, the speaker is present, while writing occurs precisely because the writer is absent. *See* WRITING.

A Derrida Reader (1990), edited by Peggy Kamuf, contains representative selections of his work.

lost generation   A term used to describe a group of young American writers of the 1920s who experienced ALIENATION and the loss of ideals resulting from World War I and its aftermath. The term derives from an anecdote that Gertrude Stein related to Ernest Hemingway. While traveling in the French countryside after the end of World War I, she had had trouble with her car. She stopped at a small village, where a local mechanic skillfully repaired the vehicle. When she reported her satisfaction to the owner of the shop, he explained that he had trained the mechanic, who had been too young to have served in the war. He was not like the war veterans; they were untrainable, "*une genération perdu*." Stein's conclusion, "You are all a lost generation" became the epigraph to Hemingway's novel *The Sun Also Rises* (1926), which recounts the disillusionment of a group of young people in the wake of the war.

There are at least three slightly different versions of Stein's story. The one recalled by Hemingway in his memoir *A Moveable Feast* (1964) is designed to reflect badly on Stein and may not be reliable. The above account is derived from James Mellow's *Charmed Circle: Gertrude Stein and Company* (2003), which contains a detailed account of the anecdote.

love In literature a term of such surpassing significance and varied meanings that no summary could do it justice. One approach to the topic is to distinguish among the Greek terms *agape*, *eros*, and *philia*. These three forms of love divide into two categories, human (*eros* and *philia*) and divine (*agape*).

Within the category of divine love lies much of Western mystical and religious writing, in which the union of the soul with God, famously represented in the conclusion to Dante's *Divine Comedy*, is the manifestation of God's love. As Plato expresses it in his *Symposium*: "God mingles not with man; but through love all the intercourse of God with man is carried on."

But it is in the domain of human love—*philia* (friendship) and *eros* (sexual love)—that the vast majority of the world's literature falls. Love of every type, from love between and within the sexes to the love of parent and child, of king and subject, individual and nation, forms the heart of literature. For example, *love* is the third most commonly used noun in the works of Shakespeare.

In the Western tradition a key development occurred in 12th-century France with the emergence of COURTLY LOVE, a code of behavior that transformed sexual desire into a noble, unrequited passion. This tradition represented the first example in Western literature of romantic love, and provided the thematic foundation of the medieval ROMANCE and the SONNET.

The courtly love tradition elevated the significance of love to the status of a religion, a concept that was intensified in 19th-century ROMANTICISM. In the Romantic tradition, love is the highest expression of spiritual longings, the source of feelings that reach an unparalleled depth and intensity. The key to this notion is the idea of love as a function of "sympathetic imagination," the capacity to enter into another's feelings, enabling the move toward a basic unity of self and other. As a result, love is a path that leads to fundamental truths of reality. Love purifies (in William Blake's poetry even *deifies*) the lover. The distinction between the older religious view and the Romantic view has been summarized by the philosopher Irving Singer: "For Medieval Christianity, God is love; for Romantic ideology, love is God."

A concurrent 19th-century development, the full emergence of capitalism, helped to create a new ideal, centered on marriage as a contract motivated by love (and threatened by ADULTERY), which had the effect of suppressing sexual motives, while, as in Jane Austen, slyly hinting at economic ones. The "love marriage" came to be seen as the only suitable form, exemplified by Queen Victoria in her devotion to her husband, Prince Albert. Nevertheless, as Joseph Boone has argued in *Tradition Counter Tradition* (1987), "the literary ideal of romantic marriage" also produced an anti-romantic reaction, reflected in the writings of Kate Chopin. Chopin, an early feminist, depicts in her stories and novels a more realistic portrait of marriage, in which the wife is frequently the prisoner of the love-marriage convention and of her own internalization of that convention.

In the 20th century, romantic love has been seriously challenged by the Freudian theory that sexuality is a feature of all forms of love, rooted in infancy and the desire for the mother. Freud focuses less on the emotion of love and more on the "drive" that he calls the "libido" and modern psychoanalytical critics term "desire." Some critics, such as Vivian Gornick, argue that love is no longer viable as a literary theme. Nevertheless love, in all its forms, continues to dominate, to the extent of defining, literature and life. This pervasiveness is tellingly represented in Jean Hagstrum's *Esteem Enlivened by Desire* (1992), a sensitive and perceptive study of the couple in Western literature.

One example of the continuing appeal of romantic love is the worldwide success of the film *Titanic* (1997). One source of its appeal is that *Titanic* exemplifies the *liebestod* tradition, the association of love and DEATH, a motif central to romantic tragedies such as *Romeo and Juliet*. While elevating *liebestod* in his tragedies (*Antony and Cleopatra* is another example), in his comic mode Shakespeare was capable of satirizing it: witness Rosalind's remark in *As You Like It*, "Men have died from time to time, and worms have eaten them, but not for love."

Shakespeare also introduced another comic perspective on love, the view of it as a "merry war" between two proud, witty, intelligent people. Beatrice and Benedick in *Much Ado About Nothing* (1598) gave birth to a long line of battling lovers that has included Millamant and Mirabell in William Congreve's *The Way of the World* (1700), Sir Peter and Lady Teazle in Richard Sheridan's *The School for Scandal* (1777) and, more recently, in a number of Spencer Tracy/Katharine Hepburn films, such as *Adam's Rib* (1949).

For yet another view of love, *see* MIMETIC DESIRE.

Denis de Rougemont's *Love in the Western World* (1966, 1984, 1987) and *Love Declared* (1964) offer a social history of love growing out of the courtly love tradition. Irving

Singer's *The Nature of Love* (3 vols., 1966, 1984, 1987) is a comprehensive treatment of the subject from the perspective of literature and philosophy. Vivian Gornick develops her thesis in *The End of the Novel of Love* (1997).

lyric   A type of poetry in which the "voice" of the poem (not necessarily that of the poet) records a specific feeling or attitude. In its original form, the lyric was designed for musical accompaniment. As the term evolved, however, it came to embrace a wide range of different poetic forms including the SONNET, ODE, ELEGY, and ECLOGUE.

m

macaronic verse   A type of poetry in which two or more languages or dialects are mixed for comic or satiric effect. Macaronic verse (from the Italian word for macaroni) originated in the MIDDLE AGES and achieved wide popularity in the RENAISSANCE.

The mingling of two languages—particularly the insertion of a line from another poet—is a common feature of modernist poetry, as in the poems of Ezra Pound and T. S. Eliot. In his poem "Mauberley," for example, Pound inserts several phrases in Greek and one prose passage in French.

macguffin   A term coined by the film director Alfred Hitchcock to describe a PLOT device that helps to initiate the action of a film, but subsequently proves to be of no importance. Hitchcock employed a number of macguffins in his films, for example, a dying man's secret message in *The Man Who Knew Too Much* (1935) and stolen money in *Psycho* (1960).

Machiavel   An ELIZABETHAN term for a cunning, deceitful villain. The name derives from Niccolò Machiavelli (1469–1527), the Italian political philosopher whose *The Prince* (1513), an analysis of political power, was regarded as ruthless and immoral. Machiavelli hoped to bring the principles of historical objectivity and pragmatic realism to his treatment of the nature of politics. His conception of the political sphere as an amoral realm created a popular view that he was the embodiment of evil. As a consequence Machiavelli's name became synonymous with diabolical political intrigue. In *Henry VI, Part Three*, Shakespeare has the villainous Gloucester (later to be crowned Richard III) assert that he will "set the murderous Machiavel to school." Other of Shakespeare's Machiavellian villains include Iago in *Othello* and Edmund in *King Lear*, both of whom share their villainy in direct addresses to the audience.

madness   Despite ongoing debates over its proper definition, madness serves as a useful, if highly generalized, term to describe people suffering from serious mental disorders. In relation to literature, madness appears in two forms: as a characteristic associated with poets and creative writers, and as a theme in literature. The view of madness as a feature of the poetic personality dates to classical times and the association of poetry with Dionysus, the god of irrational behavior (*See* APOLLONIAN/DIONYSIAN). Shakespeare's grouping of "the lunatic, the lover and the poet" reflects an extension of this notion, although he reminds us that the visions of the madman, the lover, and the poet often yield "something of great constancy" that lie beyond the grasp of "cool reason." (*See* IMAGINATION/FANCY).

Celebrated 20th-century examples of the "mad poet" include Antonin Artaud, exponent of the THEATER OF CRUELTY, and Ezra Pound, who, after collaborating with Italian Fascists during World War II, was declared insane by a panel of doctors and committed to a hospital for the criminally insane for nearly 13 years.

As a theme in literature, madness takes on a variety of forms. Greek mythology alone exhibits the full range from the haunted madness of Orestes, pursued by the Furies for the crime of matricide, to the prophetic madness of Cassandra, whose prophecies are never believed, to the mad god Dionysus, who induces in his followers orgiastic frenzies, memorably represented in Euripides' *Bacchae* (407 B.C.)

While depicting madness with great skill, Shakespeare also introduced the idea of pretended madness, notably in *Hamlet* and *King Lear*. Hamlet's feigned madness, his "antic disposition," enables him to verbally attack his enemy Claudius with riddles and double entendres. That he succeeds in getting under Claudius's skin is evident in the latter's remark, "like the hectic in my blood he rages." In *King Lear*, Edgar's assumption of the role of Tom O'Bedlam, a deranged beggar and former inmate of the famous asylum, allows for a powerful counterpoint to Lear's genuine madness. The climax of the play occurs in the "duet of madness" in act three, scene four. Taking refuge in a home on the storm-tossed heath, Lear encounters poor, naked Tom and asks him, "Has thou given all to thy two daughters?/And art thou come to this?" In the words of the critic R.G. Moulton, ". . . the centerpiece of the play is occupied with the contact of two madnesses . . . that of Lear, gathering up into a climax trains of passion from all three tragedies of the main plot and that of Edgar, holding a similar position to the three tragedies of the underplot."

The other great RENAISSANCE representation of madness is Miguel Cervantes's *Don Quixote* (1605, 1615). The author's sympathy for his mad hero does not lead him to elevate madness into an exalted state. That conception would emerge later, in the Romantic era, in which madness becomes a privileged condition. Celebrating instinct over intellect, feeling over rationality, Romantic writers in Germany and England strove for an ideal loss of the self. According to Friedrich

Nietzsche, both tragic and comic art was rooted in "Dionysian madness," the Greek festival whose participants strove to achieve ecstasy.

Probably the greatest poet of the period associated with madness was William Blake. His contemporaries frequently used the term in describing his work, but later students of Blake's poetry and art have come to see them as visionary and prophetic, which as reinterpreted by Northrop Frye and other critics, reveals a remarkably comprehensive and coherent poetic vision.

The critic Lillian Feder traces the Apollonian/Dionysian conflict in the figure of Gustave Von Aschenbach in Thomas Mann's *Death in Venice* (1912). An Apollonian artist who succumbs to madness, Aschenbach dies a victim of his long battle against his own instincts, which finally erupt in revolt against him.

World War II, whose central figure, Adolf Hitler, was a madman, offered some writers the opportunity to depict the world as a madhouse whose only retreat was an asylum. Thus in Günter Grass's *The Tin Drum* (1959), the narrator Oskar Matzerath records the story of Germany's lapse into madness from the safety of a mental hospital. Similarly, Tamura, a mental patient and the NARRATOR of Shohei Ooka's *Fires on the Plain* (1953), tells the story of Japanese soldiers reduced to cannibalism. Finally and famously, Joseph Heller's novel *Catch 22* (1961), exemplified the absurdity and madness of war.

Three films that engage the subject from perspectives that reflect the periods in which they were made are Anotle Litvak's *The Snake Pit* (1948), which explores the treatment of patients in large state-run mental hospitals; Phillipe De Broca's *King of Hearts* (1966), a parable contrasting the insanity of war with the benign hallucinations of madness, and Milos Forman's *One Flew Over the Cuckoo's Nest* (1976), based on Ken Kesey's novel, in which the anarchic hero McMurphy challenges the deadly oppressive force of the institution, embodied in the figure of Big Nurse.

Lillian Feder's *Madness in Literature* (1980) offers a comprehensive cultural history of the subject. *Dionysus in Literature* (1994) is a wide-ranging collection of essays on the topic.

madrigal   A lyric poem set to MUSIC, usually for several voices. The form, which originated in 14th-century Italy, was very popular in ELIZABETHAN England. One of the foremost Elizabethan composers of madrigals, John Morley, also composed the music for "It was a lover and his lass," a song from Shakespeare's *As You Like It*.

magazine   A periodical containing articles, stories, poems, and various other features. In addition to the LITTLE MAGAZINE, a journal that emphasizes criticism and literature, general magazines have also played a role in literary history. In the 19th century a number of major novels originally appeared in magazines in serialized form, which influenced the STRUCTURE of those novels. Included among those were Charles Dickens's *A Tale of Two Cities* (1859) and *Great Expectations* (1860–61), and Wilkie Collins's *The Woman in White* (1859–60) and *The Moonstone* (1868). *The Moonstone* first appeared in *All the Year Round*, a magazine owned and edited by Dickens.

Several 19th-century American magazines originally owned and produced by book publishers—*Harper's, Scribner's, Putnam's,* and *The Atlantic Monthly*—included distinguished literary sections. These journals featured contributions from such notable writers as Henry David Thoreau, Herman Melville, Henry Wadsworth Longfellow, Mark Twain, and Henry James. Among 20th-century American magazines that have consistently published good FICTION and POETRY, the most notable are *The New Yorker* and *Esquire. See* ZINES.

magic realism   A term referring to fiction that integrates realistic elements with supernatural or fantastic experiences. The term was originally used in the 1920s in art circles in Europe and America to describe a kind of realist painting less interested in representing the art object than in capturing its aura, as, for example, in the paintings of Henri Rousseau.

Latin American writers later employed the term to characterize the "marvelous real," seeing everyday life as if for the first time. The most celebrated example of magic realism is Gabriel García Márquez's *One Hundred Years of Solitude* (1971), an extraordinary blend of realism, myth, comedy, and history, rendered in lush, poetic language. Other sources of magic realism are the stories of Jorge Luis Borges, Mario Vargas Llosa, and Julio Cortazar. The technique is artfully represented in European literature by Milan Kundera's *The Unbearable Lightness of Being* (1984).

In American literature, magic realism, evident earlier in the stories of Bernard Malamud and in John Cheever's short story "The Enormous Radio," has become a prominent feature in contemporary works by Toni Morrison (*Beloved*, 1987), Donald Barthelme (*The Dead Father*, 1975), Alice Walker (*The Color Purple*, 1982) and William Kennedy (*Quinn's Book*, 1988).

The appeal of magic realism lies in its effective resolution of the tension between REALISM and experimentation, overcoming the limitations of the former while providing an anchor for the latter.

Post Modern Fiction: A Bio-Bibliographical Guide (1986), edited by Larry McCaffrey, includes a chapter on magic realism. *Magical Realism* (1995), edited by Lois Zamora and Wendy Faris, is a collection of essays dealing with the history and theory of the device.

malapropism   An unconscious PUN, the misuse of a word sounding like the appropriate word. The term derives from Mrs. Malaprop, a character in Richard

Brinsley Sheridan's comedy *The Rivals* (1775). An even earlier malapropist is Dogberry, the bumbling constable in Shakespeare's *Much Ado About Nothing*, who insists that "comparisons are odorous." Notable modern malapropists include Samuel Goldwyn ("in two words, impossible") and television's Archie Bunker ("imported Ricans").

manifesto   In literary politics, a statement by a group of writers or critics announcing their theoretical position. Twentieth-century examples include the manifestoes of FUTURISM (1909), IMAGISM (1915), SURREALISM (1924), and PROJECTIVISM (1950).

mannerism   In its general literary sense, a term for an eccentric self-conscious style. In art history it refers to a late 16th-century style of painting that relied on distortion of scale and perspective. Its literary sense has been applied to such stylistic experiments as EUPHUISM, the SENTIMENTAL NOVEL, and AESTHETICISM.

manuscript   A written or typed copy of a text as opposed to a published version. When the manuscript is written in the AUTHOR's hand it is said to be a *holograph*. In the MIDDLE AGES, many manuscripts were "illuminated," exhibiting an initial letter or a page with a colorful design.

marinism   An elaborate poetic style developed by the Italian poet Gianbattista Marino (1569–1625). Marino specialized in love poems that featured highly sensuous, ornate descriptions laden with lush metaphors. Marinism is a striking, if somewhat excessive, example of the BAROQUE style. *See* GONGORISM.

Marprelate controversy   In ELIZABETHAN England, a lively religious controversy, sparked by a series of pamphlets written in 1588–89 by the pseudonymous "Martin Marprelate." In attacking the episcopal structure of the Church of England, the pamphlets were applauded by the growing number of Puritans in London while being condemned by the authorities at Court. The Anglican bishops hired a number of professional writers to answer the pamphlets, which were written in a lively, often scurrilous style. With notably witty writers, such as Thomas Nashe and Robert Greene entering the fray, the controversy became even more intense and scurrilous until the Marprelate printers were arrested.

Referring to the racy, fleering, cockney manner of the controversy, the writer C. S. Lewis says of Martin Marprelate, "His importance as a controversial theologian is small. His real place is in the history of prose."

C. S. Lewis,' comments appear in his *English Literature in the 16th Century* (1954).

Marxist criticism   The application of the theories of Karl Marx, Friedrich Engels, and their successors to the study of literature. For the Marxist critic, literature must be understood in relation to the determining forces of society: history, economics, class, and IDEOLOGY. The Marxist critic thus serves two functions: to expose the underlying connection of literature and society, and to prescribe a type of literature that will serve the interests of a Marxist revolution, although many contemporary Marxist critics have abandoned this second position.

One formulation of the pro-revolutionary role is the doctrine of SOCIALIST REALISM, which became the official state-sponsored critical orthodoxy in the Soviet Union. Although under Stalin socialist realism became a form of thought control, its theoretical position received some validation in Bertolt Brecht's EPIC THEATER and his concept of the ALIENATION EFFECT, as well as in the critical analysis of the 19th-century novel developed by the Hungarian critic Georg Lukacs.

In the 1930s and '40s, the FRANKFURT SCHOOL repudiated the reduction of Marxist criticism to socialist realism. Defending in particular modernist and experimental art forms (condemned as decadent by both Communist and Nazi regimes), these Marxist critics saw the AVANT-GARDE as the enemy of totalitarianism, including the totalitarian system of capitalism. By depicting alienation and despair as the modern social reality, seemingly apolitical writers, such as Samuel Beckett, revealed the void that lies at the heart of modern capitalist culture.

The advent of STRUCTURALISM in the 1960s had a strong impact on Marxist criticism. Structuralists and Marxists share the belief that the idea of the free individual is a myth disguising the systems that govern individual thought and behavior. An early example of the fusion of Marxism and structuralism is the work of the French theorist Louis Althusser, whose concept of "ideological state apparatuses" argues that IDEOLOGY is not merely a set of ideas but a system of social practices (embracing the family, the school, the church and the agencies of the state) that create an individual's self-definition. Although literature is included as one of these "apparatuses," certain works stand apart, providing the reader with a glimpse into the working of ideology.

For the English Marxist Terry Eagleton, the task of criticism is to delve beneath the apparent consistency of a literary text to uncover its internal dissonances and contradictions, thereby revealing its open-minded, deconstructed character. The literary text in its superficially unified state functions as an agent of ideology. At its fractured, decentered core it subverts that ideology.

The structuralist influence on Marxist thought is checked in Fredric Jameson's *The Prison House of Language* (1982), which argues that the flaw in the structuralist model lies in its ahistorical analysis of social reality. In *The Political*

Unconscious (1981), Jameson incorporates a range of poststructuralist and traditional critical approaches within an overarching Marxist framework.

Jameson's eclectic approach has become a marked feature of Marxist criticism as it joins with various other schools (CULTURAL STUDIES, FEMINIST CRITICISM, PSYCHOANALYTICAL CRITICISM, POSTSTRUCTURALISM) in a general critique of the status quo that Eagleton describes as "political criticism."

The central texts of contemporary Marxist criticism include George Lukacs's *The Historical Novel* (1963); Louis Althusser's "Ideological State Apparatuses" in his *Lenin and Philosophy* (1971); Terry Eagleton's *Marxism and Literary Criticism* (1976), and *Literary Theory* (1983); and Fredric Jameson's *Marxism and Form* (1971) and *The Political Unconscious* (1981).

masque In the RENAISSANCE, an elaborate entertainment that combined DRAMA, POETRY, and MUSIC. Although employed in Italy and France, the masque achieved its most elaborate development in England during the JACOBEAN and CAROLINE periods. In those years, playwrights were commissioned to write masques for the royal court to mark ceremonial occasions, such as the visit of a foreign dignitary or the wedding of a member of the court. The greatest of the masques were those produced by the collaboration of the playwright Ben Jonson and Inigo Jones, the court architect who created scenic spectacles that served as the settings for the dramatic action. Among the products of their collaboration were *Hue and Cry After Cupid* (1608) and *The Masque of Queens* (1609).

The structure of the masque centered on the dancing of a group of elaborately costumed members of the aristocracy whose movements, interspersed with poetry and song, enacted the "plot." Their appearance was preceded by an "antimasque," in which professional performers would enact scenes of disorder and ribaldry. These performers would then be banished by a verse announcing the arrival of the masquers. At the conclusion of the entertainment the audience would be invited to join in the dance.

John Milton's *Comus* (1634) is a famous example of the form. Shakespeare's *Cymbeline* and *The Winter's Tale* include brief masques while the *The Tempest* contains a masque followed by Prospero's famous speech that begins "Our revels now are ended."

Inigo Jones: The Theatre of the Stuart Court (1973), edited by Stephen Orgel and Roy Strong, is a scholarly edition of the masques that emphasizes Jones's contributions.

medieval drama A general term used to describe the various dramatic forms of theatrical presentation in the MIDDLE AGES, including the MIRACLE PLAY, MORALITY PLAY, MYSTERY PLAY, SAINT PLAY, and LITURGICAL DRAMA.

O. B. Hardison's *Christian Rite and Christian Ritual* (1965) details the relationship among the various types of medieval drama.

medieval romance   A type of story popular in Europe from the 12th century to the RENAISSANCE, focusing on the ARTHURIAN LEGEND and the conventions of COURTLY LOVE.

mediology   A term coined by the French theorist Régis Debray to describe the study of the interplay between culture and technology, between an idea and its transmission. The effect is to reinforce the 1960's argument of Marshall McLuhan that the media is the message. In *God: An Itinerary* (2004), Debray develops his argument that the Judeo-Christian God's appearance in history is the consequence of two critical technological advances, the invention of the wheel and, most important, alphabetical writing. According to Debray, the God of Abraham and his later transformation into the figure of the son of God are inextricably interwoven with the development of writing as a tool for persuasion and conversion. With the coming of the digital age, he suggests, the "alphabetical God" is becoming obsolete, to be replaced by a new form of spirituality. *See also* GODS.

melodrama   A type of DRAMA that highlights suspense and romantic sentiment, with characters who are usually either clearly good or bad. As its name implies, the form frequently uses a musical background to underscore or heighten the emotional tone of a scene.

Melodrama first achieved great popularity on the 19th-century stage. Its appeal continues today in many films and television plays.

memoir   A form of AUTOBIOGRAPHY that subordinates the AUTHOR's personal life to the public events in which he or she has participated. In some cases, as in Simone de Beauvoir's *Memoirs of a Dutiful Daughter* (1958), the public "event" is the representative character of the life—in de Beauvoir's case, the degree to which her early life typified the upbringing of a young girl in her time. More usually, the form serves as a vehicle for a personal account of specific public events. An example is *Present at the Creation* (1978), the memoirs of Dean Acheson, the secretary of state during the establishment of the United Nations and the conduct of the Korean War.

Mermaid Tavern   The 17th-century London Tavern frequented by actors and playwrights, including Shakespeare, Ben Jonson and Francis Beaumont. Beaumont left a memorable description of the witty exchanges that took place there, as though ". . . a man had meant to put his whole wit in a jest/ and had resolved to live a fool/ the rest of his life."

metafiction   Fiction that calls attention to its own fictionality. The classic example is Laurence Sterne's *Tristram Shandy* (1759–67), in which the narrator berates his reader at one point for failing to pick up on a clue that he had planted in a previous chapter. A prominent feature of POSTMODERNISM, forms of metafiction appear in Vladimir Nabokov's *Pale Fire* (1962); John Barth's *Lost in the Funhouse* (1968); Donald Barthelme's *SnowWhite* (1973); Italo Calvino's *If on a Winter's Night a Traveler* (1979), and A. S. Byatt's *Possession* (1989).

Patricia Waugh's *Metafiction: The Theory and Practice of Self-Conscious Fiction* (1984) focuses on recent examples of the form.

metaphor   In its narrow sense, a figure of speech in which something (A) is identified with something else (B) in order to attribute to A a quality associated with B. In the phrase "Life is but a dream," for example, the idea of a transient illusion or unreality traditionally associated with dreams is carried over to the subject "life." In its broader sense, the term serves as a general category for all figures of speech, such as SIMILE, METONYMY, and SYNECDOCHE. This is the sense of the term employed when we speak of language as either literal or metaphorical.

Metaphors are characterized as either direct or indirect. "You're the cream in my coffee" is a direct metaphor. The primary subject (the "tenor") is "You" and the secondary subject (the "vehicle") is "cream in my coffee." What the metaphor creates is the sense of "You" as a unique source of continual pleasure. (In its use of an unusual vehicle to express romantic love, this popular song of the 1920s resembles the characteristic lyrics of metaphysical poetry.) An indirect metaphor is one in which the comparison is implied but not stated directly. In the line from T. S. Eliot's "The Love Song of J. Alfred Prufrock" (1915), "The yellow fog that rubs its back upon the window panes," the implied equation is: "fog"="cat." Or, when we speak of someone having "the luck of the draw," we are comparing an element of life to a card game, but that comparison is not stated directly.

This last example illustrates that language is riddled with *dead metaphors*, phrases whose original, metaphorical character has been blunted by everyday use. Thus, although always perceived to be a central element of poetry, metaphor has only recently come to be seen as a pervasive presence in all forms of language. *See* METAPHOR/METONYMY.

On Metaphor (1979), edited by Sheldon Sacks, is a collection of essays on the various aspects of the modern sense of the term.

metaphor/metonymy   In traditional usage, METAPHOR is based upon the principle of similarity, and METONYMY on the principle of association. Thus the metaphor "sleep" for "death" is based upon a certain similarity between the two states, while the metonymy "White House" for "President" is based upon a recognized convention connecting the two terms.

In 1956 the linguist Roman Jakobson used the two terms to describe two fundamental features of language. He maintained that using language involves two procedures, selection and arrangement. We select words from our vocabulary and rearrange them in phrases and sentences. Jakobson argued that these two processes are controlled by specific brain functions and that metaphor is identified with the process of selection and metonymy with arrangement.

Jakobson further maintained that literary movements could be classified on the basis of their being primarily metaphorical or metonymical. Thus Romanticism is based on metaphor and realism on metonymy. One way of interpreting this distinction is to assert that metonymy, like realism, is "referential," keyed to the extra-linguistic world, while metaphor, like Romanticism, is a purely linguistic process. *See* PARADIGM.

David Lodge's *The Mode of Modern Writing* (1979) provides a detailed, interesting application of Jakobson's ideas.

metaphysical poetry   A type of 17th-century English poetry characterized by witty, ingenious metaphors drawn from widely disparate areas of life, an intellectually challenging mode of argument reminiscent of the fine distinctions of scholastic philosophy, and a forceful, colloquial style, as in this opening line from a poem by John Donne: "For God's sake, hold your tongue and let me love."

Donne was the first and preeminent metaphysical poet. Later followers included George Herbert, Henry Vaughan, Andrew Marvell, Richard Crashaw, Abraham Cowley, and Thomas Traherne. The metaphysicals primarily focused on two subjects, romantic love and religious faith, sometimes treating the one in terms of the other, as in Donne's "The Canonization" in which two lovers are treated as saints. The distinctive feature of this poetry is its WIT, in the 17th-century sense of the term: the balancing of strong feeling and intellectual play.

Later in the century, the metaphysicals fell out of fashion and remained so until the beginning of the 20th century. Among their most important modern supporters was T. S. Eliot, who proclaimed these poets' capacity to integrate such seeming opposites as sexual love and science. He saw in them examples of the unified sensibility sorely lacking in later literature (*see* DISSOCIATION OF SENSIBILITY). Eliot's praise, along with its compatibility with the principles of NEW CRITICISM, sparked an enthusiasm for metaphysical poetry in the 1940s and '50s that now appears to have been an overestimation. One recent critique forms the basis of Margaret Edson's Pulitzer Prize–winning *Wit* (1998), a drama about an English professor dying of cancer after having devoted her life to the poetry of Donne. Confronting death, she discovers that, neither in poetry nor in life, is "wit" the supreme value she had assumed it to be.

T. S. Eliot's influential essay "The Metaphysical Poets" appears in his *Selected Essays* (1932). Joan Bennett's *Five Metaphysical Poets* (1963) is a perceptive study.

metaphysics of presence   In DECONSTRUCTION, the argument that Western thought rests upon the assumption of a presence or center existing outside of language that is always a "given" and therefore unexamined. The belief in truth as an absolute principle is an example of logocentric thinking.

In the sphere of language, the metaphysics of presence functions as LOGOCENTRISM.

metatheatre   A term coined by the critic Lionel Abel to describe a dramatic form that focuses on the "dramatic consciousness" of its characters—the consciousness, that is, of being characters in a play. They usually demonstrate this awareness by stepping out of their characters to speak directly to the audience. Abel argues that metatheatre represents a modern alternative to TRAGEDY, as a form of serious drama that offers the audience the opportunity to reflect on the action from an aesthetic distance. In this respect, metatheatre bears a resemblance to Bertolt Brecht's ALIENATION EFFECT.

For Abel, the earliest example of the form is Shakespeare's *Hamlet*: "For the first time in the history of drama the problem of the protagonist is that he has a playwright's consciousness." Other examples are Pedro Calderón de la Barca's *Life Is a Dream* (1635) and, in modern drama, Luigi Pirandello's *Six Characters in Search of an Author* (1921), Jean Genet's *The Balcony* (1956), and Tom Stoppard's *Rosencrantz and Guildenstern Are Dead* (1967).

In Woody Allen's film *The Purple Rose of Cairo* (1985), a character in a film, tired of repeating the same lines, steps out of the screen and asks to experience real life.

Lionel Abel's *Metatheatre* (1963) contains a full account of the term.

meter   In POETRY, the regular recurrence of a rhythmic sound pattern. The pattern is created by the repetition of a certain number of accented or stressed syllables together with a number of unaccented or unstressed syllables. In scanning a line of poetry it is conventional to mark the accented syllables with a slanted dash (/) and the unaccented with a breve (˘), as in this line from Alexander Pope:

> ˘ / ˘ / ˘ / ˘ / ˘ /
> *To wake the soul by tender strokes of art.*

This process of marking lines of verse is called SCANSION. When we scan an entire poem, we can determine its prevailing meter as well as its rhyme scheme.

In English verse, lines are divided into a number of individual units, each one known as a FOOT, which includes a particular combination of accented and unaccented syllables. Pope's line (above) has five feet, each one featuring an unaccented syllable followed by an accented one. A line of poetry in English is characterized by the pattern of accent and by the number of feet. In this sense an English verse line is both accentual and quantitative. In other languages, Greek and Latin for example, poetry is only quantitative.

The most common types of poetic feet are the following:

iambic   One unaccented syllable followed by an accented syllable, as in the line quoted above.

trochaic   One accented syllable followed by an unaccented one:

/ ˘ / ˘ / ˘ /
Life is but an empty dream.

dactylic   One accented syllable followed by two unaccented syllables:

/ ˘˘ / ˘˘ /
Hickory dickory dock.

anapestic   Two unaccented syllables followed by one accented. Anapests are a feature of the LIMERICK, as in this concluding line describing limericks:

˘ ˘ / ˘ ˘ / ˘ ˘ / ˘˘
And the clean ones are seldom so comical.

spondaic   Two stressed and no unstressed syllables, as in this line from Shakespeare's *The Winter's Tale*:

/ / / / / / / /
Good Queen, my Lord, I say, Good Queen.

A line of verse is also characterized by the number of feet it contains. The terms for poetic feet are the following:

One foot	MONOMETER
Two feet	DIMETER
Three feet	TRIMETER
Four feet	TETRAMETER
Five feet	PENTAMETER
Six feet	HEXAMETER
Seven feet	HEPTAMETER

Thus, a poetic line in which an accented syllable is followed by an unaccented syllable four times is in trochaic tetrameter, as in this line from W. H. Auden:

/ ⌣ / ⌣ / ⌣ /
Earth receive an honored guest.

A line in which one accented syllable is followed by two unaccented syllables three times is in dactylic trimeter:

/ ⌣ ⌣ / ⌣ ⌣ / ⌣ ⌣ / ⌣
Half a league, half a league, half a league onwards.

The best-known meter in English verse is iambic pentameter. Unrhymed iambic pentameter is also known as BLANK VERSE, the meter of Shakespeare's plays and John Milton's *Paradise Lost.*

It is important to remember that poets generally vary their meter both within a poem and even within a line. Thus in Cole Porter's lyric,

/ ⌣ / ⌣ / ⌣ / / /
Even educated fleas do it.

the trochaic pattern of the line is altered at the end by a spondaic foot. Poetry without a fixed meter is characterized as FREE VERSE.

Paul Fussell's *Poetic Meter and Poetic Form* (1965) offers an excellent guide to metrical forms.

Method acting   Term for a type of acting (also known as the Stanislavski Method) derived from the teachings of Konstantin Stanislavski (1863–1938), a Russian director and acting teacher. Method acting consists of a series of exercises designed to help actors empathize with the characters they play. Specifically the term refers to the adaptation of Stanislavski developed by Lee Strasberg while teaching at the Actors' Studio in New York from 1947 to 1956.

The essence of the Method is to have the actor discover a psychological motivation for the character he is playing. In so doing the Method emphasizes not the effect the actor creates but instead the cause of that effect. In his adaptation of Stanislavski, Strasberg developed a number of exercises to help the actor find within her own experience a connection with the motivation of the character she was portraying.

The Method was introduced and adapted during the heyday of dramatic REALISM, in which the techniques were particularly effective. Critics have charged that the Method works less well in nonrealist forms, such as classical or Shakespearean drama. Supporters of the Method maintain that the technique relates to every type of acting.

Denounced in its time as the source of a mumbling, inaudible style of speech, the Method has now been accepted as a valid approach to modern acting and has continued to exert a powerful influence, either directly or indirectly, through the performances of its many gifted students, the best known of whom are Julie Harris, Geraldine Page, Montgomery Clift, James Dean, and Marlon Brando.

Robert Lewis's *Method and Madness* (1958) offers a detailed rationale of the Method by one of the founders of the Actors Studio.

metonymy   A figure of speech in which a word is used to apply to something conventionally associated with it. Metonymy can take a number of forms, such as identifying the container with the thing contained ("He drank the whole bottle"), or an article of dress with a person ("hard hat" for a construction worker), or a writer for her work ("She read all of Jane Austen").

SYNECDOCHE, a figure of speech in which a part stands for the whole or vice versa ("All hands on deck" for a ship's crew) is sometimes considered a form of metonymy.

For a special use of the term *see* METAPHOR/METONYMY.

Middle Ages   The period of European history from the fall of Rome (A.D. 476) to the beginning of the RENAISSANCE. The first half of this period (from the fifth to the 10th centuries) is sometimes known as the Dark Ages, a disparaging term reflecting its lack of distinction in literature and the arts. The second half, often called the medieval period, is the period of Gothic architecture, SCHOLASTICISM, FEUDALISM, and in literature, the development of forms such as the ROMANCE, the SONNET, the CHANSON DE GESTE, and the MYSTERY PLAY. The two great poets of the period were Dante and Chaucer.

Basic to the understanding and appreciation of medieval literature is an awareness of the model of the universe that it embraces.   In the medieval view, everything that exists is an integrated part of a grand and beautiful design, in which nothing is irrelevant or accidental. As a result, the modern reader needs to recognize the reason for, in the words of C. S. Lewis, "the most typical vice and the most typical virtue" of the literature of the Middle Ages. The most typical vice is "dullness," long boring digressions, in which, as Lewis explains it, "The writer feels everything to be so interesting in itself that there is no need for him to make it so." On the other hand, the most typical virtue derives from the same sense of security, "the absence of strain . . . the story seems to be telling itself, medieval authors have a complete confidence in the intrinsic value of their matter. The telling is for the sake of the tale." (*See* MEDIEVAL ROMANCE.)

C.S. Lewis's *The Discarded Image* (1964) offers a description of the medieval world view that is as vivid and witty as it is educational.

Middle Comedy   A type of COMEDY that flourished in Greece in the fourth century B.C. Middle Comedy, which succeeded the Old Comedy associated with Aristophanes, frequently satirized Greek mythological figures. No complete examples of this form have survived.

Middle English   In English literature the period from the middle of the 14th century to the beginning of the 16th. The major figure of the period is Geoffrey Chaucer, regarded by many as the second greatest poet in the history of English literature. The period also saw the major achievements of the MYSTERY PLAYS, remarkable products of religious faith and popular imagination.

Other significant works of the age are William Langland's *Piers Plowman* (1367–90), an allegorical dream vision in verse; Sir Thomas Malory's *Morte D'Arthur* (1485), an important collection and re-telling of the legends of King Arthur; and *Sir Gawain and the Green Knight* (c. 1370), a verse ROMANCE dealing with the adventures of a knight defending the chivalric code of honor.

The language of Middle English was an amalgam of Old English, French, and, to a lesser extent, Latin. The GRAMMAR and syntax were largely English, the vocabulary heavily influenced by French. English, largely Germanic in its roots, was the language of the common people, French the language of the government, and Latin the language of the learned. By the end of the 14th century, when Chaucer was writing *The Canterbury Tales* (1376–1400) the language was recognizably English, but a considerable distance from modern English, as the opening lines of Chaucer's great poem illustrate:

> *Whan that April with his showres soote*
> *The droughte of March hath perced to the roote*

The lines in modern English are "When April with its showers sweet / The drought of March has pierced to the root."

Robert Ackerman's *Backgrounds to Medieval English Literature* (1966) offers a useful introduction to the literature of the period; D. W. Robertson's *A Preface to Chaucer* (1963) is an insightful guide to the poet and his age.

miles gloriosus   *See* BRAGGART WARRIOR.

mime   A play with no dialogue, in which the actor or actors rely on the skillful employment of bodily movements or facial gestures. In classical Roman times, *mime* described a form of early comedy consisting of broad slapstick and obscene dialogue. As such it attained great popularity in the waning years of the Roman Empire, but the obscenity eventually resulted in the suppression of these plays by the church in the sixth century A.D. In the Renaissance, the COMMEDIA DELL'ARTE and other groups of itinerant players incorporated some of the slapstick features of the mime tradition.

In 18th-century France, these popular troupes were forbidden to employ dialogue. As a result, the modern definition of *mime* as acting without words came into use and established a tradition that has had a long life in French theater. Great mime artists have included the 19th-century performer Jean Gaspard Deburau, and, in the 20th century, Marcel Marceau and Jacques Tati. In Marcel Carne's celebrated film *Children of Paradise* (1944), Jean-Louis Barrault appeared as Deburau and performed a portion of a mime play.

mimesis   In his *Apologie for Poetrie* (1595), Sir Philip Sidney describes POETRY as "an art of imitation, for so Aristotle termeth it in his word Mimesis, that is to say a representing, counterfeiting, or figuring forth; to speak metaphorically, a speaking picture."

Sidney's definition of mimesis is one example among many of the influence of the Aristotelian idea that literature—indeed all of art—is an imitation of life. This mimetic theory has dominated Western thought from the Renaissance to the present day, although it has been seriously challenged at various times: by ROMANTICISM, which defined art as an expression of the artist; by NEW CRITICISM, which viewed the literary text as an autonomous, self-referential object, and by DECONSTRUCTION and POSTSTRUCTURALISM, which tend to question the referential character not only of literature, but of language in general.

Nevertheless the traditional view of literature as holding, in Hamlet's words, "A mirror up to nature" retains its prominence, whether in the formulation of MARXIST CRITICISM, or in the practice of REALISM, or as demonstrated in classical critical texts such as Erich Auerbach's *Mimesis* (1953).

For another conception of Mimesis, *see* DIEGESIS/MIMESIS.

———————

Kendall Williams's *Mimesis as Make-Believe* (1990) is a theoretical discussion of the role of imagination in mimetic art and literature.

mimetic desire   Term coined by the myth critic and theorist René Girard, asserting that certain sexual, political or social drives are not instinctive but are imitations learned by copying another. The "other" who is being copied represents a model or mediator through which a human relationship is filtered. Thus "mimetic desire" represents triangular desire, in which the desiring one is motivated more to be like the model than to achieve the ostensible object of desire. One literary example is the story of Paolo and Francesca in Dante's *Inferno*. The two lovers succumb not directly to each other, but as a result of reading the love story of Lancelot and Guinevere. According to Girard, "The written word . . . impels the two young lovers to act as if determined by fate; it is a mirror in which they gaze, discovering in themselves the semblances of their brilliant models."

Girard extends his "mimetic desire" concept to challenge Freud's crucial principle, the OEDIPAL COMPLEX. In Girard's reading, the child's attraction to the mother is an imitation of the father, not a wish to eliminate him. However, if the father experiences the child as a threat, mimetic desire can lead to conflict and competition between the two. For Girard, plays featuring mixed-up pairs of lovers, such as Shakespeare's *A Midsummer Night's Dream* or Oscar Wilde's *The Importance of Being Earnest*, exhibit mimetic desire. *See* ENVY.

Girard's theories are developed in his *A Theater of Envy: William Shakespeare* (1991).

minimalism   A style in contemporary literature and art that aims at reducing the elements in a text to a bare minimum. An outstanding example is Samuel Beckett, who progressively subtracted from his work story line, physical movement, and, in his MIME plays, even dialogue.

Minimalist fiction tends to represent characters who are isolated, immobile, and sceptical about any possibilities life may appear to offer. The term has been used to describe the stories of contemporary American writers such as Raymond Carver (*Will You Please Be Quiet, Please?*, 1976) and Ann Beattie (*The Burning House*, 1982).

Frederick Karl's *American Fictions, 1940–1980* (1983) discusses the minimalist style in contemporary American fiction.

mind as mirror   According to the philosopher Richard Rorty, the metaphor of the human mind as a mirror reflecting reality has dominated Western philosophy since the later 17th century. As a result, the belief that "to know is to represent accurately what is outside the mind" led to the emergence of EPISTEMOLOGY as the central feature of philosophy, and the acceptance of representation—with the mind as the mirror of nature—as its organizing principle. Rorty calls for the abandonment of the theory of REPRESENTATION. Once that occurs, he suggests, philosophy will be forced to cede its position as the final arbiter of value and truth and take a more modest place in the ongoing "conversation of mankind." In his book *Contingency, Irony and Solidarity* (1989), Rorty makes an effective argument for the role of literature as an edifying force in society. *See* PRAGMATISM, SOCIAL CONSTRUCTION.

Rorty's arguments regarding representation are detailed in his *Philosophy and the Mirror of Nature* (1979).

265

minnesingers   Medieval German poet/musicians, who composed songs in the COURTLY LOVE tradition. Like their French counterparts, the TROUBADOURS, the minnesingers not only composed but also performed their songs. The most celebrated of the minnesingers was Walther von der Vogelweide (1170?–1230), who, in addition to his love lyrics, also produced political and religious songs.

Ronald Taylor's *The Art of the Minnesinger* (1968) provides a history and analysis of the subject.

minstrel   In medieval Europe, a traveling entertainer, who sang ballads and recounted folktales and other traditional stories. *See also* JONGLEUR; TROUBADOURS.

miracle play   A form of medieval drama centered on a miracle performed either by the Virgin Mary or a saint. The earliest known miracle play in French is *Le jeu de Saint Nicholas* (c. 1200) by Jean Bodel. The play depicts the adventures of a crusader whose life is saved by the miraculous intervention of Saint Nicholas.

This type of play resembles the SAINT PLAY but differs in that the latter focuses on the life or martyrdom of a saint. The term *miracle play* is also sometimes used to describe the English cycle plays more commonly referred to as MYSTERY PLAYS, although the latter term is usually reserved for plays based upon biblical incidents.

mise-en-scène   *See* SETTING.

mock epic   A term, sometimes known as *mock heroic*, for a form that employs the "high style" associated with EPIC poetry in order to satirize a trivial subject. The best example in English poetry is Alexander Pope's *The Rape of the Lock* (1712–14), in which the cutting of a lock of a woman's hair by an ardent admirer is treated in the manner of Homer's *Iliad*.

modernism   A development in literature and the arts that began in the late 19th century and, in a variety of evolving forms, dominated the cultural landscape until the 1950s when it began to be displaced by POSTMODERNISM.

Perhaps the distinguishing feature of modernism is its determination to dispense with the past, in Ezra Pound's phrase "to make it new." In one sense this impulse lies at the basis of every literary movement in history, but what distinguished modernism was the profound sense of intellectual crisis in which it developed.

Modernism was a response to the shift in thought and belief precipitated by intellectual developments and discoveries associated with, but not limited to, the names Charles Darwin, Karl Marx, Friedrich Nietzsche, Sigmund Freud, and Albert Einstein. Darwin's *On the Origin of Species* (1859) uprooted the traditional view of "man made in the image and likeness of God," replacing it with one of man as the descendant of an ape. Marx's view of the economic determinism that governed western history and culture directly challenged the idealist philosophy of its time. Nietzsche's declaration of "the death of God" summarized the dismissal of the very ground of the Hebraic/Christian tradition, while Freud's representation of the significance of the UNCONSCIOUS called into question the notion of rational free choice, and Einstein's conception of space/time uprooted the straightforward chronological NARRATIVE forms of the 19th century.

One consequence of this intellectual crisis was a turn toward the inner self. As the critic Denis Donoghue has expressed it, "Modernism is concerned with the validity of one's feelings and the practice of converting apparently external images and events into inwardness, personal energy." Thus one of the most influential terms in modern literature was James Joyce's EPIPHANY, which implied that truth was at best a fleeting, impermanent, intensely personal moment that the artist could strive to capture. Another was the focus on the literary SYMBOL, frequently employed as the outward sign of an interior condition. Symbolism became a major feature of modern art and literature and of the criticism it fostered.

Modernism suffered a decline in reputation in the 1970s and 1980s, attacked by feminists, Marxists, and popular culture adherents as being sexist, reactionary, and elitist. Now those groups are taking a second look. (*See* LIBERAL/CONSERVATIVE IMAGINATION.)

Malcolm Bradbury's *The Modern World: Ten Great Writers* (1988) examines modernism through its leading literary figures.

monologue   A long speech by one speaker. If the speaker is alone such a speech is called a SOLILOQUY. If the speaker addresses someone absent or an abstract idea, it is an APOSTROPHE. If the speech is addressed to someone present, it is a DRAMATIC MONOLOGUE. An INTERIOR MONOLOGUE represents a character's fleeting thoughts and impressions, or inner speech.

monometer   A line of verse consisting of one FOOT, as in Ogden Nash's airy dismissal of one of New York City's five boroughs:

The Bronx?
No Thonx.

montage   A film term that in its general sense is a synonym for editing, the process of putting together the scenes that will make up the completed film. In this sense montage is an essential feature of filmmaking. In a more specialized sense, the term refers to a sequence of quick dissolves employed to convey an element of the story. Examples of the latter include the peeling away of calendar pages to suggest the passage of time, and the speeding wheels of a train to indicate a journey.

mood   The emotional atmosphere of a literary work. The term is similar to TONE, differing in that tone alludes to the author's attitude to the subject, while mood usually refers to the reader's experience. For example, the tone of T. S. Eliot's *The Waste Land* (1922) is ironic while the mood is one of despair.

moral   In popular usage, the ethical lesson of a literary work, as in the phrase "the moral of the story." Modern critics tend to use the term only in reference to explicitly didactic texts such as SERMONS or FABLES. *See* ETHICAL CRITICISM.

morality play   A form of English drama of the 15th and early 16th centuries in which characters exemplify moral or religious abstractions. Morality plays were didactic in intent, designed to instill fear of damnation while showing the path to salvation. The best known is *Everyman* (c. 1500), in which, in response to a summons from Death, Everyman tries to enlist various allegorical figures such as Fellowship, Beauty, Five Wits, and Knowledge to accompany him on his journey. By the time he reaches his grave all have deserted him, except for Good Deeds, who stays with him as he prepares for God's judgment.

Some Elizabethan dramas, such as Christopher Marlowe's *Dr. Faustus* (1588–92) and Ben Jonson's *Volpone* (1605–6), employ features of the morality play.

morpheme   In linguistics, the smallest meaningful unit of a language. Some words, such as *work*, constitute a single morpheme; they cannot be broken down any further. Others, such as *worker*, contain two morphemes, *work* and *er*, a person who works.

A parallel term in relation to sound instead of meaning is PHONEME.

morphology   In LINGUISTICS, the study of the forms of words, of the ways in which they are made up of MORPHEMES.

Moscow Art Theater   A repertory theater founded by Konstantin Stanislavski (1863–1938) and Vladimir Nemirovich-Danchenko in 1897, famous for its acting style and its association with the great Russian dramatist Anton Chekhov. Its early production of Chekhov's *The Sea Gull* (1895), *Three Sisters* (1901), and *The Cherry Orchard* (1904) established its preeminence in the performance of his plays. The theater exercised a powerful influence on modern theories of acting, particularly the technique known as the METHOD.

motif   An element that appears in a number of literary works. It differs from a THEME, which it closely resembles, in that it is a concrete example of a theme. Hamlet's apostrophe to "poor Yorick" is an expression of the *memento mori* ("remember you must die") motif, part of the play's larger theme of DEATH. *See also* LEITMOTIF.

motion pictures   *See* FILM.

motivation   The determining forces of a character's behavior. A motivation may be psychological, social, circumstantial, or, more likely, a combination of these. The assumption of realist literature is that there is always an underlying motivation, a "cause" or "reason" that explains a person's behavior. The implicit DETERMINISM in this idea of motivation has led some modern writers to reject this notion in the name of human freedom. A celebrated example is the novelist André Gide, who in his novel *The Counterfeiters* (1926) postulates the *acte gratuit* ("the gratuitous act"), the representation of an unmotivated act.

Another famous example of an anti-motivation position is Samuel Taylor Coleridge's description of critics' search for Iago's motivation in Shakespeare's *Othello* as "the motive hunting of a motiveless malignity." *See* BANALITY OF EVIL.

In the DETECTIVE STORY the term *motive* is frequently used to designate the reason for the crime.

Movement, the   The name given to a group of English poets in the 1950s who stressed irony, restraint, self-doubt, and the celebration of ordinary life. Among its practitioners were Donald Davie, Thom Gunn, Elizabeth Jennings, and, most notably, Philip Larkin. These poets were consciously reacting against what they regarded as the pretentious, ornate poetry of the 1940s, represented by the verse of Dylan Thomas and the NEW APOCALYPSE MOVEMENT.

muckrakers   A term coined by Theodore Roosevelt to describe (and disparage) a group of American writers in the first decade of the 20th century who exposed the corrupt practices of certain big businesses and government officials. Among the best known of the muckrakers were Upton Sinclair, Frank Norris, Lincoln Steffens, and Ida Tarbell. Norris's *The Octopus* (1901) and Sinclair's *The*

Jungle (1906) helped to bring about social reforms in agriculture and the meat industry. Steffens's *The Shame of the Cities* (1904) dealt with corruption in municipal governments, while Ida Tarbell's *The History of the Standard Oil Company* (1904) exposed the ruthless, monopolistic tactics of John D. Rockefeller.

multiculturalism   A contemporary movement in the United States based upon the assumption that traditional, mainstream culture has overlooked many of the literary contributions of ethnic and minority groups. As an educational movement, multiculturalism argues that students acquire enhanced self-esteem when they study their own cultures. In reference to literature, multiculturalists argue for the inclusion of ethnic and minority literature in the CANON, the basic literary texts taught in schools and colleges. The question of the "opening up" of the canon has sparked a continuing debate.

mummers' play/mumming play   A form of folk play performed during Christmas time in English villages in the 16th and 17th centuries. Many of the plays feature the folk hero of the Red Cross, St. George. The basic plot involves a fight between St. George and the Turkish Knight, one of whom is killed. The dead man is brought back to life by the Doctor, who is also Father Christmas. The plot suggests the ancient roots of these plays, probably stretching back to pre-Christian times, in which the original "Green Man" was a vegetation deity. Mummers' plays continue to be performed in some remote villages of Northern England and Scotland.

muse   The traditional term for the source of poetic inspiration. In Greek mythology, the nine muses were goddesses who presided over the arts and other fields of learning. The names of the muses and the fields they governed are the following: Calliope, epic poetry; Clio, history; Erato, LYRIC and love poetry; Euterpe, flute music; Melpomene, TRAGEDY; Thalia, COMEDY; Polymnia, sacred music; Terpischore, dancing; and Urania, astronomy.

The INVOCATION to the muse is a traditional feature of EPIC poetry.

music   The relation of music and literature is most intense when the two join in the various forms of OPERA and SONG. This connection is underscored when the collaborators are distinguished writers and composers, as in the collaborations of Richard Strauss and Hugo von Hofmannstahl (*Der Rosencavalier*, 1911), Kurt Weill and Bertolt Brecht (*The Threepenny Opera*, 1928), and Igor Stravinsky and W. H. Auden (*The Rake's Progress*, 1951). However, there are other points of contact that can be grouped under the headings of Literature in Music and Music in Literature.

The category of Literature in Music includes "program music," compositions that attempt to "verbalize" music by relying on the emotional connotations that the arrangement of notes can produce. One example is the "tone poem," an orchestral composition that attempts to "tell a story," as in Richard Strauss's *Don Quixote* (1897).

In the category of Music in Literature belong many of the experiments that aimed to reproduce a "musical" element. The French SYMBOLIST POETS advocated this attempt "to aspire to the condition of music," using as one of their models Edgar Allan Poe's experiments with ONOMATOPOEIA.

Still another form of Music in Literature is the attempt to introduce structural features of music into POETRY and FICTION. Among these are the musical features of LEITMOTIF, notably adopted as a central principle in Marcel Proust's *Remembrance of Things Past* (1913–27). Other examples include Thomas Mann's story "The Kreutzer Sonata," Aldous Huxley's novel *Point Counterpoint* (1928), and T. S. Eliot's series of poems *The Four Quartets* (1936–42).

A common instance of poetry and music is the presence of JAZZ rhythms in the work of African-American and many other contemporary poets.

Calvin S. Brown's *Music and Literature: A Comparison of the Two Arts* (1948) is an invaluable survey of the subject. John Hollander's *The Untuning of the Sky* (1961) is an analysis of the relation of music to English poetry before the 18th century. Steven Paul Scher's "Literature and Music" appears in *Interrelations of Literature* (1982), edited by J. P. Barricelli and J. Gibaldi.

musical   A form of theatrical entertainment, derived in part from OPERETTA, that evolved chiefly in England and the United States in the 20th century. Formerly "musical comedy," the form has undergone a name change to reflect the increasingly serious tone of these plays.

Along with operetta, the chief forerunner of the musical in the United States was the revue, a variety show that included a series of unrelated musical scenes. Some revues, such as *Shuffle Along* (1921), the first all-black revue, and *Pins and Needles* (1936), sponsored by the International Ladies Garment Workers Union, had unifying themes, but the great majority merely strung together a series of unrelated skits and songs. Despite these frivolous settings, many of the best American show tunes were composed for revues, including Rodgers and Hart's "Manhattan," Schwartz and Dietz's "Dancing in the Dark," and Cole Porter's "Let's Do It."

The first significant attempt to integrate the songs with the script and dialogue ("the book") was Jerome Kern and Oscar Hammerstein's *Show Boat* (1927), which dealt in its subplot with the theme of race, memorably encapsulated in the song "Ol' Man River." Among celebrated successors to *Show Boat* in the 1930s were George and Ira Gershwin's *Of Thee I Sing* (1933) and their distinguished folk opera *Porgy and Bess* (1935).

Rodgers and Hart's *Pal Joey* (1940), its leading character the first example of an anti-hero in a musical, set the stage for the musical's coming of age in the 1940s. Beginning with Rodgers and Hammerstein's *Oklahoma!* (1943) and *Carousel* (1945), the next two decades saw the most impressive musicals in the history of the genre, including Cole Porter's *Kiss Me Kate* (1948), Frank Loesser's *Guys and Dolls* (1950), Lerner and Loewe's *My Fair Lady* (1956), Bernstein and Sondheim's *West Side Story* (1957), and Styne and Sondheim's *Gypsy* (1959).

Since that time, the most successful musicals artistically have been those created by Stephen Sondheim (*Company*, 1970; *A Little Night Music*, 1973; *Sweeney Todd*, 1979; and *Sunday in the Park with George*, 1984), while the greatest popular successes have been the English and American productions of Andrew Lloyd Webber (*Evita*, 1978; *Cats*, 1981; and *Phantom of the Opera*, 1986).

Another important development has been the increased significance of dance in musicals, a trend epitomized in *A Chorus Line* (1975). In 2000, comedy came back to the musical with a vengeance in Mel Brooks's *The Producers*, one of the funniest shows in the history of the form.

Film musicals were among the most popular American films from the 1930s to the 1960s. Aside from the adaptation of Broadway musicals, which have always provided the basis for the genre, movies produced a new and distinctive form of musical from their ability to create a fantasy world covering a range from real people in imaginary settings to animated cartoon figures.

The first filmed musical was fittingly the first sound film, or talkie, *The Jazz Singer* (1927), but the first films to make imaginative use of the camera were those choreographed by Busby Berkeley (*42nd Street*, *Footlight Parade*, and *Gold Diggers of 1933*, all produced in 1933). Other outstanding musical films of the 1930s were those featuring Fred Astaire and Ginger Rogers, animated films such as *Snow White and the Seven Dwarfs* (1937), and the film that made the greatest use of the visual potential of FILM, *The Wizard of Oz* (1939).

The 1940s saw the innovative all-black musical *Stormy Weather* (1943), as well as the memorable *Yankee Doodle Dandy* (1942) and *Meet Me in St. Louis* (1944). Outstanding among '50s musicals were *An American in Paris* (1951) with an all-Gershwin score, and the remarkably choreographed *Seven Brides for Seven Brothers* (1954). The musical that appears to offer the most effective integration of music, dancing, and story is *Singin' in the Rain* (1952). The demise of the STUDIO SYSTEM and high production costs brought an end to the Hollywood musical, except for the occasional adaptation of a Broadway hit.

Lehman Engel's *The American Musical Theater* (1967, 1975) provides an expert's overview of the genre until 1970; Stanley Green's *Hollywood Musicals* (1990) is an entertaining history. Raymond Knapp's *The American Musical and the Formation of National Identity* (2004) examines its 19th century roots.

music hall   In Great Britain, a form of variety theater popular in the 19th and early 20th centuries. Similar to American VAUDEVILLE, music hall acts included jugglers, acrobats, comedians, singers, and dancers. When singers performed, the audience was encouraged to join in. In John Osborne's *The Entertainer* (1956), the fading music hall performer Archie Rice comes to stand for postwar England, still clinging to its old glory days as it loses its place on the world stage.

mystery plays   Medieval plays that depict scenes from the Bible. The plays were made up of individual episodes that formed a cycle covering the range of biblical history from the story of Adam to the Last Judgment. The productions were extraordinary spectacles, performed in cities throughout Europe in connection with certain feast days, particularly the feast of CORPUS CHRISTI.

In England, the mysteries were produced by the local trade guilds of the town in which they appeared. Each guild was assigned the task of presenting a particular sequence from the cycle. The plays were performed on floats that were moved to various stations in the town or set up in circles or semicircles. The area between the platform and the audience, known as the *platea* (place), was also used as a performing space. The movement of the actors from the platform to the *platea* would signal a shift to a new scene.

The traditional belief that mystery plays "evolved" directly from LITURGICAL DRAMA has been challenged substantially in recent years. There is little doubt, however, that the plays performed a primary religious function, although one that incorporated the subversive principle of CARNIVAL. A complete cycle might represent major scenes from the Old and New Testaments, concluding with the Last Judgment. Performed from the 14th through the 16th centuries, the mystery cycles came to an end with the advent of Protestantism in England.

The manuscripts of the four English cycles that have been preserved are named for the towns in which they were produced: York, Wakefield, Chester, and N-Town, the last one so designated because the town is not known. Of the four cycles the most famous is that of Wakefield, because of the consummate skill of the anonymous playwright known as the Wakefield Master. The Master is the author of the best known episode of the English mysteries, *The Second Shepherd's Play*, a marvelous mixture of the solemn and the comic, the sacred and the profane.

In France the most famous of the mysteries is Arnold Greban's *Passion* (c. 1450), written for performance in the city of Le Mans, a cycle that included depictions of the life of Adam and the passion and resurrection of CHRIST.

In Spain mystery plays were also known as *autos* (one-act plays). Dealing with the lives of the saints as well as biblical stories, they were eventually replaced by the form known as *AUTO SACRAMENTAL*.

In 1951, the English mysteries were revived for performance at the Festival of Britain. Since that time, they have been regularly presented in Great Britain and have been recorded on video cassette. These presentations have brought home to many the realization that the mysteries are not a form of "primitive" drama but remarkable and powerful examples of popular art.

An excellent anthology is *Medieval Drama*, edited by David Bevington (1975). For a comprehensive treatment of the English cycles, see Martin Stevens's *Four Middle English Mystery Cycles* (1987).

mysticism   The spiritual discipline that enables an individual to experience union with God or a divine principle. An aspect of many of the world's religions, mystical experience has been the source of literature from antiquity to the present. Among the great Western classics in the mystical tradition are the KABBALAH, Thomas à Kempis's *Imitation of Christ* (1426), the autobiography of Saint Theresa of Avila, and the poetry of St. John of the Cross.

Mysticism is a feature of the work of a number of writers, including the 17th-century poets Richard Crashaw, George Herbert, and Thomas Traherne. *See also* ZEN.

myth   Stories belonging to a specific culture recounting supernatural or paradoxical events designed to reflect that culture's view of the world. Despite their seemingly endless variety, myths tend to have an underlying consistency of action, theme, and character.

The relation of myth to literature has been one of the chief concerns of literary study in the 20th century. Are the origins of literature rooted in myth? If so, what are the consequences of that history? Does the influence of myth extend beyond random traces in modern literature to include the basic structure of literature itself? These are some of the questions that literary scholars have been investigating while at the same time absorbing an increasingly complex definition of myth from the fields of anthropology, psychology, and philosophy. At the convergence of these disciplines, myth stands at the magnetic center.

Myth has occupied a central role in the psychologies of Sigmund Freud and Carl Jung and among philosophers such as Ernst Cassirer and Suzanne Langer, who argue that mythic thinking is a fundamental aspect of human consciousness. The traditional anthropological view of myth, as a collection of stories that incorporate the beliefs of a given culture, has been redefined by STRUCTURALISM as a manifestation of the way in which the human mind creates culture. All of these influences have helped to shape the divergent approaches to literature grouped under the heading of MYTH CRITICISM.

Martin Day's *The Many Meanings of Myth* (1984) examines the pervasiveness of the concept of myth in contemporary thought.

myth criticism   Central to the conception of myth criticism is the notion of "archetypal" patterns. An archetype is a basic apprehension of, or response to, an aspect of life embedded within the collective UNCONSCIOUS of every human being. Archetypes are evident in certain myths and rituals that underlie the forms of narrative literature and are the source of our profound response to certain stories and plays. An archetype can be found in literature in either the setting (for example, the forest); the plot (the descent into the underworld); or the character (the maimed or wounded hero).

In their use of the archetype, myth critics are heavily indebted to Carl Jung's theory of the collective UNCONSCIOUS and to the work of the anthropologist James Frazier, whose multi-volumed *The Golden Bough* (1890–1915) is a collection of myths and rituals exhibiting archetypal patterns from a wide variety of cultures.

The most celebrated of myth critics is Northrop Frye, whose *Anatomy of Criticism* (1957) is an impressive attempt to encompass all of literature within a mythic frame. Frye sees literature as rooted in the myths of the seasons: comedy, spring; romance, summer; tragedy, autumn; irony, winter. As a result, these four genres are indelibly marked by their mythic origins.

The appearance of Frye's book in 1957 marked the high point of myth criticism, at which time it deposed NEW CRITICISM as the dominant critical school, particularly in the study of American literature. Works such as R. W. B. Lewis's *The American Adam* (1955) and Leslie Fiedler's *Love and Death in the American Novel* (1960) were among the many attempts to analyze the archetypal pattern that defined the American tradition. The mythic approach also flourished in Shakespearean criticism, where C. L. Barber's *Shakespeare's Festive Comedy* (1959) and Northrop Frye's *A Natural Perspective* (1965) were notable achievements.

In recent years the mythic approach has been criticized by feminists and structuralists. FEMINIST CRITICISM argues that the Jungian concept of the archetypal hero assumes the centrality of the male and the secondary role of the woman. STRUCTURALISM calls for an emphasis not on the content of myth but on its structure.

Despite its critics, myth criticism in general, and Frye's version in particular, continues to play a prominent role in practical criticism.

Other notable examples of the mythic approach include Maud Bodkin's *Archetypal Patterns in Poetry* (1937), Robert Graves's *The White Goddess: A Historical Grammar of Poetic Myth* (1948) and Joseph Campbell's *The Hero with a Thousand Faces* (1949). Jacqueline De Weever's *Metaphor And Mythmaking In Black Women's Fiction* (1992) applies this approach to African-American women's literature.

naive/sentimental   A set of terms that attempts to distinguish POETRY that is direct and unself-conscious (naive) from that which is self-conscious and conflicted because of the poet's inability to reconcile thought and feeling (sentimental). The terms were coined by the German dramatist and critic Friedrich Schiller in his *On Naive and Sentimental Poetry* (1795–96), in which he contrasts the literature of classical Greece with that of his own time. Schiller argues that the Greeks lived in harmony with nature and produced a poetry that was more natural and less tortured by the ethical doubts and idealized goals of late 18th-century poets. He calls for a union of the naive and sentimental, exemplified for him by his great contemporary Johann von Goethe.

René Wellek's *A History of Modern Criticism: 1750–1950* (Volume 1, 1955) contains an informative discussion of Schiller's ideas.

narcissism   The theme of self-love, named after Narcissus, the figure in Greek mythology who fell in love with his own image while gazing into a pool of water. The Narcissus myth was adapted by Ovid in his *Metamorphoses* (first century A.D.). Ovid's version formed the basis for many medieval and Renaissance renderings of the story, most of them focusing on frustration and isolation as the fruits of self-love. A Shakespearean example is Malvolio in *Twelfth Night*, "sick of self-love," the only character not reconciled at the end of the play.

Narcissism plays an important role in Romantic poetry, in which it is allied with introspection and self-knowledge. The poetry of William Wordsworth, in particular, exhibits this acute self-centeredness, criticized by another Romantic poet, John Keats, as an example of the "egotistical sublime."

In the 20th century, Sigmund Freud's re-assignment of narcissism to that stage of infantile development in which the child's own body is the object of erotic desire has had a profound influence. Narcissistic personalities are adults "arrested" at this early stage. Viewed through the psychoanalytical theory known as "object relations" (the analysis of the capacity to love and care for another), certain literary figures present interesting examples of narcissism. In his object-relations study *Hamlet and Narcissism* (1995), John Russell argues that Shakespeare's Hamlet is a character trapped in a narcissistic illusion generated by his ambivalence toward his dead father. He contrasts Hamlet's failure to move beyond narcissism to Edgar's successful reconciliation with his father, the earl of Gloucester, in *King Lear.*

narratee   In a NARRATIVE, the figure to whom the story is told. The narratee is distinct from the implied reader of a fictional work in that the narratee is a character in the text. (*See* IMPLIED AUTHOR/READER.) In *The Catcher in the Rye* (1955), the narratee is apparently a psychiatrist whose silent presence testifies to the emotional condition of the narrator. In Albert Camus's *The Fall* (1957), the narratee is a lawyer who listens to the narrator's "confession" and is asked for a judgment. Another example of the narratee is the silent emissary to the duke in Browning's *My Last Duchess* (1842).

When, as in most narratives, the narratee is not explicitly indicated, the line between narratee and implied reader becomes difficult to distinguish.

Gerald Prince's *A Dictionary of Narratology* (1987) provides a discussion of the term.

narrative   An account of actual or imagined events told by a NARRATOR. A narrative is made up of events, the STORY, and the arrangement of those events, the PLOT. Narratives may be as simple as a joke or anecdote or as complex as a multivolumed history or NOVEL. The term applies to nonfiction as well as FICTION.

Narrative poetry refers to poems that tell a story, such as the EPIC, BALLAD, or LAY.

narratology   The systematic analysis of the elements that make up a NARRATIVE. Narratology differs from ordinary literary criticism in that it focuses on how the story is told—on the structural elements of narrative or on such features as the NARRATOR, the NARRATEE, and the IMPLIED AUTHOR/READER.

Gerald Prince's *A Dictionary of Narratology* (1987) is an excellent introduction to this field.

narrator   The voice that recounts the story in a NARRATIVE, usually understood to be a person and, in nonfiction narrative, identified with the AUTHOR. In fictional narratives, the identity of the narrator can raise complicated questions. In first-person narratives, for example, the narrator is a fictional character within the story. In third-person narratives the narrator may be invisible, in that the reader is unaware of anything but a voice, detached or intrusive, making comments on the characters or events. In either case the narrator may be identified with, or seen as separate from, the implied author or the author. (*See* IMPLIED AUTHOR/READER.)

Narrators may also be classified as reliable or unreliable. Reliable narrators, the most common form, are those whose account the reader does not doubt. Unreliable narrators may be doubted for any number of reasons including their lack of sophistication (Huck in *Adventures of Huckleberry Finn,* 1884) or their lack of sanity (Charles Kinbote in Vladimir Nabokov's *Pale Fire,* 1962). *See* NARRATEE.

Gerald Prince's *A Dictionary of Narratology* (1987) provides a thorough treatment of the term.

Native American literature   When Columbus arrived in North America there were no fewer than 350 languages spoken there. That fact should dispel any easy generalizations about Native Americans and their diverse cultures. What we can say is that their literature was oral—meant to be performed not read—and consisted mainly of MYTHs. Many of their stories and songs, resting on the belief in the power of language to affect nature, were designed to guarantee the continued orderly processes of life. Others were accounts of the creation of the world or guides to proper behavior. English translations of this literature inevitably fail to convey their tone and texture, or their oral, performative essence.

The first writings in English by Native Americans were autobiographical. The earliest of these was William Apess's *A Son of the Forest* (1829). Apess was a "mixedblood" and an orphan, who as a child worked as an indentured servant of white families. Other autobiographies were Luther Standing Bear's *My People, the Sioux* (1929) and John Rogers's *A Chippewa Speaks* (1957).

The first NOVEL by a Native American, Sophia Alice Callahan's *Wynema*, was published in 1891, but it was not until the 1960s that native authors began to win a wide readership. The turning point was the publication in 1968 of N. Scott Momaday's Pulitzer Prize–winning *House Made of Dawn*. Momaday's success opened the door for a number of talented writers, including Leslie Marmon Silko (*Ceremony*, 1977), Louise Erdrich (*Love Medicine*, 1984), and James Welch (*Fools Crow*, 1986) in fiction. In poetry, Simon Ortiz (*From Sand Creek*, 1981), Joy Harjo (*In Mad Love and War*, 1990), and Sherman Alexie (*The Business of Fancydancing*, 1992) have won critical acclaim. In nonfiction, Vine Deloria's *Custer Died for Your Sins* (1969) and Dee Brown's *Bury My Heart at Wounded Knee* (1974) are classics.

A. Lavonne Ruoff's *American Indian Literatures* (1990) is an excellent survey of the field.

naturalism   A late 19th-century movement in literature and art that grew out of the theory of REALISM. The basic effort of naturalism lay in the attempt to produce a scientifically accurate depiction of life even at the cost of representing ugliness and discord. The foremost spokesman of the naturalist school was Émile Zola, who expressed these ideas in two works, *The Experimental Novel* (1880) and *Naturalism in the Theatre* (1882). According to Zola, the artist must bring the scientist's objectivity to the depiction of his subjects. The motives and behavior of characters are determined by heredity and environment. The artists' task is to reveal the role of these factors in the lives of the characters.

Beyond his own work, Zola's ideas exerted considerable influence in the early decades of the 20th century. In American literature naturalism was evident in the works of Stephen Crane (*Maggie: A Girl of the Streets*, 1893), Frank Norris (*The Octopus*, 1901), Theodore Dreiser (*Sister Carrie*, 1900; *An American Tragedy*, 1925), and James T. Farrell (*Studs Lonigan*, 1932–34).

In drama, naturalist classics include Zola's *Thérèse Raquin* (1873), Maxim Gorky's *The Lower Depths* (1902), and Eugene O'Neill's early plays, such as *The Long Voyage Home* (1917).

Y. H. Krikorian's *Naturalism and the Human Spirit* (1944) attempts to explore the wider implications of the movement.

nature/art   Two important, contrasting terms in the history of literature. Since at least as early as classical Greece, people employed these terms to describe aspects of both external and internal reality. Externally, *nature* stands for all that was not made by man, while *art* represents the products of human invention. Internally, *nature* stands for all that is spontaneous, instinctive, "natural" within the individual; *art* stands for the product of thought and discipline. The attempt to determine the relationship of nature to art, specifically the primacy of one or the other, initiated a centuries-long debate that had important bearing on literature from classical times to the RENAISSANCE.

The view held by Plato and Aristotle was that nature and art were not oppositional but complementary. Aristotle's famous dictum "Art imitates nature" suggests the primacy of the "real" to the "artificial," but implicit in Aristotle's formula is the suggestion that the imitation might "perfect" or improve nature. For example, he would probably agree that Sophocles' *Oedipus Rex* represents a kind of perfection of the tragic action that it imitates.

The division between art and nature showed most clearly in the development of pastoralism as a literary form. (*See* PASTORAL.) In celebrating the simple, natural life of shepherds, pastoralism promoted the view of nature that was later to reappear in 19th-century ROMANTICISM. Nevertheless, pastoral poetry was itself art, not nature, its lyrical shepherds a clear idealization of the real thing.

In the Renaissance, the reports of travelers to the New World spurred the debate further. In these reports, the natives of North and South America were described in conflicting terms that provided evidence for both sides of the nature/art controversy. On the one hand, the natives were noble savages "who know no other wealth but Peace and Pleasure"; on the other, they were, in Captain John Smith's words, "perfidious, inhuman, all savage."

In *The Tempest*, a play based in part on reports of travels to the New World, Shakespeare dramatizes these ideas in the character of Caliban, the natural man and slave of Prospero, who controls Caliban through his magical art. As the critic Frank Kermode puts it, "Prospero is, therefore, the representative of Art, as Caliban is of Nature." In this scheme, nature without art is less than human. But Shakespeare also explores the question in a more didactic fashion in *The Winter's Tale*. There, in a debate between Polixenes and Perdita on the subject of cross-fertilization of flowers, Polixenes maintains that in cross-fertilization nature and art mutually interact. Thus, "art itself is nature."

Shakespeare was not alone in being of two minds on the subject. Succeeding centuries saw the pendulum swing from art to nature and back. The neoclassical ideal saw the dominance of reason and wit (as in Alexander Pope's line "True Wit is Nature to advantage dressed"), while Romanticism invested nature with a quasi-divine status. This is particularly true in 19th-century America, where the vast beauty of the landscape led writers to proclaim it "Nature's Nation." By the end of the century, on the other hand, AESTHETICISM proclaimed the superiority of art to all aspects of life.

In the 20th century, the traditional division of nature and art gave way to the opposition of nature and industrialization. Industrial and technological progress seem to many a betrayal of nature. *See also* ECOCRITICISM and PRIMITIVISM.

Edward Tayler's *Nature and Art in Renaissance Literature* (1964) is an excellent treatment of the subject. Frank Kermode's "Introduction" to the Arden edition of *The Tempest* (1954) contains a detailed and incisive treatment of nature and art in relation to the play.

negative capability A term coined by the poet John Keats to describe the poet's capacity to negate oneself in order to enter into and become one with his or her subject. For Keats, this was the quality "which Shakespeare possessed so enormously . . . capable of being in uncertainties, mysteries, doubts, without any irritable reaching after fact and reason." Keats appears to be suggesting that the willingness to suspend one's own ideas in order to open oneself to experience is the mark of the great poet. Keats is apparently responding to Shakespeare's capacity to think and feel like his characters.

negritude A movement initiated in the 1930s by black writers residing in French colonies in Africa and the West Indies. The term refers to the preservation of traditional African culture, which in the 1930s was becoming absorbed by European values and standards. In this respect the movement anticipated the position of many POSTCOLONIAL literatures.

Among the leading writers of this movement were Léopold Senghor, poet, statesman, and first president of the republic of Senegal; and Aimé Césaire, poet and playwright from Martinique. Senghor, the first black member of the Académie Française, published his complete poems (*Oeuvre poétique*) in 1990. Césaire's works include poetry and plays. One example of the latter is *A Season in the Congo* (1966), a drama set against the background of the assassination in 1960 of Patrice Lumumba, the Congolese president.

neoclassicism A style in European literature, in which WIT, reason, formal control, and order assumed a privileged place. These principles, codified in certain rules, dominated literary production in 17th- and 18th-century Europe. In England, the style had a somewhat shorter reign, from 1660 to the 1780s.

Neoclassicism was a later development of the rediscovery of the great Greek and Latin classics in the RENAISSANCE. The neoclassical reverence for classical texts established the "Ancients" as the norms against which all other writing was to be tested. Among classical authors, none wielded greater authority than Aristotle. Neoclassical critics transformed Aristotle's observations on Greek tragedy into prescriptions for all plays, and his comments on unity of action into rules governing the UNITIES, which all plays were exhorted to imitate. Despite the rigidity of this format, French drama flourished during this period, which saw the great tragedies of Pierre Corneille and Jean Racine and the comic masterpieces of Jean-Baptiste Molière.

In English literature neoclassical principles triumphed during the AUGUSTAN AGE, particularly in poetry where Alexander Pope's masterly employment of HEROIC COUPLETS constituted the standard until the first stirrings of ROMANTICISM in the last decades of the 18th century.

The neoclassical period is frequently identified with the ENLIGHTENMENT in its emphasis on the principles of rationality, order, and logic. It celebrated the development of reason as the ultimate human achievement in art as well as in life, a position that the Romantic emphasis on imagination later challenged.

Hugh Honour's *Neoclassicism* (1969) offers a concise summary of the movement.

neoconservative   A term used to describe a group of American intellectuals, former liberals, who viewed with increasing skepticism and alarm social and political developments associated with liberal Democratic policies and positions. The position was first articulated in the late 1960s by Irving Kristol and Daniel Bell, the editors of *Public Interest*, a periodical. Dismayed by what they viewed as the excesses of the '60s radicals, they issued a defense of the American system as it had evolved to that point.

Subsequently, neoconservatives found a home in the pages of *Commentary* and *The Partisan Review* and took on, especially in the former journal, a more stridently conservative tone.

Chief among the American writers associated with this movement was the novelist Saul Bellow. Two of Bellow's later novels, *Mr. Sammler's Planet* (1970) and *The Dean's December* (1982) reflect an increasingly neoconservative TONE. For a possible earlier anticipation of this development, see LIBERAL/CONSERVATIVE IMAGINATION.

Irving Kristol's *Neocon: The Autobiography of an Idea* (1995) traces the development of the movement.

neologism   A word or phrase recently introduced into a language or an old word that has been given a new meaning. A well-known recent example is the word *quark*, a subatomic particle, adapted by the physicist Murray Gell-Mann from a phrase ("three quarks for Mr. Marx") in James Joyce's *Finnegans Wake* (1939).

Neoplatonism   A philosophical system based on the doctrines of Plato. The system was established by the philosopher Plotinus in the third century B.C. in the city of Alexandria. Incorporating elements of Asian mysticism with the ideas of Plato, Neoplatonism set up a vision of existence in which all things emanate from The One or The Good.

Neoplatonism exerted a powerful influence on the MIDDLE AGES and the RENAISSANCE, in which it frequently combined with Christian MYSTICISM. Neoplatonic themes have been identified in a number of important Renaissance texts, including Castiglione's *The Courtier* (1528) and Shakespeare's *Sonnets* (1609).

neorealism   A movement in the Italian cinema of the late 1940s. Focusing on the social upheaval and suffering that emerged in post–World War II Italy, neorealist films gained international favor for the sense of raw reality they communicated to film audiences throughout the world. The first celebrated neorealist film was Roberto Rossellini's *Open City* (1945), shot while the German army was evacuating Rome. Other postwar neorealist films included Rossellini's *Paisan* (1946), and Vittorio de Sica's *Shoeshine* (1946) and *The Bicycle Thief* (1948). The latter film, regarded as a masterpiece of neorealism, was filmed with non-professional actors. The last great example of neorealism is de Sica's *Umberto D.* (1951), a moving account of old age and despair in postwar urban Italy.

With the return of relative stability and prosperity in Italy during the late 1950s, the neorealist film gave way to more conventional entertainment films.

Springtime in Italy: A Reader on Neo-Realism (1978), edited by David Overbey, is a collection of appreciative essays on the movement.

neo-Scholasticism   In American criticism, a movement of the 1940s and '50s that adapted the aesthetic theories of St. Thomas Aquinas and other medieval scholastic philosophers. Its chief figure was Jacques Maritain, whose *Creative Intuition in Art and Poetry* (1953) was highly regarded by followers of NEW CRITICISM and of the CHICAGO SCHOOL.

One of the best known features of Aquinas's aesthetic theory is his characterization of the beautiful as consisting of wholeness, harmony, and radiance. This definition receives a detailed analysis in the final chapter of James Joyce's *A Portrait of the Artist as a Young Man* (1916).

new apocalypse movement   An overblown name for a group of British poets in the 1940s, whose poems, essays, and stories reflected their intense subjectivity and ornate language. Their work appeared in three anthologies, *The New Apocalypse* (1940), *The White Horseman* (1941), and *The Cross and the Sickle* (1941), edited by two of its leading members, J.T . Hendry and Henry Treece.

Not a member but a model for the group was Dylan Thomas, whose rich, rhetorical verse delivered in the author's sonorous voice, achieved great popularity in England and America. In the 1950s the group was displaced by the MOVEMENT.

New Criticism   A type of Anglo/American criticism that arose in the 1920s and '30s and became the dominant form of academic criticism until well into the 1960s. The basic principle of New Criticism was to locate the meaning of a literary work not in the intention of the author nor in the experience of the reader, but in "the text itself," the internal relations of language that constitute a "poem." (The New Critics tended to employ the term *poem* to describe any type of literature, perhaps a reflection of their greater success in analyzing poems than fiction or drama.) The reader gained critical understanding through a process of "close reading," strict attention to the characteristics of a literary work as conveyed by such elements as IRONY, PARADOX, TENSION, IMAGERY, and SYMBOL. Among the errors to be avoided were the INTENTIONAL FALLACY, the attempt to locate meaning in the author's intention, and the AFFECTIVE FALLACY, the attempt to search for meaning in the experience of the reader.

Also to be avoided, or at least subordinated to close reading, were "extrinsic" (that is, not dealing exclusively with the language of the text) approaches to the study of literature: social, psychological, economic, political, or historical.

New Criticism can be said to have begun with the publication in 1924 of I. A. Richards's *Principles of Literary Criticism* and the same author's *Practical Criticism* (1929). The earlier work offered a theoretical framework, while practical criticism argued for a close study of the language of a poem in order to analyze it properly. In England, William Empson's *Seven Types of Ambiguity* (1930) is a classic New Critical text and a striking example of the "close reading" technique advanced by Richards.

Apart from Richards, the single most important figure in the development of the school was T. S. Eliot, who lent his prestige as a poet to the movement, frequently endorsing its principles in his own criticism.

The term *New Criticism* was coined by the American critic John Crowe Ransom in a book of that title published in 1941. Of far greater influence, however, was a textbook edited by Robert Penn Warren and Cleanth Brooks in 1938. Brooks and Warren's *Understanding Poetry* had a profound effect on the teaching of literature in American colleges for the next two decades. As a consequence, the study of literature was frequently sealed off from social, historical, and political concerns in favor of a rigorous, eminently teachable, FORMALISM. In recent years this aspect of New Criticism has been critiqued for its alleged hidden agenda: a defense of traditional religious and cultural values under the guise of advocating the autonomy of literature.

The principles of New Criticism were challenged by the BEAT and PROJECTIVISM movements and by MYTH CRITICISM in the '50s, by the student movement of the '60s, and by the emergence of THEORY in the '70s.

Despite the decline and, to some extent, disrepute into which it later fell, New Criticism made a major contribution to the vocabulary, understanding, and teaching of literature, particularly in its insistence on the need for a close reading of the literary text.

For a new critical overview of literary studies, see William K. Wimsatt and Cleanth Brooks's *Literary Criticism: A Short History* (1957). In addition to the authors cited above, other prominent new critics were R. P. Blackmur (*Form and Value in Modern Poetry*, 1957),

Joseph Frank (*The Widening Gyre*, 1963), and Alan Tate (*The Forlorn Demon*, 1953). Grant Webster's *The Republic of Letters: A History of Postwar American Literary Opinion* (1979) contains a sharp attack, characterizing the movement as "Tory Formalism."

New Formalism   A movement in American poetry of the 1980s to revive traditional formal verse. A reaction to the dominance of FREE VERSE in contemporary poetry, the New Formalists called for a return to traditional craftsmanship and the cultivation of a wider poetic audience. Among its practitioners are Dana Gioia, Molly Peacock, Charles Martin, and Timothy Steele.

Expansive Poetry (1989), edited by Frederick Feirstein, is an anthology of New Formalist verse.

New Historicism   A general term for a loosely organized approach to literary study that looks at the historical context of a work from a perspective influenced by POSTSTRUCTURALISM: New Historicism rejects the traditional distinction between the TEXT and the CONTEXT—that is, between the play or poem and the historical conditions existing at the time it was written. Where traditional historical criticism sees a literary text against a backdrop of historical events, New Historicism views the text as a participant in a historical or political process that it "reconceives." In the words of the New Historicist Louis Montrose, this approach is interested in "the historicity of texts and the textuality of history."

New Historicist thought has been strongly influenced by the theories of the French poststructuralist Michel Foucault, particularly his conception of the shifting dynamics of POWER, and the methods of the American anthropologist Clifford Geertz, whose "thick descriptions" of cultural practices (*see* ETHNOGRAPHY) provide a procedural model. A New Historicist analysis often begins with an anecdote describing an event seemingly far removed from literature—an account of a dream, for example. The analysis will then relate the anecdote to a literary text, not in terms of a direct connection, but as a parallel experience, or key both text and event to a political or social question.

A well-known example is Stephen Greenblatt's essay on *King Lear,* "Shakespeare and the Exorcists." Traditional scholarship has recognized for a long time that an anti-Catholic pamphlet, written by an Elizabethan contemporary, Samuel Harsnett, is a minor SOURCE of Shakespeare's tragedy. Harsnett's pamphlet sets out to expose the fraudulence of certain exorcisms performed by Jesuit priests in 16th-century England.

In Greenblatt's analysis, both the source and the play emerge as "part of an intense struggle to redefine the central values of that society. At the heart of this struggle . . . was the definition of the sacred." Out of this interaction, Shakespeare, according to Greenblatt, reconceives this Protestant/Catholic conflict in terms of a religion of the theater. The play offers us a fictional encounter with EVIL, not unlike the exorcists', to satisfy our need for such an experience. As removed as this appears to be from the usual view of *King Lear*, Greenblatt's analysis, if not his conclusion, convincingly illuminates both the play and its source.

Although it began as a movement among students of Renaissance texts, New Historicism has won wide approval among younger scholars and has moved into other literary periods and various other disciplines, including art history and anthropology.

The New Historicism (1989), edited by Harold A. Veeser, is a collection of essays by participants in the movement. Stephen Greenblatt's essay on *King Lear* appears in his *Shakespearean Negotiations* (1988). Louis Montrose's "New Historicisms" in *Redrawing the Boundaries* (1992), edited by Stephen Greenblatt and Giles Gunn, provides an overview of the movement.

New Humanism   An American critical movement in the first three decades of the 20th century that set itself against the dominance of scientific thought and modern skepticism. Stressing the virtues of discipline, order, and the ethical mean, New Humanists endorsed the classical virtues of restraint and clarity against what they perceived as the excesses of ROMANTICISM and the social anarchy of MODERNISM.

In literary study they extolled the classics for their moral seriousness, but they eschewed the rigid adherence to arbitrary rules of NEOCLASSICISM. They were criticized as reactionary, somewhat in the political sense, but more so in the aesthetic sphere because of their rejection of almost all modern art and literature.

The leading figures of New Humanism were Irving Babbit (*The New Laokoon*, 1910) and Paul Elmer More (*The Demon of the Absolute*, 1928). The movement was overshadowed in the 1930s by the NEW CRITICISM and the MARXIST CRITICISM of the period, but some of its positions re-emerged in the NEOCONSERVATIVE trends of the 1980s.

J. David Hoeveler's *The New Humanism* (1977) traces the influence of the movement in American life.

new journalism   A form of news reporting developed in the 1960s that incorporated some of the features associated with fiction, lending an imaginative, literary character to the traditional, fact-based report. Among these features was an emphasis on the distinctive style and personality of the authors. The figure most closely identified with new journalism is Tom Wolfe, whose *The Kandy-Kolored*

Tangerine-Flake Streamline Baby (1965) inaugurated the movement. Others included Jimmy Breslin (*The Gang that Couldn't Shoot Straight*, 1969), Hunter Thompson (*Fear and Loathing in Las Vegas*, 1972), and Joan Didion (*The White Album*, 1979).

Closely allied to new journalism is the NONFICTION NOVEL, in which novelists such as Norman Mailer and Truman Capote treat factual events in a novelistic mode.

Michael Q. Johnson's *The New Journalism* (1971) explores the early years of the movement.

new novel *(nouveau roman)*   A term referring to a post–World War II French literary movement designed to question the assumptions undergirding traditional REALISM. Adherents of the new novel argued against the view that a novel should be lifelike and that its plot should unfold in a linear, sequential fashion. The emphasis in the new novel is on technical experimentation, self-consciousness, and the profound "suspicion" that human experience is finally unknowable. This refusal to make any authorial claims of knowledge forces the reader to participate in the creation of the text's meaning by filling in the blanks of the story. In this respect the new novel anticipated those developments in contemporary literature and criticism associated with POSTMODERNISM.

Among the practitioners of the new novel, the best known are Alain Robbe-Grillet (*Jealousy*, 1959), Nathalie Sarraute (*The Age of Suspicion*, 1963), and Robert Pinget (*Le Libera*, 1968).

For a readable description of the movement, see Vivian Mercier's *The New Novel: From Queneau to Pinget* (1971).

newspeak   A term coined by George Orwell in his anti-Utopian novel *1984* (1949). In the totalitarian world of the novel, language is controlled by the government so that its citizens automatically "spray forth the correct opinions" in government slogans, designed to make lies sound truthful by inverting the traditional meanings of words. As currently used, the term refers to evasive, bureaucratic euphemisms—sometimes referred to as "doublespeak"—often alluded to in the controversy over POLITICAL CORRECTNESS.

New Wave *(nouvelle vague)*   A movement in the 1950s and '60s that introduced new techniques and subject matter to French filmmaking. The New Wave began in 1954 with the publication of an essay in the film journal *Cahiers du Cinema* by the future director François Truffaut. Truffaut's article contained a strong attack on the "quality films" then being produced in France. He argued that these films exhibited literary rather than cinematic values and, as such, did justice neither to literature nor to FILM. Truffaut called for a recognition of the film director as AUTEUR (author), a title that would imply the equal status of literature and film, rather than endorsing the view of literature as superior to film. From Truffaut's perspective, the auteur was a writer using a camera instead of a pen.

New Wave films employed unusual camera work and editing, while their scripts revealed complex characterizations. New Wave directors were fond of inserting allusions to earlier films and of creating ambiguous, "open" endings.

The most celebrated of the New Wave theorists/practitioners were Truffaut (*The 400 Blows*, 1959), Jean-Luc Godard (*Breathless*, 1959), Jacques Rivette (*Paris Belongs to Us*, 1959), Claude Chabrol (*Les Cousins*, 1959), Alain Resnais (*Last Year at Marienbad*, 1961), and Eric Rohmer (*My Night at Maud's*, 1969).

James Monaco discusses the theory and practice of the movement in *The New Wave* (1976).

New Yorker, The   A weekly magazine distinguished by the quality of its FICTION, ESSAYS, REVIEWS, and, not least, cartoons. Founded in 1925 by its first editor, Harold Ross, the magazine in its early years was noted for its humorous and satirical pieces, submitted by regular contributors such as James Thurber, E. B. White, Alexander Woollcott, S. J. Perelman, Dorothy Parker, Ogden Nash, and the cartoonists Helen Hokinson, Charles Addams, and Peter Arno.

While maintaining its urbane, sophisticated style, *The New Yorker* gradually began to introduce more serious and socially conscious contributions, notably in 1946, when it devoted an entire issue to the publication of John Hersey's *Hiroshima*, an account of the aftereffects of the first atomic bombing, and in 1962 with the publication of Rachel Carson's *The Silent Spring*, a description of the environmental dangers of insecticides.

Among the notable regular contributors to the magazine have been, in fiction, John Cheever, J. D. Salinger, John Updike, Maeve Brennan, and Alice Munro; in poetry, Pablo Neruda, Seamus Heaney, Zbigniew Herbert, and Joseph Brodsky; for criticism and reviews, Lewis Mumford, Edmund Wilson, George Steiner, and Pauline Kael.

Brendan Gill's *Here at the New Yorker* (1974) is a history of the magazine by a longtime contributor.

New York intellectuals   A general term for the writers and critics associated with the monthly journal *Partisan Review* from the 1930s through the 1960s. Coming together as a group of anti-Stalinist Marxists, figures such as Mary

McCarthy, Lionel Trilling, Sidney Hook, Harold Rosenberg, Dwight McDonald, and Philip Rahv used the pages of *Partisan Review* initially to establish a left wing journal of opinion that clearly distinguished itself from the party line rigidity of orthodox communism.

In the ensuing years their literary criticism reflected interest in major modernist writers such as James Joyce and thinkers such as Sigmund Freud and Friedrich Nietzsche. Their cultural essays frequently focused on popular culture and the role of the artist in American society.

Later critics identified with the group included Irving Howe, Alfred Kazin, Elizabeth Hardwick, William Barrett, and Delmore Schwartz. Many of these were the children of Jewish immigrants from Eastern Europe, and a recognition of those roots played an increasingly important role in their writing. By the time of the student disruptions of the 1960s, they had begun to reject their endorsement of the AVANT-GARDE and the political radicalism associated with it. Before ceasing publication in 2003, *Partisan Review* developed an increasingly NEOCONSERVATIVE tone, its earlier tradition having been absorbed to some extent by *The New York Review of Books*. (*See also* LIBERAL/CONSERVATIVE IMAGINATION.)

Alan Wald's *The New York Intellectuals* (1987) details the history of the group.

New York Review of Books, The   A bi-weekly journal devoted primarily to reviews of recent books, with occasional special articles. Founded in 1963 in the midst of a newspaper strike, the review soon emerged as a forum for serious, lengthy discussions of new books and contemporary social and political questions. In the 1960s, its political position was mockingly characterized by Tom Wolfe as "the definitive theoretical organ of radical chic," Wolfe's term for a trendy radicalism popular among certain celebrities and intellectuals at the time. In subsequent years, its politics appear to be moderate-to-liberal.

Philip Nobile's *Intellectual Skywriting: Literary Politics and the New York Review of Books* (1974) is a behind-the-scenes account of the review.

New York school   In the 1950s, a group of poets based in New York City who opted for a more informal and unpretentious poetic style than that of their contemporaries. Influenced by ACTION PAINTING, these poets emphasized the process of creation rather than its product.

Among the group's prominent practitioners were Frank O'Hara, whose witty, optimistic, and moving poems celebrated the ordinary ("I like songs about hat-check girls, elevators, bunions, syphilis, all the old sentimental things"); Kenneth Koch, whose professed poetic goal was to be "funny and lyrical at the same time"; and James Schuyler, who, despite his Manhattan residence, is a skilled nature poet. The best-known member of the group was John Ashbery, whose early POETRY anticipated the postmodern sense of INDETERMINACY.

nihilism   A term that offers at least two definitions. The first refers to a social doctrine, developed in 19th-century Russia, that called for the eradication of existing social, religious, and political institutions, including prevailing ideas of morality, justice, and private property. This type of nihilism endorsed only the truths of science. Memorable portraits of nihilists in this sense form important elements of Ivan Turgenev's *Fathers and Sons* (1862) and Fyodor Dostoyevsky's *The Possessed* (1871–72).

A broader and more commonly used sense of the term refers to the view of life that sees all existence, including that which rests on a faith in science, as empty and meaningless. Much of modern literature exhibits an attempt either to overcome or to validate this nihilistic vision. Some modern writers defiantly assert their nihilism, while others view it as the ultimate challenge, the experience of total negation that must be endured in order to emerge with an affirmation of life, however qualified an affirmation it may be.

The figure that stands at the center of modern nihilism is the 19th-century philosopher Friedrich Nietzsche, who diagnosed the search for "truth" as an illusion. Reduced at times to utter despair and ultimately to madness, he nevertheless attempted to overcome his nihilistic vision by affirming the strength of the human will and the power of creative art. Thus Nietzsche embodies the fundamental contradiction of nihilism: it usually results in some paradoxical affirmation of life.

Among the few writers whose nihilism seems to be absolute, unfettered by an internal contradiction, are its two most gifted exponents, Franz Kafka and Samuel Beckett. In his two novels, *The Trial* (1925) and *The Castle* (1926), Kafka creates ironic parables of human life in which simple existence is guilt. Beckett's plays (*Waiting for Godot,* 1952; *Endgame,* 1957) and novels (*Malone Dies,* 1951; *The Unnameable,* 1953), filled with black humor, depict a world in which the affirmation of life celebrated by Nietzsche and others is itself negated.

Charles Glicksberg's *The Literature of Nihilism* (1975) looks at the nihilist presence in a number of modern writers. Robert Martin Adams's *Nil* (1966) explores the theme of the void in 19th-century literature.

Nō   A highly ritualized form of Japanese theater, whose fixed repertory of plays has remained unchanged for 400 years. Nō plays incorporate music, dance, and poetry in austerely beautiful presentations that aim not at representing reality, but at creating a mood through visual and verbal imagery. The plays are religious in tone, echoing the doctrines of Shinto, the national religion of Japan, or Buddhism. They strive to achieve a serene, meditative pleasure and peace.

The oldest and most widely performed Nō play is *Okina,* dating from the 12th century and still presented at New Year's celebrations. Of the more than 200 plays in the Nō repertory, many of them were written by two 14th-century artists, Kwanami (1333–84) and his son Zeami Motokiyo (1363–1443). The latter is the author of close to 100 Nō plays, nearly half of those in the current repertory.

The Irish poet William Butler Yeats adapted the Nō form in a number of short plays, including *At the Hawk's Well* (1916) and *Fighting the Waves* (1929).

An excellent anthology of Nō plays in English is *Twenty Plays of the Nō Theatre,* edited by Donald Keene (1970). Keene has also written a general study of the form, *Nō: The Classical Drama of Japan* (1966).

Nobel Prize   In literature, an annual prize originally awarded to the outstanding work produced during the year, but now given in acknowledgment of a writer's entire career.

noble savage   *See* PRIMITIVISM.

nom de plume (pen name)   A name adopted by a writer to disguise his or her real name. Writers have assumed pen names for a variety of reasons. Many women, for example, employed noms de plume to avoid the long-standing prejudice against women writers. Examples include George Sand (Amandine Dupin); George Eliot (Mary Ann Cross); and Currer, Ellis, and Acton Bell (the Brontë sisters).

nonfiction novel   A term coined by the writer Truman Capote to describe a type of writing in which novelistic techniques are used to relate factual events. A notable example is Capote's *In Cold Blood* (1965), the account of a brutal murder of a Kansas family and the subsequent flight, capture, and execution of the murderers.

Another notable example of the form is Norman Mailer's account of the "March on the Pentagon" protesting the Vietnam War, *Armies of the Night* (1968), the subtitle of which characterizes the genre: "History as a Novel; The Novel as History." *See* NEW JOURNALISM.

nouveau roman   *See* NEW NOVEL.

nouvelle vague   *See* NEW WAVE.

novel   Usually a book-length fictional prose NARRATIVE, although recent years have seen the development of the NONFICTION NOVEL, and some novels have been written in verse. The traditional novel exhibits a fairly detailed PLOT and a number of characters. The emphasis may fall on a character, as in the psychological novel; on action, as in the ADVENTURE STORY; on a social problem, as in the sociological novel; or any combination of these.

Historically the novel developed from the prose ROMANCE and the PICARESQUE novel. Cervantes's *Don Quixote* (1605, 1615) is an early embodiment of the form, as is the Countess de Lafayette's *La Princesse de Clèves* (1678). The English novel came of age in the 18th century, setting a standard imitated throughout Europe. In addition to the era's novels typified by the work of such writers as Daniel Defoe (*Robinson Crusoe,* 1719) and Laurence Sterne (*Tristram Shandy,* 1759–67), the English also initiated the popular form known as the GOTHIC NOVEL.

In the 19th century the novel came into its own as the most popular and important literary form. Best able to express the prevailing doctrines of REALISM and NATURALISM, the novel achieved its high watermark in France in the work of Honoré de Balzac, Gustave Flaubert, Stendahl, and Émile Zola; in Russia with Aleksandr Pushkin, Ivan Turgenev, Fyodor Dostoyevsky, and Leo Tolstoy; in England with Jane Austen, Sir Walter Scott, William Makepeace Thackeray, Charles Dickens, George Eliot, and Thomas Hardy; and in the United States, with James Fenimore Cooper, Nathaniel Hawthorne, Herman Melville, Mark Twain, and Henry James.

The early 20th century saw the formal innovations of INTERIOR MONOLOGUE, stream of consciousness, and FREE INDIRECT STYLE and a willingness to speak frankly of sexuality and social oppression. James Joyce, Marcel Proust, Franz Kafka, Thomas Mann, Virginia Woolf, William Faulkner, and D. H. Lawrence not only brought the novel into the new century, they also revitalized and enhanced it. In the aftermath of World War II, the novel has been declared both dead and reborn in the NEW NOVEL and as a vehicle of POSTMODERNISM in the GRAPHIC NOVEL.

Ian Watt's *The Rise of the Novel* (1957) is an exemplary analysis of the impact of social conditions on the development of the English novel. Wayne Booth's *The Rhetoric of Fiction* (1961) explores the interaction of author and audience.

novel of ideas   A novel in which the focus is less on character and action than on philosophical questions that are debated and discussed at length. Although most novels contain abstract ideas in one form or another, in the "novel of ideas" they play a central role. Such novels, when they successfully integrate characters and narrative action along with ideas, can ascend to the highest level of fiction, as in Fyodor Dostoyevsky's *The Brothers Karamazov* (1879–80) and Thomas Mann's *The Magic Mountain* (1924).

When the ideas overwhelm the story, however, novels of ideas can appear tendentious and thesis-ridden, reflected in the French term for such novels, *roman à thèse* (novel with a thesis).

novel of manners   A type of novel in which the social conventions of a given society—its speech, habits, and values—play significant roles. The main focus of the form is summarized in the title of Anthony Trollope's novel of manners *The Way We Live Now* (1875). As a novelist of manners, Trollope followed in the tradition of Jane Austen, Honoré de Balzac, and William Makepeace Thackeray.

The American version of the form is best exemplified in the novels of Henry James and Edith Wharton. But the relatively stable societies depicted in their novels seem to be a thing of the past, with the result that the novel of manners appears to have been neglected in favor of questions of moral, even metaphysical problems. According to Tom Wolfe, the task of depicting "the way we live now" has fallen to the NEW JOURNALISM, and to the novels growing out of that development such as Wolfe's *The Bonfire of the Vanities* (1987) and *A Man in Full* (1998).

In *The New American Novel of Manners* (1986), Jerome Klinkowitz has argued that the form has been revived with an emphasis on the SEMIOTICS of contemporary life in the novels of Dan Wakefield (*Going All the Way,* 1970), Richard Yates (*Disturbing the Peace,* 1975), and Thomas McGuane (*Nobody's Angel,* 1981).

James Tuttleton's *The Novel of Manners in America* (1972) discusses the earlier examples of the form.

novelette   *See* NOVELLA.

novella   A term for a story that is longer than a short story and shorter than a novel. Other terms used to describe the form are *novelette* or simply *short novel.* An Italian term meaning "novelty," novella (and its plural form *novelle*) was used to describe a type of short story popular in the Renaissance. Matteo Bandello's multi-volume *Novelle* (1554–73) contained 214 such stories, one of which is a source of Shakespeare's *Romeo and Juliet.*

Distinguished 20th-century examples of the form include Thomas Mann's *Death in Venice* (1912), Joseph Conrad's *The Heart of Darkness* (1902), and Ernest Hemingway's *The Old Man and the Sea* (1952).

In the late 18th century, the great German writer J. W. Goethe employed the term *novelle* to describe a short novel such as his *The Sorrows of Young Werther* (1774, 1787). As a result, *novelle* has become the standard German word for a short novel.

Novy Mir ("Our World")   An important literary journal from 1925 to the breakup of the Soviet Union, continuing today in contemporary Russia. During the Soviet years, *Novy Mir* was the organ of the Soviet Writers Union and, as such, officially sanctioned by the government. Under the editorship of Alexander Tvardovsky, the journal strove to loosen the strict bonds of Soviet censorship. Its finest hour occurred in 1962, when Tvardovsky convinced government authorities, including Premier Nikita Khruschev, to approve the publication of Alexandr Solzhenitsyn's *One Day in the Life of Ivan Denisovich*, the first novel to expose the reality of Stalin's monstrous labor camps. Some years later, in his account of that event, Solzhenitsyn disparaged Tvardovsky's efforts, causing a controversy over Solzhenitsyn's apparent ingratitude. The novelist's reply was that as an individual he was grateful to his editor, but as a spokesman for the millions who died in the camps he could not speak well of anyone who had been complicit, however indirectly, with a monstrous regime. As Solzhenitsyn expressed it "Tvardovsky needed that fire-resistant hardness which is cultivated only in the Archipelago of the Zeks [concentration camp prisoners]."

Solzhenitsyn's account appears in his *The Calf and the Oak* (1974).

Edward Brown's *Russian Literature Since the Revolution* (1982) discusses the controversy.

nuclear war   The literature of nuclear war is divided between the historical—FICTION and POETRY based upon the 1945 attacks on Hiroshima and Nagasaki—and the hypothetical, which often crosses over into SCIENCE FICTION. John Hersey's *Hiroshima* (1946), a nonfictional description of the attack from the standpoint of six survivors, was the first and most influential treatment of the dropping of the atomic bomb. A major aspect of its influence was that its American readers were forced to come to the TEXT from the point of view of the victims rather than the victors. Published first in *THE NEW YORKER*—the magazine devoted the entire issue to the book—it left its readers, accustomed to thinking of the bombing as a triumph of American science, in a state of shock. The view that the bombing had saved thousands of American soldiers' lives now had to be balanced by the recognition that the bomb had been dropped on civilian targets of no military importance with catastrophic long-range consequences from the effects of radiation.

A similar effort is achieved in *Black Rain* (1966, trans. 1969) by the Japanese novelist Masuji Ibuse. The novel opens four years after the bombing. Shigematsu

Shizuma begins reading the diary he kept at the time of the bombing in the hope he will find information regarding his niece Yasuko, who had been exposed to "black rain," the radiation-contaminated rain that fell on Hiroshima the day after the bombing. The novel's title effectively captures the theme of the perversion of nature—that rain, the source of rebirth and regeneration, should become the agent of death.

In the 1950s, the nuclear war scenario shifted from the historical event to the apocalyptic, stories in which nuclear catastrophe forms the subject of the novel. Many of these have become classics of modern SCIENCE FICTION: Ray Bradbury's *Martian Chronicles* (1950), Arthur Clarke's *Childhood's End* (1953), and Walter Miller's *A Canticle for Leibowitz* (1959). In the 1960s and '70s, many were learning "to live with the bomb," as the threat of nuclear warfare, with the notable exception of the Cuban missile crisis of 1962, receded from consciousness somewhat, although never very far. This inattention was reflected in the literary output as well. The one work that stands out in the period is Stanley Kubrick's darkly comic, satiric film *Dr. Strangelove* (1964).

The 1980s saw the beginning of a renewed concern, sparked by the nuclear disasters at Three Mile Island (1979) and, most significant, Chernobyl (1986), as examples of the catastrophic capabilities of atomic power. Russell Hoban's *Riddley Walker* (1980) and Denis Johnson's *Fiskadoro* (1985), offered two powerful depictions of a postnuclear holocaust world. *Riddley Walker* takes place four centuries after a nuclear attack on England, in a world where written language has been all but obliterated. *Fiskadoro*, set in postnuclear Florida, describes the efforts of three characters to establish a new civilization against what appears to be overwhelming odds. Both novels feature teenage protagonists grappling to restore a lost order.

The Chernobyl disaster resulted in a departure from the hypothetical novel and a return to the historical in Vladimir Gubaryev's *Sarcophagus* (1986, trans. 1987), a tragic drama set in a medical station receiving the victims; and Christa Wolf's *Accident* (1987; trans. 1989), a novel recording the impact on the consciousness of a woman writer living in an area in East Germany that will be contaminated by radiation.

Albert Stone's *Literary Aftershocks: American Writers, Readers and the Bomb* (1994) is a thoughtful survey of the literature that emerged from the bombing of Hiroshima.

numerology   In literature, the incorporation of numerical patterns in a literary work, designed to suggest certain meanings. Such patterns are present in the BIBLE, in classical works (Virgil's *Aeneid*), in many medieval texts (Dante's *The Divine Comedy*), and in the RENAISSANCE poetry of Edmund Spenser.

One example of biblical numerology is the Book of Revelation, which contains 22 chapters, corresponding to the 22 books of the Old Testament, which in turn are based upon the 22 letters of the Hebrew alphabet. This numerical correspondence suggests that John, the author of Revelation, is presenting a history of the world from beginning to end, an idea reinforced by the inclusion in it of Christ's statement "I am the Alpha and Omega," the first and last letters of the Greek alphabet.

The practice of number symbolism was revived in the Renaissance. The most striking example of its use is in the poetry of Edmund Spenser, who employed numbers in almost all of his poems. His "Epithalamion," for example, contains 24 stanzas for each hour of the day, 365 long lines for the days of the year, and 68 short lines for the sum of the months (12), weeks (52), and seasons (4) of the year. In his SONNET sequence the *Amoretti,* he had each sonnet correspond to the successive days in the liturgical calendar. There is even evidence to suggest the presence of number symbols in his epic *The Faerie Queene,* but scholars have not as yet fully deciphered them.

A. Kent Hieatt's *Short Time's Endless Monument* (1960) is the pioneering study of Spenser's use of numerology.

O

objective correlative   A term coined by T. S. Eliot to describe an AUTHOR's
need to represent a character's internal emotion as an objective person or thing.
Eliot used the term in an essay called "Hamlet and His Problems," in which he
maintained that Hamlet's inner turmoil was objectified in the play in the person
of Gertrude, Hamlet's mother. Eliot argued that Gertrude herself is too bland
and banal a character to serve as an adequate objective correlative of Hamlet's
feelings. As a result, Eliot concluded, the play, rather than being a masterpiece, is
"almost certainly a failure."

While few have accepted Eliot's view of Shakespeare's *Hamlet*, the term
enjoyed considerable popularity in the 1940s and '50s among practitioners of
NEW CRITICISM.

T. S. Eliot's essay "Hamlet and His Problems" is included in his *The Sacred Wood* (1920);
Eliseo Vivas's *Creation and Discovery* (1955) contains a detailed critique of the objective
correlative.

objectivism   A movement among American poets that began in 1931 as a
further development of IMAGISM. Its leading figure was William Carlos Williams,
who argued that "the poem . . . is an object, an object that formally presents its
case and its meaning by the very form it assumes." This principle marked a further step in the direction, first expressed in Imagism, away from the subjectivism
of Romantic poetry. This principle was to be developed further in the movement known as PROJECTIVISM. An outstanding example of an objectivist poem
is Williams's "The Great Figure" (1921), a description of a fire truck moving
through the city on a rainy evening.

obligatory scene   A term in DRAMA, adapted from the French *scène à faire*
(scene to do), to describe a scene conventionally required by the GENRE of the
play or film in which it occurs. Examples include the chase sequence in a FARCE,
or the shootout in a WESTERN.

occasional verse   Poetry written in response to a historical occasion or in commemoration of a public event, such as a national holiday or the death of a celebrated person. Walt Whitman's "When Lilacs Last in the Dooryard Bloomed," written in response to the assassination of Abraham Lincoln, is an example of occasional verse. Other famous examples include Ben Jonson's "On Shakespeare," written as a dedicatory poem to the FIRST FOLIO (1623); Andrew Marvell's "An Horatian Ode Upon Cromwell's Return From Ireland" (1650); W. B. Yeats's "Easter 1916," in praise of the Irish uprising in 1916, and W. H. Auden's "On the Death of Yeats" (1939).

occult, the   In literature, the term *occult* refers to the presence of magical, mysterious, or supernatural influences in a literary work. Broadly defined in this way, Western literature from classical times to the RENAISSANCE exhibited strong occult strains, evident in stories and folklore dealing with witchcraft, magic, astrological influences, alchemy, and NUMEROLOGY. Many of these were based on a world view that assumed correspondences and analogies between humankind and nature. The pre-modern mind took for granted a close harmonious relationship between the order of the universe and human experience with "man as the measure of all things." Thus the world was literally a magical place.

A literary work that might stand as the culmination of this world view is Shakespeare's *The Tempest*, in which the magician Prospero controls and dominates the action of the play. At the conclusion, however, Prospero promises to "drown his book," abjure his magic, in order to re-enter the ordinary world. Prospero's renunciation of magic might stand as a symbol for the replacement of the oldworld view by modern science in the 17th century.

Nevertheless, occultism did not disappear entirely. It is manifest in the work of at least two great poets, William Blake and William Butler Yeats. Blake's prophetic books, such as *The Marriage of Heaven and Hell* (1791), exhibit a wide range of mystical and visionary thought. Yeats explicitly detailed his occultist philosophy in his *A Vision* (1925), in which he outlines his ideas of cyclical recurrences every 2,000 years, a notion powerfully expressed in his great poem "The Second Coming."

A figure associated with modern occult literature in a less acceptable sense is the English poet Aleister Crowley, famous for his dabbling in black magic rituals, which he described in his *The Diary of a Drug Fiend* (1922).

Literature and the Occult, edited by Luanne Frank (1977), is a collection of essays on various aspects of the subject.

octave   A poetic stanza containing eight lines. *See* OTTAVA RIMA.

ode   A lyric poem of any length that addresses a person or treats a theme in a dignified, serious manner. In English poetry there are three types of odes: the Pindaric, the Horatian, and the irregular. The Pindaric ode is named after the Greek poet Pindar (fifth century B.C.), whose poems, written to commemorate athletic victories, were sung by a chorus. The Horatian odes, after the Roman poet Horace (65–6 B.C.), are more personal and reflective. Both types employed regular stanzaic and metrical patterns. The irregular ode, associated with the 17th-century English poet Abraham Cowley, broke with the tradition of regular stanzas, permitting variation.

Examples of these types of odes in English POETRY include Ben Jonson's "Ode to Sir Lucius Cary and Sir Henry Morrison" (Pindaric), John Keats's "Ode on a Grecian Urn" (Horatian), and William Wordsworth's "Ode: Intimations of Immortality" (irregular).

Two notable modern American odes are Allen Tate's "Ode to the Confederate Dead" and Robert Lowell's "For the Union Dead."

Carol Maddison's *Apollo and the Nine: A History of the Ode* (1960) is a useful survey of the form.

Odysseus/Ulysses theme   The most complex and interesting of the Homeric heroes, Odysseus plays an important role in the *Iliad* and is the central figure in the *Odyssey*. From these origins he has emerged as a distinctive, universal archetype, the intelligent survivor, the hero as thinker. In the *Iliad* he is depicted as shrewd, not without courage, and exhibiting self-discipline to conform to the heroic code of the poem's warrior world. In the *Odyssey*, however, many readers think that his penchant for lying and secrecy and his suspicion of his wife, Penelope, diminish his heroic stature. This appears to be the view of later Greek authors such as Sophocles in his *Philoctetes* and Euripides in his *Hecuba*.

In Virgil's account of the Trojan War in Book II of the *Aeneid* there is, of course, a pro-Trojan bias to the depiction of the Greeks, since Romans traced their origins to the Trojan refugees led by Aeneas. As a result, according to the scholar W. B. Stanford, "Virgil . . . contrived to blacken Ulysses' character for the next fifteen hundred years." (From the Roman era on, Odysseus became known by his Roman name Ulysses.)

In the 26th canto of Dante's *Inferno*, the poet and his guide, Virgil, encounter Ulysses, represented as a tongue of flame. Here Dante creates a new ending to Homer's account. Ulysses explains that he did not go home, but that his thirst for knowledge and adventure led him to continue sailing beyond the Pillars of Hercules, the prescribed limit of exploration, only to be drowned in a whirlwind. As Stanford phrases it, "Ulysses now becomes a symbol of sinful desire for forbidden knowledge." Dante's view of Ulysses as a FAUST (*see* FAUSTIAN THEME) figure, although not endorsing his character, lent it a greater dignity than Virgil's wily trickster.

In *Troilus and Cressida*, Shakespeare assigns Ulysses two major speeches: the "degree speech" (1,3,78–137), in which he pleads the case for a hierarchical order in society, lest it be plunged into anarchy; and the rhetorical gem (3,3,145–89), in which Ulysses urges Achilles to reenter combat to avoid being forgotten ("Time hath, my lord, a wallet at its back"). They combine to suggest a conservative figure and a keen psychologist.

Another powerful poetic representation of complexity is evidenced in Alfred, Lord Tennyson's poem "Ulysses" (1833), which evokes the Faustian image that Dante suggests. Ulysses is determined "to follow knowledge like a sinking star" and concludes with its famous exhortation, "To strive, to seek, to find, and not to yield."

All of these partial perspectives on the Ulysses myth contributed to two remarkable 20th-century representations, James Joyce's *Ulysses* (1922) and Nikos Kazantzakis's *The Odyssey* (1938), a poetic sequel to the original. Joyce's *Ulysses* continues, regardless of the critical weather, to maintain its position as one of the greatest novels of modern and postmodern times. No small part of its appeal and of the author's genius is the transformation of the epic hero into a modest Jewish advertising canvasser, Leopold Bloom, making his way around the city of Dublin on a single day, June 16, 1904. At first glance, the contrast could not be more extreme; at a closer look, the two figures live parallel lives in radically different spheres. They are both exiles from their true home, wanderers longing to experience the world at large, both intellectually curious, resourceful, adaptable, courageous when the occasion arises, given to weaknesses of the flesh, but primarily impelled, above all, to return home. When Joyce was asked what he thought of Odysseus, he replied, "a good man." In Leopold Bloom he created a good man and one of literature's great characters.

Kazantzakis's sequel echoes the Dante/Tennysonian view of the character. As the 33,333-line poem opens, the restored wanderer beginning to feel restless, sails away from Ithaca, vowing never to return. His first stop is Sparta, from which he escapes with Helen, bored living with bloated Menelaus; however, Odysseus's motive is not erotic but political. He wishes to employ Helen's symbolic value for political purposes. He accomplishes this at his next stop, Crete, where he organizes the overthrow of King Minos's dynasty. From there he sails to Egypt, continuing onward into Africa in search of the source of the Nile. Still unsatisfied, he plans to build an ideal city, but it is no sooner finished than it is destroyed by a volcanic eruption. Left alone, he abandons the active life, becoming a holy man. His last journey takes him to Antarctica, where he dies peacefully alone on an ice cap. His final place as holy man makes the final movement from heroic warrior, restless wanderer and political force in his search for freedom. He finds it in death, for absolute freedom does not exist. Freedom is, as Kazantzakis's translator Kimon Friar phrases it, "the last cage" imprisoning the mind. Only death can release him from that cage.

W. B. Stanford's *The Ulysses Theme* (1954) offers an illuminating survey of the history of the hero.

Oedipal complex   The theory advanced by Sigmund Freud that very young children experience an intense love for the parent of the opposite sex and a consequent hatred and fear of the other parent, whom they view as a rival. If this emotion is not resolved in childhood, it becomes a determining factor in later adult life. To illustrate his theory, Freud chose Sophocles' *Oedipus Rex,* the tragedy of a man who unwittingly killed his father and married his mother. For Freud the universal appeal of the Oedipus story confirmed the universality of its underlying theme. Subsequently, in an early example of PSYCHOANALYTICAL CRITICISM, Freud suggested that Shakespeare's *Hamlet* illustrated the presence of the Oedipal conflict in its main character—and implicitly in its AUTHOR. Freud's observation was developed into a full-length study (*Hamlet and Oedipus,* 1949) by his disciple Ernest Jones.

As a consequence of Freud's insight, a number of commentators discovered the Oedipal pattern underlying literary texts as in D. H. Lawrence's *Sons and Lovers* (1913), the very title of which summarizes the conflict. According to the critic William Kerrigan, the complex reemerges at two later stages of a man's life: when, as a young man, he wins from another father "a successor to his original love object" and when, as a father of a daughter, he, in turn loses her to a suitor. The last two phases constitute a key theme of COMEDY.

The Oedipal complex plays a key role in the revision of Freud developed by the French psychoanalyst Jacques Lacan. Lacan suggests that the Oedipal phase of a child's development coincides with the entry into the "symbolic order," Lacan's term for the child's acquisition of language. This process results in the repression of the child's prior identification with the mother and the decentering of individual identity. Lacan's view has played a key role in recent FEMINIST CRITICISM.

The Oedipal theme is given a unique twist in Harold Bloom's argument that the "strong" poet (and critic) engages in a conflict (*see* AGON) with a great writer of the past, whom he first misreads and later rewrites.

For a critique of the Oedipal theory and its influence see Gilles Deleuze and Felix Guattari's *Anti Oedipus* (1983). Harold Bloom's theory is developed in a number of his books, notably *The Anxiety of Influence* (1973). Kerrigan's comments appear in "Life's IAMB" in *Memory and Desire*, ed. Kathleen Woodward and Murray Schwartz (1986).

off Broadway   A term for the less expensive, more experimental alternatives to commercial Broadway theaters in New York City. Off Broadway emerged as an important outlet for theatrical experimentation in the years following World War II. Centered in Greenwich Village, but soon spreading to small theaters throughout the city, the movement presented various forms of AVANT-GARDE drama, as well as revivals of classics, and neglected plays by celebrated contemporary playwrights, such as Eugene O'Neill. The production of O'Neill's *The Iceman Cometh,* staged in 1956 by the Circle in the Square Theatre, was a milestone in the development of off Broadway.

Eventually, off Broadway began to assume a more traditional and commercial character, giving birth to off-off-Broadway, a venue for experimental fare, represented by theaters such as La Mama and the Ridiculous Theater.

Old English   A term for English language and literature dating from the fifth century to the Norman invasion of England in 1066. As a language, Old English was based upon the vernaculars of the Angles, Saxons, and Jutes, German tribes that invaded the country in the fifth century, mixed with that of the Celts, whom they displaced. Later in the ninth and 10th centuries, Scandinavian invaders settled in parts of the country and contributed to the linguistic mix.

In literature the most celebrated Old English work is the epic *Beowulf,* composed some time in the eighth century. The only complete folk epic in English literature, *Beowulf* is a gloomy, episodic account of the feats of the warrior Beowulf, written in unrhymed, alliterative verse.

The era is also distinguished by religious verse, such as Caedmon's Hymn, the earliest extant English lyric. An important prose writer was the monk Aelfric, whose *Catholic Homilies* (989–94) and *Lives of the Saints* (996) exhibit rhetorical mastery and piercing intelligence. Among works translated from the Latin, the most important was Bede's *Ecclesiastical History of the English People* (731). One prominent translator was King Alfred (848–99), whose reign was marked by the unification of England. Alfred's greatest legacy is the *Anglo-Saxon Chronicle,* a history of England from the Roman invasion to the fifth century. Commissioned by Alfred in 890, the *Chronicle* was continued and updated until the 12th century.

Stanley Greenfield's *A Critical History of Old English Literature* (1966) surveys the poetry and prose of the period while David Wilson's *The Anglo-Saxons* (1971) provides a historical context. Randolph Quirk and C. L. Wrenn's *An Old English Grammar* (1958) is a useful guide to grammar and syntax. Seamus Heaney's *Beowulf* (2002) is a recent excellent modern English version of the epic.

Old Vic A theater famous in the 20th century for its productions of Shakespeare's plays. From 1963 to 1976, it served as the headquarters of the British National Theatre Company, under the direction of Laurence Olivier. *See* ROYAL NATIONAL THEATER COMPANY.

omniscient narrator A term for a type of FICTION in which the third-person NARRATOR has complete knowledge of the actions and thoughts of the characters. Frequently taken to be the "voice" of the author, the omniscient narrator is the most common type of storytelling. It is used, for example, in most of the novels of Charles Dickens. For other types of narration, *see* POINT OF VIEW.

onomatopoeia A word whose sound hints at its meaning, such as *bang, zap,* and *hiss.* The term is also used to describe a group of words in which sound and sense reinforce each other. Witness these lines from Alfred, Lord Tennyson's "The Princess," which capture the sounds made by doves and bees:

> The moan of doves in immemorial elms,
> And murmuring of innumerable bees.

ontology In philosophy, the study of being in general, frequently regarded as an aspect of metaphysics. As formulated by the German philosopher Martin Heidegger, it deals with the question "Why is there something rather than nothing?" Heidegger's ontological orientation has played a prominent role in the modern development of HERMENEUTICS. *See* DASEIN.

opera A musical DRAMA in which all of the dialogue is sung. Opera traces its roots back to classical Greek drama, which contained chanted dialogue, but its modern form was developed in RENAISSANCE Italy. The LIBRETTO or "book" of an opera is always subordinated to its music.

Joseph Kerman's *Opera as Drama* (Revised Edition, 1988) looks at the dramatic dimension of the form.

operetta A form of light or comic opera in which the dialogue is spoken. It achieved great popularity in the late 19th and early 20th centuries in the works of Johann Strauss; Sir William Gilbert and Sir Arthur Sullivan; and Franz Lehar. Operetta played an influential role in the development of the modern MUSICAL.

orality/literacy   A pairing of terms designed to emphasize the distinctive differences in form, use, authorship, and thought between oral and written literature. Beyond this specific interest lies the question of the distinctions between oral and literate societies and their importance in the immediate future.

The great majority of the world's literature has been the product of oral cultures. Included within that category are many great masterpieces that cannot be fully understood without an awareness of the oral/literate distinction. Homer's *Iliad* and *Odyssey,* for example, were viewed through the lens of literacy until the 1920s, when the American scholar Milman Parry demonstrated that the essential features of these epics were rooted in oral characteristics, such as their heavy reliance on formulaic thought and expression (what a literate mind would regard as clichés).

Parry's work has been extended to a variety of areas, including Serbo-Croatian epic poetry, studied by Albert Lord (*A Singer of Tales,* 1960) and the African epic, analyzed by Isidore Okpewho (*The Epic in Africa,* 1979). These and many other studies of oral literature focus on its essential features: mnemonic devices, repetition, formulas, epithets, and syntactic structures that feature "adding on" rather than subordination (in grammatical terms, compound rather than complex sentences). Even the concept of a climactic linear PLOT (as outlined, for example, in FREYTAG'S PYRAMID) is alien to oral literature, which relies on an essentially episodic structure.

Recent commentary has examined the stages of development from an oral to a chirographic (manuscript) to a print, and, most recently, to an electronic culture in an attempt to measure the influence of technological innovations on the forms and nature of literature. The EPIC, for example, is an oral form; ROMANCE, a chirographic one; the NOVEL, a product of print culture; and the various experimental techniques associated with POSTMODERNISM reflect the influence of an electronic culture.

These strictly literary concerns form a part of some of the large issues that are at stake in viewing history from the perspective of orality/literacy. Some of its implications were evident in the work of Marshall McLuhan, who argued that, as a consequence of the dominance of television, we are entering a new phase of human history which he characterized as the GLOBAL VILLAGE. McLuhan's former colleague, Walter J. Ong, looks at television culture as one of "secondary orality," as distinguished from the orality of preliterate cultures. Such a society will presumably incorporate features of literate culture (linearity, visuality, abstract thinking) with that of oral culture (cyclicality, sound, concrete thinking.)

Oral/literate distinctions have had a significant impact on educational questions as well. The widely held impression that writing skills have deteriorated, and with it cognitive capacities for abstraction and analysis, is a hotly debated subject in the society at large and within the field of COMPOSITION STUDIES. Inevitably, this debate touches upon questions concerning the technology-driven society thought to be around the corner, if not already here. Should we be educating students to assume a more active and participatory role in society? If so, what are the various "literacies" they will need to acquire?

Milman Parry's work is available in *The Making of Homeric Verse: The Collected Papers of Milman Parry* (1971); Walter J. Ong's *Orality and Literacy: The Technologizing of the Word* (1982) offers a valuable synthesis of the state of knowledge in this area.

ordinary language   An approach to traditional philosophical problems through an analysis of the language that frames these problems. Among the (primarily British) philosophers associated with this approach are Gilbert Ryle, P. F. Strawson, and John Austin. Austin is also well known for his formulation of SPEECH ACT THEORY.

organic form   An argument that a literary work evolves and develops like a plant or other organism, naturally and internally. This development is opposed to the view that form is imposed from without. The term was originally employed by Samuel Taylor Coleridge in defending Shakespeare from neoclassical critics' charges of formal flaws in his plays. Coleridge argues that Shakespeare's works exhibit "organic" rather than "mechanic" form: "The form is mechanic when, on any given material, we impress a predetermined form. The organic form, on the other hand, is innate; it shapes as it develops itself from within, and the fullness of its development is one and the same with the perfection of its outward form."

The idea of the literary text as a living organism has been an influential concept in the 20th century, particularly in NEW CRITICISM.

Coleridge's Shakespearean Criticism, edited by Thomas M. Raysor (2 vols., second edition, 1960), contains the complete text of Coleridge's description of organic form.

orientalism   In its neutral sense, a term used to describe Western scholarship's dealing with the Orient. In its second sense, it refers to Western perceptions of Eastern cultures and social practices. Implicit in the second sense of the term, a consequence of the influence of the publication of Edward Said's *Orientalism* (1978), is the implication of bias and misreading on the part of Western observers. Said's work is a powerful critique both of Western scholarship and its interconnections with the imperialist designs of Western nations, particularly England and France. According to Said, a major historical benchmark for this process was the invasion of Egypt by Napoleon Bonaparte in 1798. Napoleon was accompanied by a group of scholars enlisted to explain the importance of the East to the West. However, these scholars employed their scholarship in the essential colonialist task, "dominating, restructuring, and having authority over the Orient," and their work set the standard until the present day.

Said's book stands as an outstanding example of postcolonial criticism. (*See* POSTCOLONIAL STUDIES.)

original sin The Christian doctrine that Adam's sin implicated all mankind and that, as a result, human beings are born with a flaw or stain that limits our knowledge and our freedom. A prevailing doctrine among both Catholics and Protestants through the 17th century, the doctrine came under heavy criticism with the liberalization of thought among certain Protestant sects during the ENLIGHTENMENT. Among the defenders of the doctrine was the Puritan theologian Jonathan Edwards, whose *Original Sin* (1758) rebuked opponents of the traditional belief.

A number of critics of American literature have argued for the importance of the theme of original sin in the work of Nathaniel Hawthorne, Herman Melville, and Henry James in the 19th century and William Faulkner and Robert Penn Warren in the 20th century. (*See also* FALL, THE; FORTUNATE FALL.)

For a discussion of the conception see R. W. B. Lewis's *The American Adam* (1955) and Ihab Hassan's *Radical Innocence* (1961).

Ossian Name given to the alleged AUTHOR of ancient EPIC poems thought to be written in Gaelic. In fact these poems were fabricated by James Macpherson, an 18th-century Scottish poet who claimed that his *Fingal* (1762) and *Temora* (1763) were translations of Ossian's epics. Before the exposure of Macpherson's fraud, "Ossian's" poems won wide popularity in Europe, particularly in Germany, where they exercised considerable influence on the burgeoning ROMANTICISM of the late 18th century.

other *See* SELF/OTHER.

ottava rima An eight-line stanza (octave) with an a-b-a-b-a-b-c-c rhyme scheme. In its original Italian version each line consists of 11 syllables. As adapted into English, it is written in iambic pentameter. The 16th-century poet Sir Thomas Wyatt was the first poet to employ the form in English. In the 19th century, Lord Byron used it with great success in his *Don Juan* (1819–24). Among modern poems employing the stanza, one of the best known is William Butler Yeats's "Among School Children."

Oxford English Dictionary (OED) A dictionary described by its publishers, the Oxford University Press, as "the most authoritative and comprehensive dictionary of English in the world." The dictionary has had a fascinating history. In 1857, members of the Philological Society of London began planning a dictionary that would provide a history of every word included in it; it would show the meaning of a word as it first appeared in the language and any subsequent meanings it acquired in the course of its history. These various meanings would be validated by dated quotations from various writings. The original title was *A New English Dictionary on Historical Principles*. It was published in serial form, its first issue appearing in 1884.

In 1928, 71 years after it was begun, the dictionary was completed. In 1933, the complete edition, in 12 volumes that included a one-volume supplement, was published under its new name, *The Oxford English Dictionary*. The OED, as it is commonly known, was republished in 1989, having integrated within it a number of its supplementary volumes. The complete work now consists of 20 volumes.

The chief editor of the OED was James Murray. One of his most important and prolific contributors was William Chester Minor, an American surgeon "residing" in England. Although Murray and Minor had not met, they formed a friendship through their correspondence. Only after many years did Murray discover that Minor was a convicted murderer, confined to a hospital for the criminally insane. Simon Winchester's *The Professor and the Madman* (1998) is a poignant account of the relationship between the two men.

John Willinsky's *Empire of Words: The Reign of the OED* (1994) offers a history and analysis of the dictionary.

Oxford Movement A 19th-century reform movement within the Anglican Church (the Church of England). Alarmed by the degree to which skepticism and materialism had emerged in English religious life, leaders of the movement, who included John Henry Newman, John Keble, E. B. Pusey, and R. H. Froude, advocated a return to the Catholic rituals of the MIDDLE AGES. They wrote a series of papers (*Tracts for the Times*, 1831–41) designed to clarify "the relation of the Church of England to the Catholic Church at large." The result, for Newman and some other members of the movement, was eventual conversion to Catholicism. Newman recorded this experience in his *Apologia pro Vita Sua, or a History of My Religious Opinions* (1864), commonly regarded as a masterpiece of 19th-century English prose.

After Newman, the movement was led by E. B. Pusey, who incorporated some of the changes advocated in *Tracts for the Times*. In its emphasis on the medieval roots of the Church, the movement exerted some influence on the medievalism of the PRE-RAPHAELITES.

Oxford theory   *See* ANTI-STRATFORDIAN THEORIES.

oxymoron   A contradictory term, such as Milton's "darkness visible," employed to highlight an ambiguous condition.

In the first act of Shakespeare's *Hamlet,* Claudius employs a number of oxymora to explain his hasty marriage to Gertrude so soon after the death of Hamlet's father:

> *Therefore our sometime sister, now our queen,*
> *The imperial jointress to this warlike state,*
> *Have we, as 'twere with a defeated joy,*
> *With an auspicious and a dropping eye,*
> *With mirth in funeral and with dirge in marriage*
> *In equal scale, weighing delight and dole,*
> *Taken to wife.*

See also PARADOX.

paean A song of rejoicing, often used to describe any intense expression of joy or praise.

pageant An elaborate spectacle or procession. In the MIDDLE AGES, a pageant was a moveable platform on which MYSTERY PLAYS were performed. In the Elizabethan Age, processional pageants, celebrating a visit of the queen or other dignitary, frequently included small dramatic skits.

palindrome A word, group of words, or sentence that reads the same backward and forward. Among famous examples: "Madam, I'm Adam" and the complaint, falsely attributed to Napoleon, "Able was I ere I saw Elba."

palinode A retraction of something written earlier. A celebrated example is Chaucer's retraction at the conclusion of *The Canterbury Tales* in which he asks forgiveness for the "worldly vanitees" of virtually all of his writings.

pamphlets Short works, separately published, on a variety of themes. In 16th-century England, pamphlets played an important role in social and literary life. An early example are the polemical exchanges of pamphlets between Sir Thomas More and William Tyndale in the early days of the REFORMATION: More defended the traditional Catholic position and Tyndale the then-new creed of Protestantism. Later in the century, Elizabethan pamphleteers achieved great popularity, depicting or satirizing social and cultural conditions. Among them was Robert Greene, whose *Greene's Groatsworth of Wit* (1592) is notable for containing the first printed reference to Shakespeare. Greene attacks the newly arrived playwright as "an upstart crow beautified with our feathers . . . that supposes he is well able to bombast out a blank verse as the best of you, and . . . is in his own conceit the only Shake-scene in a country." Greene's attack offers a taste of the lively, spirited, and often scurrilous language of these pamphlets.

The 17th century in England saw the conflict between Parliament and Charles I that resulted in the overthrow of the monarchy and the establishment of the COMMONWEALTH PERIOD. This conflict was fueled by a pamphlet war, whose most notable participant was the poet John Milton. Milton's contributions included his *Areopagitica* (1644), a classic plea for freedom of the press.

Among the famous 18th-century pamphlets, none outshines Jonathan Swift's satirical masterpiece *A Modest Proposal for Preventing the Children of the Poor People in Ireland from Becoming a Burthen to Their Parents or Country, and for Making Them Beneficial to the Publick* (1729), in which he suggests that poor Irish children should be killed and sold as food. As a final touch, the pamphlet includes a number of recipes.

Pamphlets also played important roles in the early years of the French and American Revolutions, setting the precedent in which all subsequent major political upheavals were accompanied by a profusion of pamphlets. In American history, the name most closely associated with the pamphlet is Thomas Paine, whose *The American Crisis* (1776–83) was a series of 16 pamphlets, the first of which included the famous opening line, "These are times that try men's souls."

British Pamphleteers, Vol. I, edited by George Orwell and Reginald Reynolds (1941), and *Vol. II,* edited by Reginald Reynolds with an introduction by A. J. P. Taylor (1951), collect notable English pamphlets from the 16th century to the 1930s.

panegyric   Extended praise of a subject. In RHETORIC, the term is used as a synonym for "epideictic" speech, language designed more to display the skill of the speaker than to establish an argument.

pantaloon (pantalone)   In COMMEDIA DELL' ARTE, a stock character who is a greedy, suspicious old man, the father of the heroine, determined to marry her off to a wealthy suitor. The figure of Harpagon in Molière's *The Miser* (1668) is an example of the type adapted to formal COMEDY.

pantoum   A poetic form made up of QUATRAINS, in which the second and fourth lines of one stanza are repeated as the first and third lines in the next stanza.   In the final stanza the second and fourth lines repeat the first and third lines of the first stanza. The form was adopted by 19th-century French poets from Malaysian poetry. Twentieth century examples in English include Donald Justice's *Pantoum of the Great Depression.*

parable   A tale designed to teach a moral lesson. Usually, as in the parables of Jesus in the New Testament, the story involves human beings whose actions are clarified by the concluding moral. The parable differs from ALLEGORY, in which the characters represent abstract qualities, and from FABLE, in which the moral is unstated because it is presumed to be self-evident.

paradigm   In LINGUISTICS, the set of possible words from which a speaker chooses to form a statement. In the sentence John loves Mary, John and Mary are selected from the paradigm of possible nouns, loves from the paradigm of verbs. The arrangement of the sentence according to the rules of grammar (John in the subject position, Mary the object) is called the syntagm. The linguist Roman Johnson argued that paradigm/syntagm corresponds to METAPHOR/METONYMY as basic features of language.

In *The Structure of Scientific Revolutions* (1962), the historian of science Thomas Kuhn maintains that scientific knowledge moves not in a continuous line of development but by occasional revolutionary jumps, such as the displacement of the Ptolemaic by the Copernican system or of Newtonian by Einsteinian physics. These extraordinary occurrences he characterized as "paradigm shifts." Despite Kuhn's caveat that his theory could be applied only to the natural sciences, the terms *paradigm* and *paradigm shift* began to appear in every discipline, not least in literary THEORY as it emerged in the 1970s and '80s.

paradox   An apparent contradiction that asserts a truth. It is a frequent feature of religious language, as in the biblical injunction "The last shall be first." For the Romantic essayist Thomas de Quincey, paradox is inherent in the nature of reality: "No man needs to search for paradox in this world of ours. Let him simply confine himself to the truth, and he will find paradox growing everywhere. . . ."

In NEW CRITICISM, paradox represents a central feature of POETRY. In the view of the new critic Cleanth Brooks, the language of a poem is profoundly paradoxical in its emphasis on the reconciliation of opposites. He argues that "the truth which the poet utters can be approached only in terms of paradox." In *The Well Wrought Urn* (1947), Brooks discusses the importance of paradox in a series of poems from John Donne's "The Canonization" to William Butler Yeats's "Among School Children."

Rosalie Colie's *Paradoxia Epidemica* (1966) is a study of the importance of paradox in English Renaissance thought.

parallelism   The principle of representing equal ideas in the same grammatical form, for example, "government of the people, by the people, and for the people." Parallelism produces a sense of balance and order, and is frequently employed as a feature of the PERIODIC SENTENCE.

paraphrase A restatement in different words of the plot or meaning of a literary text. Paraphrases are frequently used in literary criticism as a springboard to critical comments. Cleanth Brooks, a prominent exponent of NEW CRITICISM, characterized any suggestion that the meaning of a poem could be expressed in language other than that of the poem itself as "the heresy of the paraphrase."

Cleanth Brooks's *The Well Wrought Urn* (1947) is a series of essays illustrating new critical principles.

parataxis In RHETORIC, clauses or phrases arranged in coordinate rather than subordinate constructions. In *Orality and Literacy* (1982), Walter Ong has argued that parataxis is a feature of oral culture and subordination ("hypotaxis"), a characteristic of print culture. Ong offers as evidence a passage from two translations of the BIBLE, the Douay version (1610), produced in a culture with a largely oral tradition, and the New American Bible, published in 1970:

1610 version
In the beginning God created heaven and earth. And the earth was void and empty, and darkness was upon the face of the deep; and the spirit of God moved over the waters. And God said: Be light made. And light was made. And God saw the light that it was good; and he divided the light from the darkness. And he called the light Day, and the darkness Night; and there was evening and morning one day.

1970 version
In the beginning, when God created the heavens and the earth, the earth was a formless wasteland, and the darkness covered the abyss, while a mighty wind swept over the waters. Then God said, 'Let there be light,' and there was light. God saw how good the light was. God then separated the light from the darkness. God called the light 'day' and the darkness he called 'night.' Thus evening came, and morning followed—the first day.

Ong points out that the earlier passage contains nine introductory "ands" as opposed to the subordinating "when," "while," "then," and "thus" constructions of the modern text. Print culture requires more elaborate and flexible structures because it cannot rely on the interpersonal contact of speech to enforce its meaning. (*See* ORALITY/LITERACY.)

Parnassians A school of 19th-century French poets who reacted against what they took to be the excesses of ROMANTICISM. As a result they chose a name that represented a classical ideal. Mount Parnassus in Greece was the legendary home of the MUSES.

The Parnassians advocated the use of traditional verse forms including RHYME, calling for a POETRY of control and precision. They were also identified with the ART FOR ART'S SAKE movement.

Prominent Parnassians included Leconte de Lisle, Théophile Gautiér, and François Coppée.

parody Imitation of a particular style or genre for the purposes of satirizing it. The object of satire may be an AUTHOR with a distinctive style, such as Ernest Hemingway, or a formulaic structure, such as SOAP OPERA.

Parody is an ancient form. Aristophanes parodied both Aeschylus and Euripides in *The Frogs* (405 B.C.). In the late MIDDLE AGES, Rabelais parodied the language of SCHOLASTICISM. Jane Austen's *Northanger Abbey* (1818) is a parody of the popular GOTHIC NOVELS of her day.

In recent years, parody appears as an increasingly significant form. As exemplified in two novels, Miguel de Cervantes's *Don Quixote* (1605, 1615) and Laurence Sterne's *Tristram Shandy* (1759–67), it has come to be seen as an important, even central, example of the principle of INTERTEXTUALITY in fiction. As represented in the fiction of Jorge Luis Borges (*Ficciones,* 1962), Vladimir Nabokov (*Pale Fire,* 1962), Malcolm Bradbury (*Who Do You Think You Are? Stories and Parodies,* 1976), Umberto Eco (*The Name of the Rose,* 1983), and David Lodge (*Nice Work,* 1988), parody has assumed a defining role in the formation of literary POSTMODERNISM.

Dwight McDonald's *Parodies: An Anthology* (1960) offers a rich array of parodies from Chaucer to the present. A comprehensive study of the subject is Margaret Rose's *Parody: Ancient, Modern and Post-Modern* (1993).

parousia A Greek word, meaning "arrival," used in the New Testament to refer to the second coming of CHRIST, which will signal the end of the world. In the early years of the Christian era, the parousia was thought to be imminent. Since that time the idea of the APOCALYPSE, the belief that "the end is near," has played a significant role in literary culture. William Butler Yeats's "The Second Coming," for example, is one of the most frequently quoted poems in the English language: "And what rough beast, its hour come round at last, / Slouches towards Bethlehem to be born?" (*See also* "LEFT BEHIND" NOVELS.)

Partisan Review   *See* NEW YORK INTELLECTUALS.

passion play   A play dealing with the suffering, death, and resurrection of Christ. Originating in the MIDDLE AGES, passion plays frequently formed a part of CORPUS CHRISTI celebrations in many European countries. Since 1634, a passion play has been performed at Oberammergau in Bavaria. This production has been altered in recent years in response to charges of ANTI-SEMITISM in the original TEXT.

pastiche   In literature, a text made up of material from other texts. Traditionally a disparaging term designed to characterize a work as derivative, pastiche has assumed a more respectable status with the advent of POSTMODERNISM. Pastiche is now seen, along with PARODY, as an acknowledgment of INTERTEXTUALITY.

pastoral   Originally a literary form idealizing the lives of shepherds (the Latin for shepherd is *pastor*), more recently used to describe celebrations of innocent country or small town life. Implicit in the idea of pastoral is the identification of happiness with simple, natural existence, associated in classical times with the GOLDEN AGE, and in modern times with images such as "the little house on the prairie" or "Grover's Corners," the locale of Thornton Wilder's play *Our Town* (1938).

Early examples of the form are the Greek pastorals, notably Theocritus's *Idylls* (third century B.C.), which established the convention of shepherds whiling away beautiful days by composing love songs, or elegies for departed friends (*see* ELEGY), or engaging in poetic contests with each other (*see* DEBAT). Theocritus's pastoralism was adapted by the Roman poet Virgil, whose *Eclogues* (37 B.C.) profoundly influenced subsequent literature. A century later, the New Testament used the metaphor of Christ as the "Good Shepherd," a figure of speech later to be transferred to members of the clergy.

Fusion of the Virgilian and Christian elements (intensified by the belief that Virgil's sixth eclogue contained a prophecy of the coming of Christ) was evident in the various forms pastoral assumed in the Renaissance. Examples include Spenser's *The Shepherd's Calendar* (1590), Philip Sidney's *Arcadia* (1590), and Shakespeare's *As You Like It* (1599)—which celebrates the form while occasionally tweaking its nose with lighthearted parodies of pastoral conventions—and *The Winter's Tale* (1610). The outstanding adaptation of the pastoral elegy is John Milton's *Lycidas* (1637), echoed in the 19th century in Percy Bysshe Shelley's *Adonais* (1821), a lament on the death of the poet John Keats.

In the 20th century the term has undergone considerable expansion, beginning with the critic William Empson's *Some Versions of Pastoral* (1935). Empson saw pastoral as a mode that enables one "to talk about complex people by a complete consideration of simple people"—just as traditional pastoral always implicitly critiqued urban or courtly life by focusing on the shepherd's life. Empson's definition has led to a broader use of the term, particularly in American literature where the WESTERN or novels of the rural South (for example, Eudora Welty's *The Delta Wedding,* 1945, and *The Ponder Heart,* 1954) create a world in which the natural and the human exist in fragile harmony.

The expansion of the term has extended even into what is, from a pastoral view, the heart of darkness, New York City. J. D. Salinger's novel *The Catcher in the Rye* (1951) is often regarded as an "urban" pastoral, a contradiction justified here by the young hero's attempt to wrest innocence and honesty from the jaws of corrupt experience. The pastoral ideal is represented in the meaning of the title, Holden Caulfield's vision of himself as saving children from falling as they play in a field of rye.

Another distinctive sub-genre of American pastoral is the writing on baseball, both FICTION and nonfiction. For an increasingly (sub)urbanized America, BASEBALL has come to represent the eternal summer of youth, the myth of innocence, the Edenic garden where the central goal is "coming home." Among the literature dealing with the subject are Bernard Malamud's *The Natural* (1952), Robert Coover's *The Universal Baseball Association* (1968), and the writings of Roger Angell.

W. W. Greg's *Pastoral Poetry and Pastoral Drama* (1906) is a classic study of the traditional use of the form; Frederick Karl's "The Persistence of Pastoral" in his *American Fictions 1940–1980* (1983) provides an overview of the modern American pastoral. Among Roger Angell's books on baseball is *The Summer Game* (1972).

pathetic fallacy   A term coined by the art critic John Ruskin in his *Modern Painters* (1856) to describe the poetic attribution of human feelings to natural objects, such as trees and mountains. Ruskin uses the term in a derogatory sense in reference to ordinary poets for whom the fallacy is a sign of careless thinking. He acknowledges, however, that for such poets as Shakespeare, who employ it to exploit the idea of nature as a vital force, the fallacy can be a powerful poetic instrument.

pathos   In literature and drama, the evocation in an audience of the feelings of pity and sorrow. In RHETORIC, the term is used to refer to the emotional appeal of an argument that supplements its ethical (ethos) and logical (logos) appeals. In literature, pathos is associated with EMPATHY and is a part of an audience's reaction to TRAGEDY. In its negative or excessive form it is identified with SENTIMENTALITY.

patriarchy   Literally, rule by the father and, by extension, a social system controlled by men. Patriarchy is a central target of FEMINIST CRITICISM, which takes as one of its goals the unveiling of patriarchal structures in societies past and present. Feminists argue that many pervasive aspects of patriarchy are disguised by the assumption of natural differences between men and women. For feminists, the biological difference between male and female, the difference of sex, has been extended to the social and cultural sphere of GENDER. Thus, they argue that the traditional notion of "women's work," both inside and outside the home, as a seemingly "natural" condition was in fact part of a systematic retention of POWER within the patriarchal system.

Within literature, patriarchy is evident in the overwhelming prominence of male writers in the CANON, and in the consequent representation of the woman as "the other" in much of the world's literature (*See* SELF/OTHER).

The Feminist Reader (1989), edited by Catherine Belsey and Jane Moore, provides a thorough introduction to the topic.

pentateuch   A term for the first five books of the BIBLE: Genesis, Exodus, Leviticus, Numbers, and Deuteronomy. The Hebrew term *Torah* often serves as a synonym for pentateuch. Tradition has ascribed the authorship to Moses, but recent scholarship has discredited this notion.

periodic sentence   A long, complex sentence in which the main clause appears near or close to the end, creating suspense about its outcome. The sentence usually includes a number of parallel, subordinate clauses or phrases, as in this sentence from Samuel Johnson's *The Preface to Shakespeare* (1765):

> To bring a lover, a lady, and a rival into the fable; to entangle them in contradictory obligations, perplex them with oppositions of interest, and harass them with violence of desires inconsistent with each other; to make them meet in rapture and part in agony, to fill their mouths with hyperbolical joy and outrageous sorrow, to distress them as nothing human ever was distressed, to deliver them as nothing human ever was delivered, is the business of a modern dramatist.

periods, literary   A system for arranging the history and teaching of literature. Chronologically arranged, literary periods provide convenient categories for historically oriented approaches to literature. The names assigned to periods are frequently arbitrary: some derived, in England, from the names of sovereigns (ELIZABETHAN, JACOBEAN, VICTORIAN), some from historical periods

(RESTORATION, Romantic, Modern). The chief English and American periods are the following:

English	American
OLD ENGLISH (fifth cent.–1100)	COLONIAL (1607–1765)
ANGLO NORMAN (1100–1350)	REVOLUTIONARY (1765–1789)
MIDDLE ENGLISH (1350–1500)	EARLY NATIONAL (1789–1828)
EARLY TUDOR (1500–1558)	AMERICAN RENAISSANCE (1828–1865)
ELIZABETHAN (1558–1603)	REALISTIC (1865–1900)
JACOBEAN (1603–1625)	NATURALISTIC (1900–1914)
CAROLINE (1625–1649)	MODERN (1914–1950)
COMMONWEALTH (1649–1660)	POSTMODERN (1950–)
RESTORATION (1660–1710)	
AUGUSTAN (1710–1750)	
AGE OF JOHNSON (1750–1798)	
ROMANTIC (1798–1832)	
VICTORIAN (1832–1901)	
EDWARDIAN (1901–1914)	
MODERN (1914–1950)	
POSTMODERN (1950–)	

(*See also* ETHNIC LITERATURE.)

peripeteia   In DRAMA or NARRATIVE, a reversal in fortune, either, as in comedy, the move from bad to good, or in tragedy from good to bad or, occasionally, from bad to worse.

persona   A term for a character in DRAMA or FICTION. In the criticism of lyric poetry, the term is used to distinguish the speaker in the poem from the AUTHOR. By using persona, the critic implies that the "I" speaking the poem is a character, not necessarily the author.

The DRAMATIS PERSONAE is the list of characters in a play, printed at the beginning of the text.

personification   A figure of speech in which human qualities are attributed to an inanimate or abstract entity. As George Lakoff and Mark Turner explain, "Personification permits us to use our knowledge about ourselves to maximal effect, to use insight about ourselves to help us comprehend such things as forces of nature, common events, abstract concepts, and inanimate objects."

Personification is a common feature of POETRY from Virgil ("the tears of things") to Emily Dickinson ("Because I could not stop for Death/He kindly stopped for me") to popular songs ("April played the fiddle").

Personification is an essential component of ALLEGORY.

George Lakoff and Mark Turner's *More than Cool Reason: A Field Guide to Poetic Metaphor* (1989) is a stimulating treatment of metaphorical language.

perspectivism   The view that knowledge of a subject is limited by the perspective from which it is viewed. In literature and criticism, the term refers to the process of acquiring knowledge by viewing it from different perspectives. A common practice in modern FICTION and DRAMA is to relate the action from more than one POINT OF VIEW or to mix points of view through such devices as INTERIOR MONOLOGUE or FREE INDIRECT STYLE. Another technique is to develop an overarching metaphor such as the world-as-stage or life-as-a-dream.

Still another approach is famously associated with two films, Orson Welles's *Citizen Kane* (1942) and Akira Kurosawa's *Rashomon* (1950). In the former, a variety of NARRATORs all contribute their individual pieces to the puzzle that is the core of the main character, but none of them is able to penetrate the mystery surrounding Kane's last words. In *Rashomon*, the story is told through the eyes of the three protagonists, each one contradicting the others. Finally, an eyewitness provides a fourth version, which may or may not be the "truthful" one. One example of perspectivism in criticism is Stanley Edgar Hyman's *Iago: Five Approaches to the Illusion of His Motivation* (1970) in which the AUTHOR offers critical readings of Iago's character from the perspective of major schools of modern criticism.

Charles Glicksberg's *Modern Literary Perspectivism* (1970) relates the approach to various modernist texts.

Petrarchan sonnet   *See* SONNET.

phallocentrism   A term for a mode of thinking and behavior that locates the source of personal or social POWER in the phallus. A key term in FEMINIST CRITICISM, where it is viewed as synonymous with PATRIARCHY, phallocentrism is nevertheless a term of ambiguous reference. The sense in which the phallus is identical with the penis is the dominant one in the use of the term. However, the secondary meaning of phallus—the sexually indistinguishable tissue within the embryo that forms either the penis or the clitoris—suggests that at some fundamental levels, phallocentrism is common to both men and women. This is the view reflected in the PSYCHOANALYTICAL CRITICISM of the French poststructuralist Jacques Lacan.

Jacques Derrida, the leading exponent of DECONSTRUCTION, has taken the idea of phallocentrism a step further in coining the phrase "phallogocentrism." The term is an amalgam of phallocentrism and LOGOCENTRISM, the belief that language is rooted in an authority external to it. Phallogocentrism suggests that this external authority is the phallus, that every aspect of language reflects male dominance and female oppression. *See* WRITING.

Toril Moi's *Sexual/Textual Politics* (1985) provides ample discussion of the issue.

phenomenology A philosophical method that describes objects as they are registered in the consciousness of an observer. The founder of phenomenology is Edmund Husserl, who described its aim as a description of what is given in experience. One major implication of Husserl's approach is that it rejected the traditional dualism, the separation of subject and object, that had dominated Western philosophy since the time of Descartes. In place of the basic distinction of subject and object, Husserl focused on phenomena, things as experienced by human consciousness. Thus the phenomenological method involved a close analysis of mental processes.

The phenomenological method was incorporated into the philosophy of EXISTENTIALISM or, as is it more precisely known, Existential Phenomenology, by Husserl's disciple Martin Heidegger. Where Husserl had developed a general theory of how we know, Heidegger employed it to explore a way of knowing human existence and ultimately Being itself.

In its application to literature, phenomenology focuses attention on the experience of the reader, a position first outlined by the Polish theorist Roman Ingarden, who argued that a literary TEXT was "concretized" in the act of reading. Ingarden's idea was developed further by Wolfgang Iser, who set out to give a detailed phenomenological description of the reading process. Iser's description focuses on the conventional codes that govern our reading and influence the preconceptions we bring to a given text. For Iser the superior texts are those that force us to revise and reconsider those preconceptions. As we go about reading we constantly make assumptions that are later proven to be wrong, or at least only partly right. In the meantime we are constantly "filling in the gaps"—imagining, for example, that the first character we meet in a story is the main character until we discover otherwise. In this continuing process of making assumptions, "gap-filling," and correcting those assumptions, the reader is constructing the text, "concretizing" it in different ways. Iser's work has played a major role in the development of READER RESPONSE CRITICISM.

Also heavily influenced by phenomenological theory has been the so-called GENEVA SCHOOL of criticism. Known as "critics of consciousness," this group treats the literary text as the expression of the consciousness of its author in intersubjective relationship with its reader. One prominent American critic, J. Hillis Miller, began his career as a disciple of the Geneva School before switching allegiance to DECONSTRUCTION.

Phenomenology bears a close relation to HERMENEUTICS, the analysis of interpretation. Both approaches operate from the basic phenomenological premise of the intersubjectivity of reader and text.

Robert Magliola's *Phenomenology and Literature* (1977) offers a reliable introduction to the topic. Wolfgang Iser's *The Act of Reading* (1978) provides a phenomenological description of the reading process.

philistine   A boorish, uncultivated person. Matthew Arnold used the term in his *Culture and Anarchy* (1869) to describe the prosperous middle class that had come to power in industrialized Europe. Arnold regarded this new middle class as interested solely in material possessions and therefore as a threat to genuine culture. *See* ARNOLDIAN CRITICISM.

In biblical times, the Philistines were a warlike people who co-occupied territory in Palestine and were consistent enemies of the Hebrews.

philology   The historical study of language. In the 19th and early 20th centuries, the term was used to include in one category the study of both language and literature. Since that time the study of language has been called LINGUISTICS while literary study is designated as either scholarship, CRITICISM, or THEORY.

philosophes   A group of 18th-century French thinkers who advanced the principles of rationalism, the belief in reason as the chief source of knowledge. Among the early philosophes were Voltaire and Montesquieu. In the latter part of the 18th century, the term became attached to the group of thinkers associated with the Encyclopedia (*Encyclopédie* [1751–65]), one of the most important works of the ENLIGHTENMENT.

phoneme   In linguistics, the smallest unit of speech that distinguishes one word from another. A phoneme is always seen in relation to other phonemes. Thus the b in *big* and the p in *pig* are phonemes. According to many linguists, these phonemic differences form the basis of language, which they see as a system of differences. (*See* STRUCTURALISM.)

picaresque   A term for a form of NARRATIVE that recounts the adventures of a *pícaro* (Spanish for "rogue"). Usually exhibiting an episodic structure, in which the *pícaro* moves from one situation to another, the form generally satirizes the characters or societies it depicts. In this respect the picaresque embodies a reaction to the social/cultural conflicts that arose in Spain (and the rest of Western Europe) as it shifted from a feudal to a monarchial society in the 16th century. Among other social disruptions, the change created a class of vagabonds or beggars. The picaresque gave voice to this class, offering an outsider's view of society.

As a result the form found fertile ground in other countries as well as Spain. The prototype is the anonymous *Lazarillo de Tormes* (1554), but Mateo Alemán's *Guzmán de Alfarache* (1599–1604) is the first to include the picaro as first person NARRATOR, a feature that became a defining characteristic of the genre.

The form was imitated in the rogue literature of ELIZABETHAN England, as well as in France and Germany. A notable German picaresque was Johannes Von Grimmelshausen's *The Adventurous Simplicissimus* (1669), a picaresque with a religious resolution.

Not only did the picaresque contribute significantly to the early development of the NOVEL, it has had a continued life as a minor form in modern literature. Examples of the modern picaresque include such distinguished works as Herman Melville's *The Confidence Man* (1857), Joyce Cary's *The Horse's Mouth* (1944), Ralph Ellison's *Invisible Man* (1952), Saul Bellow's *The Adventures of Augie March* (1953), and Thomas Mann's *The Adventures of Felix Krull, Confidence Man* (1954).

Richard Bjornson's *The Picaresque Hero in European Fiction* (1977) traces the form from its beginning through the 18th century; Alexander Blackburn's *The Myth of Picaro* (1979) focuses on the symbolic significance of the hero.

pirated edition   An edition published without the permission of the AUTHOR or holder of the copyright. A notable example of a pirated edition is the first edition of Shakespeare's *Hamlet*, which was published in 1603, containing the following corrupted version of the "To be or not to be" soliloquy:

> To be or not to be, Aye, there's the point,
> To be, to sleep, is that all? Aye all.

plagiarism   The act of representing as one's own the writing of another person. The opposite of plagiarism is the literary forgery, the act of representing one's own writing as the work of another. In contemporary theory, the questioning of authorial privilege (*see* AUTHOR) has led to a re-examination of the legal definitions of copyright and plagiarism.

The Construction of Authorship, edited by Martha Woodmansee and Peter Jaszi (1990), is a collection of essays on the history of the subject.

Platonism   Ideas developed by the Greek philosopher Plato. The central doctrine of Plato's thought is the belief in the reality of Ideas or Forms, of which the world of ordinary experience is but a shadow or imitation. Plato's teachings, both in themselves and as they were adapted in NEOPLATONISM, exercised a profound influence on Western thought and literature, including the theology of Christianity, the development of Renaissance HUMANISM, the philosophical foundations of ROMANTICISM, even the modern theory of mathematics.

The concept of Platonic Love—the transcendence of mere physical pleasure through the apprehension of the spiritual beauty of the beloved—played a key role in the COURTLY LOVE tradition and in the development of the SONNET.

play   A composition written to be performed. In the more special sense of leisure, play is conceived of as the opposite of work, as the essence of freedom. As the philosopher George Santayana put it, "For it is in the spontaneous play of his faculties that man finds himself and his happiness."

For many of those who have written on the subject, there is an important distinction between play and game. Game is rule-governed and structured while play, as in "free play," is open-ended and self-reflexive, but for many others the terms are used interchangeably to indicate activity indulged in for its own sake.

In contemporary literary study *play* has become a virtual synonym for DECONSTRUCTION. For deconstructionists, a final definitive meaning of a TEXT can never be achieved. All that is available is the free play of alternative meanings. For the Russian theorist Mikhail Bakhtin, on the other hand, play in the form of CARNIVAL serves a serious, subversive role in society.

The playful, in the carnivalesque and the deconstructionist senses, is a dominant feature of literary POSTMODERNISM, in which it functions as an expression of irresistible vitality and the dance of language.

Johan Huizinga's *Homo Ludens: A Study of the Play Element in Culture* (1950) is a classic study of the importance of play in Western culture. Jacques Derrida's "Structure, Sign and Play in the Discourse of the Human Sciences," an important statement of deconstructionist principles, is reprinted in *A Derrida Reader* (1990).

plot   The design and ordering of incidents in a NARRATIVE or dramatic work. The plot should not be confused with a simple outline of the events in a narrative. The plot portrays events in terms of their impact on CHARACTER. For example, an outline such as "Boy meets girl, boy loses girl" might be translated into a plot as "Boy meets girl but, because of his jealous nature, boy loses girl." Although plot and character frequently are treated as separable parts of a narrative, these elements are in fact interfused: plot requires characters to enact it; characters always engage in acts, however minimal. In recent years the concept of plot has been examined closely by students of NARRATOLOGY, the study of narrative.

plurisignation   A term referring to the capacity of a particular word or text to exhibit a variety of meanings. The term is essentially a synonym for the more commonly used AMBIGUITY.

poetaster   In ELIZABETHAN drama, a disparaging term for an inferior poet. Ben Jonson's *The Poetaster* (1600) was a satiric attack directed at two rival playwrights, John Marston and Thomas Dekker. Marston and Dekker retaliated with a lampoon of Jonson in *Satiromastix* (1601).

poète maudit (cursed poet)   A French term used to describe a writer who is regarded as a social outcast. It was originally used to refer to the 19th-century SYMBOLIST poets, Charles Baudelaire, Arthur Rimbaud, and Paul Verlaine, all of whom led lives marked by scandal and excess. The term has been extended to characterize writers as diverse as Edgar Allan Poe and Ezra Pound.

poetic diction   Diction refers to the choice of words used in a literary work. Poetic diction refers to the special use of language in POETRY, its order, arrangement, and, in some cases, vocabulary. The history of poetry in English records the shifts in poetic diction that have occurred in each literary period. John Donne's "For God sake hold your tongue and let me love," for example, introduced a colloquial diction that was replaced in the late 17th and 18th centuries by a highly artificial and ornate language. In reaction, the Romantic poets declared their intention, in William Wordsworth's preface to *Lyrical Ballads* (1798) to "speak a language really used by men." Romantic diction in turn was replaced by the diction of modern poetry, which strives to incorporate a wide range of language from technical scientific terms to common obscenities. One example of postmodern diction is the effort of the LANGUAGE POETS to produce deliberately distorted words and phrases.

poetic justice   The doctrine that a literary work ought to end with the good characters rewarded and the evil ones punished. The term was coined by Thomas Rymer, a disciple of NEOCLASSICISM, who dismissed Shakespeare's *Othello* as "a Bloody Farce, without salt or savor." In calling for morally appropriate endings, Rymer acknowledged that such justice is not necessarily true to life but that literature should be superior to life in the moral sphere.

In *Poetic Justice* (1996), the critic Martha Nussbaum has adapted the term to argue that fiction makes available to its readers the feelings of individuals existing on the margins of society and in so doing serves the interests of social justice. *See also* ETHICAL CRITICISM.

Rymer's views are available in *The Critical Works of Thomas Rymer* (1956), edited by Curt Zimansky.

poetic license   In the general sense, the freedom granted to writers to manipulate the historical facts of NARRATIVE in the interests of producing a more compelling story. For example, in his history play *Henry IV, Part One,* Shakespeare chose to make Prince Hal and Hotspur the same age in order to heighten the parallel between the two. Historically, Hotspur (Henry Percy) was 23 years older than Hal.

In its narrower and original sense, poetic license refers to the poet's freedom to depart from the rules of METER, DICTION, and RHYME.

poetry   In its most common use, any type of literature that employs some principle of METER. In this sense it is distinguished from prose and from nonpoetic DRAMA, except in those cases, common until the 19th century, when the term was also used to refer to all forms of imaginative writing. *Poetry* in this second sense has been replaced by the term *literature,* thus limiting *poetry* to a type of literature.

As a literary type, poetry is marked by three subdivisions—lyric, epic, and dramatic—and by its reliance on sound as well as sense in creating its impact. With the emergence of the PROSE POEM, the distinction between poetry and prose has been difficult to maintain, but even here the prose poem exhibits the cadence and rhythms of poetry, printed as prose, whereas "poetic prose" (for example, certain descriptive passages in the novels of John Updike) remains PROSE.

point of view   The perspective from which the action in a story is viewed. Common points of view include:

first person   in which the "I" of the story is a participant or observer.

second person (rarely used) designed to draw the reader in more closely, it is in effect a novel way of presenting a first-person narration, as in Jay McInerney's *Bright Lights, Big City* (1984).

third person the most traditional form of third-person NARRATIVE is that of the OMNISCIENT NARRATOR, in which the narrative voice (usually identified with that of the AUTHOR) is presumed to know everything there is to know about the characters and action. This is the technique employed in most traditional novels.

A more limited third-person perspective is that viewed through the consciousness of a particular character, as in the novels of Henry James, in which the story is told from the main character's point of view. In *Ulysses* (1922), James Joyce took this process a step further by perfecting the stream of consciousness technique.

Still another technique is the multiple point of view, which relates the story from the perspective of a number of characters.

Peter Lamarque's *Fictional Points of View* (1996) examines the subject in considerable detail.

political correctness (PC) A term popularized around 1990 to describe the imposition of liberal or leftist ideas on the campuses of American universities. To its critics, such as Allan Bloom (*The Closing of the American Mind,* 1982) and Dinesh D'Souza (*Illiberal Education,* 1991), political correctness represents a form of totalitarian thought control. They cite, as examples of PC, codes of behavior and speech, in which efforts to avoid offending minorities and women result in the stifling of free expression. The critics of these critics, on the other hand, argue that the term represents a conservative backlash designed to restore the HEGEMONY of the white, male patriarchy.

In literary studies, political correctness has been an issue in the debate over the attempts to change, or do away with, the traditional literary CANON. One influential compromise position is the critic Gerald Graff's suggestion "to teach the conflicts"—that is, to make the debate part of the subject of classroom instruction. *See also* CAMPUS NOVEL.

Gerald Graff develops his position in *Professing Literature: An Institutional History* (1987).

politics Strictly defined as practices and ideas relating to government, politics has played an important but limited role in literary history. In the broader sense—the sense in which "political" embraces questions of race, gender, and class—politics is present in virtually all literary texts from landscape POETRY to such seemingly apolitical novels as J. D. Salinger's *The Catcher in the Rye* (1951). In

FEMINIST CRITICISM, the representations of women in literary history are viewed as profoundly political acts, extensions and reinforcements of patriarchal power. A leading Marxist critic, Fredric Jameson, argues for the need to recognize the political content even of fantasy and dreams, of what he calls the "political unconscious."

Nevertheless, critics still debate whether overtly political literature constitutes, in the words of the 19th-century novelist Stendhal, "a pistol shot in the middle of a concert, something loud and vulgar and yet a thing to which it is not possible to refuse one's attention." In other words, is the presence of explicit political ideas an intrusion of abstract ideology into the concrete experience of a literary text, bringing with it the threat of didacticism and PROPAGANDA? If so, it is generally agreed that such a threat is overcome in most successful political literature. Examples in poetry include Andrew Marvell's "An Horatian Ode upon Cromwell's Return from Ireland" (1650), a poem that does not so much advocate a single position as measure the necessary price paid for political power.

As Irving Howe maintains in *The Political Novel* (1957), however, the NOVEL is the form best suited to the treatment of politics, since it enables political ideas "to seem to become characters." Among the classic political novels of the 19th century are Stendhal's *The Red and the Black* (1830), Dostoyevsky's *The Possessed* (1872), and Henry James's *The Princess Casamassima* (1886).

Major 20th-century political novels include Joseph Conrad's *The Secret Agent* (1907) and André Malraux's *Man's Fate* (1935), two penetrating portraits of the revolutionary mind; Arthur Koestler's *Darkness at Noon* (1940); George Orwell's *1984* (1949); and Alexander Solzhenitsyn's *Cancer Ward* (1972), three indictments of totalitarian socialism.

The most celebrated of the political views of literature is Percy Bysshe Shelley's argument (in his *Defense of Poetry*, 1821) that the poet is "the unacknowledged legislator of the world." Shelley's view is consistent with the view of the poet as a visionary who helps to create the future he envisions. (*See* LIBERAL/CONSERVATIVE IMAGINATION.)

Fredric Jameson's *The Political Unconscious* (1981) is a thoughtful and searching Marxist analysis.

popular culture   A term describing forms of cultural expression that exhibit wide popularity, such as a DETECTIVE STORY, a WESTERN, or a television SITCOM. Popular culture is usually distinguished from "folk culture," a term reserved for older cultural practices rooted in the oral tradition of a community.

A related distinction is the line between "serious" or "high" culture and popular culture. In literature, the distinction is not entirely clear since texts such as

Shakespeare's plays and Charles Dickens's novels were parts of the popular culture of their day. Nevertheless, the traditional view holds that works of popular culture are transient and time-bound, while works of high culture transcend the limitations of time.

More recently, popular culture has been viewed from two contrasting perspectives. For the theorists of the FRANKFURT SCHOOL, a group of Marxist-oriented intellectuals who fled Nazi Germany and settled in the United States, popular culture was an arm of capitalist IDEOLOGY, functioning as the cultural equivalent of its economic practices. These critics saw popular culture as a commodity to be consumed by the population like any other commercial product. The result, in their view, was that the spread of popular culture was destroying the last vestiges of independent, critical thinking among the masses. The term they frequently employed was *mass culture.*

An alternative view is that associated with the movement known as CULTURAL STUDIES. Like the Frankfurt School, many of the proponents of Cultural Studies have a leftist or neo-Marxist point of view, but they differ from the Frankfurt School in asserting that popular culture is not a simple case of mindless consumerism by an unquestioning mass. Instead, they argue that a close study of examples of culture should include not just the products themselves but also what use people make of them. That is, Cultural Studies critics argue that popular culture is the site of a negotiation between the individual and the product. The individual may, and frequently does, subvert the intended "meaning." Thus Madonna is a "text," according to the critic John Fiske, "circulated among some feminists as a reinscription of patriarchal values, among men as an object of voyeuristic pleasure, and among many girl fans as an agent of empowerment and liberation." In this respect Cultural Studies is a companion to READER RESPONSE CRITICISM in its emphasis on the role of the reader/audience as the co-creator of the meaning of the text.

Another interesting aspect of popular culture is the process by which certain popular items become enshrined as high culture. Recent examples include certain Hollywood films, such as FILM NOIR, and certain musical forms such as JAZZ. The historian Lawrence Levine has traced a reversal of this process: the transformation of Shakespeare's plays from popular to high culture in American society at the turn of the 20th century.

A particularly important popular culture phenomenon is the Russian theorist Mikhail Bakhtin's idea of CARNIVAL, which challenges authority by introducing alternative voices into literature. The traditional popular carnival, according to Bakhtin, infused a literary genre such as the NOVEL with contending points of view, allowing popular values an equal voice with those sanctioned by the governmental or ecclesiastical authorities.

John Fiske's *Understanding Popular Culture* (1989) provides a useful introduction. Lawrence Levine's study is *Highbrow-Lowbrow* (1988). Mikhail Bahktin's analysis of Carnival appears in his *Rabelais and His World* (1965).

pornography   Derived from a Greek word meaning "writing about prostitutes," the term refers to literature and art intended to create sexual arousal. Pornography has to be distinguished from literature that features explicit sexual scenes which are subordinate to the overall NARRATIVE. In pornography, the story is subordinate to the sexual scenes.

Central to the discussion of pornography are the shifting standards of what constitutes obscenity and which works call for CENSORSHIP. The most celebrated example is James Joyce's *Ulysses* (1922), banned in the United States until a court decision in 1933. That decision helped to create a standard for distinguishing pornographic from sexually explicit work that exhibits redeeming social or aesthetic value. The best known test of this definition are the novels of the Marquis de Sade (1746–1814), unquestionably obscene by most standards, yet regarded by many contemporary writers as profound explorations of the conflicting, perverse labyrinth of the inner self.

The issue of pornography has created a controversy within FEMINIST CRITICISM between those who see it as a degradation of women and those who view censorship in general as inimical to feminist interests.

Steven Marcus's *The Other Victorians* (1966) provides an incisive cultural commentary on the use of pornography in the Victorian age.

Port-Royal   An abbey in the Chevreuse Valley in France that became the center of a 17th-century Catholic reform movement known as JANSENISM. Originally the home of a community of nuns, the abbey attracted a number of pious laymen and intellectuals who opened a school on the grounds. Here students were taught the religious ideas associated with Jansenius, the bishop of Ypres and author of a controversial work on the doctrine of grace that hewed somewhat closely to the position of CALVINISM.

Jansenism eventually was condemned by Rome and Port-Royal was closed down, its buildings destroyed by order of Louis XIV.

In its brief life Port-Royal won the support of the great theologian and mathematician Blaise Pascal, whose *Provincial Letters* (1656–67) and *Pensées* (1670) defended the community's ideas. Among the pupils of Port-Royal was the celebrated tragedian Jean Racine. The Marxist critic Lucien Goldmann has argued that both the *Pensées* and Racine's tragedies reflect the Jansenist attempt to define a position somewhere between the Catholic belief in free will and the Calvinist

329

doctrine of predestination. As a Marxist, Goldmann argues that this conception is, in turn, rooted in 17th-century social conditions. Published in 1964, Goldmann's study is regarded as an early example of "French New Criticism," a critical movement that was a forerunner of POSTSTRUCTURALISM.

The English title of Goldmann's study is *The Hidden God: A Study of Tragic Vision in the Pensées of Pascal and the Tragedies of Racine* (1964).

postcolonial studies A term for literary and cultural studies that emphasize the impact of the culture of European empires on their former colonies. The approach involves the critical examination of European representations of colonial peoples and the production of a "counter discourse" designed to resist the continued encroachment of European/American culture on former colonies. The term encompasses such categories as Third World, British Commonwealth, and Middle Eastern countries.

Rooted in earlier colonial movements such as NEGRITUDE and the writings of Frantz Fanon (*Black Skin, White Masks,* 1950; *The Wretched of the Earth,* 1961), postcolonial studies surfaced in Anglo-American circles with the publication in 1978 of Edward Said's *Orientalism,* an account of how Western scholarship's "myth of the Orient" provided the justification for the political imperialism that followed in its wake. Since that time the impact of colonialism has been explored in French-and English-speaking Africa and the Caribbean, in India and Southeast Asia, and in the cultures of indigenous populations affected by European settlers, such as the Australian aborigines.

Novelists associated with postcolonial literature include Chinua Achebe (*Things Fall Apart,* 1958), Wole Soyinka (*A Dance of the Forests,* 1960), and Salman Rushdie (*Midnight's Children,* 1981). Well-known postcolonial critics include Gayatri Spivak (*In Other Worlds,* 1987), Henry Louis Gates (*The Signifying Monkey,* 1980), and Kwame Appiah (*In My Father's House,* 1992). These critics have integrated their studies with techniques derived from contemporary THEORY and, in varying degrees, from MARXIST CRITICISM.

Terry Eagleton's *Nationalism, Colonialism and Literature* (1988) offers a useful account of the subject.

postmodernism In literature, a term used to describe characteristics of some contemporary literature that distinguish it from the literature of MODERNISM. Where modernist literature was characterized by its commitment to the value of a unified, coherent work of art employing SYMBOL and MYTH, exhibiting ALIENATION from ordinary life, postmodernism celebrates incoherence, discontinuity, parody, popular culture, and the principle of METAFICTION.

Postmodernism appears to have passed through at least two phases. In its earliest phase—identified with the 1950s and 1960s—its characteristic tone was one of PLAY, a delight in language and the intellectual puzzle reflected in works such as Jorge Luis Borges's *Ficciones* (1962), Vladimir Nabokov's *Pale Fire* (1962), the poetry of the NEW YORK SCHOOL, and plays, such as Tom Stoppard's *Rosencrantz and Guildenstern Are Dead* (1967).

The second phase was signaled by Gabriel García Márquez's *One Hundred Years of Solitude* (1970), where techniques such as MAGIC REALISM provided a bridge between experimentalism and the traditional realistic novel. *One Hundred Years of Solitude* demonstrated that the playful element of postmodernism could be effectively wielded to explore social, historical, and political issues. In novels such as Thomas Pynchon's *Gravity's Rainbow* (1973), Donald Barthelme's *The Dead Father* (1976), Toni Morrison's *Beloved* (1987), and Martin Amis's *Time's Arrow* (1991), postmodernism has combined formal experimentalism with powerful social and cultural criticism.

Postmodern Fiction (1986), edited by Larry McCaffery, offers a useful "bio-bibliographical guide" to the movement.

poststructuralism   An intellectual movement, associated primarily with a group of French thinkers, derived from STRUCTURALISM but departing from it in certain key respects. Its most celebrated practitioners have been Jacques Lacan in psychoanalysis, Michel Foucault in philosophy, Roland Barthes in semiotics, Julia Kristeva in criticism, Jean-François Lyotard in political theory, and Jacques Derrida, whose DECONSTRUCTION theory represents the best-known aspect of poststructuralism. Despite a wide range of specific differences, these thinkers share, at a minimum, the view that meaning is indeterminate since any given TEXT can be interpreted in various, even conflicting ways.

The major outgrowth of this position is a radical critique of the "human subject," the term poststructuralists prefer to the traditional "self" or "individual." The notion of the rational, unified, autonomous "I" (as in Descartes's "I think, therefore I am") has been a staple of Western thought since the Renaissance. The poststructuralist "Subject" carries with it a grammatical sense (as in "subject of the sentence") which reinforces the poststructuralist point: the centers of consciousness that we think of as "ourselves" are linguistic constructs "subject to" the shaping force of language.

In literary theory, Derrida and Barthes have been the most influential figures. Derrida's celebrated 1966 essay "Structure, Sign, and Play in the Discourse of the Human Sciences" inaugurated the poststructuralist critique of structuralism. Barthes's contributions to the poststructuralist mode included a distinction between two types of text: the "readerly" text, which invites passive acceptance, and the "writerly" TEXT, which requires that the reader be an active producer of meaning.

Barthes is also responsible for the controversial position summarized in the title of one of his essays, "The Death of the Author." Barthes's point here is that the term "author" assumes a controlling "authority" who bestows coherence and unity on the text. Barthes argues that the author is merely an effect of the language he or she brings into being. In attacking the traditional idea of the author, Barthes assumes a basic poststructuralist position: The meaning of a text cannot be determined by tracing it to its apparent source. According to Barthes, the power that has been assigned in the past to the author must be given over to the reader, who will experience, not "the meaning," but the indeterminate play that is the "pleasure of the text."

Lacan's adaptation of Freud constitutes a revolution in psychoanalysis, while Julia Kristeva's term INTERTEXTUALITY has had a powerful influence on contemporary criticism.

Strains of poststructuralism are evident in recent critical movements. Michel Foucault's work has exercised a strong influence on NEW HISTORICISM. Kristeva and Lacan have played important roles in the development of FEMINIST CRITICISM and PSYCHOANALYTICAL CRITICISM.

Richard Harland's *Superstructuralism* (1987) is a clear and insightful account of the movement.

poulter's measure   A poetic form employing rhyming lines of 12 and 14 syllables (*see* FOURTEENER). Popular in the verse of the early- and mid-Tudor period, it produced a plodding, dreary effect, captured by the writer C. S. Lewis when he referred to mid-Tudor poetry as the "Drab Age."

C. S. Lewis, *History of English Literature in the Sixteenth Century* (1954).

power   In the sense of the ability to exercise control, this term, for some literary theorists, represents the primary base from which to interpret a TEXT. This position is most prominently identified with the French poststructuralist Michel Foucault (1926–84). For Foucault, power is not a quality possessed by an individual or a government; it is a network of social relations governed by language. As a result, even those in positions of authority are "in power" in an ironic sense, trapped within the web of power. Foucault maintains that power in action is translated into DISCOURSE, the use of language to determine the proper subjects and objects of knowledge, what is known and what is knowable in a given discipline. In this sense, power and knowledge are intimately entwined with each other.

Foucault's view of power has played a significant role in contemporary MARXIST CRITICISM and FEMINIST CRITICISM and particularly in the development of NEW HISTORICISM.

Feminists see the power relationships of men and women embedded in a language in which "man" can be used to stand for all human beings and the masculine pronoun (he/his) to represent any individual. Marxists seek to expose the dominance (see HEGEMONY) of capitalist discourse operating under the form of liberal HUMANISM. New Historicists generally employ Foucault's conception in analyzing the power relations between institutions—for example, the Elizabethan monarchy and the theater of the time.

Edward Said's "Foucault and the Imagination of Power" in *Foucault: A Critical Reader,* edited by David Hay (1986), analyzes the place power occupies in Foucault's thought.

practical criticism   A type of criticism that emphasizes the analysis of a particular TEXT. The term is associated with the critic I. A. Richards, whose *Practical Criticism* (1929) had a profound impact on the teaching of literature in the United States and Britain from the 1930s to the 1960s. The term is also used to describe criticism that operates without any conscious theoretical orientation. *See* NEW CRITICISM.

pragmatism   An American philosophical movement which holds that the meaning of an idea is equal to the practical consequences of adopting it. The more general meaning of the term, as a synonym of *practical*, has developed from this philosophical position. For pragmatists the measure of a concept's meaning lies in its practical value to human beings. As a movement, pragmatism is associated with the American philosophers Charles Peirce, William James, and John Dewey.

The major pragmatist statement on questions of literature and art is Dewey's *Art as Experience* (1934), which holds that the purpose of art is to enhance and enrich the experience of its observers, enabling them to cope with life more effectively. Thus art is both an end in itself and a valuable social instrument. This position has been refashioned by the contemporary pragmatist Richard Rorty, who argues that art offers "more and more possibilities, to be constantly learning." Rorty suggests that literature makes a greater contribution to our culture than traditional philosophy, and that our model for emulation should not be the traditional seer, the repository of "truth," but the poet, the creator of new metaphors, and the novelist, the creator of characters who are unique and diverse. As an example Rorty cites Charles Dickens, whose characters, in their distinctive idiosyncrasies, "do an enormous amount for equality and freedom," in that they teach us "to be comfortable with a variety of different sorts of people." Art, according to Rorty, represents as close to a meaningful morality as is possible in a de-centered, antifoundationalist world. Rorty's views have won wide acceptance by a number of American critics, frustrated by what they see as the dead end of POSTSTRUCTURALISM and DECONSTRUCTION.

In *Poetry and Pragmatism* (1992), Richard Poirier argues that the roots of pragmatism extend back to Ralph Waldo Emerson and that Emerson's pragmatist INFLUENCE is evident in the poetry of Robert Frost, Gertrude Stein, and Wallace Stevens. *See also* ANARCHISM.

Richard Rorty's views are available in his *Consequences of Pragmatism* (1982) and *Philosophical Papers, Vols. I and II* (1991). Giles Gunn's *Thinking across the American Grain* (1992) traces the "intellectual renaissance" of pragmatism in contemporary theory.

Prague School Term for a group of linguists at Charles University in Prague from 1926 to 1948 who laid the groundwork for French STRUCTURALISM. A key figure in the group was the linguist Roman Jakobson, who emigrated to Prague from Moscow, bringing with him the ideas of RUSSIAN FORMALISM. The Prague School extended the work of the Formalists by integrating it with the linguistic theories of Ferdinand de Saussure, whose theory of the SIGN was to have a profound impact on Structuralism.

Another important theorist of the Prague School was Jan Mukarovsky, who developed the concept of FOREGROUNDING, the use of self-referential language within a TEXT.

J. G. Merquior's *From Prague to Paris: A Critique of Structuralist and Post-Structuralist Thought* (1986) explores the role of the Prague School in the development of Structuralism.

précis A summary of the PLOT of a literary work.

preface The introduction to a literary work, in which the author explains the background, scope, or intention of the work. Significant prefaces include Samuel Johnson's preface to his edition of Shakespeare's plays (1765); William Wordsworth's preface to the second edition of *Lyrical Ballads* (1800), commonly regarded as the manifesto of Romanticism; Joseph Conrad's preface to *The Nigger of the "Narcissus"* (1897), in which he delineates his artistic creed; Henry James's valuable prefaces to a collected edition of his novels (1907–9); and

George Bernard Shaw's wide-ranging, provocative, and entertaining prefaces to his plays.

pre-Raphaelites   A group of English artists who in 1848 founded a movement protesting the conventional academic art of the time. The pre-Raphaelites called for a simpler, less sophisticated form of painting than that which followed in the wake of the RENAISSANCE painter Raphael (1483–1520).

In literature the movement is associated with the POETRY of Christina and Dante Rossetti, A.C. Swinburne, and William Morris. Their poetry strove to capture the sensuous religious character of pre-Raphaelite painting. A typical pre-Raphaelite poem is Dante Rossetti's "The Blessed Damozel" (1850), with its combination of sensuous detail, religious feeling, and dreamlike mood.

Characterized by critics as the "Fleshly School of Poetry," these poets contributed to the development of AESTHETICISM at the close of the 19th century.

primitivism   A belief that simpler so-called primitive societies are superior to those of the contemporary world. This assumption is present in many literary periods, reflected in the popularity of PASTORAL and in various forms of ROMANCE.

Primitivism assumed a central role in the doctrines of ROMANTICISM, particularly in the influential writings of the 18th-century French philosopher Jean-Jacques Rousseau. Rousseau argued that the "natural man" is essentially good but in time becomes corrupted by civilization. This conception played a key role in the Romantic veneration of nature found in the idea of the "Noble Savage," the belief in the innate dignity and goodness of primitive people (*see* NATURE/ART).

Primitivism inaugurated a central theme in 19th-century American literature, reflected in the portrayal of Native Americans in the novels of James Fenimore Cooper and Herman Melville and in the philosophy and practice of Henry David Thoreau. This association of the natural and the good continued to play a strong role in 20th-century American literature—for example, in the writings of Ernest Hemingway, whose spare, simple prose style created the literary equivalent of primitive art.

prison literature   As a literary theme, prison or imprisonment appears both in autobiographical accounts by people who have been imprisoned and as an occasion in fiction to explore the psychological and/or social dimensions of enforced confinement. The popularity of these themes, depicting people subjected to extreme pressures, have brought into existence a number of sub-genres: political, criminal, debtor, prisoner of war, innocent victim, all testifying to the fascination the subject holds for readers.

Prison literature has a particularly distinguished lineage in Russia. Fyodor Dostoyevsky's novel *The House of the Dead* (1861), based upon the few years he spent as a prisoner in Siberia, is the prototype of the novels that were to emerge in the era of Joseph Stalin's reign in the 20th century. Dostoyevsky's 20th-century descendant in this respect is Aleksandr Solzhenitsyn, who recorded the horror of the Stalinist GULAG, the infamous prison camps where millions of Soviet citizens perished. Using both FICTION and nonfiction, Solzhenitsyn set the stage for his relentless exposure in his novel *One Day in the Life of Ivan Denisovich* (1962), which depicts a representative "good" day in the life of a prisoner: "A day without a dark cloud, Almost a happy day." Ivan is an honorable man, who recognizes that honor and dignity are essential to survival. Solzhenitsyn's next novel, *The First Circle,* (1968, 1978) (the title is a reference to the least horrible of the circles in Dante's *Inferno*) deals with a prison that also serves as a research laboratory. As a result, its prisoners are relatively well-treated, but morally tortured by the realization that their work benefits the regime they despise. His *The Gulag Archeipelago,* whose publication in Paris in 1973 led to the author's arrest and expulsion from the Soviet Union, is an enormously detailed history of the Gulag Penal System, camps of which ranged across the length of the country, forming an imagined archipelago. The enormity of the crimes, the official lies and corruption that the volumes record, in the words of scholar Edward Brown, "serves to undermine our normal notion of civilized limit and tears to shreds all comfortable stereotypes."

Notable English examples of prison literature include Lord Byron's narrative poem *The Prisoner of Chillon* (1816), cast as a dramatic monologue delivered by Francis Bonjonist, a 16th-century French satirist. An entirely different type of prison is brought to life in Charles Dickens's *Little Dorrit* (1847), whose chief character, Amy Dorrit, works for years in a desperate effort to free her father from the Marshalsea debtors' prison, where Dickens's own father had been imprisoned when the novelist was a child (*see* ADVERTISING).

The Irish playwright Brendan Behan spent two years in an English borstal (reform school) for his involvement with the Irish Republican Army. His imprisonment formed the subject of his memoir *Borstal Boy* (1958). After his release, he returned to Ireland, to be arrested there for his participation in an action in which a policeman was wounded. Sentenced to 14 years in Dublin's Mountjoy Jail, he was released in a general amnesty. Behan used his experience in Mountjoy as the basis of *The Quare Fellow* (1954), a depiction, in raucous comitragic prose, of a prison on the evening before an execution. Behan's *The Hostage* (1958) considers another form of imprisonment: A British soldier is held hostage by the IRA in an effort to prevent the execution of one of their own men. The plot of *The Hostage* bears a close relation to one of the best-known stories of the Irish short story writer Frank O'Connor, "Guests of the Nation."Yet another variation of a British soldier taken as a hostage is reflected in the opening segments of the Neil Jordan film *The Crying Game* (1992).

In his studies of American prison literature, the critic H. Bruce Franklin designates SLAVE NARRATIVES as an early example of what he calls "the history of literature by convicts in America." Treating "the criminal as artist," Franklin focuses on those who dealt with prison experience in their writing, thus Franklin does not consider the works of O. Henry (William Porter), who wrote many of his stories while in prison, though he acknowledges the importance of O. Henry as a model for future convict authors. One of the best-known accounts of prison life was Robert Burns's *I Am a Fugitive from a Georgia Chain Gang!* (1932), a horrific account of how Burns, a World War I shell-shocked veteran, was convicted of the robbery of $5.80 and sentenced to a chain gang, from which he escaped. Seven years later, after having established a successful career as a journalist, he was recaptured and returned to one of the worst chain gang prisons in Georgia, from which he again escaped. When the book was published, he was still in hiding. Burns's description of the brutality of the prisoners' treatment brought the reality of prison life to a large audience as the book became a best seller, and was later transformed into an ACADEMY AWARD–nominated film.

Among women convicts a notable name is Agnes Smedley, imprisoned for political acts in New York City's "Tombs." She included an account of the effects of imprisonment on her mind in the revised edition of her novel *Daughter of the Earth* (1935).

For the period leading up to the 1960s, Franklin pays particular attention to the novels of two writers, one white, one black, Malcolm Braly and Chester Himes. Braly, convicted four times for burglary, was the author of a number of novels dealing with prison life, the most successful of which is *On the Yard* (1967), covering a six-month period in San Quentin during which futility, random violence, desperate scheming, and official abuse of power characterize life in prison. For Chester Himes, best known for his detective novels, a prison experience as a young black man, captured in some early stories and his novel *Cast the First Stone* (1952), left a profound impression on all of his subsequent work.

Undoubtedly the most significant example of American prison literature is *The Autobiography of Malcolm X* (1965), in which the transformation of Malcolm in prison begins with his determination to read with deep understanding, becoming in the process a powerful international figure.

In H. Bruce Franklin's *The Victim as Criminal and Artist* (1978), the condemnation of the American penal system, particularly in respect to the racism that has characterized its history is effectively documented. Less convincing is his application of Marxist themes to his argument. Edward Brown's *Russian Literature Since the Revolution* (rev. ed. 1982) contains an important chapter on "Solzhenitsyn and the epic of the camps."

problematic In contemporary THEORY, a term used (as a noun) to designate a group of related ideas that represents one aspect or subset of an IDEOLOGY. Identifying a work's problematic enables a reader to recognize its limitations as well as its strengths.

problem play A form of drama that raises controversial social questions. An example of the questioning of tradition that marked the early 19th century, the modern problem play was first developed by the French playwright Alexandre Dumas (the son of the author of *The Three Musketeers*) in a series of plays attacking social evils. The most celebrated name associated with the form is that of the great Norwegian playwright Henrik Ibsen. Ibsen focused on social problems in *A Doll's House* (women's rights), *An Enemy of the People* (the moral individual in an immoral society), and *Ghosts* (religious hypocrisy and venereal disease). Later practitioners of the form included George Bernard Shaw (*Mrs. Warren's Profession*, 1893), Lillian Hellman (*The Children's Hour*, 1934), and Arthur Miller (*All My Sons*, 1947).

Shakespearean critics use the term in a different way, to characterize plays that have created problems of interpretation for readers and viewers, particularly *All's Well That Ends Well* (1602), *Troilus and Cressida* (1602), and *Measure for Measure* (1604).

Eric Bentley's *The Playwright as Thinker* (1946) provides a distinctive analysis of the problem play, and Ernest Schanzer's *The Problem Plays of Shakespeare* (1963) offers a controversial approach to the topic.

process/product Two ways of looking at literature that constitute the basic terms of a controversy extending back to the classical period. In his *Anatomy of Criticism* (1957), Northrop Frye speaks of "a distinction between two views of literature that has run all through the history of criticism, . . . the view of literature as product and the view of literature as process." The product critic sees literature as an aesthetic object, the process critic as the occasion for a creative response "in which the reader, the poem and sometimes . . . the poet also, are involved." Frye identifies Aristotle as the progenitor of the product view, and the third century rhetorician Longinus as the initiator of the process approach.

To focus on a written work as an artifact, a completed construct, is to view it as a product. This is the perspective adopted in NEOCLASSICISM and NEW CRITICISM. To view it as a process, a creative activity that achieves completion in the experience of its readers, is a principle associated with ROMANTICISM and POSTMODERNISM, particularly such process-oriented approaches as READER RESPONSE CRITICISM and ACTION PAINTING. Roland Barthes's view of READERLY/WRITERLY texts represents another version of the process/product debate.

The two terms play a large role in COMPOSITION STUDIES, where the teaching of writing is debated by those who emphasize the "composing process" and those who focus on the finished product.

projectivism   A term for a movement among American poets triggered by the poet Charles Olson in his essay "Projective Verse" (1950). Writing during the hegemony of NEW CRITICISM, when the dominant model of contemporary poetry was that associated with T. S. Eliot and Wallace Stevens, Olson called for a rejection of this type of poetry on the grounds that it was written for the eye rather than the ear. In its place he endorsed poetic principles associated with the theories and practice of Ezra Pound and William Carlos Williams (*see* IMAGISM and OBJECTIVISM). Olson argued for a biological basis of poetry characterized by one of his disciples, Robert Duncan, as "muscular poetry." In this "physical verse," the poet's breath governs the length of each poetic line. Contending that poetry conforming to the New Critical mode was too cerebral, Olson invoked a poetry that would restore the lost unity of mind and body, of subject and object.

In the 1950s, Olson, Duncan, and Robert Creeley all served on the faculty of Black Mountain College, a community in North Carolina that existed from 1933 to 1956 for the encouragement of experimentation in the arts. As a result the Projectivist poets are sometimes referred to as the "Black Mountain Poets," but the influence of Olson, Duncan, and Creeley extended well beyond the confines of Black Mountain to constitute an important influence on contemporary American poetry.

The best-known example of Projectivist verse is Olson's *Maximus* poems (1960, 1968), a series of communications from Maximus, a Ulysses-like voyager, to his Ithaca, Gloucester, Massachussetts.

Sherman Paul's *Olson's Push* (1978) analyzes Olson's poetic techniques.

prolepsis   A term for the anticipation of events that appear later. *See* FORESHADOWING.

proletarian literature   FICTION, DRAMA, and POETRY that focuses on the experience of working-class people. A particularly popular form in the 1930s, it tended to represent the working class in idealized terms, as in the plays of

Clifford Odets (*Waiting for Lefty*, 1935) and the novels of John Steinbeck (*The Grapes of Wrath*, 1939). Examples in film include Stephen Frears's *My Beautiful Laundrette* (1985) and John Sayles's *Matewan* (1987).

prologue An introduction to a literary work. The best-known example in English literature is the Prologue to Chaucer's *The Canterbury Tales* (1389–1400), but the term is most often used in DRAMA. In Greek drama, the prologue is an inherent feature of the structure of the play, usually serving as the EXPOSITION. In ELIZABETHAN drama, the prologue commented on the action or theme of the play.

prompt book The annotated script of a play, used by the prompter to assist the actors with their lines and cues. Textual evidence suggests that prompt books served as the printer's texts for some of the plays in the FIRST FOLIO of Shakespeare's plays (1623).

propaganda An organized attempt to influence public opinion on political, religious, social, or cultural issues. Propaganda is most visible during wartime, but is generally more effective when it is disguised as something else. Literature and films can be most effective disguises, and the question of where to draw the line between what is and is not propaganda is a controversial one. The contemporary view that argues against the possibility of objectivity suggests that all language is rhetorical and that propaganda is merely an extreme point on a continuous spectrum. Certain genres, such as the film DOCUMENTARY, tend to veer close to propaganda. In these cases the question is usually resolved not by determining the author's "objectivity," but by the complexity and artistry of the specific text.

A. P. Foulkes's *Literature and Propaganda* (1983) discusses the topic from the perspective of literary theory.

proscenium In most theaters, the area "in front of the scenery," that is, in the conventional modern theater, the playing space where the actors perform before an audience sitting in front of the stage. The structure that frames the playing space is called the "proscenium arch." Alternative stages include the "thrust" stage, in which the audience sits on three sides, and the "arena" or "theater in the round" stage, in which the audience surrounds the stage.

prose A type of language not organized according to a regular metrical principle or pattern, as is POETRY. As a literary vehicle, prose developed later than poetry and was—and, for some people, still is—regarded as an inferior form. Like poetry, prose exhibits a rhythm, but one that is, in the critic Northrop Frye's words, "continuous, not recurrent, a rhythm that is particularly conducive to NARRATIVE forms, where the usual aim is to move the reader along without calling attention to itself."

Northrop Frye's essay "The Rhythm of Continuity: Prose" appears in his *Anatomy of Criticism* (1957).

prose poem   A composition that, while printed as prose, displays the rhythms and types of imagery usually found in verse. The prose poem was developed in 19th-century France by the symbolist poets Charles Baudelaire (*Paris Spleen,* 1869) and Arthur Rimbaud (*Illuminations,* 1886). See SYMBOLISTS.

The prose poem has become increasingly common in the work of contemporary poets including the American John Ashbery (*Three Poems,* 1972) and the Irish poet Seamus Heaney (*Station Island,* 1984).

prosody   In literature, the study of the metrical characteristics of verse, such as METER, RHYME, and RHYTHM.

protagonist   The chief CHARACTER in a DRAMA or STORY. The rival or opposing figure of the protagonist is termed the antagonist. In many cases the protagonist is the HERO and the antagonist the VILLAIN. The reverse may be the case, however, as in Shakespeare's *Richard III,* where Richard is the protagonist/villain and the earl of Richmond the antagonist/hero. In many modern psychological plays and stories, the protagonist/antagonist opposition is represented as an internal conflict within the same character.

Protestant reformation   *See* REFORMATION.

proverb   A short saying expressing a point of view commonly held to be true within the culture in which it is cited. The Old Testament Book of Proverbs, traditionally attributed to King Solomon, was a rich source of later proverbial lore.

pseudepigrapha   A group of about 65 TEXTs falsely ascribed to Old Testament figures, but in fact written by Jews and Christians in the last three centuries before Christ and in the first two centuries of the Christian era.

In a more general sense the term refers to any text that has been falsely attributed to a well-known author. Thus from the standpoint of an ANTISTRATFORDIAN, the complete works of Shakespeare are pseudepigrapha.

psychoanalytical criticism   A general term for a number of critical approaches that derive from the theories of Sigmund Freud and his followers, notably the French theorist Jacques Lacan.

Freud's ideas, such as the concept of the UNCONSCIOUS and the relation of dreams, repression, and sublimation to the artistic process, were developed in the early decades of the 20th century, the heyday of literary MODERNISM. As a result, many modern artists were heavily influenced by Freudianism. Psychoanalytic insights into human behavior constituted the basis for entire movements such as EXPRESSIONISM and SURREALISM and informed the work of modern writers, including James Joyce, D. H. Lawrence, Thomas Mann, and Eugene O'Neill. A measure of Freud's impact is evident in Lionel Trilling's claim in "Freud and Literature" (1947): "Freudianism is the only systematic account of the human mind which in point of subtlety and complexity, of interest and tragic power, deserves to stand beside the chaotic mass of psychological insights which litera- ture has accumulated through the centuries."

But often the enthusiasm with which Freud's ideas were taken up led critics, particularly professional psychologists, to apply them to literature in a manner that reduced either the writer or the TEXT (or both) to a psychologi- cal case study, thereby missing the rich complexity of the literature itself. The result was a tendency to subordinate literature to psychoanalysis, a position manifestly at odds with Freud's own view that "the poets and the philosophers discovered the unconscious long before I did." Lacan's revision of Freud has helped to restore the influence and prestige of the psychoanalytic approach among literary critics.

The critical application of Freudian concepts generally falls into three cat- egories: emphasis on the AUTHOR's psychological conflicts as evidenced in his work, analysis of the characters in a story as if they were real people, and focus on the appeal of the work as the working out of the hidden desires and fears of its readers. In the first category belong many biographical studies of writers. An important early example of this approach is Marie Bonaparte's 1933 study of Edgar Allan Poe. The best-known example of the psychoanalysis of a literary character is Ernest Jones's treatment of Hamlet as suffering from an OEDIPAL COMPLEX (*Hamlet and Oedipus,* 1949).

As for the psychoanalysis of the reader, the most prominent proponent of this view is Norman Holland, who argues that the reader brings into the text his or her fantasies, anxieties, and unacknowledged biases. In addition to these more or less programmatic approaches, many critics of the '40s and '50s employed Freudian ideas selectively, using them where they seemed appropriate, as in Edmund Wilson's interpretation of Henry James's *The Turn of the Screw* (1898).

Jacques Lacan's revision of Freud employs some of the principles of POSTSTRUCTURALISM, specifically in his emphasis on the linguistic character of the unconscious. (Lacan's most celebrated utterance is "The unconscious is structured like a language.") Two central terms for Lacan are the Imaginary, the pre-Oedipal phase of human development when the infant imagines himself at one with the world, and the Symbolic phase, when he acquires language and with it the sense of separateness and loss. For Lacan, the Imaginary phase is associated with the Mother and the Symbolic with "the name of the father."

Lacan's ideas have been taken up by many modern critics, particularly those associated with FEMINIST CRITICISM. One example is the work of Julia Kristeva, a practicing psychoanalyst, novelist, and literary theorist, who has developed Lacan's theory of the Imaginary and Symbolic phases to suggest that in the early "pre-Oedipal" phase the child employs a "feminine" language that is rich in verbal play, such as is found in James Joyce's *Finnegans Wake* (1939).

A recent critique by Gilles Deleuze and Felix Guattari (*Anti-Oedipus*, 1983) argues that Freud and Lacan have set up the Oedipal theme as a master code that reduces the full range of human social experience to the study of "mama, papa, and me."

Another major psychological thinker who has influenced modern literature is Carl Jung. Jung began as a disciple of Freud but broke away from traditional psychoanalysis to develop his own theories of the collective unconscious and of archetypes, both of which play a major role in MYTH CRITICISM.

Literature and Psychoanalysis, edited by Edith Kurzweil and William Phillips (1983), offers a comprehensive anthology of psychoanalytical criticism. Norman Holland's studies include *The Dynamics of Literary Response* (1968) and *Five Readers Reading* (1975). For a critique of psychoanalytic criticism by a former practitioner, see Frederick Crews's *Out of My System* (1975); for the influence of Lacan, see James Mellard's *Using Lacan, Reading Fiction* (1992).

psychobiography   A type of BIOGRAPHY that stresses the psychological development of its subject, frequently employing Freudian insights in order to explain certain behavior. Examples include David Riggs's *Ben Jonson: a Life* (1989) and Louise Kaplan's *The Family Romance of the Impostor Poet Thomas Chatterton* (1987).

psychomachia (war for the soul)   In medieval literature, the representation of the forces of good and evil contending for the soul of mankind. Usually rendered in allegorical form as a struggle between the "Good Angel" and the diabolical VICE figure in MORALITY PLAYS, the psychomachia motif influenced later literature.

Shakespeare invokes the psychomachia tradition in "Sonnet 144" when he casts the "Dark Lady" and the "Young Man" of the sonnets as evil and good angels:

Two loves have I of comfort and despair,
Which like two spirits do suggest me still:
The better angel is a man right fair,
The worser spirit a woman colour'd ill.
To win me soon to hell, my female evil
Tempteth my better angel from my side. . . .

Bernard Spivack's *Shakespeare and the Allegory of Evil* (1958) offers an interesting argument concerning Shakespeare's use of the psychomachia in *Othello.* Spivack sees Iago as an example of the Vice figure and Desdemona as a "Good Angel" contending for Othello's soul, a point emphasized by Othello when, near the end of the play, he asks:

Will you, I pray, demand that demi-devil
Why he hath thus ensnared my soul and body?

Ptolemaic/Copernican   Two historical views of the structure of the universe. The Ptolemaic system, derived from the second-century astrologer Ptolemy, conceived of the earth as the center of the universe, around which the sun, moon, and planets rotated in a harmonious and beautiful order. This view of the universe persisted well into the RENAISSANCE until it was contradicted by the theories of Copernicus, a Polish astronomer whose work was published in 1453. Copernicus demonstrated that the sun was the center of the universe and that the earth revolves around it.

The Copernican system shattered a world view that had undergirded most of the cultural, political, and religious views of the MIDDLE AGES and early Renaissance. Its impact is summarized in John Donne's line "And new philosophy calls all in doubt."

public/private theaters   Terms for two types of ELIZABETHAN playhouses. The first public theater, erected in 1576, was called The Theatre. Several other playhouses were built later. In 1599 the original Theatre was torn down and its materials used to construct the GLOBE THEATRE, the home of Shakespeare's company.

The public theaters were located in the suburbs of the city of London because of Puritan opposition to plays. These outdoor theaters were large, accommodating as many as 3,000 people. They featured a platform or thrust stage, bordered on three sides by the audience. Scenery and costumes were minimal.

The private theaters were smaller indoor institutions, located within London because the influence of their more wealthy and aristocratic patrons outweighed the Puritan opposition. In their early years, private theater plays were performed by boy actors. These children's companies created such a vogue that they forced many of the adult companies to leave London and go on tour. This rivalry is alluded to in Shakespeare's *Hamlet* where the children's companies are described as "little eyases [young hawks] that cry out on the top of question and are most tyrannically clapped for it."

In 1608, Shakespeare's company came to occupy one of these theaters, the Blackfriars. Some have attributed Shakespeare's shift from comedy and tragedy to the ROMANCE form at this time as his adaptation to his new theater and its more select audience. In any case, Shakespeare's company (The King's Men) continued to perform in both theaters, the outdoor Globe in the summer, and indoor Blackfriars in winter.

Andrew Gurr's *The Shakespearean Stage, 1574–1642,* third edition (1992) is a highly authoritative study.

pulp fiction A type of popular fiction published on cheap pulp paper from the 1920s through the 1940s. Like the DIME NOVEL of an earlier period, these magazines featured early, often primitive examples of later genres such as the DETECTIVE STORY, SCIENCE FICTION, and the WESTERN.

The term reappeared in the title of Quentin Tarantino's *Pulp Fiction* (1994), a film that offers a postmodernist treatment of pulp fiction elements.

pun A play on words, usually for comic effect, but sometimes for a serious purpose, as in the first act of Shakespeare's *Hamlet*:

KING: *And now our cousin Hamlet and our son.*
HAM: *A little more than kin and less than kind.*

Hamlet's pun on "kin" can be read as "I'm not your son," while "less than kind" contains a pun on the word "kind" meaning "natural," a reference to the "unnatural" union of the King and Hamlet's mother.

Doctor Johnson chided Shakespeare for his fondness for the pun, calling it "the fatal Cleopatra for which he was lost the world—and was content to lose it." In modern times the pun has come to be seen as an important device for exhibiting IRONY, AMBIGUITY, and the inherent instability of language. As a result the pun is a feature not only of modern literature, notably in the work of James Joyce, but also of contemporary theory and criticism.

Jonathan Culler's *On Puns: The Foundation of Letters* (1988) argues for the pun as a central feature of literary language.

Puritanism   A religious reform movement beginning in mid-16th-century England that went on to play a major role in the shaping of American literature. The original Puritans focused on the reform of practices and services of the Church of England. Eventually the movement grew to the point where, in alliance with Presbyterianism, the Anglo-Scottish version of CALVINISM, it controlled Parliament, deposed and executed King Charles I, and established the Puritan Commonwealth (1649–60). English Puritanism produced one of the towering figures of literature, John Milton, and one of the most popular religious texts, John Bunyan's *The Pilgrim's Progress* (1678).

While still a persecuted minority, one group of Puritans had emigrated and settled the New England colonies. These Puritans produced a body of essentially religious literature which has come to be recognized as a formidable achievement. Two significant poets, Anne Bradstreet and Edward Taylor, were members of the Puritan community. Bradstreet's poetry reveals the struggle to resolve the claims of this world and the next, while Taylor's poems exhibit a sensuous humanism not normally associated with the Puritans. In prose the histories of William Bradford and John Winthrop and the religious writings of Jonathan Edwards are outstanding.

The impact of Puritanism on American culture, particularly in its emphasis on the centrality of the BIBLE, has been profound and powerful. *The Bay Psalm Book* (1640), a translation of the Book of Psalms for congregational singing (and the first book printed in America) was enormously popular and influential throughout the Colonial period. Within writers such as Nathaniel Hawthorne (*The Scarlet Letter,* 1850) and Herman Melville (*Billy Budd,* 1890) the struggle with Puritan ideas is a continuing theme. For them as for many others American writers, the "Puritan Heritage" was both a boon and a form of bondage.

Two important and divergent views of the Puritan impact on American culture are Perry Miller's *The New England Mind* (2 vols. 1939, 1953) and Sacvan Bercovitch's *The American Jeremiad* (1978).

purple prose   A perjorative term for a passage or an entire work that is stylistically extravagant or overdone. The American novelist of the 1930s Thomas Wolfe frequently employed purple prose in his fiction.

9

quadrivium   *See* TRIVIUM-QUADRIVIUM.

quantitative verse   The term for poetic METER based on quantity, the length of time it takes to pronounce a syllable. Greek and Latin verse, for example, is quantitative: Its verse is composed of syllables that are designated "long" if they contain a long vowel sound and "short" if they contain a short one. It takes twice as long to utter a long syllable as a short one. This system differs from English PROSODY, which measures a line in terms of the number of stresses in it. Occasional experiments in rendering English poetry in quantitative verse have demonstrated only the intractably accentual character of English.

quarto   In printing, a book size produced by folding a printer's sheet twice, thereby forming four leaves or eight pages of print. Approximately half of Shakespeare's plays were originally printed as quartos, later collected in the larger size folio. *See* FIRST FOLIO.

quatrain   A four-line stanza of verse, generally exhibiting a rhyme scheme. The traditional BALLAD was usually composed in quatrains, in which the second and fourth lines rhyme.

queer theory   A term adopted by some gays and lesbians to describe their theoretical orientation. They use the word *queer* to transform a word meant as an insult into a term of defiant pride. Moreover, in the other sense of *queer,* meaning *unusual* or *not ordinary,* the term emphasizes their distinctive approach to cultural theory. The chief distinction of this approach is its stress on sexuality not as a natural occurrence, but as a historical construction, as depicted in Michel Foucault's *The History of Sexuality* (three vols., 1978–86). Foucault argues that sexuality represents a powerful, anarchic force that always threatens authority, so that the history of sexuality is the history of the various forms the repression of it takes. One aspect of repression, according to Foucault, was the gradual marginalization and criminalization of homosexuality, which moved from being "a category of forbidden acts" to being a form of identity: "The nineteenth-century homosexual became a personage, a past, a case history. . . . The sodomite had been a temporary aberration; the homosexual was now a species."

Foucault's formulation has become the springboard for the work of queer theorists, who use the marginalized position of the homosexual as a vantage point from which to critique the heterosexual norm in Western culture. Notable examples include Judith Butler's *Gender Trouble* (1989), an analysis of the heterosexual bias implicit in general definitions of gender; and Eve Kosofsky Sedgwick's *The Epistemology of the Closet* (1990), a study of the ways in which the repression of homosexuality has affected modern culture.

quintain   A five-line stanza of verse, the usual stanza for the LIMERICK.

Qumran manuscripts   Manuscripts rediscovered between 1947 and 1956 in Qumran near the Dead Sea. Popularly known as the Dead Sea Scrolls, the manuscripts contain fragments of nearly all the books of the Old Testament, along with some biblical apocrypha. The most interesting fragments are the commentaries written by the Jewish sect, the Essenes, who originated the manuscripts. These were a group of people who, in the first century A.D., had retreated to the remote area of Qumran to separate themselves from what they regarded as the corrupt practices of the religion in Jerusalem. One important part of these commentaries was their emphasis on the imminent arrival of the Messiah. It is thought that these writings influenced John the Baptist in his later teaching of the coming of the Messiah in the figure of Jesus.

Rabelaisian   A term for extravagant, licentious, satiric language in the manner of François Rabelais's five-part satirical work *Gargantua and Pantagruel* (1532–64).

radio drama   Plays written for radio represented a unique development in the history of DRAMA in that its performers were unseen. As a result, radio dramas acquired certain distinctive characteristics, such as the frequent use of a NARRA-TOR, along with a heavy reliance on music, sound effects, and most important, the spoken word. Embracing a wide range of dramatic forms, radio drama gave birth, on the one hand, to the SOAP OPERA and, on the other, to the recondite and difficult plays of Samuel Beckett. Between these extremes lay a range of work, the sheer volume of which has never before been matched. In Great Britain, for example, more than one thousand plays a year were produced on the BBC during radio's golden age. Even today, despite the common view in the United States that radio drama died with the advent of television, radio plays are regularly produced in Europe.

With its concentration on the spoken voice, radio plays were able to develop the long neglected form of poetic drama, which attracted many of the leading poets of the time. Notable examples include Archibald MacLeish's *The Fall of the City* (1937), and Louis MacNeice's *Christopher Columbus* (1942) and *The Dark Tower* (1947).

Among celebrated radio dramas in prose (all produced for the BBC) are Dorothy L. Sayers's *The Man Born To Be King* (1941), Dylan Thomas's *Under Milk Wood* (1954), Samuel Beckett's *All That Fall* (1957), Harold Pinter's *A Slight Ache* (1959), and Tom Stoppard's *The Dog It Was That Died* (1982).

Probably the best known of radio dramas, testifying to the power of the form, is Orson Welles's 1938 adaptation of H. G. Wells's *The War of the Worlds*. Welles's version dramatized an invasion from Mars as though it were an eyewitness news account and precipitated widespread panic throughout the United States.

Eric Barnouw's *Mass Communication* (1956) includes a useful history of radio plays. *Radio Drama* (1981), edited by Peter Lewis, is a collection of essays on the history and present state of the form.

raisonneur (reasoner)   A French term for a character in a novel or play whose calm, rational behavior contrasts sharply with the intense passion of other characters. The contrast is often underscored by the fact that the *raisonneur* frequently also functions as the confidant or close friend of the protagonist. A well-known example is Horatio, the confidant of Shakespeare's Hamlet. The Prince pays this tribute to his *raisonneur* friend:

> *. . . and blest are those*
> *Whose blood and judgment are so well commingled*
> *That they are not a pipe for fortune's finger*
> *To sound what stop she please. Give me that man*
> *That is not passion's slave, and I will wear him*
> *In my heart's core—aye, in my heart of heart,*
> *As I do thee.*

rap   A term in African-American slang that has acquired a variety of meanings still in use. At first, it referred to a prison term (as in "take the rap"). Later it came to mean a conversation, as in *A Rap on Race* (1967), an exchange between novelist James Baldwin and anthropologist Margaret Mead. More recently it has come to refer to a rhymed monologue set to music (also known as hip-hop). Rap lyrics frequently contain angry statements about racism, violence, and other negative social conditions. In one celebrated example (Ice T's "Copkiller") the lyric appeared to advocate the murder of police officers. Other rap lyrics have been accused of being sexist and obscene.

Rap's defenders have described it as an information network for African-American youth or, in the words of rapper Chuck D. of the rap group Public Enemy, a "Black CNN."

An exciting development of rap's literary aspects is *Russell Simmons Def Poetry Jam*, a performance poetry event that was seen first on television and later on the Broadway stage, where it won a Tony award in 2003.

Aleks Pate's "Rap: The Poetry of the Streets" in *USA Weekend* (February 5–7, 1993) places rap within the general tradition of African-American poetry. Nelson George's *Hip-Hop America* (1998) analyzes the movement within the social and political context of America in the last two decades of the 20th century.

rape   Sexual violence against women is not as pervasive in literature as in life, partly because of censorship and partly, as FEMINIST CRITICISM suggests, as a result of male silence on the subject. Even when present, "representations of rape. . . are almost always framed by a masculine perspective, premised on men's fantasies about male sexuality and their fears of false accusation."

One of the primary literary TEXTs on the subject is the STORY in Ovid's *Metamorphoses* of the rape of Philomela by King Tereus, who, to conceal his guilt, had her tongue cut out. Philomela weaves the story of the rape into a tapestry, enabling her sister Procne, the wife of Tereus, to take revenge on the king.

A similar motif of rape, disfigurement, and revelation occurs in Shakespeare's *Titus Andronicus,* where after raping Lavinia, the daughter of Titus, her two assailants cut off her tongue and hands so that she will not be able to reveal their identity. Lavinia exposes the culprits by using the stumps of her arms to turn to the pages in Ovid that recount the story of Philomela. Then she writes the names of the rapists on the ground, using a stick that she holds in her mouth. Another classical legend adapted by Shakespeare is the story of Lucrece, a Roman matron, who after being raped by Tarquin, recounts her story and concludes by committing suicide. Lucrece's family and friends defeat the Tarquins, a victory that leads to the founding of the Roman republic. The question raised by feminist critics is whether these stories, despite their moral condemnation of rape, establish a pattern that sanctions male power and rationalizes violence against women.

In modern American literature, the subject of rape intersects with a number of other social forces. One of these is the massive historical evidence of sexual violence against women slaves by slavemasters, poignantly delineated in Toni Morrison's *Beloved* (1987). Another is the false rape charge that forms the central incident in Harper Lee's *To Kill a Mockingbird* (1960).

Rape and Representation (1991), edited by Lynn Higgins and Brenda Silver, is a collection of essays offering a feminist perspective on the subject.

readerly/writerly (*lisible/scriptible*) Contrasting terms used by the French theorist Roland Barthes to describe a fundamental distinction between two types of TEXT. The readerly (*lisible*) text is the conventional narrative with a beginning, middle and end, a finished product that leaves the reader in the position of a passive consumer. The writerly (*scriptible*) text, on the other hand, is process rather than product, an open, pluralist, linguistic experience which the reader is asked not to consume but to co-produce.

Barthes is unclear about whether the writerly text actually exists or represents an ideal. Many critics now use the term to refer to difficult, demanding texts, such as James Joyce's *Finnegans Wake* (1939).

Roland Barthes explains his use of the term in his *S/Z* (1970).

reader response criticism   A critical movement that focuses on the belief that the meaning of a literary work "has no effective existence outside of its realization in the mind of a reader." The range of this criticism focuses on such questions as, in the critic Jane Tompkins's formulation, "the kind of readers various texts seem to imply, the role actual readers play in the determination of literary meaning, the relation of reading conventions to textual interpretation, and the status of the reader's self."

The modern reader response movement began in the 1970s, but it rested on a long tradition, allied to RHETORICAL CRITICISM, of judging a work in terms of its effect upon a reader. It was this approach that was critiqued as the AFFECTIVE FALLACY during the reign of the NEW CRITICISM.

Central to the reader-oriented approach is the definition of the term *reader*. For many, "reader" denotes the hypothetical response a TEXT seems to require or "imply" (*see* IMPLIED AUTHOR/READER). For others the term refers to actual readers. Critics who focus on actual readers tend to emphasize the psychology of reading, while others examine the cultural, social, or historical contexts in which reading occurs. Feminist critics have called attention to the importance of the reader-as-woman.

A crucial distinction in reader response theory turns on the question of the text as an objective entity. Clearly the words exist on the paper independent of a reader. However, the meaning of those words must be activated by the reader. Once the interaction of reader and text takes place, the text can no longer be thought of as separate, but becomes part of an interactive process. The literary text, on this view, is not an object or artifact; it is an event. (*See* TRANSACTIONAL THEORY.) The traditional question to be asked of a text has been "*what* does it mean?"; the New Critics altered that to "*how* does it mean?", but in reader response criticism the question becomes "what does a reader do in order to 'co-create' a meaning?"

To the charge that this approach invites an anarchic relativism in which a text can mean anything a given reader wants it to mean, these critics argue that both reader and writer are governed by a common grammar, a language system of rules and connections that proscribe radically aberrant interpretations. Another answer, supplied by the European approach known as RECEPTION THEORY, is to look at the reception of the text over time. Still another approach, adopted by the critic Stanley Fish, is to suggest "interpretive communities," groups of readers with shared assumptions which they bring to the reading of a text.

A representative collection is the anthology *Reader Response Criticism* (1980), edited by Jane Tompkins. Elizabeth's Freund's *The Return of the Reader: Reader Response Criticism* (1987) offers an overview and analysis. Stanley Fish's arguments for "interpretive communities" can be found in his *Is There A Text in This Class?* (1980).

realism   In art and literature, a term covering a broad range of views centered on the attempt to depict life as it is usually experienced, without recourse to miraculous events, larger-than-life characters, or supernatural intervention. In a realistic text, the emphasis is on the way things are for ordinary people, whose behavior and speech mirror their social position and cultural attitudes. In this sense realism is opposed to ROMANCE, which represents life as we would like it to be, or to other anti-realist approaches such as EXPRESSIONISM or IMPRESSIONISM.

In a strict historical sense, the term refers to a movement in 19th-century France led by novelists, such as Honoré de Balzac, who set out to produce a richly detailed account of French society. A key feature of realist literature is its emphasis on the author's objectivity. Balzac viewed himself as his society's recording secretary, observing and describing with cool detachment the "Human Comedy" (*La Comédie Humaine*), the collective title of his vast outpouring of NOVELS and SHORT STORIES.

Another characteristic feature of 19th-century realism—present in varying degrees in the works of novelists such as George Eliot, Thomas Hardy, and Leo Tolstoy—was DETERMINISM, the view that individual free will is, if not completely illusory, radically limited by cultural, environmental, and historical forces.

In theory, as opposed to practice, realism was replaced by NATURALISM, which sought to take the determinist element in realism a step further. Naturalism, as expounded by its founder Émile Zola, argued that, since heredity and environment are the sole determinants of individual character, the writer's role was to study his or her subjects as if they were experimental animals, recording one's findings with the objectivity of a scientist.

Naturalism proved to be both oversimplified science and narrow theory, but realist practice has continued to be the dominant form of the novel and drama in the 20th century. Its appeal for the playwright Bernard Shaw lay in its role in debunking the Romantic ideals that perpetuate injustice and ignorance; for other dramatists—Henrik Ibsen, for example—realism offered the most effective means of exposing social hypocrisy, while for Anton Chekhov, it provided a vehicle of revealing the tragic-comic truth of unfulfilled longings.

Among the great realistic novelists of the 20th century—Henry James, D. H. Lawrence, and Thomas Mann—realism offered a form flexible enough to accommodate experimentation and representation. Nevertheless, realism's broad appeal as a vehicle of both popular and serious fiction and drama has not prevented many of its critics from seeing it as an "exhausted" form, one that is too conventional for the expression of distinctively new and fresh literary experiences.

Adherents of experimental writing decry what they see as the tyranny of MIMESIS, the insistence that a work be judged solely in terms of its correspondence to the ordinary sense of what is real. An example of realist tyranny is the fate of SOCIALIST REALISM, which, as the officially sanctioned literary form of the Soviet Union, proved to be an artistic strait-jacket. In place of realist criteria, the experimentalists would substitute the principles of pleasure and play: They, along with many visual artists, argue that any attempt to reproduce the appearance of outside reality is merely dealing with the surface of life.

One happy compromise in the conflict of realism and anti-realism is the development, particularly in Latin American literature, of MAGIC REALISM, in which the fantastic and the realistic are juxtaposed. But beyond this development, the debate between the two factions continues: writing in the wake of his successful, satirical realist novel *Bonfire of the Vanities* (1988), Tom Wolfe has called for a return to the traditional realist novel of society. He sees contemporary novelists as retreating to subjective experience and, as a result, contributing to the view of contemporary fiction as irrelevant.

A significant contribution to realist criticism is Erich Auerbach's *Mimesis* (1953), a study of "the literary treatment of reality." Auerbach sees realism rooted in two distinct traditions, the classical and the biblical. His attention to the linguistic details of the texts he examines underscores his larger concern: the history of the changing conceptions of reality from classical times to the present.

In literary theory the reaction against realism is founded on skepticism over whether a literary text can mirror a world outside itself. In the famous phrase of Jacques Derrida, the principal exponent of DECONSTRUCTION, "there is no outside the text." Derrida's point seems to be that any linguistic text refers only to itself. A related position is reflected in the concept of INTERTEXTUALITY, in which a given text is simply, in Julia Kristeva's words, "a permutation of text . . . several utterances, taken from other texts, [that] intersect and neutralize each other."

An example of the extremes to which the anti-realist position appears to be moving is the prediction of the critic Raymond Federman that future fiction will not "pretend any longer to pass for reality, for truth, or for beauty. Consequently, fiction will no longer be regarded as a mirror to life, as a pseudorealistic document that informs us about life."   .

In the development of FILM THEORY, the realist debate has assumed a major role. The notion that film provides at its core a picture of reality has been generally an unexamined assumption. In an earlier period, theorists argued over whether film positions a viewer before a "window" (realism) or a "frame" (formalism). In recent years, the SEMIOTICS approach to film has focused on the ways in which the illusion of experience is created by the technique of film—how, for example, the movement of the camera mirrors the act of visual perception as it unfolds within the observer.

Theory aside, the experience of most people who see a film, whether as "realistic" as a DOCUMENTARY or as "unrealistic" as an animated film, is that it presents a "world" of its own. That world may bear a sharp resemblance to the world we perceive, as in Italian NEOREALISM, but its ultimate reality resides in the recognition that an audience's response confers on it.

F. W. J. Hemmings's *The Age of Realism* (1974) covers the realist movement in the 19th century; *Documents of Modern Realism,* edited by George Becker (1963), collects the basic writings in the case for realism while John Kuehl's *AlternateWorlds:A Study of Postmodern Anti-Realist American Fiction* (1989) offers the rationale of the antirealist position. The debate among film theorists is analyzed in Dudley Andrew's *Concepts in Film Theory* (1984).

realist/naturalist A period in American literature extending approximately from the end of the Civil War to the beginning of World War I. In American literature, realism was a gradually developing process, stirred by the spread of scientific and rationalist thought. One of its earliest appearances is in the work of regionalist writers, such as Bret Harte and Sarah Orne Jewett, who emphasized the details of daily living in the lives of their characters. These characteristics, coupled with psychological and social observations, were elevated to a higher plane in the work of Mark Twain (*The Adventures of Huckleberry Finn,* 1884), William Dean Howells (*The Rise of Silas Lapham,* 1885), Henry James (*Washington Square,* 1881), and Edith Wharton (*The House of Mirth,* 1905). In poetry, the descriptive poems of Walt Whitman, such as "Crossing Brooklyn Ferry," reflected his enthusiasm for ordinary life.

The naturalist movement dominated the second half of the period, from 1890 to 1914. The movement owed much to its European origins, particularly the principle of DETERMINISM, in which the social, economic, and biological forces at work in the formation of the individual assumed great importance (*see* NATURALISM). Among the most important American naturalist writers were Stephen Crane (*Maggie: A Girl of the Streets,* 1896), Harold Frederic (*The Damnation of TheronWare,* 1896), Frank Norris (*McTeague,* 1899), and Jack London (*The Call of the Wild,* 1903).

Warner Berthoff's *The Ferment of Realism:American Literature 1884–1918* (1965) traces the main currents of thought in the period.

recension An edition of a TEXT that has been edited to include the most plausible readings.

reception theory   A German critical movement that focuses on the social/ historical contexts within which a literary work is received. Designed to integrate the opposed camps of FORMALISM and historical criticism, reception theory argues that the work of literature is a historical phenomenon, not something transcendent or "timeless," and that the reader's perception plays the critical role without which the work is incomplete. Central to this conception is the idea of the reader's "horizon of expectations": Every reader approaches a literary text with assumptions about the type or GENRE it represents, its relation to other works of its time, and the reader's own experience of life. These horizons shift over time so that classical texts, such as Shakespeare's plays, develop a reception history of their own, which to some extent becomes part of a later generation's horizon in regard to the work.

Reception theory is associated with Hans Robert Jauss, who formulated his theory in 1967, at which time he focused on readers in the collective sense. Since that time, he has placed more attention on the individual reader. In this respect the movement appears to have moved closer to READER RESPONSE CRITICISM.

Hans Robert Jauss's *Toward an Aesthetic of Reception* (1982) and *Aesthetic Experience and Literary Hermeneutics* (1982) are two of his works that have been translated into English.

redaction   An edition of a TEXT that has been revised or edited. It also refers to the selection and arrangement of the older Hebrew texts into what became the Hebrew Bible.

referent   A term for that to which a word or literary text refers. In REALISM the referent is usually assumed to be the nonliterary world of experience. An alternative view, associated with DECONSTRUCTION and many postmodernist texts, asserts that literary texts are self-referential, closed in upon themselves.

Reformation   The 16th-century religious movement that rejected the authority of the Roman Catholic Church. Its religious consequences, the establishment of Protestantism, led to, or accompanied, a series of important political and social changes in European and American history. *See* CALVINISM and PURITANISM.

refrain   A passage that is repeated at various points in a poem or song. Frequently the refrain will be repeated with a slight variation in the last line, as in Stephen Sondheim's "We Had a Good Thing Going" in which the title/refrain is finally repeated as "We had a good thing going, going, gone."

reification   In MARXIST CRITICISM, the condition of passivity in the face of the capitalist transformation of the products of labor—and the laborers themselves—into things. (To reify is to turn someone or something into a thing.) According to Marx, reification separates the product from the sociopolitical conditions that govern the labor process. Thus the thing becomes more important than the laboring process that brought it into being. The result is a profound ALIENATION experienced by the modern worker.

In a markedly different but substantively similar sense of the term, reification plays a central role in the religious EXISTENTIALISM of the theologian Martin Buber. Basic to Buber's thought is the distinction between the "I" and the "Thou." Ideally, we have an I/Thou relationship with another living person while the I/It describes the relationship with an inanimate object. However, we can and often do, treat a person as an "It." An I/It relationship to another person is not in fact a relationship at all, since the "I" is alone, trapped within himself, alienated because he has reified the other in turning a "Thou" into an "It". In the I/It relation, only a part of the "I" is present, the other part is outside, observing or judging, while in the I/Thou relationship the total being of the persons are involved.

The English translation of Buber's central work is *I and Thou* (1950).

religious faith   In Western European civilization, the dominant role of literature, in relation to religion, has been either to question, as in the Book of Job, or to justify, in John Milton's words, "the ways of God to man." Although theology has offered elaborate explanations for the grounds of faith and for the facts of suffering, EVIL, and injustice in the world, it has remained for literature to ask and sometimes answer these questions in terms of concrete individual human experience. The biblical Job and the classical Prometheus embody the individual petitioning or defying the heavens from the perspective of faith, doubt, or despair.

From the perspective of faith, the great affirmations include Aeschylus' *Oresteia,* which sees the GODS as both merciful and just but demanding of humankind the price of suffering; Dante's *Divine Comedy,* which offers a mystical vision of unified Christendom; Milton's *Paradise Lost,* which invokes the paradox of the FORTUNATE FALL; T. S. Eliot's *Four Quartets,* which explores the relation of time to eternity; Georges Bernanos's *Diary of a Country Priest* (1936) with its fierce and stark view of the internal struggle of a religious man; Flannery O'Connor's SHORT STORIES, comic and macabre, but rooted in and exemplifying a belief in the Incarnation; and Marilynne Robinson's *Gilead* (2004) depicting the serenity and beauty of a life celebrating God's creation.

From the perspective of doubt, Shakespeare's great tragedies *Hamlet* and *King Lear* offer a challenge to make what we can of the "ripeness" and "readiness" that is "all"; Herman Melville's *Moby-Dick* represents his ongoing "quarrel with God"; and the novels of John Updike persistently probe questions of faith and religion in contemporary life.

From the perspective of despair, there arise those distinctly modern and postmodern texts, Franz Kafka's *The Trial* (1925), Samuel Beckett's *Waiting for Godot* (1952), and, in the wake of the HOLOCAUST, André Schwartz-Bart's *The Last of the Just* (1960).

In 20th-century literary criticism, these strains are evident in critical approaches that see literature as either validating, critiquing, or offering an alternative to religion. Among movements associated with the validation of religious values in literature are NEW CRITICISM, NEO-SCHOLASTICISM, and the concept of religious EXISTENTIALISM. Critical movements offering a negative view of religion's relation to literature are the NEW YORK INTELLECTUALS, MARXIST CRITICISM, and, to the extent that it views religion as overwhelmingly patriarchal in its orientation, FEMINIST CRITICISM. Among the movements that see literature as an alternative to religion (a position first articulated by Matthew Arnold) or who see the two as fusing in a common identity, are MYTH CRITICISM and one branch of HERMENEUTICS.

Hoxie Neale Fairchild's *Religious Trends in English Poetry* (six vols., 1939–68) is a comprehensive history of religious thought in English poetry from the 18th through the 20th centuries. Two valuable anthologies covering the many sides of the subject are *Spiritual Problems in Contemporary Literature* (1952), edited by Stanley Romaine Hopper, and *Literature and Religion* (1971), edited by Giles Gunn.

Renaissance   The period from approximately 1400 to 1650 when Western Europe underwent a series of radical changes in art, literature, religion, and politics. In the 19th century, under the influence of the historian Jacob Burckhardt's *The Civilization of the Renaissance in Italy* (1860), the era was regarded as one in which a miraculous "rebirth" took place. From Burckhardt's perspective, it was a time when the religious trappings of the MIDDLE AGES were discarded and "modern man" came into existence. More recently, scholars have recognized the extent to which the seeds of the Renaissance were sown in the later Middle Ages, and some predate the Renaissance as far back as the 12th century. For example, in English literature it has become common to view Chaucer as a direct SOURCE of some ELIZABETHAN poetry.

Recently some contemporary scholars and historians have argued that the term *Renaissance* (literally "re-birth") overemphasizes the beginnings of the period and fails to recognize its anticipation of modern thought. This group prefers the designation EARLY MODERN PERIOD. Nevertheless, Renaissance remains a legitimate historical term and period, one that looked back as well as forward.

The term was first used to describe the rediscovery of the classics of Greece and Rome associated with the 15th-century movement known as HUMANISM. One outgrowth of the humanist movement was its emphasis on individual as opposed to collective identity. This development was evident in religion in the Protestant emphasis on individual interpretation of the BIBLE; in economics, in the rise of business and banking entrepreneurs; in science, in the discoveries that led to the validation of Copernicus's view that the sun was the center of the universe; and in art, in the discovery of perspectivism (the representation of three-dimensional objects on a flat surface), which led to an emphasis on the individual human form.

In Italian literature, the Renaissance is associated with the names of Petrarch, whose SONNETS to his unattainable beloved, Laura, established a poetic tradition throughout Western Europe, and with Torquato Tasso whose *Jerusalem Delivered* (1580) was a heroic attempt to adapt the classical EPIC.

In France, the dominant Renaissance figures are Rabelais, whose *Gargantua and Pantagruel* (1532–64) celebrates the life of both the senses and the intellect, and Michel de Montaigne, the creator of the ESSAY. In Holland, Desiderius Erasmus, the greatest of the humanists and author of the wide-ranging satire *In Praise of Folly* (1511), was a leader in the development of the Renaissance in Northern Europe. In Spain, the Renaissance saw the creation of the PICARESQUE, the great dramatic achievements of Calderón and Lope de Vega, and in fiction a unique masterpiece, Cervantes's *Don Quixote* (1605–15).

In England, the term Renaissance connotes the humanist and martyr Thomas More, whose *Utopia* (1516) created a new genre of utopian fiction, and the great Elizabethan and Jacobean writers, including Edmund Spenser, Christopher Marlowe, Ben Jonson, and Shakespeare. The period comes to a glorious conclusion with John Milton's epic, *Paradise Lost* (1660).

Among the many historical studies of the period is John R. Hale's *Renaissance* (1965). Stephen Greenblatt's *Renaissance Self-Fashioning* (1980) looks at the era through the lens of NEW HISTORICISM. Vernon Hall's *Renaissance Literary Criticism: A Study of its Social Context* (1945) establishes the relation of literature to the prevailing views of the time.

repetition   A technique in literature and film that serves a variety of purposes. In its simplest use, repetition functions as a form of emphasis, as, for example, in advertising or propaganda, designed to imprint their messages on the minds of their audiences. In poetry and song, a comparable emphasis occurs with the use of the REFRAIN, the words of which are sometimes slightly altered depending on the changes in context set up by the preceding stanza. Thus, in William Blake's "The Tyger," the last lines of the first stanza

What immortal hand or eye
Could frame thy fearful symmetry?

appears in the final stanza as

What immortal hand or eye
Dare frame thy fearful symmetry?

Other examples of the use of repetition are the employment of repeated images, contributing to the IMAGERY of the work, or to the repetition of keywords, such as the use of *honest*, in Shakespeare's *Othello*. Its repeated use in reference to Iago becomes an ironic incantation. Repetition also can be a feature of a work's structure, as in Samuel Beckett's *Waiting for Godot* (1952), in which the second act repeats the first with only slight modifications. This sense of sameness recreates for the audience the very act of waiting that is the subject of the play.

Repetition, as enshrined in ritual, is a central feature of MYTH. As the scholar Mircea Eliade points out, the repetition of certain archetypal actions frees certain societies from the burden of history by creating the sense that with each enactment of ritual, the community is "beginning again" (*see* ETERNAL RETURN).

The use of repetition as a means of transcending time is evident in Marcel Proust's *Remembrance of Things Past* (1914–28), in which the NARRATOR's experience of "involuntary memory" enables him to recapture the past. On the other hand, repetition in the form of compulsive behavior can signal a character neurotically trapped in the past, as it does, in a comic vein, for the narrator of Philip Roth's *Portnoy's Complaint* (1969).

Another important use of repetition occurs in Eastern religions, such as Hinduism. Believers use repeated mantras and other incantations to free themselves from the illusion of change and difference through the recognition of the oneness of all things.

Bruce Kawin's *Telling it Again and Again* (1972) is a thoughtful, wide-ranging study of repetition in literature and film.

representation   A term referring to the belief that the mind "represents" the objective world in the manner that a mirror reflects its object, and that there is a natural connection between a word and its REFERENT. This traditional conception of knowledge and language has been challenged by the American philosopher Richard Rorty (*Philosophy and the Mirror of Nature*, 1979) and the French poststructuralist Michel Foucault (*The Order of Things*, 1970). Their anti-representational views are reflected in the literature of POSTMODERNISM. *See* MIND AS MIRROR.

reputation   Literary scholars study AUTHORs' historical reputations—not simply to discover more about the writers—but also to learn about the popular tastes and critical standards of particular eras. A case study in the fluctuations of a historical reputation on the literary stock market is that of John Donne, a poet admired in his own time, reflected in his position as the foremost practitioner of METAPHYSICAL POETRY in early 17th-century literature. However, in the latter half of the century, Donne's distinctive use of complex conceits and images drawn from philosophy, science, theology, as well as ordinary life, drew the fire of neoclassical poets, such as John Dryden, for being too intellectual, particularly in his love poems. In the 18th century, Samuel Johnson in his *Lives of the Poets* chided Donne and the other metaphysicals for employing "heterogeneous ideas . . . yoked by violence together."

It was not until the early 20th century that Donne's POETRY found an admiring audience, largely as a result of T. S. Eliot's laudatory essay "The Metaphysical Poets" (1921). The key point in Eliot's praise was that these poets were the last to exhibit a unified sensibility, integrating thought with feeling and feeling with thought. He maintained that by the end of the 17th century, Dryden's era, the triumph of scientific modes of thought had resulted in the DISSOCIATION OF SENSIBILITY, severing thought from feeling, and, by extension, truth from poetry. Eliot's case for the Metaphysicals helped restore Donne to the status of major English poet, a position that was solidified by the compatibility of his poetry with the principles of NEW CRITICISM. Since then, Donne has suffered a slight devaluation (not nearly as severe, ironically enough, as Eliot has), reflected indirectly in Margaret Edson's Pulitzer Prize–winning drama *Wit* (1999), in which a Donne scholar discovers on her deathbed the limitations of his poetry and her life.

In *Hemingway and Faulkner in Their Time* (2005), Earl Rovit and Arthur Waldhorn bring an original and provocative approach to the study of reputations. Choosing as their subjects Ernest Hemingway, the best-known and most influential American writer of his time, and William Faulkner, generally regarded as the most important American novelist of the 20th century, the editors have delved into the diaries, letters, and interviews of the writers who were contemporaries of the two titans. What emerges from these off-the-record sources is a compilation of comments that range from mean-spirited envy to perceptive critical insight, all the more readable because the editors have supplied brief biographical introductions to all of the quoted writers. The book is topped off by Hemingway's comments on Faulkner (often unkind) and Faulkner's on Hemingway (extremely generous). The result is a study that looks behind the scenes of the public reputations, offering glimpses of what their peers privately thought of them, what they thought of each other, and how accurate Shakespeare is when he speaks of "the bubble reputation."

The question of reputation has taken on new significance in light of the continuing controversy regarding the literary CANON. The charge made by those who would significantly alter or completely disregard the canon suggests that those in support of the existing canon are critics and academics with a vested interest in the status quo. However, the examples of Donne and *Hemingway and Faulkner in Their Time* opens up another possibility, that the judgments of other writers have the greatest influence on literary reputations in or out of the canon: in Donne's case, Dryden, Johnson, Eliot, and Edson; in *Hemingway and Faulkner in Their Time,* as Rovit and Waldhorn explicitly underscore, it is first their fellow writers. Of course these judgments have finally to be confirmed by readers, who may be, as John Milton described his audience, "fit though few," or they may continue to enjoy a wide readership, like Jane Austen or Charles Dickens. Either way, their status is first confirmed by their peers.

T. S. Eliot's analysis of Donne and the Metaphysical Poets is available in his *Collected Essays* (1932).

Restoration   A period in English literature covering the years 1660 to 1710. The name refers to the restoration to the English throne of the Stuart king, Charles II, following the death of Oliver Cromwell and the end of the Commonwealth government. The king and his court had spent their exile in France, and the cultural attitudes they brought back with them were heavily influenced by French standards. In literature, this meant a preference for neoclassical forms, such as HEROIC DRAMA, EPIC, satire, and the period's most notable achievement, RESTORATION COMEDY.

But the age also saw notable contributions in prose. The year 1662 saw the founding of the Royal Society, a group dedicated to the study of "natural philosophy and other parts of human learning." One of the Society's aims was to make English prose simpler, clearer, and closer to speech. As a result, modern English prose was born. Some notable examples of the style are the diary of Samuel Pepys (1660–69), the essays of Sir William Temple, and the literary criticism of John Dryden.

John Milton, who stands outside the period ideologically and stylistically, nevertheless made two great contributions with his sequel to *Paradise Lost, Paradise Regained* (1671) and his blank verse tragedy *Samson Agonistes* (1671). Another anomaly in the Restoration age is John Bunyan's Puritan classic *The Pilgrim's Progress* (1678).

George Clark's *The Later Stuarts, 1660–1714* (1961) provides a comprehensive history of the period.

Restoration comedy   A type of English comedy associated with the last decades of the 17th and the first decade of the 18th centuries. Indebted to some extent to the French comedies of Molière, Restoration comedies were witty, sophisticated, elegant exercises, designed to reflect and occasionally satirize the manners, mores, and taste of its elite audience. Plots usually turned on the efforts of social climbers to gain advantageous marriages and their defeat by young, clever protagonists. Among the best of these plays are William Wycherley's *The Country Wife* (1673), George Etherege's *The Man of Mode* (1676), John Vanbrugh's *The Relapse* (1697), Richard Farquhar's *The Beaux' Stratagem* (1707), and, commonly regarded as the finest example of the genre, William Congreve's *The Way of the World* (1700).

Robert Hume's *The Development of English Drama in the Late Seventeenth Century* (1976) studies the interaction of social change and theatrical fashions in the period.

revenge   Revenge is a major theme in Aeschylus' *Oresteia* and in the plays of Seneca, but it achieved its most concentrated expression in the revenge tragedies of ELIZABETHAN and JACOBEAN drama, where the action usually focused on the hero's revenge for the murder of a family member. Among the conventions of the form were the real or feigned madness of the hero, disguise, intrigue, and the appearance of the ghost of the original victim.

Thomas Kyd's *The Spanish Tragedy* (1589) was an early influential example of the form. Others include Cyril Tourneur's *The Revenger's Tragedy* (1607), John Marston's *Antonio's Revenge* (1599), and George Chapman's *The Revenge of Bussy d'Ambois* (1610).

Both representing and transcending the genre is Shakespeare's *Hamlet,* in which the idea of revenge presents the hero with a moral conflict he must resolve before acting on his revenge.

Charles and Elaine Hallett's *The Revenger's Madness* (1981) surveys the conventions and themes of revenge tragedy.

review   A form of criticism that attempts to evaluate and, to some extent, analyze a recent publication or performance. The term also refers to a type of periodical in which critical articles and reviews appear. Two contemporary examples are *The NEW YORK REVIEW OF BOOKS* and *The London Review of Books.*

revision   The process of correcting or changing a TEXT, either in the act of writing or later. Regarded by many as a central feature of the writing process, its centrality is captured in the expression, "All writing is re-writing." The term revised edition implies substantial changes in a published text.

Recent developments in COMPOSITION STUDIES have seen a movement away from the attempt to heighten the critical (that is social and political) consciousness of student writers to an emphasis, in the words of the scholar Joseph Harris, on helping them "to more powerful forms of reading and writing, not to repeat our [the teacher's] positions and interpretations but to form their own." To this end, Harris stresses the importance of revision in helping students define their goals as writers.

revolutionary/early national period   The period in American literature between 1765 and 1828. This was an era in which American writers attempted to define a distinctly American literature, striving for artistic as well as political independence from England. In the first phase of the period (1765–89), the effort bore little fruit. The POETRY of the time represented, for the most part, pale imitations of its neoclassical English models, particularly the poetry of Alexander Pope. Representative was a group of writers known as the CONNECTICUT WITS, whose members included John Trumbull, the author of a satirical mock epic *M'Fingal* (1776), heavily indebted in its form to Pope's poems. The most accomplished poet of the period was Philip Freneau, "the poet of the American Revolution," who wrote sharp, satirical attacks on the British army. Historically important was the poetry of Phillis Wheatley (*Poems on Various Subjects,* 1773), a black slave who mastered the conventions of neoclassical poetry in an incredibly short time.

The period also saw the publication of the first novel written by an American, William Hill Brown's *The Power of Sympathy* (1789). The most important prose writings of the period, however, were Thomas Jefferson's *Declaration of Independence* and Benjamin Franklin's *Autobiography* (published in 1818).

The second phase of the period (1789–1828) saw the first stirrings of a new and distinctive national literature. The chief figures were the poet William Cullen Bryant, whose *Thanatopsis* (1817) marks the beginning of the poetry of nature in American literature, and the novelist James Fenimore Cooper, whose *The Last of the Mohicans* (1826) and *The Prairie* (1827) inaugurate the theme of the WESTERN.

The Columbia Literary History of the United States (1988), edited by Emory Elliott, contains a perceptive account of the period.

rhetoric   In popular use a word associated with pompous language devoid of real content, as in the phrase "mere rhetoric." In education, it is used as an alternative term for courses in speech or composition, in which context it refers to using language to inform or persuade an audience. (*See* COMPOSITION STUDIES.) Traditionally, rhetoric also has been synonymous with the study of classical figures of speech, such as METAPHOR, METONYMY, and SYNECDOCHE.

Recently a much broader conception of the term has come into use, spurred by theories of language that emphasize the transactional nature of communication or the views of language associated with POSTSTRUCTURALISM. The other position, traditional since the 18th century, operated on the assumption that, except for POETRY, literal language was superior to figurative language, that "rhetoric" was the fancy clothing disguising the honest, bare-bones reality revealed by logic. The postmodern position, first articulated by the 19th-century philosopher Friedrich Nietzsche, is that all language is fundamentally rhetorical. It is not capable of revealing truth but only of persuading another that it speaks truth. As a consequence of this view, "rhetoric" has been elevated to a privileged place, above logic, in contemporary THEORY.

The principles of rhetoric were developed in classical Greece and Rome and enshrined in the educational curriculum of the MIDDLE AGES as one of the subjects of the TRIVIUM/QUADRIVIUM. The subject of rhetoric was divided into five parts: Invention, Arrangement, Style, Memory, and Delivery. The category "memory" should remind us that the term applied largely to the art of oratory. With the invention of the printing press in the Renaissance, and the subsequent development of wide-scale literacy, rhetorical principles were applied to writing.

Aristotle laid the foundation of rhetorical study. His *Rhetoric* established the three essential categories of proof: the appeal to reason (*logos*), the appeal to emotion (*pathos*), and the ethical appeal, exemplified in the character of the orator (*ethos*).

Among other great classical rhetoricians were Cicero, who broadened the scope of rhetorical study to embrace a wide range of knowledge, and Quintilian, who insisted that the rhetorician must be a person of strong moral character. In the fourth century, St. Augustine adopted rhetorical theory to emphasize its instructional as well as its persuasive function, the "rhetoric of the sermon."

In the RENAISSANCE the most influential figure in rhetoric was Erasmus, whose textbooks dominated rhetorical education for two hundred years. The other significant figure of the era was Peter Ramus, a French scholar who argued that the categories of Invention and Arrangement should be taught as subdivisions of Logic, thus reducing the significance of rhetorical study. The Ramist doctrine helped contribute to the decline of rhetoric's prestige in favor of scientific (allegedly a-rhetorical) discourse.

The 18th century produced two notable rhetoricians, the Scotsmen George Campbell and Hugh Blair. Campbell's *Philosophy of Rhetoric* (1776) and Blair's *Lectures on Rhetoric and Belles Lettres* (1783) attempted to stem the anti-rhetorical tide ushered in with the triumph of science. But by the 19th century, the study of rhetoric had declined into a concentration on figures of speech.

In the 20th century, the field was revived by two important major redefinitions, Kenneth Burke's *Rhetoric of Motives* (1950) and Chaim Perelman and Lucie Olbrechts-Tyteca's *The New Rhetoric* (1969). Burke's method incorporates his theory of DRAMATISM and the process of identification with one's audience. *The New Rhetoric* explores the interaction of audience and arrangement in the fashioning of an argument. The postmodern adaptation of rhetoric has been spurred by the example of Burke, who took literary criticism out of its traditionally narrow confines into the wider context of human DISCOURSE.

George Kennedy's *Classical Rhetoric and Its Christian and Secular Tradition from Ancient to Modern Times* (1980) is a valuable history. An admirable, brief account of the history of rhetoric is included in Edward Corbett's *Classical Rhetoric for the Modern Student* (second edition, 1971).

rhetorical criticism   A term with two meanings: the application of the study of RHETORIC to literature, and the analysis of examples of "pure" rhetoric, such as ADVERTISING and political speeches.

1. The rhetorical criticism of literature represents an ancient tradition. Its earliest notable contribution is a document that has come to be known as *Longinus On the Sublime* (third century A.D.), a rhetorical analysis of the emotional response to literature. The idea of the SUBLIME has played a major role not only in the critical theory underlying ROMANTICISM, but also in contemporary criticism.

Other recent examples of rhetorical criticism include Wayne Booth's pioneering study *The Rhetoric of Literature* (1961), an analysis of certain novels in terms of their intended effect upon their readers. Along with Louise Rosenblatt's pioneering *Literature as Exploration* (1938), *The Rhetoric of Literature* helped to spark the reader response movement (*see* READER RESPONSE CRITICISM) and other theories of language as a form of action, in which the interaction of writer, reader, TEXT, and context create highly complex communications whose meaning is neither fixed nor limited.

2. The other sense of the term focuses on overtly persuasive texts, such as the wartime oratory of Winston Churchill, television ADVERTISING, and, in a subtler form, the "management" of news reporting and the creation of images. Common to both forms of rhetorical criticism is an emphasis on the way in which language can shape human behavior.

Rhetorical Analysis of Literary Works, edited by Edward Corbett (1969), contains rhetorical analyses on figures from John Donne to Wallace Stevens. Kenneth Burke's *A Rhetoric of Motives* (1950) contains many examples of his unique critical approach.

rhetorical question   A question asked for rhetorical effect rather than as a request for an answer. In effect, a rhetorical question is a statement in the form of a question. Literary examples include Christopher Marlowe's "Was this the face that launched a thousand ships / And burnt the topless towers of Ilium?"—a reference to Helen of Troy—and William Butler Yeats's conclusion to "Among School Children," "How shall we know the dancer from the dance?"

rhyme   The duplication of sounds, usually at the end of a line of verse. The most common form of rhyme occurs when the last accented vowel is repeated with a different preceding sound, as in labor-neighbor or Jill hill.

When the rhyme falls on the last syllable (include-intrude), it is said to be a masculine rhyme; a rhyme falling on the next-to-last, penultimate, syllable (baby-maybe) is a feminine rhyme.

In the broad sense of the term, rhyme may include *assonance,* the rhyming of vowel sounds (blame-mate), or *consonance,* rhymes in which the vowels are the same but pronounced differently (love prove).

rhyme royal   A seven-line stanza rhyming a-b-a-b-b-c-c in iambic pentameter (*see* METER). Chaucer's *Troilus and Criseyde* (1370) is in rhyme royal.

rhythm   The pattern of sounds and pauses that are a feature of POETRY, PROSE, and ordinary speech. The basic unit of rhythm in English poetry is the FOOT, the repeated pattern of which constitutes the METER of a poem. But in addition to the regular repetition of meter, rhythm embraces nonmetrical forms such as FREE VERSE and PROSE. The rhythms of William Faulkner's prose, for example, might be measured in terms of the alternating lengths of his sentences, along with his use of subordinate clauses, parallel structures, repetitions, and cadences.

SPRUNG RHYTHM, a technique developed by the Victorian poet Gerard Manley Hopkins, emphasizes the number of accents in a poetic line while ignoring the number of unaccented syllables.

ritual   A ceremony, either religious or cultural, enacting in specifically prescribed forms behavior designed to benefit the society within which it is practiced. It has long been recognized that DRAMA, both TRAGEDY and COMEDY, is rooted in ancient rituals.

The relationship of ritual to MYTH usually turns on the question of origins. Does a given myth arise as a way of explaining an existing ritual; or does the ritual enact a NARRATIVE that already exists? A compelling thesis in favor of the priority of ritual is René Girard's argument that ritual sacrifice of the SCAPEGOAT is rooted in the effort to control mutual violence within the sacrificing community itself. *See also* CAMBRIDGE RITUALISTS.

René Girard's position is detailed in his *Violence and the Sacred* (1997).

rococo In architecture, a highly decorative style originating in early 18th-century France as a development of the BAROQUE style. As applied to literature, the term refers to an elegant, witty, graceful prose and verse style that framed certain ideas associated with the ENLIGHTENMENT, an era that celebrated free thought. Among works that qualify as rococo are Alexander Pope's *The Rape of the Lock* (1712–14), Voltaire's *Candide* (1759), and Tobias Smollett's *Humphrey Clinker* (1771).

Helmut Hatzfield's *The Rococo* (1972) is a comprehensive treatment of the subject.

roman à clef (novel with a key) A French term for a novel in which actual, sometimes well-known people or institutions are presented with fictional names. Often associated with satire, the roman à clef is a frequent feature of satirical novels such as Evelyn Waugh's *The Loved One* (1948), a merciless look at Forest Lawn Cemetery in Los Angeles, and Mary McCarthy's *The Oasis* (1949), a satiric view of the NEW YORK INTELLECTUALS.

In more recent years the form has been a regular feature in popular fiction, as in the novels of Jacqueline Susann.

roman à thèse (thesis novel) A French term for a novel that advocates a specific position on a social or moral question. It is frequently used interchangeably with the term *protest novel*. Examples include John Steinbeck's *The Grapes of Wrath* (1939), an indictment of the treatment of migrant laborers in the 1930s, and Alexander Solzhenitsyn's *One Day in the Life of Ivan Denisovich* (1962), a protest against the inhumanity of Soviet concentration camps.

romance A type of NARRATIVE featuring adventures in exotic places, love stories, and/or the celebration of simple rustic life. In Northrop Frye's words, "the romance is nearest of all literary forms to the wish-fulfillment dream. . . ." As a result, romance has been a staple of popular literature from the time of the Greek romances (second and third centuries A.D.) to contemporary Harlequin novels.

Although a typical romance may involve any number of minor adventures, its focus usually falls on one major action. In *The Wizard of Oz,* for example, the many adventures of Dorothy and her friends are subordinate to Dorothy's overarching desire to return to her home in Kansas.

An early prominent model is the medieval romance, which celebrates the ideal of chivalry, as represented in the legends surrounding Arthur of Britain and Charlemagne of France. (*See* MEDIEVAL DRAMA.)

Romance is associated with the two greatest names of Renaissance literature, Shakespeare and Cervantes. Shakespeare's contribution lies in his later plays, *Pericles* (1607), *Cymbeline* (1609), *The Winter's Tale* (1610), and *The Tempest* (1613). All of these plays employ improbable events, strange coincidences, and an episodic structure central to the romance form. In *Don Quixote* (1605, 1615), Cervantes moves the traditional romance into a new dimension by suggesting a connection between the ideals of romance and the brute facts of reality. The Don's commitment to the world of romance is the subject of ridicule and satire, but at the same time it is an endorsement of the romantic world as an imaginative ideal.

ROMANTICISM revived the romance in verse form. The exotic world that is the genre's traditional setting is rendered with rich sensuality in the opening passage of Samuel Taylor Coleridge's "Kubla Khan" (1816):

In Xanadu did Kubla Khan
A stately pleasure dome decree:
Where Alph, the sacred river, ran
Through caverns measureless to man
   Down to a sunless sea.

Other outstanding examples of verse romances include John Keats's "The Eve of St. Agnes" (1820), Alfred, Lord Tennyson's *Idylls of the King* (1859), and William Morris's *Earthly Paradise* (1868–70). All of these works invoke a past implicitly contrasted to urban, industrial, 19th-century England, a period in which the values of romance never seemed more threatened.

In 19th-century fiction, romance appears in yet another form in works such as Nathaniel Hawthorne's novel *The House of the Seven Gables: A Romance* (1851). In the preface, Hawthorne declares, "When a writer calls his work a Romance, it need hardly be observed that he wishes to proclaim a certain latitude. . . which he would not have felt himself entitled to assume had he professed to be writing a novel."

These words call attention to a distinction that was to remain in force throughout the century. The novel became associated with REALISM, the romance with a world suggestive of a reality within or beyond the "real world."

The 20th century saw a marked tendency to identify romance with stories in which love forms the central action. Defined this way, romance becomes a capacious category embracing the majority of FICTION, FILMs, and popular songs of Western culture. Recent FEMINIST CRITICISM has examined some of the tacit assumptions of the form, looking critically, for instance, at the genre's traditionally prescribed endings: either marriage or death.

Gillian Beer's *The Romance* (1970) surveys the history of the form; Janice Radway's *Reading the Romance: Women, Patriarchy and Popular Culture* (1984) offers a telling critique of popular romance fiction.

romantic comedy   In DRAMA and FILM, a popular form of light entertainment that focuses on a love affair. Early examples of this form include Shakespeare's *As You Like It* and *Twelfth Night*, in the original productions of which, boy actors played the women who, in the play, disguised themselves as boys.

Romantic comedy was reborn in the films of the 1930s and '40s. The distinction between a romantic comedy and the modern sense of ROMANCE is apparent in a comparison of Leo McCrary's *A Love Affair* (1939), which the director remade as *An Affair to Remember* (1957). Both of these films are unequivocally modern romances, while Nora Ephron's *Sleepless in Seattle* (1993), a film that pays extensive homage to *An Affair to Remember*, is clearly a romantic comedy.

Romanticism   A broad literary, artistic, and intellectual movement that developed in Western Europe and America in the late 18th and early 19th centuries. Although scholars have debated the usefulness of a term that is frequently seen as self-contradictory, *Romanticism* and *Romantic* continue to be essential words in the vocabulary of literary history. They designate not only a historical period, but also a fundamental, recurring attitude toward literature and life, in which the emotional and intellectual freedom of the individual is elevated over the traditional norms and strictures of society. Thus the term can be used to describe contemporary writers as well as those associated with the Romantic movement.

The Romantic movement developed as a reaction against the narrow rationalism of the early and mid-18th century. Among the first manifestations of the new impulse were the philosophical and personal writings of Jean-Jacques Rousseau in France, the appearance of the STURM UND DRANG movement in Germany, and the developments of the cult of SENSIBILITY and the GOTHIC NOVEL in England. An important historical progenitor of the movement was the French Revolution, particularly in its emphasis on liberty and equality.

A central tenet of Romanticism was the belief in nature as a source of poetic inspiration. The interaction of the poet's creative imagination and the underlying spirit of nature produced an intense, subjective experience, communicated to readers in fresh, spontaneous language. Thus the Romantics enshrined the natural genius, the child of nature, whose creative understanding of the world-as-symbol provided readers the opportunity to explore their own "inner worlds." For the Romantics, the prototype of the natural genius was Shakespeare.

The first stirrings of Romanticism occurred in Germany in the doctrines of the philosopher Immanuel Kant and in the poems and plays and stories of Goethe and Friedrich von Schiller. English Romanticism is identified principally with the POETRY of William Blake, William Wordsworth, Samuel Taylor Coleridge, Percy Bysshe Shelly, Lord Byron, John Keats, and with the novels of Sir Walter Scott.

Despite the early influence of Madame de Stael, French Romanticism was slow to develop, emerging in the 1820s and '30s in the poetry of Lamartine and the novels of Victor Hugo. In Russia, Romanticism is reflected in the work of Aleksandr Pushkin and Mikhail Lermontov. American Romanticism first emerged in James Fenimore Cooper's Leatherstocking novels, prototypes of the WESTERN, and in the New England–based movement known as TRANSCENDENTALISM.

In the latter half of the 19th century Romanticism was opposed by REALISM, and in the 20th century by the doctrines of NEW HUMANISM and, to some extent, NEW CRITICISM. In contemporary THEORY, on the other hand, the Romantics have assumed a central role in illustrating critical positions, such as DECONSTRUCTION.

Romanticism: Points of View (1970), edited by Robert Gleckner and Gerald Enscoe, offers a collection of important essays on conflicting definitions of the term. *Romanticism and Contemporary Criticism* (1986), edited by Morris Eaves and Michael Fischer, explores the relation of Romanticism to modern literary theory.

Royal National Theatre Company   Formed from the nucleus of the OLD VIC company, the National Theatre came into existence in 1962 (the "royal" charter was granted in 1988). Laurence Olivier served as its first artistic director. The theatre is subsidized by the government, a situation that allows for more experimentation and less pressure to produce commercially successful productions.

Royal Shakespeare Company (RSC)   The principal contemporary acting company focusing on the plays of Shakespeare. The company received its royal charter in 1925, appearing at the Shakespeare Memorial Theatre in Stratford-on-Avon. In the spring of 1961, under the direction of Peter Hall, the Stratford Theatre was renamed the Royal Shakespeare Theatre, but the company also acquired a permanent London home, first at the Aldwych and later at the Barbican.

Although its chief focus is Shakespeare, the company has expanded its reper-
toire to include other works, resulting in such notable productions as *Marat / Sade*
(1966) and *Nicholas Nickleby* (1982).

Russian formalism   A school of criticism that flourished in Russia from about
1915 to 1932. The Formalists concentrated on determining the distinction
between language as it is used in literature and the ordinary use of language. They
approached their analyses with scientific rigor, freed from what they regarded as
the emotional excesses of symbolism and FUTURISM. Among their practitioners
were the distinguished linguist Roman Jakobson and Vladimir Propp, a prominent analyst of folk literature.

Two critical terms introduced by the Formalists are still employed today:
DEFAMILIARIZATION, the disruption of a reader's usual expectations, and
FOREGROUNDING, the use of language that calls attention to itself. The movement
came to an end in 1932 when SOCIALIST REALISM was installed as the official critical doctrine in the Soviet Union.

Victor Erlich's *Russian Formalism* (third edition, 1981) is the standard history of the
movement.

saga   In its original sense, a medieval Scandinavian or Icelandic NARRATIVE poem depicting the adventures of legendary figures. Elaborate and intricate stories, the sagas were derived from earlier oral accounts, which were transcribed in the 13th century, at which time certain literary features of that period were incorporated into the stories. One type of saga involved the action of legendary figures and their families and were known as family sagas. This sense of the term was continued in modern literature, where it has come to mean a long narrative dealing with the fortunes of a family over a number of generations. Thus the term has been used to describe John Galsworthy's *The Forsyte Saga* (1922), Gabriel García Márquez's *One Hundred Years of Solitude* (1970), and John Updike's *In the Beauty of the Lilies* (1996).

saint play   A type of medieval drama that focused on the life or martyrdom of a saint. Saint plays were popular in England, France, and Italy from the 13th to the 16th centuries. In England, a common form of the saint play was the Saint George play, which depicted the defeat of the dragon and the subsequent martyrdom of George, the legendary patron saint of England. In France, a number of plays celebrated the life of Saint Nicholas, and in Italy the lives of Saint Anthony and Saint Dominic were frequently enacted.

A celebrated example of a modern saint play is T. S. Eliot's *Murder in the Cathedral* (1935), a verse rendering of the assassination of Saint Thomas à Becket.

The Saint Play in Medieval Europe (1986), edited by Clifford Davidson, provides a wide-ranging account of the genre.

salon   In literature, a term for a place, usually the home of a well-to-do person, where writers and artists met regularly for informal discussions. The earliest salons were held in 17th-century Paris.

samizdat   In Russian, a word that carries the meaning of "self as publisher." Under the government of the Soviet Union, censorship was a powerful and pervasive repressive force. Revolting against these restrictions, some Soviet writers, denied access to regular publishing, began distributing carbon copies of their manuscripts that were passed along from one sympathetic reader to another. The best-known example is Boris Pasternak's novel *Doctor Zhivago*, which served as a samizdat text before being published in Italy in an Italian translation in 1957. The following year an English translation was published in England, and Pasternak was awarded the Nobel Prize.

Other major works that appeared in samizdat include Alexander Solzhenitsyn's *The Gulag Archipelago* (1973) and the POETRY of Osip Mandelstam and Joseph Brodsky. All of these works were published abroad and smuggled back into the Soviet Union. As the scholar Edward Brown summarizes it, "Books that moved in this weird manner were, as we know, among the greatest of the century."

Edward Brown's *Russian Literature Since the Revolution* (rev. ed., 1982) is a masterly treatment of its subject.

San Francisco renaissance   A period in the early 1950s when San Francisco became the center of experimental POETRY associated with the BEAT poets and PROJECTIVISM. Among the poets living in San Francisco during this period were Robert Duncan, Kenneth Rexroth, Kenneth Patchen, and William Everson, a poet who was also a Dominican lay brother, publishing many of his works under his religious name, Brother Antoninus. Their work coalesced when Lawrence Ferlinghetti, an original member of the Beats, moved to San Francisco and opened the City Lights Bookshop in 1953. In 1956, City Lights published Allen Ginsberg's *Howl*. The popularity of *Howl* soared when local authorities seized copies of the poem, declaring it obscene. Ginsberg won the trial that ensued in more ways than one—the publicity helped to make *Howl* a best seller.

Sapphics   Verse stanzas of four lines, of which the first three have 11 syllables and the fourth, five syllables. The pattern is named after the Greek woman poet Sappho (seventh century B.C.). A common form in classical poetry, it is rarely used in English.

satire   A type of literature that aims to ridicule folly or vice in a society, an institution, or an individual. Satire uses laughter as a weapon against any target that the satirist considers silly, stupid, or vicious. As such it is an attack, but an attack ameliorated by the element of play. The aim is to be entertaining as well as censorious, to create fun by poking fun. Thus satire is a negotiation between the judgmental and the joyous. These two poles are represented in classical Latin literature by Juvenal and Horace. Juvenal stands for slash-and-burn, harsh, biting satire; Horace for the genial, sophisticated, tolerant form.

Satiric passages enhance and enliven many plays, poems, and novels that are not themselves satires, but there are also outstanding examples of works that are pure satires. In England the golden age of the form was the neoclassical period, when John Dryden (*MacFlecknoe*), Alexander Pope (*The Dunciad*), and Jonathan Swift (*Gulliver's Travels*) raised satire to the highest levels, establishing a tradition kept alive in the Romantic period in the POETRY of Lord Byron (*Don Juan*).

In the 20th century, many of the most notable satirists have been journalists. Outstanding among them have been the Austrian writer Karl Kraus, who published and was the sole contributor to a journal, *Die Fackel* (*The Torch*), that for 25 years lacerated the follies of Viennese society. His American equivalent was H. L. Mencken, the editor of *The American Mercury*, whose principal target was the "booboisie," Mencken's term for middle-class Americans. Their English equivalent was George Orwell, best known for his fable *Animal Farm* (1945) and the novel *1984* (1949), two satires aimed at totalitarian governments.

Satire: A Critical Anthology ed. John Rusell and Ashley Brown (1967) offers a representative selection. George Test's *Satire, Spirit and Art* (1991) looks at satire from a broad perspective that includes, but is not limited to, its literary manifestations.

satyr play   In the classical Greek dramatic festival of Dionysus, the comic afterpiece that followed the tragic trilogy and implicitly mocked the high seriousness of the preceding plays. Satyrs were pleasure-seeking hedonists dressed in goatskins, masks, tails, and pointed ears. Their performance usually represented a BURLESQUE of a popular myth. The only complete satyr play that has survived is Euripides' *Cyclops* (438 B.C.).

Satan   *See* EVIL.

scansion   A method of describing a poem by analyzing the METER and RHYME of its lines. The most common form of scansion divides a metrical FOOT into stressed and unstressed syllables. A stress is indicted by a virgule (/) or dash (-) and an unstressed syllable by a breve (˘) or x. Scansion also attends to a pause or CAESURA within a line, indicated by a double vertical line (||) and to its rhyme scheme, indicated by small letters a, b, c, and so on.

A scansion of the opening lines of Alexander Pope's "Essay on Criticism," written in HEROIC COUPLETS:

˘　／　˘　／　　˘　／　˘　／　˘　／
'Tis hard to say | | if greater want of skill
˘　／　˘　／　˘　　／　˘　／　˘　／
Appear in writing | | or in judging ill.

scapegoat　A figure who suffers for the crimes or sins of others. In literature, the term is frequently associated with MYTH CRITICISM, in which the scapegoat figure occupies a central place in both tragedy and comedy. The word *tragedy* means "goat song" and is thought to refer to an early ritual involving the sacrifice of a goat. From this perspective the tragic hero can be seen as a scapegoat figure, a sacrificial victim whose death redeems the community and, in Hamlet's words, "sets right" the time that is "out of joint." In comedy the scapegoat is related to the figure of Misrule, who thrives during the period of CARNIVAL, but is later cast out, once the society resumes its ordinary rules and practices.

A distinguished fictional rendering of the scapegoat ritual is Shirley Jackson's SHORT STORY "The Lottery" (1944). An interesting critical treatment is Edmund Wilson's *The Wound and the Bow* (1941). Wilson argues that the artist is the ultimate scapegoat: "The artist who renders himself abhorrent to society. . . is also the master of a superhuman art which everybody has to respect and the normal man finds he needs."

scenario　An outline of the plot of a film or play, as distinguished from the TREATMENT, which is a detailed summary.

scene　In DRAMA, a subdivision of an ACT or of an entire play. In literature, in general, the term refers to the place in which an action occurs, as in "the scene of the crime."

Scholasticism　The theological and philosophical thought of the late MIDDLE AGES, from the 12th through the 14th centuries. The chief goal of Scholastic thinkers was to reconcile Christian belief and classical philosophical understanding, debating such questions as whether reason should be grounded in faith ("I believe in order that I may understand") or faith grounded in reason ("I understand in order that I may believe").

The rediscovery of Aristotle's works in the Middle Ages led to a rigorous, comprehensive synthesis of classical and medieval thought, magisterially summarized in Thomas Aquinas's *Summa Theologica* (1265–74). Aquinas's position was challenged by the Scottish theologian Duns Scotus, who argued for a greater reliance on faith and less on reason.

The coming of the RENAISSANCE, the emergence of HUMANISM, and the growth of scientific thought led to the eclipse of Scholasticism. In the mid-20th century it experienced a revival as NEO-SCHOLASTICISM.

Two modern authors influenced by Scholasticism were Gerard Manley Hopkins, who derived a key concept of INSCAPE/INSTRESS from Duns Scotus, and James Joyce, whose debt to the aesthetics of Aquinas is recorded in the fifth chapter of *A Portrait of the Artist as a Young Man* (1916).

science   Traditionally regarded as polar opposites, literature and science have always interacted, either absorbing each other's insights or correcting the other's imbalances. The view of the two as oppositional most recently emerged in the TWO CULTURES controversy, in which the novelist C. P. Snow and the critic F. R. Leavis engaged in an acrimonious debate over Snow's charge that most humanists are inexcusably ignorant of the most elementary scientific knowledge.

But the early history of the two disciplines reveals a time when literature, science, and philosophy were united. An example from the first century B.C. is Lucretius's *De Rerum Natura* ("On the Nature of Things"), a six-volume work setting out an atomic theory of matter. The work is also a poem, written in dactylic hexameter and containing highly lyrical passages, while formulating a theory that has won the respect of modern physicists.

Similarly, the Italian novelist and critic Umberto Eco has called Galileo the greatest Italian prose writer because of the unique quality of his scientific-poetic imagination, producing a language that is both elegant and precise.

Ironically, the 17th-century scientific revolution that Galileo helped to usher in created the split between the two cultures, lamented by T. S. Eliot as the DISSOCIATION OF SENSIBILITY, the rigid compartmentalizing of thought and feeling. By the end of the 17th century, modern scientific language had begun to take shape: objective, detached, transparent, the opposite of "poetic language."

Nevertheless, the gap closed somewhat in the 19th century with the advent of REALISM, which offered a model, at least in prose, in which the author functioned as a detached observer, a "recording secretary" in Balzac's term. Another example of the growing prestige of science in the literary community is the impact of Darwin's theories on the literary world. The VICTORIAN novelists George Eliot, Thomas Hardy, and Joseph Conrad were directly influenced by Darwin. One example is Conrad's *Lord Jim* (1899), in which Jim's decision to save himself from a sinking ship ironically illustrates the "survival of the fittest." As the critic George Levine has pointed out, even in the novels of avowedly "anti-scientific" novelists such as Charles Dickens and Anthony Trollope there are remarkable correspondences to Darwinian concepts.

Similarly, in the 20th century, Einstein's theories have had a marked influence on literary representations of TIME.

More recently, scientists have become aware that their ideal of an objective, value-free language is largely illusory. From the other side, a number of postmodernist writers, particularly the novelist Thomas Pynchon (*Gravity's Rainbow,* 1973), have employed the terminology and ideas of quantum physics and other sciences as part of the conceptual scheme of their work. *See also* CONSCIOUSNESS and SCIENCE FICTION.

Beyond the Two Cultures (1990), edited by Joseph Slade and Judith Lee, is a collection of essays dealing with questions of the relation between science, technology, and literature. George Levine's *Darwin and the Novelists* (1988) is an important study of Darwin's influence on Victorian literature.

science fiction   A type of fiction based on future possibilities, derived from scientific discoveries. Chief among these have been interstellar travel, closely followed by stories dealing with the aftermaths of nuclear war and environmental disasters, altered states of consciousness, extraterrestrial visitors to earth, and artificial intelligence. These and many other scenarios have contributed to the international popularity of the genre, both in its printed form and as dramatized on film and television.

The acknowledged forerunner of *sci fi* or *sf,* as it is commonly known, is Mary Shelley's *Frankenstein* (1818), in which a man-made monster suggests the possibility of scientific discovery going too far, taking on a God-like power that leads to disaster. This motif has always played a prominent role in science fiction. Another important precursor of the genre was Jules Verne, whose *Voyage to the Center of the Earth* (1864) and *Around the World in Eighty Days* (1873) introduced the theme of exploration through scientific technology. But the true father of science fiction is H. G. Wells, a trained scientist and an accomplished realistic novelist. Wells combined these skills in *The Time Machine* (1895), with its depiction of travel through time; *The War of the Worlds* (1898), the prototype of alien invasion fiction; and *The First Men on the Moon* (1901), a prophecy fulfilled some 60 years later.

Wells referred to these fictions as "scientific romances." The term *science fiction* was popularized in America by Hugo Gernsback, the editor of *Amazing Stories,* the first magazine devoted to science fiction. From its humble origins as a form of PULP FICTION in the 1920s, the genre gained increasing prestige with the contributions of writers such as Aldous Huxley (*Brave New World,* 1932) and C. S. Lewis (*Out of the Silent Planet,* 1938).

Following World War II and the development of nuclear weapons (*see* NUCLEAR WAR), science fiction began to sound less like fantasy and more like realism, a fact that contributed to its great popularity. The Russian and American space programs, along with the appearance of a number of gifted and skillful writers, only intensified the appeal. Among these were Arthur Clarke (*Childhood's End,* 1953), Ray Bradbury (*Fahrenheit 451,* 1953), Robert Heinlein (*Starship Troopers,* 1959), Frank Herbert (*Dune,* 1965), Ursula K. Le Guin (*The Left Hand of Darkness,* 1969), and Kurt Vonnegut (*Slaughterhouse Five,* 1969).

Outstanding achievements in FILM include Stanley Kubrick's *2001* (1968), featuring HAL, a villainous computer; George Lucas's *Star Wars* (1977), which balances technical effects with a human drama; and Stephen Spielberg's *Close Encounters of the Third Kind* (1977), with its stunning, ethereal concluding segment. Also notable is the *Star Trek* film series (1979–), adapted from the enormously successful, ongoing television series.

Recent innovations in the genre include Octavia Butler's *Kindred* (1979), in which a 20th-century American black woman time travels back to the 1830s where she lives as a free black in a slave state, and William Gibson's *Necromancer* (1984), which introduces cyberspace into the world of science fiction. (*See also* ZINES.)

Brain Aldiss's *Billion Year Spree* (1973) is a lively history of the genre.

scop   A term in Anglo-Saxon literature for a minstrel who was attached to the royal court. The *scop* composed and performed his own works, which were drawn from legends and biblical stories.

screenplay   The script that forms the basis of a film. Usually preceded by a SCENARIO and/or TREATMENT, the screenplay generally undergoes a number of major revisions, often at the hands of another writer, before it emerges as the shooting script. Even here, many changes will be introduced into the script, often the product of the collaboration of director and writer. Frequently the number of people with a hand, or at least a finger, in a script can be quite large. For example, according to film critic Pauline Kael, 20 different people participated in the writing of scripts that eventually became the successful comedy *Tootsie* (1982).

screwball comedy   A type of Hollywood comedy of the 1930s and '40s that featured two lovers, one of whom is a madcap zany (usually the woman), and the other a naive stuffed shirt with little experience of real life. Combining fast action, smart dialogue, and many of the features of classical farce, these comedies were ideally suited to the talents of such performers as Carole Lombard, Irene Dunne, Jean Arthur, Katharine Hepburn, Cary Grant, and James Stewart. Some of the best examples of the genre include Frank Capra's *It Happened One Night* (1934), William Wellman's *Nothing Sacred* (1937), and Howard Hawks's

Bringing Up Baby (1938). In the 1970s, Peter Bogdanovich revived the form in his *What's Up, Doc?* (1972).

scriptures   The sacred writings of any religion, most commonly used in reference to the BIBLE.

Scrutiny   An influential literary journal published in England from 1932 to 1953. Its editor was the powerful critic F. R. Leavis, and it numbered among its contributors T. S. Eliot. The title of the journal reflects its emphasis on "close reading," a central tenet of NEW CRITICISM.

self/other   Two terms that have taken on unusual connotations in contemporary THEORY. The new sense of *self* no longer suggests the unified, autonomous individual of traditional HUMANISM, or even the divided self later conceived in EXISTENTIALISM. In contemporary theory, *self* has given way to the term SUBJECT to suggest a being "constructed" by our language-determined, culturally-driven modes of thinking. Among the illusions entertained by the "subject" is that he or she possesses an inner, autonomous "self."

Other is now frequently used to describe traditional attitudes towards minorities, colonized peoples, or marginalized groups, such as gays or lesbians. In FEMINIST CRITICISM, the term summarizes the process by which male literature depicts women as, in various ways, either inferior or threatening. First articulated by Simone de Beauvoir in *The Second Sex* (1949) and later developed by French feminists in the notion of *écriture féminine* ("feminine writing"), the feminist response to this position stresses the positive sides of "otherness."

For the French psychoanalyst Jacques Lacan, the child in its "symbolic stage," the phase in which it begins to acquire language, perceives itself as not a being identical with the self, but as "other," a "subject" of "the name of the father." Thus, according to Lacan, the sense of otherness is part of the universal human condition in which the self is experienced as fragmented and lacking a true center. *See* PSYCHOANALYTICAL CRITICISM.

semantics   The study of meaning in language. Semantics is a major area of LINGUISTICS. In its modern form, semantics deals with meaning not as some abstract, independent entity, but as an event that occurs within a specific linguistic context.

In the 1930s and '40s, an approach known as "general semantics" attempted to offer solutions to existing social and intellectual problems by demonstrating that they were linguistic in nature. In *Science and Society* (1939), Alfred Korzybski argued that flawed linguistic systems resulted in misperceptions and misunderstandings among people, creating discord and conflict. Korzybski called for a "scientific" approach to language and thought. Korzybski's ideas were popularized by S. I. Hayakawa in *Language in Action* (1941), later revised as *Language in Thought and Action* (1949).

semiotics/semiology   The study of SIGNS. The American philosopher Charles Peirce coined the term *semiotics* in 1867; *semiology* is the coinage of the Swiss linguist Ferdinand de Saussure. Both terms are employed interchangeably, but semiotics is the preferred usage in the United States. In semiotics, "signs" are not only words, linguistic signs, but also any object or form of activity that may indicate something else. Thus the Eiffel Tower, a television commercial, shaking hands, wearing jeans, or the McDonald's arch are all signs that communicate messages according to a conventional CODE.

Literary semiotics focuses on verbal signs, although it acknowledges the presence of nonverbal signification in literature. There are two traditions of literary semiotics, one originating with Saussure and culminating in STRUCTURALISM and POSTSTRUCTURALISM, and the other deriving from Peirce. The latter group looks not simply at the structure of signs, but also at their impact on their audience and their implications within a given society. This so-called pragmatic approach explores the relation of signs to social and political forces and their importance in fields such as advertising and POPULAR CULTURE.

Semiotics has produced a number of studies of theater and FILM, designed to penetrate the mystique of these two forms by locating and analyzing the code systems that govern them. The critic Marvin Carlson, for example, analyzes the role of the audience in absorbing the semiotic clues within the play and within the theater itself. In film, the feminist critic Tessa de Lauretis frames each character in a film as coded along the lines of sexual difference, where the male represents the human, and the female, forms of nature.

Robert Scholes's *Semiotics and Interpretation* (1982) offers a clear, well-reasoned introduction to the field. Marvin Carlson's study is *Theatre Semiotics: Signs of Life* (1990); Tessa de Lauretis's analysis is *Alice Doesn't: Feminism, Semiotics Cinema* (1984).

Senecan style   A term for the style of English prose developed in the late 16th and early 17th centuries. Named for the Roman philosopher and dramatist Seneca, the style was a reaction against the highly formal, ornate CICERONIAN STYLE that had dominated formal English prose in the 16th century. The Senecan style was comparatively plain and epigrammatic, creating sentences of irregular lengths and variations. The new style better suited the emerging form of the ESSAY, as in this example from Francis Bacon's essay "Of Death":

> Men fear death, as children fear to go in the dark; and as that natural fear in children is increased with tales, so is the other. Certainly the contemplation of death, as the wages of sin and passage to another world, is holy and religious, but the fear of it, as a tribute due unto nature, is weak.

The adoption of the Senecan, sometimes known as the "Attic," style marked a major step toward the development, in the latter half of the 17th century, of modern English prose. (*See* RESTORATION.)

George Williamson's *The Senecan Amble* (1951, 1966) provides an excellent scholarly treatment of the style.

sensibility   In early 18th-century England, a term used to describe sensitivity to the sorrows of others. In the literature of the last half of the century, sensibility referred to the importance of emotion and the ideal of the "inspired" poet who transcended the rules of NEOCLASSICISM. Sensibility acquired a kind of cult status during this period, prominent enough to lead to the suggestion that the last half of the 18th century in England can be characterized as "The Age of Sensibility." The effects of the movement in literature are evident in SENTIMENTAL COMEDY and the SENTIMENTAL NOVEL. The parallel term SENTIMENTALITY is usually seen as a debased form of sensibility. Jane Austen's *Sense and Sensibility* (1811) offers a satiric portrait of extreme "sensibility."

   In the 20th century the term has been used to denote an intellectual and emotional perceptiveness, the sense employed by T. S. Eliot when he described the DISSOCIATION OF SENSIBILITY.

Janet Todd's *Sensibility* (1986) provides a concise introduction to the term.

sententia   A Latin term referring to a short statement expressing a commonly held truth, similar to a PROVERB. In *Hamlet*, Polonius's advice to his son, Laertes, contains a number of sententiae: "The apparel oft proclaims the man," and "Neither a borrower or lender be . . . to thine own self be true."T. S. Eliot's poem "The Love Song of J. Alfred Prufrock" (1917) contains an allusion to Polonius as "full of high sentence, but a bit obtuse."

sentimental comedy   A type of 18th-century English comedy emphasizing the virtues, rather than the foibles, of its major characters and celebrating the triumph of good over evil. Conceived in reaction to the cynical and amoral tone of RESTORATION COMEDY, the comedy of SENSIBILITY, as sentimental comedy was known, was notably short on laughs, but rich in "warmth." In this respect it was a precursor of 19th-century MELODRAMA and of the television SITCOM of the 1950s. (*See* COMÉDIE LARMOYANTE.)

sentimental novel   A type of novel popular in late 18th-century Europe. The aim of the sentimental novel, as described by the critic Janet Todd, was "the arousal of pathos through conventional situations, stock familiar characters, and rhetorical devices." In the hands of more accomplished writers, this excessive emotionalism was tempered with irony and humor, as in Oliver Goldsmith's *The Vicar of Wakefield* (1766) and Laurence Sterne's *A Sentimental Journey* (1768).

The "novel of sensibility," as it was known, had a powerful impact on European literature. In France, Jean-Jacques Rousseau's *La Nouvelle Héloïse* (1761) initiated a new literary mode. In Germany, Goethe's *The Sorrows of Young Werther* (1774) took the nation by storm.

Janet Todd's *Sensibility* (1986) examines the popularity of the form.

sentimentality   In literature, an excessive display of the emotion of pity or sympathy. It also refers to the easy manipulation of the reader's or audience's emotions by formulaic novels or films characterized as "tear jerkers." The history of literature reveals the radical relativity of the term: one generation's estimate of honest realism is frequently another generation's sentimentality. *See* SUFFERING/SYMPATHY.

sequel   A PLAY, FILM, or NARRATIVE which, complete in itself, is designed to follow a previous work. A Shakespearean example includes *Henry IV, Part Two,* which is generally regarded as a less powerful and original work than *Part One.* This negative judgment is the usual fate of sequels.

In films, the sequel has been popular since the 1970s when the success of films such as *The Godfather* (1972), *Jaws* (1975), and *Rocky* (1976) spawned multiple sequels.

serial   In film, a term for the brief, weekly chapters that flourished in movie theaters from the 1920s to the 1950s. Filled with incredible adventures and demonic villains, each chapter ended in a cliffhanger in which the hero, heroine, or both were tied up, about to be done in by some fiendish device. The succeeding chapter always began with their miraculous escape. Among the most famous of the serials were *The Perils of Pauline,* starring Pearl White, the first and most popular of serial heroines. Other serial heroes of note included Dick Tracy, Flash Gordon, and the Lone Ranger.

Steven Spielberg paid elaborate homage to the form in his highly successful films *Raiders of the Lost Ark* (1981), *Indiana Jones and the Temple of Doom* (1984), and *Indiana Jones and the Last Crusade* (1989).

sermon   A form of religious discourse not normally regarded as literature, although many sermons have been celebrated for their artistic as well as religious values. Among these are John Donne's "Death's Duel," preached before King Charles I shortly before Donne's death in 1631, and John Cotton's "God's Promise to His Plantation," delivered in 1630 on the occasion of John Winthrop's departure from England to establish the Massachusetts Bay Colony.

Notable sermons in literature include Father Mapple's preaching in *Moby-Dick* (1850) and Father Arnall's vision of eternity in James Joyce's *A Portrait of the Artist as a Young Man* (1916).

sestet   A poem or stanza of six lines. The term is also used to describe the final six lines of a Petrarchan SONNET, in which the sestet offers a response to the proposition in the first eight lines.

sestina   An unrhymed 39-line poem consisting of six stanzas of six lines each and a final three-line ENVOY, an addition to a poem addressed to a person or an abstraction. Adding to the complexity of the form is the requirement that each stanza use the same end words, but always in a different order.

Considered to be the invention of the TROUBADOUR poet Arnaut Daniel, the sestina was used throughout the MIDDLE AGES. In modern times, the form has been employed by a number of poets, including Ezra Pound ("Sestina: Altaforte") and W. H. Auden ("Paysage Moralisé"). Rudyard Kipling's "Sestina of the Tramp-Royal" (1896) is a sestina in which an itinerant laborer expresses his philosophy of life, concluding with an envoy to God:

> *Gawd, bless this world! Whatever she hath done—*
> *Except where awful long—I've found it good.*
> *So write, before I die, "'E liked it all."*

setting   The time and place of a NARRATIVE and DRAMA and, by extension, the social and political context of the action. The French term for setting is *mise en scène*.

seven deadly sins   Pride, covetousness, lust, anger, ENVY, gluttony, and sloth. The earliest reference to the sins as a group is in the quasi-biblical "Testament of the Twelve Patriarchs" (109–106 B.C.). The most important Christian source is St.

Gregory the Great's *Moralia* (sixth century A.D.), which prescribed the order of the sins; pride was first, since it was considered the source of all the others. The list was popularized through sermons and penitence manuals, books designed to guide the faithful in examining their conscience.

The sins were often personified in medieval and RENAISSANCE literature, notably in Dante's *Divine Comedy,* William Langland's *Piers Plowman* (1362–94), and Christopher Marlowe's *Doctor Faustus* (1588–92). In *The Castle of Perseverance,* an early 15th century MORALITY PLAY, the Deadly Sins are pitted against the Seven Cardinal Virtues: Meekness, Charity, Chastity, Patience, Generosity, Abstinence, and Industry.

The Seven Deadly Sins is the title of an ELIZABETHAN play now lost, but the "plot" of which has been recovered. In the Elizabethan theater *plot* referred to an outline of the play, listing the entrances and exits of the actors. This play's plot is important in that it supplies the names of the leading actors of a troupe that was to become Shakespeare's company—the Lord Chamberlain's Men, later to be known as The King's Men (*see* CHAMBERLAIN'S/KING'S MEN).

Morton Bloomfield's *The Seven Deadly Sins* (1952) is the definitive scholarly study of the subject.

Sewanee Review   Periodical published since 1892 by the University of the South in Sewanee, Tennessee. Since the early 1940s, the *Review* has been noted for the quality of the essays, criticism, and fiction. During those years, it was closely identified with the NEW CRITICISM particularly the Southern writers Robert Penn Warren, Allen Tate and Cleanth Brooks, but long after the demise of that school, the journal has continued to maintain its reputation as a distinguished literary quarterly, one with a particular interest in Southern American literature. *See* SOUTHERN RENAISSANCE.

shadow theater   A form of entertainment in which shadows are projected onto a screen by puppets placed behind the screen. It is not certain whether shadow theater originated in India, China, or Indonesia. In its Indonesian form, the plays are performed by a single puppeteer who speaks all the parts and sings all the songs, while manipulating as many as 40 or 50 different puppets in the course of an evening's performance. As adapted in Turkey, where it is known as *Karegoz* ("Black Eye"), the name of one of the two principal characters, shadow theater frequently comments on or satirizes features of contemporary life.

Shakespearean apocrypha   Plays attributed to Shakespeare at various times but not now generally accepted as having been written by him. Among these are *Edward III* (1595), a history play which Shakespeare may have revised, if not written entirely, and *Edmund Ironside* (1585–90), a play never published in its own day.

Shakespeare's sonnets   A variation on the Petrarchan sonnet (*see* SONNET), the Shakespearean form retains the 14 line length, while altering the original structure to include three questions and one concluding couplet. The couplet epitomizes the point of the preceding QUATRAINS. The form was introduced by Sir Thomas Wyatt and developed by Henry Howard, the earl of Surrey. The sonnets of both poets appeared in a famous anthology *Tottel's Miscellany: Songs and Sonnets* (1557). Other significant sonnet collections called Sonnet Sequences, included Philip Sidney's *Astrophel and Stella* (1591), Edmund Spenser's *Amoretti* (1594), and John Donne's *Holy Sonnets* (1617).

But Shakespeare's collection of 154 sonnets is unique both in the range and quality of the verse and in the intense biographical speculation they have generated. Here we are speaking not of the formal or aesthetic qualities, significant as they are, but of their alleged relevance to Shakespeare's biography. Most of the sonnets seem to be addressed not to some fair Petrachan maiden but to a young man, son of a noble family, urging him to marry, while 24 appear to be addressed to a "Dark Lady," who has become the mistress of both the young man and the poet.

Further complicating the situation is the dedication to the first edition (1609) of the poems "to the onlie begetter of these ensuring sonnets, Mr. W. H." The attempt to identify "Mr. W. H" and the young man (assuming them to be the same person) has yielded two candidates. One is the earl of Southampton, whose name, Henry Wriothesly reverses the W. H. The second candidate is William Herbert, the earl of Pembroke, to whom (along with his brother) the actors in Shakespeare's company dedicated the FIRST FOLIO in 1623.

Looming over these and numerous other possibilities is the chance that the sonnets bear no significant relationship to the poet's life. This position also applies to persistent speculation that the sonnets reveal a homosexual connection between Shakespeare and the young man. None of these possibilities should overshadow the poems' power as works of art, representations of intense personal experiences, but not necessarily related to the author's biography, at least in any obvious sense. It is not unreasonable to suppose that the poet who could create such complex and varied characters as Iago, Cleopatra, and Shylock in the crucible of his imagination could perform similar magic in the lyric mode.

The finest critical work on the sonnets is Stephen Booth's *Shakespeare's Sonnets* (1977), which combines on facing pages a facsimile of the original with a modernized text and a textual, critical commentary for each poem. Equally commendable are Helen Vendler's illuminating readings in *The Art of Shakespeare's Sonnets* (1997).

short story   A fictional NARRATIVE, the length of which varies, but which rarely exceeds 20,000 words. Any longer work is usually classified as a NOVELLA or short novel. A short story usually contains two or three characters and frequently focuses on a simple incident or a moment of sudden insight, characterized by James Joyce as an EPIPHANY.

Although the form contains ancestors that include PARABLE, FABLE and FOLKTALE, the modern short story was developed in the 19th century and came into its own in the 20th century, published in both the general MAGAZINE and the LITTLE MAGAZINE. Many of the greatest novelists of the past century have written short stories, but writers who have dedicated themselves exclusively to this form of fiction include O. Henry, Isaak Babel, Katherine Mansfield, Frank O'Connor, Jorge Luis Borges, Raymond Carver, and Alice Munro.

Frank O'Connor's *The Lonely Voice* (1964) is a study of the form.

shot   In FILM, a single, uninterrupted running of the camera. *See also* ESTABLISHING SHOT; TRACKING SHOT; ZOOM SHOT.

sign   In LINGUISTICS, any element, verbal or nonverbal, that can be taken to represent something. As formulated by the Swiss linguist Ferdinand de Saussure, a verbal sign is made up of two aspects, the SIGNIFIER/SIGNIFIED. The signifier is the sound or written letters, while the signified represents the idea or concept. Note that both the signifier and the signified are linguistic entities, not the extra-linguistic object called the REFERENT. Thus the sign *table* is made up of the sound (signifier) and the idea of a table (signified). Saussure suggested that not only was the relationship of the sign to the referent an arbitrary one, so too was the relation of the signifier to the signified.

Saussure's distinction proved to be a key element in the development of STRUCTURALISM and POSTSTRUCTURALISM. These movements suggested that words do not refer to the real world; instead, they indicate concepts and, as Robert Scholes phrases it, "Concepts are aspects of thought, not reality."

Robert Scholes's *Semiotics and Interpretation* (1982) offers a detailed discussion of these ideas.

signifier/signified   According to the Swiss linguist Ferdinand de Saussure, the two component parts of a linguistic SIGN. The signifier is the sound of a word or, in writing, the marks on a page. The signified is its concept or meaning. The signifier of the word *cat* is a one-syllable sound that rhymes with the sound "bat." The signified are the mental images of a four-legged animal. It is important not to confuse the signified with the object referred to, the REFERENT—in our example, an actual cat. The signified is a concept, a linguistic entity.

Saussure argues that just as the relation of the whole sign to its referent is an arbitrary convention, so too is the relation between the signifier (the sound image) and the signified (the concept generated by the sound).

As a result of this arbitrary relation, some theorists, notably Jacques Derrida, the leading exponent of DECONSTRUCTION, have maintained that language is a self-referential system with no direct connection to reality.

signifyin(g)   In African-American speech, a term describing the use of metaphorical language for a variety of purposes, including parody, persuasion, ridicule, or provocation. Rhetorical features such as "rapping" (*see* RAP), "testifying" (acknowledging one's faults), and "playing the dozens" (exchanging insults in rhyme) are subdivisions of signifying. Its folklore roots are traced in stories of the signifying monkey, a trickster figure. The monkey's equivocal language invariably causes trouble for his friend the lion, who takes the monkey's language literally.

According to Henry Louis Gates, signifyin[g] is the central feature of African-American novels, such as Zora Neale Hurston's *Their Eyes Were Watching God* (1937) and Ishmael Reed's *Mumbo Jumbo* (1972).

Henry Louis Gates's *The Signifying Monkey: A Theory of Afro-American Criticism* (1988) contains a comprehensive account of the practice.

silence   A literary theme with a wide range of references. Silence can connote holiness, beauty, fear, repression, or the inexpressible. The desire for it can be the subject of comic ridicule, as in Ben Jonson's *Epicoene or the Silent Woman* (1609), or it can represent the victor's confidence, as in August Strindberg's *The Stronger* (1889). Silence has played a central role in the plays of Samuel Beckett, in which it represents the empty void that is reality.

In FEMINIST CRITICISM, the analysis of "silence" has assumed an increasingly important role. In *Silences* (1978), the American SHORT STORY writer Tillie Olsen pointed to the relative absence of women's voices in literature—the result of the demanding roles played by most women, and by their exclusion from the CANON of classical works. Olsen's theme was echoed by Adrienne Rich in *On Lies, Secrets and Silence* (1979).

One outgrowth of these observations has been a critical focus on "silences," things that are not said in TEXTs written by women, which might indicate signs of oppression or strategies of resistance. Although most feminist critics focus on women writers, an interesting example of strategic silence comes at the end of Shakespeare's *Measure for Measure*. At the conclusion of this play, Duke Vincentio "proposes" to Isabella, a religious novice, in a manner that takes her acceptance for granted. He is greeted by her silence, an ambiguity that has led to a variety of directorial choices in productions of the play, including one in which she turns and silently walks away.

Listening to Silences (1994), edited by Elaine Hedges and Shelley Fisher Fishkin, is a collection of recent feminist criticism on the theme. Ihab Hassan's *The Literature of Silence* (1969) studies the theme in the works of Henry Miller and Samuel Beckett.

simile   A comparison between two dissimilar things, usually connected by the words *like* or *as*. In this respect a simile is very close to METAPHOR, with which it is frequently paired. "My love is like a red, red rose" is a simile; "My love is a red rose" is a metaphor. Both simile and metaphor aim to provide a vivid description and clarity of meaning, as in Lord Byron's line "She walks in beauty like the night."

sitcom   A shortened form of *situation comedy,* a term used to describe the serialized, half-hour comedies that have been the staple of popular television since its earliest years. A sitcom is rooted in a particular context (usually house or workplace) in which clearly identified, predictable characters experience a series of plot complications and reversals before moving to a happy ending. The laughter-inducing features of the story may depend upon the comic talent of the star (*I Love Lucy*), the quality of the scripts (*M*A*S*H, Barney Miller, Seinfeld*), the ensemble playing of the cast (*The Honeymooners, The Mary Tyler Moore Show*), or the shock value of the subject matter (*All in the Family*). The plot normally centers on a threat to the real or extended family, which consists of the regular cast. The threat may take the form of an outsider disrupting the group or an insider aspiring to move outside it. The resolution invariably endorses the central value of the family's continued existence. In the efficiency of its construction, a good sitcom qualifies as a species of WELL-MADE PLAY.

Rick Mintz's *The Great TV Sitcom Book* (1980) provides a history and description of the form.

skeltonics   An irregular verse form used by the early Tudor poet John Skelton (1460–1529). It features short lines with varying numbers of stresses and a rhyming technique in which, as C. S. Lewis put it, "any given rhyme may be repeated as long as the resources of language hold out." Here is a sample from Skelton's anticlerical, satirical poem "Colin Clout".

> For though my rhymes be ragged
> Tattered and jagged,
> Rickety rain-beaten
> Rusty and mold-eaten
> If ye take fell therewith
> It hath in it some pith

Contemporary practitioners of RAP and hip-hop may be surprised to discover an ancestor in John Skelton.

C. S. Lewis's *English Literature in the Sixteenth Century* (1954) contains a perceptive appreciation of Skeltonics.

skepticism   A critical attitude that calls into question any claim of certitude or truth made by an individual or group. As a philosophical position, skepticism played a prominent role in the intellectual history of the West, beginning with Plato's ACADEMY. It emerged as a powerful intellectual tool in the RENAISSANCE, principally in the essays of Michel de Montaigne, one of which, *Apology for Raymond Sébond*, summarized the case against the validity of rational thought. The challenge of skepticism was met by the 17th-century philosopher René Descartes, who accepted all of the skeptics' doubts, including the doubting of one's own existence. But Descartes turned the table, asserting that the very act of doubting proves that one does exist: "I think, therefore I am." Descartes' victory over the skeptics was reinforced by Immanuel Kant.

A recent manifestation of radical skepticism has been the belief that there is an unbridgeable gap between the structure of reality and the capacity of the human mind to discern that structure, most evident in the analysis of language. The result is the contemporary skeptical position, characterized by the phrase attributed to Jacques Derrida, "There is no outside the text," the human mind is trapped by language, which is unstable and lacking any foundation. The only alternative is to expose, deconstruct, and demystify the metaphorical fictions that have passed as absolutes (*see* DECONSTRUCTION).

By the 1990s, the inevitable antiskeptical reaction set in, rejecting the "hermeneutics of suspicion," the philosopher Paul Ricoeur's term for the perceived arrogant nihilism of radical skepticism. The result has led to a renewed respect for pluralism and, in literature, a renewed commitment to the IMAGINATION as a mode of knowledge. Another effect has been a return to aesthetic appreciation of a type represented in Harold Bloom's *The Western Canon* (1994), the view that in its relentless negativity, the "hermeneutics of suspicion" had reached an impasse (*see* HERMENEUTICS). As the philosopher George Santayana put it, ". . . life and even discussion forces me to break away from a complete skepticism. . . . I have frankly taken nature by the hand, accepting as a rule in my farthest speculations the animal faith I live by from day to day."

Don Cameron Allen's *Doubt's Boundless Sea* (1964) is a valuable history of the growth of skepticism in the Renaissance; George Santayana's *Skepticism and Animal Faith* (1923; repr't, 1955) contains his final views on the value and limitations of skepticism.

slave narratives   Nineteenth-century, autobiographical accounts by escaped slaves. In the years leading up to the Civil War, slave NARRATIVEs became, in the words of the critic Henry Louis Gates, "the most popular form of written discourse in the country." These narratives vividly recreated the dehumanizing conditions of slave life. The best known of these accounts is *Narrative of the Life of Frederick Douglass* (1845). Douglass's eloquent description of his experiences amounted to a damning indictment of slavery.

Some of the narratives that followed in Douglass's wake appear to be inauthentic, written either by ardent white abolitionists or people trying to capitalize on a popular form. A number of them, however, including Harriet Jacobs's *Incidents in the Life of a Slave Girl* (1861) and *Scenes in the Life of Harriet Tubman* (1869), are authentic, moving representations of slave life.

The most powerful fictional account of the lives of slaves is Toni Morrison's *Beloved* (1987).

Henry Louis Gates's *Figures in Black* (1987) contains a subtle and perceptive analysis of slave literature. Gates is also the editor of *The Classic Slave Narratives* (1987), a collection of the most significant examples of the genre.

soap opera   A term for serialized radio or television DRAMAs presented in the United States every weekday afternoon or, in Great Britain, every evening. The earliest of these series, produced for radio in the 1930s, were sponsored by soap manufacturers, and became known as soap operas. Among the best-known soap operas in radio were *One Man's Family* (1932–59), *Ma Perkins* (1933–60), and *The Romance of Helen Trent* (1933–52), which announced its theme at the beginning of each episode: "That because a woman is 35, romance in life need not be ended, that romance can exist at 35, and even beyond."

Outstanding television soaps include *The Guiding Light* (1952–   ), which began as a radio serial in 1937 and is the longest running soap opera; *General Hospital* (1963–   ), a series that achieved an unusually high degree of popularity;

and *All My Children* (1970–   ), the series credited with being the most sophisticated of the soaps.

One of the remarkable features of soap operas is their capacity for eliciting intense devotion from their audience. Many soap opera fans are self-confessed addicts of their favorite shows, devoting years of their lives not only to watching but also to worrying about the various fates of their characters. Another common element of soap opera fandom is the tendency to confuse the character with the actor playing the role.

Soaps rely on a store of plot elements derived from traditional MELODRAMA: amnesia, blackmail, adultery, and the Wicked Woman. The characters, including members of racial and ethnic minorities, tend to be members of the professional middle class. The setting is generally an idealized small town.

In contrast, English soap operas tend to represent working-class urban life. They are presented in the early evening and draw proportionately an even larger share of the audience than their American counterparts. Among the long running English soaps are *Coronation Street* and *East Enders*.

Manuel Soares's *The Soap Opera Book* (1978) covers both the television and radio eras; Ruth Rosen's "Search for Yesterday" in *Watching Television* (1987), edited by Todd Gitlin, offers a trenchant analysis of the appeal of the soaps.

social class   *See* CLASS.

social construction   The argument that in everyday life, conceptions of "reality" and "truth"—often covered by the term *common sense*—are socially constructed, that is formed by interactions within human communities. The idea was first advanced in 1966 by the sociologists Peter Burger and Thomas Luckmann, who examined the phenomenon from the vantage point of the sociology of knowledge. That perspective was broadened and deepened by the philosopher Richard Rorty in *Philosophy and the Mirror of Nature* (1979). (*See* MIND AS MIRROR.) Viewed from the perspective of the anthropologist Clifford Geertz, "Human thought is consummately social, social in its origins, social in its function, social in its application." Thus such seemingly "natural" terms as *childhood* or that keystone of secular HUMANISM, the autonomous SELF can be seen to be socially constructed terms.

In literary theory, social construction emerges in such concepts as Stanley Fish's idea of "interpretive communities," that the meaning of a TEXT is fixed by a community of readers, who create a meaning based upon a shared set of beliefs and interpretative practices, as one would find, for example, in a literature classroom. Its extension into COMPOSITION STUDIES as well is evident in the idea of COLLABORATIVE LEARNING.

Peter Berger and Thomas Luckmann's pioneering study is *The Social Construction of Reality* (1966).

socialist realism   A form of realism designed to represent the superiority of socialism as a form of government. The term was defined in 1934 at the First Soviet Writers Conference as "the basic method of Soviet literature and literary criticism" in which "artistic representation of reality must be combined with the task of ideological remolding and education of the working people in the spirit of socialism." As adopted by the regime of Joseph Stalin, this position was sufficiently vague to permit easy adaptation to the shifting policies and demands of the government. In short, literature was seen as an agency of PROPAGANDA. *See* REALISM.

soliloquy   In DRAMA, a MONOLOGUE in which a character appears to be thinking out loud, thereby communicating to the audience his inner thoughts and feelings. It differs from an ASIDE, which is a brief remark directed to the audience. In performing a soliloquy, the actor traditionally acts as though he were talking to himself, although some actors directly address the audience.

The soliloquy achieved its greatest effect in English RENAISSANCE drama. When employed in modern drama, it is usually as the equivalent of the INTERIOR MONOLOGUE in FICTION. Filmed versions of Shakespearean plays, for example, often represent a soliloquy through a voiceover.

song   A term for a type of LYRIC poem, not necessarily designed to be set to music. In this sense it serves as a synonym for a lyric poem, as in William Blake's "Songs of Innocence and Experience" (1794) and Walt Whitman's "Song of Myself" (1855).

In DRAMA, songs play significant roles in nonmusical plays. Shakespeare employs songs to establish a mood ("The Willow Song" in *Othello*), to advance the plot ("Tell me where is fancy bred" in *The Merchant of Venice*), to summarize the action ("A Great While Ago, the World Began" in *Twelfth Night*), or to underscore a theme ("The Gravedigger's Song" in *Hamlet*). In John Osborne's *The Entertainer* (1957) the songs of the main character Archie Rice serve all of these purposes, as they do in Bertolt Brecht's *Mother Courage and Her Children* (1941).

In Richard Powers's novel *The Time of Our Singing* (2003), a divided family survives the polarizing fissures of modern life through its shared love of song. In FILM, the song "As Time Goes By" famously constitutes the linchpin of the love story in *Casablanca* (1943). In many of the films of John Ford songs contribute to their strong masculine ethos, while in Dennis Potter's television series, later made into films, *Pennies from Heaven* (1981) and *The Singing Detective* (1986), they provide both a historical context and an ironic subtext.

sonnet A 14-line lyric poem usually written, for sonnets in English, in iambic pentameter. Since its origins in 12th-century Italy, the sonnet has been one of the most popular poetic forms.

There are two distinct rhyme schemes for the sonnet, the Petrarchan and the Shakespearean. The Petrarchan sonnet, named for the 14th-century Italian poet Petrarch, is divided into two parts: the octave (the first eight lines), with an a-b-b-a a-b-b-a rhyme scheme, and the sestet (the final six lines), rhyming either c-d-e c-d-e or c-d-c c-d-c. The Shakespearean form consists of three quatrains (a-b-a-b c-d-c-d e-f-e-f) and a final couplet (g-g). (*See* SHAKESPEARE'S SONNETS.)

In the Petrarchan sonnet, the more commonly employed form, the octave states the general subject of the poem, the basic idea or emotion, and the sestet offers a resolution. The sonnets written by Petrarch himself are addressed to his unattainable beloved, Laura. Their appeal spawned imitations throughout Europe.

In 16th-century England, the sonnet fad took the form known as the sonnet sequence, a series of sonnets that trace the development of the relationship between the poet and his idealized beloved. Shakespeare departed from this convention in a sequence of 154 poems, of which 1 through 126 are addressed to a young man and the remainder, with the exception of the last two, to a "dark lady." More important, Shakespeare used the sonnets to reflect on such themes as TIME and POWER. John Donne's "Holy Sonnets" expanded the subject to embrace spiritual concerns.

The popularity of the sonnet declined in the 18th century but was revived by the Romantics. William Wordsworth wrote more than 500 sonnets and John Keats wrote two of the best-known sonnets in the English language, "On First Looking into Chapman's Homer" and "When I have fears that I may cease to be." The VICTORIAN period saw the publication of Elizabeth Barrett Browning's *Sonnets from the Portuguese* (1850), a sequence celebrating her love for her husband, Robert Browning.

Celebrated 20th-century sonnets include Thomas Hardy's "Hap," William Butler Yeats's "Leda and the Swan," and Robert Frost's "Acquainted with the Night."

The Sonnet (1965), edited by Robert Bender and Charles Squier, is an anthology of sonnets in English with a critical introduction by the editors.

source A TEXT used by a writer for a PLOT, ideas, or stylistic devices. According to the principle of INTERTEXTUALITY, all texts have sources, but the more traditional use of the term focuses on specific texts whose presence can be detected in another text. For example, almost all of Shakespeare's plays are adaptations of pre-existing sources. The chief source of *King Lear* (1605) is an earlier play on the subject, but additional sources of the play include Sir Philip Sidney's *Arcadia* (1590), John Florio's translation of Montaigne's *Essays* (1603), and Samuel Harsnett's *A Declaration of Egregious Popish Impostures* (1603). (*See* NEW HISTORICISM.) Reading these sources leaves one with an increased admiration for Shakespeare. In the words of the critic Stephen Greenblatt, "the closer Shakespeare comes to a source. . . the more devastating and decisive his transformation of it."

A related term, *INFLUENCE,* refers to the impact of a writer on others.

Stephen Greenblatt's comments are part of his discussion of *King Lear* in *Shakespearean Negotiations* (1988).

Southern renaissance   In American literature, the period from 1920 to 1960, which saw the emergence of important writers who drew on the culture and conflicts of the American South in their work. Preeminent among them was William Faulkner, whose position as the greatest American novelist of the 20th-century remains unchallenged. Faulkner's fictional Yoknapatawpha County constitutes a microcosmic picture of Southern life and history including its heritage of racial inequity.

Other figures include Thomas Wolfe, whose autobiographical novels, the best known of which is *Look Homeward, Angel* (1929), deal with the conflict within a Southern writer who has left his roots for life in the North; Eudora Welty, whose stories and novels create an authentic picture of life in a small town in Mississippi and Robert Penn Warren, whose *All the King's Men* (1946) provided an incisive portrait of a Louisiana politician modeled on Huey Long.

A second generation of Southern writers continued the depiction of Southern life, including Carson McCullers (*The Heart is a Lonely Hunter*, 1940), Walker Percy (*The Moviegoer*, 1961), William Styron (*The Confession of Nat Turner*, 1967), Alice Walker (*The Color Purple*, 1982) and, second only to Faulkner, Flannery O'Connor, who used the South as the setting for stories and novels with profound and passionate religious conviction.

For an account of important critical movements of the Southern Renaissance, *see* FUGITIVE AGRARIANS, and *SEWANEE REVIEW.*

Louis Rubin and Robert Jacobs's collection *Southern Renaissance, The Literature of the Modern South* (1953) provides a reliable, informative guide.

speech act theory   A philosophical analysis of language as a mode of human behavior rather than as an abstract system. In classical terms, speech act theory sees language as rooted in rhetoric rather than logic. From this perspective, any linguistic utterance can be analyzed not just in terms of its "locution," its noncontextual meaning, but as an "illocution," an "act" designed to reassure, promise, or threaten, or as a "perlocution," an effect a speaker wishes to produce in a listener. From this perspective, there are two types of utterances: the "performative," statements that perform the acts they designate, as when the preacher says, "I now pronounce you husband and wife"; and the "constative," statements that describe a situation, as in "He lives on 86th Street." But implicit in the constative is a performative ("I affirm that he lives on 86th Street"), and implicit in the performative is a constative (the just-married couple really are husband and wife).

The English philosopher J. L. Austin first developed these ideas in his book *How to Do Things With Words* (1962). They were subsequently elaborated by a number of philosophers, notably John Searle (*Speech Acts: An Essay in the Philosophy of Language,* 1969) and famously "deconstructed" by Jacques Derrida. Derrida argued that the constative/performative intermixture lies at the root of the basic instability of language.

In literary study, speech act theory has contributed to the recent tendency to focus on a literary text as "performative." Literary language does not describe an existing condition. It brings into existence something that was not there before. In this sense it is performative. Looking at it in this manner, we can say that literature not only says something, it also does something, resulting in a "perlocutionary" impact on its readers. These actions are to some extent predetermined, to some extent improvisational, but in all cases they constitute a "performance." In this respect, the theory bears a resemblance to Kenneth Burke's conception of DRAMATISM.

Mary Louise Pratt's *Toward a Speech Act Theory of Literary Discourse* (1977) and Charles Altieri's *Act and Quality: A Theory of Literary Meaning and Humanistic Understanding* (1981) explore the relevance of this theory to the study of literature. Derrida's critique is reprinted in his *Limited Inc.* (1988).

Spenserian stanza   A stanza consisting of nine lines, the first eight of which are 10-syllable iambic pentameters, while the last line contains an 11th syllable. The rhyme scheme is a-b-a-b-b-c-b-c-c. This is the stanza of Edmund Spenser's *The Faerie Queene* (1590–96) and of a number of other major English poems including Lord Byron's *Childe Harold's Pilgrimage* (1812), John Keats's "The Eve of St. Agnes" (1820), and Percy Bysshe Shelley's *Adonais* (1821).

spondee   *See* METER.

sprung rhythm   A distinctive variation of normal meter, in which any num-
ber of stressed syllables may occur without intervening unstressed syllables.
According to the VICTORIAN poet Gerard Manley Hopkins, who devised this
technique, sprung rhythm approximates the rhythm of ordinary English speech.
An example from Hopkins's poetry is a line from his poem "The Wreck of the
Deutschland":

/   ˘   ˘   /   /   /
Christens her wild worst best.

stage   The space where a theatrical performance occurs. The three major types
of stage currently used are the arena, thrust, and proscenium stages.
   The arena stage is one in which the audience surrounds the playing area.
Also known as the "theater in the round," the arena was the form of the classical
theater of Greece and Rome and is frequently employed today by small experimental theater groups, such as the Arena Stage in Washington, D.C.
   The thrust or apron stage is one in which the audience is seated on three
sides of a platform. The most celebrated example of this type of stage is the GLOBE
THEATRE, where Shakespeare's plays were originally performed.
   The proscenium stage—the most common form in use—is one in which the
audience sits in front of the stage which is framed like a picture that is revealed by
the opening of the curtain. When the setting of the play is a specific interior, the
effect is that of watching a room from which the fourth wall has been removed.

George and Portia Kernodle and Edward Pixley examine the different stages in *Invitation
to the Theater* (1985).

stage directions   Information added to the text of a play to describe an action
("enter," "exit"), the delivery of a line ("quietly," "laughing") and the opening and
closing of the play, as in Arthur Miller's *Death of a Salesman* (1948), which begins
and ends with directions for a melody played upon a flute.

stand-up   A form of comedy in which a comedian, usually working alone,
delivers a monologue offering observations on an array of topics: politics, sex,
the media, ethnic and racial characteristics, the ordinary details of life, or the
comedian's own personal history. The founding father of the form—not as
the funniest comedian, but the figure who extended the idea of comedy to its
limits—is generally considered to be Lenny Bruce.
   Trevor Griffith's *The Comedians* (1976), a DRAMA using a night class for aspiring comedians as its setting, explores the tension between those who see stand-up

as a collection of easy laughs and those, like Lenny Bruce, who see it as a vehicle for speaking the truth.

stanza In verse, the basic division of a poem, the equivalent of a paragraph in PROSE. Stanzas are designated according to the number of lines they contain:

COUPLET (2 lines)	SESTET (6 lines)
TERCET (3 lines)	SEPTET (7 lines)
QUATRAIN (4 lines)	OCTET (8 lines)
QUINTAIN (5 lines)	NONET (9 lines)

Many modern poems have either irregular stanza lengths or no stanzas at all.

stereotype A highly generalized idea, situation, or character, derived from an oversimplified treatment in a work. More commonly, it refers to the reliance on generalizations about racial, national, or sexual groups in the depiction of certain characters. The rendering of Irish Americans as drunken and pugnacious in 19th-century political cartoons, or of African Americans in the films of the 1930s and '40s as shuffling and slow witted, qualify as stereotypes. Occasionally a character will have stereotypical features, but these will be subordinated to the distinctively individualized features of the character. Shakespeare's Shylock in *The Merchant of Venice* is a notable example (*see* ANTI-SEMITISM.)

Stereotypes should not be confused with STOCK CHARACTERS. The latter term refers to character types who perform certain conventional functions in stories and plays.

stichomythia In DRAMA, a dialogue in which two characters respond to each other in rapid, hostile repartee. The effect is that of a verbal duel, in which each character parries the other's words while thrusting home with a cutting remark. A Greek term, stichomythia was a feature of classical drama, notably in the exchange of Oedipus and Tiresias in *Oedipus Rex*. Shakespeare gives it a comic turn in this exchange between the clownish figures Don Armado and Moth in *Love's Labour's Lost*:

> Armado: *Pretty and apt.*
> Moth: *How mean you, sir, I pretty and my saying apt? or I apt,*
> *and my saying pretty?*
> Armado: *Thou pretty, because little.*
> Moth: *Little pretty, because little. Wherefore apt?*
> Armado: *And therefore apt, because quick.*

Repartee is the modern term for stichomythia.

stock character   A CHARACTER type who serves a particular function in the literary genre in which he or she appears. A typical example from COMEDY, which regularly employs a number of stock characters, is the *miles gloriosus* (BRAGGART WARRIOR), a comic figure from the classical period to modern DRAMA. The RAISONNEUR in FICTION and drama, and the plodding, unimaginative "chief inspector" in the traditional DETECTIVE STORY are other examples of stock characters.

stoicism   A philosophical school that stressed the suppression of passionate emotion in favor of self-control, the performance of one's duty, and living according to the rules of nature. Founded by the Greek philosopher Zeno around 300 B.C., stoicism was adapted and adopted by Roman thinkers and writers, notably the Roman emperor Marcus Aurelius and the tragedian Seneca.

Stoic philosophy influenced ELIZABETHAN dramatists, particularly George Chapman. T. S. Eliot analyzed Shakespeare's debt to Seneca in a well-known essay "Shakespeare and the Stoicism of Seneca."

Stoic principles are still very much alive in the modern novels of Walker Percy (*The Thanatos Syndrome*, 1987) and in Tom Wolfe's *A Man in Full* (1998).

story   In its usual sense, a NARRATIVE, usually fictional, or the PLOT of such a narrative. Many contemporary critics distinguish between story and plot, however. The story, in this sense, is the chronological sequence of events; the plot, those events as actually ordered in the narration. Thus the story of Shakespeare's *Hamlet* begins with the murder of Hamlet's father by Claudius, but the plot consists of the events as they unfold in the play. This distinction is sometimes referred to by the Latin term *fabula* (story) and the Russian term *sjuzet* (plot). RUSSIAN FORMALISM was the original source of the distinction.

stream of consciousness   *See* INTERIOR MONOLOGUE.

structuralism   An intellectual movement that originated in linguistic theory and eventually spread to a variety of disciplines, such as anthropology, psychology, and literary criticism. Structuralism developed from the work of the Swiss linguist Ferdinand de Saussure, who rejected the traditional view of language, in which words acquire meaning because of their connection to things in the world. For Saussure a word is a SIGN, consisting of two parts, the signifier (the noise or mark we make when we speak or write the word) and the signified (the idea generated by the sound or mark). (*See* SIGNIFIER/SIGNIFIED.)

The relation between the signifier and the signified is strictly arbitrary. For example there is no necessary relation between the letters KEY and the image it creates in our mind. The association is purely conventional, not natural. Thus, meaning is found not in the inherent relationship between the signifier and the signified, nor between the sign as a whole and the thing it refers to. Meaning emerges in the interrelation of signs within a given language system. This interrelation is based upon difference, the difference, for example, between KEY and all the other signs in the language.

While language is a system of differences, "meaning" is a structure of consciousness—a "text" we carry around in our heads—that has been formed by our language system. Structuralists reject the view that language is a tool employed by human beings. They see language as a force that shapes our notion of reality, not the other way around. As the influential philosopher Martin Heidegger expressed it, "language speaks us."

Put another way, the traditional view sees the mind as the source of language, which functions as its instrument. The structuralist view sees any given individual "mind," not as the root and source of reflection, but as the consequence of possibilities inherent in a given linguistic system.

Saussure employed two important terms to distinguish particular uses of a language from the overall language system. The latter he designated *langue* and the former *parole*. Saussure draws an analogy from chess: He likens langue to the abstract rules that govern chess and parole to the actual games of chess that people play. Langue therefore plays a shaping role in every example of parole. He advises linguists to focus their studies on the synchronic (limited to a particular point in time) langue rather than the diachronic (changing over time) parole. (*See* LANGUE/PAROLE.)

In literary studies the effect of this emphasis has been to redirect interpretation. Structuralist critics disregard approaches to literary analysis that look for the meaning of a work in the intention of the author or in its alleged truth about human life, or, as in NEW CRITICISM, within the text itself. Structuralists are less interested in the individual work (which corresponds to the parole of Saussure's formula) than in the system (Saussure's langue). They view both author and reader as not-always-conscious participants in genres, codes, and conventions that radically limit and shape their roles. To return to Saussure's analogy, every player, whether conscious of it or not, is playing by the rules.

Structuralist interests lie in the underlying "grammar of literature," that is, the general principles that govern literary structure. As a consequence, the most important direct contribution of structuralist thought to literary studies has been in the analysis of genres, such as narrative (*see* NARRATOLOGY), or in linguistically related concepts, such as METAPHOR and METONOMY.

The most significant contributions of structuralism in literary studies, however, have been indirect. The key structuralist principles—the arbitrary relation of the signifier and the signified, the priority of language over thought, the emphasis on relations between entities rather than on the isolated entities themselves, and the consequence of this emphasis for the traditional view of the individual—have been incorporated into the intellectual fabrics of POSTSTRUCTURALISM, POSTMODERNISM, and DECONSTRUCTION. As a result, while only briefly viable as a movement in the '60s, structuralism appears to have contributed to a permanent alteration of intellectual life in the latter half of the 20th century.

A good introduction to the literary uses of structuralism is Robert Scholes's *Structuralism in Literature* (1974); Fredric Jameson's *The Prison-House of Language: A Critical Account of Structuralism and Russian Formalism* (1972) critiques the structuralists from a Marxist perspective.

structure   In literature, the skeleton or internal relations of a TEXT. Sometimes used interchangeably with the older term FORM, the two terms can be distinguished by treating form as the overall effect and structure as the underlying principles. In this sense, form might be seen as the concrete and glass, and structure as the steel girders, of an office building.

Where used interchangeably, structure has become the preferred term of many contemporary theorists on the grounds that *form* carries connotations of philosophical idealism, while *structure* appears to connote the material quality of language.

studio system   In American FILM, the practice in which the control of film production was vested in seven major studios, Metro Goldwyn Mayer, 20th Century Fox, Paramount, Warner Brothers, Columbia, Universal, and RKO, as well as a number of minor studios, such as Republic and Monogram. The latter specialized in "second features," in an age when double features were the norm. Most of the major studios owned their own distribution chains of theaters, giving them a virtual monopoly. In 1948, the Supreme Court ruled that they would have to sell their theaters, a development, along with the growing popularity of television, that led to the eventual dissolution of the major studios.

Sturm und Drang (storm and stress)   A German literary movement in the 1770s. A reaction to the prevailing 18th-century NEOCLASSICISM, this movement of young writers strove to achieve an emotional intensity and freedom from the restrictions of neoclassical conventions. Another important influence was the political and social unrest in Europe that was to issue in the French Revolution.

The movement, led by Johann Herder, Friedrich Schiller, and Johann Goethe, looked to Shakespeare as their model of a natural genius, untrammeled by rigid rules. Their works, primarily DRAMAs, exhibited intensity, emotionalism, and exaggerated language. Among the major works of the movement were Goethe's *Götz von Berlichingen* (1773), Schiller's *The Robbers* (1781), and the play that gave the movement its name, Friedrich Klinger's *Confusion or Storm and Stress* (1776). *See also* ROMANTICISM.

style   In literature, a particular manner of employing language. The term may refer to a period of literary history (VICTORIAN style), or a genre (tragic style), a profession (legal style), or to an individual writer (Jane Austen's style). In the last case, the style is usually regarded as an index to the mind or personality of the writer.

stylistics   A subdivision of LINGUISTICS that studies variations in sound, syntax, and vocabulary that produce a distinctive STYLE. One subdivision, stylometry or stylometrics, uses statistical- and computer-based analyses of texts to determine disputed cases of authorship.

subject   A key term for exponents of POSTSTRUCTURALISM and THEORY. In the language of these movements, *subject* plays a number of roles. Serving as a substitute for the older terms *person, individual,* and *self,* the term also can serve as a synonym for "that which is subjected," the product of certain historical and social forces. The point of these changes in terminology is to dispute the notion that the *subject*—under whatever name—designates a unified center of consciousness that is the free originator of thought. Instead, these theorists argue that the subject is a fractured, "decentered," language-shaped creature. In some versions of feminist and Marxist theory, the subject also is seen as capable of resistance and self-assertion.

Paul Smith's *Discerning the Subject* (1988) argues for a definition of the subject that includes the idea of an active agent.

subjective criticism   A form of READER RESPONSE CRITICISM which argues that the personality of the reader is the most important element in interpreting a text. Unlike other forms of reader-oriented criticism, subjective criticism focuses not on implied or ideal readers, but on the readings of actual individuals.

The most prominent exponent of subjective criticism is David Bleich, whose *Reading and Feelings* (1975) examines the interpretations of specific students in his classes and traces the relation between their personalities and their interpretations. In *Five Readers Reading* (1975), Norman Holland uses PSYCHOANALYTICAL CRITICISM to explore the written interpretation of his students.

sublime   A characteristic of nature and art that embodies grandeur and nobility and evokes in its audience a sense of awe. In literature, the term derives from the treatise *On the Sublime* (first century A.D.), traditionally attributed (almost certainly erroneously) to Longinus, a Greek rhetorician and philosopher. For "Longinus," the sublime is the emotional response to a spoken or written utterance of great power, which at first overwhelms and later creates in the reader/listener a feeling of transcendence.

Interest in sublimity in art and literature re-emerged in late 18th-century England with the publication of Edmund Burke's *Philosophical Enquiry into the Origins of Our Ideas of the Sublime and Beautiful* (1757). Burke's distinction between the awesome power of the sublime and the more constrained and decorous appeal of the beautiful played an influential role in the development of English ROMANTICISM. Many Romantic poets strove to achieve the effects of sublimity by conceiving of literature as an ORGANIC FORM, having, potentially at least, the force and grandeur of nature.

The *American sublime* is a term for the distinctive role that the concept has played in the works of Ralph Waldo Emerson, Emily Dickinson, Walt Whitman, and Wallace Stevens.

The American Sublime (1986), edited by Mary Arensberg, is a collection of critical essays on the topic.

subplot   A subordinate sequence of events in a PLAY or NOVEL. A given subplot may be designed to mirror, intensify, or enhance the main PLOT, as in the subplot of Bottom and the amateur actors in *A Midsummer Night's Dream*, or it may be unrelated to it, as in Touchstone's wooing of the rustic Audrey in *As You Like It*. Both of these plays also show that a play or novel may have more than one subplot.

substitution   In PROSODY a reference to a FOOT in a line of verse that varies from the rest of the line. Many iambic lines, for example, begin with a trochee, a two-syllable foot in which the first syllable is stressed:

   / ˘ ˘ / ˘ / ˘ /   ˘ /
Not from the stars do I my judgment pluck

Other variations might include the insertion of a three-syllable foot, two unstressed syllables (pyrrhic) or two stressed syllables (spondee). Thus, the first line of SHAKESPEARE'S SONNET " Whén tŏ thĕ séssiŏns ŏf swéet sílĕnt thóught," contains an opening trochee and a spondee.

subtext   A term used in contemporary DRAMA to suggest the implied, rather than explicit, meaning of statements that a character makes. In the plays of Anton

Chekhov and Harold Pinter, for example, dialogue is frequently disjointed and incomplete. As a result, the characters' remarks are on one level inappropriate or irrelevant, but on another evocative of their hidden feelings.

success manual   A term for a type of nonfiction designed to show people how to succeed in life. The prototype of the genre was Samuel Smiles's *Self-Help,* an enormously successful book published in England in 1849.

Post–Civil War America proved to be fertile ground for the success manual. With such titles as *Room at the Top* (1884) and *The Secret of Success* (1889), these manuals were addressed to young men and told them how to achieve fame and fortune. Although many of these books were published, their format was generally uniform. Written in inspirational style, they celebrated the habits of self-reliance, hard work, frugality, and old-fashioned virtue. The historian Judy Hilkey has analyzed the success manuals of this period, suggesting that these books inadvertently depicted American life in the GILDED AGE as a jungle in which survival constituted success.

Celebrated later examples of the success manual were Dale Carnegie's *How to Win Friends and Influence People* (1936) and Norman Vincent Peale's *The Power of Positive Thinking* (1952). Shepherd Mead's *How to Succeed in Business without Really Trying* (1962) successfully spoofed the genre and formed the basis of Frank Loesser's Broadway and film MUSICAL of the same title.

Judy Hilkey's study of the success manual is *Character is Capital* (1997).

suffering/sympathy   From a literary perspective, suffering and sympathy reflect an interaction in which the depiction of the former by the writer creates the latter response in the reader. But within that broad statement lie a number of specific questions, many of which fall within the concern of ETHICAL CRITICISM. Is the depiction of suffering in Dante's *Inferno*, for example, altered by the appearance that the writer is "settling scores" with old enemies? Is Dr. Samuel Johnson's response to the death of Cordelia in King Lear—"I was so shocked by Cordelia's death that I know not whether I ever endured to read again the last scenes of the play till I undertook to revise them as an editor"—an appropriate or excessive reaction? Is the sympathy extended to the horribly burned victim in Michael Ondaatje's *The English Patient* (1992) modified or withheld because of the knowledge that he is not English but a Hungarian working for the German army in an attempt to save his lover's life? These are examples of the complexity residing in authorial intention, individual sensitivity, or the social context of work.

The archetypal sufferer is the biblical Job. Job's friends assume that his suffering is punishment for his sins, while Job himself attributes it to personal malevolence on God's part. But the book itself seems merely to ratify the mystery of the ways of God to man. Unlike John Milton, who in *Paradise Lost* (1667) set out to "justify" those ways, the AUTHOR(s) of the Book of Job suggests that the divine/human relation is being played out on a vast stage beyond our comprehension. In the Romantic era, William Wordsworth stands out as the poet most profoundly concerned with the sadness of human life and its impact upon the mind of the poet coming to terms with it. In *Lyrical Ballads* (1798), Wordsworth confronts the moral question surrounding the depiction of suffering: Does it exploit the poor and the wretched in the interest of gratifying the emotional desires of the reader? Wordsworth grapples with this problem—one that would emerge in the next century in connection with literary depictions of the HOLOCAUST. In his later poems, he shifts his attention away from questions involving the morality of aesthetic pleasure derived from suffering to general questions of a metaphysical nature.

Suffering/sensitivity constitutes a central subject in the works of the great master of psychological fiction, Fyodor Dostoyevsky. In *Crime and Punishment* (1866), the young protagonist Raskolnikov successfully atones for the murder he has committed by suffering. In his notebooks, Dostoyevsky states it as a general truth: "Man must earn his happiness and only through suffering."

In his book-length study of suffering and sympathy in modern literature, the critic Walter Slatoff takes as his central text W. H. Auden's powerful poem "Musee des Beaux Arts." Auden's poem is inspired by Peter Breugel's painting "Landscape with the Fall of Icarus," which hangs in the Musee Royaux des Beaux Arts in Brussels. The famous line that begins the poem—"About suffering they were never wrong/The Old Masters. . ."—establishes Auden's theme: the lack of affect that is evident when we perceive suffering from afar. The painting provides a kind of panoramic view of the scene in which Icarus plunges to his death as an assortment of people go about their business, oblivious to the tragedy.

On the other hand, there are those who make the pain of others their own, and Slatoff analyzes literary examples of this type. In Nathaniel West's *Miss Lonelyhearts* (1933), for example, "Miss Lonelyhearts" is a newspaper man, an agony columnist, one who answers the letters of desperate people seeking advice in coping with their lives. Driven to near madness by the massive unhappiness of the city and the diabolic commentary of his editor, Shrike, he attempts to take upon himself the punishment that may redeem others, but his efforts fail, as his compassion invariably turns into violence. His violent reactions have the effect, in turn, of negating any sympathy the reader might feel for him, since his compassion appears to be the servant of a destructive force.

In contrast, Slatoff cites the example of Major Scobie, the Catholic protagonist of Graham Greene's *The Heart of the Matter* (1948). Scobie is a man so acutely aware of the pain of others and so ready to experience another's guilt, that he takes his own life despite his religious conviction that, in doing so, he is damning himself.

Miss Lonelyhearts and *The Heart of the Matter* are appropriately modern in their shifting the focus of suffering from the body to the mind, but that should not blind us to the unparalleled physical pain endured by millions in this 20th century and the horrors of the Holocaust, the GULAG, AIDS, and genocide that raged through the last century and continues in the new one.

James Averild's *Wordsworth and the Poetry of Human Suffering* (1980) offers an intelligent account of suffering as a poetic subject in Wordsworth. Walter Slatoff's *The Look of Distance* (1985) is a subtly shaded, often highly personal response to the subject of suffer-ing/sympathy. Susan Sontag's *Regarding the Pain of Others* (2004) reflects upon the subject in the light of atocities that occurred during the Bosnian War (1992–95).

supplement (*supplément*) In DECONSTRUCTION, a term used to describe the ambiguous role of WRITING. The French term *supplément* carries the meaning of "substitute" as well as an "addition," For the French theorist Jacques Derrida, writing is a *necessary* addition to speech, one that reveals the actual working of lan-guage and thought. Derrida sees writing as both a substitute for speech—that is, it is employed and read when the author is not present—and as an enhancement of speech. In this respect, writing is to speech as culture is to nature, something initially added on that eventually comes to dominate the original. Thus writing captures the "truth" of language, that it is a system of negative differences, while speech fosters the illusion of direct human contact. (*See* DECONSTRUCTION.)

surrealism An artistic and literary movement that stressed the importance of the UNCONSCIOUS in artistic creativity. The French poet and critic André Breton founded the movement in 1924, after breaking away from DADA, another highly experimental AVANT-GARDE development. Breton defined surrealism as "pure psychic automatism by means of which we propose to express either verbally, or in writing, or in some other fashion, what really goes on in the mind. Dictation by the mind unhampered by conscious control and having no aesthetic or moral goals." Out of this program the surrealists developed a series of principles that stressed the importance of dreams, the underlying logic of apparent contradic-tions, the suspect character of abstract ideals (such as those that led to World War I), and the importance of the Freudian "id" as the source of creativity for the reader as well as the writer (*See* UNCONSCIOUS, THE).

Among the leading surrealists of the '20s and '30s were the dramatist Jean Cocteau, the poet Paul Éluard, the painter Salvador Dalí, and the filmmaker Luis

Buñuel. Dalí and Buñuel collaborated on two celebrated surrealist films, *Un Chien Andalou* (1928) and *L'Age d'Or* (1930).

Like dada, surrealism proved to be more significant in its general impact than in the specific achievements of surrealist painters and writers. Surrealist techniques, such as automatic writing, discontinuous images, and extended dream sequences have exerted an important influence on contemporary literature and film. Surrealism also figured as a major influence in the formation of the leading European avant garde journal of the '60s and '70s, TEL QUEL.

Wallace Fowlie's *The Age of Surrealism* (1950) provides an insightful survey of the movement.

suspense Uncertainty about the outcome of a particular action or of the entire STORY, NOVEL, or PLAY. There are two types of suspense. The most common occurs when the audience is uncertain about what is going to happen. The second type is the suspense of FORM, in which the uncertainty lies not in *what* will happen, but *how* or when it will happen.

sweetness and light A phrase, popularized by the poet and critic Matthew Arnold in his *Culture and Anarchy* (1869), to describe the aim of high culture. For Arnold, who wrote at a time when religion was losing its power to influence behavior, the purpose of culture and literature was to emphasize the life of the spirit ("sweetness") and the mind ("light") against the chief enemy of culture, identified by Arnold as 19th-century industrialism, as embodied in the PHILISTINE.

syllepsis In RHETORIC, the use of a word that appears to be in the same relation to two or more other words, but turns out not to be. This example is from Alexander Pope's *The Rape of the Lock*:

Here thou, great Anna! whom three realms obey
Dost sometimes counsel take—and sometimes tea.

Counsel and *tea* are the direct objects of the verb *take,* but the wit of the lines is that the two words are mutually incompatible because of the double meaning of the verb.

The rhetorician Richard Lanham argues, however, that the above definition should be applied to another figure of speech, ZEUGMA. Syllepsis, according to Lanham, should be restricted to cases in which a verb does not agree with at least one of its subjects.

Richard Lanham states his position in his *A Handlist of Rhetorical Terms* (second edition, 1991).

symbol   A widely used term in many disciplines, referring to the process by which a person, place, object, or event comes to stand for some abstract idea or condition. As normally used in literary study, symbol suggests a connection between the ordinary sense of reality and a moral or spiritual order. It differs from METAPHOR in that the connection between the subject and its referent is never explicit; it is left for the reader to discover. For example, in what is probably the most famous symbol in American literature, the White Whale in Herman Melville's *Moby-Dick* (1851), the reader is never told what the whale specifically represents. Instead, the figure seems to radiate a range of shifting, fragile meanings, some specific, others infinite in their extension, aspects of existence that would be otherwise inexpressible.

The example of the whale suggests another important aspect of the symbol: it should not be an arbitrary intrusion into the TEXT but should have a function on the literal level of the STORY. Whatever else the whale represents, it should never cease to be a whale.

Critics frequently employ the verb "embody" to suggest the action of the symbol: It does not so much point to its meaning as embody it. In the words of Samuel Taylor Coleridge, "It partakes of the reality that it renders intelligible." Thus the symbol is by definition mysterious and unresponsive to any attempts to establish a one-to-one relationship. Paul De Man, a prominent exponent of DECONSTRUCTION, takes exception to this view. In an essay titled "The Rhetoric of Temporality," he distinguishes the symbol from ALLEGORY, rejecting the idea that in the symbol, language and reality unite in a mystical fashion. For De Man, ALLEGORY is a superior FORM in that it clearly marks the gap between language and what it refers to. In fact, says De Man, so-called symbols are really allegories.

The practice of employing symbols is called *symbolism,* a term also used to describe a group of symbols within a particular text. For example, an account of the symbolism in *Moby-Dick* would include Ahab's wooden leg, the coin fixed to the mast, the names of the major characters, all combining to suggest a religious, moral, philosophical, and finally unfathomable mystery. The term *Freudian symbolism* refers to the assignment of particular significance to objects as they appear in dreams.

The mysteriousness of a symbol often makes it difficult for the reader to recognize whether a given image or event is literal or symbolic. This uncertainty is further complicated by the possibility that a symbol may be a product of the author's UNCONSCIOUS, and thus vigorously denied by that author. Another source of uncertainty is that, as Freud is alleged to have said, "Sometimes a cigar is just a cigar."

An insightful treatment is William York Tindall's *The Literary Symbol* (1965). Paul De Man's essay appears in his *Allegories of Reading* (1979).

symbolic action   A term coined by the critic Kenneth Burke to argue that a literary work is a special FORM of act, comparable to a physical act. Thus, for example, a dramatic tragedy is not just, as in Aristotle's definition, "an imitation of an act"; the imitation is itself an act, moving through a series of dialectical transitions of "purpose, passion, and perception." *See also* SPEECH ACT THEORY.

Kenneth Burke's *Language as Symbolic Action* (1966) is a collection of essays illustrating his theory.

symbolists   A term used to describe a group of 19th-century French poets who had a powerful effect on 20th-century literature. The chief aim of the symbolists was to render POETRY as a FORM of MUSIC—that is, to make it an art of immediate presentation, evoking in its readers a mood rather than a moral or intellectual response. The goal of poetry was not to represent nature; neither was it to be the expression of the poet. The symbolist view is that a poem should be an aesthetic object formed from the union of imagination and nature.

A central feature of this union was the principle of correspondence, articulated by Charles Baudelaire, the poet usually identified as the originator of the symbolist movement. Correspondence argues that everything in the mind corresponds to something in nature and that everything in nature corresponds to something in the world of spirit. It is this principle that implies the idea carried by the term SYMBOL.

Baudelaire's poetic successors included Arthur Rimbaud, Paul Verlaine, and Stephané Mallarmé. Their influence extended well into the 20th century in the poetry of Paul Valéry and Paul Claudel and in the fiction of Marcel Proust. The doctrine of the symbolists has had a profound effect as well on the poetry of Ezra Pound, T. S. Eliot, William Butler Yeats, Wallace Stevens, and the FICTION of D. H. Lawrence. In DRAMA, the movement flourished in France at the turn of the century. Among notable symbolist plays are Villiers de Lisle-Adam's *Axel* (1884) and Maurice Maeterlinck's *Pelléas and Mélisande* (1892).

Two classic studies of the subject are Arthur Symons's *The Symbolist Movement in Literature* (1899) and Edmund Wilson's *Axel's Castle* (1931).

syncope   In PROSODY, a form of contraction in which a consonant is dropped from the middle of a word in order to conform to the regular meter of a line. Words such as *o'er* and *ne'er* that contract two-syllable words into one syllable are common examples, as in Alexander Pope's definition of WIT:

What oft was thought but ne'er so well expressed

The above line, in using *oft* for *often* illustrates another common metrical feature, apocope, subtraction from the end of a word rather than the middle. The elision of a syllable from the beginning of a word, usually a vowel, is termed aphaeresis.

synecdoche   A figure of speech in which the part stands for the whole or the whole for the part. Examples include hearts or hands for people, as in "We need brave hearts and steady hands." Whole-for-the-part synecdoche is evident in expressions such as "The police are investigating the case" for "some police."

Synecdoche is sometimes included under the general heading of METONYMY.

synoptic gospels   A term for the gospels of Matthew, Mark, and Luke (but not John), which give slightly different views of the same material. As a result, most scholars agree that the earliest gospel (Mark) serves as a direct source for Matthew and Luke although some recently have argued for the primacy of Matthew. In 1776, the German biblical scholar J. J. Griesbach set out the texts in three parallel columns, enabling scholars to study their differences and similarities.

tableau In theater, a silent, static grouping of people, frequently used at the conclusion of an act or PLAY. In films the equivalent phenomenon is known as a FREEZE FRAME.

tale A loose term for any type of STORY, frequently used to describe very simple NARRATIVEs, such as a FAIRY TALE. A "tall tale" is an exaggerated or fantastic story, usually comic in its intention.

Talmud In Judaism, the body of laws known as the Mishna, as received from the PENTATEUCH, and the commentary upon those laws.

Taoism A religious/philosophical system originating in China in the sixth century B.C. The Tao is, broadly speaking, the law of nature which one follows by abandoning the illusions of the world and choosing a path of mystic contemplation.

tautology In logic and RHETORIC, a statement in which the predicate is already contained in the subject ("All bachelors are men."), or the inclusion of unnecessary words, such as the phrase, repeatedly used during the Watergate hearings, "at this point in time" for "at this time."

television drama In the early years of the medium, from the mid-1940s through the '50s, drama on television reflected two important conditions: the size of the screen and the fact that most presentations were "live," telecast as they were performed.

The small size of the early TV sets dictated an intimate, "indoors" type of drama with an emphasis on character and dialogue rather than action. In this respect, TV plays were closely allied to stage drama. With the coming of videotape in 1958, and the increased use of film, TV dramas moved closer to feature films, a shift resulting in an opening up of the action, but with a consequent loss of intimacy and immediacy. It also moved from being a playwright/actor's to a director/editor's medium.

During the early years, the so-called golden age of television drama in the United States, the medium attracted a number of distinctive new playwrights and plays. Among these were Paddy Chayevsky's *Marty* (1953), Reginald Rose's *Twelve Angry Men* (1954), Rod Serling's *Patterns* (1955), William Gibson's *The Miracle Worker* (1957), and J. P. Miller's *The Days of Wine and Roses* (1958). All of these television plays were later to be transformed into successful films.

Since the '60s, this type of independent work within a format dictated only by length has given way to the dominant mode of television drama, the serial. Either in the form of SOAP OPERA or in weekly comic episodes, the SITCOM, or in series related to a pre-existing genre such as the WESTERN or the DETECTIVE STORY, television drama is essentially serial drama. One variation of this fact is the mini-series and the movie of the week, which are essentially films created with the requirements of television in mind, such as commercial breaks. Among the outstanding examples of the mini-series are *Roots* (1977) and the Western *Lonesome Dove* (1989). Outstanding European examples include the BBC's *The Glittering Prizes* (1978) and Ingmar Bergman's *Scenes from a Marriage* (1973).

According to some critics, however, beyond the plays that are literal dramas, everything that appears on TV tends to be dramatized: news events, sports, commercials, even talk shows are more "scripted" than they appear to be. For some observers this has led to the observation that the power of TV rests on its ability to present all of life as a form of drama, a power that raises the question formulated by the critic Martin Esslin, "Can reality be mastered by a population nurtured on daydreams?"

Max Wilk's *The Golden Age of Television* (1976) celebrates the early years of the medium. Martin Esslin's *The Age of TV* (1982) offers a thoughtful analysis of later developments.

Tel Quel (As Is) A literary journal, begun in Paris in 1960, that became the leading voice of the AVANT-GARDE in Europe for the next two decades. From a beginning in which it remained aloof from any specific political or philosophical position, *Tel Quel* moved in the late '60s to an endorsement of radical Maoist politics, a position it repudiated in 1976. In its final issues the journal, which had spearheaded the avant-garde for 20 years, called for an end to the idea of the avant-garde, dismissing its adherents as the parrots of those in power. *Tel Quel* ceased publication in 1982. In literary theory, *Tel Quel* occupied a prominent position as the ideological home of POSTSTRUCTURALISM. The theorist Julia Kristeva was particularly associated with the journal, in whose pages she first articulated her concept of INTERTEXTUALITY.

tenor/vehicle   Two terms coined by the critic I. A. Richards to describe the two constituents of a METAPHOR. *Tenor* is Richards's term for the subject to which the metaphor applies; *vehicle,* the figure that illustrates the idea. In John Donne's "No man is an island," *man* is the tenor, *island* the vehicle.

tension   In NEW CRITICISM, a term used to describe the synthesis of conflicting elements that constitutes the unity of a poem. In this view, a poem is an example of dramatic conflict in which the play of conflicting elements is resolved in the form of PARADOX. The words of a poem, in the New Critical view, incorporate intractable, warring elements—the conflict, for example, between concrete and abstract language or between literal and metaphorical meaning. The successful poem creates a synthesis out of these conflicts.

An excellent discussion from a New Critical perspective is available in William Wimsatt and Cleanth Brooks's *Literary Criticism: A Short History* (1957).

terrorism   In its simplest sense, the use of unexpected violent force to achieve a political or social goal. In this sense it has existed throughout history in the form of individual terrorism (assassinations, the Oklahoma City bombings), state terrorism, in which the official government pursues a policy of terrorizing its own citizens (the reign of terror in the French Revolution; the government of Idi Amin in Uganda; the rule of Raphael Trujillo in the Dominican Republic; the Nazi and Stalinist governments); and organized groups seeking a specific political goal (the Basque separatists of the group ETA, the IRA, the Weatherman of the 1960s). The problem of definition is reflected in the relativism of history, in which three leaders characterized as terrorists at one point in their lives, Menachem Begin, Yassir Arafat, and Nelson Mandela, later went on to win the Nobel Peace Prize. Nevertheless, there are certain acts that can be accurately described in most of the world as terrorist. Of these an outstanding example is the September 11th, 2001, attacks on the World Trade Center and the Pentagon, which constituted a surprise attack on a civilian population working within institutions of enormous symbolic and commercial value, calculated to capture the attention of the world's media.

In this last sense of the term, modern terrorism may be said to begin in the 1860s with the repeated bombings in various English cities, set off by the Fenians, a radical subgroup of the Irish Republican Brotherhood dedicated to the principle of Irish Home Rule, that is, not independence but local rule. The bombings produced a number of novels, pro and con, one of which, *The Dynamiter* (1885) was written by Robert Louis Stevenson and his wife, Fanny. *The Dynamiter*'s title was well-chosen. Dynamite, invented by Alfred Nobel in 1863, created powerful, pervasive fear, for it could explode as if from out of nowhere, a fact that lent it a kind of demonic status in the popular imagination, producing precisely the goal the terrorists were seeking—widespread terror.

Among literary efforts to explore the mind of the terrorist, two outstanding novels are Joseph Conrad's *The Secret Agent* (1907) and *Under Western Eyes* (1911). In *The Secret Agent*, the PLOT turns on a terrorist attempt to blow up the Greenwich Observatory. The deviser of the plot explains that to engender terror, the act must seem to be entirely gratuitous, ". . . an act of destructive ferocity so absurd as to be incomprehensible, inexplicable, almost unthinkable, in fact, mad." In other words, the true terrorist act should seek targets beyond government buildings and military installations in order to enter into the lives of ordinary people, so that no place and no person feels safe. In *Under Western Eyes*, the protagonist Razumov is trapped between revolutionary terrorism and the autocratic government of the czar, a conflict Conrad describes as "senseless desperation provoked by senseless tyranny." Caught between these two extremes, Razumov, forced into becoming an undercover government agent, joins the revolutionaries and falls in love with the sister of a man he has betrayed. He undergoes penitential suffering, eventually is redeemed, but not Russian society, which Conrad sees as inevitably moving toward revolution, led by murderers and hypocrites.

In modern Northern Ireland, injustice helped to beget terrorism, especially when British troops fired on a peaceful civil rights demonstration in 1972, killing 13 civilians. This "Bloody Sunday" massacre led to the revitalization of the Irish Republican Army (IRA), whose terrorist tactics gave birth to two militant Protestant groups, whose brutality matched that of the IRA. The subsequent career of these three groups provide a powerful demonstration of the corrupting effect of prolonged terrorist activity on the community involved and on the terrorists themselves. Nurtured on violence from birth, some have difficulty managing without it. They become hard-liners, who find the traditional paramilitary groups too staid and tame. They form anarchic breakaway groups, actually more criminal than political. Two novels dealing with such groups are James Hynes's *The Wild Colonial Boy* (1990) and Eoin McNamee's *Resurrection Man* (1994). In *The Wild Colonial Boy*, a young American is duped into thinking he's aiding the IRA, when in fact he is the tool of a fanatical breakaway group determined to check any move in the direction of a peace settlement. In *Resurrection Man*, on the other hand, a young Protestant protagonist forms a group of killers, who murder people at random, carving them up as if they were statues. The two novels bring to mind William Butler Yeats's characterization of the sectarian violence in Ireland. "We have fed the heart on fantasy/ The heart has grown brutal from the fare."

In Don DeLillo's *Mao II*, (1991), the terrorist forms one side of a triangle that also includes the writer and, linking the two, their images. Bill Gray, a reclusive novelist, becomes ensnared with a terrorist group in Beirut during the Lebanese civil war in the 1980s. The terrorists, who acknowledge Mao Tse-tung as their model, are holding a well-known French poet as a hostage. The terrorist thrives on publicity, his image reproduced on the shirts his young followers (just as Andy Warhol's silk screen portraits of Mao form the cover design of the novel). The novelist seeks solitude, but his attempt to avoid publicity makes him more famous than he otherwise might be. He, too, consents to sit for a series of photographs by a woman photographer who comes to play a significant role. DeLillo creates a complex network of comparisons and contrasts between the terrorist and the novelist, with the image always a central factor until it seems to replace the real. . . . The novel concludes with the woman photographer, standing on a balcony in Beirut, watching in the dark the flash of fire from automatic weapons, only to realize that it is not the flash of automatic weapons. "Someone is out there with a camera and a flash unit. . . The dead city photographed one more time."

Alex Houen's *Terrorism and Modern Literature* (2002) explores the responses of some English and American writers, from Joseph Conrad to the Belfast poet Ciaran Carson, to terrorism. Margaret Scanlan's *Plotting Terror* (2001) examines at the literature of terror with particular attention to Northern Ireland.

tetralogy Four NOVELS or PLAYS focusing on the same characters, as in John Updike's four novels representing stages in the life of Rabbit Angstrom, or a connected series of actions, as in Shakespeare's three *Henry VI* plays and *Richard III*.

tetrameter A line of verse consisting of four feet (*see* FOOT).

text Traditionally, the words that make up a composition. With the advent of DECONSTRUCTION and POSTSTRUCTURALISM, text has taken on a much broader significance. Assuming that we are enclosed within the "prison house of language," these theorists argue that we are always inside a text whenever we use language. In this sense we can never get outside the text; for, in the famous phrase of Jacques Derrida, "There is no outside-the-text." Thus historical events, human relations, even an individual's sense of self, are "textualized," available to us only in the form of language.

The pervasiveness of textuality extends to literary texts themselves which are seen as largely constituted by other texts, the phenomenon known as INTERTEXTUALITY.

textual criticism A term for the analysis of a TEXT with the goal of determining its most authentic FORM, usually regarded as that identified with the

AUTHOR's final intention. Textual criticism often takes place as part of the process of preparing an edition of a text for publication. Errors or other corruptions, such as physical decay of the manuscripts, complicate the task of the textual critic or editor. So too can the existence of variant texts. Celebrated examples of the latter are the QUARTO and Folio versions of Shakespeare's plays. In *Othello,* for example, was it the "base Indian" (Quarto) or the "base Judean" (Folio) who threw away a pearl richer than all his tribe? This type of problem is known as a "CRUX." (*See* FIRST FOLIO.)

Nor are textual problems limited to older texts. William Butler Yeats, for example, constantly revised his poems long after their original publication. Sometimes textual editors have defied the wishes of the author and published the unauthorized version, as in the famous example of the two endings to *Great Expectations* (1860–61). When Dickens read the galley proofs of the novel, he changed the original unhappy ending, but the unanimous opinion of subsequent editors is that the original ending is superior.

In his novel *Pale Fire* (1962), Vladimir Nabokov satirizes the language and some of the assumptions of textual criticism.

James Thorpe's *Principles of Textual Criticism* (1972) provides an excellent introduction to the field.

texture   Traditionally, the distinctive, external features of a literary TEXT, those characteristics, such as IMAGERY and TONE, that are separate from its organizing principles, its FORM or STRUCTURE. In NEW CRITICISM, the density and complexity of the texture of a poem are marks of its value.

theater of cruelty   A theory of theatrical performance, designed to return theater to its primitive, ritualistic origins. The phrase was coined in the 1920s by the French dramatist Antonin Artaud. Artaud called for a theater that would liberate its audience from the repressive character of modern society, a theater not tied to a script, but one in which spontaneous improvisation would be the dominant mode of presentation.

In the 1950s and '60s, Artaud's ideas played a formative role in the development of the Living Theater in the United States and in the productions of director Jerzy Grotowski in Poland.

Antonin Artaud's *The Theater and Its Double* (1938) contains a full account of his theory.

theater of the absurd   *See* ABSURD.

theatrum mundi (theatre of the world)   A basic metaphor suggesting that the most appropriate analogy for the world is that of a vast theater in which human history is played out. In this conception, human beings play their parts—"have their exits and their entrances"—guided by a divine, invisible AUTHOR. The germ of the idea is found in Plato's *Philebus,* where he speaks of "the comedy and tragedy of life," but the first sustained treatment is in a medieval text, John of Salisbury's *Policraticus* (1159), which extends this idea to include God as both author and audience, witnessing the comedy and tragedy of human existence.

The world-as-theater conception became a dominant theme in the golden age of Spanish DRAMA in the 17th century. As the German scholar Ernst Curtius phrases it, "this theatrical metaphor, nourished on the antique and the medieval tradition, reappears in a living art of the theater and becomes the expression of a theocentric concept of human life, which neither the English nor the French drama knows." The best-known examples are the plays of Calderón de la Barca, particularly his *Life Is a Dream* (1635) and *The Great World Theatre* (1649).

The conception of the world as stage is continually invoked in the plays of Shakespeare, notably in the speeches of Jaques in *As You Like It* ("All the world's a stage"), Prospero in *The Tempest* ("Our revels now are ended"), and with piercing pessimism in Macbeth's description of life as "a poor player/That struts and frets his hour upon the stage/And then is heard no more."

In the 20th century, the Austrian dramatist Hugo von Hofmannstahl regenerated the tradition. His *The Salzburg Great Theater of the World* (1922) and *The Tower* (1925) are based upon Calderón's plays. In the former play, God summons The Rich Man, The Peasant, The Beggar, and assorted other allegorical figures to perform for him the drama of human life.

Ernst Curtius's *European Literature in the Latin Middle Ages* (1953) offers an excellent discussion of the term.

theme   A significant idea in a literary TEXT, sometimes used interchangeably with MOTIF. Theme is also used to describe a recurring idea in a number of texts. (It is used in this sense in this book in the entries on ALIENATION, DEATH, LOVE, and TIME, for example.) One problem with the varied uses of the term is the tendency to employ it as the equivalent of MORAL, as in "The theme of this novel is that mindless conformity is the greatest threat to freedom."

As a result of its ambiguous and imprecise uses, some critics have advocated abandoning the term, but its usefulness as a way of organizing the reading of a text, of connecting one text to another (*see* INTERTEXTUALITY), and of applying reading to the experience of life, appears to be indispensable to understanding literature. This is particularly true in contemporary literature, in which PLOT and CHARACTER are often obscure, while theme offers a consistent thread through which the reader can unify the narrative.

Thematic criticism (also known as "Thematics") is the term for a critical approach to literature through themes. Significant examples of the range of thematic criticism include Georges Bataille's *Literature and Evil* (1973); Leslie Fiedler's *Love and Death in the American Novel* (1966); Susan Sontag's *Illness as Metaphor* (1979), and *AIDS and Its Metaphors* (1989); and Toni Morrison's *Playing in the Dark: Whiteness and the Literary Imagination* (1992).

A perceptive overview is Russell Brown's "Theme" in *Encyclopedia of Contemporary Literary Theory*, edited by Irena Makaryk (1993). *The Return of Thematic Criticism*, edited by Werner Sollors (1993), is a collection of essays on theory and practice.

theology *See* RELIGIOUS FAITH.

theory In literature, a term used to describe the assumptions that underlie literary study. Theory should be distinguished from CRITICISM, the analysis of particular literary texts, but the two frequently overlap, if only because every act of criticism rests, consciously or unconsciously, upon a theory. Literary theory is as old as Plato and dominated for over a thousand years by Aristotle, whose *Poetics* (fourth century B.C.) is easily the most influential text in the history of literary theory.

In its current use, theory refers to the examination of basic critical principles from a variety of perspectives that include POSTSTRUCTURALISM, feminism (*see* FEMINIST CRITICISM), HERMENEUTICS, NEW HISTORICISM, and DECONSTRUCTION. These movements all focus on the way in which language shapes and orders not only the experience of literature but the totality of human experience. As a result these positions make large, quasi-philosophical claims that extend well beyond traditional literary concerns. Deriving their view of language from the writings of the Swiss linguist Ferdinand de Saussure and the adaptation of Saussure within French STRUCTURALISM, advocates of theory have cultivated an acutely critical view of the assumptions underlying traditional criticism, assumptions that include the idea of the AUTHOR, the makeup of the CANON, the nature of NARRATIVE, the roles of GENDER, CLASS, and race, and the definition of LITERATURE.

In the course of this critique, theory has given birth to a bewildering array of contesting schools of thought, each with its own terminology, as well as cultural and political agenda. In its pluralist, fragmented and de-centered character, theory might be seen as the critical handmaiden of POSTMODERNISM, which takes as its central principle a break with the "meta-narratives" or sustaining myths of the past. In their place, theory argues for the recognition that we are enclosed within "the prison house of language" where RHETORIC, not reason, governs our lives.

In the 1980s a reaction "against theory" developed that resulted in a number of critical developments, one of which was the revival of PRAGMATISM.

By the turn of the new century, the reign of theory seemed to be over, toppled by the weight of its own SKEPTICISM. Its relentless exposure of the sustaining beliefs of past and present societies had taken on a relentlessly negative, scolding tone, wittily characterized by Harold Bloom as "the school of resentment." Theory had lost sight of the fact that a major purpose of reading literature was pleasure, that people read novels and poems for the SONG, not just the sermon. Nevertheless, the effects of theory are still powerfully present, some of which give every evidence of being permanent, not least in the gains won by feminists, gays and lesbians, Marxists, and post-colonialists. Theory had escorted them to the dance.

René Wellek and Austin Warren's *Theory of Literature* (1949) is a comprehensive treatment of the subject from the standpoint of New Criticism. Terry Eagleton's *Literary Theory* (1983) is a highly readable introduction to the subject from a Marxist point of view. Eagleton's *After Theory* (2004) looks back at the weaknesses of theory and offers a program for building on its achievements.

thick description   The term used by the cultural anthropologist Clifford Geertz to describe the anthropologist's goal, that is, to probe a particular practice in a society in order to uncover the layers of meaning that underlie the practice. A number of contemporary literary critics, particularly adherents of NEW HISTORICISM, have adopted Geertz's procedures.

threnody   A lament spoken or sung on the occasion of a funeral. The concluding 15 lines of Shakespeare's "The Phoenix and the Turtle" is a threnody, celebrating the fusion of beauty (the phoenix) and fidelity (the turtle dove). The birds presumably stand for a recently deceased married couple, but the identity of the couple remains unknown.

through line   In the acting theory of Konstantin Stanislavski, the persistent goal that summarizes a character's specific purpose. The actor's task is to discover his/her character's deep intention. As treated by a dramatic critic, such a goal can assume a somewhat abstract character. Francis Ferguson, for example, describes Macbeth's through line as "to outrun the pauser, reason."

Ferguson's discussion appears in his *The Idea of a Theater* (1953).

419

time   In Western literature, two fundamental distinctions have governed the conception of time. The one, deriving from classical Greek philosophy, is the distinction between time and eternity. The other, the heritage of Hebraic thought, is the historical conception of time as a linear, uni-directional, unrepeatable series. The latter conception was significantly modified by Saint Augustine, who made a distinction between historical time and psychological time, or, as Virginia Woolf was to phrase it some 15 centuries later, "the extraordinary discrepancy between time on the clock and time in the mind." Augustine perceived historical time to be directed by Divine Providence, and, since psychological time rendered all experience in a continuous present, even "time in the mind" was a mirror of eternity.

In the RENAISSANCE this coherent and comforting compatibility of two temporal orders began to dissolve. As individual life on earth assumed greater importance (a central principle of HUMANISM), time came to be seen as a threat, the enemy of life, the agent of death. This is a view that receives its most memorable expression in Shakespeare's plays and sonnets. Here life is, in the dying Hotspur's words, "time's fool" and, even more despairingly, in Macbeth's time-obsessed expression of meaninglessness:

> To-morrow, and to-morrow, and to-morrow
> Creeps in this petty pace from day to day
> To the last syllable of recorded time,
> And all our yesterdays have lighted fools
> The way to dusty death.

The shift in interest from external to psychological time begins in the 18th-century novel, notably in Laurence Sterne's *Tristram Shandy* (1759–67). Sterne locates the action of his novel not as chronological sequences of events, but as an act of consciousness in which past, present, and future are collapsed into a continuous present. According to the critic Dorothy Van Ghent, "Sterne's project was not to have a parallel. . . until Proust wrote *Remembrance of Things Past*." Written over a period of 10 years, from 1912 to 1922, the year of his death, Proust's novel incorporated the concept of "involuntary memory," positing memory as a basic form of reality and thereby a means of transcending time.

If he anticipated Proust, Sterne directly influenced another great 20th-century novelist, his fellow Irishman James Joyce. Sterne's emphasis on the psychic dimension of time was translated by Joyce into the stream of consciousness, a technique designed to capture the temporal flow of awareness and perception. Joyce's other forays into the problem of temporality are evident in his conception of EPIPHANY, the realization of a moment that freezes time, and in the cyclical view of history that underlies his *Finnegans Wake* (1939).

The preoccupation with time—both its concept and its representation—haunts the literature of MODERNISM. This almost obsessive concern reveals itself in the preoccupation with history ("the nightmare from which I am trying to awake," as Joyce's Stephen Dedalus describes it) and the sense of coming to an end, caught, in T. S. Eliot's *The Waste Land*, in the pub owner's last call: "Hurry up, please. It's time."

Certainly one major influence on the representation of time in 20th-century literature is the theory of Albert Einstein regarding the inseparability of time and the state of motion of its observers. The relativity theory thus discarded the notion of time and space as separate entities. A highly imaginative novelistic rendering of this theory is Alan Lightman's *Einstein's Dreams* (1993), which depicts the speculative stages through which Einstein progresses to arrive at his theory. In Martin Amis's *Time's Arrow* (1991), the entire story is told in reverse, some sentences even written backwards. These experiments are responses to the imaginative challenge raised by Einstein's redefinition of time.

The obsession with time is radically evident in the uniquely 20th-century form, FILM. The process of MONTAGE renders simultaneity as sequence by cross-cutting from one perspective to another. Other basic filmic techniques such as the FLASHBACK and the DISSOLVE also invite experiments with time. Alain Resnais's *Hiroshima Mon Amour* (1959) and *Last Year at Marienbad* (1961) adroitly interweave past and present, rendering them at times indistinguishable.

In postmodern theory, time has been closely linked with the theory of narrative, particularly by the French philosopher Paul Ricoeur. Ricoeur's three-volume study *Time and Narrative* (1983–85) argues that time "becomes human time" only when it is represented in either historical or fictional narrative, a fact that gives narrative a special claim to truth.

Aspects of Time (1976), edited by C. A. Patrides, is a collection of essays on the theme of time in various authors, with an excellent overview by the editor. Ricardo Quinones's *The Renaissance Discovery of Time* (1972) looks at the theme in major writers from Dante to Milton. Patricia Tobin's *Time and the Novel* (1978) analyzes the patrilineal nature of the novel and its ramifications in novelists as diverse as Thomas Mann, Vladimir Nabokov, and Gabriel Garcia Marquez.

Times Literary Supplement (TLS)   Weekly British journal specializing in reviews of new and important books and general essays in a variety of fields.

tone   In literature, the attitude toward the subject expressed in a work. Tone usually is understood as the AUTHOR's attitude, but need not be identified with the author. When the language is ambiguous, for example, as in SHAKESPEARE'S

SONNET 94 ("They that have power to hurt"), the tone becomes increasingly difficult to determine. A common tone in contemporary literature is IRONY.

Tone should be distinguished from mood, the feeling the reader experiences. Although often identical, there are times when the tone and mood are significantly different.

topos (topic) In RHETORIC, both the material that makes up an argument and the form these arguments might take. The term is derived from the Greek word for place, which reinforces the idea that in oral cultures aids to memory were conceived of in spatial terms. The plural of *topos* is *topoi*. In his *Rhetoric,* Aristotle lists 28 valid and 10 invalid examples of *topoi*.

In literary study, *topos* is used to describe conventional literary motifs, such as CARPE DIEM or THEATRUM MUNDI.

Richard Lanham's *A Handlist of Rhetorical Terms* (second edition, 1991) provides a lively account of "the topics."

touchstone A term for a method developed by the 19th-century poet and critic Matthew Arnold "for detecting the presence or absence of high poetic quality. . ." Arnold argues (in *The Study of Poetry*, 1880) that certain lines or passages written by Homer, Dante, Shakespeare, and John Milton constitute infallible criteria for judging the value of lines placed alongside them. An example of an Arnoldian touchstone is Hamlet's dying plea to Horatio not to commit suicide:

> *If thou didst ever hold me in thy heart,*
> *Absent thee from felicity a while*
> *And in this harsh world draw thy breath in pain*
> *To tell my story.*

Among the objections of modern critics to Arnold's proposal is that its emphasis on small excerpts ignores the work as a whole. *See* ARNOLDIAN CRITICISM.

tracking shot In FILM, a SHOT in which the camera moves as it surveys a scene or follows the movement of a character. Orson Welles's *The Magnificent Ambersons* (1942) provides a number of imaginative examples of tracking shots.

tradition The idea that legitimate and identifiable lines of descent exist in literature has long been an assumption underlying literary history. Identifying the tradition, however, has often created controversy. Early in the 20th century, T. S. Eliot and other modernist writers allotted tradition a privileged place. In "Tradition and the Individual Talent," Eliot argued that the great tradition in literature is always under attack by commercial and secular forces in the modern world. The preservation of the tradition is a critical responsibility of the writer, whose innovations within the tradition keep it alive. This position was reinforced by the critic F. R. Leavis, whose *The Great Tradition* (1948) attempted to establish a clear line of English novelists who represented the tradition. Part of the controversy related to the CANON stems from the sense that the Eliot/Leavis sense of the tradition represented an attempt to dictate the terms of inclusion within the tradition.

tragedy   A form of literature that depicts the downfall of the leading character whose life, its disastrous end notwithstanding, represents something significant. In this sense, tragedy may be seen as rooted in the human need to extract a value from human mortality. Viewed from this perspective, tragedy has a positive side in its search for meaning in individual life. As a result, tragedy may be less pessimistic than COMEDY, with the latter's more limited view of individual human possibility, a fact that has become evident in recent years when the most nihilistic forms of drama are written in the comic mode (*see* ABSURD).

Like comedy, tragedy is not limited to DRAMA. Its values can appear in FICTION and POETRY, but drama is its natural expression since, as is commonly believed, it has its origins in rituals that enacted myths of dying gods and heroes. In Western literature, tragedy originated in the Greek festival of Dionysus and reached its apex in the fifth century B.C. in the plays of Aeschylus, Sophocles, and Euripides.

Classical Greece was also the site of the great analysis of tragedy, the comments of Aristotle in his *Poetics* (fourth century B.C.), which includes his famous definition of tragedy: "an imitation of an action that is serious, complete in itself, and of a certain magnitude. . . in the form of action, not narrative, through pity and fear effecting the proper purgation of these emotions." The "proper purgation" referred to in Aristotle's definition is CATHARSIS, a term that has sparked considerable controversy over the centuries. The chief conflict focuses on whether the term refers to the experience of the characters or of the audience.

Also controversial is Aristotle's concept of HAMARTIA, a mistake of judgment on the part of the hero, frequently translated as "tragic flaw." But for Aristotle plot or action is "the soul of tragedy" and character, while important, is secondary. Two other key Aristotelian terms are reversal (PERIPETEIA) and discovery (ANAGNORISIS). Discovery is the revelation to the hero of an important fact, and reversal the sudden downturn in the hero's fortunes. The two events are usually interrelated, as when Oedipus's discovery of his true identity precipitates his disaster.

The sole example of tragedy in Roman literature are the plays of Seneca. Adaptations of the Greek tragedies heavily influenced by the doctrine of

STOICISM, Seneca's dramas derive their historical importance from the role they played in RENAISSANCE tragedy, both in the ELIZABETHAN theater and in the plays of Jean Racine. The Senecan presence in Elizabethan tragedy is evident in the five-act structure and the fondness for scenes of horror and mutilation, as in Shakespeare's most Senecan play, *Titus Andronicus*. The other source of Elizabethan tragedy is its medieval heritage, which bequeathed, in narrative rather than in dramatic form, the image of life on earth as ruled by the goddess Fortune, as in John Lydgate's long narrative poem *The Fall of Princes* (c. 1438). Striving for life's prizes, one becomes attached to what Shakespeare in *Henry V* calls "Fortune's furious, fickle wheel," which moves one up to triumph and down to disaster. This description of tragedy as a "fall" was given added emphasis by its association with the primal fall of Adam. (*See* FORTUNATE FALL.)

The tradition of mixing comedy and tragedy in medieval drama was exemplified in the "merry devil" or Vice figure, who, in the Elizabethan age, was transformed into Iago, Richard III, Edmund in *King Lear,* and Bosola in John Webster's *The Duchess of Malfi.*

The next major contribution to tragedy comes in late 17th-century France in the plays of Pierre Corneille and Jean Racine, highly formal neoclassical texts that achieved a singular power and beauty.

In the 19th century the most important tragic drama appears first in Germany and later in Scandinavia. The historical tragedies of Friedrich Schiller, such as *Mary Stuart* (1800), and Goethe's *Faust Part I* (1808) exemplify the use of tragic settings for the "drama of ideas." Later in the century tragedy moves into a new mode in the realistic drama of Henrik Ibsen (*Ghosts,* 1882; *Hedda Gabler,* 1891) and the NATURALISM of August Strindberg (*The Father,* 1887; *Miss Julie,* 1889).

Despite the impressive achievements of Eugene O'Neill (*A Long Day's Journey into Night,* 1940; *The Iceman Cometh,* 1946), many critics have declared 20th-century tragedy a "dead" form, its ritualistic and metaphysical worldview now considered incompatible with modern experience. Others have argued that the tragic vision has merely shifted from stage to page, from drama to the novel. Among the great 19th- and 20th-century novels that lay claim to the designation *tragic* are Gustave Flaubert's *Madame Bovary* (1857), Leo Tolstoy's *Anna Karenina* (1875–77), Herman Melville's *Moby-Dick* (1851), Thomas Hardy's *Tess of the D'Urbervilles* (1891), Joseph Conrad's *Nostromo* (1907), and William Faulkner's *The Sound and the Fury* (1929). But the absence of novels written since World War II that have achieved tragic status suggests that the death of tragedy, replaced by a more disturbing, less dignified view of human existence, has finally occurred.

Tragedy: Vision and Form (1965), edited by Robert Corrigan, is an excellent anthology of criticism on tragedy. Among the classical theories of tragedy are Friedrich Nietzsche's

The Birth of Tragedy (1872); G. W. F. Hegel's *Aesthetics* (1835–38), translated by T. M. Knox (1975); and A. C. Bradley's *Shakespearean Tragedy* (1904). George Steiner's *The Death of Tragedy* (1961) exemplifies the argument for tragedy's demise.

tragicomedy   A play that generally incorporates both tragic and comic elements, and specifically one with a serious, even tragic, TONE that ends happily. An early type of tragicomedy was developed in 16th-century Italy and transported to JACOBEAN England, where Francis Beaumont and John Fletcher created a vogue for plays involving disguised heroines, romantic settings, and sudden reversals that warded off impending disaster. Among Beaumont and Fletcher's most popular tragicomedies were *Philaster* (1610) and *A King and No King* (1611). Shakespeare employed the form in his late "romances" such as *Cymbeline* and *The Winter's Tale*.

Tragicomedy reappeared in the German drama of the early 19th century in Georg Büchner's *Leonce and Lena* (1836) and Heinrich von Kleist's *The Prince of Homburg* (1811), both plays influenced by Shakespeare. Later in the century Henrik Ibsen experimented with the form, and Anton Chekhov revolutionized it by adopting the features of drawing room comedy but adding a tragic ending and penetrating psychological insight.

As a result tragicomedy exhibited what George Bernard Shaw called "a much deeper and grimmer entertainment than tragedy." This notion of getting beyond tragedy via comedy became a prominent feature of 20th-century drama, and of films such as Jean Renoir's *Rules of the Game* (1939). In the 1950s and '60s, the tragicomic/comitragic interplay became the dominant feature of those plays associated with the Theater of the ABSURD. As Samuel Beckett was to put it, with characteristic irony, "There's nothing funnier than unhappiness."

J. L. Styan's *Dark Comedy: The Development of Modern Comic Tragedy* (1962) analyzes the modern form. Eric Bentley's *The Life of the Drama* (1964) includes an analysis of the form.

transactional theory   A theoretical approach to literature that emphasizes the interaction of the reader and the TEXT. The critic Louise Rosenblatt first put forth the theory in *Literature as Exploration* (1938). Rosenblatt argued that literary experience is reciprocal, its meaning not to be found exclusively in the reader, as in some versions of SUBJECTIVE CRITICISM, nor in the text, as in NEW CRITICISM. Her thesis is that meaning is to be located in the transaction between the reader and text. "Under the guidance of the text, out of his own thoughts, and feelings and sensibilities, the reader makes a new ordering, the formed substance which is for him the literary work of art." Much of Rosenblatt's book focuses on the pedagogical aspects of her theory, its implications for teachers of literature.

Rosenblatt has refined her theory further in *The Reader, the Text, the Poem* (second edition, 1994).

transcendentalism   An American literary and philosophical movement that developed in New England in the 1830s and '40s. Based upon some of the ideas of the German philosopher Immanuel Kant and a variety of other sources, transcendentalism emphasized individual intuition as a central means of understanding reality. Keyed to this idea was a belief in the presence of God in nature. God's imminence produces a microcosmic world, in which everything contains within itself the laws of the universe. Thus the individual's soul mirrors the world's soul, and we can arrive at these truths by communing with the beauty and goodness of nature.

As the leading transcendentalist, Ralph Waldo Emerson, wrote in his essay *Nature* (1836), nature "is the apparition of God. . . the organ through which the universal spirit speaks to the individual and strives to lead the individual back to it." This communion with nature was the source of the term *transcendental,* as Kant had described it in his *Critique of Pure Reason* (1788): "I call all knowledge *transcendental* which is concerned, not with objects, but with our mode of knowing objects, as far as that is possible. . . ."

The dissemination of these ideas began with formation of the "Transcendental Club," an informal group that met, usually at Emerson's house in Concord, Massachusetts, between 1836 and 1844. One direct outgrowth of these meetings was the establishment of *The DIAL,* a quarterly journal that served as a vehicle of transcendentalist thought. Among the members of the club were Margaret Fuller, the first editor of *The Dial;* the novelist Nathaniel Hawthorne; Bronson Alcott, the father of Louisa May Alcott; and Henry David Thoreau, whose *Walden* (1854) exhibited a philosophy of nature and of individualism that proved to be the most important and effective expression of the movement's ideals.

American Transcendentalism (1973), edited by Brian Barbour, is a collection of critical essays on the movement.

transition   An AVANT-GARDE periodical, published in Paris from 1927 to 1938. The journal, edited by Eugène Jolas and Elliott Paul, is best known for its serialized publication of "Work in Progress," the working title of James Joyce's *Finnegans Wake* (1939).

Other contributors to the periodical included Gertrude Stein, Ernest Hemingway, and William Carlos Williams.

travel   The literature of travel has played an important role in the history of the West. In the MIDDLE AGES and the RENAISSANCE, the reports of early travelers, such as Marco Polo, made Europeans aware of the existence of people very different from themselves. These reports also excited the imaginations of readers and writers, fueling the desire for exploration and discovery.

Ironically, some of the most successful of these accounts were fictitious. One celebrated example was Sir John Mandeville's *Travels* (c. 1370). Mandeville selected an indiscriminate mix of stories and legends from various travelers, occasionally adding sensational elements, and cast the entire book as adventures he himself had undergone. The result was a book that achieved great popularity. Originally written in French, it was translated into English in 1375 and remained popular for centuries.

The Renaissance saw the reports of voyagers and explorers to the Americas, among them Sir Walter Raleigh's *The Discovery of the Large, Rich, and Beautiful Empire of Guiana* (1596) and Captain John Smith's *General History of Virginia, New England and the Summer Isles* (1624). Many of these accounts have drawn the recent attention of the practitioners of NEW HISTORICISM, who look at these texts for the cultural and imperialist values implicit in them.

The two great travel books of the 18th century are fictional, Daniel Defoe's *The Adventures of Robinson Crusoe* (1719) and Jonathan Swift's *Gulliver's Travels* (1726), but both drew on existing travel books for factual details.

The Victorian age saw a prolific outpouring of travels to exotic lands: Sir Richard Burton's *Pilgrimage to El-Medinah and Mecca* (1855–56) and Charles Doughty's *Travels in Arabia Deserta* (1888) provided an inside view of Arab life.

Frances Trollope, the mother of the novelist Anthony Trollope, wrote a very critical account of American life (*Domestic Manners of the Americans*, 1832), which created a storm of controversy. Charles Dickens's *American Notes* (1842) presented a largely complimentary picture of the emerging nation but criticized the practice of slavery. More important, however, was the account written by a French visitor, Alexis de Tocqueville. His *Democracy in America* (1838) is a classic analysis of the American experiment in democracy.

In the 20th century, the period between the two world wars saw travel literature raised to a new level. As the critic Paul Fussell points out in his *Abroad: British Literary Traveling Between the Wars* (1980), modern travel literature had integrated elements of the comic novel, the moral essay, the romance, and the war memoir. The results were engrossing and subtle narratives. Among these are T. E. Lawrence's *Seven Pillars of Wisdom* (1926), an account of his activities in fomenting a rebellion of Arab tribes against the Turks during World War I; Graham Greene's *Lawless Roads* (1939), a description of Mexico in the 1930s, and Evelyn Waugh's travel books, collected under the title *When the Going Was Good* (1946).

Among contemporary travel writers, Paul Theroux (*The Great Railway Bazaar,* 1975 and *The Old Patagonian Express,* 1979) and V. S. Naipaul (*The Middle Passage,* 1962) are outstanding.

The Art of Travel (1982), edited by Philip Dodd, is a collection of essays covering the field from early travel narratives to the present.

treatment   In FILM, the term generally used for a detailed narrative account of a proposed SCREENPLAY. The treatment includes all of the characters and scenes that would appear in the film, but omits the dialogue. Three interesting examples of the form, written by William Faulkner while employed by Warner Bros. Pictures in the 1940s, have been published as *Country Lawyer and other Stories for the Screen* (1987), edited by Louis Brodsky and Robert Hamblin.

trilogy   Three related NOVELs or DRAMAs. In classical Greek dramatic festivals, playwrights submitted three connected plays for consideration. The only extant trilogy from this period is Aeschylus's *Oresteia*, consisting of the *Agamemnon*, *Cheophoroi,* and *Eumenides*. In 20th-century American literature, a surprisingly large number of narrative trilogies were written in the first half of the 20th century by ethnic American writers. Most, but not all, of the works focused on the immigrant experience of specific ethnic groups.

trimeter   A line of verse consisting of three feet (*see* FOOT).

trivium/quadrivium   In medieval and Renaissance education, the seven liberal arts were divided into two parts: the lower division, the Trivium, consisting of grammar, rhetoric, and logic; and the upper division, the Quadrivium, which included arithmetic, geometry, astronomy, and music.

trochee   A metrical FOOT of one stressed syllable followed by an unstressed syllable.

trope   In RHETORIC, a term for figurative language that changes the meaning of words. Derived from the Greek word for "twist" or "turn," the term refers to the turning of the meaning of a word or phrase away from its literal meaning. Contemporary theorists argue that tropes exert a profound influence on many forms of thought and experience. The theorist and critic Kenneth Burke has argued that there are four "master tropes," METAPHOR, METONYMY, SYNECDOCHE, and IRONY, which help to shape all of human thought.

An entirely different sense of the term is found in LITURGICAL DRAMA, in which a trope is an elaboration of a liturgical text.

Kenneth Burke's argument is contained in "Appendix D" of his *A Grammar of Motives* (1945).

troubadours   The term for a group of poets from the 12th to the 14th centuries in the Provence section of France who composed poems and songs in praise of love. The troubadours composed the music as well as the lyrics of their songs, which celebrated the idea of COURTLY LOVE.

trouvères   Medieval poets in northern France who were influenced by the TROUBADOURS. The best known of the trouvères is Chrétien de Troyes, whose *Lancelot, or The Knight of the Cart* (c. 1170) and *Percival, or the Story of the Grail* (c. 1190) are the first important literary treatments of the ARTHURIAN LEGEND.

two cultures   A phrase coined in 1959 by the English novelist and scientist C. P. Snow to dramatize the gap in knowledge that exists between scientists and humanists. Snow charged that the traditional humanist was guilty of an anti scientific bias rooted in ignorance of scientific method. His argument was answered by F. R. Leavis, the most influential English critic of his day, in a spirited *ad hominem* attack: *Two Cultures: The Significance of C. P. Snow* (1963). The controversy helped to foster the contemporary movement toward interdisciplinary studies. *See* SCIENCE.

Beyond the Two Cultures (1990), edited by Joseph Slade and Judith Lee, is a collection of essays exploring the interaction of science, technology, and literature.

typology   A mode of interpreting the BIBLE in which a character or event in the Old Testament is viewed as an anticipation, or *type,* of a character or event in the New Testament. Thus biblical interpreters saw Melchizedek, the high priest who blessed Abraham, as a *type* of Jesus Christ. Another term for this practice is figuration.

U

Ulster cycle   In early Irish literature, the term for a group of myths and legends set in Ulster, the northernmost of the four provinces of Ireland. The Ulster cycle deals with the exploits of the legendary hero Cuchullan. In the best-known of these tales, "The Cattle Raid at Cooley," Cuchullan singlehandedly defeats an invading army. *See* FENIAN CYCLE.

ultraism (*ultraismo*)   A literary movement founded in 1919 by a group of Spanish poets who argued for a "pure" poetry free from the constraints of logic or traditional form. The ultraists employed FREE VERSE and favored unusual discon- nected images. In the 1920s, the Argentinian writer Jorge Luis Borges introduced the movement to South America. Best known for his stories and essays, Borges's early poems exhibit a strong ultraistic influence.

unconscious, the   The theory, developed by Sigmund Freud, that a significant dimension of the human psyche is hidden from the conscious mind, because the rational consciousness is merely the tip of an iceberg made up largely of an unconscious, instinctual force.

For Freud, the mind in its totality is divided into three major areas: the ordinarily rational, though partly unconscious, governing principle (designated the "ego" by Freud); the force of instinctive energy (the "id"); and another largely unconscious element, the censoring voice of parent and society (the "superego").

The task of psychoanalysis, in Freud's words, is "to strengthen the ego, make it more independent of the superego. . . and so to extend its organization that it can take over new portions of the id. Where id was, there shall ego be."

The impact of this view on literature, as on life in the 20th century, has been profound and pervasive. Of particular note is Freud's view that dreams represent the conflict of id, ego, and superego in narrative form, thus suggesting that, like dreams, literature fulfills a seminal purpose: gratifying instinctual wishes in a disguised, sublimated form.

The Swiss psychologist Carl Jung moved Freud's concept of a personal unconscious in a striking direction by positing the existence of a "collective unconscious"—the seat of certain psychic instincts that are inherent in all human beings. Jung's theories have formed the basis of modern MYTH CRITICISM.

The French psychologist Jacques Lacan has created the most important development in the theory of the unconscious since Jung. For Lacan, the "unconscious is structured like a language." That is, the language of the superego, the language of parent and society, occupies the unconscious like an invading army. Thus, for Lacan, the shaping power of language operates at the deepest level of the human mind (see PSYCHOANALYTICAL CRITICISM).

Although most of modern literature has been affected by these theories, the one work regarded as extraordinary in its attempt to represent the unconscious is James Joyce's audacious, pun-filled *Finnegans Wake* (1939), a novel that, at one point, describes a character as "jung and easily freudened."

Sigmund Freud's *An Outline of Psychoanalysis* (1940), Carl Jung's *The Structure and Dynamics of the Psyche* (1960), and Jacques Lacan's *Écrits* (1977) are three basic texts on the unconscious.

underground   In current use, a term denoting 1) AVANT-GARDE movements in film, or 2) a psychological state of resistance to prevailing modes of thought and behavior.

1. *Underground cinema* is a term for the experimental, avant-garde films designed to shock, exasperate, or bore viewers. Andy Warhol's *Empire* (1964), a film that shows a view of the Empire State Building from a stationary camera for eight hours, is an extreme example of the form.

2. As a psychological condition depicting ALIENATION, *underground* is a metaphor sustaining three important modern texts: Dostoyevsky's *Notes from the Underground* (1864), Richard Wright's "The Man Who Lived Underground" (1949), and Ralph Ellison's *Invisible Man* (1952).

underworld, the   In classical mythology, the world of the dead. The underworld, ruled by the god Hades (Pluto) and his wife Persephone (Proserpina), was the domain of all dead people, both good and bad, although beneath Hades lay Tartarus, reserved for those who had been thoroughly evil. Visitations to the underworld form major episodes in the classical epics, Homer's *Odyssey* and Virgil's *Aeneid*. In mythology, the 12th labor of Heracles (Hercules) required a descent into the underworld to rescue Theseus. Orpheus's attempt to rescue Eurydice is another celebrated myth. In Euripides' tragicomedy, *Alcestis,* Heracles rescues the self-sacrificing Alcestis from the underworld.

unities, the   In DRAMA, a term for the three categories of single time, place, and action that neoclassical critics insisted were necessary elements in all tragedies. These critics invoked the authority of Aristotle's *Poetics* to support their claim that a tragedy should take place in a single day, in a single setting, focusing on a single action. Although these "rules" misrepresented Aristotle, whose comments were descriptive, not prescriptive, they played a powerful role in French drama during the 17th and 18th centuries. (*See* NEOCLASSICISM.)

universality   Traditionally in literary studies, the claim that great literature transcends the limits of time and place. A celebrated expression of this view is Ben Jonson's tribute to Shakespeare, "He was not of an age but for all times." This view has been vigorously contested by Marxist critics (*see* MARXIST CRITICISM) who view the claim of universality as an attempt to aestheticize and de-historicize literature and, therefore, to render it an unacknowledged servant of bourgeois ideology.   In a similar fashion, proponents of NEW HISTORICISM see literature as inextricably caught up in a network of interactive social practices existing in a particular time and place. In *Textual Power* (1988), Robert Scholes puts the case succinctly, "If human nature is always and everywhere the same, then it follows that every literary text may express aspects of that great universal truth. But if human beings are constituted differently in different cultural situations, then the varieties of literature must be seen as temporal rather than eternal." Scholes goes on to assert that the limits of time and place apply as well to "a loss of faith in the universal wisdom of the author. . ."

Defenders of the traditional view concede that Ben Jonson overstated the case in his "not of an age" phrase. All authors are, of course, shaped and fashioned by their particular culture. But as Aristotle long ago pointed out, the universality of the author and his work is rooted in the historical here and now. That is, the nature of literature is to express the presence of the universal in the particular, a phenomenon expressed in literary study by the term SYMBOL. This, according to Aristotle, is what distinguishes literature from history, the latter representing the particular in the particular. Moreover, the principle of universality refers to the capacity not to reveal an imagined truth but to engage continuing generations of readers or viewers to the extent that they create new meanings, rather than echoing traditional ones. (*See also* CONCRETE UNIVERSAL.)

University Wits   A term used to describe a group of Oxford and Cambridge graduates who descended on London at the height of the ELIZABETHAN age and contributed significantly to the era's great achievements in DRAMA and POETRY. The wits were not an organized school or movement; they stand as prototypes of the young writer determined to make his mark in the big city.

The greatest of the wits was Christopher Marlowe, whose "mighty line" established BLANK VERSE as the standard form in Elizabethan drama. Others included John Lyly, George Peele, Thomas Nashe, Thomas Lodge, Samuel Daniel, and Robert Greene. Greene is the author of *Greene's Groatsworth of Wit* (1592), a pamphlet in which he warns his fellow university men of the appearance of an "upstart crow, beautified with our feathers, that with his tiger's heart wrapped in a player's hide, supposes he is well able to bombast out a blank verse as the best of you. . . [who] is in his own conceit the only Shake-scene in a country." Greene's remark represents the first reference to Shakespeare as a London playwright.

For a concise account of the Greene reference to Shakespeare, see S. Schoenbaum's *William Shakespeare: A Compact Documentary Life* (1977).

utopia   A generic term for a work that describes an ideal community or state. The term itself derives from St. Thomas More's *Utopia* (1516), but the form dates back to Plato's *Republic* (fourth century B.C.). Plato envisions a state ruled by philosopher-kings in which the family, religion, and poetry are de-emphasized if not eliminated altogether. More's *Utopia,* on the other hand, is notable for its benign socialism, toleration of religious differences and contempt for money. It also introduces a recurrent feature of utopian literature: the implied critique of the actual society in which the author lives.

Later utopias have included Tommaso Campanella's *City of the Sun* (1623), Francis Bacon's *New Atlantis* (1626), Edward Bellamy's *Looking Backward* (1887), William Morris's *News From Nowhere* (1891), and H. G. Wells's *A Modern Utopia* (1905).

Twentieth-century literature, more skeptical about ideal states and fearful of totalitarian thought control, has emphasized the anti-utopian or dystopian novel. Among these are Aldous Huxley's *Brave New World* (1932), George Orwell's *1984* (1949), Evelyn Waugh's *Love Among The Ruins* (1953), and Ursula K. LeGuin's *The Dispossessed* (1974). In these novels the future is depicted as a nightmare world of state or corporate control and of de-humanized mechanization.

Peter Ruppert's *Reader in a Strange Land: The Activity of Reading Literary Utopias* (1986) is an interesting account given from the perspective of the reader's experience.

$\mathcal{V}$

---

value judgment   A judgment rooted in one's personal principles or cultural taste. In literary study the problem of values focuses on two questions: the relationship of INTERPRETATION to value judgments—the connection, if any, between one's understanding of a text and one's sense of its quality—and the validity of value judgments in general. In some situations interpretation and evaluation obviously interact, as in a newspaper or magazine REVIEW of a book or film. The reviewer's evaluation is usually part of her interpretation, as in Pauline Kael's evaluative description of the film *Dances With Wolves* (1990): "a nature boy movie, a kid's dream of being an Indian." But many interpretations strive to suspend evaluation, operating on the principle that value judgments are, in Northrop Frye's words, "the donkey's carrot of literary criticism" which always turns out to be "an illusion of the history of taste." According to Frye, the statement that Shakespeare is one of the great poets of the world is a value judgment disguised as a fact and "not a shred of systematic criticism can ever be attached to it."

   This objection to value judgments has taken a more aggressive stance in some MARXIST CRITICISM, which sees the critical preference for FORM over CONTENT as an example of the HEGEMONY of the dominant classes, their controlling role in the formation of cultural opinion. For others, the questions concerning value judgments (Who makes them? Who benefits from them?) is relevant to the debate over the CANON or the distinction between high and popular culture, a central concern of CULTURAL STUDIES.

Northrop Frye's position is detailed in *Anatomy of Criticism* (1957). The Marxist position is rendered in Pierre Bourdieu's *Distinction: A Social Critique of the Judgement of Taste* (1984). Barbara Herrnstein Smith's *Contingencies of Value* (1988) is a subtle and comprehensive treatment of the subject.

vampirism   The theme of a dead person come back to life to suck the blood of a living person appears in ancient folklore, but the vampire figure is a relatively recent addition to Western folklore. The modern birth of the vampire may be said to begin in 1816 at a soirée hosted by Lord Byron in his home in Geneva. At the party, Byron asked each of his guests to write a horror story. Out of that invitation emerged two novels, Mary Shelley's *Frankenstein* (1818) and John Polidoris's *The Vampyre* (1829), the former justly famous in itself, the latter for its status as the first vampire novel in English. A much more accomplished example of the genre is Sheridan Le Fanu's *Camilla* (1872), a short novel in which both vampire and victim are women, giving rise to the suspicion that the story exhibits an unacknowledged lesbian theme. Twenty-five years later appeared the novel that continues to dominate and define the genre, Bram Stoker's *Dracula* (1897). A classic example of gothic fiction (*see* GOTHIC NOVEL), Dracula is set in a ruined castle in Transylvania, presided over by an evil count, intent on drinking the blood of virginal young women.

The continuation of the Dracula story owes much to two classic films based on Stoker's novel. The first of these is F. W. Murnau's *Nosferatu* (1922). Murnau changed the names of the characters and its setting in an attempt to avoid paying royalties to Stoker's widow. He failed and in the process almost destroyed his great example of cinematic EXPRESSIONISM. The second film, familiar to all moviegoers, is Tod Browning's *Dracula* (1931), with Bela Lugosi as the count. Though lacking the artistic merit of *Nosferatu*, this film and Lugosi's performance captured a worldwide audience. The result has been a host of sequels on stage as well as screen. Notable among these is Frank Langella's *Dracula* in a 1977 stage production and 1979 film.

The popularity of Dracula has played a major role in the resurgence of popular vampire fiction in the latter half of the 20th century. Notable examples are Stephen King's *'Salem's Lot* (1975) and Chelsea Quinn Yarbro's vampire novels, such as *Hotel Transylvania* (1977), in which the vampire is presented as a good man, who must have blood in order to survive and limits himself to willing victims.

But the most significant of recent vampire fiction is Anne Rice's five-volume *The Vampire Chronicles* (1985–95), featuring the vampire Lestat and told in passionate language that offers explicit descriptions of the erotic-verging-on-religious texture of vampiric existence.

Leonard Wolf's *Dracula: The Connoisseur's Guide* (1997) is a lively, well-informed celebration of vampirism.

vaudeville   The American equivalent of the British MUSIC HALL, vaudeville entertainment enjoyed great popularity in the late 19th and early 20th centuries. A true variety show, a vaudeville performance might include singers, dancers, animal acts, jugglers, acrobats, magicians, dramatic soliloquies, and slapstick comedy.

The popularity of motion pictures, particularly "talkies" spelled the end of vaudeville in the 1920s, although the format survived on television for many years on the *Ed Sullivan Show*. Neil Simon's play (later film) *The Sunshine Boys* (1972, 1975) evokes the era through the aging eyes of two former comics.

vernacular theory   Term used to describe the exposure of the cultural assumptions underlying social practices by ordinary people, not just academic theorists. First employed by the African-American critic Houston Baker to describe RAP music as a form of resistance to, and DECONSTRUCTION of, popular culture, the term has been adapted by the critic Thomas McLoughlin to refer to various grassroots movements, as examples of the shrewd, incisive, independent thinking associated with the term *street smarts*.

Houston Baker's position is developed in his *Blues, Ideology and Afro American Literature* (1984). Thomas McLoughlin's case is outlined in *Street Smarts and Critical Theory: Listening to the Vernacular* (1996).

verse   Term with a number of definitions, some of them overlapping. In its most general sense it is a synonym for POETRY but in its more restricted sense it refers to poems written in more or less regular METER, as opposed, for example, to FREE VERSE. In yet another sense it refers to a less intense, less serious form of poetry, as in LIGHT VERSE. In relation to the Bible, it refers to a basic subdivision of the book.

vers libre   *See* FREE VERSE.

Vice, the   In the medieval MORALITY PLAY, a villainous character. He often functioned as a diabolical figure, seducing and corrupting other characters by trickery and deceit. In asides to the audience, he frequently displayed a cynical wit that made him paradoxically appealing. The Vice is thought to be the prototype of some of Shakespeare's most notable villains, such as Iago in *Othello* and Edmund in *King Lear*.

Bernard Spivack's *Shakespeare and the Allegory of Evil* (1958) offers a detailed account of the Vice.

Victorian   In English literature, the period covered by the reign of Queen Victoria from 1837 to 1901. During these 64 years, England experienced the apex of its ascendancy as a world power, having established an empire "on which the sun never set." At home, England became the first nation to become fully industrialized, which turned out to be a mixed blessing, creating as it did massive social problems brought about by urban slums and social dissension.

In literature, the social upheaval proved grist for the mill of novelists who probed the connections between the individual and his or her rapidly changing society. The major novels of the period suggest its literary wealth: William Makepeace Thackeray's *Vanity Fair,* George Eliot's *Middlemarch,* Charlotte Brontë's *Jane Eyre,* Emily Brontë's *Wuthering Heights,* Thomas Hardy's *Tess of the D'Urbervilles,* George Meredith's *The Ordeal of Richard Feverel,* Anthony Trollope's *The Warden,* Joseph Conrad's *Lord Jim,* and any one of a half dozen novels by Charles Dickens.

In poetry, the great Victorian names include Alfred, Lord Tennyson, Robert Browning, Elizabeth Barrett Browning, Gerard Manley Hopkins, Matthew Arnold, Dante Rossetti, Algernon Swinburne, and the young William Butler Yeats.

This was also the age of the "Victorian sage," distinguished thinkers and men of letters such as Thomas Carlyle, Cardinal Newman, John Stuart Mill, John Ruskin, William Morris, and the man whose theories traumatized and transformed the age, Charles Darwin.

Jerome Buckley's *The Victorian Temper* (1951) provides a concise, perceptive summary of the period. J. Hillis Miller's *The Forms of Victorian Fiction* (1968) is an early example of a poststructuralist approach to its subject. Elaine Showalter's *A Literature of Their Own: British Women Novelists from Brontë to Lessing* (1977) is a challenging feminist reading, particularly of *Jane Eyre.*

villain   The chief evil CHARACTER in a DRAMA or story. Usually, the villain is the antagonist to the HERO but sometimes is the PROTAGONIST or chief character, as in Shakespeare's *Richard III* and *Macbeth.* The villain/hero is also a regular feature of the GANGSTER FILM.

villanelle   A short poem on a pastoral subject, introduced to France from Italy in the 16th century. The original form of the villanelle was open and unrestrained, but as it developed it assumed a fixed form: a 19-line poem consisting of five three-line stanzas and one quatrain.

Among 20th-century poets who have employed the form are Ezra Pound ("The Psychological Hour"), Dylan Thomas ("Do not go gentle into that good night"), and Theodore Roethke ("The Waking").

Vulgate, the   A term for the Latin translation of the BIBLE, completed at the beginning of the fifth century by Saint Jerome. The first printed book, the Gutenberg Bible of 1456, was an edition of the Vulgate.

war   The opening line of Virgil's _Aeneid,_ "Of arms and the man, I sing," reminds us that, along with Homer's _Iliad,_ it stands as the great source of war literature in the Western tradition. Until the 20th century, that tradition has tended to celebrate, frequently to romanticize and idealize, war. For the greatest part of its existence, war literature has played a role comparable to martial music, stirring the emotions and heating the blood. In its defense, much of traditional war literature has praised not war, but instead the warrior, "the man" in Virgil's line. The heroic virtues of courage in the face of danger, the endurance of suffering, and the willingness to face death are always evident in war, frequently obscuring the senselessness of the war itself.

The genre linked closely to war is the EPIC, since it offers the scope for the depiction of battles and heroism on a grand scale. Such are the depictions in the medieval epics _Beowulf, El Cid,_ and _Song of Roland._ In that tradition is the work commonly regarded as the greatest war novel, Tolstoy's _War and Peace_ (1865–69). A panoramic vision of a society at war, the novel ranges from domestic scenes to the battlefield, from the experience of the soldier to the deliberations of the generals, bringing it all to life with a master's touch. In Tolstoy's hands, war becomes a subdivision of history, part of a vast impersonal force, that defines, even as it destroys, human life.

On a much smaller scale, but with no less poignance, is an American masterpiece, Stephen Crane's _The Red Badge of Courage_ (1895), with its description of a young boy's awakening from the dream of war to the reality. Crane's realism anticipated the great antiwar reaction that followed World War I, described by Ernest Hemingway as "the most colossal, murderous, mismanaged butchery that has ever taken place on earth." Capturing that experience in poetry laced with anger and irony were a group of young English poets including Siegfried Sassoon, Wilfred Owen, Isaac Rosenberg, and David Jones. Their vivid descriptions of life in the trenches, written both as poetry and in memoir form, created a picture that validates Hemingway's comment, as did his own novel _A Farewell to Arms_ (1929).

Little of that anger is apparent in the literature of World War II, an indication of the all but unanimous view of that particular war as a necessary, unavoidable event.

The following lines from Norman Mailer's *The Naked and the Dead* (1948) could describe war's primitive appeal:

> It was all covered with tedium and routine, regulation and procedure, and yet there was a naked quivering heart to it, which involved you deeply when you were thrust into it. All the deep, dark urges of man . . . weren't all of them contained in the shattering screaming burst of a shell, the man-made thunder and light?

A more influential view of war emerged from Joseph Heller's *Catch-22* (1961), which depicted it as the deadly setting for an all-powerful bureaucracy. Heller's novel became one of the touchstones of resistance to the draft in the 1960s.

Among the books that have emerged from the Vietnam War, the most celebrated are Michael Herr's nonfictional *Dispatches* (1977), an impressionistic journal, and Tim O'Brien's powerful novel *Going after Cacciato* (1978).

FILM

Many war films are designed to serve as PROPAGANDA, but the best of them have been produced from a postwar, and usually more balanced, realistic perspective. Thus a typical American film made during World War I was titled *The Kaiser: Beast of Berlin* (1918), while years later King Vidor's *The Big Parade* (1925) captured that war as experienced by ordinary soldiers. Similarly in World War II, *Back to Bataan* (1945) depicted a machine gun–toting John Wayne triumphing over impossible odds, while the postwar *Twelve O'Clock High* (1949) captured the nerve-wracking intensity of airmen flying bomber attacks over Germany, and Stephen Spielberg's *Saving Private Ryan* (1998) vividly rendered the large-scale slaughter and dismemberment of the battlefield. In the Vietnam War the contrast was evident in the vast difference in tone and attitude between *The Green Berets* (1968), directed by and starring John Wayne, and Oliver Stone's *Platoon* (1986), a powerful critique of America's involvement in Vietnam.

Platoon also represents a sub-genre, the antiwar film, the most notable examples of this type being Lewis Milestone's *All Quiet on the Western Front* (1930), Jean Renoir's *Grand Illusion* (1937), and Stanley Kubrick's *Paths of Glory* (1957). *Grand Illusion* might also stand for another sub-genre, the prisoner-of-war film, another outstanding example of which is David Lean's *The Bridge on the River Kwai* (1957).

Still another sub-genre is the historical war film. Among examples of this type are D. W. Griffith's *The Birth of a Nation* (1915), Sergei Eisenstein's epic

Alexander Nevsky (1938), and John Huston's *The Red Badge of Courage* (1951). The Griffith and Huston films focus on the American Civil War, which is represented most memorably in the Ken Burns documentary *The Civil War* (1990).

A spectacularly successful hybrid of war film and SCIENCE FICTION is the original Star Wars trilogy: *Star Wars* (1977), *The Empire Strikes Back* (1981), and *Return of the Jedi* (1984).

Men at War, edited by Ernest Hemingway (1942), is an interesting wartime collection of war stories from the classical period to modern times, containing a lengthy introduction by Hemingway. Jeffrey Walsh's *American War Literature 1914 to Vietnam* (1982) covers the relevant fiction and poetry of the period. Brock Garland's *War Movies* (1987) provides a brief history of the genre and entries on 450 films.

well-made play (*pièce bien faite*)   A play that is skillfully constructed to please the audience, but lacks the substance and complexity of serious DRAMA. The term originally described the 19th-century plays of Eugène Scribe, a phenomenally successful French playwright. Scribe's formula included a plot based upon a secret that is not revealed until the climactic moment of the play, and the building up of suspense by such tried and true devices as mistaken identities, hidden clues, and letters delivered to the wrong person. Immediately prior to the climactic revelation, the protagonist would be reduced to despair, only to emerge triumphant once the secret is revealed. Scribe produced literally hundreds of plays, very few of which are ever revived; nevertheless he exerted a powerful influence on subsequent drama, not only in France but throughout Europe. Among the major playwrights influenced by Scribe was Henrik Ibsen, who employed many of his techniques in his own plays (*Hedda Gabler,* 1882; *A Doll's House,* 1886).

The popularity of Scribe's plays was matched by that of his disciple Victorien Sardou, whose well-made plays include *La Tosca* (1887), later (1900) the basis of Puccini's opera of the same name.

John Russell Taylor's *The Rise and Fall of the Well-Made Play* (1967) traces the history of the form in 19th- and 20th-century drama.

western, the   In literature and film, fictional accounts of life on the American western frontier, usually focusing on the adventures of a cowboy hero. Western literature combines action and romance so that the individual's relation to his natural environment and his sense of his own integrity play significant roles. The western hero is typically a man with a personal code of behavior and a strong attachment to the outdoors. The prototypes of the GENRE are James Fenimore

Cooper's *Leatherstocking Tales* (1823–41), five novels depicting life on the frontier. Cooper's novels gained an international audience and were widely imitated. One form the imitation took was the popular DIME NOVEL, which offered a more sensationalized and simplified view of the West. Dime novels commanded a large readership until well into the 1890s.

By the beginning of the new century, the sense of the end of the frontier created a nostalgia for the Old West that was fed by the highly successful Owen Wister novel *The Virginian* (1902). This novel offered for the first time a hero who was to be the model for subsequent Westerns: a free spirit and rugged individualist whose reaction to an insult was to draw his pistol and reply "When you call me that, smile." Popular successors to Wister have included Zane Grey (*Riders of the Purple Sage*, 1912), Ernest Haycox (*The Border Trumpet*, 1939), Luke Short (the pen name of Frederick Gildedden), and Louis L'Amour (*Where the Long Grass Grows*, 1976).

While these novels continued the cowboy formula created by Wister, a significant departure from this type is evident in the work of Walter Van Tilburg Clark (*The Oxbow Incident*, 1940), A. B. Guthrie (*The Big Sky*, 1947), and Larry McMurtry (*Lonesome Dove*, 1985). An extraordinary new figure who might transform the genre is Cormac McCarthy. His *All the Pretty Horses* (1992) and *The Crossing* (1994) combine powerful descriptive prose with a bleak and desolate vision of the ultimate western scene: a human being astride a horse, alone in nature.

FILM

Although there are earlier examples of the genre, the film western achieved its first notable expression in E. S. Porter's *The Great Train Robbery* (1903), a 12-minute silent one-reeler, filmed in the wilds of New Jersey. The first of the great cowboy heroes was William S. Hart, whose many films were distinguished by a gritty realism that to some extent deglamorized the western myth.

Hart's realism gave way to heroes like Tom Mix, whose character was as unspotted as his costume. With sound came the singing cowboys, Roy Rogers and Gene Autry. Their yodeling banality marked a sharp contrast to the films of the western's greatest director, John Ford. Ford's best work (*Stage Coach*, 1939; *My Darling Clementine*, 1946; *Fort Apache*, 1948; *The Searchers*, 1956; *The Man Who Shot Liberty Valance*, 1961) maintained the traditional conventions while infusing them with the vitality of his personal vision of the West, a land in which natural grandeur and human heroism merged.

The post-Ford western saw the innovations of Sam Peckinpah (*The Wild Bunch*, 1969). Foreign imitations, the spaghetti Westerns of the 1960s (so called because they were Italian productions), introduced Clint Eastwood, the successor to John Wayne as the prototypical cowboy hero. Eastwood's *The Unforgiven* was the most honored film of the year in 1992, serving as a reminder of the seemingly inexhaustible vitality of the genre. Another example of that vitality: Ang Lee's *Brokeback Mountain* (2005), centering on a homosexual love affair between two ranch hands.

A pioneering study of the West from the mythic perspective is Henry Nash Smith's *Virgin Land: The American West as Symbol and Myth* (1950); Will Wright offers an interesting and provocative analysis in his *Six Guns and Society: A Structural Study of the Western* (1975); George Feinim and William Everson's *The Western: From Silence to Cinerama* (1962) offers a useful survey of the film genre.

willing suspension of disbelief   A phrase coined by Samuel Taylor Coleridge in his *Biographia Literaria* (1817). Coleridge argued that, in dealing with supernatural figures in literature, it was necessary "to procure for these shadows of imagination that willing suspension of disbelief for the moment which constitutes poetic faith." The phrase is now commonly used to indicate the necessary predisposition on the part of a reader or audience to accept the initial hypothesis of a work of literature.

wit   As currently used, the ability to express an insight in an ingenious and amusing manner. The term has undergone several changes in the course of its history. In the RENAISSANCE, it represented a kind of lively intelligence, as in the term UNIVERSITY WITS or, in its negative sense, as the calculating rationality of Iago in Shakespeare's *Othello*. In the 17th century, wit described a blend of intellect and imagination, reflected in the IMAGERY of METAPHYSICAL POETRY.

From the late 17th to the mid-18th century, wit was prized as the highest example of poetic skill. During this period, it was given its most enduring definition in Alexander Pope's *Essay on Criticism* (1711): "What oft was thought, but ne'er so well expressed." In the late 18th century, wit began to be viewed as mere superficial cleverness, an attitude that continued throughout the 19th century.

T. S. Eliot reaffirmed the value of wit to POETRY in his writings on the metaphysical poets and in his doctrine of the DISSOCIATION OF SENSIBILITY. Wit has continued to play an important role in 20th-century poetry, because of its close identification with the principle of IRONY. Margaret Edson's drama *Wit* (1998) enacts the limitation of wit as a guiding principle of life and literature.

womanist   A term coined by the novelist Alice Walker to make a distinction between a feminist and a "feminist of color," to point up the differences in the history and perspectives of the two groups.

women's writing (*écriture féminine*) In FEMINIST CRITICISM, an argument that the female body plays an important role in a woman's use of language, particularly in a literary context. Derived from the PSYCHOANALYTICAL CRITICISM of Jacques Lacan, which views traditional language, logic, and rationality as expressions of PHALLOCENTRISM, women's writing is viewed by many French feminists as rooted in a richer, unrepressed, pre-Oedipal phase of language development.

Some of the leading feminist theorists in France, including Hélène Cixous, Luce Irigaray, and Julia Kristeva, have advanced this argument. Many Anglo-American feminists, however, have dissented from this position on the grounds that it represents another version of ESSENTIALISM, the idea that there is a uniquely "female" essence that transcends cultural conditioning. This, of course, is a notion that underlies traditional male sexism. The French feminists reply that they are describing a future form of writing available to men as well as women once they have cast off the patriarchal rationality of phallocentric language. As if to illustrate this point they cite as one example of "women's writing" James Joyce's *Finnegans Wake*.

The New Feminist Criticism (1985), edited by Elaine Showalter, offers a variety of views in relation to the topic.

work The contrasting views of work as something burdensome, unpleasurable, forced and something useful, natural and a source of gratification are reflected in literature from its beginning. In Eden, Adam and Eve, tending to the garden in their prelapsarian state, experience the joy of labor. After the FALL, work becomes a central element of Adam's curse, while Eve must undergo painful "labor" in giving birth. The BIBLE also includes ethical issues related to work in the parable of the Laborers in the Vineyard and the Unjust Steward, and in the distinction between the active, work-oriented mode of life and the contemplative mode, in the New Testament account of Mary and Martha.

The development of guilds and trades in the MIDDLE AGES offered still another view, in which one's trade defined oneself more profoundly than one's name, as reflected, for example, in Chaucer's *Canterbury Tales*. There the pilgrims are known by their work—miller, parson, clerk, cook, man of law, etc., their personal names, if used at all, appearing as an afterthought. In the 16th-century REFORMATION, the emergence of the Protestant ethic, reinforced the commitment to work, of whatever kind, as a means to, and a manifestation of, membership in the elect, those predestined to be saved.

The rise of industrialism in the late 18th and early 19th centuries gives birth to the alienated worker in the factory as well as the slave in the cotton fields, deriving no satisfaction from their labor. Their plight is captured in 19th-century novels such as Elizabeth Gaskell's *Mary Barton* (1848) and Charles Dickens's *Hard Times* (1854).

But a more psychologically complex study of a worker is rendered in Herman Melville's *Bartleby the Scriviner* (1853). Bartleby's enigmatic refusal to do the work assigned to him—significantly expressed as a matter of free will, "I prefer not to"—has triggered an inexhaustible supply of interpretations. Those that connect to the theme of work usually highlight the story's subtitle "A Story of Wall Street."

The movement from the "wage slave" status of the industrial or clerical worker to that of actual slavery was one of incalculable qualitative depth. As recounted in *Narrative of the Life of Frederick Douglass, an American Slave* (1845), Douglass was "apprenticed" to a slave breaker and in a short time became "broken in body, soul and spirit." But finally driven to desperation, he fought back and from that time until his escape north, he was a "slave in form but not in fact."

Two critical figures in altering the view of work in the VICTORIAN period were John Ruskin and William Morris. Ruskin established as his criterion of ideal work the building of medieval cathedrals, where the workers were engaged in the creation of something beautiful and meaningful, along with the freedom to express their own creativity in forging the hideous gargoyles atop the cathedrals.

Morris develops Ruskin's insights in his novel *News from Nowhere* (1890), set in the year 2090, in an England that has evolved into a socialist paradise, where labor and art are indistinguishable. Both Ruskin and Morris looked to art as the key element in restoring vitality to labor. Just as the craftsman and the artist share a sense of creative freedom, so, too, must the industrial worker be admitted into the circle of those for whom life is organic, where work and play interact. This is also the doctrine espoused by D. H. Lawrence in *Women in Love* (1925).

The 1930s saw the emergence of two forms that stressed the experience of working class people, PROLETARIAN LITERATURE in the United States and SOCIALIST REALISM in the Soviet Union. Both forms illustrated the danger of attempting to force literature into the service of a political agenda. Ironically, the redemptive quality of work is reflected, not in the boy-meets-tractor formulas of state prescribed fiction, but in the most searing exposure of Stalinism, Alexandr Solzhenitsyn's *One Day in the Life of Ivan Denisovich* (1962). Ivan, imprisoned in the hell of the GULAG, snatches a shred of satisfaction from having done a good day's work.

Somewhat more successful, because less narrowly ideological, was the 1950's British movement ANGRY YOUNG MEN and KITCHEN SINK DRAMA. A more recent contribution to working-class literature has been James Kelman's portraits of working-class life in contemporary Glasgow, Scotland (*A Disaffection*, 1989; *How Late It Was, How Late*, 1994).

David Meakin's *Men and Work* (1976) looks at encounter over the centuries. David Sprague Herreshoff's *Labor into Art: The Theme of Work in Nineteenth Century American*

Literature (1991) examines work as a theme in Thoreau, Melville, Douglass, and Dickinson.

writing   Traditionally, either the process of putting words on a page or the result of that process. In the wake of DECONSTRUCTION and POSTSTRUCTURALISM, this seemingly self-evident and simple term (frequently referred to by the French word *écriture*) has emerged as an important and complex theoretical concept.

The most controversial of these new conceptions of writing is that associated with Jacques Derrida, the leading exponent of DECONSTRUCTION. Derrida argues that Western thought has been dominated by "phonocentrism," the priority of speech over writing. According to Derrida, writing has been seen as an imitation of speech, lacking the force, immediacy, and presence of speech. In this sense, writing is a SUPPLEMENT to speech, but Derrida points out that in French the word *supplément* implies, not just a later addition, but also a necessary addition, an addition that enhances the original. Thus writing is a better realization of what language in fact does. It stresses absence not presence, difference not identity, pluralistic not single meanings.

Writing is also seen as less "author-itarian" because of the absence of the AUTHOR for the reader. As a result, the reader is free to read in a manner that moves beyond the author's intention and to absorb the physical facts of writing, such as margins, capital letters, and the spaces between letters and words. This liberty of interpretation can generate a more skeptical, subversive response than speech permits. Such a view is reflected in some feminists's concept of WOMEN'S WRITING (*écriture féminine*), which works out a theory of specifically female writing.

Barbara Johnson's "Writing" in *Critical Terms for Literary Study* (1990), edited by Frank Lentricchia and Thomas McLaughlin, offers an insightful discussion of the term.

writing across the curriculum   Term for a movement in COMPOSITION STUDIES, growing out of the awareness that effective instruction in writing should not be limited to English classes but should be an aspect of teaching in all the disciplines. The underlying principle is that writing of any kind is, in William Zinsser's words, "thinking on paper," a mode of learning, requiring concentration, logic, imagination, and physical activity, combining to produce a product that can be analyzed and altered through revision. The other basis for the emphasis on writing in all disciplines is based on the recognition that skill in writing is a critical part of a professional career of any type. From research chemist to personnel manager, professionals all testify the importance of writing,—whether it be a lab notebook, a grant proposal, a prospectus, customer correspondence or any of a hundred other writing tasks—in their jobs.

The major problem in implementing WAC, as it is known, is convincing non-English faculty to agree to a shared set of assumptions about the teaching of writing. The practice of faculty workshops involves a number of obstacles, professorial egos being not the least, but after years of trial and error many campuses have found that the cooperative research and teaching that has grown out of these workshops have at least brought a heightened consciousness of the importance of writing.

Writing Across the Disciplines, ed. Art Young and Toby Fulwiler (1986), provides a collection of essays on the theory and practice of the movement.

y

Yale critics   A group of critics, associated with DECONSTRUCTION in the 1970s and '80s, who were on the faculty of Yale University. The group included J. Hillis Miller, Geoffrey Hartman, and Paul De Man, the latter regarded as the leading exponent of deconstruction in the United States. Paul De Man died in 1983, and four years later he was revealed to have written articles for a Nazi newspaper during the war years in Belgium. The result was a serious discrediting of De Man's ideas in particular and deconstruction in general.

Another Yale professor who sometimes was linked with this group is Harold Bloom. Bloom, however, describes himself as "against, in turn, the neo-Christian New Criticism of T. S. Eliot and his academic followers; the deconstruction of Paul De Man and his clones; the current rampages on the New Left and the Old Right on the supposed inequities and, even more dubious, moralities of the literary canon."

Harold Bloom's comments appear in his *The Western Canon* (1994).

yellow journalism   A general term for newspapers and magazines that emphasize scandal and lurid stories. The term dates from 1894, when the New York *World* newspaper introduced the first comic strip in color. The strip, "Hogan's Alley" by R. F. Outcault, featured a street urchin, The Yellow Kid, who enjoyed great popularity. When Outcault was hired by a rival paper, William Randolph Hearst's New York *Journal,* the ensuing competition between the two papers led each to try to outdo the other in reporting sensational stories.

young adult literature   A literary genre designed to appeal to middle and high school students. It has replaced the term *adolescent literature*, since *adolescent* has acquired some negative connotations. Young adult is also distinguished from CHILDREN'S LITERATURE, designed for elementary school students; however, overlapping categories is a common practice in this field, notably when universally appealing stories, such as the *Harry Potter* series, find an audience among children, young adults, and adults.

One of the major features of young adult novels is the presentation of the story from the perspective, and often in the language of, teenagers. The use of this feature owes much to the adult novel that has long since become a young adult classic, J. D. Salinger's *The Catcher in the Rye* (1951). Its crossover career has been facilitated by main character and narrator Holden Caulfield's distinctive voice, which still evokes a shock of recognition among young people more than 50 years after its publication.

The Catcher in the Rye is also one of the novels that contributes to the development of adult themes in young adult literature. Emerging from a background of strict censorship, young adult novels and stories now deal directly with race relations, sexual mores, social justice, and the complexities of inter-family relationships. This new openness has not emerged without a struggle. Many classic TEXTs have been banned from some local or school libraries, including Mark Twain's *Adventures of Huckleberry Finn* (1885), Harper Lee's *To Kill a Mockingbird* (1960), and, ironically but not surprisingly, *The Catcher in the Rye*.

Teenplots: A Book Talk Guide to Use With Readers Ages 12-18 (2003) is a useful source of young adult literature.

zeitgeist (spirit of the time)   A German term expressing the idea that an underlying spirit governs a given historical period, reflected in its social, intellectual, and political life. Once a popular term with historians and historical critics, *zeitgeist* has come to be seen as leading to facile generalizations about the past. Nevertheless, the idea, if not the term, continues to be employed in literary history, sometimes personified in terms of an outstanding figure, such as in the title of Hugh Kenner's study of MODERNISM, *The Pound Era* (1971).

Similar German terms sometimes employed are *Volksgeist* (the spirit of a nation) and *Weltanschauung* (worldview).

Zen   A form of Buddhism that emphasizes meditation as the key to enlightenment (*satori*). Zen masters teach the importance of moving beyond reason to achieve a direct, intuitive apprehension of reality. One of their celebrated techniques is the *koan* (a paradox or riddle, such as "What is the sound of one hand clapping?"), designed to encourage meditation.

Historically, Zen has had a close relation to POETRY. Practitioners compose a poem as an expression of their solution to a koan. These poems, along with other types of Zen poetry, such as "death poems," form an impressive body of work within Japanese and Chinese literatures.

Zen has attracted a number of literary followers in the West, notably in the BEAT movement. Jack Kerouac's *The Dharma Bums* (1958) is an example of a Beat novel, heavily influenced by Zen principles. Best known of Zen-influenced American writers is J. D. Salinger (*Franny and Zooey,* 1961), whose mysterious silence since the 1960s has been interpreted by some as evidence of his movement through a process of Zen enlightenment that requires withdrawal from the world.

Recent American Zen-ists include the novelist Robert Pirsig, whose *Zen and the Art of Motorcycle Maintenance* (1974) was an extraordinarily popular NOVEL OF IDEAS. Among poets Lucien Stryk (*Encounter with Zen,* 1981) is a prominent advocate for, and translator of, Zen poetry.

zeugma A figure of speech in which one word governs a series of succeeding words or phrases. Examples include Shakespeare's "Give them thy fingers, me thy lips to kiss" and Alexander Pope's "Who could not win the mistress, wooed the maid." In the first example the verb *give* governs the two phrases that follow; in the second, the pronoun *who* governs the following phrases.

Richard Lanham's *A Handlist of Rhetorical Terms* (second edition, 1991) provides definitions of nearly 1,000 rhetorical terms.

zines A term for alternative, self-published magazines that in recent years have become an influential publishing phenomenon. *Zine* is short, not for magazine, but for *fanzine*, a term that was first applied to SCIENCE FICTION magazines. The earliest of these magazines *Amazing Stories* (1926) encouraged its readers to communicate with one another. Fans began sending their stories to other fans. Relying heavily on mimeograph machines, they spawned an enthusiastic readership of each other's work. By the 1960s, fanzines had moved beyond the borders of science fiction, creating underground newspapers (the *Berkeley Barb*, *East Village Other*) to cover the political upheaval of the period and rock and roll, beginning with *Crawdaddy* in 1966. Meanwhile, the arrival of the Xerox machine spurred greater personal zine activity. Beginning in the 1980s, computers, with their opportunity for desktop publishing, brought self publishing to an unprecedented level as the zine began to be replaced by the *e-zine*.

The Factsheet Five Zine Reader, ed. R. Seth Friedman (1997), offers a rich selection of zine articles divided into traditional categories such as politics, sex, pop culture, work , and a few novel ones such as "fringe" and "riot grrrls."

zoom shot In FILM, a SHOT that moves rapidly toward or away from its subject while the camera remains stationary, using a special lens.

Index

Boldface numbers indicate major treatment of a topic.

A

Abbey Theatre **1**, 25, 134
Abel, Lionel 259
Abel-Cain story 172
Absolute **1–2**, 183
absolute literature 2
abstract expressionism. *See* action painting
absurd **2–3**, 18, 34, 87, 153, 160, 425
academic discourse **3–4**, 121
academic fiction. *See* campus novel
Académie française 4
Academy **4**, 390
Academy Awards **4–5**
accent **5**, 169, 259, 260. *See also* dialect
acrostic 5
act **5**, 376
action **5–6**
   in chase scene 73–74
   rising and falling 174–175
   symbolic 128, **409**
   tragic 5–6, 69, 88
action painting **6**, 290, 339
actor-manager **6–7**, 120–121
adaptation **7**
adolescent literature. *See* young adult literature
Adorno, Theodore 173
adultery **7–8**
adventure story 8
advertising **8–9**, 96, 231, 359, 381
Advertising Fictions (Wickes) 8–9
Aeschylus 62, 236, 314, 357, 363, 428
Aesop 157
aesthetic distance 10
aestheticism **9–10**, 37, 147, 244, 281

aesthetics **10**, 55, 205, 284
affective fallacy **10–11**, 285, 352
African-American literature **11–12**, 74–75, 163, 192–193, 227, 350, 388
agape 246
agent-scene ratio 128
Age of Johnson 12
Age of Reason. *See* Enlightenment
Age of Sensibility. *See* Age of Johnson
aging **13–14**
agitprop 14
agon **14**, 214, 302
agrarians/fugitive 175
AIDS **14–15**, 109, 178
alazon **15**, 85, 135, 223
alcohol **16–17**
Alexander, Meena 212
alexandrine 17
alienation **17–18**, 152, 165, 245, 330, 357, 441
alienation effect 10, **18–19**, 51, 127, 141, 254, 259
allegorical meaning 171
allegory **19–20**, 131, 343, 408
alliteration 20
allusion **20**, 73
Alter, Robert 51, 52
Althusser, Louis 205, 254
Alvarez, Julia 197–198
Amazing Stories (zine) 451
ambiguity **20–21**, 324
"Americanization" 149
American renaissance **21–22**
American sublime 403
amphibrach 169
amphimacer 169
anagnorisis **22**, 205, 423
anagogical meaning 171
analogy 22
anapest **22**, 169, 260
anaphora 23
anarchism **23–24**

anatomy 24
androgyny **24–25**
Anglo-Irish literature 25
Anglo Norman **25–26**
angry young men **26**, 445
angst 26
animated films **26–27**
anonymous discourse 27
Ansky, S. 132
antagonist **27**, 341, 437
anthology 27
anthropology **27–28**, 149, 419
anticlimax 28
anti-hero **28–29**, 192, 195
"antimasque" 255
anti-Semitism **29–31**, 199
anti-Stratfordian theories **31**, 341
antistrophe **32**
aphorism 32
apocalypse **32**, 237–238, 296, 314
apocrypha **32**, 348
   Shakespearean **385–386**
Apollonian/Dionysian 16, **32**, 183, 250
aporia **33**, 71, 111
apostrophe **33**, 267
appearance/reality **33–34**, 144
apron (thrust) stage **34**, 340, 397
Aquinas, St. Thomas 284, 376
Arab-American literature **34–35**
Arcadia 35
archetype 275
archive **35**
arena stage 340, 397
Arendt, Hannah 47, 151
argument **35**
aristocracy 80. *See also* upper class
Aristophanes 85, 263, 314
Aristotle 5, 16, 35, 69, 75, 77, 94, 123, 139, 180, 190, 205, 280, 282, 365, 376, 418, 422, 423, 432

Aristotelian criticism **35–36,** 75

Arlen, Michael 36

Armenian-American literature **36**

Arnold, Matthew 36–37, 147, 193, 321, 407, 422

Arnoldian criticism **36–37,** 321

Artaud, Antonin 416

art for art's sake 9–10, **37,** 109, 147, 167, 243, 314

Arthurian legend 7, 26, **37–38,** 59, 104, 238, 263, 429

artist/hero **38–39**

art/nature **280–281,** 370–371

Ashbery, John 291

Asian-American literature **39**

aside **39,** 97, 393

"as if" fictions **39, 158**

As Is. *See Tel Quel*

assonance **40,** 367

Astor Place riot **40**

As You Like It (Shakespeare) 86, 247, 417

aubade **40–41**

Auchincloss, Louis 67

Auden, W. H. 61, 260–261, 405

audience 18–19, 39, **41,** 97–98, 102, 127, 141, 142

Auerbach, Erich 52, 164, 354

Augustan age **41,** 95, 196, 282

Augustine, Saint 79, 420

Austen, Jane 87, 184, 247, 314, 382

auteur **42,** 121, 166, 289

author **42–43**
    Barthes (Roland) on 332
    as bricoleur 58
    external 208, 209
    Foucault (Michel) on 35
    implied **208–210,** 278, 279, 352
    internal 208, 209
    madness of 250
    psychoanalysis of 342
    reputation of 361
    tone of 421–422
    voice of 119–120, 173–174, 304

autobiography **43–44,** 181, 256, 279, 335, 391

auto sacramental **44,** 98, 274

avant-garde **44–45,** 98, 167, 244, 254, 290, 303, 406, 412, 426, 431

B

Bacon, Sir Francis 31, 146, 225, 381–382

bad faith **46**

bad quarto **46**

Baker, Houston 436

Bakhtin, Mikhail 68, 117, 180, 196, 219, 323, 328

ballad **46–47**

Balzac, Honoré de 66, 353, 377

banality of evil **47,** 151

bard **47**

bardolatry **48**

Barnes, Djuna 239

baroque **48,** 184, 253, 368

Barth, John 78

Barthes, Roland 43, 231, 339, 351

baseball **48–49,** 316

basic writing 3, **49–50**

Bataille, Georges 151

Bate, Jonathan 134

bathos **50**

Battle of the books **50**

Baudelaire, Charles 149–150, 409

Beardsley, Monroe 10, 216

beat 45, **50–51,** 178, 374, 450

Beaumont, Francis 425

Beauvoir, Simone de 153, 162, 256, 380

Beckett, Samuel 2, 87, 109, 192, 207, 265, 291, 349, 358, 360, 388, 425

"Bedroom Farce" 159–160

Behan, Brendan 336–337

belles lettres **51**

Bellow, Saul 17, 69, 283

Benjamin, Walter 173

Beowulf (epic) 303

Bergson, Henri 135

Berliner Ensemble **51**

Berryman, John 94

bestiary **51**

best seller **51**

Bible **51–53,** 317, 348, 380, 410, 438
    apocalypse in 32, 237–238, 314
    authority of 196–197
    on body 56

    canon of 64
    Darwinism and 106
    deism on 112
    demythologizing 113
    on envy 139
    fall in 158, 171
    on fratricide 172
    incest in 210
    interpretation of 42, 151, 164, 429
    parables in 311–312
    parataxis in 313
    parousia in 314
    proverbs in 341
    Puritanism on 346
    Reformation on 42, 213
    religious plays based on 98, 273
    on suffering 404–405
    on work 444

bibliography **53**

bildungsroman **53,** 80, 89, 191

bile 202

binary opposition 28, **53–54,** 70, 103

biography **54,** 190, 343

Blackfriars Theatre **54–55,** 72, 345

Black Rain (Ibuse) 295–296

Blair, Hugh 366

Blake, William 23, 32, 33, 65–66, 79, 209, 251, 299, 360

blank verse **55,** 133, 137, 162, 196, 204, 261, 433

blazon **55**

blood 202

Bloom, Allan 326

Bloom, Harold 14, 164, 214, 232, 302, 390–391, 419, 448

Bloomsbury group 54, **55–56**

Boccaccio, Giovanni 157

body **56**

body of Christ. *See* Corpus Christi

bombast **57**

book(s) **57**
    Battle of **50**
    chapbook **72**
    commonplace **89–90**
    courtesy **99–100**
    index of forbidden. *See* Index Librorum Prohibitorum
    jest **228**
    prompt **340**
    self-help **404**

Boon, James 149–150
Boone, Joseph 247
Booth, Wayne 208, 223, 366
Boswell, James 54
Boulevard theaters **57**
bourgeois (middle class) **57,** 66, 80, 96, 125, 129, 167, 205, 321, 375, 432
bourgeois drama. *See drâme bourgeois*
Bové, Paul 122
bowdlerize **57**
Bradstreet, Anne 346
braggart warrior 15, **57,** 399
Braly, Malcolm 337
brat pack **58**
Brecht, Bertolt 5, 10, 18–19, 51, 127, 141–142, 177, 254, 259
Breton, André 406
breviary **58**
bricoleur **58**
Brook Farm **58**
Brooks, Cleanth 223, 285, 312, 313
brotherhood 172
Browning, Robert 13, 127, 139
Brunietrière, Ferdinand 180
Buber, Martin 357
Bultmann, Rudolph 113
Bunraku **58–59**
Buntline, Ned 40, 120
Burckhardt, Jacob 358
Burger, Peter 392
Burke, Edmund 25, 403
Burke, Kenneth 6, 128, 217, 366, 409, 428
burlesque **59,** 375
Burns, Robert 337
busker **59**
buskin **59–60**
Byron, George Gordon Byron 126, 172, 307, 336, 375, 435
Byronic hero 38, **60**

C

Cabala. *See* Kabbalah
cacophony **61,** 150, 241
cadence **61**
caesura **61,** 375
Cahan, Abraham 149
Cain-Abel story 172
Calasso, Roberto 2, 183
Calderón de la Barca, Pedro 130, 417

Calvinism **61–62,** 65, 116, 225, 329–330, 346
Cambridge Ritualists **62**
camp **62**
campaign biography 190
Campbell, George 366
campus novel **63**
Camus, Albert 2, 153, 188, 237, 278
canon 32, **64–65,** 101, 197, 270, 317, 326, 362, 423, 434
canto **65**
caper film **65**
capitalism 42, 43, **65–67,** 96, 205, 254, 357
Capote, Truman 292
captivity narratives **67,** 84
caricature **67–68**
Carlson, Marvin 381
Carlyle, Thomas 66
carnival **68,** 85, 117, 157, 273, 323, 328, 376
Caroline **68–69,** 255
carpe diem **69,** 70
cartoons. *See* animated films
catachresis **69**
catalogues. *See* list poem
catastrophe **69**
Catcher in the Rye, The (Salinger) 205–206, 278, 316, 449
catharsis **69–70,** 423
Catholic Church 70, 99, 212, 220, 221, 225, 228, 244–245, 307, 308, 310, 329–330, 356
Cavalier Poets 68–69, **70**
Celtic literature 37, 47, **70**
Celtic Revival 70
censorship **70,** 329, 376
center/decenter **70–71,** 111
cento 83
Cervantes, Miguel de 87, 250, 293, 369
Césaire, Aimé 282
chain of being **71**
Chamberlain's/King's Men 54, **71–72,** 167, 182, 192, 385
Chandler, Raymond 115
chanson de geste **72,** 104, 163, 262
chapbook **72**
Chapman, George 172
character(s) **72–73.** *See also specific characters*
    caricature of 67–68
    in comedy 15, 57, 85, 135, 223, 311, 399

conflict between 95
consciousness in 96
dialect of 205–206
dramatic consciousness of 259
in minimalist fiction 265
motivation of 269, 280
objective correlative of feelings of 298
plot and 324
psychoanalysis of 342
through line of 419
in tragedy 423
voice of 119–120, 173–174
Charles I (king of England) 68, 70, 90, 311, 346, 384
Charles II (king of England) 362
chase **73–74,** 160, 233
Chaucer, Geoffrey 131, 138–139, 151, 157, 196, 204, 263, 310, 340, 358, 444
Chekhov, Anton 86–87, 268–269, 353
Chernobyl disaster 296
Chesterton, G. K. 115
chiasmus 74
Chicago renaissance **74–75**
Chicago school 36, **75,** 180
Chicano/Chicana literature 197
Chikamatsu Monzaemon 58–59
children's literature 8, **75–76,** 158, 190, 448
Chin, Frank 76
Chinese-American literature **76–77**
choler 202
Chomsky, Noam 91, 185
Chopin, Kate 247
choriamb 169
chorus 14, 32, **77,** 85, 95
Chrétien de Troyes 37
Christ **77–78,** 158, 171, 237–238, 245, 274, 297, 314, 315, 429. *See also* Corpus Christi
Christie, Agatha 115
chronicle play **78**
Chu, Louis 76
Church of England 253, 308
Ciceronian style **78,** 381
cinema. *See* films
cinéma verité **79,** 124

circumlocution **79**
citation 219
city **79–80**
City of God, The (Augustine) 79
Civil Rights movement 11–12
civil war 172
Clair, René 181
class **80–81,** 193–194, 205,
 322
classicism **81**
 agon in 14
 aporia in 33
 body in 56
 buskin in 59
 comedy in 85–86,
  222–223
 death in 107–108
 in medias res used in 215
 rhetoric in 365
 stichomythia in 398
 time in 420
 tragedy in 223, 423–424
climax **82,** 113, 174–175
closed context 97
closed heroic couplet 196
close reading 285
closet drama **82**
close-up **82,** 103
closure 43, 71, **82–83**
cockney school of poetry **83**
code **83,** 381
codex **83**
Coleridge, Samuel Taylor 2,
 34, 146, 191, 207, 269, 306,
 369, 408, 443
collaborative learning **83**
collage **83**
collation **84**
collective unconscious 431
Colonial period (American literature) 67, **84**
colophon **84**
Comédie-Française **84**
comédie larmoyante **84–85**
comedy **85–87**
 body in 56
 characters in 15, 57, 85,
  135, 223, 311, 399
 drawing room **129**
 farce 7, 86, **159–160**
 of humors 202
 irony in 222–223
 Middle 85, **263**
 musical. *See* musical
 New 85–86
 Old 85, 263
 Restoration **363**

romantic **370**
screwball 87, **379–380**
sentimental 85, 86,
 382–383
situation. *See* sitcom
stand-up **397–398**
tearful. *See* comédie larmoyante
tragicomedy 86, **425**
comic book. *See* graphic novel
comic novel **87–88**
comic relief **88**
coming of age 53, **88–89**
commedia dell'arte 86, **89,**
 264, 311
commemoration 299
commonplace book **89–90**
common reader **90**
common sense 392
Commonwealth period 55, 68,
 72, **90,** 182, 311, 346, 362
comparative literature **90–91**
competence/performance **91**
complaint **91**
complication **91–92**
composition studies 3, 49–50,
 83, **92,** 306, 339, 364, 446
conceit **92–93**
concordance **93**
concrete universal **94**
Condell, Henry 167
condensation 131
confessional poetry 18, **94–95,**
 109
confidant(e) **95**
conflated text **95**
conflict **95,** 100, 342. *See also*
 agon
Connecticut wits **95,** 364
connotation/denotation **113**
Conrad, Joseph 23, 106, 134,
 188, 334, 377, 414
consciousness **95–96.** *See also*
 unconscious
 dasein and 106
 dramatic 259
 in ethnography 149
 in phenomenology 320
 stream of 217, 293, 326
 structure of 400
consciousness criticism 178–
 179, 321
conservative/liberal imagination **239–240**
consonance 367
constative statements 396
consumption **96–97,** 328

content **97,** 170, 434
context **97,** 102, 286
continuous allegory 19
convention **97–98,** 111, 215,
 298
cony-catcher **98**
Cooper, James Fenimore 198,
 335, 364, 441–442
Copernican system **344,** 359
copyright 322–323
Corpus Christi 44, **98,** 273,
 315
cosmic irony 223
cothurnus. *See* buskin
counterfactual fiction **98–99**
Counter-Reformation **99**
coup de théâtre **99**
couplet **99,** 398
courtesy books **99–100**
courtly love 37, **100,** 246, 266,
 323, 429
Crane, Stephen 439
Crashaw, Richard 48
creative evolution 135
Creeley, Robert 339
crisis **100**
Criterion, The **100–101**
criticism **101**
 Aristotelian **35–36,** 75
 Arnoldian **36–37,** 321
 of canon 64
 Chicago school 36, **75,**
  180
 cultural **102**
 ecocriticism **134**
 ethical **147–148,** 404
 feminist. *See* feminist criticism
 Geneva school **178–179,**
  321
 of genre 180
 gynocriticism 162, **189**
 higher 52, **196–197**
 historical **198,** 356
 language of 121
 Marxist. *See* Marxist criticism
 myth. *See* myth criticism
 New. *See* New Criticism
 practical 101, 285, **333**
 process 338–339
 product 338
 psychoanalytical 320,
  342–343
 reader response. *See* reader
  response criticism
 review as 363–364

rhetorical 352, **366–367**
subjective **402,** 425
textual 53, 57, 84, 95, **415–416**
thematic 418
theory compared to 418
Cromwell, Oliver 90, 362
cruelty, theater of 250, **416**
Crumb, R. 185
crux **101–102,** 416
cry 91
cultural criticism **102**
cultural studies 37, **102–103,** 328
Culture and Anarchy (Arnold) 193
cursed poet. *See poète maudit*
curtal sonnet **103**
Curtius, Ernst 417
cut **103**
cyberpunk **103**
cycle **104**
Cymberline (Shakespeare) 121, 369
cynics **104**
Cyrano de Bergerac (Rostand) 203

D

dactyl **105,** 169, 260, 261
dada 98, **105,** 407
dance of death **105–106,** 108
danse macabre. See dance of death
Dante 65, 171, 239, 246, 264–265, 300–301, 357, 404
Dark Ages. *See* Middle Ages
Darwinism 52, **106,** 180, 267, 377
dasein **106,** 152, 194
date of a literary text **107**
dead metaphor 257
Dead Sea Scrolls **348**
death **107–109**
    dance of **105–106,** 108
    existentialism on 152, 153
    graveyard school on 186
    love and 108, 247
débat **109**
Debray, Régis 256
decadence **109–110,** 167
decenter/center **70–71,** 111
deconstruction **110–111**
    on Absolute 2
    on allegory 19
    aporia in 33, 111

on center/decenter 70–71, 111
on closure 82
determinism in 116
on ethical criticism 148
explication in 154
indeterminacy in 211–212
on language 110, 259, 388
logocentrism in 2, 110, 245, 259, 320
on meaning 110, 111, 218, 323
poststructuralism and 331
on realism 354
referent in 356
skepticism in 390
supplement in 406
on symbol 408
on text 33, 415
on writing 446
Yale critics 448
decorum 98, **111–112**
deep focus **112**
defamiliarization 10, **112,** 235, 372
deism **112–113,** 138
DeLillo, Don 49, 224, 414–415
De Man, Paul 111, 408, 448
demythologizing 113, 152
denotation/connotation **113**
denouement **113**
De Quincey, Thomas 28, 312
Derrida, Jacques 2, 110, 245, 320, 331–332, 354, 388, 390, 396, 406, 415, 446
Descartes, René 390
description **113–114**
desire **114**
    mimetic 139, **264–265**
detective story 113, **114–116,** 165, 168, 188, 269, 399, 412
determinism 61, **116,** 202, 269, 353, 355
deus ex machina **116**
Devil. *See* evil; Satan
Dewey, John 214, 333
diachronic/synchronic **116**
Dial, The **116–117,** 244, 426
dialect **117,** 205–206, 249
dialectic **117**
dialogism **117–118,** 219
dialogue **118,** 119, 398
diary 43, **118–119**

Dickens, Charles 8, 9, 16, 38, 66, 73, 79, 87–88, 106, 113–114, 236, 334, 336, 377, 416, 427
Dickinson, Emily 137
diction **119**
    poetic **324**
didactic literature **119**
Diderot, Denis 129
Di Donato, Pietro 223–224
diegesis/mimesis **119–120,** 173–174
dieresis **120**
dime novel **120,** 345, 442
dimeter **120,** 260
Dionysian/Apollonian 16, **32,** 183, 250
Dionysian madness 250, 251
direct cinema. *See cinéma verité*
direct metaphor 257
director 42, **120–121,** 166, 289
dirge **121**
disbelief, willing suspension of 8, 41, 98, **443**
discourse **121–122.** *See also* language
    academic **3–4,** 121
    anonymous 27
    feminist criticism on 163
    Foucault (Michel) on 138, 143, 199
discourse analysis **122**
discovery space **122**
disintegrators **122**
Disney, Walt 27
displacement 131
dissociation of sensibility **122–123,** 143, 361, 377, 443
dissolve **123,** 421
dithyramb **123**
Divine Comedy (Dante) 65, 246, 264–265, 300–301, 357, 404
"docudrama" 125, 180
documentary 79, **123–125,** 165, 200, 340
doggerel **125**
domestic tragedy **125**
Don Juan theme **125–126,** 213
Donne, John 93, 108, 123, 225, 258, 324, 344, 361, 384, 413
Donoghue, Denis 267
Don Quixote (Cervantes) 87, 250, 293, 369
doppelgänger (double) **126–127,** 172

Dostoyevsky, Fyodor 77, 153, 336, 405
doublespeak 288
Douglas, Ann 193
Douglass, Frederick 391, 445
downstage/upstage 127
Doyle, Conan 114
drama 127. *See also* act
  closet 82
  conventions in 98
  director of 120–121
  family 125, 129
  heroic 59, **196**
  kitchen sink 233, 445
  liturgical **244–245**, 273, 428
  medieval **255–256**, 266, 424
  melodrama 95, **256**, 392
  radio 349
  television 115–116, 391–392, **411–412**
dramatic consciousness 259
dramatic illusion 127
dramatic monologue **127**, 139, 267
dramatism 128
dramatis personae **128**, 318
dramatization 129
dramaturge 129
drâme bourgeois 129
drawing room comedy 129
dream **129–131**, 131–132
dream vision 129–130, **131**
dreamwork 130, **131–132**
drinking. *See* alcohol
Dryden, John 5, 196, 361, 375
D'Souza, Dinesh 326
DuBois, W. E. B. 214
Dumas, Alexandre 338
dumb show 132
Duncan, Robert 339
Dunne, Finley Peter 220
dybbuk 132

E

Eagleton, Terry 254, 255
early modern period **133**, 359. *See also* Renaissance
early national/revolutionary period 364
early Tudor **133**, 171–172, 332
eclogue 109, **133–134**
ecocriticism 134
écriture féminine. See women's writing

Edson, Margaret 258–259, 443
education novel. *See* bildungsroman
Edward VII (king of Great Britain) 134
Edwardian era **134–135**
Edwards, Jonathan 84, 307
ego 430
Einstein, Albert 267, 421
eiron 15, 85, **135**, 223
élan vital 135
elegy **135**, 315
Eliot, George 106
Eliot, T. S. 77, 81, 92, 100–101, 122–123, 127, 143, 160, 191, 192, 257, 258, 268, 285, 298, 339, 357, 361, 377, 421, 422–423, 443
Elizabeth I (queen of England) 72, 136, 150
Elizabethan era **136**
  chapbooks in 72
  chronicle plays in 78
  commercialism in 65
  cony-catchers in 98
  domestic tragedies in 125
  dream in 130
  dumb shows in 132
  five-act structure from 5
  humors in 202
  inkhornism in 215
  jig in 230–231
  madrigal in 251
  Marprelate controversy in 253
  pageant in 310
  pamphlets in 310
  picaresque in 322
  playhouses in 344
  poetaster in 324
  prologue in 340
  revenge in 363
  seven deadly sins in 385
  stage in 34, 122, 344
  stoicism in 399
  tragedy in 424
  University Wits in 432–433
emblem 136
emendation 137
Emerson, Ralph Waldo 213–214, 334, 426
empathy **137**, 316
empiricism **137**, 144
Empson, William 20–21, 315–316

end of the century. *See* fin de siècle
end-stopped line **137**
Engels, Friedrich 254
enjambment **137–138**
Enlightenment 112, **138**, 282, 307, 368
environmentalism 134
envoy (envoi) **138–139**, 384
envy **139–140**, 227
Envy (Olesha) 139–140
epic 80, 111, **140–141**, 168, 196, 215, 220, 242, 266, 307, 439
epic theater 5, 51, 127, **141–142**, 254
epicureanism 142
epideictic oratory 142
epigram 32, **142**
epigraph 142
epilogue 142
epiphany **143**, 267, 387, 420
episodic novel 143
episteme **143–144**
epistemology **144**, 265
epistle 144
epistolary novel **144–145**
epitaph 145
epithalamion 145
epithet **145**, 200
Erasmus, Desiderius 359
eros 246
erotic literature 145
escapist literature 145
esemplastic 146
essay 146
essentialism **146–147**, 444
Esslin, Martin 2
establishing shot 147
eternal return **147**, 360
ethical criticism **147–148**, 404
ethnic literature **148–149**, 205, 270
ethnography 28, **149–150**
ethos **150**
Eugenides, Jeffrey 187
euphony **150**, 241
euphuism 136, **150**
Euripides 16, 250, 300, 314
Eustace Diamonds, The (Trollope) 219
Everyman (morality play) 268
evil 47, **150–151**, 325, 343, 344. *See also* Satan; villain
evolution 106, 135
exegesis **151**
exemplum **151**

existentialism **151–154**
  on absurd 2, 153
  on alienation 18
  on bad faith 46
  on comedy 87
  dasein in 106, 152
  on death 109, 152, 153
  determinism in 116
  development of 152
  on humanism 202
  phenomenology in 320
  philosophy of 152–153
  on religion 358
  self in 380
exordium **154**
explication **154**
exposition **154**, 340
expressionism **154–155**, 342
  abstract. *See* action painting
  in films 155, 165–166, 201, 435
  realism in opposition to 353
external author 208, 209
external conflict 95
extravaganza **155**
extrinsic/intrinsic study of literature **155–156**, 285

F

Fabian society **157**
fable **157**, 159, 169
fabliau **157**
fabula 399
fade **158**
fairy tale 75, **158**, 159, 169, 411
faith
  bad **46**
  religious 114, 258, **357–358**, 376–377, 384
fall 139, **158–159**, 171, 199, 307, 357, 424
fallacy
  affective **10–11**, 285, 352
  intentional 10, 42, **216**, 285
  pathetic **316**
falling action 174–175
family drama 125, 129
family romance **159**
fancy/imagination. *See* imagination/fancy
fantasy **159**, 252
farce 7, 86, **159–160**

Farewell to Arms, A (Hemingway) 208, 209
Farrell, James T. 220
fascism 175
Fatherland (Harris) 98
fatwa 70, **160**
Faulkner, William 78, 361–362, 367, 395
Faustian theme 60, **160–161**, 213, 301
Federal Theater Project **161**
Federman, Raymond 354
felix culpa. *See* fortunate fall
feminine ending **161–162**, 367
feminist criticism 148, **162–163**, 444
  on androgyny 24–25
  on binary opposition 54
  on body 56
  on consumption 97
  on desire 114
  on erotic literature 145
  essentialism in 146, 444
  on gender 162, 178, 317
  gynocriticism in 162, 189
  identity in 205
  on myth criticism 275–276
  on patriarchy 317, 319
  on phallocentrism 319, 444
  politics in 327
  on pornography 329
  on power 317, 319, 333
  on psychoanalysis 343
  on rape 350–351
  on reader-as-woman 352
  on religion 358
  on romance 370
  on self 380
  semiotics/semiology in 381
  on silence 388–389
Fenian cycle **163**
Fetterley, Judith 209
feudalism **163**, 262
Feydeau, Georges 159–160
fiction **164**. *See also* novel(s); story
  absurdist 3
  "as if" **39**, 158
  characters in 72–73
  comic relief in 88
  conventions in 98
  counterfactual **98–99**
  horror 184, **200**, 435

interactive computer 203, **216**
metafiction **257**, 331
science. *See* science fiction
fictional films 165
Fielding, Henry 87
figural interpretation 52, **164**, 429
film noir 115, 155, **165–166**, 328
films 4–5, **165**. *See also* shot
  AIDS in 15
  alcohol in 17
  animated **26–27**
  auteur of 42, 166, 289
  caper **65**
  chase scenes in **73–74**, 160, 233
  comedies 87
  death in 109
  detective stories 115
  director of 121, 166, 289
  documentary 79, **123–125**, 165, 200, 340
  epic 141
  existentialist 153
  expressionist 155, 165–166, 201, 435
  fictional 165
  flashback in 123, **167**, 215, 421
  gangster **176–177**, 224
  homage in 20
  horror 201
  incest in 211
  Irish-American 222
  keystone (cops) comedies **232–233**
  macguffin in 249
  madness in 251
  montage in **268**, 421
  musicals 272
  neorealist **283–284**
  New Wave **288–289**
  nonfiction 165
  perspectivism in 319
  realist **354–355**
  romantic 370
  science fiction 379, 441
  screenplay of **379**, 428
  screwball comedy 87, **379–380**
  sequels 383
  serials **383–384**
  studio system 121, 272, **401**
  treatment in 428

underground 431
vampirism in 435
war 440–441
western 442–443
film theory **166–167,** 354
film truth. *See* cinéma verité
fin de siècle **167**
fine letters. *See belles lettres*
Finnegans Wake (Joyce) 130–131
First Folio 46, 53, 72, 102, 107, **167,** 340
first-person narrative 278, 325
Fish, Stanley 352, 392
Fiske, John 47, 328
Flaherty, Robert 124
flashback 123, **167,** 215, 421
flat character 73
Fleshly School. *See* pre-Raphaelites
Fletcher, John 425
Flying Dutchman **167–168**
flyting **168**
foil **168**
folio 57
folk ballads 46–47
folk culture 327–328
folklore 132, 157, **168**
folk play 270
folktale 158, 163, 168, **169**
foot **169,** 260
footnote 182
Ford, John 211
foregrounding 112, **169,** 372
foreshadowing **170**
form 97, **170,** 401
    organic 170, **306,** 403
    in value judgment 434
formalism 10, **170,** 205
    in film theory 166
    New **286**
    in reception theory 356
    Russian 112, 170, 243, 334, **372**
Forrest, Edwin 40
Forster, E. M. 134, 135, 177
fortunate fall 158, **171,** 199, 307, 357, 424
Foucault, Michel 27, 35, 43, 121, 122, 138, 143–144, 150, 199, 286, 331, 332–333, 347–348, 361
four levels of meaning 20, **171,** 239, 242
fourteener **171–172,** 194, 332
Frankfurt school **173,** 254, 328
Franklin, H. Bruce 337
fratricide **172–173**

Frazier, James 28, 62, 275
free indirect style 96, 120, **173–174,** 293, 319
free verse 61, **174,** 207, 261, 286, 367, 430, 436
freeze frame **174**
Freiligrath, Ferdinand 191
Freneau, Philip 364
Freud, Sigmund 54, 73, 113, 130, 131–132, 210, 247, 265, 267, 277, 302, 342–343, 408, 430–431
Freudian symbolism 408
Freytag, Gustav 174
Freytag's pyramid **174–175**
Frisch, Max 126
Frost, Robert 174
Frye, Northrop 19, 24, 29, 52–53, 86, 148, 180, 195, 204, 207, 223, 243, 251, 275, 276, 338, 341, 368, 434
Frykholm, Amy Johnson 238
fugitive/agrarians **175**
funeral song 121, 419
Fussell, Paul 427
futurism **175,** 372

G

Gadamer, Hans-Georg 194
Gaddis, William 66–67
Gaelic literature 163, 222, 307
Galileo 377
game 323
gangster film **176–177,** 224
García Márquez, Gabriel 252, 331
Gates, Henry Louis 391
gay literature 14–15, 62, **177–178,** 238–239, 347–348
Geertz, Clifford 28, 149, 286, 392, 419
gender 162, **178,** 317
Geneva school **178–179,** 321
genre 111, **179–180,** 298. *See also* form
Geoffrey of Monmouth 25–26, 37
georgic **180**
Gernsback, Hugo 378
Ghose, Zulfikar 212
ghost story **180–181**
ghostwriter 181
Gibran, Kahil 34
Gibson, William 103
Gide, André 177, 269
Gilded Age **181,** 404

Ginsberg, Allen 50, 374
Girard, René 139, 264, 265, 368
global village **181–182,** 305
Globe Theatre 34, 54, 71, 90, **182,** 344, 345
gloss **182**
glossary 182
god from the machine. *See* deus ex machina
gods **182–183,** 357
Goethe, Johann Wolfgang von 38, 161, 191, 213, 277, 295, 383
golden age **183–184,** 315
Golding, William 188–189
Goldmann, Lucien 329, 330
gongorism 48, **184**
Gornick, Vivian 247
gothic novel 60, **184–185,** 200, 293, 314, 370, 435
Graff, Gerald 64, 326
grammar 92, **185**
Gramsci, Antonio 193–194
graphic novel **185**
Grass, Günter 251
graveyard school 108, **186**
Greek-American literature **186–187**
Greek religion (ancient) 62, 182–183
Greenberg, Eric Rolfe 49
Greenblatt, Stephen 3, 286–287, 395
Greene, Graham 17, 74, 405–406
Greene, Robert 310, 433
grotesque **187**
Group Theatre 188
Gubaryev, Vladimir 296
Guillaume de Lorris 131
guilt **188–189,** 237, 351
gynocriticism 162, **189**

H

hagiography 54, **190**
haiku **190,** 208
hamartia **190,** 201, 423
Hamlet (Shakespeare) 18, 33–34, 88, 95, 108, 120, 154, 164, 168, 172, 179, 190, 191–192, 194, 250, 269, 278, 298, 302, 309, 322, 345, 350, 357–358, 363, 376, 382, 399, 422
Hamletism 191–192

Hamlet theme **191–192**
Hammett, Dashiell 115
happening **192**
Hardison, O. B. 216
Harlem Renaissance 11,
 192–193, 227
Harris, Joseph 364
Harris, Richard 98
Hart, William S. 442
Hartley, John 47
Hasek, Jaroslav 29
Hassidic Jewish folklore 132
Hawthorne, Nathaniel 8, 346,
 369
Hebraism/Hellenism **193**
Hebrew Bible. *See* Old
 Testament
Hegel, G. W. F. 1, 17, 18, 117
hegemony **193–194**, 205,
 326, 434
Heidegger, Martin 106, 134,
 152, 194, 304, 320, 400
Heilbrun, Carolyn 24
Heisenberg, Werner 211
Hellenism/Hebraism **193**
Heller, Joseph 29, 66, 251, 440
Heminges, John 167
Hemingway, Ernest 24–25, 83,
 208, 209, 245, 246
"Hemingway Code" 83
hendiadys **194**
Henry IV, Part 1 (Shakespeare)
 29, 56, 150, 325
Henry IV, Part 2 (Shakespeare)
 56, 69
Henry V (Shakespeare) 77, 137,
 220, 424
Henry VIII (king of England)
 133
heptameter **194**, 260. *See also*
 iambic heptameter
Heraclitus 147
hermeneutic circle 194
hermeneutics 152–153, **194–
 195**, 218, 321, 358, 390, 391
hermetic poetry **195**
hero/artist **38–39**
hero/heroine **195**. *See also*
 anti-hero; protagonist; villain
 Byronic 38, **60**
 in chanson de geste 72
 Christ as 77
 conflict with villain 95
 epic 140
 in film noir 165
 friend of 135
 in gangster film 176–177

in Odysseus/Ulysses
 theme 300
 tragic 6, 190, 376
heroic couplet 99, 137, **196,**
 204, 282, 375–376
heroic drama 59, **196**
Herring, Phillip 212
Hersey, John 289, 295
Hesiod 184
heteroglossia 68, **196**
hexameter 260
Heywood, John 217–218
high culture 102–103, 327–
 328, 434
higher criticism 52, **196–197**
Hijuelos, Oscar 197
Himes, Chester 337
Hiroshima (Hersey) 289, 295
Hirsch, E. D. 195
Hispanic-American literature
 197–198
historical criticism **198**, 356.
 See also literary history
historical novel **198**, 295–296
historical time 420
history of ideas **198–199**
Hitchcock, Alfred 249
Hoban, Russell 296
Holderlin, Friedrich 183
Holland, Norman 342
Hollander, John 242
Holmes, Oliver Wendell 241
Holocaust 31, 47, 124, 181,
 199–200, 358, 405
holograph 253
homage 20
Homer 7, 13, 140, 168, 182,
 200, 215, 220, 300, 305,
 431, 439
Homeric **200**
Homeric epithet 145, 200
homosexuality 347–348. *See
 also* gay literature; lesbian
 literature
Hooker, Richard 78
Hopkins, Gerard Manley 103,
 215, 367, 377, 397
Horace 144
Horatian ode 300
Horatian satire 375
horror fiction 184, **200**, 435
horror film **201**
Howe, Irving 327
hubris (hybris) **201**
Hughes, Langston 193
Hugo, Victor 74
human (moral) evil 150, 151

humanism **201–202**
 in early Tudor era 133
 essentialism in 146
 New 2, 202, **287**, 371
 in Renaissance 201, 359,
 420
 self in 380
humanistic existentialism 152
humors 22, **202**
Hurston, Zora Neale 193
Husserl, Edmund 152, 320
Hwang, David Harry 76
hymn 123
Hynes, James 414
hyperbole **203**
hypertext **203**
hypotaxis **203**

I

iamb 5, 17, 169, **204**, 260, 403
iambic heptameter 171–172,
 194
iambic pentameter 5, 17, 55,
 99, 194, 196, 204, 261, 307,
 367, 391, 396
Ibsen, Henrik 170, 338, 353,
 441
Ibuse Masuji 295–296
Iceman Cometh, The (O'Neill) 17
id 430
identification **204**
identity **204–205**
ideology 14, 68, 80, 82, 148,
 205, 254
idiolect **205–206**
idyll **206**
Iliad, The (Homer) 7, 13, 182,
 200, 215, 220, 300, 305, 439
illocution 396
illusion
 dramatic **127**
 theater of 141
imagery **206**, 360
imagination/fancy 146, **206–
 207**, 215, 390
imagism 45, 134, 190, **207–
 208**, 298
imitation **208**
immigrant literature. *See* ethnic
 literature
implied author/reader **208–
 210**, 278, 279, 352
impostor. *See* alazon
impressionism **210**, 353
incest **210–211**
incorporation 193–194

incunabula 211
indeterminacy 43, **211–212**
Index librorum prohibitorum 70, **212**
Indian/Pakistani American literature 212
indirect metaphor 257
individualism **213–214**, 359
induction 214
inductive reasoning 137
industrial revolution **214**
influence **214**, 395
Ingarden, Roman 320
inkhornism **215**
in medias res **215**
inscape/instress **215**, 377
inspiration **215–216**, 220, 270
intentional fallacy 10, 42, **216**, 285
interactive computer fiction 203, **216**
interdisciplinarity **216–217**
interior monologue 73, 88, 96, 120, 173–174, **217**, 267, 293, 319, 393
interlude 133, **217–218**
interment camps 226
intermittent allegory 19
internal author 208, 209
internal conflict 95
internal rhyme **218**
interpolation **218**
interpretation 42, 151, 164, **218**, 429, 434
Interregnum. *See* Commonwealth period
intertextuality 7, **218–219**, 332, 354, 394–395, 415, 417
in the middle of things. *See* in medias res
intrinsic/extrinsic study of literature **155–156**, 285
introduction 214, 334–335, 340
invention **219–220**
invocation **220**, 270
Irish-American literature **220–222**
Irish National Theatre Company 1
Irish renaissance 25, **222**
Irish Republican Army 413, 414
irony 29, 87, 88, **222–223**, 443
irregular ode 300

Irving, Washington 233
Iser, Wolfgang 209, 320–321
Islam 233
Italian-American literature **223–224**

J

Jackson, Shirley 376
Jacobean era 68, 78, **225**, 255, 363, 425
Jacobs, Harriet 391
Jakobson, Roman 243, 258, 334
James I (king of England) 72, 225
James, Henry 8, 9, 38, 96, 119, 144, 170, 180–181, 242, 294, 326, 334, 353
James, William 214
Jameson, Fredric 148, 254–255, 327
Jansenism **225–226**, 329
Japan. *See* Bunraku; haiku; Kabuki; N
Japanese-American literature 226
jargon 3, **226–227**
Jauss, Hans Robert 356
jazz 11, 50, **227**, 271
jealousy 139, **227–228**
Jenkins, Jerry 237–238
jeremiad 228
jest books 228
Jesuits 225, **228–229**
Jewish-American literature **229–230**
Jewish stereotypes 29–31
jig **230–231**
jingle 231
Johnson, Denis 296
Johnson, Roman 312
Johnson, Samuel 12, 90, 317, 334, 361
jongleur 231
Jonson, Ben 67–68, 79, 90, 167, 202, 225, 255, 300, 324, 388, 432
jouissance 231
journal 118
journalism
  new **287–288**, 294
  yellow **448**
Joyce, James 8, 9, 23, 38–39, 52, 81, 88, 96, 109, 119–120, 130–131, 141, 143, 179, 191, 212, 267, 283,

284, 301, 326, 329, 377, 420, 431
Judaism 132, 229–230, 232, 274, 411
Judson, E. Z. C. *See* Buntline, Ned
Jung, Carl 38, 275, 343, 431
justice, poetic **325**
Juvenalian satire 375
juvenilia **231**

K

Kabbalah **232**, 274
Kabuki **232**
Kadlec, David 23–24
Kafka, Franz 2, 187, 189, 237, 291, 358
Kaiser, Georg 155
Kant, Immanuel 390, 426
Kazan, Elia 186
Kazantzakis, Nikos 13, 78, 172, 301–302
Keats, John 223, 277, 281–282, 300, 369, 394
Kennedy, William 49
kenning **232**
Kermode, Frank 281
Kerouac, Jack 50
Kerrigan, William 302
keystone (cops) comedies **232–233**
Kierkegaard, Søren 26, 152
Kim Ronyoung 233
King Lear (Shakespeare) 13, 46, 88, 93, 151, 183, 250, 278, 286–287, 357–358, 395, 404, 436
King's/Chamberlain's Men. *See* Chamberlain's/King's Men
Kingston, Maxine Hong 76
kitchen sink dramas **233**, 445
Klinkowitz, Jerome 294
Knickerbocker group 233
Koch, Kenneth 290–291
Koran 233
Korean-American literature **233–234**
Korzybski, Alfred 380–381
Kraus, Karl 375
Krieger, Murray 97
Kristeva, Julia 219, 331, 332, 343, 354, 412
Kroeber, Karl 134
Kuhn, Thomas 312
Kyd, Thomas 136

L

Lacan, Jacques 71, 114, 302, 320, 331, 332, 342, 343, 380, 431
La Fayette, Marie-Madeleine 228, 293
La Fontaine, Jean de 157
LaHaye, Tim 237–238
Lahiri, Jhumpa 212
Lake poets **235**
Lakoff, George 318–319
lamentation 91, 121
lampoon **235**
Langland, William 131
language. *See also* discourse
 deconstruction on 110, 259, 388
 dialect in 117, 205–206, 249
 endless variety of 196
 foregrounding in 169
 historical study of 321
 idiolect in 205–206
 ordinary **306**
 of poetry 324
 speech act theory on 395 396
 structuralism on 114, 399 401, 418, 431
 study of. *See* linguistics
 as "symbolic action" 128
language poets 45, **235**, 324
langue/parole **235–236,** 400
Lanham, Richard 407
Lardas, Konstantinos 187
Latino/Latina literature 197–198
law **236–237**
Lawrence, D. H. 302, 353
lay (lai) **237**
Lazarus, Emma 229
leaf 57
Leavis, F. R. 377, 380, 423, 429
Lee, Chang-rae 233–234
Le Fanu, Sheridan 435
"Left Behind" novels 52, **237–238**
legend 169, **238**
Leibniz, Gottfried 71
Leitch, Vincent 218–219
leitmotif (leitmotiv) **238,** 271
lesbian literature 163, **238–239,** 347–348
letter 43, 51, 144–145, **239**
Levine, George 106, 377

Levine, Lawrence 328
Lévi-Strauss, Claude 28, 58, 149–150
Lewis, C. S. 262, 332, 389–390
liberal/conservative imagination **239–240**
Liberty, Statue of 229
libretto 126, **240,** 304
light and sweetness **407**
light verse **241,** 436
Lillo, George 125
limerick **241,** 348
linguistic determinism 116
linguistics **241–242**
 competence/performance in 91
 discourse analysis in 122
 grammar in 185
 morphology in 268
 paradigm in 312
 phoneme in 321–322
 Prague School 334
 semantics in 380–381
 signs in 381, 387–388
 stylistics in 402
Lin Yutang 76
lisible/scriptible. *See* readerly/writerly
list poem 242
literacy/orality. *See* orality/literacy
literal **242**
literal meaning 171
literary forgery 322–323
literary history 198, **243**
literary periods. *See* periods, literary
literati **243**
literature **243–244**
litotes **244**
little magazine **244,** 387
liturgical drama **244–245,** 273, 428
locution 396
Lodge, David 63, 96, 208, 217
logocentrism 2, 110, **245,** 259, 320
Longinus 403
lost generation **245–246**
love 100, 108, 114, 227, **246–248,** 247, 258, 323
Lovejoy, Arthur 171, 198–199
Love's Labour's Lost (Shakespeare) 89, 215, 398
Lowell, Amy 208
Lowenthal, Leo 173

Lowry, Malcolm 16
Luckmann, Thomas 392
Lucretius 377
Lyly, John 150
lyric 135, 179, **248,** 251, 300, 393, 394

M

macaronic verse 249
Macbeth (Shakespeare) 16, 28, 40, 88, 107, 137–138, 206, 218, 420
"MacFlecknoe" (Dryden) 5
macguffin 249
Machiavel 249
Machiavelli, Niccolò 86, 249
Macpherson, James 307
Macready, Charles 40
madness **249–251**
madrigal 251
magazine **251–252,** 387, 451. *See also* little magazine
magic realism 49, 73, 159, 168, **252,** 331, 354
Mailer, Norman 162, 292, 440
Malamud, Bernard 49
malapropism **252–253**
Malory, Sir Thomas 37
Mandeville, Sir John 127
manifesto 253
Mankiewicz, Joseph 181
Mann, Thomas 38, 109, 161, 213, 251, 353
mannerism 253
Mansfield, Katherine 173–174
manuscript 253
March of Time, The (film) 124
Marinetti, Tommaso 175
marinism 48, **253**
Marlowe, Christopher 31, 136, 160, 161, 177, 213, 367, 433
Marprelate controversy 253
Marquand, John P. 66
Marvell, Andrew 90
Marx, Karl 17, 18, 66, 80–81, 117, 254, 267
Marxist criticism 148, 205, 244, **254–255**
 on bourgeois 57, 66, 96, 205, 432
 Brecht (Bertolt) and 19, 254
 on closure 82
 on consumption 96–97
 cultural studies in 103

on hegemony 193–194,
205, 434
historical criticism and
198
on humanism 202
New York intellectuals in
289–290, 358
politics in 327
on popular culture 173,
328
on power 333
reification in 357
on religion 358
on universality 432
value judgment in 434
masculine ending 162, 367
masque **255**
mass culture 328
Matthiessen, F. O. 21
Maus (Speigelman) 185
Mayakovsky, Vladimir 175
McCarthy, Mary 63
McCarthyism 124–125
McCourt, Frank 222
McDermott, Alice 221
McEwan, Ian 96
"McGuffey Readers" 27
McLuhan, Marshall 181–182,
305
McNamee, Eoin 414
meaning
alternative 19
deconstruction on 110,
111, 218, 323
determining 170, 216,
218
four levels of 20, **171,**
239, 242
New Criticism on 10,
218, 284, 352
poststructuralism on 332
pragmatism on 333
reader response criticism
on 218, 352
simplest 242
structuralism on 400
study of 380–381
Measure for Measure
(Shakespeare) 338, 389
medieval drama **255–256,**
266, 424
medieval romance 7, 37, 100,
104, 157, 163, 237, 246,
256, 262, 266, 369
mediology **256**
Mehlman, Jeffrey 31
melodrama 95, **256,** 392

Melville, Herman 66, 153,
177, 236, 335, 346, 358,
408, 445
memento mori motif 269
memoir 43, **256**
Mencken, H. L. 375
Merchant of Venice, The
(Shakespeare) 65, 236
Mermaid Tavern **256**
Merry Wives of Windsor, The
(Shakespeare) 7
metafiction **257,** 331
metaphor **257**
analogy as 22
brotherhood as 172
chain of being as 71
conceit as 92
connotation and 113
fall as 158
imagery in 206
kenning as 232
in metaphysical poetry 258
mind as mirror as 265
mixed 69
simile compared to 389
symbol compared to 408
tenor and vehicle of 413
underground as 431
metaphor/metonymy **257–**
258, 312
metaphysical (supernatural) evil
150, 151
metaphysical poetry 48, 92,
122–123, 225, 257, **258–**
259, 361, 443
metaphysics of presence 245,
259
metatheatre **259**
meter 5, 169, **259–261,** 375
Method acting 188, **261–262,**
269
metonymy **262,** 410
metonymy/metaphor **257–**
258, 312
Mexican American literature
197
Michalaros, Demetrios 186
Middle Ages 108, 163, **262,**
444
middle class. *See* bourgeois
Middle Comedy 85, **263**
Middle English 20, 26, **263**
Midsummer Night's Dream, A
(Shakespeare) 86, 130, 142,
206
miles gloriosus. *See* braggart
warrior

Miller, Arthur 97
Miller, J. Hillis 148, 448
Millett, Kate 162
Milton, John 69, 90, 101–102,
171, 204, 209, 261, 309,
311, 357, 362, 405
mime **263–264,** 265
mimesis 10, 35, **264,** 354
mimesis/diegesis **119–120,**
173–174
mimetic desire 139, **264–265**
mind as mirror **265,** 392
minimalism **265**
mini-series 412
minnesingers **266**
Minor, William Chester 308
minstrel **266**
miracle play **266**
mirror, mind as **265**
Mitchell, Charles 214
Mitchell, Margaret 198
mixed metaphor 69
mock epic **266**
modernism **266–267**
anarchism and 23
"as if" fictions and 39
characters in 73
early 133
in Edwardian era 134
on fratricide 172
New Humanism on 287
psychoanalysis and 342
symbolism in 19
time in 421
Molière 6, 57, 86, 89, 120,
126, 311
Momaday, N. Scott 279
monologue 119, **267**
apostrophe **33,** 267
dramatic **127,** 139, 267
interior. *See* interior
monologue
in rap 350
soliloquy 267, **393**
in stand-up 397
monometer 260, **267**
montage **268,** 421
Montaigne, Michel de 108,
146, 359, 390
Montrose, Louis 286
mood **268**
Moore, Marianne 148
moral 151, **268,** 417
moral (human) evil 150, 151
morality play 19, 30, **268,** 343,
385, 436
More, Sir Thomas 310, 359, 433

morpheme **268**
morphology **268**
Morris, William 369, 445
mortality. *See* death
Morton, Thomas 84
Moscow Art Theater 121, 188, **268–269**
motif **269**, 417
motion picture. *See* films
motivation **269**, 280
Movement, the **269**
movies. *See* films
Mozart, Wolfgang Amadeus 126
muckrakers 66, **269–270**
Mukherjee, Bharati 212
Mullan, John 227
multiculturalism 64, **270**
mummers' play/mumming play **270**
Murray, James 308
muse 215, 220, **270**
music 251, **270–271**, 304. *See also* jazz
musical 77, 240, **271–273**, 304–305
music hall **273**, 435
mystery plays 30, 86, 98, 104, 245, 262, 263, 266, **273–274**, 310
mysticism 26, **274**, 283
myth **274–275**. *See also* demythologizing
    of fall 158
    folk 169
    of golden age 183–184
    of Hamlet 191
    in Native American literature 279
    repetition in 360
    and well-being of society 39, 172
myth criticism **275–276**
    anthropology in 28
    on catharsis 69
    on characters 73
    on Christ 77
    on comedy 85
    and genre criticism 180
    on imagination/fancy 207
    irony in 223
    Jung (Carl) and 431
    literary history in 243
    and New Criticism 275, 285
    on religion 358
    on scapegoat 376
    on Shakespeare 62

N

naive/sentimental **277**
narcissism **277–278**
narratee **278**
narrative 179, **278**, 279. *See also* fiction
    captivity **67**, 84
    in epic 140
    in fable 157
    foreshadowing in 170
    in free indirect style 173–174
    on Holocaust 200
    interior monologue in 217
    in medias res in 215
    in novel 293
    in picaresque 322
    point of view in 278–279, 304, 325–326
    in saga 373
    slave 11, 22, 337, **391**, 445
narrative complaint 91
narratology 122, 208, **278**
narrator **278–279**
    dialect of 205–206
    in dream vision 131
    omniscient **304**, 326
    of radio drama 349
    reliable 279
    unreliable 279
    voice of 119–120, 173–174
Nash, Ogden 267
Native American literature **279**
Nativist Party 40
naturalism 66, 116, **280**, 293
naturalist/realist 181, 280, 353, **355**
nature
    as Absolute 2
    and art **280–281**, 370–371
    four elements of 202
Nazism 199–200, 251. *See also* Holocaust
negative capability **281–282**
negative identification 204
negritude **282**, 330
Nemoianu, Virgil 240
neoclassicism 81, **282**
    in Augustan age 41
    Battle of the books in 50
    on decorum 111
    genres in 180

nature/art in 281
New Humanism compared to 287
    poetic justice in 325
    product criticism in 338
    in Restoration era 362
    sensibility in 382
    Sturm und Drang against 401
neoconservative 240, **283**
neologism **283**
neo-noir 166
Neoplatonism 71, **283**, 323
neorealism 124, **283–284**
neo-Scholasticism **284**, 358, 377
new apocalypse movement **284**
New Comedy 85–86
New Criticism 243, **284–286**
    affective fallacy in 10, 285, 352
    classical principles of 81
    on conceit 92
    on concrete universal 94
    on context 97
    in *The Criterion* 101
    deconstruction compared to 111
    development of 20
    dissociation of sensibility in 123
    explication in 154
    extrinsic/intrinsic study in 156, 285
    on form 170
    fugitive/agrarians in 175
    on historical criticism 198
    on imagery 206
    intentional fallacy in 42, 216, 285
    irony in 223
    on meaning 10, 218, 284, 352
    on metaphysical poetry 258
    myth criticism and 275, 285
    paradox in 312
    paraphrase in 313
    product criticism in 338
    and projectivism 285, 339
    on religion 358
    on Romanticism 371
    Sewanee Review and 385
    on Shakespeare (William) 298
    tension in 413

texture in 416
transactional theory compared to 425
New Formalism **286**
New Historicism **286–287**. *See also* literary history
on context 97, 286
definition of 74
ethnography and 28, 150
historical criticism and 198
poststructuralism and 286
on power 333
on text 102, 286
thick description in 419
on travel accounts 427
on universality 432
New Humanism 2, 202, **287**, 371
new journalism **287–288**, 294
Newman, John Henry 308
new novel **288**, 293
newspeak 288
New Testament 52, 113, 152, 164, 171, 273, 297, 311–312, 314, 429. *See also* Bible
New Wave 42, 166, **288–289**
New Yorker, The **289**, 295
New York intellectuals 230, **289–290**, 358
New York Review of Books, The **290**
New York school 6, 178, **290–291**
Nietzsche, Friedrich 32, 43, 114, 147, 152, 183, 250–251, 267, 291, 365
nihilism 207, **291**
N **291–292**
Nobel Prize **292**
nom de plume **292**
nonet 398
nonfiction films 165
nonfiction novel 164, 288, **292**, 293
nouveau roman. *See* new novel
nouvelle vague. *See* New Wave
novel(s) **293**
in Augustan age 41
campus **63**
comic **87–88**
dialogism in 117
dime **120**, 345, 442
education. *See* bildungsroman
episodic **143**
epistolary **144–145**
gothic. *See* gothic novel

graphic **185**
historical **198**, 295–296
"Left Behind" 52, **237–238**
new **288**, 293
nonfiction 164, 288, **292**, 293
protest 368
sentimental 382, **383**
short. *See* novella
thesis. *See* roman à thèse
novella **294–295**, 387
novel of ideas **293–294**
novel of manners **294**
novel with a key. *See* roman à clef
Novy Mir **295**
nuclear war 99, **295–296**, 378–379
numerology **296–297**, 299
Nussbaum, Martha 325
Nuyorican Poetry 197

O

objective correlative **298**
objectivism 208, **298**
obligatory scene **298**
occasional verse **299**
occult **299**
O'Connor, Flannery 88, 170, 221, 357
octave **299**, 307, 394
octavo 57
octet 398
ode 107, **300**
Odysseus/Ulysses theme **300–302**
Odyssey, The (Homer) 182, 200, 300, 305, 431
Odyssey, The (Kazantzakis) 301–302
OED. *See* Oxford English Dictionary
Oedipal complex 113, 210, 214, 265, **302–303**, 342, 343
Oedipus Rex (Sophocles) 188, 223, 280, 302
off Broadway **303**
O'Hara, Frank 6, 290
Okada, John 226
Olbrechts-Tyteca, Lucie 366
Old Comedy 85, 263
Old English 20, **303–304**
Old Testament 52, 164, 171, 210, 228, 273, 297, 341, 348, 429. *See also* Bible

Old Vic **304**, 371
Olesha, Yuri 139–140
Olsen, Tillie 388
Olson, Charles 339
omniscient narrator **304**, 326
Ondaatje, Michael 404
O'Neill, Eugene 17, 48, 155, 221, 303
Ong, Walter J. 305, 313
onomatopoeia 271, **304**
On the Origin of Species (Darwin) 106, 267
ontology **304**
Ooka, Shohei 251
opera 240, 270, **304**
operetta 271, **304**
opposition, binary 28, **53–54**, 70, 103
orality/literacy 57, 140, 158, 163, 168, 169, 279, **305–306**, 373
ordinary language **306**
organic form 170, **306**, 403
orientalism **306–307**
original sin 158, **307**
Orwell, George 288, 375
"Oscar." *See* Academy Awards
Ossian 70, 163, **307**
Othello (Shakespeare) 7, 47, 102, 139, 151, 227, 228, 269, 325, 344, 360, 416, 436
other/self 162, **380**
ottava rima **307**
"Our World." *See* Novy Mir
Outcault, R. F. 448
Ovid 351
Oxford, Edward de Vere 31
Oxford English Dictionary (OED) **308**
Oxford Movement **308–309**
oxymoron **309**

P

paean **310**
Pafko at the Wall (DeLillo) 49
pagan gods 182–183, 357
pageant **310**
Paine, Thomas 311
palindrome **310**
palinode **310**
pamphlets **310–311**
panegyric **311**
pantaloon (pantalone) **311**
pantoum **311**
parable **311–312**
paradigm **312**

paradigm shift 312
paradox 194, 223, 291, **312,** 413
parallelism **312**
paraphrase **313**
parataxis **313**
Parnassians **314**
parody 59, **314**
parole/langue **235–236,** 400
parousia **314**
Parry, Milman 305
Partisan Review 289, 290
Pascal, Blaise 225, 329–330
Passage to Ararat (Arlen) 36
passion play **315**
Pasternak, Boris 374
pastiche **315**
pastoral 35, 109, 133–134, 135, 280 281, **315–316,** 335
pathetic fallacy **316**
pathos **316**
patriarchy 162, 178, **317,** 319
PC. *See* political correctness
Peirce, Charles 381
pen name. *See* nom de plume
pentad 128
pentameter 260. *See also* iambic pentameter
pentateuch **317, 411**
Perelman, Chaim 366
performance/competence **91**
performative statements 396
Pericles (Shakespeare) 77, 211, 369
periodic sentence 312, **317**
periods, literary **317–318**
peripeteia 22, 205, **318,** 423
periphrasis 79
perlocution 396
persona **318**
personal allusion 20
personification 19, **318–319**
perspectivism 52, **319**
Petrakis, Harry Mark 149, 186–187
Petrarch 359, 384, 386, 394
phallocentrism 114, 162, **319–320,** 444
phallogocentrism 320
phenomenology 34, 152, 178, 209, 210, **320–321**
philia 246
philistine **321,** 407
philology 241, **321**
philosophes **321**
phlegm 202

phoneme 268, **321–322**
phonocentrism 245, 446
phonology 241
picaresque 143, 221–222, 293, **322,** 359
pièce bien faite. See well-made play
Pindaric ode 300
Pinker, Steven 95–96
pirated edition **322**
Piscator, Erwin 141
pity 383
plagiarism **322–323**
Plath, Sylvia 94, 109
Plato 4, 24, 33, 56, 71, 108, 117, 118, 170, 280, 283, 323, 390, 417, 418, 433
Platonism **323**
play(s) **323,** 331
   absurdist 2
   chronicle **78**
   miracle **266**
   morality 19, 30, **268,** 343, 385, 436
   mummers' **270**
   mystery *See* mystery plays
   passion **315**
   problem 179, **338**
   sacramental. *See* auto sacramental
   saint 266, **373**
   satyr **375**
   well-made **441**
plot 95, 113, 249, 293, 324, 399, 403
plurisignation 21, **324**
Poe, Edgar Allan 22, 114, 200, 243, 271
poetaster **324**
poète maudit 151, **324**
poetic diction **324**
poetic justice **325**
poetic license **325**
Poetics (Aristotle) 16, 35, 69, 75, 123, 190, 205, 418, 423, 432
poetry **325.** *See also* meter; rhyme; verse
   alliteration in 20
   apocalyptic 32
   cockney school of **83**
   confessional 10, **94 95,** 109
   graveyard school of 108, **186**
   hermetic **195**
   language of 324

metaphysical. *See* metaphysical poetry
New York school of 6, 178, **290–291**
pre-Raphaelite 335
symbolists. *See* symbolists
point of view 319, **325–326**
Poirier, Richard 334
Polidoris, John 435
political censorship 70, 374
political correctness (PC) 63, 64, 288, **326**
politics 14, 205, **326–327**
Pope, Alexander 5, 61, 71, 99, 112, 137, 144, 196, 204, 259, 266, 282, 364, 375–376, 407, 409, 443, 451
popular culture 47, 97, 102–103, 173, 194, **327–329,** 381, 434
pornography 70, 145, **329**
Porter, Cole 261
Port-Royal 225, **329–330**
positive identification 204
postcolonial studies 282, **330**
postmodernism **330–331,** 418–419
   characters in 73
   development of 173, 331
   episodic novel in 143
   on imagination/fancy 207
   intertextuality in 219
   play in 323, 331
   poetic diction in 324
   process criticism in 339
   on representation 361
   on rhetoric 365
poststructuralism **331–332**
   on author 42–43, 332
   binary opposition in 54, 70, 103
   on center/decenter 70–71
   cultural studies in 103
   development of 243–244, 331–332
   episteme in 143–144
   ethnography and 149, 150
   existentialism compared to 146
   on fiction 164
   on humanism 202
   intertextuality in 218–219, 332, 415
   on meaning 332
   psychoanalysis and 343

semiotics/semiology
in 381
on signs 387
on subject 402
on text 218–219, 415
on writing 446
Poulet, Georges 179
poulter's measure 172, **332**
Pound, Ezra 23, 30–31, 65,
207–208, 249, 250, 266, 339
power 286, 317, 319, **332–333**
Power and the Glory, The (Greene)
74
practical criticism 101, 285,
333
pragmatism 23, 214, **333–334,**
419
Prague School 169, **334**
Praz, Mario 108
précis **334**
preface **334–335**
pre-Raphaelites 38, **335**
prescriptive grammar 185
presence, metaphysics of 245,
259
presupposition 219
primary epic 140
primitivism **335**
prison literature **335–338**
private/public theaters
344–345
problematic **338**
problem play 179, **338**
process criticism **338–339**
process/product **338–339**
product criticism 338
Prohibition 16, 176
projectivism 45, 208, 298,
339, 374
prolepsis **339**
proletarian literature 66,
339–340, 445
proletariat 80, 81
prologue 214, **340**
prompt book **340**
propaganda 14, 124, 327, **340,**
359, 393, 440
proscenium 34, 127, **340,** 397
prose **340–341,** 367
prose poem 325, **341**
prosody 17, **341,** 347, 403,
409
protagonist 6, 27, 95, 195, 205,
341. *See also* hero/heroine
Protestantism 42, 356, 359. *See
also* Calvinism; Puritanism;
Reformation

protest novel 368
Proulx, E. Annie 29
Proust, Marcel 228, 360, 420
proverb **341,** 382
pseudepigrapha **341**
psychoanalysis. *See also* unconscious
in biography 54
and character depic-
tion 73
on desire 114
on dreams 130, 131–132
on family romance 159
on guilt 188
on incest 210
on jealousy 227
on narcissism 277
on sexuality 247
psychoanalytical criticism 320,
342–343
psychobiography **343**
psychological evil 150
psychological time 420
psychomachia **343–344**
Ptolemaic system **344**
public/private theaters
344–345
pulp fiction **345,** 378
pun 252–253, **345–346**
puppet theater 58–59, 385
Puritanism 61–62, 65, 67, 68,
72, 84, 90, 182, 253, 307,
344, 345, **346**
purple prose **346**
Puzo, Mario 224

Q

quadrivium/trivium 365, **428**
quantitative verse 169, 260,
347
quarto 57, **347**
quatrain 103, 311, **347,** 386,
394, 398
queer theory **347–348**
question, rhetorical **367**
Quinones, Ricardo 172
quintain **348,** 398
Qumran manuscripts **348**

R

Rabelais, François 16, 236,
314, 349, 359
Rabelaisian **349**
Racine, Jean 211, 329–330
Radcliffe, Anne 184

radio drama **349**
raisonneur **350,** 399
Ramus, Peter 365
Ransom, John Crowe 94, 285
rap **350,** 388, 436
rape **350–351**
rationalism 137, 144, 370
reader. *See also* audience
computer user as 216
expectations of 356
implied **208–210,** 278,
279, 352
psychoanalysis of 342
in transactional theory
425
readerly/writerly 332, 339,
351
reader response criticism **352**
on closure 82
development of 75, 352,
366
on empathy 137
on imagery 206
on implied author/reader
209, 352
on meaning 218, 352
phenomenology in 321
on popular culture 328
on process/product 339
subjective 402
realism **353–355**
Bible and 52–53
on capitalism 66
deconstruction on 354
in film theory 166, 354
in fin de siècle 167
and genres 180
in historical novel 198
in kitchen sink dramas
233
magic 49, 73, 159, 168,
252, 331, 354
in Method acting 261
metonymy in 258
on motivation 269
neorealism **283–284**
in new novel 288
in novels 293
referent in 356
romance in opposition to
353, 369
on Romanticism 371
and science in literature
377
socialist 119, 140, 175,
254, 354, **393,** 445
theatrical 127

realist/naturalist 181, 280, 353, **355**
reality/appearance **33–34**, 144
reasoner. *See raisonneur*
recension **355**
reception theory 218, 352, **356**
redaction **356**
referent **356**, 360, 387, 388
Reformation 42, 52, 99, 213, 310, **356**. *See also* Calvinism; Puritanism
refrain **356**, 360
reification **357**
Reilly, Patrick 188
reliable narrator 279
religious censorship 70
religious existentialism 152
religious faith 114, 258, **357– 358**, 376–377, 384
Renaissance 133, **358–359**
  ancient gods in 183
  anti Semitism in 30
  appearance/reality in 33–34
  authority in 42
  chain of being in 71
  on city 79
  comedy in 86
  Copernican system in 344, 359
  courtesy books in 99
  on death 108
  dialogue in 118
  epithalamion in 145
  genres in 180
  homosexuality in 177
  humanism in 201, 359, 420
  individualism in 213, 359
  invention in 219
  macaronic verse in 249
  on madness 250
  masque in 255
  nature/art in 281
  Neoplatonism in 283
  occult in 299
  opera in 304
  rhetoric in 365
  skepticism in 390
  time in 420
  tragedy in 424
  travel in 426–427
  use of anatomy as term in 24
repartee 398
repetition 356, **359–360**
representation 265, **360–361**

reputation 92, **361–362**
Restoration comedy **363**
Restoration era 86, 126, 196, **362–363**
"retribalization" 181–182
revenge **363**
review **363–364**, 434
revision **364**
revolutionary/early national period **364**
revue 271
rhetoric 241, **365–366**
  anaphora in 23
  argument in 35
  catachresis in 69
  chiasmus in 74
  circumlocution in 79
  connotations of words in 113
  epideictic oratory in 142
  ethos in 150
  exordium in 154
  hendiadys in 194
  hypotaxis in 203
  invention in 219
  panegyric in 311
  parataxis in 313
  pathos in 316
  syllepsis in 407
  tautology in 411
  topos in 422
  trope in 428
rhetorical criticism 352, **366–367**
rhetorical question **367**
rhyme 260, **367**
  analyzing 375
  assonance **40**, 367
  internal **218**
  lack of 174
  Parnassians on 314
  in quatrain 347
rhyme royal **367**
rhythm **367**
  sprung 367, **397**
Richards, I. A. 333, 413
Richardson, Samuel 144
Ricoeur, Paul 195, 390, 421
Riefenstahl, Leni 124
Rihani, Ameen 34
"ripple dissolve" 123
rising action 174–175
ritual **367–368**
Robbe-Grillet, Alain 227–228
rococo **368**
Roethke, Theodore 94
roman à clef **368**

roman à thèse **368**
romance **368–370**
  adventure in 8
  family **159**
  in fantasy 159
  in historical novel 198
  medieval. *See* medieval romance
  and novel 293
  realism in opposition to 353, 369
Roman religion (ancient) 182–183
"Romantic agony" 108
romantic comedy **370**
Romantic irony 223
Romanticism **370–371**
  on Absolute 2
  on alienation 18
  ancient gods in 183
  artist/hero in 38
  as avant-garde 45
  Byronic hero in 60
  on capitalism 65–66
  on city 79
  classicism in opposition to 81
  on courtly love 100
  on death 108
  Don Juan theme in 126
  empathy in 137
  Faustian theme in 161
  on fratricide 172
  genres in 180
  gothic novel in 184, 370
  Hamlet theme in 191, 192
  imagism compared to 207
  on incest 211
  Lake poets in **235**
  on love 246–247
  on madness 250–251
  metaphor in 258
  narcissism in 277
  nature/art in 281, 370–371
  New Humanism on 287, 371
  Parnassians against 314
  pastoral in 281
  poetic diction in 324
  primitivism in 335
  process criticism in 339
  romance in 369
  sonnets in 394
  sublime in 403
  suffering/sympathy in 405

Romeo and Juliet (Shakespeare) 77, 108, 129, 247
Roosevelt, Theodore 269
Rorty, Richard 265, 333–334, 361–362, 392
Rosenberg, Harold 6
Rosenblatt, Louise 425
Rostand, Edmond 203
Roth, Philip 230
round character 73
Roundheads 70
Rousseau, Jean-Jacques 335, 370, 383
Rowlandson, Mary 67
Royal National Theatre Company 371
Royal Shakespeare Company (RSC) 371–372
Rushdie, Salman 70, 160
Ruskin, John 316, 445
Russell, John 278
Russian formalism 112, 170, 243, 334, 372
Rymer, Thomas 325

S

sacramental play. *See* auto sacramental
sacrifice 172, 368, 376
saga 373
Said, Edward 306–307, 330
saint play 266, 373
Salinger, J. D. 205–206, 278, 316, 449, 450
salon 373
samizdat 374
San Francisco renaissance 374
Santayana, George 323
Sapphics 374
Saroyan, William 36
Sartre, Jean-Paul 46, 153, 188, 202
Satan 151, 160–161
Satanic Verses, The (Rushdie) 160
satire 374–375
  in burlesque 59
  in campus novel 63
  in comic novel 87
  by Connecticut wits 95
  cynical 104
  by Dickens (Charles) 79
  in fabliau 157
  of Gilded Age 181
  in grotesque 187
  Horatian 375
  Juvenalian 375

  in lampoon 235
  of law 236
  in macaronic verse 249
  in mock epic 266
  in parody 314
  in picaresque 322
  by Rabelais (François) 349
  in realism 354
  in roman à clef 368
  by Shakespeare (William) 179
  by Swift (Jonathan) 50, 311, 375
satyr play 375
Saussure, Ferdinand de 116, 235–236, 242, 334, 381, 387–388, 399, 400, 418
scansion 61, 260, 375–376
scapegoat 85, 368, 376
Scarlet Letter, The (Hawthorne) 8
scenario 376
scene 376
Schiller, Friedrich 277
Scholasticism 71, 262, 284, 314, 376–377
Scholes, Robert 432
Schuyler, James 291
science 377–378, 429
science fiction 99, 103, 112, 134–135, 159, 184, 201, 295, 296, 378–379, 441, 451
scientific determinism 116
scop 379
Scott, Sir Walter 198
screenplay 379, 428
screwball comedy 87, 379–380
Scribe, Eugène 441
scriptible/lisible. *See* readerly/writerly
scriptures 380
Scrutiny 380
secondary epic 140
second-person narrative 326
secularism 201, 202
seize the day. *See* carpe diem
self
  autonomous 205
  "centered" 71
  modernism on 267
self-help book 404
self-love 277
self/other 162, 380
semantics 380–381
semiotics/semiology 166, 294, 354–355, 381
Senecan style 5, 78, 381–382, 423–424

Senghor, Léopold 282
sensibility 370, 382
  dissociation of 122–123, 143, 361, 377, 443
sentence, periodic 312, 317
sententia 382
sentimental comedy 85, 86, 382–383
sentimentality 316, 382, 383
sentimental/naive 277
sentimental novel 382, 383
septet 398
sequel 383
serial 8, 251–252, 383–384, 391–392, 412
sermon 84, 384
sestet 103, 384, 394, 398
sestina 384
setting 384
seven deadly sins 139, 384–385
Seven Types of Ambiguity (Empson) 20–21
Sewanee Review 385
sex 162, 178
Sexton, Anne 94
sexuality 100, 210–211, 246, 247, 329, 350–351
shadow theater 385
Shadwell, Thomas 126
Shakespeare, William. *See also* specific plays
  accent of performers of 112
  acting company of 54, 71–72, 167, 182, 192, 344, 345, 385
  on adultery 7
  on aging 13
  on alienation 18
  on ancient gods 183
  on androgyny 24
  anticlimax used by 28
  anti-heroic characters of 29
  anti-Stratfordian theories on 31, 341
  on appearance 33–34
  biography of 3
  on body 56
  bowdlerization of plays of 57
  canon of works of 122
  catastrophe used by 69
  chorus used by 77
  chronology of plays of 107

climax used by 82
on colonialism 84
comedies of 86, 89
comic relief used by 88
on commercialism 65
concordance to 93
conflict used by 95
on cony-catcher 98
on death 108
devotion to 48
dieresis used by 120
as director 120
dirge by 121
on dream 129, 130
on drinking 16
in Elizabethan era 136
emendation of work of 137
enjambment used by 137–138
on envy 139
epilogue used by 142
euphuism used by 150
on evil 151, 344
exposition used by 154
feminine ending used by 161–162
First Folio of works of 46, 53, 72, 102, 107, 167, 340
foil used by 168
on fratricide 172
on genre 179
hamartia used by 190
hendiadys used by 194
imagery used by 206
on imagination/fancy 206
on incest 211
inkhornism used by 215
interpolation used by 218
invocation used by 220
in Jacobian era 225
on jealousy 227, 228
on law 236
on love 247
on madness 250
memento mori motif used by 269
metatheatre used by 259
meter of 204, 261
myth criticism on 62
on narcissism 278
on nature/art 281
New Criticism on 298
New Historicism on 286–287
on occultism 299

Odysseus/Ulysses theme used by 301
organic form by 306
oxymoron used by 309
pirated edition of work of 322
on poetic justice 325
poetic license used by 325
problem plays by 338
psychoanalytical criticism on 302
pun used by 345
raisonneur used by 350
on rape 351
on religious faith 357–358
repetition used by 360
on revenge 363
romantic plays by 369, 370
on scapegoat 376
sententia used by 382
silence used by 389
sonnets by 21, 55, 91, 99, 177, 344, 386–387, 394, 403, 422
sources of 395
stichomythia used by 398
on suffering/sympathy 404
textual criticism on 416
theaters of 54–55, 71–72, 90, 182, 344, 345
on theatrum mundi 417
threnody by 419
on time 420
tomb of 145
tone of 421–422
touchstone used by 422
tragedies by 424
universality of 432
villains created by 47, 139, 213, 249, 269, 341, 344, 436, 437
zeugma used by 451
Shakespearean apocrypha 385–386
Shaw, George Bernard 66, 87, 126, 135, 335, 353, 425
Shelley, Mary 378, 435
Shelley, Percy Bysshe 108, 327
Shklovsky, Viktor 112
short novel. See novella
short story 387
shot 387
close-up 82, 103
cut from 103
deep focus 112

dissolve 123, 421
establishing 147
fade 158
freeze frame 174, 411
tracking 422
zoom 451
Showalter, Elaine 189
Sidney, Sir Philip 264
sign 166, 381, 387, 399
signifier/signified 387–388, 399–400, 401
signifyin[g] 388
silence 388–389
simile 22, 206, 389
sin(s)
original 158, 306
seven deadly 139, 384–385
sitcom 389, 412
sjuzet 399
Skelton, John 389–390
skeltonics 389–390
skepticism 390–391, 419
slang 169, 350
Slatoff, Walter 405–406
slave narratives 11, 22, 337, 391, 445
Smedley, Agnes 337
Snow, C. P. 377, 429
soap opera 349, 391–392, 412
social construction 83, 128, 392–393
socialism 157
socialist realism 119, 140, 175, 254, 354, 393, 445
Socrates 108, 117, 118, 135
Socratic irony 222–223
soliloquy 267, 393
Solzhenitsyn, Alexandr 295, 336, 368, 374, 445
Sone, Monica 226
song 270, 393–394
song of deeds. See chanson de geste
sonnets 394
curtal 103
Elizabethan 136
on love 246, 323
Petrarchan 359, 384, 386, 394
Shakespeare's 21, 55, 91, 99, 177, 344, 386–387, 394, 403, 422
Sontag, Susan 62
Sophocles 107, 188, 223, 236, 280, 300, 302
source 7, 214, 394–395

Southern renaissance 395
Soviet Union 140, 175, 254, 295, 336, 354, 374, 393, 445
speech act theory 6, 306, **395–396**
Speigelman, Art 185
Spenser, Edmund 297
Spenserian stanza **396**
spirit of the time. *See* zeitgeist
Spivack, Bernard 344
spondee 169, 260, 261
sprung rhythm 367, **397**
stage **397**
    apron **34,** 340, 397
    arena 340, 397
    discovery space on 122
    downstage/upstage **127**
    in Elizabethan era 34, 122, 344
    proscenium 34, 127, **340,** 397
stage directions **397**
stand-up **397–398**
Stanford, W. B. 300–301
Stanislavski, Konstantin 121, 261, 268, 419
stanza **398**
    Spenserian **396**
Stein, Gertrude 238–239, 245–246
Steinbeck, John 77, 368
stereotype **398**
Sterne, Laurence 420
Stevens, Wallace 339
Stevenson, Robert Louis 413–414
stichomythia **398**
stock character 73, 85, 398, **399**
stoicism **399**
Stoker, Bram 435
Stoppard, Tom 192
storm and stress. *See* Sturm und Drang
story **399**
    adventure **8**
    detective. *See* detective story
    ghost **180–181**
    short **387**
Strachey, Lytton 54
stream of consciousness 217, 293, 326
Strindberg, August 154–155, 388
stroke of theater. *See* coup de théâtre

strophe 32
structuralism 170, **399–401**
    anthropology and 28
    binary opposition in 53
    deconstruction compared to 111
    development of 116, 236, 242, 334
    ethnography and 149
    foregrounding in 169
    on language 114, 399–401, 418, 431
    and Marxist criticism 254
    on meaning 400
    on myth 275
    on myth criticism 275, 276
    and poststructuralism 331, 332
    semiotics/semiology in 381
    on signs 387, 399–400, 401
structure 170, 252, **401**
studio system 121, 272, **401**
Sturm und Drang 370, **401–402**
style 242, **402**
stylistics 242, **402**
subject **402**
    "decentered" 71
subjective criticism **402,** 425
sublime 366, **403**
subplot **403**
substitution **403**
subtext **403–404**
success manual **404**
suffering **404–406**
Suffrage Movement 134
Sunday Mass 244–245
superego 430
supernatural (metaphysical) evil 150, 151
supplement *(supplément)* **406**
surrealism 105, 342, **406–407**
suspense **407**
sweetness and light **407**
Swift, Jonathan 25, 50, 311, 375
syllepsis **407**
symbol 267, **408**
symbolic action 128, **409**
symbolism 372, 408. *See also* numerology
symbolists 10, 18, 19, 45, 110, 174, 271, 324, **409**
sympathetic imagination 246

sympathy 137, 383, **404–406**
synchronic/diachronic **116**
syncope **409–410**
synecdoche 262, **410**
synoptic gospels 52, **410**
syntax 241–242
synthesis 117

T

tableau **411**
tale **411**
Talmud **411**
Tan, Amy 149
Tanner, Tony 7
Taoism **411**
tautology **411**
Taylor, Edward 346
tearful comedy. *See* comédie larmoyante
television 47, 180, 181–182, 305, 389
television documentaries 124–125
television drama 115–116, 391–392, **411–412**
Tel Quel **412**
Tempest, The (Shakespeare) 84, 281, 299, 369, 417
Tennyson, Alfred Tennyson 301, 304, 369
tenor **413**
tension **413**
tercet 398
terminology 226–227
terrorism 23, **413–415**
tetralogy **415**
tetrameter 260, 261, **415**
text **415**. *See also* meaning
    deconstruction on 33, 415
    New Criticism on 216
    New Historicism on 102, 286
    poststructuralism on 218–219, 415
    readerly/writerly 332, 351
    in transactional theory 425
textual criticism 53, 57, 84, 95, **415–416**
texture 206, **416**
theater(s)
    of the absurd 2, 87, 160, 425
    actor-manager of 6–7, 120–121

Boulevard **57**
of cruelty 250, **416**
epic 5, 51, 127, **141–142,**
254
of illusion 141
in Japan. *See* Bunraku;
Kabuki; N
public/private **344–345**
shadow **385**
of the world. *See* theatrum
mundi
Yiddish 132
theatrical realism 127
theatrum mundi 130, **417**
thematic criticism 418
theme 97, 238, 269,
417–418
Theocritus 315
theology 357
theory **418–419**
thesis novel. *See roman à thèse*
thick description **419**
third-person narrative 278–
279, 304, 326
Thomas, Dylan 284
Thompson, Francis 74
Thoreau, Henry David
213–214
threnody **419**
through line **419**
thrust stage. *See* apron (thrust)
stage
time 147, 152, **420–421**
Times Literary Supplement (TLS)
421
Titanic (film) 247
Titus Andronicus (Shakespeare)
351, 424
Todd, Janet 383
Tolkien, J. R. R. 158
Tolstoy, Leo 23, 77, 109, 153,
439
Tompkins, Jane 352
tone 91, 268, **421–422,** 425
tone poem 271
topical allusion 20
topos (topic) **422**
Torah 317
touchstone **422**
tracking shot **422**
tradition **422–423**
tragedy **423–425**
action in 5–6, 69, 88
Aristotle on 5, 69, 77,
123, 423
catastrophe in 69
characters in 423

for children 75–76
comic relief in 88
death in 107–108
determinism in 116
domestic **125**
gangster film as 176–177
irony in 223
law in 236
Nietzsche (Friedrich) on
32, 183
tragic farce 160
tragic flaw 190
tragic hero 6, 190, 376
tragicomedy 86, **425**
transactional theory 352,
425–426
transcendentalism 21, 58, 116,
244, **426**
transformational grammar 185
transition **126**
translation, literal 242
travel **426–428**
treatment **428**
Trilling, Lionel 239–240, 342
trilogy **428**
trimeter 260, 261, **428**
trivium/quadrivium 365, **428**
trochee 169, 260, 261, 403,
428
Troilus and Cressida
(Shakespeare) 301, 338
Trollope, Anthony 106, 219,
294, 377
trope **428**
tropological meaning 171
troubadours 100, 231, 266,
384, **429**
trouvères 37, 100, **429**
Truffaut, François 288–289
Trumbull, John 364
Turner, Mark 318–319
Tvardovsky, Alexander 295
Twain, Mark 181
Twelfth Night (Shakespeare) 16,
24, 89
two cultures 377, **429**
Tyndale, William 310
typology **429**
Tzara, Tristan 105

U

Ulster cycle **430**
ultraism *(ultraismo)* **430**
Ulysses (Joyce) 9, 39, 52,
81, 88, 119–120, 141,
191, 301, 326, 329

Ulysses/Odysseus theme
300–302
uncertainty. *See* indeterminacy
unconscious 73, 105, 130,
131, 267, 275, 342, 343,
406, 408, **430–431**
underground **431**
Under the Volcano (Lowry) 16
underworld **431**
unities 282, **432**
universality 94, **432**
University Wits **432–433,** 443
unreliable narrator 279
Updike, John 8, 14, 63, 358,
415
upper class 80, 129
upstage/downstage **127**
utopia 58, **433**

V

Vaihinger, Hans 39, 158
value judgment 64, **434**
vampirism **434–435**
Van Ghent, Dorothy 420
vaudeville 273, **435–436**
vehicle **413**
vernacular theory **436**
Verne, Jules 378
verse **436**. *See also* poetry
blank. *See* blank verse
free. *See* free verse
light **241,** 436
macaronic **249**
occasional **299**
quantitative 169, 260, **347**
Vice 343, **436**
Victoria (queen of Great
Britain) 436
Victorian era 134, 377, 394,
436–437, 445
Vidal, Gore 67
villain 95, 150, 188, 213, 249,
269, 344, 436, **437**. *See also*
antagonist
villanelle **437**
Virgil 184, 300, 315, 431,
439
vital impulse. *See* élan vital
vorticism 155
Vulgate 52, **438**

W

WAC. *See* writing across the
curriculum
Wace (Norman writer) 37

Waiting for Godot (Beckett) 2, 87, 192, 360
Waldhorn, Arthur 361–362
Walker, Alice 163, 443
Walpole, Hugh 184
war **439–441**
Warner, Charles Dudley 181
Warren, Austin 156
Warren, Robert Penn 285
Warshow, Robert 176
Watt, Ian 213
wedding poem 145
Weisinger, Herbert 171
Wellek, René 156
Welles, Orson 167
well-made play **441**
Wells, H. G. 134–135, 349, 378
Welty, Eudora 395
West, Nathaniel 405
western 73, 116, 198, 316, 364, 412, **441–443**
"what if" fiction. *See* counterfactual fiction
Wheatley, Phillis 364
White, T. H. 38
Whitman, Walt 97, 174, 177, 299
Wickes, Jennifer 8–9
Wilde, Oscar 10, 86
Williams, Raymond 103

Williams, Roger 84
Williams, William Carlos 214, 298, 339
willing suspension of disbelief 8, 41, 98, **443**
Wilson, Edmund 376
Wilson, J. Dover 122
Wilson, Sloan 66
Wimsatt, William 10, 94, 216
Winter's Tale, The (Shakespeare) 7, 77, 98, 227, 281, 369
Wister, Owen 442
wit 95, 142, 230, 241, 258–259, 282, 363, 364, 368, 409, 432–433, **443**
Wittig, Monique 163
Wolf, Christa 296
Wolfe, Tom 67, 290, 294, 346, 354, 395
womanist **443**
women's rights 134
women's writing 56, 162, 163, 189, 238–239, **444**
Woolf, Virginia 90, 162, 420
Wordsworth, William 33, 79, 277, 300, 324, 334, 394, 405
work **444–446**
working class 66, 80, 81, 125, 339–340, 444–445
world-as-theater. *See* theatrum mundi

writer. *See* author
writerly/readerly 332, 339, **351**
writing **446**
    basic 3, **49–50**
    women's **444**
writing across the curriculum (WAC) 3–4, 83, **446–447**

Y
Yale critics **448**
Yeats, William Butler 32, 108–109, 299, 307, 314, 416
Yellow Book, The (magazine) 244
yellow journalism **448**
Yiddish theater 132
Young, Philip 83
young adult literature **448–449**

Z
zeitgeist **450**
Zen **450**
zeugma **451**
zines **451**
Zinsser, William 446
Zola, Émile 280, 353
zoom shot **451**